Open Economy Macroeconomics

Open Economy Macroeconomics

Martín Uribe

Stephanie Schmitt-Grohé

PRINCETON UNIVERSITY PRESS • PRINCETON AND OXFORD

Published by Princeton University Press, 41 William Street, Princeton, New Jersey 08540

In the United Kingdom: Princeton University Press, 6 Oxford Street, Woodstock, Oxfordshire OX20 1TW

press.princeton.edu

ISBN 978-0-691-15877-8

British Library Cataloging-in-Publication Data is available

This book has been composed in MinionPro and MyriadPro using ZzTEX by Cohographics and Windfall Software.

Printed on acid-free paper. ∞

Printed in the United States of America

10 9 8 7 6 5 4 3 2

To Cristóbal and Imanol

Contents

10   Exchange-Rate Policy and Capital Controls   369

11   Policy Credibility and Balance-of-Payments Crises   399

Preface

The past two decades have witnessed an enormous growth in the field of open economy macroeconomics. Perhaps the most important methodological innovation has been to bring theoretical models and data together in ways that were unimaginable just a few years ago. This has been made possible by three key developments. First, we have experienced major theoretical advances introducing financial and nominal frictions into micro-founded dynamic models of the open economy. The current state of the theoretical frontier offers models that allow us to develop a much better understanding of the financial and monetary aspects of regular international business-cycle fluctuations and global crises than we had only a couple of decades ago. Second, macro and micro data for a large number of countries spanning long periods of time have become readily available through the efforts of national and international statistical agencies. Without a doubt, access to data has also been immensely facilitated by the emergence of the World Wide Web. Key global data sets, such as the World Development Indicators, the Penn World Tables, or the Eurostat databases, are reachable at the click of a mouse. Third, there has been a revolution in the tools available to simulate and estimate dynamic stochastic models. These techniques have made the computation, econometric estimation, and evaluation of competing models a common practice. Until not too long ago, model predictions and econometric analysis ran on different tracks. They belonged to different papers. Now they are both integral parts of the same research effort.

The marriage of models and data has given rise to a plethora of new theoretical and empirical insights. For example, the Eaton-Gersovitz model of imperfect enforcement of international debt contracts provides a compelling narrative of why countries lend to and borrow from one another, even though the world lacks a supranational authority capable of adjudicating and enforcing debt contracts. According to this theory, countries honor their debts because failing to do so earns them a bad reputation and exclusion from international financial markets. This theoretical framework was well understood by the mid-1980s. However, beginning only a few years ago were researchers able to produce quantitative predictions of the Eaton-Gersovitz model and confront them with data. This development revealed that under plausible parameterizations, the Eaton-Gersovitz model delivers equilibrium debt levels that are many times smaller than those observed in actual data. For example, when calibrated to Argentina, the model predicts a debt-to-output ratio of less than 1 percent, nowhere near the actual level of around 30 percent. This game-changing finding brought the literature on sovereign default back to square zero and spurred an outburst of new research.

Another example of how the scrutiny of the empirical validity of economic theories has led to rethinking how the economy works and how economic policy should be conducted is the area of exchange-rate determination. Time and time again we observe that economic crises in emerging countries end in large devaluations, sometimes as large as 200 or 300 percent. Invariably such events were explained with theories featuring some type of policy mismanagement, such as unsustainable fiscal deficits (as in models of balance-of-payments crises) or unjustified monetary expansions (as in the exchange-rate overshooting model). At the same time, the emergence of micro-founded models with nominal rigidities in product and factor prices granted the use of devaluations as a way to correct misalignments in key relative prices, such as the real wage or the real exchange rate. However, these predicted devaluations were thought to be quantitatively small, part of a fine-tuning approach to economic stabilization policy. As it turned out, when subjected to shocks of realistic size, estimated versions of these types of models tell a very different story. For they predict that the optimal response to a large real shock is often a large devaluation of the magnitude observed in actual crises. These devaluations are optimal in the sense that they maximize the welfare of agents and play the role of avoiding potentially large levels of involuntary unemployment.

A third example of how confronting model predictions with data has led to changes in paradigms is the case of the desirability of capital controls. The findings described in the previous paragraph put in perspective the pros and cons of fixed exchange-rate arrangements like the ones that the periphery of Europe is engaged in. And, in particular, these findings have fostered a revival of research on the issue of optimal stabilization policy for countries with fixed exchange rates. One important outcome of this area of research has been a re-evaluation of the role of capital controls. Once believed to be villains, they are now considered a legitimate part of the toolkit available to policymakers to stabilize the economy. A novel by-product of this line of research has been the emergence of what is now known as the theory of macroprudential policy. For example, in dynamic models with nominal rigidities in which the powers of the local monetary authority are limited by a currency peg or by membership in a monetary union, the Ramsey optimal capital control policy calls for restricting capital inflows during good times instead of waiting until after a crisis has occurred to pick up the broken pieces. This profound reassessment of the role of policy instruments would have been impossible without the use of welfare-based quantitative models amenable to econometric estimation.

More generally, the aforementioned methodological developments in open economy macroeconomics allow us to answer central questions. What shocks are important for understanding movements in real activity, the current account, and exchange rates? What frictions are the most relevant for transmitting disturbances within and across borders? What are the welfare consequences of alternative exchange-rate and fiscal policies? What is the shape of the optimal policy regime in the context of economies with multiple frictions and disturbances? Our hope is that this book will impart to careful readers the theories and techniques necessary to understand the workings of the global economy and to formulate and tackle new research challenges in open economy macroeconomics.

This book covers more topics than fit in a one-semester course. However, because each chapter is largely self-contained, it can be used quite flexibly. For instance, at Columbia we have taught Chapters 1–4, which cover the foundations of modern open economy macroeconomics, in half a semester of the first-year Ph.D. sequence in macroeconomics. In the second-year Ph.D. open economy macro course, we cover selected advanced topics from Chapters 5–13. These chapters cover business-cycle analysis for open economies, interest-rate shocks, terms-of-trade and commodity-price shocks, the determination of the real exchange rate, optimal exchange-rate policy in models with nominal rigidities, optimal capital controls, balance-of-payments crises, financial frictions, and sovereign default. In a number of master programs, especially in Europe, Asia, and Latin America (but increasingly also in the United States, as standalone master programs continue to emerge), different combinations of chapters of this book are used in macroeconomics courses.

We believe that an essential element of any scientific activity is replicability. For this reason, we have made an effort to make available to readers many of the data sets and computer codes necessary to replicate the results reported in the book. Over the years that we have taught the material in this book, we have accumulated a large number of exercises, which range in scope from proving analytical properties of the models studied in the body of the book to small research projects that involve theoretical, computational, and econometric work. In our experience, students have found these exercises helpful in mastering the material of the book and in easing their transition into the production of original work. For this reason, we have included them in the book and placed them at the end of the relevant chapters. In addition, we have made available online slides that we hope will be useful to instructors and students alike. These slides, computer programs, and other materials are available on the book's Web site, which can be accessed through http://press .princeton.edu/titles/11032.html.

Acknowledgments

Over our careers we have benefited from the mentorship, advice, and assistance from more people than we can acknowledge here. We have learned from our current and former colleagues, co-authors, academic advisors, and a large number of scholars who do not belong to any of these categories but have nonetheless, through their academic contributions, shaped our own ways of analyzing economic problems. At the risk of being unfair to many, we single out just a few. Much of our interest in the fields of open economy macroeconomics and macroeconomics in general stems from reading and interacting with our current and former colleagues Guillermo Calvo, Enrique Mendoza, and Michael Woodford. Guillermo Calvo's work on lack of credibility of exchange-rate policy was one of our first exposures to the field and, to this day, represents to us a standard of how important ideas in economics can be delivered in simple and elegant models. Enrique Mendoza's work on open economy business-cycle theory in the early 1990s is reflected in various parts of the book. As our dissertation advisor at the University of Chicago, Michael Woodford always encouraged us to pursue our interest in open economy macroeconomics even though it forced him to step out of his theoretical comfort zone. This book is encrusted with the analytical approach and modeling techniques we learned from our longstanding interaction with him. We have also benefited from the comments and suggestions of innumerable students at the University of Pennsylvania, Duke University, and Columbia University, who read and reread various chapters of this book at different stages of completion. Special thanks go to Marco

Airaudo, Ozge Akinci, Ryan Chahrour, Javier García-Cicco, Yang Jiao, Yoon Joo Jo, Arthur Xuan Liu, Wataru Miyamoto, Seunghoon Na, Pablo Ottonello, Samer Shousha, Vivian Yue, and Sarah Zubairy. For helpful comments and corrections, we thank Francisco Ciocchini, Stéphane Dupraz, Felix Hammermann, Manfred Jager-Ambrozewicz, and Krisztina Orban. We are especially grateful to our editor, Seth Ditchik of Princeton University Press, for asking us to develop into a book a set of lecture notes that were growing and gaining interest among students and colleagues but were otherwise sleeping the sleep of the just. We are also grateful to Peter Dougherty, the director of Princeton University Press, for kindly stepping in as our editor after Seth's departure to pursue other goals, and to Cyd Westmoreland for superb copyediting. Last but not least, we thank our mothers, Delia Neuman and Barbara Schmitt-Grohé, for their unconditional love and support.

Business-Cycle Facts Around the World

Open economy business-cycle theory aims to answer some fundamental questions about movements of aggregate indicators in and across countries. How volatile is output? Do the components of aggregate demand (consumption, investment, government spending, and exports) move pro or countercyclically? How persistent are movements in aggregate activity? Are economic expansions and contractions associated with deficits or surpluses in the trade balance? Is aggregate consumption less or more volatile than output? Are emerging countries more or less volatile than developed countries? Does country size matter for business cycles? The answers to these questions form a basic set of empirical facts about business cycles that one would like macroeconomic models of the open economy to be able to explain. Accordingly, the purpose of this chapter is to document these facts using aggregate data on economic activity spanning time and space.

1.1 Measuring Business Cycles

In the theoretical models we study in this book, the basic economic units are the individual consumer, the firm, and the government. The models produce predictions for the consumers' income, spending, and savings and for firms' investment and production decisions. These decisions are then aggregated across agents, yielding predicted macroeconomic indicators. To compare the predictions of theoretical models to actual data, it is therefore natural to consider time series and cross-country evidence on per capita measures of aggregate activity, spending, and cross-border trade in goods and assets. Accordingly, in this chapter we describe the business-cycle properties of output per capita, denoted y; total private consumption per capita, denoted c; investment per capita, denoted i; public consumption per capita, denoted g; exports per capita, denoted x; imports per capita, denoted m; the *trade balance* per capita, denoted $tb \equiv (x - m)$; and the current account per capita, denoted ca.

We use annual and quarterly cross-country time-series data. We begin by analyzing the annual data. The source is the World Bank's World Development Indicators (WDI) database.[1] All time series are expressed in real per capita terms. We include only countries

---

1. The WDI database is publicly available at databank.worldbank.org. We made some corrections to the WDI data as described in the online appendix. The data used in this chapter are in the file `data_annual.xls` available on the book's Web site via http://press.princeton.edu/titles/11032.html.

with at least 30 uninterrupted years of data for y, c, i, g, x, and m. The resulting sample contains 120 countries and covers, on average, the period from 1965 to 2010.[2]

Before proceeding to display business-cycle facts, a word on the consumption data is in order. The WDI database contains information on household final consumption expenditure. This time series includes consumption expenditure on nondurables, services, and durables. Typically, business-cycle studies remove expenditures on durables from the definition of consumption. The reason is that from an economic point of view, expenditures on durable consumption goods, such as cars and washing machines, represent an investment in household physical capital. For this reason, researchers often add this component of consumption to the gross investment series. From a statistical point of view, there is also a reason to separate durables from nondurables and services in the definition of consumption. Expenditures on durables are far more volatile than expenditures on nondurables and services. For example, in the United States, durable consumption is about three times as volatile as output, whereas consumption of nondurables and services is less volatile than output. Even though expenditure on durables represents only 13 percent of total consumption expenditure, the standard deviation of total consumption is 20 percent higher than that of nondurables and services. Unfortunately, the WDI data set does not provide consumption data disaggregated into durables and nondurables. One should therefore keep in mind that the volatility of consumption reported later in this chapter is likely to be somewhat higher than the one that would result if our measure of consumption excluded expenditures on durable goods.

The focus of our analysis is to understand aggregate fluctuations at the business-cycle frequency. We must therefore find a way to extract the cyclical component from the raw time series. The existing literature suggests a variety of methods for isolating the cyclical component of a time series. The most popular ones are log-linear detrending, log-quadratic detrending, Hodrick-Prescott (HP) filtering, first differencing, and band-pass filtering. The following analysis uses quadratic detrending, HP filtering, and first differencing.

To extract a log-quadratic trend, we proceed as follows. Consider, for instance, the case of output. Let y_t denote the natural logarithm of real output per capita in year t for a given country, y_t^c the cyclical component of y_t, and y_t^s the secular (or trend) component of y_t. Then we have

$$y_t = y_t^c + y_t^s. \tag{1.1}$$

The components y_t^c and y_t^s are estimated by running the regression

$$y_t = a + bt + ct^2 + \epsilon_t,$$

and setting

$$y_t^c = \epsilon_t$$

and

$$y_t^s = a + bt + ct^2.$$

We use the same procedure to detrend the natural logarithms of consumption, investment, government spending, exports, and imports, and the levels (not the logs) of the trade-balance-to-output ratio and the current-account-to-output ratio.[3] We analyze two

---

2. Only 94 countries contained 30 uninterrupted years of current account data.
3. The reason we detrend the levels and not the logs of the latter two variables is that they can take negative and positive values.

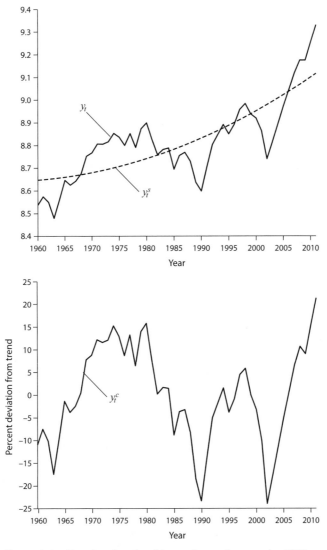

Figure 1.1 Trend and cycle of Argentine real per capita GDP.

Source: Authors' calculations based on WDI data.

additional variables, the level of the trade balance (tb) and the level of the current account (ca). Before quadratically detrending these two variables, we divide them by the secular component of output ($e^{y_t^s}$).[4] We perform the decomposition into cycle and trend for every time series and every country separately.

To illustrate the workings of the log-quadratic filter, Figure 1.1 displays the trend and cyclical components of Argentine real GDP per capita from 1960 to 2011. The top panel

---

4. The reason we divide these two series by the secular component of output is that, although the levels of these variables typically do not have a clear trend, the absolute deviations from their respective means do. After doing this, detrending is not absolutely necessary, but we do it for consistency.

of the figure shows with a solid line the raw data and with a dashed line the estimated quadratic trend y_t^s. The bottom panel shows the cyclical component y_t^c. The detrending procedure delivers three well-marked cycles if one measures them from peak to peak in y_t^c: one from the beginning of the sample until 1980, a second one from 1980 to 1998, and a third one from 1998 to the end of the sample. In particular, the log-quadratic filter succeeds in identifying the two major contractions in postwar Argentina, namely, the one associated with the hyperinflation of the late 1980s and the one associated with the demise of the Convertibility Plan in 2001. In the first of these contractions, real GDP per capita fell by about 40 percent from the peak in 1980 to the trough in 1990, giving the 1980s the well-deserved nickname of the lost decade.

The behavior of the business-cycle component of real GDP suggests that the Argentine economy has been highly volatile over the past 50 years. The standard deviation of y_t^c is 10.8 percent per year. The cyclical component is also quite persistent. The serial correlation of y_t^c is 0.85.

In the next section, we expand this analysis to all macroeconomic aggregates and countries included in our data set.

1.2 Business-Cycle Facts Around the World

To characterize the average world business cycle, we compute business-cycle statistics for each country in the sample and then take a population-weighted average of each statistic across countries. The resulting average summary statistics appear in Table 1.1 under the heading "All Countries."[5]

The table displays standard deviations, correlations with output, and serial correlations. Relative standard deviations are cross-country averages of country-specific relative standard deviations. The table also displays averages of the trade-balance-to-output ratio and the openness ratio, defined as $(x + m)/y$.

According to Table 1.1, the world is a pretty volatile place. The average standard deviation of output across all countries is 6.2 percent. To put this number into perspective, we contrast it with the volatility of output in the United States. The standard deviation of the cyclical component of U.S. output is 2.9 percent, half as large as the average volatility of output across all countries in the data set.

Fact 1 (High Global Volatility) The cross-country average standard deviation of output is twice as large as its U.S. counterpart.

One statistic in Table 1.1 that might attract some attention is that on average across countries, private consumption is 5 percent more volatile than output. This fact might seem at odds with the backbone of optimizing models of the business cycle, namely, consumption smoothing. However, recall that the measure of consumption used here includes

---

5. Country-by-country statistics for a selected number of emerging and rich countries are shown in Table 1.8 in the appendix. The online appendix (available on the book's Web site) presents country-by-country statistics for all countries.

Table 1.1   Business Cycles in Poor, Emerging, and Rich Countries

Statistic	United States	All Countries	Poor Countries	Emerging Countries	Rich Countries
Standard Deviations					
σ_y	2.94	6.22	6.08	8.71	3.32
σ_c/σ_y	1.02	1.05	1.12	0.98	0.87
σ_g/σ_y	1.93	2.26	2.46	2.00	1.73
σ_i/σ_y	3.52	3.14	3.24	2.79	3.20
σ_x/σ_y	3.49	3.07	3.08	2.82	3.36
σ_m/σ_y	3.24	3.23	3.30	2.72	3.64
$\sigma_{tb/y}$	0.94	2.34	2.12	3.80	1.25
$\sigma_{ca/y}$	1.11	2.16	2.06	3.08	1.39
Correlations with y					
y	1.00	1.00	1.00	1.00	1.00
c	0.90	0.69	0.66	0.75	0.76
g/y	−0.32	−0.02	0.08	−0.08	−0.39
i	0.80	0.66	0.60	0.77	0.77
x	−0.11	0.19	0.14	0.35	0.17
m	0.31	0.24	0.14	0.50	0.34
tb/y	−0.51	−0.15	−0.11	−0.21	−0.26
tb	−0.54	−0.18	−0.14	−0.24	−0.25
ca/y	−0.62	−0.28	−0.28	−0.24	−0.30
ca	−0.64	−0.28	−0.28	−0.26	−0.31
Serial Correlations					
y	0.75	0.71	0.65	0.87	0.76
c	0.82	0.66	0.62	0.74	0.75
g	0.91	0.76	0.71	0.80	0.89
i	0.67	0.56	0.49	0.72	0.67
x	0.75	0.68	0.65	0.74	0.74
m	0.63	0.65	0.61	0.74	0.69
tb/y	0.79	0.61	0.59	0.62	0.69
ca/y	0.79	0.57	0.55	0.52	0.71
Means					
tb/y	−1.5	−1.3	−1.6	−1.4	−0.0
$(x+m)/y$	18.9	36.5	32.5	46.4	40.4

Source: Authors' calculations based on WDI data.

Notes: The variables $y, c, g, i, x, m, tb \equiv (x - m)$, and ca denote, respectively, output, total private consumption, government spending, investment, exports, imports, the trade balance, and the current account. All variables are expressed in real per capita terms. The variables y, c, g, i, x, and m are quadratically detrended in logs and expressed as percentage deviations from trend. The variables $tb/y, g/y$, and ca/y are quadratically detrended in levels. The variables tb and ca are scaled by the secular component of y and quadratically detrended. The sample contains 120 countries and covers, on average, the period 1965–2010 at annual frequency. Moments are averaged across countries using population weights. The sets of poor, emerging, and rich countries are defined as all countries with average PPP converted GDP per capita in U.S. dollars of 2005 over the period 1990–2009 in the ranges 0–3,000, 3,001–25,000, and 25,001–∞, respectively. The lists of poor, emerging, and rich countries are presented in the appendix to this chapter.

expenditures on consumer durables, which are highly volatile. The fact that expenditure on durables is highly volatile need not be at odds with consumption smoothing, because it represents an investment in household capital rather than direct consumption. For example, a household that buys a new car every 5 years displays a choppy path for expenditures on cars but might choose to experience a smooth consumption of the services provided by its car, as measured by, for example, miles driven per year.

> Fact 2 (Excess Consumption Volatility) On average across countries, private consumption including durables is more volatile than output.

The government does not appear to smooth its own consumption of goods and services either. On average, the standard deviation of public consumption is more than twice that of output.

Investment, exports, and imports are by far the most volatile components of the national income and product accounts, with standard deviations around three times as large as that of output. The trade-balance-to-output ratio and the current-account-to-output ratio are also highly volatile, with standard deviations of more than 2 percent of GDP.

> Fact 3 (Global Ranking of Volatilities) The ranking of cross-country average standard deviations from top to bottom is imports, investment, exports, government spending, consumption, and output.

We say that a variable is *procyclical* when it has a positive correlation with output. Table 1.1 reveals that consumption, investment, exports, and imports are all procyclical. Private consumption is the most procyclical component of aggregate demand.

> Fact 4 (Procyclicality of the Components of Aggregate Demand) On average, consumption, investment, exports, and imports are all positively correlated with output.

In contrast, the trade balance, trade-balance-to-output ratio, current account, and current-account-to-output ratio are all *countercyclical*. This means that countries tend to import more than they export during booms and to export more than they import during recessions.

> Fact 5 (Countercyclicality of the Trade Balance and the Current Account) On average across countries, the trade balance, trade-balance-to-output ratio, current account, and current-account-to-output ratio are all negatively correlated with output.

Table 1.1 shows that the government-spending-to-output ratio is roughly acyclical. This empirical regularity runs contrary to the traditional Keynesian stabilization policy prescription, according to which the share of government spending in GDP should be increased during contractions and cut during booms.

Fact 6 (Acyclicality of the Share of Government Consumption in GDP) On average across countries, the share of government consumption in output is roughly uncorrelated with output.

This fact must be qualified along two dimensions. First, here the variable g denotes government consumption of goods. It does not include government investment, which may be more or less procyclical than government consumption. Second, g does not include transfers. To the extent that transfers are countercyclical and directed to households with high propensities to consume—presumably low-income households—total government spending may be more countercyclical than government consumption.

A standard measure of persistence in time series is the first-order serial correlation. Table 1.1 shows that on average across countries, output is quite persistent, with a serial correlation of 0.71. All components of aggregate demand as well as imports are broadly as persistent as output.

Fact 7 (Persistence) The components of aggregate supply (output and imports) and aggregate demand (consumption, government spending, investment, and exports) are all positively serially correlated.

Later in this chapter, we will investigate whether output is a persistent stationary variable or a nonstationary variable. This distinction is important for choosing the stochastic processes of shocks driving theoretical models of the macroeconomy.

1.3 Business Cycles in Poor, Emerging, and Rich Countries

An important question in macroeconomics is whether business cycles look differently in poor, emerging, and rich economies. For if this were the case, then a model that is successful in explaining business cycles in, say, rich countries, may be less successful in explaining business cycles in emerging or poor countries. One difficulty with characterizing business cycles at different stages of development is that any definition of the terms poor, emerging, and rich country is necessarily arbitrary. For this reason, it is particularly important to be as explicit as possible when describing the classification method adopted.

As the measure of development, we use the geometric average of purchasing power parity (PPP)–converted GDP per capita in U.S. dollars of 2005 over the period 1990–2009. Loosely speaking, PPP-converted GDP in a given country is the value of all goods and services produced in that country evaluated at U.S. prices. By evaluating production of goods in different countries at the same prices, PPP conversion makes cross-country comparisons more sensible. To illustrate the concept of PPP conversion, suppose that in a given year country X produces 3 haircuts and 1 ton of grain and that the unit prices of these items inside country X are 1 and 200 dollars, respectively. Then the nonconverted measure of GDP is 203 dollars. Suppose, however, that because a haircut is not a service that can be easily traded internationally, its price is very different in country X and the United States (few people are willing to fly from one country to another just to take advantage of differences in haircut prices). Specifically, assume that a haircut costs 20 dollars in the

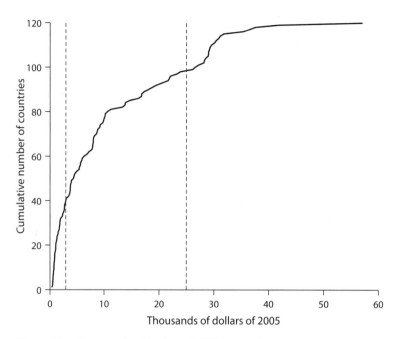

Figure 1.2   Country distribution of GDP per capita.

Source: Authors' calculations based on WDI data.
Notes: The *x*-axis is the geometric average of PPP-converted GDP per capita
in U.S. dollars of 2005 during 1990–2009. The *y*-axis indicates the cumulative
number of countries. The total number of countries is 120. The dashed vertical
lines mark the groups of poor, emerging, and rich countries.

United States, twenty times more than in country X. Assume also that, unlike haircuts, grain
is freely traded internationally, so its price is the same in both country X and the United
States. Then, the PPP-converted measure of GDP in country X is 260. In this example, the
PPP-adjusted measure is 28 percent higher than its unadjusted counterpart, reflecting the
fact that nontraded services are more expensive in the United States than in country X.

We define the set of poor countries as all countries with annual PPP-converted GDP
per capita of up to 3,000 dollars, the set of emerging countries as all countries with PPP-
converted GDP per capita between 3,001 and 25,000 dollars, and the set of rich countries
as all countries with PPP-converted GDP per capita above 25,000 dollars. This definition
delivers 40 poor countries, 58 emerging countries, and 22 rich countries in our data set. The
lists of countries in each category appear in the appendix to this chapter. Figure 1.2 displays
the distribution of PPP-converted GDP per capita across countries. The strong concavity
of the plotted line suggests that output is unevenly distributed across countries. There are
few high-income countries and many low- and medium-income countries.

Table 1.1 displays standard deviations, correlations with output, and serial correlations
by income level. Statistics for each income group are population-weighted averages of
the corresponding country-specific statistics. There are significant differences in volatility
across income levels. Compared to rich countries, the rest of the world is a roller coaster.

A simple inspection of Table 1.1 makes it clear that the central difference between business cycles in rich countries and business cycles in either emerging or poor countries is that rich countries are about half as volatile as emerging or poor countries. This is true not only for output, but also for all components of aggregate demand.

> Fact 8 (Excess Volatility of Poor and Emerging Countries) Business cycles in rich countries are about half as volatile as business cycles in emerging or poor countries.

Explaining this impressive fact is perhaps the most important unfinished business in business-cycle theory. Are poor and emerging countries more volatile than rich countries because they face more volatile shocks (such as terms of trade, country risk premia, productivity disturbances, or animal spirits)? Or is their elevated instability the result of precarious economic institutions (manifested in, for example, poorly designed monetary and fiscal policies, political distortions, fragile financial systems, or weak enforcement of economic contracts) that tend to exacerbate the aggregate effects of changes in fundamentals? One of the objectives of this book is to shed light on these two non-mutually exclusive views.

A second important fact that emerges from the comparison of business-cycle statistics across income levels is that consumption smoothing is increasing with income per capita. Table 1.1 shows that in rich countries consumption is 13 percent less volatile than output, whereas in poor countries it is 12 percent more volatile than output. In emerging countries, consumption and output are about equally volatile.

> Fact 9 (Less Consumption Smoothing in Poor and Emerging Countries) The relative consumption volatility is higher in poor and emerging countries than in rich countries.

Table 1.1 shows that the trade-balance-to-output ratio is countercyclical for poor, emerging, and rich countries. That is, fact 5 holds not only unconditionally, but also conditional on the level of economic development.

An important difference between business cycles in rich countries and the rest of the world that emerges from Table 1.1 is that in rich countries the share of government consumption in GDP is significantly more countercyclical than in emerging or poor countries. Rich countries appear to adhere more to the classic Keynesian dictum of boosting (reducing) the share of government spending during economic contractions (expansions) than do poor or emerging economies.

> Fact 10 (The Countercyclicality of Government Spending Increases with Income) The share of government consumption is countercyclical in rich countries, but acyclical in emerging and poor countries.

1.4 Country Size and Observed Business Cycles

Table 1.2 presents business-cycle facts disaggregated by country size. Countries are sorted into three size categories: small, medium, and large. These three categories are defined,

Table 1.2 Business Cycles in Small, Medium, and Large Countries

	All Countries			Poor Countries			Emerging Countries			Rich Countries		
	S	M	L	S	M	L	S	M	L	S	M	L
Standard Deviations												
σ_y	8.00	7.92	5.55	8.17	9.46	5.63	9.50	8.99	7.86	4.31	3.05	3.29
σ_c/σ_y	1.12	0.96	1.07	1.39	1.05	1.11	0.97	0.93	1.08	0.92	0.93	0.84
σ_g/σ_y	2.22	2.21	2.28	2.92	2.86	2.40	1.85	2.05	1.99	1.66	1.71	1.76
σ_i/σ_y	3.65	3.23	3.06	4.68	4.01	3.08	2.97	2.86	2.58	3.07	3.07	3.28
σ_x/σ_y	2.46	3.29	3.07	2.81	3.94	3.01	2.23	2.92	2.95	2.23	3.33	3.56
σ_m/σ_y	2.55	3.12	3.33	2.96	3.45	3.30	2.25	2.68	3.02	2.36	3.80	3.77
$\sigma_{tb/y}$	4.29	3.64	1.76	5.62	3.82	1.77	4.00	4.39	2.75	2.29	1.47	0.98
$\sigma_{ca/y}$	3.68	2.97	1.84	4.84	3.40	1.87	3.55	3.45	2.39	2.37	1.47	1.23
Correlations with y												
y	1.00	1.00	1.00	1.00	1.00	1.00	1.00	1.00	1.00	1.00	1.00	1.00
c	0.64	0.71	0.69	0.58	0.74	0.66	0.73	0.70	0.84	0.55	0.70	0.82
g/y	−0.03	−0.01	−0.02	0.02	0.24	0.07	0.03	0.00	−0.26	−0.26	−0.40	−0.40
i	0.60	0.70	0.66	0.45	0.55	0.61	0.72	0.76	0.82	0.63	0.74	0.81
x	0.54	0.42	0.08	0.53	0.58	0.08	0.53	0.36	0.25	0.58	0.37	0.00
m	0.59	0.57	0.11	0.53	0.62	0.07	0.62	0.57	0.34	0.63	0.47	0.23
tb/y	−0.12	−0.24	−0.13	−0.04	−0.25	−0.10	−0.21	−0.24	−0.17	−0.11	−0.24	−0.29
tb	−0.21	−0.26	−0.15	−0.18	−0.33	−0.12	−0.32	−0.24	−0.21	−0.04	−0.24	−0.29
ca/y	−0.17	−0.22	−0.30	−0.17	−0.11	−0.30	−0.20	−0.34	−0.11	−0.11	−0.08	−0.44
ca	−0.21	−0.25	−0.30	−0.23	−0.17	−0.29	−0.25	−0.36	−0.13	−0.08	−0.10	−0.43
Serial Correlations												
y	0.83	0.83	0.66	0.76	0.84	0.62	0.89	0.84	0.90	0.83	0.80	0.74
c	0.67	0.69	0.66	0.61	0.61	0.62	0.70	0.71	0.81	0.73	0.75	0.75
g	0.73	0.80	0.75	0.61	0.74	0.72	0.78	0.80	0.81	0.87	0.89	0.90
i	0.66	0.66	0.53	0.62	0.64	0.47	0.67	0.70	0.79	0.71	0.61	0.70
x	0.67	0.75	0.67	0.58	0.73	0.65	0.74	0.76	0.70	0.68	0.75	0.74
m	0.69	0.70	0.63	0.68	0.68	0.60	0.71	0.72	0.80	0.66	0.71	0.68
tb/y	0.54	0.58	0.63	0.50	0.51	0.61	0.52	0.58	0.74	0.67	0.68	0.70
ca/y	0.42	0.50	0.60	0.36	0.42	0.57	0.40	0.46	0.65	0.56	0.67	0.75
Means												
tby	−5.6	−1.5	−0.8	−10.4	−5.4	−0.7	−5.2	−0.0	−1.7	3.1	0.0	−0.6
xmy	73.9	48.6	29.0	57.7	48.9	29.5	69.2	49.7	29.9	116.8	45.2	25.3

Notes: See Table 1.1. The sets of small (S), medium (M), and large (L) countries are defined as countries with 2011 populations of, respectively, less than 20 million, between 20 and 80 million, and more than 80 million.

respectively, as all countries with population in 2011 of less than 20 million, between 20 and 80 million, and more than 80 million. The first regularity that emerges from Table 1.2 is that conditional on size, rich countries are at least half as volatile as emerging or poor countries. This means that fact 8 is robust to controlling for country size. To further characterize the partial correlations of output volatility with economic development and country size, we regress the standard deviation of output per capita of country i, denoted $\sigma_{y,i}$, onto a constant, the logarithm of country i's population in 2009, denoted $\ln \text{pop}_i$ ($\ln$ denotes the natural logarithm), the logarithm of country i's average PPP-converted output per capita over the period 1990–2009, denoted $\ln y_i^{PPP}$, and country i's openness share, denoted xmy_i. All 120 countries in the sample are included. The regression yields

$$\sigma_{y,i} = 15.0 - 0.08 \ln \text{pop}_i - 0.78 \ln y_i^{PPP} + 0.86 \, xmy_i + \epsilon_i,$$

$$t\text{-stat:} \quad (3.5) \qquad (-0.4) \qquad (-2.9) \qquad (0.9)$$

$$R^2 = 0.07.$$

This regression shows that both higher income per capita and larger country size tend to be associated with lower output volatility. At the same time, more open economies appear to be more volatile. Note, however, that population and openness are statistically insignificant, and the overall explanatory power of the regressors is low. Further, this regression is mute with respect to the direction of causality.

Table 1.2 suggests that the consumption-output volatility ratio falls with income per capita and, less strongly, also with country size. This relationship is corroborated by the following regression:

$$\ln \left(\frac{\sigma_{c,i}}{\sigma_{y,i}} \right) = 1.8 - 0.06 \ln \text{pop}_i - 0.11 \ln y_i^{PPP} + 0.14 \, xmy_i + \epsilon_i,$$

$$t\text{-stat:} \quad (4.1) \qquad (-2.7) \qquad (-3.8) \qquad (+1.4)$$

$$R^2 = 0.19.$$

According to this regression, more populous and richer countries tend to have a lower relative volatility of consumption. Taking into account that the volatility of output falls with size and income, this means that the volatility of consumption falls even faster than that of income as size and income increase. These results generalize fact 9, according to which consumption smoothing increases with income.

Finally, Table 1.2 shows that smaller countries are more open than larger countries. This result holds unconditionally as well as conditional on the level of income.

1.5 Hodrick-Prescott (HP) Filtering

We now consider an alternative detrending method developed by Hodrick and Prescott (1997), known as the Hodrick-Prescott, or HP, filter. The HP filter identifies the cyclical component y_t^c and the trend component y_t^s of a given series y_t, for $t = 1, 2, \ldots, T$, as the solution to the minimization problem

$$\min_{\{y_t^c, y_t^s\}_{t=1}^T} \left\{ \sum_{t=1}^{T} (y_t^c)^2 + \lambda \sum_{t=2}^{T-1} \left[(y_{t+1}^s - y_t^s) - (y_t^s - y_{t-1}^s) \right]^2 \right\} \quad (1.2)$$

subject to (1.1). The appendix to this chapter provides the first-order conditions and solution to this problem. According to this formula, the HP trend is the result of a trade-off between minimizing the variance of the cyclical component and keeping the growth rate of the trend constant. This trade-off is governed by the parameter λ, known as the smoothing parameter. The larger is λ, the more penalized changes in the growth rate of the trend will be. In the limit as λ goes to infinity, the trend component associated with the HP filter coincides with the linear trend. At the other extreme, as λ goes to zero, all variation in the time series is attributed to the trend, and the cyclical component is nil. Business-cycle studies that use data sampled at an annual frequency typically assume a λ value of 100.

Figure 1.3 displays the trend in Argentine real per capita GDP implied by the HP filter for λ equal to 100. The HP filter attributes a significant fraction of the output decline during the lost decade (1980–1989) to the trend. In contrast, the log-quadratic trend is monotonically increasing during this period, implying that the lost decade was a cyclical phenomenon.

Figure 1.4 presents a closer comparison of the cyclical component of Argentine GDP implied by the HP and log-quadratic filters. The correlation between the two cyclical components is 0.70, indicating that for the most part they identify the same cyclical movements. However, the two filters imply quite different amplitudes for the Argentine cycle. The standard deviation of the cyclical component of output is 10.8 percent according to the log-quadratic filter, but only 5.7 percent according to the HP filter. The reason for this large reduction in the volatility of the cycle when applying the HP filter is that under this filter the trend moves much more closely with the raw series.

The value of λ plays an important role in determining the amplitude of the business cycle implied by the HP filter. Ravn and Uhlig (2002) suggest a value of λ of 6.25 for annual data. Under this calibration, the standard deviation of the cyclical component of Argentine GDP drops significantly to 3.6 percent. Figure 1.5 displays the actual Argentine GDP and the trend implied by the HP filter when λ takes the value 6.25. In this case, the trend moves much more closely with the actual series. In particular, the HP filter now attributes the bulk of the 1989 crisis and much of the 2001 crisis to the trend. This is problematic, especially for the 2001 depression. For this was a V-shaped, relatively short contraction followed by a swift recovery. This suggests that the 2001 crisis was a business-cycle phenomenon. In contrast, the HP trend displays a significant contraction in 2001, suggesting that the crisis was to a large extent noncyclical. For this reason, we calibrate λ at 100 for the subsequent analysis.

Table 1.3 displays business-cycle statistics implied by the HP filter for $\lambda = 100$. The central difference between the business-cycle facts derived from quadratic detrending and HP filtering is that under the latter detrending method, all standard deviations fall by

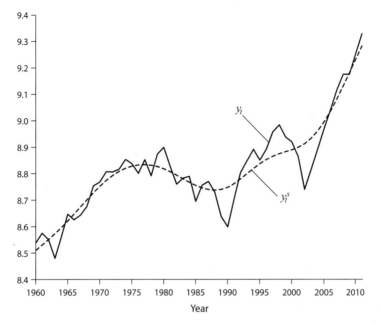

Figure 1.3   HP filtered trend of Argentine output ($\lambda = 100$).

Source: Authors' calculations based on WDI data.

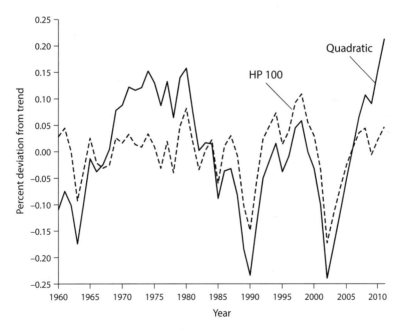

Figure 1.4   Cyclical component of Argentine GDP HP filter 100 versus quadratic trend.

Note: See Figures 1.1 and 1.3.

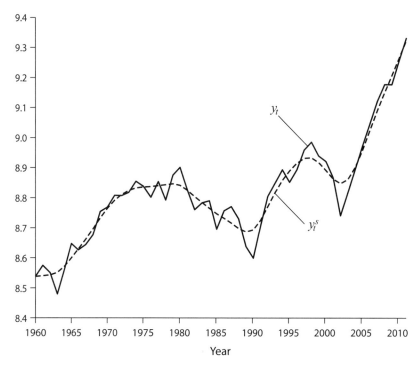

Figure 1.5   Trend of Argentine output according to the HP filter 6.25.

Source: Authors' calculations based on WDI data.

about a third. For example, the average standard deviation of output falls from 6.2 percent under quadratic detrending to 3.8 percent under HP filtering. In all other respects, the log-quadratic and HP filters produce very similar business-cycle facts. In particular, facts 1–10 are robust to applying the HP filter with $\lambda = 100$.

1.6 Growth Rates

Thus far, we have detrended output and all other components of aggregate demand using either the log-quadratic filter or the HP filter. An alternative to these two approaches is to assume that the variables in question are nonstationary in levels but stationary in growth rates. In other words, this approach assumes that the logarithms of output and the components of aggregate demand are integrated of order one.

Table 1.4 displays two statistical tests that provide evidence in favor of modeling these time series as stationary in growth rates and nonstationary in levels. The top panel of the table displays the results of applying the Augmented Dickey-Fuller (ADF) test to the logarithm of real per capita GDP. The ADF test evaluates the null hypothesis that a univariate representation of the time series in question has a unit root against the alternative hypothesis that it does not. The table displays population-weighted cross-country averages of the decision value. The decision value is unity if the null hypothesis is rejected and zero if it

Table 1.3   HP-Filtered Business Cycles

Statistic	All Countries	Poor Countries	Emerging Countries	Rich Countries
Standard Deviations				
σ_y	3.79	4.12	3.98	2.07
σ_c/σ_y	1.08	1.09	1.23	0.87
σ_g/σ_y	2.29	2.53	2.29	1.23
σ_i/σ_y	3.77	3.80	3.79	3.62
σ_x/σ_y	3.50	3.47	3.67	3.42
σ_m/σ_y	3.65	3.70	3.52	3.63
$\sigma_{tb/y}$	1.79	1.64	2.92	0.89
$\sigma_{ca/y}$	1.78	1.71	2.63	1.02
Correlations with y				
y	1.00	1.00	1.00	1.00
c	0.60	0.53	0.68	0.82
g/y	−0.08	0.02	−0.06	−0.56
i	0.69	0.65	0.71	0.86
x	0.19	0.18	0.13	0.30
m	0.32	0.23	0.46	0.58
tb/y	−0.18	−0.08	−0.34	−0.37
tb	−0.20	−0.11	−0.36	−0.36
ca/y	−0.32	−0.29	−0.39	−0.38
ca	−0.33	−0.29	−0.41	−0.37
Serial Correlations				
y	0.46	0.39	0.60	0.55
c	0.36	0.29	0.44	0.53
g	0.51	0.48	0.52	0.65
i	0.34	0.27	0.45	0.46
x	0.47	0.47	0.44	0.46
m	0.42	0.43	0.44	0.33
tb/y	0.39	0.36	0.42	0.47
ca/y	0.39	0.36	0.39	0.54
Means				
tb/y	−1.3	−1.6	−1.4	0.0
$(x+m)/y$	36.5	32.5	46.4	40.4

Notes: See Table 1.1. The variables y, c, g, i, x, and m are HP filtered in logs and expressed as percentage deviations from trend, and the variables tb/y and ca/y are HP filtered in levels and expressed as percentage points of output. The variables tb and ca were scaled by the secular component of GDP and then HP filtered. The parameter λ of the HP filter takes the value 100.

Table 1.4   ADF and KPSS Tests for Output in Poor, Emerging, and Rich Countries

Lags	All Countries	Poor Countries	Emerging Countries	Rich Countries
ADF Test				
0	0.5	0.7	0.1	0.3
1	0.3	0.3	0.0	0.3
2	0.3	0.4	0.0	0.3
3	0.2	0.3	0.0	0.1
AIC for Lag Length	0.8	0.9	1.0	0.5
KPSS Test				
0	1.0	1.0	1.0	1.0
1	1.0	1.0	0.9	0.9
2	1.0	1.0	0.9	0.9
3	0.9	0.9	0.8	0.9
AIC for Lag Length	0.0	0.0	0.0	0.0

Notes: See notes to Table 1.1. Entries correspond to population-weighted decision values for the Augmented Dickey-Fuller (ADF) and Kwiatkowski-Phillips-Schmidt-Shin (KPSS) tests. For each country, a decision value of 1 indicates rejection of the null at 5 percent confidence level and a decision value of 0 indicates failure to reject the null. The null hypothesis is unit root under the ADF test and all roots in the unit circle in the KPSS test. Decision values are based on an F test. AIC stands for the population weighted cross-country average of the lag length suggested by the Akaike information criterion.

cannot be rejected. The table shows that the null hypothesis is rejected in 30 percent of the countries at the lag length of 1 year suggested by the Akaike information criterion (AIC), providing support to the unit-root hypothesis.

The lower panel of Table 1.4 displays the results of applying the Kwiatkowski-Phillips-Schmidt-Shin (KPSS) test to the logarithm of real output. This test evaluates the null hypothesis that the univariate representation of the logarithm of output has no unit root versus the alternative hypothesis that it does. For the lag length favored by the AIC test, the decision value is unity for virtually all countries, which suggests that the hypothesis of stationarity in levels is strongly rejected.

The results of the ADF and KPSS tests have to be interpreted with caution. The reason is that they both are based on the assumption that the time series in question has a univariate representation. As we will see in the following chapters, in general, theoretical models of the business cycle do not imply that output has a univariate representation.

Table 1.5 displays standard deviations, correlations with output growth, and serial correlations of the growth rates of output, private consumption, government consumption, investment, exports, and imports. Most of the ten business-cycle facts obtained under quadratic detrending also hold true when stationarity is induced by first-differencing the data. For example, world business cycles are highly volatile (fact 1). The cross-country average volatility of output growth is twice as large as the volatility of U.S. output growth (not shown). Poor and emerging countries are twice as volatile as rich countries (fact 8). The volatility of consumption growth relative to output growth is much higher in emerging and

Table 1.5 First Differenced Business Cycles

Statistic	All Countries	Poor Countries	Emerging Countries	Rich Countries
Standard Deviations				
$\sigma_{\Delta y}$	4.39	4.94	4.08	2.38
$\sigma_{\Delta c}/\sigma_{\Delta y}$	1.14	1.14	1.34	0.85
$\sigma_{\Delta g}/\sigma_{\Delta y}$	2.14	2.28	2.39	1.17
$\sigma_{\Delta i}/\sigma_{\Delta y}$	3.81	3.80	4.06	3.49
$\sigma_{\Delta x}/\sigma_{\Delta y}$	3.37	3.22	3.98	3.22
$\sigma_{\Delta m}/\sigma_{\Delta y}$	3.60	3.50	3.84	3.76
$\sigma_{tb/y}$	2.34	2.12	3.80	1.25
$\sigma_{ca/y}$	2.16	2.06	3.08	1.39
Correlations with Δy				
Δy	1.00	1.00	1.00	1.00
Δc	0.60	0.54	0.64	0.79
g/y	−0.10	−0.02	−0.18	−0.32
Δi	0.64	0.59	0.66	0.83
Δx	0.21	0.18	0.15	0.42
Δm	0.33	0.26	0.40	0.57
tb/y	−0.10	−0.08	−0.20	−0.07
ca/y	−0.07	−0.06	−0.12	−0.07
Serial Correlations				
Δy	0.29	0.28	0.29	0.32
Δc	0.02	−0.03	0.02	0.27
Δg	0.18	0.14	0.11	0.48
Δi	0.01	−0.01	0.03	0.08
Δx	0.07	0.08	−0.00	0.10
Δm	0.04	0.08	−0.02	−0.04
tb/y	0.61	0.59	0.62	0.69
ca/y	0.57	0.55	0.52	0.71

Notes: See notes to Table 1.1. The variables Δy, Δc, Δg, Δi, Δx, and Δm denote, respectively, the log differences of output, consumption, government consumption, investment, exports, and imports. The variables g/y, tb/y, and ca/y are quadratically detrended in levels. All variables are expressed as percentages.

poor countries than in rich countries (fact 9). The trade-balance share is negatively correlated with output growth (fact 5). Finally, we note that, predictably, the serial correlations of growth rates are much lower than their (detrended) level counterparts.

1.7 Business-Cycle Facts with Quarterly Data

Thus far, we have empirically characterized business cycles around the world using annual data. Because annual data on national income and product accounts are readily available, this choice made it possible to derive business-cycle facts for a large set of countries and for a relatively long period of time. Many business-cycle studies, however, especially those focused on developed economies, use quarterly data. For this reason, in this section we characterize business-cycle facts using quarterly data.

Gathering data at a quarterly frequency turns out to be much more difficult than doing so at an annual frequency. Most countries have some quarterly data, but often sample periods are short, typically less than 20 years. The problem with such short samples is that it becomes difficult to separate the trend from the cyclical component. For this reason, to be included in our quarterly data set, we continue to require that a country have at least 30 years (or 120 quarters) of quarterly data for output, consumption, investment, exports, imports, and public consumption. This restriction reduces significantly the number of countries for which data are available relative to the case of annual data. Specifically, our quarterly panel contains no poor countries, 11 emerging countries, and 17 rich countries. By comparison, our annual panel contains 40 poor countries, 58 emerging countries, and 22 rich countries. The sample period is from 1980:Q1 to 2012:Q4 with two exceptions, Uruguay and Argentina.[6] The quarterly data are available on the book's Web site in the file usg_data_quarterly.xls.

Table 1.6 displays business-cycle statistics at quarterly frequency for emerging and rich countries and for three different ways of measuring the cyclical component, namely, log-quadratic detrending, HP filtering with $\lambda = 1,600$, and first differencing. Overall, the business-cycle facts that emerge from quarterly data are similar to those identified using annual data. In particular, Table 1.6 shows that:

1. Investment, government spending, exports, and imports are more volatile than output, and private consumption is about as volatile as output (fact 3).

2. Consumption, investment, exports, and imports are all procyclical, whereas the trade balance is countercyclical (facts 4 and 5).

3. Output, consumption, investment, exports, and imports are all positively serially correlated (fact 7).

4. Emerging countries are more volatile than rich countries (fact 8).

5. Consumption is more volatile than output in emerging countries, but less volatile than output in rich countries (fact 9).

6. The share of government spending in output is more countercyclical in rich countries than in emerging countries (fact 10).

As expected, the serial correlation of all macroeconomic indicators is higher in quarterly data than in annual data. Table 1.9 in the appendix presents business-cycle statistics for each individual country in the sample.

---

6. The data for Uruguay begins in 1983:Q1, and the time series for private and public consumption in Argentina begin in 1993:Q1.

Table 1.6   Business Cycles in Emerging and Rich Countries, Quarterly Data, 1980:Q1–2012:Q4

Statistic	*Log-Quadratic Time Trend*			*HP Filter* ($\lambda = 1,600$)			*First Differences*		
	All	Emerging	Rich	All	Emerging	Rich	All	Emerging	Rich
Standard Deviations									
σ_y	3.26	4.27	2.74	1.80	2.60	1.38	1.12	1.70	0.81
σ_c/σ_y	0.99	1.23	0.87	1.01	1.32	0.85	1.18	1.48	1.03
σ_g/σ_y	1.46	2.07	1.15	1.30	2.02	0.93	2.07	3.33	1.41
σ_i/σ_y	3.44	3.67	3.31	3.73	3.88	3.65	4.32	4.95	3.99
σ_x/σ_y	3.77	3.97	3.67	4.01	3.80	4.11	4.38	4.65	4.25
σ_m/σ_y	3.52	3.55	3.51	4.44	3.65	4.84	4.60	4.26	4.77
$\sigma_{tb/y}$	1.80	2.93	1.21	1.09	1.95	0.64	1.80	2.93	1.21
Correlations with *y*									
y	1.00	1.00	1.00	1.00	1.00	1.00	1.00	1.00	1.00
c	0.83	0.72	0.88	0.78	0.78	0.78	0.61	0.62	0.61
g/y	−0.43	−0.11	−0.59	−0.58	−0.22	−0.78	−0.16	−0.17	−0.15
i	0.86	0.82	0.88	0.84	0.77	0.87	0.65	0.57	0.70
x	0.17	−0.00	0.26	0.43	−0.05	0.67	0.33	0.04	0.48
m	0.60	0.48	0.66	0.68	0.52	0.76	0.44	0.37	0.47
tb/y	−0.44	−0.52	−0.41	−0.39	−0.56	−0.31	−0.02	−0.11	0.02
tb	−0.44	−0.51	−0.40	−0.39	−0.56	−0.31			
Serial Correlations									
y	0.94	0.91	0.95	0.84	0.80	0.85	0.33	0.24	0.37
c	0.91	0.87	0.93	0.76	0.74	0.76	0.11	0.07	0.13
g	0.87	0.79	0.91	0.56	0.44	0.62	−0.14	−0.25	−0.09
i	0.91	0.87	0.93	0.78	0.71	0.82	0.14	−0.01	0.22
x	0.92	0.90	0.93	0.80	0.73	0.83	0.25	0.06	0.35
m	0.90	0.88	0.91	0.80	0.72	0.84	0.27	0.05	0.38
tb/y	0.88	0.85	0.89	0.70	0.71	0.69	0.88	0.85	0.89
Means									
tb/y	−0.1	0.2	−0.2						
(x + m)/y	43.8	45.7	42.8						

Notes: The variables *y*, *c*, *g*, *i*, *x*, *m*, and $tb \equiv (x - m)$ denote, respectively, output, total private consumption, government spending, investment, exports, imports, and the trade balance. All variables are real and per capita. For quadratic detrending or HP filtering, the variables *y*, *c*, *g*, *i*, *x*, and *m* are detrended in logs and expressed as percentage deviations from trend. For first differencing, *y*, *c*, *g*, *i*, *x*, and *m* denote log differences. The variables *tb/y* and *g/y* are detrended in levels. The variable *tb* is scaled by the secular component of *y* and detrended. The sample contains 11 emerging and 17 rich countries. Moments are averaged across countries using population weights. The sets of emerging and rich countries are defined as all countries with average PPP-converted GDP per capita in U.S. dollars of 2005 during 1990–2009 in the ranges 3,000–25,000 and 25,001–∞, respectively. Rich countries: Australia, Austria, Belgium, Canada, Denmark, Finland, France, Germany, Hong Kong, Italy, Japan, Netherlands, Norway, Sweden, Switzerland, the United Kingdom, and the United States. Emerging countries: Argentina, Israel, Mexico, New Zealand, Peru, Portugal, South Africa, South Korea, Spain, Turkey, and Uruguay. The data sources are presented in the appendix to this chapter.

1.8 Duration and Amplitude of Business Cycles in Emerging and Developed Countries

We have documented that emerging countries display significantly more output volatility than developed countries (fact 8). We now decompose business cycles into contractions and expansions and estimate for each of these phases of the cycle its duration and amplitude. Calderón and Fuentes (2010) adopt a classical approach to characterizing business cycles in emerging and developed countries, consisting of identifying peaks and troughs in the logarithm of real quarterly GDP. They define a peak as an output observation that is larger than the two immediately preceding and succeeding observations. Formally, letting y_t denote the logarithm of real GDP, a peak takes place when $y_t > y_{t+j}$, for $j = -2, -1, 1, 2$. Similarly, a trough is defined as an output observation that is lower than its two immediately preceding and succeeding observations, that is, as a level of y_t satisfying $y_t < y_{t+j}$, for $j = -2, -1, 1, 2$. The duration of a cycle is the period of time between one peak and the next. The duration of a contraction is the period of time between a peak and the next trough. And the duration of an expansion is the period of time that it takes to go from a trough to the next peak. The amplitude of a contraction is the percentage fall in output between a peak and the next trough. The amplitude of an expansion is the percentage increase in output between a trough and the next peak.

Table 1.7 displays the average duration and amplitude of business cycles in two groups of countries, one consisting of 12 Latin American countries and the other of 12 OECD countries. We identify the former group with emerging countries and the latter with developed countries. The table shows that contractions in emerging and developed countries have equal durations of 3–4 quarters. However, the amplitude of contractions is much larger in emerging countries than in developed countries (6.2 versus 2.2 percent of GDP). Comparing the durations of expansions to those of contractions indicates that expansions are much longer than contractions and that expansions are relatively shorter in emerging countries than in developed countries (16 versus 23.8 quarters). At the same time, the amplitude of expansions is about the same in both groups of countries (about 20 percent of GDP). Finally, emerging countries are more cyclical than developed countries in the sense

Table 1.7   Duration and Amplitude of Business Cycles in Emerging and Developed Economies

Group of Countries	Duration		Amplitude	
	Contraction	Expansion	Contraction	Expansion
Latin America	3.5	16.0	6.2	21.3
OECD	3.6	23.8	2.2	20.2

Source: Calderón and Fuentes (2010).
Notes: The data are quarterly real GDP from 1980:Q1 to 2006:Q4. The countries included in the Latin American group are: Argentina, Bolivia, Brazil, Chile, Colombia, Costa Rica, Ecuador, Mexico, Paraguay, Peru, Uruguay, and Venezuela. The countries included in the OECD group are Australia, Canada, France, Germany, Italy, Japan, New Zealand, Portugal, Spain, Sweden, the United Kingdom, and the United States.

that in the former, complete cycles are shorter (20 quarters versus 27 quarters). Summarizing, the general pattern that emerges from this analysis is that emerging countries are more cyclical and experience deeper contractions.

1.9 Appendix

1.9.1 Countries with at Least 30 Years of Annual Data

The sample consists of 120 countries. There are 22 small poor countries, 11 medium-sized poor countries, 7 large poor countries, 41 small emerging countries, 14 medium-sized emerging countries, 3 large emerging countries, 14 small rich countries, 5 medium-sized rich countries, and 3 large rich countries. The individual countries belonging to each group are listed below.

Small Poor Countries Benin, Bhutan, Burkina Faso, Burundi, Central African Republic, Comoros, Gambia, Guyana, Honduras, Lesotho, Malawi, Mali, Mauritania, Mongolia, Niger, Papua New Guinea, Rwanda, Senegal, Sierra Leone, Togo, Zambia, Zimbabwe.

Medium-Sized Poor Countries Cameroon, Congo (Democratic Republic of), Côte d'Ivoire, Ghana, Kenya, Madagascar, Mozambique, Nepal, Sri Lanka, Sudan, Uganda.

Large Poor Countries Bangladesh, China, Ethiopia, India, Indonesia, Pakistan, Philippines.

Small Emerging Countries Albania, Antigua and Barbuda, Bahrain, Barbados, Bolivia, Botswana, Bulgaria, Chile, Costa Rica, Cuba, Cyprus, Dominica, Dominican Republic, Ecuador, El Salvador, Fiji, Gabon, Greece, Grenada, Guatemala, Hungary, Israel, Jordan, Malta, Mauritius, Namibia, New Zealand, Panama, Paraguay, Portugal, Puerto Rico, Seychelles, St. Kitts and Nevis, St. Lucia, St. Vincent and the Grenadines, Suriname, Swaziland, Tonga, Trinidad and Tobago, Tunisia, Uruguay.

Medium-Sized Emerging Countries Algeria, Argentina, Colombia, Iran, Malaysia, Morocco, Peru, South Africa, South Korea, Spain, Syria, Thailand, Turkey, Venezuela.

Large Emerging Countries Brazil, Egypt, Mexico.

Small Rich Countries Austria, Belgium, Denmark, Finland, Hong Kong, Iceland, Ireland, Luxembourg, Macao, Netherlands, Norway, Singapore, Sweden, Switzerland.

Medium-Sized Rich Countries Australia, Canada, France, Italy, United Kingdom.

Large Rich Countries Germany, Japan, United States.

1.9.2 Derivation of the HP Filter

The first-order conditions associated with the problem of choosing the series $\{y_t^c, y_t^s\}_{t=1}^T$ to minimize (1.2) subject to (1.1) are

$$y_1 = y_1^s + \lambda(y_1^s - 2y_2^s + y_3^s),$$

$$y_2 = y_2^s + \lambda(-2y_1^s + 5y_2^s - 4y_3^s + y_4^s),$$

$$y_t = y_t^s + \lambda(y_{t-2}^s - 4y_{t-1}^s + 6y_t^s - 4y_{t+1}^s + y_{t+2}^s); \quad t = 3, \ldots, T-2,$$

$$y_{T-1} = y_{T-1}^s + \lambda(y_{T-3}^s - 4y_{T-2}^s + 5y_{T-1}^s - 2y_T^s),$$

and

$$y_T = y_T^s + \lambda(y_{T-2}^s - 2y_{T-1}^s + y_T^s).$$

Letting $Y^s \equiv [y_1^s \, y_2^s \, \ldots \, y_T^s]$ and $Y \equiv [y_1 \, y_2 \, \ldots \, y_T]$, the above optimality conditions can be written in matrix form as

$$Y = (I + \lambda A)Y^s,$$

where I is the $T \times T$ identity matrix, and A is the following $T \times T$ matrix of constants:

$$A = \begin{bmatrix}
1 & -2 & 1 & 0 & 0 & 0 & 0 & 0 & \cdots & 0 \\
-2 & 5 & -4 & 1 & 0 & 0 & 0 & 0 & \cdots & 0 \\
1 & -4 & 6 & -4 & 1 & 0 & 0 & 0 & \cdots & 0 \\
0 & 1 & -4 & 6 & -4 & 1 & 0 & 0 & \cdots & 0 \\
0 & 0 & 1 & -4 & 6 & -4 & 1 & 0 & \cdots & 0 \\
\vdots & & & & & & & & & \vdots \\
0 & \cdots & 0 & 1 & -4 & 6 & -4 & 1 & 0 & 0 \\
0 & \cdots & 0 & 0 & 1 & -4 & 6 & -4 & 1 & 0 \\
0 & \cdots & 0 & 0 & 0 & 1 & -4 & 6 & -4 & 1 \\
0 & \cdots & 0 & 0 & 0 & 0 & 1 & -4 & 5 & -2 \\
0 & \cdots & 0 & 0 & 0 & 0 & 0 & 1 & -2 & 1
\end{bmatrix}.$$

Solving for Y^s, one obtains

$$Y^s = (I + \lambda A)^{-1} Y.$$

Finally, letting $Y^c \equiv [y_1^c \, y_2^c \, \ldots \, y_T^c]$, we have that

$$Y^c = Y - Y^s.$$

1.9.3 Country-by-Country Business-Cycle Statistics at Annual and Quarterly Frequency

Tables 1.8 and 1.9 present annual and quarterly data on business-cycle statistics for various emerging and rich countries. Further information on these data can be found in the online appendix to this chapter, available on the book's Web site.

Table 1.8 Business Cycles, Log-Quadratic Detrending, Annual Data, 1965–2011

Country	Standard Deviations							Correlations with y							Serial Correlations							Means	
	σ_y	$\frac{\sigma_c}{\sigma_y}$	$\frac{\sigma_g}{\sigma_y}$	$\frac{\sigma_i}{\sigma_y}$	$\frac{\sigma_x}{\sigma_y}$	$\frac{\sigma_m}{\sigma_y}$	$\sigma_{tb/y}$	c	$\frac{g}{y}$	i	x	m	$\frac{tb}{y}$	tb	y	c	g	i	x	m	$\frac{tb}{y}$	$\frac{tb}{y}$	$\frac{x+m}{y}$
Emerging Countries																							
Argentina	10.76	0.86	3.88	2.55	2.15	2.06	3.18	0.71	0.49	0.92	0.19	0.63	−0.40	−0.31	0.85	0.61	0.78	0.83	0.63	0.59	0.60	1.83	20.49
Israel	5.35	1.03	4.31	3.44	4.10	5.86	6.26	0.47	0.61	0.80	0.58	0.67	−0.63	−0.70	0.83	0.44	0.89	0.70	0.87	0.89	0.79	−11.19	77.62
Korea, Rep.	6.09	0.92	1.75	2.39	3.67	2.56	3.44	0.75	−0.07	0.48	−0.62	−0.45	−0.03	−0.09	0.84	0.71	0.77	0.51	0.83	0.78	0.51	−2.42	59.61
Mexico	6.02	0.75	2.49	2.26	2.88	2.64	2.69	0.73	0.49	0.85	−0.20	−0.31	0.04	0.03	0.85	0.61	0.88	0.73	0.78	0.81	0.72	−0.69	35.46
New Zealand	3.86	0.89	1.06	3.61	1.91	2.76	2.64	0.87	−0.31	0.88	0.39	0.57	−0.56	−0.55	0.82	0.77	0.70	0.72	0.68	0.67	0.44	−0.39	56.69
Peru	12.78	1.07	1.79	1.96	2.23	1.76	3.78	0.84	0.57	0.57	0.72	0.84	0.10	0.05	0.92	0.89	0.88	0.67	0.80	0.71	0.63	−0.92	36.65
Portugal	6.67	0.77	1.38	2.48	2.19	1.62	2.82	0.60	0.23	0.59	0.27	0.65	−0.28	−0.41	0.88	0.80	0.84	0.63	0.72	0.53	0.68	−7.41	55.92
South Africa	9.13	0.84	1.14	2.93	1.88	2.36	3.48	0.80	−0.19	0.96	0.70	0.87	−0.47	−0.42	0.96	0.83	0.89	0.89	0.86	0.84	0.65	2.52	52.46
Spain	6.43	0.67	0.58	2.37	1.96	2.44	1.98	0.72	−0.79	0.71	0.50	0.79	−0.57	−0.59	0.93	0.85	0.78	0.85	0.84	0.76	0.70	−1.84	38.12
Turkey	4.92	1.15	3.04	3.45	5.58	4.09	2.46	0.76	0.29	0.78	−0.41	0.04	−0.54	−0.58	0.68	0.72	0.86	0.51	0.72	0.54	0.41	−2.91	29.26
Uruguay	7.12	1.38	1.85	4.66	2.55	2.76	3.17	0.82	−0.09	0.51	−0.11	0.44	−0.67	−0.67	0.81	0.58	0.62	0.37	0.59	0.64	0.71	0.18	39.15
Rich Countries																							
Australia	3.21	0.92	1.52	2.82	2.07	2.32	1.27	0.62	−0.41	0.78	0.24	0.12	0.04	0.03	0.85	0.84	0.84	0.64	0.42	0.49	0.30	−0.93	32.90
Austria	2.81	0.89	1.39	2.51	3.23	3.17	1.13	0.47	−0.34	0.41	0.84	0.88	0.10	0.09	0.83	0.67	0.88	0.58	0.80	0.74	0.55	0.49	71.41
Belgium	3.08	0.65	2.59	3.22	2.23	2.55	1.58	0.25	0.13	0.55	0.62	0.58	−0.11	−0.08	0.85	0.71	0.95	0.67	0.54	0.56	0.81	1.51	120.82
Canada	3.71	0.59	2.01	2.78	3.31	2.65	1.72	0.62	−0.17	0.80	0.34	0.36	0.12	0.14	0.86	0.70	0.93	0.69	0.85	0.78	0.76	1.35	55.43
Denmark	2.98	0.91	2.20	4.23	2.18	2.74	1.95	0.71	−0.49	0.89	0.24	0.43	−0.28	−0.25	0.72	0.62	0.93	0.67	0.62	0.73	0.73	1.08	72.33
Finland	5.35	0.90	0.91	3.39	2.59	2.59	2.86	0.86	−0.65	0.94	0.45	0.75	−0.42	−0.37	0.84	0.80	0.86	0.78	0.81	0.78	0.83	1.68	58.26
France	3.08	0.59	1.17	2.65	3.19	3.65	1.29	0.50	−0.55	0.57	0.65	0.73	−0.31	−0.30	0.89	0.77	0.92	0.59	0.78	0.74	0.76	0.08	42.03
Germany	1.93	0.87	2.43	4.34	4.28	5.24	1.10	0.57	−0.38	0.79	0.15	0.17	−0.07	−0.06	0.54	0.67	0.89	0.66	0.65	0.73	0.68	0.50	54.83
Hong Kong	6.29	1.01	1.30	3.05	2.00	1.98	4.93	0.85	−0.62	0.67	0.78	0.88	−0.14	−0.09	0.78	0.77	0.83	0.71	0.80	0.77	0.82	3.82	237.14
Italy	2.26	0.99	1.86	3.70	4.62	6.12	1.68	0.88	−0.43	0.73	0.29	0.35	−0.17	−0.17	0.64	0.63	0.81	0.50	0.77	0.74	0.67	0.45	41.11
Japan	4.99	0.39	0.89	2.01	3.27	4.13	0.99	0.79	−0.62	0.86	0.17	0.07	0.10	0.15	0.85	0.88	0.88	0.79	0.79	0.77	0.49	1.11	22.23
Netherlands	4.39	0.94	1.86	2.04	1.60	1.51	1.27	0.62	0.01	0.46	0.45	0.47	0.02	0.12	0.90	0.89	0.95	0.77	0.58	0.52	0.57	3.60	108.67
Norway	2.89	1.65	1.34	4.57	2.80	2.47	3.82	0.42	−0.54	0.31	0.52	0.42	0.14	0.19	0.84	0.68	0.50	0.74	0.62	0.64	0.60	4.84	73.25
Sweden	4.44	0.57	1.71	2.61	2.33	2.48	1.44	0.75	−0.03	0.75	0.58	0.66	−0.20	−0.09	0.87	0.77	0.96	0.65	0.78	0.72	0.66	2.95	64.99
Switzerland	2.34	0.54	1.37	3.60	2.62	3.32	0.98	0.40	−0.34	0.94	0.70	0.71	−0.24	−0.16	0.74	0.72	0.77	0.67	0.61	0.66	0.56	4.35	77.53
United Kingdom	3.36	1.39	2.02	3.17	2.71	2.86	1.40	0.83	−0.32	0.89	0.22	0.51	−0.55	−0.57	0.80	0.86	0.92	0.67	0.78	0.69	0.68	−0.78	51.21
United States	2.94	1.02	1.93	3.52	3.49	3.24	0.94	0.90	−0.32	0.80	−0.10	0.31	−0.51	−0.54	0.75	0.82	0.91	0.67	0.75	0.63	0.79	−1.54	18.89

Notes: The variables y, c, g, i, x, m, and $tb \equiv (x - m)$ denote, respectively, output, total private consumption, government spending, investment, exports, imports, and the trade balance. All variables are real and per capita. The variables y, c, g, i, x, and m are detrended in logs and expressed as percentage deviations from trend. The variables tb/y and g/y are detrended in levels. The variable tb is scaled by the secular component of y and detrended. This table includes all countries for which we have not only 30 years of annual data but also 30 years of quarterly data. The country-specific sample periods and data sources are given in the online appendix to this chapter, available on the book's Web site.

Table 1.9 Business Cycles, Log-Quadratic Detrending, and Quarterly Data, 1980:Q1–2012:Q4

Country	Standard Deviations σ_y	$\frac{\sigma_c}{\sigma_y}$	$\frac{\sigma_g}{\sigma_y}$	$\frac{\sigma_i}{\sigma_y}$	$\frac{\sigma_x}{\sigma_y}$	$\frac{\sigma_m}{\sigma_y}$	σ_{tb}/y	Correlations with y: c	$\frac{g}{y}$	i	x	m	$\frac{tb}{y}$	tb	Serial Correlations: y	c	g	i	x	m	$\frac{tb}{y}$	Means $\frac{tb}{y}$	$\frac{x+m}{y}$
Emerging Countries																							
Argentina	7.71	1.11	1.41	3.04	2.38	4.24	3.72	0.75	0.13	0.91	−0.47	0.52	−0.88	−0.87	0.95	0.95	0.71	0.93	0.88	0.96	0.93	2.18	23.91
Israel	2.63	2.08	2.06	4.84	4.00	3.54	2.88	0.33	−0.30	0.54	−0.02	−0.03	0.08	0.03	0.81	0.91	0.71	0.92	0.88	0.84	0.78	−7.53	77.87
Mexico	3.44	1.29	2.40	3.51	5.53	4.34	3.04	0.75	0.02	0.82	−0.09	0.43	−0.45	−0.43	0.92	0.87	0.77	0.88	0.90	0.90	0.91	1.11	41.79
New Zealand	3.99	0.85	0.94	3.54	1.97	2.66	1.87	0.86	−0.61	0.85	0.30	0.44	−0.37	−0.36	0.90	0.86	0.61	0.94	0.87	0.88	0.69	0.07	57.95
Peru	7.26	0.97	2.51	2.53	2.58	2.02	3.66	0.81	0.45	0.71	0.28	0.61	−0.18	−0.20	0.92	0.87	0.82	0.88	0.90	0.75	0.84	0.13	38.08
Portugal	4.43	1.11	1.75	3.00	1.92	1.96	3.11	0.90	0.44	0.86	−0.17	0.71	−0.72	−0.78	0.89	0.89	0.93	0.95	0.91	0.88	0.94	−8.14	64.79
South Africa	2.80	1.30	2.67	4.83	4.62	5.19	3.03	0.82	0.01	0.61	0.41	0.54	−0.28	−0.26	0.95	0.89	0.89	0.67	0.83	0.88	0.73	2.35	52.51
South Korea	3.05	1.51	1.42	4.07	3.38	2.42	3.57	0.37	−0.26	0.90	−0.25	0.34	−0.49	−0.47	0.87	0.90	0.82	0.86	0.88	0.79	0.85	1.35	71.75
Spain	4.16	0.97	1.15	3.69	3.00	3.06	2.12	0.94	−0.59	0.93	0.24	0.76	−0.79	−0.80	0.98	0.95	0.54	0.95	0.96	0.96	0.94	−1.83	47.68
Turkey	4.46	1.15	2.51	3.67	3.91	2.73	2.08	0.66	−0.38	0.87	−0.01	0.39	−0.61	−0.62	0.86	0.75	0.77	0.88	0.93	0.84	0.77	−1.12	36.80
Uruguay	7.40	1.39	0.96	3.35	1.77	2.66	3.18	0.94	−0.35	0.78	0.73	0.89	−0.65	−0.66	0.96	0.91	0.84	0.78	0.80	0.86	0.68	−1.33	47.54
Rich Countries																							
Australia	2.46	1.24	0.93	3.42	3.17	3.09	1.21	0.69	−0.68	0.78	0.33	0.73	−0.46	−0.47	0.95	0.96	0.64	0.88	0.82	0.88	0.82	−1.18	36.83
Austria	2.04	0.63	0.89	2.37	4.35	3.75	1.36	0.71	−0.79	0.63	0.83	0.84	0.39	0.41	0.94	0.81	0.88	0.96	0.96	0.95	0.84	1.31	83.28
Belgium	2.27	0.65	1.21	3.75	3.06	3.19	1.19	0.71	−0.47	0.74	0.53	0.58	−0.14	−0.11	0.96	0.91	0.79	0.96	0.89	0.87	0.44	2.18	138.62
Canada	3.48	0.66	1.16	2.18	4.16	3.10	2.02	0.84	−0.80	0.84	0.54	0.52	0.44	0.46	0.97	0.95	0.96	0.96	0.97	0.96	0.93	1.86	62.22
Denmark	3.12	0.94	0.88	4.33	2.40	2.91	1.49	0.78	−0.60	0.89	0.62	0.81	−0.59	−0.52	0.92	0.87	0.93	0.88	0.92	0.94	0.81	3.66	79.42
Finland	5.70	0.67	0.81	3.27	2.73	1.91	2.79	0.83	−0.73	0.86	0.34	0.61	−0.04	0.02	0.97	0.95	0.96	0.77	0.93	0.85	0.82	3.30	66.20
France	2.06	0.75	0.73	4.27	4.09	3.90	0.90	0.84	−0.82	0.86	0.65	0.79	−0.17	−0.18	0.97	0.92	0.96	0.94	0.96	0.95	0.89	−0.18	48.71
Germany	2.17	0.72	0.91	3.24	3.66	3.60	1.09	0.73	−0.66	0.88	0.34	0.44	−0.11	−0.08	0.90	0.80	0.78	0.93	0.91	0.92	0.89	1.38	61.22
Hong Kong	6.35	1.05	0.87	2.69	2.23	2.16	4.83	0.87	−0.88	0.59	0.90	0.93	0.01	0.09	0.96	0.96	0.75	0.88	0.96	0.95	0.89	5.44	288.07
Italy	2.44	0.98	1.80	3.07	4.14	4.33	1.28	0.91	−0.26	0.93	0.43	0.72	−0.55	−0.56	0.96	0.93	0.93	0.97	0.94	0.93	0.87	0.63	46.54
Japan	2.92	0.68	0.76	2.88	4.12	5.13	0.96	0.90	−0.87	0.95	0.16	0.26	−0.30	−0.27	0.95	0.89	0.83	0.96	0.90	0.93	0.92	1.37	23.17
Netherlands	3.23	1.34	0.76	2.45	2.09	2.13	1.13	0.91	−0.72	0.67	0.62	0.66	−0.13	0.00	0.96	0.97	0.86	0.82	0.92	0.92	0.72	5.22	121.34
Norway	3.41	1.16	1.27	3.66	3.01	1.98	4.12	0.38	−0.63	0.45	0.64	0.61	0.26	0.32	0.93	0.85	0.81	0.84	0.90	0.82	0.87	8.91	72.44
Sweden	3.92	0.77	0.69	3.29	2.84	2.54	1.46	0.87	−0.73	0.83	0.57	0.69	0.02	0.15	0.95	0.95	0.88	0.88	0.95	0.94	0.76	4.66	75.52
Switzerland	2.45	0.54	1.36	3.63	2.69	3.27	1.13	0.44	−0.36	0.89	0.69	0.70	−0.16	−0.08	0.95	0.92	0.95	0.91	0.93	0.94	0.69	4.51	78.06
United Kingdom	3.64	0.97	1.35	3.06	1.77	1.86	1.25	0.95	−0.24	0.79	0.30	0.57	−0.40	−0.43	0.98	0.96	0.94	0.87	0.86	0.85	0.85	−0.87	54.67
United States	2.60	0.97	1.34	3.57	3.90	3.21	1.12	0.95	−0.50	0.91	0.02	0.85	−0.73	−0.75	0.96	0.96	0.97	0.95	0.96	0.90	0.68	−2.56	22.31

Notes: The variables y, c, g, i, x, m, and $tb = (x - m)$ denote, respectively, output, total private consumption, government spending, investment, exports, imports, and the trade balance. All variables are real and per capita. The variables y, c, g, i, x, and m are detrended in logs and expressed as percentage deviations from trend. The variables tb/y and g/y are detrended in levels. The variable tb is scaled by the secular component of y and detrended. Only countries with at least 30 years of quarterly data are included. The country-specific sample periods and data sources are given in the online appendix to this chapter, available on the book's Web site.

1.10 Exercises

1.1 (Business-Cycle Regularities in South Korea and the United States) In this exercise, you are asked to analyze the extent to which the numbered business-cycle facts discussed in this chapter apply to South Korea and the United States. To this end compute the relevant business-cycle statistics for the following four alternative detrending methods: (i) log-linear detrending; (ii) log-quadratic detrending; (iii) HP filtering with $\lambda = 100$; and (iv) HP filtering with $\lambda = 6.25$. Make a 2×2 graph showing the natural logarithm of real per capita GDP and the trend, one panel per trend. Discuss how the detrending method influences the volatility of the cyclical component of output. Also discuss which detrending method identifies recessions for the United States most in line with the NBER business-cycle dates. The data should be downloaded from the World Bank's WDI database. As the sample period for South Korea use 1960–2011, and for the United States use 1965–2011. Specifically, use the following time series to construct the required business-cycle statistics:

GDP per capita (constant LCU)	NY.GDP.PCAP.KN
Household final consumption expenditure, etc. (percentage of GDP)	NE.CON.PETC.ZS
Gross capital formation (percentage of GDP)	NE.GDI.TOTL.ZS
General government final consumption expenditure (percentage of GDP)	NE.CON.GOVT.ZS
Imports of goods and services (percentage of GDP)	NE.IMP.GNFS.ZS
Exports of goods and services (percentage of GDP)	NE.EXP.GNFS.ZS

An Open Endowment Economy

The purpose of this chapter is to build a canonical dynamic, general equilibrium model of the open economy and contrast its main predictions with the data.

The model economy we study here is simple enough to allow for a full characterization of its equilibrium dynamics using pen and paper. The economy is inhabited by households that receive an exogenous but stochastic endowment of perishable goods each period. In addition, households have access to an internationally traded bond, which they use to smooth consumption in response to random income disturbances. In turn, consumption smoothing gives rise to equilibrium movements in the trade balance and the current account.

2.1 The Model Economy

Consider an economy populated by a large number of infinitely-lived households with preferences described by the utility function

$$E_0 \sum_{t=0}^{\infty} \beta^t U(c_t), \tag{2.1}$$

where c_t denotes consumption; $\beta \in (0, 1)$ denotes the subjective discount factor; U denotes a period utility function, assumed to be continuously differentiable, strictly increasing, and strictly concave; and E_t denotes the mathematical expectations operator conditional on information available in period t.

Each period, households receive an endowment of goods and have the ability to borrow or lend in a risk-free internationally traded bond. The sequential budget constraint of the representative household is given by

$$c_t + (1+r)d_{t-1} = y_t + d_t, \tag{2.2}$$

where d_{t-1} denotes the debt position assumed in period $t-1$ and due in period t, r denotes the interest rate, assumed to be constant, and y_t is an exogenous and stochastic endowment of goods. The endowment process represents the sole source of uncertainty in this economy. The above constraint states that the household has two sources of funds, the endowment, y_t, and debt, d_t. It uses those funds to purchase consumption goods, c_t, and pay back the principal and interest on its outstanding debt, $(1+r)d_{t-1}$. Households are assumed to be subject to the following sequence of borrowing constraints that prevents them from engaging in Ponzi games:

$$\lim_{j\to\infty} E_t \frac{d_{t+j}}{(1+r)^j} \leq 0. \tag{2.3}$$

This limit condition states that the household's debt position must be expected to grow at a rate lower than the interest rate r in the long run.

The optimal allocation of consumption and debt will always feature the no-Ponzi-game constraint (2.3) holding with strict equality. To see this, suppose, contrary to this claim, that at some $t \geq 0$, the optimal allocation $\{c_{t+j}, d_{t+j}\}_{j=0}^\infty$ satisfies

$$\lim_{j\to\infty} E_t \frac{d_{t+1}}{(1+r)^j} = -\alpha; \quad \alpha > 0.$$

Then consider the alternative consumption process

$$c'_{t+j} = \begin{cases} c_{t+j} + \alpha & \text{if } j = 0 \\ c_{t+j} & \text{if } j > 0. \end{cases}$$

Clearly, because the period utility function is assumed to be strictly increasing, the process $\{c'_{t+j}\}_{j=0}^\infty$ must be preferred to the process $\{c_{t+j}\}_{j=0}^\infty$. Now construct the associated alternative debt process, $\{d'_{t+j}\}_{j=0}^\infty$, as follows. For $j = 0$, the budget constraint (2.2) dictates

$$\begin{aligned} d'_t &= (1+r)d_{t-1} + c'_t - y_t \\ &= (1+r)d_{t-1} + c_t + \alpha - y_t \\ &= d_t + \alpha. \end{aligned}$$

Note that the right-hand side of the first equality features d_{t-1} and not d'_{t-1}. This is because we are not disturbing the equilibrium allocation before period t. For $j = 1$, the budget constraint (2.2) implies that

$$\begin{aligned} d'_{t+1} &= (1+r)d'_t + c'_{t+1} - y_{t+1} \\ &= (1+r)(d_t + \alpha) + c_{t+1} - y_{t+1} \\ &= d_{t+1} + (1+r)\alpha. \end{aligned}$$

Continuing with this argument, we have that for $j \geq 0$,

$$d'_{t+j} = d_{t+j} + (1+r)^j \alpha.$$

We have constructed the alternative process for debt to ensure that it satisfies the sequential budget constraint (2.2) for all dates and states. It remains to check that it also satisfies the no-Ponzi-game constraint (2.3). To see that this is the case, use the above equation to write

$$\lim_{j \to \infty} E_t \frac{d'_{t+j}}{(1+r)^j} = \lim_{j \to \infty} E_t \frac{[d_{t+j} + (1+r)^j \alpha]}{(1+r)^j}$$

$$= \lim_{j \to \infty} E_t \frac{d_{t+j}}{(1+r)^j} + \alpha$$

$$= -\alpha + \alpha$$

$$= 0.$$

Since the consumption process $\{c'_{t+j}\}_{j=0}^{\infty}$ is preferred to the process $\{c_{t+j}\}_{j=0}^{\infty}$ and satisfies all constraints of the household, we have that the latter process cannot be optimal. This completes the proof that at the optimal allocation, the no-Ponzi-game constraint (2.3) must hold with equality. When the no-Ponzi-game constraint holds with equality, it is called the *transversality condition*.

The household chooses processes for c_t and d_t for $t \geq 0$, so as to maximize (2.1) subject to (2.2) and (2.3). The Lagrangian of this problem in period 0 is given by

$$\mathcal{L}_0 = E_0 \sum_{t=0}^{\infty} \beta^t \{U(c_t) + \lambda_t[d_t + y_t - (1+r)d_{t-1} - c_t]\},$$

where $\beta^t \lambda_t$ denotes the Lagrange multiplier associated with the sequential budget constraint in period t. The optimality conditions associated with this problem are (2.2), (2.3) holding with equality,

$$U'(c_t) = \lambda_t,$$

and

$$\lambda_t = \beta(1+r)E_t\lambda_{t+1}.$$

The last two conditions are, respectively, the derivatives of the Lagrangian with respect to c_t and d_t set equal to zero. Combining these expressions to eliminate λ_t yields the following optimality condition, often referred to as the *Euler equation*:

$$U'(c_t) = \beta(1+r)E_tU'(c_{t+1}). \tag{2.4}$$

The interpretation of this expression is that at the margin, the household is indifferent between consuming a unit of good today or saving it and consuming it the next period along with the interest. To see this, note that if the household reduces consumption by one unit in period t, its period-t utility falls by approximately $U'(c_t)$. If instead the household invests this unit of consumption in the international bond market, in period $t+1$ it will receive $1+r$ units of consumption, which, if consumed, increase the period-$(t+1)$ utility by approximately $(1+r)U'(c_{t+1})$. From the perspective of period t the expected present value of this increase in period-$(t+1)$ utility equals $\beta(1+r)E_tU'(c_{t+1})$.

All households are assumed to have identical preferences, realizations of the endowment process, and initial asset holdings. Therefore, we can interpret c_t and d_t as the aggregate per capita levels of consumption and net foreign liabilities, respectively. Then a rational expectations equilibrium can be defined as a pair of processes $\{c_t, d_t\}_{t=0}^{\infty}$ satisfying (2.2), (2.3) holding with equality, and (2.4), given the initial condition d_{-1} and the exogenous driving process $\{y_t\}_{t=0}^{\infty}$.

Combining the household's sequential budget constraint (2.2) and the no-Ponzi-game constraint (2.3) holding with equality yields an intertemporal resource constraint. To see this, begin by expressing the sequential budget constraint in period t as

$$(1+r)d_{t-1} = y_t - c_t + d_t.$$

Eliminate d_t by combining this expression with itself evaluated one period forward:

$$(1+r)d_{t-1} = y_t - c_t + \frac{y_{t+1} - c_{t+1}}{1+r} + \frac{d_{t+1}}{1+r}.$$

Repeat this procedure s times to obtain

$$(1+r)d_{t-1} = \sum_{j=0}^{s} \frac{y_{t+j} - c_{t+j}}{(1+r)^j} + \frac{d_{t+s}}{(1+r)^s}.$$

Apply expectations conditional on information available at time t, and then take the limit for $s \to \infty$ using condition (2.3) holding with equality, to get the following intertemporal resource constraint:

$$(1+r)d_{t-1} = \sum_{j=0}^{\infty} \frac{E_t(y_{t+j} - c_{t+j})}{(1+r)^j}, \tag{2.5}$$

which says that at every point in time, the economy must be expected to put aside a stream of resources, $\{y_{t+j} - c_{t+j}\}_{j=0}^{\infty}$, large enough in present discounted value to cover the outstanding external debt.

A key macroeconomic indicator in open economy business-cycle analysis is the *trade balance,* which is defined as the difference between exports and imports of goods and services. In the present model, there is a single good. Therefore, in any given period, the country either exports or imports this good, depending on whether the endowment is higher or lower than consumption. It follows that the trade balance is given by the difference between output and consumption. Formally, letting tb_t denote the trade balance in period t, we have that

$$tb_t \equiv y_t - c_t. \tag{2.6}$$

Combining this definition with equation (2.5) yields

$$(1+r)d_{t-1} = \sum_{j=0}^{\infty} \frac{E_t tb_{t+j}}{(1+r)^j}.$$

Intuitively, this equation says that the country's initial net foreign debt position must equal the present discounted value of current and future expected trade surpluses. Can a country run a perpetual trade deficit? The answer to this question depends on its initial debt position. If the country is a debtor (i.e., if $d_{t-1} > 0$), then it must be expected to run a trade surplus in at least one period; that is, $E_t tb_{t+j}$ must be positive for at least one $j \geq 0$. However, if the economy starts as a net creditor of the rest of the world (i.e., if $d_{t-1} < 0$), then it could in principle expect to run a perpetual trade deficit; that is, tb_{t+j} could in principle be negative for all $j \geq 0$.

We now make two additional assumptions that greatly facilitate the analysis. First, we require that the subjective and market rates of discount, β and $1/(1+r)$, respectively, be equal to each other:

$$\beta(1+r) = 1.$$

This assumption eliminates long-run growth in consumption when the economy features no stochastic shocks.

Second, we assume that the period utility index is quadratic and given by

$$U(c) = -\frac{1}{2}(c - \bar{c})^2, \tag{2.7}$$

with $c \leq \bar{c}$, where $\bar{c} > 0$ is a satiation point. This specification has the appealing feature of allowing for a closed-form solution of the model. After imposing the above two assumptions, our model becomes essentially Hall's (1978) permanent income model of consumption. In particular, the Euler condition (2.4) now becomes

$$c_t = E_t c_{t+1}, \tag{2.8}$$

which says that consumption follows a *random walk:* at each point in time, households expect to maintain a constant level of consumption next period. Indeed, households expect all future levels of consumption to be equal to its present level. To see this, lead the Euler equation (2.8) one period to obtain $c_{t+1} = E_{t+1} c_{t+2}$. Take expectations conditional on information available at time t, and use the law of iterated expectations to obtain $E_t c_{t+1} = E_t c_{t+2}$. Finally, again use the Euler equation (2.8) to replace $E_t c_{t+1}$ by c_t, which gives $c_t = E_t c_{t+2}$. Repeating this procedure j times, we can deduce that

$$E_t c_{t+j} = c_t,$$

for all $j \geq 0$.

To find the closed-form solution for consumption, use the above expression to get rid of expected future consumption in the intertemporal resource constraint (2.5) to obtain, after rearranging terms,

$$c_t = \frac{r}{1+r} \sum_{j=0}^{\infty} \frac{E_t y_{t+j}}{(1+r)^j} - r d_{t-1}. \tag{2.9}$$

The first term on the right-hand side is known as *nonfinancial permanent income,* and we denote it by y_t^P:

$$y_t^P \equiv \frac{r}{1+r} \sum_{j=0}^{\infty} \frac{E_t y_{t+j}}{(1+r)^j}. \tag{2.10}$$

The nonfinancial permanent income is a weighted average of the lifetime stream of expected endowments. To see this, note that the weights multiplying the expected endowments, $\frac{r}{1+r} \frac{1}{(1+r)^j}$, for $j \geq 0$, are all positive and add up to 1: $\frac{r}{1+r} \sum_{j=0}^{\infty} \frac{1}{(1+r)^j} = 1$. Thus, equation (2.9) states that every period the optimal contingent plan is to spend the permanent income on consumption and interest payments,

$$c_t + r d_{t-1} = y_t^P. \tag{2.11}$$

Because d_{t-1} is predetermined in t and y_t^P is exogenously given, this expression represents the closed-form solution for c_t. Combining the above expression with the sequential budget constraint (2.2) yields the closed-form solution for the equilibrium level of the country's external debt:

$$d_t - d_{t-1} = y_t^P - y_t. \tag{2.12}$$

Intuitively, the economy borrows from (lends to) the rest of the world when permanent income is higher (lower) than current income.

The *current account* is defined as the sum of the trade balance and net investment income on the country's *net foreign asset position,* $-r d_{t-1}$. Formally, letting ca_t denote the current account in period t, we have that

$$ca_t \equiv tb_t - r d_{t-1}. \tag{2.13}$$

Combining this expression with the definition of the trade balance given in (2.6) and with the sequential budget constraint (2.2), we obtain the following alternative expression for the current account:

$$ca_t = -(d_t - d_{t-1}). \tag{2.14}$$

This expression, known as the fundamental balance-of-payments identity, says that the current account equals the change in the country's net foreign asset position. In other words, a current account deficit (surplus) is associated with an increase (reduction) in the country's external debt of equal magnitude. Combining (2.12) and (2.14) yields

$$ca_t = y_t - y_t^P, \tag{2.15}$$

which says that the country runs current account surpluses (deficits) when current income is higher (lower) than permanent income. Recalling that the current account equals the trade balance plus interest income, $ca_t = tb_t - rd_{t-1}$, we can use equation (2.15) to obtain the equilibrium trade balance

$$tb_t = y_t - y_t^p + rd_{t-1}, \qquad (2.16)$$

which states that the trade balance responds countercyclically (procyclically) to changes in current income if permanent income increases by more (less) than current income in response to increases in current income.

Because expectations of future income, as embedded in the definition of permanent income, feature so prominently in the determination of the current account, the present model is known as the *intertemporal approach to the balance of payments*. It is clear from the analysis conducted thus far that the equilibrium behavior of the current account and external debt depends crucially on the interaction between current income and permanent income. In turn, this interaction is governed by the properties of the stochastic process followed by the endowment. We address this issue next.

2.2 Stationary Income Shocks

Assume that the endowment follows a first-order autoregressive (AR(1)) process of the form

$$y_t = \rho y_{t-1} + \epsilon_t,$$

where ϵ_t denotes an i.i.d. innovation, and the parameter $\rho \in (-1, 1)$ defines the serial correlation of the endowment process. The larger ρ is, the more persistent the endowment process will be. Given this autoregressive structure of the endowment, the j-period-ahead forecast of output in period t is given by

$$E_t y_{t+j} = \rho^j y_t.$$

Using this expression to eliminate expectations of future income from identity (2.10) delivers the following expression for permanent income when the endowment follows an AR(1) process:

$$y_t^p = \frac{r}{1 + r - \rho} y_t. \qquad (2.17)$$

If the endowment process is highly persistent ($\rho \to 1$), permanent income is close to the endowment itself. This makes sense, because any innovation in the current endowment is expected to affect all future endowments. At the other extreme, if the endowment is highly transitory ($\rho \to 0$), only a small fraction $r/(1 + r)$ of the current endowment is regarded as permanent. Combining the above expression (2.17) with equation (2.11), we obtain

$$c_t = \frac{r}{1 + r - \rho} y_t - rd_{t-1}. \qquad (2.18)$$

Consider now the effect of an innovation in the endowment. Because ρ is less than unity, we have that a unit increase in y_t leads to a less-than-unit increase in consumption. The remaining income is saved to allow for higher future consumption.

Combining equation (2.18) with the definitions of the trade balance (2.6) and of the current account (2.13), we can write

$$tb_t = rd_{t-1} + \frac{1 - \rho}{1 + r - \rho} y_t \tag{2.19}$$

and

$$ca_t = \frac{1 - \rho}{1 + r - \rho} y_t. \tag{2.20}$$

Note that the current account inherits the stochastic process of the underlying endowment shock. Because the current account equals the change in the country's net foreign asset position—that is, $ca_t = -(d_t - d_{t-1})$—it follows that the equilibrium evolution of the stock of external debt is given by

$$d_t = d_{t-1} - \frac{1 - \rho}{1 + r - \rho} y_t. \tag{2.21}$$

According to this expression, external debt follows a random walk and is therefore non-stationary. A temporary increase in the endowment produces a gradual but permanent decline in the stock of foreign liabilities. Because the long-run behavior of the trade balance is governed by the dynamics of external debt (see equation (2.19)), a temporary increase in the endowment leads to a long-run deterioration in the trade balance.

Let's examine in more detail the response of the endogenous variables of the model to an unanticipated increase in output. Two polar cases are of interest: purely temporary endowment shocks ($\rho = 0$) and permanent endowment shocks ($\rho \to 1$). When endowment shocks are purely transitory, equation (2.18) implies that only a small part of the increase in the endowment, a fraction $r/(1 + r)$, is allocated to current consumption. Most of the endowment increase, a fraction $1/(1 + r)$, is saved in the form of foreign bonds. As a result the trade balance and the current account both increase by $1/(1 + r)$ (see equations (2.19) and (2.20)) and the external debt falls by $1/(1 + r)$ (see equation (2.21)). The intuition behind this result is clear. Because income is expected to return quickly to its long-run level, households smooth consumption by eating a tiny part of the current windfall and leaving the rest for future consumption. In this case, the current account plays the role of a shock absorber. The economy saves in response to positive income shocks via current account surpluses and borrows from the rest of the world to finance negative income shocks via current account deficits. Importantly, the current account is procyclical. That is, it improves during expansions and deteriorates during contractions. This prediction of the model is at odds with the data. As documented in Chapter 1, in small open economies the current account is countercyclical and not procyclical as predicted by the model studied here.

At the other extreme, when endowment shocks are permanent ($\rho \to 1$), households allocate all increase in output to current consumption (see equation (2.18)). As a result, the trade balance, the current account, and the stock of external debt remain unchanged (see equations (2.19), (2.20), and (2.21)). Intuitively, when endowment shocks are permanent, an increase in output today is accompanied by an increase in output of the same magnitude in all future periods. As a result, the household does not need to save part of the current increase in output to smooth consumption. In this case, the current account does not play the role of a shock absorber. Rather, households adjust consumption up or down in response to output shocks.

The two polar cases suggest that the role of shock absorber of the current account increases with the temporariness of the endowment shock. In turn, this implies that the more temporary the endowment shock is, the more volatile the current account will be. This implication can be clearly seen from equation (2.20). When $\rho = 0$, the standard deviation of the current account equals $\sigma_y/(1 + r)$, which is close to the volatility of the endowment itself, denoted σ_y, for small values of r. At the other extreme, when $\rho \to 1$, the standard deviation of the current account is zero.

The intermediate case of a gradually trend-reverting endowment process, which takes place when $\rho \in (0, 1)$, is illustrated in Figure 2.1. It displays the economy's response to a positive endowment shock, assuming that the initial external debt is zero. In response to the endowment shock, consumption experiences a once-and-for-all increase. This expansion is smaller than the initial increase in income. As a result, the trade balance and the current account improve. After their initial increase, these two variables converge gradually to their respective long-run levels. The trade balance converges to a new long-run level lower than the preshock one. This is because in the long run the economy settles at a lower level of external debt, whose service requires a smaller trade surplus. Thus, a positive endowment shock produces a short-run improvement but a long-run deterioration in the trade balance.

Before moving on, let us take stock of the key results derived thus far. The open economy model we are studying captures the essential elements of what has become known as the intertemporal approach to the current account. In equilibrium, consumption, external debt, the trade balance, and the current account are driven by perceived differences between current and permanent income. A central implication of this theory is that external borrowing is guided by the principle "finance temporary shocks and adjust to permanent shocks." When output is assumed to follow an AR(1) process, a weakness of the model is the counterfactual prediction of procyclical trade and current account balances.

Equation (2.15) provides the clue for why the present model fails to deliver a countercyclical current account when the endowment process is AR(1). It says that the current account deteriorates in response to an increase in current income if and only if the increase in current income is smaller than the associated increase in permanent income. But if the endowment process is AR(1), with $0 < \rho < 1$, an increase in y_t is always accompanied by the expectation of a declining path of income, and thus by an increase in permanent income that is less than the increase in current income. Specifically, equation (2.17) shows that an increase in y_t increases y_t^p by a fraction $r/(1 + r - \rho) < 1$. This result suggests that one way to generate a countercyclical current account would be to formulate an endowment process with the property that, in response to an increase in current income, permanent income increases by more than current income. We turn to this task next.

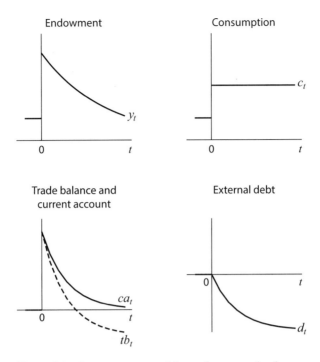

Figure 2.1   Response to a positive endowment shock.

2.3 Stationary Income Shocks: AR(2) Processes

Suppose the endowment process is autoregressive of order two (AR(2)). Specifically, assume that

$$y_t = \rho_1 y_{t-1} + \rho_2 y_{t-2} + \epsilon_t, \tag{2.22}$$

where ϵ_t denotes an i.i.d. shock, and the parameters ρ_1 and ρ_2 are such that this process is stationary, or mean reverting. By mean reversion, we mean that the conditional expectation $E_t y_{t+j}$ exists for all $j \geq 0$ and that

$$\lim_{j \to \infty} E_t y_{t+j} = 0$$

for all $t \geq 0$ and for any initial condition (y_{t-1}, y_{t-2}). To establish the conditions under which this endowment process is mean reverting, let's begin by writing it as a first-order vector autoregressive process. To this end, define

$$Y_t = \begin{bmatrix} y_t \\ y_{t-1} \end{bmatrix}.$$

Then we can write the endowment process (2.22) as

$$Y_{t+1} = R\, Y_t + \begin{bmatrix} \epsilon_{t+1} \\ 0 \end{bmatrix},$$

with

$$R \equiv \begin{bmatrix} \rho_1 & \rho_2 \\ 1 & 0 \end{bmatrix}.$$

Then we have that

$$E_t Y_{t+j} = R^j Y_t. \tag{2.23}$$

Thus, the mean-reversion condition $\lim_{j \to \infty} E_t y_{t+j} = 0$ is satisfied if and only if both eigenvalues of the matrix R lie within the unit circle. Therefore, we need both roots of the characteristic equation

$$\lambda^2 - \rho_1 \lambda - \rho_2 = 0$$

to be less than unity in absolute value. This latter requirement is satisfied as long as

$$\rho_2 < 1 - \rho_1,$$

$$\rho_2 < 1 + \rho_1,$$

and

$$\rho_2 > -1$$

(see, for example, Zellner 1971, 196).

Figure 2.2 presents an impulse response of output to a unit innovation in period 0 when $\rho_1 > 1$ and $\rho_2 < 0$. In this case, the impulse response is hump shaped, that is, the peak output response occurs several periods after the shock occurs. (In the figure the peak response is reached three periods after the shock.) The case of a hump-shaped path for income is of particular interest, because it implies that the current level of output may rise by less than permanent income, that is, the change in y_t may be less than the change in y_t^p. In this case, the trade balance and the current account would deteriorate in response to an increase in output, bringing the model closer to the data.

To establish whether there exist parameterizations of the AR(2) endowment process for which the trade balance and the current account respond countercyclically to an endowment shock, let us calculate permanent income. To this end, multiply both sides of (2.23) by $(1+r)^{-j}$ to obtain

$$\left(\frac{1}{1+r} \right)^j E_t Y_{t+j} = \left(\frac{1}{1+r} R \right)^j Y_t.$$

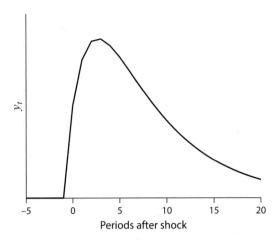

Figure 2.2 Impulse response of endowment, AR(2) process.

Summing this expression, we have

$$\sum_{j=0}^{\infty}\left(\frac{1}{1+r}\right)^j E_t Y_{t+j} = \sum_{j=0}^{\infty}\left(\frac{1}{1+r}R\right)^j Y_t$$

$$= \left(I - \frac{1}{1+r}R\right)^{-1} Y_t$$

$$= \frac{1+r}{(1+r-\rho_1)(1+r)-\rho_2}\begin{bmatrix} 1+r & \rho_2 \\ 1 & 1+r-\rho_1 \end{bmatrix} Y_t.$$

Now multiplying the first row of this vector by $r/(1+r)$, we find that nonfinancial permanent income is

$$y_t^p \equiv \frac{r}{1+r}\sum_{j=0}^{\infty}\frac{E_t y_{t+j}}{(1+r)^j}$$

$$= \frac{r\left[(1+r)y_t + \rho_2 y_{t-1}\right]}{(1+r-\rho_1)(1+r)-\rho_2}. \tag{2.24}$$

Using this expression to replace permanent income in equations (2.11), (2.15), and (2.16) yields the following expressions for consumption, the trade balance, and the current account, respectively:

$$c_t = \frac{r\left((1+r)y_t + \rho_2 y_{t-1}\right)}{(1+r-\rho_1)(1+r)-\rho_2} - rd_{t-1},$$

$$tb_t = y_t - \frac{r\left((1+r)y_t + \rho_2 y_{t-1}\right)}{(1+r-\rho_1)(1+r)-\rho_2} + rd_{t-1},$$

and

$$ca_t = y_t - \frac{r\left((1+r)y_t + \rho_2 y_{t-1}\right)}{(1+r-\rho_1)(1+r) - \rho_2}.$$

When $\rho_2 = 0$, that is, when the endowment follows an AR(1) process, these expressions collapse to (2.18), (2.19), and (2.20), respectively. In this case, as we established earlier, there is no chance for an innovation in the endowment to generate a countercyclical response either in the trade balance or in the current account. But when $\rho_2 \neq 0$, the dynamic properties of the model can change substantially. To see this, assume that in period t the economy experiences an unanticipated unit increase in the endowment. To find out whether the trade balance and the current account deteriorate on impact, we have to find out by how much permanent income increases. Equation (2.24) implies that the change in permanent income is equal to $\frac{r(1+r)}{(1+r-\rho_1)(1+r)-\rho_2}$. Thus, permanent income will increase by more than current income if $r(1+r) > (1+r-\rho_1)(1+r) - \rho_2 > 0$ (the last inequality is needed for consumption to increase in response to a positive income innovation). Because $r = \beta^{-1} - 1 > 0$, and because $\rho_2 < 1 - \rho_1$, it follows that a necessary condition for permanent income to increase by more than current income is that $\rho_1 > 1$ and $\rho_2 < 0$.

The requirement that $\rho_1 > 1$ is intuitive, because it implies that the impulse response of output is hump shaped. The requirement that $\rho_2 < 0$ ensures that the endowment process is stationary given that ρ_1 is greater than 1. But simply requiring $\rho_1 > 1$ and $\rho_2 < 0$ does not guarantee a countercyclical response of the trade balance. The necessary and sufficient conditions for this are the restrictions given above and $\rho_2 > (1+r)(1-\rho_1)$. These conditions put a restriction on how negative ρ_2 can be for a given value of $\rho_1 > 1$. The reason ρ_2 cannot become too negative is that smaller values of ρ_2 reduce the response of permanent income to a positive innovation in the endowment. Specifically, the more negative ρ_2 is, the smaller the hump and the persistence of the endowment response become. We note that for sufficiently large negative values of ρ_2 (i.e., values close to -1) the impulse response of the endowment process starts to oscillate. In this case a positive output shock will first drive the endowment up but then down below its average value.

The AR(2) example shows that a higher-order autoregressive endowment process allows the model to predict a countercyclical trade balance response. Notice that in the example the endowment process is stationary, or mean reverting. Hence the example demonstrates that the counterfactual prediction of the model of a procyclical trade balance is a consequence of assuming an AR(1) structure for the endowment process rather than of assuming that the endowment process is stationary. In the next section we show that allowing the endowment to follow a nonstationary process is an alternative mechanism to induce the model to predict that permanent income increases by more than current income.

2.4 Nonstationary Income Shocks

Suppose now that the rate of change of output, rather than its level, displays mean reversion. Specifically, let

$$\Delta y_t \equiv y_t - y_{t-1} \tag{2.25}$$

denote the change in endowment between periods $t-1$ and t, and suppose that Δy_t evolves according to the autoregressive process

$$\Delta y_t = \rho \Delta y_{t-1} + \epsilon_t, \qquad (2.26)$$

where ϵ_t is an i.i.d. shock with mean zero and variance σ_ϵ^2, and $\rho \in [0, 1)$ is a constant parameter. According to this process specification, the level of income is nonstationary, in the sense that a positive output shock ($\epsilon_t > 0$) produces an increasing expected path of output leading to a permanently higher long-run value. To see this, suppose that $\Delta y_{t-1} = 0$ and that $\epsilon_t > 0$. Then the expected path of output conditional on information available in period t is given by

$$y_t = y_{t-1} + \epsilon_t,$$

$$E_t y_{t+1} = y_{t-1} + (1+\rho)\epsilon_t,$$

$$E_0 y_{t+2} = y_{t-1} + (1+\rho+\rho^2)\epsilon_t,$$

$$\vdots$$

$$E_t y_\infty = y_{t-1} + \frac{1}{1-\rho}\epsilon_t.$$

It follows that

$$y_t < E_t y_{t+1} < E_t y_{t+2} < \ldots < E_t y_\infty.$$

Faced with such an increasing income profile, consumption-smoothing households in period t have an incentive to borrow against future income, thereby producing a countercyclical response in the current account. Figure 2.3 provides a graphical representation of this intuition.

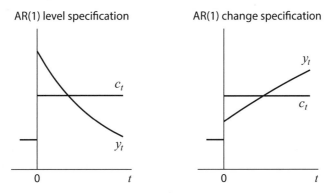

Figure 2.3   Consumption response to an output shock: AR(1) level specification versus AR(1) change specification of the endowment process.

Aside from the endowment process, all other aspects of the model economy are as before. In particular, we continue to assume that preferences are described by the utility function (2.7). Therefore, in equilibrium the current account is given by the difference between current income and permanent income, $y_t - y_t^p$. Combining definitions (2.10) and (2.25), we can write

$$y_t - y_t^p = -\sum_{j=1}^{\infty} \frac{E_t \Delta y_{t+j}}{(1+r)^j}. \qquad (2.27)$$

Note that in deriving this expression, we have not used the assumed stochastic properties of output. Therefore, the above expression is valid regardless of whether output follows a stationary or a nonstationary process.

Now combining equations (2.15) and (2.27) yields the following expression for the current account:

$$ca_t = -\sum_{j=1}^{\infty} \frac{E_t \Delta y_{t+j}}{(1+r)^j}. \qquad (2.28)$$

This formula states that the current account equals the present discounted value of future expected income decreases. If output is expected to fall over time, then the current account is positive. In this case, households save part of their current income to allow for a smooth path of future consumption. The opposite happens if income is expected to increase over time. In this case, the country runs a current account deficit to finance present spending.

The assumed autoregressive structure for the change in the endowment, given in equation (2.26), implies that

$$E_t \Delta y_{t+j} = \rho^j \Delta y_t.$$

Using this result to eliminate $E_t \Delta y_{t+j}$ from equation (2.28), we can write the equilibrium current account as

$$ca_t = \frac{-\rho}{1+r-\rho} \Delta y_t.$$

According to this formula, the current account deteriorates in response to a positive innovation in output. This prediction is in line with the cross-country time series evidence presented in Chapter 1. We note that the countercyclicality of the current account in the model with nonstationary shocks depends crucially on output changes being positively serially correlated, or $\rho > 0$. When ρ is zero or negative, the current account ceases to be countercyclical. The intuition behind this result is clear. For an unexpected increase in income to induce an increase in consumption larger than the increase in income itself, it is necessary that future income be expected to be higher than current income, which happens only if Δy_t is positively serially correlated.

Are implied changes in consumption more or less volatile than changes in output? This question is important, because as we saw in Chapter 1, developing countries are characterized by consumption growth being more volatile than output growth. Formally, letting $\sigma_{\Delta c}$

and $\sigma_{\Delta y}$ denote the standard deviations of $\Delta c_t \equiv c_t - c_{t-1}$ and Δy_t, respectively, we wish to find out conditions under which $\sigma_{\Delta c}$ can be higher than $\sigma_{\Delta y}$ in equilibrium.[1] We start with the definition of the current account:

$$ca_t = y_t - c_t - rd_{t-1}.$$

Taking differences, we obtain

$$ca_t - ca_{t-1} = \Delta y_t - \Delta c_t - r(d_{t-1} - d_{t-2}).$$

Noting that $d_{t-1} - d_{t-2} = -ca_{t-1}$ and solving for Δc_t, we obtain:

$$\Delta c_t = \Delta y_t - ca_t + (1+r)ca_{t-1}$$

$$= \Delta y_t + \frac{\rho}{1+r-\rho}\Delta y_t - \frac{\rho(1+r)}{1+r-\rho}\Delta y_{t-1}$$

$$= \frac{1+r}{1+r-\rho}\Delta y_t - \frac{\rho(1+r)}{1+r-\rho}\Delta y_{t-1}$$

$$= \frac{1+r}{1+r-\rho}\epsilon_t. \tag{2.29}$$

Thus, the change in consumption is white noise. This result is not surprising, nor is it a consequence of the assumed stochastic process for the endowment. Rather it is an implication of the Euler equation (2.8), which states that the level of consumption is a random walk. However, the precise value of the coefficient multiplying ϵ_t in equation (2.29) does depend on the assumed specification of the endowment process. This coefficient is important for the purpose of the present analysis, because it governs the magnitude of the standard deviation of consumption changes. Specifically, equation (2.29) implies that the standard deviation of consumption changes is given by

$$\sigma_{\Delta c} = \frac{1+r}{1+r-\rho}\sigma_\epsilon.$$

In turn, equation (2.26) implies that $\sigma_{\Delta y}\sqrt{1-\rho^2} = \sigma_\epsilon$. Then we can write the ratio of the standard deviation of consumption to the standard deviation of output as

$$\frac{\sigma_{\Delta c}}{\sigma_{\Delta y}} = \left[\frac{1+r}{1+r-\rho}\right]\sqrt{1-\rho^2}. \tag{2.30}$$

This expression suggests that the persistence of output changes, embodied in the parameter ρ, is a key determinant of the relative volatility of consumption changes. When $\rho = 0$, consumption and output changes are equally volatile. This result is intuitive. When

---

1. Strictly speaking, this exercise is not comparable to the data displayed in Chapter 1, because here we are analyzing changes in the levels of consumption and output (i.e., Δc_t and Δy_t), whereas in Chapter 1 we reported statistics pertaining to the growth rates of consumption and output (i.e., $\Delta c_t/c_{t-1}$ and $\Delta y_t/y_{t-1}$).

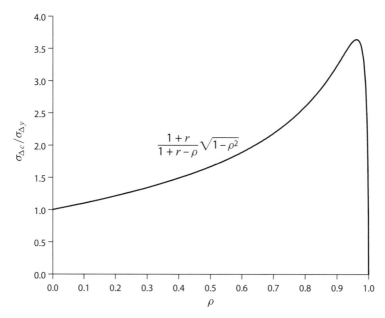

Figure 2.4   Excess volatility of consumption changes and the persistence of output changes.

Note: This figure plots equation (2.30) as a function of ρ for an interest rate of 4 percent ($r = 0.04$).

$\rho = 0$, we have that $y_{t+j} = y_t + \epsilon_{t+1} \ldots \epsilon_{t+j}$, so $E_t y_{t+j} = y_t$. That is, when $\rho = 0$, current income is equal to permanent income. Since in the present model the current account equals the difference between current and permanent income, we have that when $\rho = 0$, the current account is nil at all times. Households do not need to save or borrow in response to changes in current income, because future income is expected to change by exactly the same amount. Now if the current account is zero at all times, consumption must move in tandem with output at all times, implying that consumption and output changes must be equally volatile.

For positive values of ρ, consumption changes can become more volatile than output changes. To see this, note that the right-hand side of (2.30) is increasing in ρ at $\rho = 0$. Since consumption and output changes are equally volatile at $\rho = 0$, it follows that there are values of ρ in the interval $(0, 1)$ for which the volatility of consumption changes is higher than that of output changes. This property ceases to hold as Δy_t becomes highly persistent. This is because as $\rho \to 1$, the variance of Δy_t becomes infinitely large as changes in income become a random walk, whereas, as expression (2.29) shows, Δc_t follows an i.i.d. process with finite variance for all values of $\rho \in [0, 1]$. Figure 2.4 displays the volatility ratio $\sigma_{\Delta c}/\sigma_{\Delta y}$ as a function of ρ for an interest rate of 4 percent ($r = 0.04$). The consumption-change to output-change volatility ratio increases steadily from unity to almost 4 as ρ increases from 0 to about 0.9, before dropping quickly to 0. Thus, in principle, a model with nonstationary income shocks can predict that changes in consumption are more volatile than changes in output.

2.5 Testing the Intertemporal Approach to the Current Account

Hall (1978) was the first to explore the econometric implications of the simple model developed in this chapter. Specifically, he tested the prediction that consumption follows a random walk. Hall's work motivated a large literature devoted to testing the empirical relevance of the random-walk hypothesis by examining its predictions for the equilibrium dynamics of variables other than consumption. In particular, Campbell (1987) deduced and tested a number of theoretical restrictions on the equilibrium behavior of national savings. In the context of the open economy model studied in this chapter, Campbell's restrictions are readily expressed in terms of the current account. Here we review these restrictions and their empirical validity.

The starting point is equation (2.28), which we reproduce for convenience:

$$ca_t = -\sum_{j=1}^{\infty}(1+r)^{-j}E_t\Delta y_{t+j}. \tag{2.28 R}$$

Recall the intuition behind this expression. It states that the country borrows from the rest of the world (i.e., runs a current account deficit) when income is expected to grow in the future. Similarly, the country chooses to build up its net foreign asset position (i.e., it runs a current account surplus) when income is expected to decline in the future. In this case, the country saves for a rainy day. It is important to recall that the derivation of this equation does not require the specification of a particular stochastic process for the endowment y_t.

Consider now an empirical representation of the time series Δy_t and ca_t. Define

$$x_t = \begin{bmatrix} \Delta y_t \\ ca_t \end{bmatrix}.$$

Consider estimating the following vector autoregression (VAR) in x_t:

$$x_t = Dx_{t-1} + \epsilon_t, \tag{2.31}$$

where D is a matrix of coefficients, and ϵ_t is a mean-zero i.i.d. process. In general, the model is silent on whether x_t has a VAR representation of this form. An example in which such a representation exists is when Δy_t itself is a univariate AR(1) process like the one assumed in Section 2.4.

Let H_t denote the information contained in the vector x_t. Then, from the above VAR system, we have that the forecast of x_{t+j} given H_t is given by

$$E_t[x_{t+j}|H_t] = D^j x_t.$$

It follows from this expression that

$$\sum_{j=1}^{\infty}(1+r)^{-j}E_t[x_{t+j}|H_t] = \left[I - \frac{D}{1+r}\right]^{-1}\frac{D}{1+r}\begin{bmatrix} \Delta y_t \\ ca_t \end{bmatrix}.$$

The left-hand side of this expression is a 2×1 vector whose first element is $\sum_{j=1}^{\infty}(1+r)^{-j}E_t[\Delta y_{t+j}|H_t]$. Thus, we can write

$$\sum_{j=1}^{\infty}(1+r)^{-j}E_t[\Delta y_{t+j}|H_t] = \begin{bmatrix} 1 & 0 \end{bmatrix}\left[I - \frac{D}{1+r}\right]^{-1}\frac{D}{1+r}\begin{bmatrix} \Delta y_t \\ ca_t \end{bmatrix}.$$

Let

$$F \equiv -\begin{bmatrix} 1 & 0 \end{bmatrix}\left[I - \frac{D}{1+r}\right]^{-1}\frac{D}{1+r}.$$

Now consider running separate regressions of the left- and right-hand sides of equation (2.28) onto the vector x_t. That is, consider regressing separately ca_t onto x_t and $\sum_{j=1}^{\infty}(1+r)^{-j}E_t[\Delta y_{t+j}|H_t]$ onto x_t. Since x_t includes ca_t as its second element, we obtain that the regression coefficient of the left-hand-side regression is the vector [0 1]. The regression coefficient of the right-hand-side regression is F. So the model implies the following restriction on the vector F:

$$F = [0 \ 1].$$

Nason and Rogers (2006) perform an econometric test of this restriction. They estimate the VAR system (2.31) using Canadian data on the current account and GDP net of investment and government spending. The estimation sample is 1963:Q1 to 1997:Q4. The VAR system that Nason and Rogers estimate includes 4 lags. In computing F, they calibrate r at 3.7 percent per year. Their data strongly rejects the above cross-equation restriction of the model. The Wald statistic associated with the null hypothesis that $F = [0 \ 1]$ is 16.1, with an asymptotic p-value of 0.04. This p-value means that if the null hypothesis were true, then the Wald statistic, which reflects the discrepancy of F from [0 1], would take a value of 16.1 or higher only 4 out of 100 times.

Consider now an additional testable cross-equation restriction on the theoretical model. From equation (2.28), it follows that

$$E_t ca_{t+1} = -\sum_{j=1}^{\infty}(1+r)^{-j}E_t E_{t+1}\Delta y_{t+1+j}$$

$$= -\sum_{j=1}^{\infty}(1+r)^{-j}E_t\Delta y_{t+1+j}$$

$$= E_t\Delta y_{t+1} - E_t\Delta y_{t+1} - \sum_{j=1}^{\infty}(1+r)^{-j}E_t\Delta y_{t+1+j}$$

$$= E_t\Delta y_{t+1} - (1+r)\sum_{j=1}^{\infty}(1+r)^{-j}E_t\Delta y_{t+j}$$

$$= E_t\Delta y_{t+1} + (1+r)ca_t,$$

which provides the testable implication

$$E_t ca_{t+1} - (1+r)ca_t - E_t\Delta y_{t+1} = 0. \tag{2.32}$$

According to this expression, the variable $ca_{t+1} - (1+r)ca_t - \Delta y_{t+1}$ is unpredictable in period t. In particular, if one runs a regression of this variable on current and past values of x_t, all coefficients should be equal to zero.[2] Nason and Rogers (2006) find that this hypothesis is rejected with a p-value of 0.06. This restriction is not valid in a more general version of the model featuring private demand shocks. Consider, for instance, a variation of the model economy where the bliss point, $\bar{c}$, is a random variable. Specifically, replace $\bar{c}$ in equation (2.7) by $\bar{c} + \mu_t$, where $\bar{c}$ is still a constant, and μ_t is an i.i.d. shock with mean zero. In this environment, equation (2.32) becomes

$$E_t ca_{t+1} - (1+r)ca_t - E_t \Delta y_{t+1} = \mu_t.$$

Clearly, because in general μ_t is correlated with ca_t, the orthogonality condition, which states that $ca_{t+1} - (1+r)ca_t - \Delta y_{t+1}$ ought to be orthogonal to variables dated t or earlier, will not hold. Nevertheless, in this case we have that $ca_{t+1} - (1+r)ca_t - \Delta y_{t+1}$ should be unpredictable given information available in period $t-1$ or earlier.[3] This orthogonality condition is also strongly rejected by the data. Nason and Rogers (2006) find that a test of the hypothesis that all coefficients are zero in a regression of $ca_{t+1} - (1+r)ca_t - \Delta y_{t+1}$ onto past values of x_t has a p-value of 0.01.

We conclude that the propagation mechanism invoked by the canonical intertemporal model of the current account does not provide a satisfactory account of the observed behavior of current account dynamics, regardless of whether the underlying endowment shock is stationary or nonstationary.

To bring closer together the observed and predicted behavior of the current account and other macroeconomic aggregates, in the following chapters, we will enrich both the model's sources of fluctuations and its propagation mechanism.

2.6 Exercises

2.1 (Consumption Innovations) In the economy with AR(1) endowment shocks studied in Section 2.2, we found that $E_t c_{t+1} = c_t$, which means that $c_{t+1} = c_t + \mu_{t+1}$, where μ_{t+1} is a white noise process that is unforecastable given information available in t. Derive the innovation μ_{t+1} as a function of r, ρ, and ϵ_{t+1}.

2.2 (An Economy with Endogenous Labor Supply) Consider a small open economy populated by a large number of households with preferences described by the utility function

$$E_0 \sum_{t=0}^{\infty} \beta^t U(c_t, h_t),$$

where U is a period utility function given by

$$U(c, h) = -\frac{1}{2}\left[(\bar{c} - c)^2 + h^2\right],$$

---

2. Consider projecting the left- and right-hand sides of this expression on the information set H_t. This projection yields the orthogonality restriction $[0\ 1][D - (1+r)I] - [1\ 0]D = [0\ 0]$.

3. In particular, one can consider projecting $E_t ca_{t+1} - (1+r)ca_t - E_t \Delta y_{t+1} = \mu_t$ onto Δy_{t-1} and ca_{t-1}. This yields the orthogonality condition $[0\ 1][D - (1+r)I]D - [1\ 0]D^2 = [0\ 0]$.

where $\bar{c} > 0$ is a satiation point. The household's budget constraint is given by

$$d_t = (1+r)d_{t-1} + c_t - y_t,$$

where d_t denotes real debt acquired in period t and due in period $t+1$, and $r > 0$ denotes the world interest rate. To avoid inessential dynamics, we impose

$$\beta(1+r) = 1.$$

The variable y_t denotes output, which is assumed to be produced by the linear technology

$$y_t = Ah_t.$$

Households are also subject to the no-Ponzi-game constraint

$$\lim_{j \to \infty} E_t d_{t+j}/(1+r)^j \le 0.$$

1. Compute the equilibrium laws of motion of consumption, debt, the trade balance, and the current account.
2. Assume that in period 0, unexpectedly, the productivity parameter A increases permanently to $A' > A$. Establish the effect of this shock on output, consumption, the trade balance, the current account, and the stock of debt.

2.3 (An Open Economy with Habit Formation, I) Consider a two-period small open economy populated by a large number of identical households with preferences specified by the utility function

$$\ln c_1 + \ln(c_2 - x),$$

where c_1 and c_2 denote, respectively, consumption in periods 1 and 2, and (as always) ln denotes the natural logarithm. Households are endowed with $y > 0$ units of goods each period and are born in period 1 with no assets or debts. In period 1, households can borrow or lend at a zero interest rate. Derive the equilibrium level of consumption and the trade balance under the following three formulations:

1. $x = 0$ (no habits).
2. $x = 0.5c_1$ (internal habit formation).
3. $x = 0.5\tilde{c}_1$, where $\tilde{c}_1$ denotes the economy's per capita level of consumption in period 1 (external habit formation).

Compare economies (1) and (2) and provide intuition. Similarly, compare economies (2) and (3) and provide intuition.

2.4 (An Open Economy with Habit Formation, II) Section 2.2 characterizes the equilibrium dynamics of a small open economy with time-separable preferences driven by stationary endowment shocks. It shows that a positive endowment shock induces an improvement in the trade balance on impact. This prediction, we argued, was at odds with the empirical evidence presented in Chapter 1. Consider now a variant of the aforementioned model economy in which the representative consumer has time-nonseparable preferences described by the utility function

$$-\frac{1}{2}E_t \sum_{j=0}^{\infty} \beta^j [c_{t+j} - \alpha \tilde{c}_{t+j-1} - \bar{c}]^2; \quad t \geq 0,$$

where c_t denotes consumption in period t; $\tilde{c}_t$ denotes the cross-sectional average level of consumption in period t; E_t denotes the mathematical expectations operator conditional on information available in period t; and $\beta \in (0, 1)$, $\alpha \in (-1, 1)$, and $\bar{c} > 0$ are parameters. The case $\alpha = 0$ corresponds to time-separable preferences, which is studied in the main text. Households take as given the evolution of $\tilde{c}_t$. Households can borrow and lend in international financial markets at the constant interest rate r. For simplicity, assume that $(1 + r)\beta$ equals unity. In addition, each period $t = 0, 1, \ldots$, the household is endowed with an exogenous and stochastic amount of goods y_t. The endowment stream follows an AR(1) process of the form

$$y_{t+1} = \rho y_t + \epsilon_{t+1},$$

where $\rho \in [0, 1)$ is a parameter and ϵ_t is a mean-zero i.i.d. shock. Households are subject to the no-Ponzi-game constraint

$$\lim_{j \to \infty} \frac{E_t d_{t+j}}{(1+r)^j} \leq 0,$$

where d_t denotes the representative household's net debt position at date t. At the beginning of period 0, the household inherits a stock of debt equal to d_{-1}.

1. Derive the initial equilibrium response of consumption to a unit endowment shock in period 0.
2. Discuss conditions (i.e., parameter restrictions), if any, under which a positive output shock can lead to a deterioration of the trade balance.

2.5 (Anticipated Endowment Shocks) Consider a small open endowment economy enjoying free capital mobility. Preferences are described by the utility function

$$-\frac{1}{2}E_0 \sum_{t=0}^{\infty} \beta^t (c_t - \bar{c})^2,$$

with $\beta \in (0, 1)$. Agents have access to an internationally traded bond paying the constant interest rate r^*, satisfying $\beta(1 + r^*) = 1$. The representative household starts period zero with an asset position b_{-1}. Each period $t \geq 0$, the household receives an endowment y_t, which obeys the law of motion, $y_t = \rho y_{t-1} + \epsilon_{t-1}$, where ϵ_t is an i.i.d. shock with mean zero and standard deviation σ_ϵ. Notice that households know already in period $t - 1$ the level of y_t with certainty.

1. Derive the equilibrium process of consumption and the current account.
2. Compute the correlation between the current account and output. Compare your result with the standard case in which y_t is known only in period t.

2.6 (Anticipated Interest Rate Decline)

Consider a small open endowment economy enjoying free capital mobility. Preferences are described by the utility function

$$\sum_{t=0}^{\infty} \beta^t \ln c_t,$$

with $\beta \in (0, 1)$. Agents have access to an internationally traded bond paying the interest rate r_t when held from period t to period $t + 1$. The representative household starts period zero with an asset position b_{-1}. Each period $t \geq 0$, the household receives an endowment y_t. Households know the time paths of $\{r_t\}$ and $\{y_t\}$ with certainty. The sequential budget constraint of the household is given by $c_t + b_t/(1 + r_t) = y_t + b_{t-1}$. And the household's borrowing limit is given by $\lim_{j \to \infty} \frac{b_{t+j}}{\prod_{s=0}^{j}(1+r_{t+s})} \geq 0$.

1. Derive the household's present value budget constraint.
2. Derive the equilibrium paths of consumption and assets in terms of y_t, r_t, and b_{-1}.

Assume now that in period 0 it is learned that in period $t^* \geq 0$ the interest rate will decline temporarily. Specifically, the new path of the interest rate is

$$r_t' = \begin{cases} r_t & \text{for all } t \geq 0 \text{ and } t \neq t^* \\ r_{t^*}' < r_{t^*} & \text{for } t = t^* \end{cases}.$$

3. Find the impact effect of this anticipated interest rate cut on consumption; that is, find $\ln c_0'/c_0$, where c_t' denotes the equilibrium path of consumption under the new interest rate path, and c_t denotes the equilibrium path of consumption under the old interest rate path. Distinguish two cases. First consider a storage economy with $y_t = 0$ for all t and $b_{-1} > 0$. Discuss whether the anticipated future rate cut stimulates demand at the time it is announced. Provide intuition. Then consider an endowment economy with $b_{-1} = 0$ and $y_t = y > 0$ for all t. Analyze whether the response of consumption in period 0 is equal in size to the anticipated rate cut and whether it depends on the anticipation horizon t^*. In particular, do anticipated interest rate cuts have a smaller stimulating effect on current consumption the further in the future they will take place, that is, the larger t^* is? Provide intuition for your findings.
4. Relate the insights obtained in this exercise to the debate on Forward Guidance as a monetary policy strategy. In particular, interpret the present real economy as a monetary economy with rigid nominal prices and a central bank that deploys the necessary monetary policy to fully control the real interest rate r_t. Address in particular the question of whether forward guidance is an effective tool to stimulate aggregate demand.

2.7 (Predicted Second Moments) In Chapter 1, we showed that two empirical regularities that characterize emerging economies are the countercyclicality of the trade-balance-to-output ratio and the fact that consumption growth appears to be more volatile than output growth. In this chapter, we developed a simple small open endowment economy and provided intuitive arguments suggesting that this economy fails to account for these two stylized facts. However, that model does not allow for closed-form solutions of second moments of output growth, consumption growth, or the trade-balance-to-output ratio. The goal of this exercise is to obtain these implied statistics numerically.

To this end, consider the following parameterization of the model developed in the present chapter:

$$y_t - \bar{y} = \rho(y_{t-1} - \bar{y}) + \epsilon_t,$$

with $\rho = 0.9$, $\bar{y} = 1$, and ϵ_t distributed normally with mean 0 and standard deviation 0.03. Note that the parameter $\bar{y}$, which earlier in this chapter was implicitly assumed to be zero, represents the deterministic steady state of the output process. Assume further that $r = 1/\beta - 1 = 0.1$, $d_{-1} = \bar{y}/2$, and $y_{-1} = \bar{y}$.

1. Simulate the economy for 100 years.

2. Discard the first 50 years of artificial data to minimize the dependence of the results on initial conditions.

3. Compute the growth rates of output and consumption and the trade-balance-to-output ratio.

4. Compute the sample standard deviations of output growth and consumption growth and the correlation between output growth and the trade-balance-to-output ratio. Here we denote these three statistics by σ_{gy}, σ_{gc}, and $\rho_{gy,tby}$, respectively.

5. Replicate steps 1 to 4 1,000 times. For each replication, keep record of σ_{gy}, σ_{gc}, and $\rho_{gy,tby}$.

6. Report the average of σ_{gy}, σ_{gc}, and $\rho_{gy,tby}$ over the 1,000 replications.

7. Discuss your results.

2.8 (Empirical Plausibility of an AR(2) Output Specification) The purpose of this exercise is to obtain econometric estimates of the AR(2) output process given in equation (2.22) and then check whether the estimated values of ρ_1 and ρ_2 satisfy the requirement for permanent income to increase by more than current income in response to an innovation in current income. The satisfaction of this condition guarantees a countercyclical response of the trade balance and the current account to output innovations in the model.

1. Download the quarterly data for Chapter 1 posted on the book's Web site. For each country, extract GDP per capita at constant local currency units (LCU). Denote this series $\tilde{y}_t$.

2. For each country, obtain a log-quadratically detrended output series, denoted $\hat{y}_t$, by running the ordinary least squares (OLS) regression

$$\ln \tilde{y}_t = a_0 + a_1 t + a_2 t^2 + \hat{y}_t,$$

where $\hat{y}_t$ is the regression residual.

3. In the model, output is defined in levels. So, for each country, produce the transformed variable

$$y_t \equiv \exp(\hat{y}_t).$$

4. For each country, use the time series y_t to estimate the AR(2) process

$$y_t = \rho_0 + \rho_1 y_{t-1} + \rho_2 y_{t-2} + \epsilon_t$$

by OLS.

5. Ignore the parameter ρ_0. Set the interest rate r at 2 percent per quarter. Using the analysis of Section 2.3, establish, for each country, whether the condition for permanent income to increase by more than current income in response to an innovation in current income is met. Present your results in the form of a table, with one row for country and columns displaying, in this order, ρ_1, ρ_2, and yes/no to indicate whether the condition is met or not. Discuss your findings.

6. Change the quarterly interest rate to 1 percent, and recalculate the table. What do you learn, and what is the intuition behind your results?

7. Redo the exercise using the annual data for real GDP per capita at constant LCU used in Chapter 1 and available on the book's Web site. Make sure to adjust the interest rate in accordance with the change of frequency. Discuss your results.

2.9 (Expected Output Changes and Permanent Income) Equation (2.27) expresses the difference between current and permanent income, $y_t - y_t^p$, as the present discounted value of future expected changes in the endowment. Present a step-by-step derivation of equation (2.27) starting from definitions (2.10) and (2.25). Comment on the cyclical properties of $y_t - y_t^p$ depending on whether the level or the change of y_t follows an AR(1) process.

2.10 (Impatience and the Current Account, I) Consider a small open endowment economy populated by a large number of identical consumers with preferences described by the utility function

$$\sum_{t=0}^{\infty} \beta^t \ln(c_t - \bar{c}),$$

with the usual notation, except that $\bar{c} > 0$ denotes a subsistence level of consumption. Consumers have access to the international debt market, where the interest rate, denoted by r, is positive, constant, and satisfies

$$\beta(1+r) < 1.$$

Consumers start period 0 with an outstanding debt, including interest, of $(1+r)d_{-1}$. It is forbidden to violate the constraint $\lim_{j \to \infty}(1+r)^{-j}d_{t+j} \leq 0$. Each period, everybody receives a positive amount of consumption goods $y > 0$, which is nonstorable.

1. State the optimization problem of the representative consumer.

2. Derive the consumer's optimality conditions.

3. Derive a maximum value of initial debt, d_{-1}, beyond which an equilibrium cannot exist. Assume that d_{-1} is less than this threshold.

4. Characterize the steady state of this economy. In particular, calculate the steady-state values of consumption, debt, the trade balance, and the current account. Note that in this economy the steady-state level of external debt is not history dependent. Comment on the factors determining this property of the model.

5. Derive explicit formulas for the equilibrium dynamic paths of consumption, debt, the trade balance, and the current account as functions of $t, d_{-1}, r, \beta, \bar{c}$, and y.

6. Now assume that in period 0 the outstanding debt, d_{-1}, is at its steady-state level, and that, unexpectedly, all consumers receive a permanent increase in the endowment from y to $y' > y$. Compute the initial response of all endogenous variables. Discuss your result, paying particular attention to possible differences with the case $\beta(1+r) = 1$.

7. Characterize the economy's dynamics after period 0.

2.11 (Impatience and the Current Account, II) Consider an open economy inhabited by a large number of identical, infinitely-lived households with preferences given by the utility function

$$\sum_{t=0}^{\infty} \beta^t \ln c_t,$$

where c_t denotes consumption in period t, $\beta \in (0, 1)$ denotes the subjective discount factor, and ln denotes the natural logarithm operator. Households are endowed with a constant amount of goods y each period and can borrow or lend at the constant world interest rate $r > 0$ using one-period bonds. Let d_t denote the amount of debt acquired by the household in period t, and $(1+r)d_t$, the associated gross obligation in $t+1$. Assume that households start period 0 with no debts or assets ($d_{-1} = 0$) and that they are subject to a no-Ponzi-game constraint of the form $\lim_{t\to\infty} (1+r)^{-t} d_t \leq 0$. Suppose that

$$\beta(1+r) < 1.$$

1. Characterize the equilibrium path of consumption. In particular, calculate c_0, c_{t+1}/c_t for $t \geq 0$, and $\lim_{t\to\infty} c_t$ as functions of the structural parameters of the model, β, r, and y. Compare this answer to the one that would obtain under the more standard assumption $\beta(1+r) = 1$ and provide intuition.

2. Characterize the equilibrium path of net external debt. In particular, deduce whether debt is increasing, decreasing, or constant over time, and calculate $\lim_{t\to\infty} d_t$. Solve for the equilibrium level of d_t as a function of t and the structural parameters of the model.

3. Define the trade balance, denoted tb_t, and characterize its equilibrium dynamics. In particular, deduce whether it is increasing, decreasing, or constant; positive or

negative; and compute $\lim_{t\to\infty} tb_t$, as a function of the structural parameters of the model.

2.12 (Global Approximation of Equilibrium Dynamics) This exercise is concerned with numerically approximating the equilibrium dynamics of a small open endowment economy by value-function iterations.

1. Consider an endowment, y_t, following the AR(1) process

$$y_t - 1 = \rho(y_{t-1} - 1) + \sigma_\epsilon \epsilon_t,$$

where ϵ_t is an i.i.d. innovation with mean zero and unit variance, $\rho \in [0, 1)$, and $\sigma_\epsilon > 0$.

   Discretize this process by a two-state Markov process defined by the 2×1 state vector $Y \equiv [Y_1 \ Y_2]'$ and the 2×2 transition probability matrix Π with element (i, j) denoted π_{ij} and given by $\pi_{ij} \equiv \text{Prob}\{y_{t+1} = Y_j | y_t = Y_i\}$. To reduce the number of parameters of the Markov process to two, impose the restrictions $\pi_{11} = \pi_{22} = \pi$, $Y_1 = 1 + \gamma$, and $Y_2 = 1 - \gamma$. Pick π and γ to match the variance and the serial correlation of y_t. Express π and γ in terms of the parameters defining the original AR(1) process.

2. Calculate the unconditional probability distribution of Y (this is a 2×1 vector).

3. Assume that $\rho = 0.4$ and $\sigma_\epsilon = 0.05$. Evaluate the vector Y and the matrix Π.

4. Now consider a small open economy populated by a large number of identical households with preferences given by

$$E_0 \sum_{t=0}^{\infty} \beta^t \frac{c_t^{1-\sigma} - 1}{1 - \sigma}.$$

Suppose that households face the sequential budget constraint

$$c_t + g + (1 + r)d_{t-1} = y_t + d_t,$$

where c_t denotes consumption in period t, d_t denotes one-period debt assumed in period t and maturing in $t + 1$, g denotes a constant level of domestic absorption that yields no utility to households (possibly wasteful government spending), and r denotes the world interest rate, assumed to be constant and exogenous. Households are subject to the no-Ponzi-game constraint $\lim_{j\to\infty}(1 + r)^{-j} E_t d_{t+j} \leq 0$. Express the household's problem as a Bellman equation. To this end, drop time subscripts and use instead the notation $d = d_{t-1}$, $d' = d_t$, $y = y_t$, and $y' = y_{t+1}$ for all t. Denote the value function in t by $v(y, d)$. [Here it suffices to use the notation y and y', because the endowment process is AR(1). Higher-order processes would require an extended notation.]

5. Let $\sigma = 2$, $r = 0.04$, $\beta = 0.954$, and $g = 0.2$. And assume that the endowment process follows the two-state Markov process given in item 3. Discretize the debt state, d, using 200 equally spaced points ranging from 15 to 19. Calculate the

value function and the debt policy function by value function iteration (these are 2 vectors, each of order 400×1). Calculate also the policy functions of consumption, the trade balance, and the current account (each of these policy functions is a 400×1 vector). Calculate the transition probability matrix of the state (y, d) (this is a 400×400 matrix, whose rows all add up to unity; each row has only 2 nonzero entries).

6. Define the impulse response of the variable x_t to a one-standard-deviation increase in output as $E[x_t|y_0 = Y_1] - E[x_t]$ for $t = 0, 1, 2, \ldots$ (note that these expectations are unconditional with respect to debt; alternatively, we could have conditioned on some value of debt, but we are not pursuing this definition here). Make a figure with 4 subplots (in a 2×2 arrangement) showing the impulse responses of output, consumption, the trade balance, and debt for $t = 0, 1, \ldots, 10$.

7. Plot the unconditional probability distribution of debt.

8. Finally, suppose that government spending, g, increases from 0.2 to 0.22. Plot the resulting unconditional distribution of debt. For comparison superimpose the one corresponding to the baseline case $g = 0.2$. Provide intuition for the differences you see.

2.13 (Determinants of the World Interest Rate) Throughout this chapter, we have studied small open economies in which the world interest rate is given. This exercise aims at illustrating the forces determining this variable.

Consider a two-period world composed of a continuum of countries indexed by $i \in [0, 1]$. Each country is populated by a large number of identical households with preferences given by

$$\ln(c_1^i) + \ln(c_2^i),$$

where c_1^i and c_2^i denote consumption of a perishable good in country i in periods 1 and 2, respectively. Households start period 1 with a nil net debt position. In period 1, they can borrow or lend in the international financial market via a debt instrument, denoted d_1^i, that matures in period 2 and carries the interest rate r. The interest rate r is exogenous to each country i. In period 1, each household receives an endowment of goods $y_1^i = y_1 + \epsilon^i$, where y^1 is the world component of the endowment, and ϵ^i is a country-specific component satisfying $\int_0^1 \epsilon^i di = 0$. In period 2, the endowment has no idiosyncratic component and is given by $y_2^i = y_2$. Finally, households are subject to a no-Ponzi-game constraint that forbids them to end period 2 with a positive debt position; that is, they are subject to the constraint $d_2^i \leq 0$, where d_2^i denotes the debt assumed in period 2.

1. Write down and solve the household's optimization problem in country i, given r.

2. Derive the equilibrium levels of the trade balance, the current account, and external debt in periods 1 and 2 in country i given r.

3. Write down the world resource constraints in periods 1 and 2.

4. Derive the equilibrium level of the world interest rate, r.

5. Suppose now that output in period 1 in country i increases by $x > 0$, that is, $\Delta y_1^i = x$. Derive the effect of this shock on the trade balance and the level of external debt in period 1 in country i and on the world interest rate under the following two alternative cases:

   a. A country-specific endowment shock, $\Delta y_1^i = \Delta \epsilon^i = x$, and $\Delta y_1 = 0$.

   b. A world endowment shock, $\Delta y_1^i = \Delta y_1 = x$, and $\Delta \epsilon^i = 0$.

   Provide a discussion of your results.

2.14 (Leontief Preferences over Discounted Period Utilities) Consider a perfect-foresight small open economy populated by a large number of identical households with preferences described by the utility function

$$\min_{t \geq 0} \left\{ \beta^t c_t \right\},$$

where c_t denotes consumption in period t, and $\beta \in (0, 1)$ is a parameter. Households have access to the international financial market, where they can borrow or lend at the constant interest rate r. Assume that

$$\beta(1+r) = 1 + \gamma,$$

where $\gamma > 0$ is a parameter. Households are endowed with a constant amount of consumption goods denoted by y each period and start period 0 with a level of debt equal to $d_{-1} > 0$. Finally, households are subject to a no-Ponzi-game constraint of the form $\lim_{t \to \infty} (1+r)^{-t} d_t \leq 0$, where d_t denotes one-period debt acquired in period t and maturing in $t + 1$.

1. Formulate the household's maximization problem.

2. Write down the complete set of optimality conditions.

3. Characterize the equilibrium paths of consumption and debt in this economy. In particular, express the equilibrium levels of c_t and d_t, for $t \geq 0$, in terms of the structural parameters (possibly β, r, γ, and y) and the initial condition d_{-1}.

4. What is the equilibrium asymptotic growth rate of the economy's net asset position? How does it compare to the equilibrium growth rate of consumption?

5. Suppose that in period 0 the economy unexpectedly experiences a permanent increase in the endowment from y to $y + \Delta y$, with $\Delta y > 0$. Derive the impact response of the trade balance. Briefly discuss your result.

6. Characterize the equilibrium under the assumption that $\gamma = 0$.

2.15 (An Economy with Labor and Technological Progress) Consider a small open economy inhabited by a large number of identical households with preferences described by the utility function

$$\sum_{t=0}^{\infty} \beta^t \ln \left(C_t - \frac{X_t}{2} h_t^2 \right),$$

where C_t denotes consumption in period t, h_t denotes hours worked in period t, $\beta \in (0, 1)$ is a subjective discount factor, and X_t is an exogenous and deterministic factor governing household and market technological progress, which evolves according to the expression

$$X_t = \mu X_{t-1},$$

for all $t \geq 0$, where $\mu > 1$ is a parameter, and $X_{-1} = 1$. Households face the sequential budget constraint

$$C_t + D_{t-1}(1 + r_{t-1}) = Y_t + D_t,$$

where D_t denotes the amount of one-period debt assumed in period t, r_t denotes the interest rate in period t, and Y_t denotes output in period t, which is produced via the technology

$$Y_t = X_t h_t.$$

Households are subject to the no-Ponzi-game constraint $\lim_{j \to \infty} D_{t+j} / \prod_{s=0}^{j-1}(1 + r_{t+s}) \leq 0$, for all t. The country interest rate, r_t, is the sum of a constant world interest rate, r^*, and a country spread, denoted $\rho\left(\tilde{D}_t / X_t\right)$, where $\tilde{D}_t$ denotes that cross-sectional average of D_t. Assume the functional form $\rho(x) = \gamma \left[\exp(x - \bar{d}) - 1\right]$, where $\gamma, \bar{d} > 0$ are parameters. Finally, assume that $1 + r^* = \mu / \beta$ and that $(1 + r_{t-1})D_{-1} / X_{-1} = (1 + r^*)\bar{d}$.

1. State the household's maximization problem.
2. Derive the optimality conditions associated with the household's problem.
3. Derive the complete set of equilibrium conditions in stationary form by appropriately scaling variables that display perpetual growth in equilibrium.
4. Derive equilibrium paths of consumption, hours, the trade balance, the current account, and external debt. Provide intuition.

2.16 (Testing the Intertemporal Approach on Emerging Market Data) Use the data posted on the book's Web site with the materials for Chapter 1 to test the empirical validity of the intertemporal approach to the current account in emerging countries. Specifically, extract quarterly data on output and the current account from an emerging country of your choice and apply the econometric tests studied in Section 2.5. Discuss your findings. Make sure to include a comparison with the results for Canada reported in the aforementioned section.

2.17 (Leontief Preferences for Consumption and Leisure) Consider a small open economy inhabited by a large number of identical households with preferences described by the utility function

$$\sum_{t=0}^{\infty} \beta^t \ln(x_t)$$

with

$$x_t = \min\{c_t, 1 - h_t\},$$

where c_t denotes consumption in period t, and h_t denotes labor effort in period t and is restricted to reside in the interval $[0, 1)$. Households produce goods with the technology

$$y_t = h_t,$$

where y_t denotes output. They can also borrow or lend in one-period bonds that pay the constant interest rate $r > 0$. Let d_t denote the debt acquired in t and maturing in $t + 1$. Assume that households start period 0 with no debts or assets inherited from the past. Borrowing is limited by the no-Ponzi-game constraint $\lim_{t \to \infty} (1 + r)^{-t} d_t \leq 0$. Finally, assume that the subjective and market discount rates are equal to each other:

$$\beta = \frac{1}{1 + r}.$$

1. Write down the household's optimization problem.
2. Derive the first-order conditions associated with the household's problem.
3. Calculate the equilibrium levels of consumption and the trade balance. These should be 2 numbers.
4. Now consider an environment in which households are relatively impatient, in the sense that the subjective discount factor is larger than the market discount factor. Specifically, assume that the interest rate is 10 percent ($r = 0.1$) and that $\beta = 1/1.2$. Calculate the equilibrium levels of consumption and the trade balance in period 0, and characterize their evolution over time.

3

An Open Economy with Capital

In this chapter we introduce capital accumulation in the open economy of Chapter 2. The purpose of introducing physical capital in the model is twofold. First, an important result derived in Chapter 2 is that for the most commonly used stationary specifications of the endowment shock process—namely, AR(1) specifications—the simple endowment economy model fails to predict the observed countercyclicality of the trade balance and the current account documented in Chapter 1. Here we show that allowing for capital accumulation can contribute to mending this problem. The second reason for introducing capital is that the assumption that output is an exogenously given stochastic process, which was maintained throughout Chapter 2, is unsatisfactory if the goal is to understand observed business cycles. For output is perhaps the main variable any theory of the business cycle should aim to explain. In this chapter we provide a partial remedy to this problem by assuming that output is produced with physical capital, which, in turn, is an endogenous variable.

3.1 The Basic Framework

Consider an open economy populated by a large number of infinitely-lived households with preferences described by the utility function

$$\sum_{t=0}^{\infty} \beta^t U(c_t), \tag{3.1}$$

where c_t denotes consumption; $\beta \in (0, 1)$ denotes the subjective discount factor; and U denotes the period utility function, assumed to be increasing and concave. Each period, households face the budget constraint

$$c_t + i_t + (1+r)d_{t-1} = y_t + d_t. \tag{3.2}$$

The left-hand side displays the uses of wealth, given by purchases of consumption goods; purchases of investment goods, denoted i_t; and payment of principal and interest on debt obligations maturing in t, denoted $(1 + r)d_{t-1}$. The right-hand side displays the sources of wealth, given by output, denoted y_t, and the acquisition of debt maturing in $t + 1$, denoted d_t. Output is produced with physical capital, denoted k_t, using the technology

$$y_t = A_t F(k_t), \tag{3.3}$$

where A_t is an exogenous and deterministic productivity factor, and F is an increasing and concave production function satisfying the Inada conditions. Capital evolves according to the law of motion

$$k_{t+1} = k_t + i_t. \tag{3.4}$$

For the sake of simplicity, we assume that capital does not depreciate. In later chapters, we relax both the assumption of no depreciation and the assumption of deterministic productivity.

Finally, households are subject to the no-Ponzi-game constraint

$$\lim_{j \to \infty} \frac{d_{t+j}}{(1+r)^j} \le 0. \tag{3.5}$$

The Lagrangian associated with the household's problem is

$$\mathcal{L} = \sum_{t=0}^{\infty} \beta^t \left\{ U(c_t) + \lambda_t \left[A_t F(k_t) + d_t - c_t - (k_{t+1} - k_t) - (1+r)d_{t-1} \right] \right\}.$$

The first-order conditions corresponding to c_t, d_t, k_{t+1}, and λ_t, respectively, are

$$U'(c_t) = \lambda_t, \tag{3.6}$$

$$\lambda_t = \beta(1+r)\lambda_{t+1}, \tag{3.7}$$

$$\lambda_t = \beta\lambda_{t+1}[A_{t+1}F'(k_{t+1}) + 1], \tag{3.8}$$

and

$$A_t F(k_t) + d_t = c_t + k_{t+1} - k_t + (1+r)d_{t-1}. \tag{3.9}$$

Household optimization implies that the borrowing constraint holds with equality:

$$\lim_{t \to \infty} \frac{d_t}{(1+r)^t} = 0. \tag{3.10}$$

As in Chapter 2, we assume that

$$\beta(1+r) = 1,$$

to avoid inessential long-run dynamics. This assumption together with optimality conditions (3.6) and (3.7) implies that consumption is constant over time,

$$c_{t+1} = c_t, \tag{3.11}$$

for all $t \geq 0$. Using this expression, the optimality conditions (3.8)–(3.10) reduce to the following two expressions:

$$r = A_{t+1}F'(k_{t+1}) \tag{3.12}$$

and

$$c_t + rd_{t-1} = \frac{r}{1+r} \sum_{j=0}^{\infty} \frac{A_{t+j}F(k_{t+j}) - (k_{t+j+1} - k_{t+j})}{(1+r)^j}, \tag{3.13}$$

for $t \geq 0$.

Equilibrium condition (3.12) states that households invest in physical capital in period t until the expected marginal product of capital in period $t+1$ equals the rate of return on foreign debt. It follows from this equilibrium condition that next period's level of physical capital k_{t+1} is an increasing function of the future expected level of productivity, A_{t+1}, and a decreasing function of the interest rate r. Formally,

$$k_{t+1} = \kappa \left(\frac{A_{t+1}}{r} \right), \tag{3.14}$$

with $\kappa' > 0$.

To obtain equilibrium condition (3.13), follow the same steps as in the derivation of its counterpart for the endowment economy, equation (2.9). The right-hand side of (3.13) is the household's nonfinancial permanent income y_t^p. It is a natural generalization of a similar expression obtained in the endowment economy (see equation (2.10)). In the present environment, nonfinancial permanent income is given by a weighted average of present and future expected output net of investment expenditure. Thus, equilibrium condition (3.13) states that each period households allocate their nonfinancial permanent income to consumption and to servicing their debt.

A *perfect-foresight equilibrium* is a set of sequences $\{c_t, d_t, k_{t+1}\}_{t=0}^{\infty}$ satisfying (3.11), (3.13), and (3.14) for all $t \geq 0$, given the initial stock of physical capital, k_0, the initial net external debt position, d_{-1}, and the deterministic sequence of productivity $\{A_t\}_{t=0}^{\infty}$. To construct a perfect-foresight equilibrium, proceed as follows. Given initial conditions k_0 and d_{-1} and a deterministic sequence $\{A_t\}$, use equilibrium condition (3.14) to obtain $\{k_t\}_{t=1}^{\infty}$. With the path of k_t in hand, evaluate condition (3.13) at $t = 0$ to obtain c_0. Then use condition (3.11) to find the time path of c_t for all $t > 0$. Finally, evaluate equation (3.13) at $t > 0$ and solve for d_{t-1} to obtain the equilibrium sequence of debt for any $t \geq 0$. We can then determine output from equation (3.3), investment from (3.4), and the marginal utility of consumption, λ_t, from (3.6).

The trade balance is given by the difference between output and domestic absorption,

$$tb_t = y_t - c_t - i_t,$$

and the current account equals the trade balance plus net investment income,

$$ca_t = tb_t - rd_{t-1}.$$

3.2 A Steady-State Equilibrium

Suppose that up until period -1 inclusive, the technology factor A_t was constant and is given by $\bar{A}$. Moreover, assume that for all $t < 0$, agents expected A_{t+j} to be equal to $\bar{A}$ for all $j \geq 0$ with certainty. This assumption gives rise to a steady state for $t < 0$ in which all endogenous variables are constant. We indicate the steady state of a variable by placing a bar over it. The fact that A_t is expected to be equal to $\bar{A}$ at all times implies, by (3.14), that the capital stock is also constant and is given by $k_t = \bar{k} \equiv \kappa(\bar{A}/r)$ for all $t \geq 0$. Similarly, output is constant and given by $y_t = \bar{y} \equiv \bar{A}F(\bar{k})$ for all $t < 0$. Because the capital stock is constant and because the depreciation rate of capital is assumed to be zero, we have by equation (3.4) that investment is also constant and equal to zero, $i_t = \bar{i} = 0$ for all $t < 0$. By the Euler equation (3.11), consumption must also be constant for all $t < 0$. Equilibrium conditions (3.2) and (3.13) then imply that d_t must also be constant for all $t < 0$, at a value denoted $\bar{d}$. Because the current account is defined as the change in the net international asset position $(ca_t = -(d_t) - (-d_{t-1}))$, we have that in the steady state, the current account equals zero, $ca_t = \overline{ca} = 0$, for all $t < 0$. Finally, recalling that the current account is also defined as the sum of the trade balance and net investment income, $ca_t = tb_t - rd_{t-1}$, we have that in the steady state, the trade balance must be constant and given by $tb_t = \overline{tb} = r\bar{d}$ for all $t < 0$.

3.3 Adjustment to a Permanent Productivity Shock

Suppose now that in period 0, unexpectedly, the technology factor increases permanently from $\bar{A}$ to $A' > \bar{A}$, that is,

$$A_t = \begin{cases} \bar{A} & \text{for } t \leq -1 \\ A' > \bar{A} & \text{for } t \geq 0. \end{cases}$$

Figure 3.1 presents the response of the model to this shock. Because k_0 and d_{-1} were chosen in period -1, when households expected A_0 to be equal to $\bar{A}$, we have that $k_0 = \bar{k}$ and $d_{-1} = \bar{d}$. In period 0, investment experiences an increase that raises the level of capital available for production in period 1, k_1, from $\bar{k}$ to $k' \equiv \kappa(A'/r) > \kappa(\bar{A}/r) = \bar{k}$. The fact that productivity is constant after period 0 implies, by (3.4) and (3.14), that starting in period 1 the capital stock is constant and investment is nil. Thus, $k_t = k'$ for $t \geq 1$, $i_0 = k' - \bar{k} > 0$, and $i_t = 0$, for $t \geq 1$. In words, investment experiences a one-time increase in period 0 and the capital stock a once-and-for-all increase in period 1. Output increases in period 0, $y_0 - y_{-1} = A'F(\bar{k}) - \bar{A}F(\bar{k}) > 0$, and then again in period 1, $y_1 - y_0 = A'F(k') - A'F(\bar{k}) > 0$. The one-period lag in the full adjustment of output is due to the fact that it takes one period for investment to become productive capital. Starting in period 1, output is constant over time, $y_t = A'F(k')$ for $t \geq 1$.

Consumption increases permanently in response to the permanent positive productivity shock. To see this, note first that by equilibrium condition (3.11), $c_t = c_0$ for all $t \geq 0$. Denote this constant level of consumption by c', so that $c_t = c'$ for all $t \geq 0$. Now, plugging

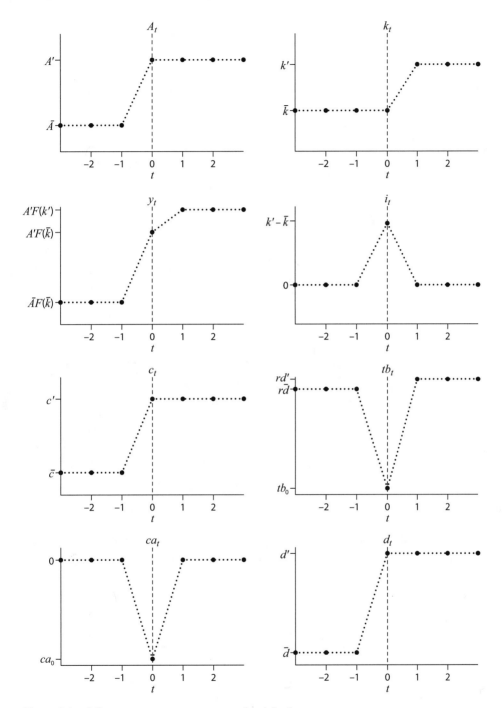

Figure 3.1 Adjustment to a permanent productivity increase.

the equilibrium path of the capital stock into the intertemporal resource constraint (3.13) and evaluating that equation at $t = 0$ yields

$$c' = -r\bar{d} + \frac{r}{1+r}\left[A'F(\bar{k}) - k' + \bar{k}\right] + \frac{1}{1+r}A'F(k').$$

Rearranging terms, we have

$$c' = -r\bar{d} + A'F(\bar{k}) + \frac{1}{1+r}\left\{A'\left[F(k') - F(\bar{k})\right] - r\left[k' - \bar{k}\right]\right\}.$$

Use equation (3.12) to replace r for $A'F'(k')$ in the expression in curly brackets to obtain

$$c' = -r\bar{d} + A'F(\bar{k}) + \frac{1}{1+r}\left\{A'\left[F(k') - F(\bar{k})\right] - A'F'(k')\left[k' - \bar{k}\right]\right\}.$$

Because F is assumed to be strictly concave and $k' > \bar{k}$, we have that $\frac{F(k')-F(\bar{k})}{k'-\bar{k}} > F'(k')$. This means that the expression in curly brackets is strictly positive. Therefore, we have that

$$c' > -r\bar{d} + A'F(\bar{k}) > -r\bar{d} + \bar{A}F(\bar{k}) = \bar{c}. \qquad (3.15)$$

This establishes that consumption experiences a once-and-for-all increase in period 0.[1]

Indeed, consumption initially increases by more than output. To see this, use the above inequality and the definition of the steady state to write

$$c_0 - c_{-1} \equiv c' - \bar{c}$$
$$= c' - [\bar{A}F(\bar{k}) - r\bar{d}]$$
$$> [A'F(\bar{k}) - r\bar{d}] - [\bar{A}F(\bar{k}) - r\bar{d}]$$
$$= A'F(\bar{k}) - \bar{A}F(\bar{k})$$
$$= y_0 - y_{-1}.$$

The inequality follows from the first inequality in (3.15). The initial overreaction of consumption is because output continues to grow after period 0. So, from the perspective of period 0, households observe an increasing path of income over time ($y_t - y_0 = A'F(k') - A'F(\bar{k}) > 0$ for all $t > 0$). As a consequence, households borrow against future income to

---

1. We thank Alberto Felettigh for providing this proof. An alternative demonstration of this result is as follows. Consider the following suboptimal paths for consumption and investment: $c_t^s = A'F(\bar{k}) - r\bar{d}$ and $i_t^s = 0$ for all $t \geq 0$. Clearly, because $A' > \bar{A}$, the consumption path c_t^s is strictly preferred to the preshock path, given by $\bar{c} \equiv \bar{A}F(\bar{k}) - r\bar{d}$. To show that the proposed allocation is feasible, let us plug the consumption and investment paths c_t^s and i_t^s into the sequential budget constraint (3.2) to obtain the sequence of asset positions $d_t^s = \bar{d}$ for all $t \geq 0$. Obviously, $\lim_{t\to\infty} \bar{d}/(1+r)^t = 0$, so the proposed suboptimal allocation satisfies the no-Ponzi-game condition (3.5). We have established the existence of a feasible consumption path that is strictly preferred to the preshock consumption allocation. It follows that the optimal consumption path must also be strictly preferred to the preshock consumption path. This result—together with the fact that, from equilibrium condition (3.11), the optimal consumption path is constant starting in period 0—implies that consumption must experience a permanent, once-and-for-all increase in period 0.

finance current consumption. This result resembles what happens in the endowment economy with AR(2) stationary endowment shocks (Section 2.3) or with AR(1) nonstationary endowment shocks (Section 2.4).

The initial increase in domestic absorption causes the trade balance to deteriorate. To see this, recall that $tb_t = y_t - c_t - i_t$, which implies that $tb_0 - tb_{-1} = (y_0 - y_{-1}) - (c_0 - c_{-1}) - (i_0 - i_{-1})$. We have already shown that $(y_0 - y_{-1}) - (c_0 - c_{-1}) < 0$ and that $i_0 - i_{-1} > 0$. It therefore follows that $tb_0 - tb_{-1} < 0$. This result is significantly different from the one obtained in the endowment economy studied in Chapter 2 in which a once-and-for-all increase in the endowment leaves the trade balance unchanged.

The trade balance improves in period 1. This is because output continues to grow from period 0 to period 1, whereas investment falls to zero and consumption is unchanged. Formally, $tb_1 - tb_0 = (y_1 - y_0) - (c_1 - c_0) - (i_1 - i_0)$. Now $y_1 - y_0 = A'F(k') - A'F(\bar{k}) > 0$, $c_1 - c_0 = c' - c' = 0$, and $i_1 - i_0 = 0 - (k' - \bar{k}) < 0$, which implies that $tb_1 - tb_0 > 0$. From period 1 on, the trade balance is constant. To see this, recall that $tb_t = y_t - c_t - i_t$ and that y_t, c_t, and i_t are all constant from period 1 on. Specifically, we have that $tb_t = tb' \equiv A'F(k') - c'$ for all $t \geq 1$.

The equilibrium stock of external debt, d_t, is constant starting in period 0. To see this, use the definition of the trade balance and equation (3.2) to write the evolution of debt as

$$d_t = (1+r)d_{t-1} - tb',$$

for $t \geq 1$. Since $r > 0$, it follows that unless $d_t = d_{t-1} = tb'/r$, this difference equation will yield a path of debt that grows or falls asymptotically at the rate r, violating the transversality condition. The fact that net foreign debt is constant from period 1 on implies that the equilibrium current account is zero, $ca_t = 0$, for all $t \geq 1$.

We next show that the current account deteriorates in period 0, that is, $\Delta ca_0 < 0$. This follows immediately from the definition of the current account, $ca_0 = tb_0 - r\bar{d}$, and the fact, as we just established, that the trade balance deteriorates in period 0. Indeed, because the current account is nil in the preshock steady state ($ca_t = 0$ for $t < 0$), we have that the level of the current account is negative in period 0: $ca_0 < 0$. In turn, this result and the identity $ca_0 = (-d_0) - (-d_{-1})$ together imply that net foreign debt must rise in period zero, that is, $d_0 > \bar{d}$. To service this elevated level of debt, the trade balance must increase after period 0 to a level exceeding the one it had prior to period 0, that is, $tb_t > tb_{-1}$ for all $t > 0$. That is, the permanent increase in the technology shock first leads to a deterioration of the trade balance and then to an improvement in the trade balance above its preshock level.

Let's take stock of the results obtained thus far. We started with the endowment economy of Chapter 2 and introduced a single modification, namely, capital accumulation. We then showed that the modified model produces very different predictions regarding the initial behavior of the trade balance in response to a positive permanent increase in productivity. In the present economy, such a shock causes the trade balance to initially deteriorate, whereas in the endowment economy a permanent output shock leaves the trade balance unchanged. What is behind the novel predictions of the present model? An important factor that contributes to causing an initial deterioration of the trade balance is the combination of a demand for goods for investment purposes and a persistent productivity shock. This factor has two implications. One direct implication is that because the positive productivity shock is expected to last, investment in physical capital increases. The fact that investment rises in response to the permanent increase in productivity causes the trade balance to deteriorate. This channel is closed in the endowment economy of Chapter 2, because investment was by assumption always equal to zero. The second implication is less direct. The combination of capital accumulation and a persistent increase in productivity implies that output increases by more in the long run than in period 0. This is so because in the period in which the productivity shock occurs, the capital stock has not yet adjusted and output only increases by the increase in productivity. But in later periods output is higher due to both a higher level of productivity and a higher level of physical capital. Consumption-smoothing households adjust consumption in period 0 taking into account the entire future path of output. Faced with an upward-sloping time path of income, households increase consumption in period 0 by more than the increase in output in that period. In the endowment economy a once-and-for-all increase in the endowment did not give rise to an upward-sloping path of income, and hence the consumption response did not exceed the output response in period 0.

The size of the increase in investment—and hence the size of the implied decline in the trade balance in response to a positive productivity shock—depends on the assumed absence of capital adjustment costs. Note that in response to the increase in future expected productivity, the entire adjustment in investment occurs in period 0. Indeed, investment falls to zero in period 1 and remains nil thereafter. In the presence of costs of adjusting the stock of capital, investment spending is spread over a number of periods, dampening the increase in domestic absorption in the period the shock occurs. The fact that the productivity shock leads to a time path of income that is increasing is the result of the productivity shock being permanent. To highlight the importance of these two assumptions (namely, absence of adjustment costs and permanence of the productivity shock) in generating a deterioration of the trade balance in response to a positive productivity shock, in the next two sections we analyze separately an economy with purely temporary productivity shocks and an economy with capital adjustment costs.

3.4 Adjustment to Temporary Productivity Shocks

To stress the importance of persistence in productivity movements in inducing a deterioration of the trade balance in response to a positive output shock, it is worth analyzing the effect of a purely temporary shock. Specifically, suppose that up until period -1 inclusive, the productivity factor A_t was constant and equal to $\bar{A}$. Suppose also that in period -1 people assigned a zero probability to the event that A_0 would be different from $\bar{A}$. In period 0, however, a zero probability event happens, namely, $A_0 = A' > \bar{A}$. Furthermore, suppose that everybody correctly expects the productivity shock to be purely temporary. That is, everybody expects $A_t = \bar{A}$ for all $t > 0$. In this case, equation (3.12) implies that the capital stock, and therefore also investment, are unaffected by the productivity shock. That is, $k_t = \bar{k}$ for all $t \geq 0$, where $\bar{k}$ is the level of capital inherited in period 0. This is intuitive. The productivity of capital unexpectedly increases in period 0. As a result, households would like to have more capital in that period. But k_0 is predetermined in period 0. Investment in period 0 can only increase the future stock of capital. At the same time, agents have no incentives to have a higher capital stock in the future, because its productivity is expected to go back down to its historic level $\bar{A}$ right after period 0.

The positive productivity shock in period 0 does produce an increase in output in that period, from $\bar{A}F(\bar{k})$ to $A'F(\bar{k})$. That is,

$$y_0 = y_{-1} + (A' - \bar{A})F(\bar{k}),$$

where $y_{-1} \equiv \bar{A}F(\bar{k})$ is the preshock level of output. This output increase induces higher consumption. Evaluating equation (3.13) for $t = 0$, recalling that $c_{-1} = -r\bar{d} + \bar{A}F(\bar{k})$, and that $d_{-1} = \bar{d}$, we have that

$$c_0 = c_{-1} + \frac{r}{1+r}(y_0 - y_{-1}).$$

Basically, households invest the entire increase in output in the international financial market and increase consumption by the interest flow associated with that financial investment.

Combining the above two expressions and recalling that investment is unaffected by the temporary shock, we get that the trade balance in period 0 is given by

$$tb_0 - tb_{-1} = (y_0 - y_{-1}) - (c_0 - c_{-1}) - (i_0 - i_{-1}) = \frac{1}{1+r}(A' - \bar{A})F(\bar{k}) > 0.$$

This expression shows that the trade balance improves on impact. The reason for this counterfactual prediction is simple: firms have no incentive to invest, as the increase in the productivity of capital is short lived. At the same time, consumers save most of the purely temporary increase in income to smooth consumption over time. As a consequence, domestic absorption increases but by less than the increase in output.

Comparing the results obtained under the two polar cases of permanent and purely temporary productivity shocks, we can derive the following principle.

Principle I   The more persistent productivity shocks are, the more likely an initial deterioration of the trade balance will be.

We will analyze this principle in more detail in Chapters 4 and 5, in the context of models featuring a more flexible notion of persistence.

3.5 Capital Adjustment Costs

Consider now an economy identical to the one analyzed thus far, except that now changes in the stock of capital come at a cost. Capital adjustment costs—in a variety of forms—are a regular feature of business-cycle models. A property of most open economy models is that in the absence of adjustment costs, investment is excessively volatile. Investment adjustment costs are therefore frequently used to dampen the volatility of investment over the business cycle (see, e.g., Mendoza 1991, and Schmitt-Grohé 1998, among many others).

Suppose that the sequential budget constraint is of the form

$$A_t F(k_t) + d_t = (1+r)d_{t-1} + c_t + i_t + \frac{i_t^2}{2k_t}. \tag{3.16}$$

Here, capital adjustment costs are given by $i_t^2/(2k_t)$ and are a strictly convex function of investment. Capital adjustment costs are nil in the steady state, that is, when $i_t = k_{t+1} - k_t = 0$. The slope of the adjustment-cost function, given by i_t/k_t, also vanishes in the steady state. As will be clear shortly, this feature implies that in the steady state the relative price of capital goods in terms of consumption goods is unity. As in the economy without adjustment costs, we assume that physical capital does not depreciate, so that the law of motion of the capital stock continues to be given by (3.4).

The household problem then consists of maximizing the utility function (3.1), subject to the law of motion of capital (3.4), to the no-Ponzi-game constraint (3.5), and to the sequential budget constraint (3.16). The Lagrangian associated with this optimization problem is

$$\mathcal{L} = \sum_{t=0}^{\infty} \beta^t \left\{ U(c_t) \right.$$

$$\left. + \lambda_t \left[A_t F(k_t) + d_t - (1+r)d_{t-1} - c_t - i_t - \frac{1}{2}\frac{i_t^2}{k_t} + q_t(k_t + i_t - k_{t+1}) \right] \right\}.$$

The variables $\beta^t \lambda_t$ and $\beta^t \lambda_t q_t$ denote Lagrange multipliers on the sequential budget constraint and the law of motion of the capital stock, respectively. The optimality conditions associated with the household problem are (3.4), (3.5) holding with equality, (3.6), (3.7), (3.16),

$$1 + \frac{i_t}{k_t} = q_t, \tag{3.17}$$

and

$$\lambda_t q_t = \beta \lambda_{t+1} \left[q_{t+1} + A_{t+1} F'(k_{t+1}) + \frac{1}{2}\left(\frac{i_{t+1}}{k_{t+1}}\right)^2 \right]. \tag{3.18}$$

The variable q_t represents the shadow relative price of capital in terms of consumption goods, and is known as *Tobin's q*. Optimality condition (3.17) equates the marginal cost of producing a unit of capital, $1 + i_t/k_t$, on the left-hand side, to the marginal revenue of selling a unit of capital, q_t, on the right-hand side. If q_t increases, agents have incentives to devote more resources to the production of physical capital, so i_t increases. In turn, the increase in investment raises the marginal cost of producing capital, i_t/k_t, which tends to restore the equality between the marginal cost and marginal revenue of capital goods.

We continue to assume that $\beta(1+r) = 1$. As in the model without investment adjustment costs, this assumption implies, by optimality conditions (3.6) and (3.7), that λ_t and

c_t are constant over time. Then optimality condition (3.18) can be written as

$$(1+r)q_t = A_{t+1}F'(k_{t+1}) + \frac{1}{2}\left(\frac{i_{t+1}}{k_{t+1}}\right)^2 + q_{t+1}. \tag{3.19}$$

The left-hand side of this expression is the return of investing q_t units of goods in bonds, and the right-hand side is the return associated with investing q_t units of goods in physical capital. Consider first the rate of return of investing in physical capital. Adding one unit to the existing stock costs q_t. The additional unit yields $A_{t+1}F'(k_{t+1})$ units of output in the next period. In addition, an extra unit of capital reduces tomorrow's adjustment costs by $(i_{t+1}/k_{t+1})^2/2$. Finally, the unit of capital can be sold next period at the price q_{t+1}. Alternatively, the agent can engage in a financial investment by purchasing q_t bonds in period t, which yields a gross return of $(1+r)q_t$ in period $t+1$. At the optimum both strategies must yield the same return.

The level of consumption can be found by solving the sequential budget constraint (3.16) forward and using the transversality condition (i.e., the no-Ponzi-game constraint (3.5) holding with equality). This yields

$$c_t = -rd_{t-1} + \frac{r}{1+r}\sum_{j=0}^{\infty}\frac{A_{t+j}F(k_{t+j}) - i_{t+j} - \frac{1}{2}(i_{t+j}^2/k_{t+j})}{(1+r)^j}.$$

This is by now a familiar expression. Households split their nonfinancial permanent income, given by the second term on the right-hand side, to service their outstanding debt and to consume. The definition of nonfinancial permanent income is adapted to include adjustment costs as one additional component of domestic absorption subtracted from the flow of output. The right-hand side of the above expression is known as *permanent income* and is given by the sum of net investment income $(-rd_{t-1})$ and nonfinancial permanent income.

3.5.1 Dynamics of the Capital Stock

Using the evolution of capital (3.4) to eliminate i_t from optimality conditions (3.17) and (3.19), we obtain the following two first-order, nonlinear difference equations in k_t and q_t:

$$k_{t+1} = q_t k_t, \tag{3.20}$$

$$q_t = \frac{A_{t+1}F'(q_t k_t) + (q_{t+1} - 1)^2/2 + q_{t+1}}{1+r}. \tag{3.21}$$

Suppose the technological factor A_t is constant and equal to $\bar{A}$. The perfect-foresight solution to these equations is depicted in Figure 3.2. The horizontal line $\overline{KK'}$ corresponds to the pairs (k_t, q_t) for which $k_{t+1} = k_t$ in equation (3.20). That is,

$$q_t = 1. \tag{3.22}$$

Above the locus $\overline{KK'}$, the capital stock grows over time, and below the locus $\overline{KK'}$, the capital stock declines over time, as indicated by the horizontal arrows.

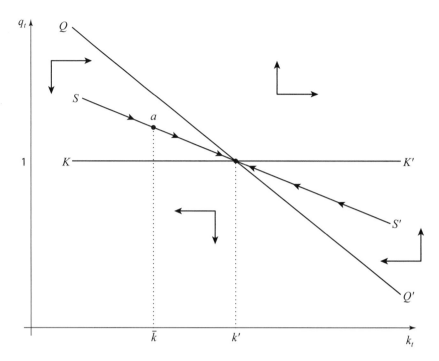

Figure 3.2   The dynamics of the capital stock.

The locus $\overline{QQ'}$ corresponds to the pairs (k_t, q_t) for which $q_{t+1} = q_t$ in equation (3.21). That is,

$$rq_t = \bar{A}F'(q_t k_t) + (q_t - 1)^2/2. \tag{3.23}$$

For q_t near unity, the locus $\overline{QQ'}$ is downward sloping (we can ignore the quadratic term, since it is second order). Above and to the right of $\overline{QQ'}$, q increases over time, and below and to the left of $\overline{QQ'}$, q decreases over time, as indicated by the vertical arrows.

Jointly, equations (3.22) and (3.23) determine the steady-state value of the capital stock and the steady-state value of Tobin's q. The steady-state value of q_t is clearly 1. The steady-state value of k_t is implicitly determined by the expression $r = \bar{A}F'(\bar{k})$. This is the same value obtained in the economy without adjustment costs, and we denoted it by $\bar{k} = \kappa(\bar{A}/r)$, with $\kappa' > 0$. This is not surprising, because, as noted earlier, adjustment costs vanish in the steady state.

The system (3.20)–(3.21) is saddle-path stable. The locus $\overline{SS'}$ represents the converging *saddle path*. If the initial capital stock is different from its long-run level, both q and k converge monotonically to their steady states along the saddle path. For example, if the economy starts with an initial capital stock below $\bar{k}$, then the transitional dynamics feature a price of capital above average, positive investment, and an increasing stock of capital.

3.5.2 A Permanent Technology Shock

Suppose now that in period 0 the technology factor Λ_t increases permanently from $\bar{\Lambda}$ to $A' > \bar{A}$. It is clear from equation (3.22) that the locus $\overline{KK'}$ is not affected by the productivity shock. Equation (3.23) shows that the locus $\overline{QQ'}$ shifts up and to the right. It follows that in response to a permanent increase in productivity, the long-run level of capital experiences a permanent increase. In contrast, the price of capital, q_t, is not affected in the long run.

Consider now the transition to the new steady state. Figure 3.2 displays the initial stock of capital, $\bar{k}$, which was the steady-state value of capital prior to the innovation in productivity. It also displays the new steady-state value of capital, k'. In the period of the shock, the capital stock does not move, since it is predetermined. The price of installed capital, q_t, jumps to the new saddle path, point a in the figure. This increase in the price of installed capital induces an increase in investment, which in turn makes capital grow over time. After the initial impact, q_t decreases toward 1. Along this transition, the capital stock increases monotonically toward its new steady state k'.

The equilibrium dynamics of investment in the presence of adjustment costs are quite different from those arising in the absence thereof. In the frictionless environment, investment experiences a one-time jump equal to $k' - \bar{k}$ in period 0. Under capital adjustment costs, the initial increase in investment is smaller, as the capital stock adjusts gradually to its long-run level.

The different behavior of investment with and without adjustment costs has consequences for the equilibrium dynamics of the trade balance. In effect, because investment is part of domestic absorption, and because investment tends to be less responsive to productivity shocks in the presence of adjustment costs, it follows that the trade balance falls by less in response to a positive innovation in productivity in the environment with frictions. The following principle therefore emerges.

> **Principle II** The more pronounced are capital adjustment costs, the smaller will be the initial trade balance deterioration in response to a positive and persistent productivity shock.

In light of principles I and II derived in this chapter, it is natural to ask what the model would predict for the behavior of the trade balance in response to productivity shocks when one introduces realistic degrees of capital adjustment costs and persistence in the productivity-shock process. We address this issue in Chapter 4.

3.6 Exercises

3.1 (Full Depreciation) Consider the model of Section 3.1. The law of motion of capital given in equation (3.4) is a special case of the specification

$$k_{t+1} = (1 - \delta)k_t + i_t,$$

where δ denotes the depreciation rate. The case considered in Section 3.1 obtains when $\delta = 0$, which implies that capital does not depreciate. Show that in response to a permanent positive productivity shock of the type analyzed in Section 3.3, the trade balance depreciates on impact. Consider first the polar case of full depreciation, which takes place when $\delta = 1$, and then the general case $\delta \in (0, 1)$.

3.2 (Anticipated Productivity Shocks) Consider a perfect-foresight economy populated by a large number of identical households with preferences described by the utility function

$$\sum_{t=0}^{\infty} \beta^t U(c_t),$$

where c_t denotes consumption; U is a period utility function assumed to be strictly increasing, strictly concave, and twice continuously differentiable; and $\beta \in (0, 1)$ is a parameter denoting the subjective rate of discount. Households are subject to the following four constraints:

$$y_t + d_t = (1+r)d_{t-1} + c_t + i_t,$$

$$y_t = A_t F(k_t),$$

$$k_{t+1} = k_t + i_t,$$

and

$$\lim_{j \to \infty} \frac{d_{t+j}}{(1+r)^j} \le 0,$$

given d_{-1}, k_0, and $\{A_t\}_{t=0}^{\infty}$. The variable d_t denotes holdings of one-period external debt at the end of period t, r denotes the interest rate on these debt obligations, y_t denotes output, k_t denotes the (predetermined) stock of physical capital in period t, and i_t denotes gross investment; F is a production function assumed to be strictly increasing, strictly concave, and to satisfy the Inada conditions, and $A_t > 0$ is an exogenous productivity factor. Suppose that $\beta(1+r) = 1$. Assume further that up until period -1 inclusive, the productivity factor was constant and equal to $\bar{A} > 0$ and that the economy was in a steady state with a constant level of capital and a constant net debt position equal to $\bar{d}$. Suppose further that in period 0 the productivity factor also equals $\bar{A}$, but that agents learn that in period 1 it will jump permanently to $A' > \bar{A}$. That is, in period 0, households know that the path of the productivity factor is given by

$$A_t = \begin{cases} \bar{A} & t \le -1 \\ \bar{A} & t = 0 \\ A' > \bar{A} & t \ge 1 \end{cases}.$$

1. Characterize the equilibrium paths of output, consumption, investment, capital, the net foreign debt position, the trade balance, and the current account.

2. Compare your answer to the case of an unanticipated permanent increase in productivity studied in Section 3.3.

3. Now assume that the anticipated productivity shock is transitory. Specifically, assume that the information available to households at $t = 0$ is

$$
A_t = \begin{cases} \bar{A} & t \leq -1 \\ \bar{A} & t = 0 \\ A' > \bar{A} & t = 1 \\ \bar{A} & t \geq 2 \end{cases}.
$$

    a. Characterize the equilibrium dynamics.

    b. Compare your answer to the case of an unanticipated temporary increase in productivity studied in Section 3.3.

    c. Compare your answer to the case of an anticipated endowment shock in the endowment economy studied in exercise 2.5 of Chapter 2.

3.3 (Adjustment Costs and Temporary Technology Shocks) In the economy with adjustment cost studied in Section 3.5, characterize the dynamics triggered by a purely temporary positive technology shock. Specifically, assume that before the shock the economy is in a steady state with capital, debt, and productivity constant at $\bar{k}$, $\bar{d}$, and $\bar{A}$, respectively. Assume that in period 0, unexpectedly, A_t increases to $A' > \bar{A}$, and returns permanently to $\bar{A}$ in period 1.

3.4 (Balanced Growth) A small open economy is populated by infinitely-lived families with preferences given by

$$
\sum_{t=0}^{\infty} \beta^t \sqrt{C_t},
$$

where C_t denotes consumption of a perishable good in period t and $\beta \in (0, 1)$ is the subjective discount factor. Households can produce goods domestically via the technology

$$
Y_t = A_t^{1-\alpha} K_t^{\alpha},
$$

with $\alpha \in (0, 1)$, where Y_t denotes output; K_t denotes the stock of physical capital; and A_t denotes a technological factor that grows at the constant gross rate $\gamma > 1$, that is,

$$
A_{t+1} = \gamma A_t,
$$

with $A_0 > 0$ given. The law of motion of the capital stock is given by

$$
K_{t+1} = K_t + I_t,
$$

with $K_0 > 0$ given, where I_t denotes net investment. Families have access to world financial markets. Each period $t \geq 0$, they can take on one-period debt, denoted D_t, that matures in period $t + 1$. The interest, denoted r, is constant and satisfies

$$\beta(1 + r) = \sqrt{\gamma}.$$

Households start period 0 with outstanding debt, including interest, of $(1 + r)D_{-1} > 0$. Debt accumulation is subject to the terminal condition $\lim_{t \to \infty}(1 + r)^{-t}D_t \le 0$.

1. Write down the household's optimization problem.
2. Derive the associated optimality conditions.
3. Characterize the equilibrium dynamics of all variables in the model. Make sure to also consider the equilibrium dynamics of the trade balance and the current account. (You might want to first devise a scaling of variables that makes the equilibrium stationary. After characterizing the equilibrium cast in scaled variables, you can go back to the original variables.)
4. What variables display a trend in equilibrium?
5. Establish whether the equilibrium displays balanced growth. That is, discuss whether consumption, investment, and the capital stock share a common trend with output. Do the trade balance, the current account, and external debt display a trend?

3.5 (Unbalanced Growth) Consider the same economy as in exercise 3.4, except that the interest rate and the subjective discount factor now satisfy

$$\beta(1 + r) = 1,$$

and $r > 0$.

1. Characterize the equilibrium dynamics of output, consumption, investment, the trade balance, the current account, and external debt.
2. What variables display a trend in equilibrium?
3. Considering jointly the results obtained in this exercise and in exercise 3.4, what general conclusion can you derive?

The Open Economy
Real-Business-Cycle Model

In the previous chapter, we built a model of the open economy driven by productivity shocks and argued that it can capture the observed countercyclicality of the trade balance. We also established that two features of the model are important for making this prediction possible. First, productivity shocks must be sufficiently persistent. Second, capital adjustment costs must not be too strong. In this chapter, we ask more questions about the ability of that model to explain observed business cycles. In particular, we ask whether it can explain the sign and magnitude of business-cycle indicators, such as the standard deviation, serial correlation, and correlation with output of output, consumption, investment, the trade balance, and the current account. To give the model a fair chance to explain the data, we extend the relatively simple structure of Chapter 3 by allowing for three features that make it more realistic: endogenous labor supply and demand, uncertainty in the technology shock process, and capital depreciation. The resulting theoretical framework is known as the Small Open Economy Real-Business-Cycle model, or, succinctly, the SOE-RBC model.

4.1 The Model

Consider an economy populated by an infinite number of identical households with preferences described by the utility function

$$E_0 \sum_{t=0}^{\infty} \beta^t U(c_t, h_t), \qquad (4.1)$$

where c_t denotes consumption; h_t denotes hours worked; $\beta \in (0, 1)$ is the subjective discount factor; and U is a period utility function, which is assumed to be increasing in its first argument, decreasing in its second argument, and concave. The symbol E_t denotes the expectations operator conditional on information available in period t.

The period-by-period budget constraint of the representative household is given by

$$d_t = (1 + r_{t-1})d_{t-1} - y_t + c_t + i_t + \Phi(k_{t+1} - k_t), \qquad (4.2)$$

where d_t denotes the household's debt position at the end of period t, r_t denotes the interest rate at which domestic residents can borrow in period t, y_t denotes domestic output, i_t denotes gross investment, and k_t denotes physical capital. The function $\Phi(\cdot)$ is meant to capture capital adjustment costs and is assumed to satisfy $\Phi(0) = \Phi'(0) = 0$ and $\Phi''(0) > 0$. Small open economy models typically include capital adjustment costs to avoid excessive investment volatility in response to variations in the productivity of domestic capital or in the foreign interest rate. The restrictions imposed on Φ and Φ' ensure that in the steady state, adjustment costs are nil and that the relative price of capital goods in terms of consumption goods is unity. Note that here adjustment costs are expressed in terms of final goods. Alternatively, one could assume that adjustment costs take the form of lost capital goods (see exercise 4.11).

Output is produced by means of a linearly homogeneous production function that takes capital and labor services as inputs,

$$y_t = A_t F(k_t, h_t), \tag{4.3}$$

where A_t is an exogenous and stochastic productivity shock. This shock represents the single source of aggregate fluctuations in the present model. The stock of capital evolves according to

$$k_{t+1} = (1 - \delta)k_t + i_t, \tag{4.4}$$

where $\delta \in (0, 1)$ denotes the rate of depreciation of physical capital.

Households choose processes $\{c_t, h_t, y_t, i_t, k_{t+1}, d_t\}_{t=0}^{\infty}$ to maximize the utility function (4.1) subject to (4.2)–(4.4) and a no-Ponzi constraint of the form

$$\lim_{j \to \infty} E_t \frac{d_{t+j}}{\prod_{s=0}^{j}(1 + r_s)} \leq 0. \tag{4.5}$$

Using equations (4.3) and (4.4) to eliminate, respectively, y_t and i_t from the sequential budget constraint (4.2) yields

$$d_t = (1 + r_{t-1})d_{t-1} - A_t F(k_t, h_t) + c_t + k_{t+1} - (1 - \delta)k_t + \Phi(k_{t+1} - k_t). \tag{4.6}$$

The Lagrangian corresponding to the household's maximization problem is

$$\mathcal{L} = E_0 \sum_{t=0}^{\infty} \beta^t \left\{ U(c_t, h_t) \right.$$

$$\left. + \lambda_t \left[A_t F(k_t, h_t) + (1 - \delta)k_t + d_t - c_t - (1 + r_{t-1})d_{t-1} - k_{t+1} - \Phi(k_{t+1} - k_t) \right] \right\},$$

where $\beta^t \lambda_t$ denotes the Lagrange multiplier associated with the sequential budget constraint (4.6). The first-order conditions associated with the household's maximization problem are (4.5) holding with equality, (4.6),

$$\lambda_t = \beta(1+r_t)E_t\lambda_{t+1}, \tag{4.7}$$

$$U_c(c_t, h_t) = \lambda_t, \tag{4.8}$$

$$-U_h(c_t, h_t) = \lambda_t A_t F_h(k_t, h_t), \tag{4.9}$$

and

$$\lambda_t[1 + \Phi'(k_{t+1} - k_t)]$$
$$= \beta E_t\lambda_{t+1}\left[A_{t+1}F_k(k_{t+1}, h_{t+1}) + 1 - \delta + \Phi'(k_{t+2} - k_{t+1})\right]. \tag{4.10}$$

Optimality conditions (4.7), (4.8), and (4.10) are familiar from Chapter 3. Optimality condition (4.9) equates the supply of labor to the demand for labor. To put it in a more familiar form, divide (4.9) by (4.8) to eliminate λ_t. This yields

$$-\frac{U_h(c_t, h_t)}{U_c(c_t, h_t)} = A_t F_h(k_t, h_t). \tag{4.11}$$

The left-hand side of this expression is the household's labor supply schedule. It is the marginal rate of substitution between leisure and consumption, which is increasing in hours worked, holding the level of consumption constant.[1] The right-hand side of (4.11) is the marginal product of labor, which in a decentralized version of this model equals the demand for labor. The marginal product of labor is decreasing in labor, holding constant the level of capital.

The law of motion of the productivity shock is assumed to be given by the first-order autoregressive process

$$\ln A_{t+1} = \rho \ln A_t + \widetilde{\eta}\epsilon_{t+1}, \tag{4.12}$$

where ϵ_t is an i.i.d. white noise process with mean zero and unit standard deviation, the parameter $\widetilde{\eta}$ is the standard deviation of innovations to productivity, and the parameter $\rho \in (-1, 1)$ governs the serial correlation of the technology shock. According to this expression, the expected value of the productivity shock in period $t + 1$ conditional on information available in period t is a fraction ρ of the current productivity shock,

$$E_t \ln A_{t+1} = \rho \ln A_t. \tag{4.13}$$

More generally, the assumed AR(1) structure of the productivity shock implies that its expected value j periods ahead conditional on current information is a fraction ρ^j of its present value:

$$E_t \ln A_{t+j} = \rho^j \ln A_t.$$

In other words, $\ln A_t$ is always expected to converge to zero at the rate ρ.

---

1. A sufficient condition for $-U_h/U_c$ to be increasing in h_t holding c_t constant is $U_{ch} < 0$, and the necessary and sufficient condition is $U_{hh}/U_h > U_{ch}/U_c$.

4.1.1 Inducing Stationarity: External Debt-Elastic Interest Rate (EDEIR)

In Chapters 2 and 3 we saw that the equilibrium of an open economy with one internationally traded bond and a constant interest rate satisfying $\beta(1 + r) = 1$ features a random walk in consumption, net external debt, and the trade balance. Under perfect foresight, that model predicts that the steady-state levels of debt, consumption, and the trade balance depend on initial conditions, such as the initial level of debt itself. This does not mean that the deterministic steady state is indeterminate. Rather, it means that the steady state is history dependent.

The nonstationarity of the one-bond open economy model complicates the task of approximating equilibrium dynamics, because available approximation techniques require stationarity of the state variables. Here, we follow Schmitt-Grohé and Uribe (2003) and induce stationarity by making the interest rate debt elastic.[2]

Specifically, we assume that the interest rate faced by domestic agents, r_t, is increasing in the country's cross-sectional average level of debt, which we denote by $\widetilde{d}_t$. Formally, r_t is given by

$$r_t = r^* + p(\widetilde{d}_t), \tag{4.14}$$

where r^* denotes the world interest rate, and $p(\cdot)$ is a country-specific interest-rate premium. Households take the evolution of $\widetilde{d}_t$ as exogenously given. For simplicity, we assume that the world interest rate, r^*, is constant. The function $p(\cdot)$ is assumed to be strictly increasing. As we will see shortly, the assumption of a debt-elastic interest-rate premium gives rise to a steady state of the model that is independent of initial conditions. In addition, this assumption ensures that a first-order approximation of the equilibrium dynamics converges to the true (nonlinearized) equilibrium dynamics as the support of the underlying shocks becomes small.

The intuition for why a debt-elastic interest rate induces stationarity is simple. As the level of debt rises above its steady-state level, the country premium also rises, inducing households to increase savings, which curbs debt growth. Similarly, if debt falls below its steady-state level, the country premium falls, inducing households to increase consumption and reduce savings, which fosters debt growth.

Here we have motivated a debt-elastic interest rate on purely technical grounds. However, this feature is also of interest for empirical and theoretical reasons. In Chapters 5 and 6 we argue on econometric grounds that data from emerging countries favor a significantly debt-sensitive interest rate. From a theoretical point of view, a debt-elastic interest rate is of interest, because it represents a simple way to capture the presence of financial frictions. In Chapter 13 we provide microfoundations to this interpretation in the context of models with imperfect enforcement of international debt contracts.

4.1.2 Equilibrium

Because agents are assumed to be identical, in equilibrium the cross-sectional average level of debt must be equal to the individual level of debt, that is,

$$\widetilde{d}_t = d_t. \tag{4.15}$$

---

2. In Section 4.10 we study various alternative ways to induce stationarity.

Use equations (4.8), (4.14), and (4.15) to eliminate λ_t, r_t, and $\tilde{d}_t$ from (4.5), (4.6), (4.7), and (4.10) to obtain

$$d_t = [1 + r^* + p(d_{t-1})] d_{t-1} + c_t + k_{t+1} - (1-\delta)k_t$$
$$+ \Phi(k_{t+1} - k_t) - A_t F(k_t, h_t), \tag{4.16}$$

$$U_c(c_t, h_t) = \beta(1 + r^* + p(d_t)) E_t U_c(c_{t+1}, h_{t+1}), \tag{4.17}$$

$$U_c(c_t, h_t)[1 + \Phi'(k_{t+1} - k_t)] \tag{4.18}$$
$$= \beta E_t U_c(c_{t+1}, h_{t+1}) \left[A_{t+1} F_k(k_{t+1}, h_{t+1}) + 1 - \delta + \Phi'(k_{t+2} - k_{t+1}) \right],$$

and

$$\lim_{j \to \infty} E_t \frac{d_{t+j}}{\prod_{s=0}^{j}(1 + r^* + p(d_s))} = 0. \tag{4.19}$$

A competitive equilibrium is a set of processes $\{d_t, c_t, h_t, k_{t+1}, A_t\}$ satisfying (4.11), (4.12), and (4.16)–(4.19), given A_0, d_{-1}, and k_0, and the process $\{\epsilon_t\}_{t=0}^{\infty}$.

Given the equilibrium processes of consumption, hours, capital, and debt, output is obtained from equation (4.3), investment from equation (4.4), and the interest rate from equation (4.14) evaluated at $\tilde{d}_t = d_t$. One can then construct the equilibrium process of the trade balance from the definition

$$tb_t \equiv y_t - c_t - i_t - \Phi(k_{t+1} - k_t), \tag{4.20}$$

where tb_t denotes the trade balance in period t. Finally, the current account is given by the sum of the trade balance and net investment income, that is,

$$ca_t = tb_t - r_{t-1}d_{t-1}. \tag{4.21}$$

Alternatively, one could construct the equilibrium process of the current account by using the fact that the current account measures the change in net foreign assets, that is,

$$ca_t = d_{t-1} - d_t.$$

4.2 Decentralization

The economy presented thus far assumes that production, employment, and the use of capital are all carried out in the household. Here we present an alternative formulation in which all of these activities are performed in the marketplace. This formulation is known as the *decentralized economy*. A key result of this section is that the equilibrium conditions of the decentralized economy are identical to those of the centralized one. The decentralized formulation is of interest because it provides predictions for the equilibrium behavior of relative prices, such as the real wage, the rental rate of capital, and the value of the stock market.

4.2.1 Households in the Decentralized Economy

We assume that each period the household supplies h_t hours to the labor market. We also assume that the household owns shares of a firm that produces physical capital and rents it to firms that produce final goods. Let w_t denote the real wage, π_t the profit generated by firms that produce capital goods, s_t the number of shares of these firms owned by the household, and p_t^s the price of each share. The household takes w_t, π_t, and p_t^s as exogenously given. Its period-by-period budget constraint can then be written as

$$d_t = (1 + r_{t-1})d_{t-1} + c_t + p_t^s(s_t - s_{t-1}) - s_{t-1}\pi_t - w_t h_t. \tag{4.22}$$

The household chooses processes $\{c_t, h_t, d_t, s_t\}_{t=0}^{\infty}$ to maximize the utility function (4.1) subject to (4.5) and (4.22), taking as given the processes $\{r_t, w_t, \pi_t, p_t^s\}_{t=0}^{\infty}$ and the initial conditions $(1 + r_{-1})d_{-1}$ and s_{-1}. The first-order conditions associated with the household's problem are (4.5) holding with equality, (4.7), (4.8), (4.22),

$$-\frac{U_h(c_t, h_t)}{U_c(c_t, h_t)} = w_t, \tag{4.23}$$

and

$$\lambda_t p_t^s = \beta E_t \lambda_{t+1}[p_{t+1}^s + \pi_{t+1}].$$

The variable p_t^s represents a stock market index, such as the S&P 500. The above Euler equation can be integrated forward to obtain

$$p_t^s = E_t \sum_{j=1}^{\infty} \beta^j \frac{\lambda_{t+j}}{\lambda_t} \pi_{t+j}, \tag{4.24}$$

which states that the value of the stock market in period t equals the present discounted value of future expected profits.

4.2.2 Firms Producing Final Goods

Firms hire labor and rent capital to produce a homogeneous final good. They operate in perfectly competitive product and factor markets. The production technology is given by

$$y_t = A_t F(k_t, h_t).$$

Profits in period t are given by

$$A_t F(k_t, h_t) - w_t h_t - u_t k_t,$$

where u_t denotes the rental rate of capital. The firm picks hours and capital to maximize profits. For firms that find it optimal to produce a positive and finite level of output, first-order conditions associated with the profit maximization problem are

$$A_t F_h(k_t, h_t) = w_t \tag{4.25}$$

and

$$A_t F_k(k_t, h_t) = u_t. \tag{4.26}$$

Because the production technology is homogeneous of degree one, these efficiency conditions imply that firms make zero profits at all times. To see this, multiply (4.25) by h_t, (4.26) by k_t, and sum the resulting expressions to obtain $A_t F_h(k_t, h_t) h_t + A_t F_k(k_t, h_t) k_t = w_t h_t + u_t k_t$. By the assumed linear homogeneity of the production function, the left-hand side of this expression is equal to $A_t F(k_t, h_t)$. It then follows that the total cost of production equals output, or, that profits equal zero.

4.2.3 Firms Producing Capital Goods

Firms producing capital invest i_t units of final goods each period and are subject to adjustment costs $\Phi(k_{t+1} - k_t)$ measured in units of final goods. Each period, these firms rent the stock of capital to firms producing final goods at the rental rate u_t per unit. Profits of firms producing capital goods are then given by

$$\pi_t = u_t k_t - i_t - \Phi(k_{t+1} - k_t). \tag{4.27}$$

The problem of the firm producing capital goods is to choose processes $\{\pi_t, i_t, k_{t+1}\}_{t=0}^{\infty}$ to maximize the present discounted value of profits

$$E_0 \sum_{t=0}^{\infty} \beta^t \frac{\lambda_t}{\lambda_0} \pi_t,$$

subject to the law of motion of the capital stock given in equation (4.4) and to the definition of profits given in equation (4.27), taking as given the processes $\{u_t, \lambda_t\}_{t=0}^{\infty}$ and the initial condition k_0. Note that profits are discounted using the factor $\beta^t \lambda_t / \lambda_0$, which is the value assigned by households to contingent payments of goods in period t in terms of units of goods in period 0. This way of discounting makes sense, because households own the firms producing capital. Note further that the objective function of the firm is identical to the right-hand side of the household's optimality condition (4.24). This means that the objective of the firm producing capital can be interpreted as maximizing the value of the firm in the stock market, given by p_t^s.

Using equation (4.4) to eliminate i_t from equation (4.27) and the resulting expression to eliminate π_t from the firm's objective function yields

$$E_0 \sum_{t=0}^{\infty} \beta^t \frac{\lambda_t}{\lambda_0} \left[(u_t + 1 - \delta) k_t - k_{t+1} - \Phi(k_{t+1} - k_t) \right].$$

The optimality condition with respect to k_{t+1} is then given by

$$\lambda_t [1 + \Phi'(k_{t+1} - k_t)] = \beta E_t \lambda_{t+1} \left[u_{t+1} + 1 - \delta + \Phi'(k_{t+2} - k_{t+1}) \right]. \tag{4.28}$$

4.2.4 The Decentralized Equilibrium

Without loss of generality, we can normalize the number of shares to be one per household at all times:

$$s_t = 1. \tag{4.29}$$

A competitive equilibrium in the decentralized economy is then a set of processes $\{d_t,$ $\tilde{d}_t, c_t, p_t^s, s_t, r_t, \pi_t, h_t, w_t, \lambda_t, y_t, u_t, k_{t+1}, i_t, A_t\}_{t=0}^{\infty}$, satisfying (4.3), (4.4), (4.7), (4.8), (4.12), (4.14), (4.15), (4.19), (4.22), (4.23), and (4.24)–(4.29), given A_0, d_{-1}, and k_0, and the process $\{\epsilon_t\}_{t=0}^{\infty}$.

It is straightforward to see that the equations included in this definition can be combined to produce all the equations of the equilibrium in the centralized economy defined in Section 4.1.2. It can also be readily established that if all the conditions for an equilibrium in the centralized economy are satisfied, then one can construct processes for market prices, profits, and share holdings, namely, processes $\{w_t, u_t, p_t^s, \pi_t, s_t\}_{t=0}^{\infty}$, so that all the equilibrium conditions of the decentralized economy listed here are satisfied. This completes the proof that the equilibrium conditions of the centralized and decentralized economies are identical.

4.3 Functional Forms

We assume that the period utility function takes the form

$$U(c, h) = \frac{G(c, h)^{1-\sigma} - 1}{1 - \sigma}, \quad \sigma > 0,$$

with

$$G(c, h) = c - \frac{h^\omega}{\omega}, \quad \omega > 1.$$

The form of the subutility index $G(c, h)$ is due to Greenwood, Hercowitz, and Huffman (1988) and is typically referred to as GHH preferences. It implies that the labor supply (the marginal rate of substitution between consumption and leisure) is independent of the level of consumption. Specifically, under GHH preferences, equilibrium condition (4.23) becomes

$$h_t^{\omega-1} = w_t. \tag{4.30}$$

This labor supply schedule has a wage elasticity of $1/(\omega - 1)$ and is independent of c_t. GHH preferences were popularized in the open economy business-cycle literature by Mendoza (1991). They were first introduced for technical reasons, as the feature that the labor supply is independent of the marginal utility of wealth facilitates the computation of the neoclassical growth model (in its open or closed economy forms) using global methods. Subsequently, GHH preferences have been embraced because, by shutting off wealth effects on labor supply, they prevent persistent positive productivity shocks from causing a decline in employment. Because employment is procyclical, this prediction is counterfactual under the hypothesis that disturbances in total factor productivity are a major source of business cycles. Finally, GHH preferences are considered appealing from an empirical point of view. For example, Schmitt-Grohé and Uribe (2012b) estimate a general preference specification that nests the GHH form as a special case and find that the income elasticity of labor supply is small at business-cycle frequency, lending support to the GHH specification for business-cycle analysis. Exercise 4.13 explores the robustness of the quantitative predictions of the present model to replacing the GHH preference specification with a Cobb-Douglas one.

The period utility function $U(c, h)$ displays constant relative risk aversion (CRRA) over the subutility index $G(c, h)$. The parameter σ measures the degree of relative risk aversion, and its reciprocal, $1/\sigma$, measures the intertemporal elasticity of substitution.

We adopt a Cobb-Douglas specification for the production function,

$$F(k, h) = k^\alpha h^{1-\alpha},$$

with $\alpha \in (0, 1)$. This specification implies a unitary elasticity of substitution between capital and labor. That is, a 1 percent increase in the wage-to-rental ratio, w_t/u_t, induces firms to increase the capital-labor ratio by 1 percent. To see this, divide equation (4.25) by equation (4.26) and use the Cobb-Douglas form for the production function to obtain

$$\left(\frac{1-\alpha}{\alpha}\right) \frac{k_t}{h_t} = \frac{w_t}{u_t},$$

which implies that in equilibrium the capital-labor ratio is proportional to the wage-to-rental ratio. The Cobb-Douglas specification of the production function is widely used in the business-cycle literature.

The capital adjustment cost function is assumed to be quadratic,

$$\Phi(x) = \frac{\phi}{2} x^2,$$

with $\phi > 0$. This specification implies that net investment, whether positive or negative, generates resource costs.

Finally, we follow Schmitt-Grohé and Uribe (2003) and assume that the country interest-rate premium takes the form

$$p(d) = \psi_1 \left(e^{d - \bar{d}} - 1\right),$$

where $\psi_1 > 0$ and $\bar{d}$ are parameters. According to this expression the country premium is an increasing and convex function of net external debt.

4.4 Deterministic Steady State

Assume that the variance of the innovation to the productivity shock, $\tilde{\eta}$, is nil. We refer to such an environment as a deterministic economy. We define a *deterministic steady state* as an equilibrium of the deterministic economy in which all endogenous variables are constant over time.

The characterization of the deterministic steady state is of interest for two reasons. First, the steady state facilitates the calibration of the model. This is because, to a first approximation, the deterministic steady state coincides with the average position of the model economy. In turn, matching average values of endogenous variables to their observed counterparts (e.g., matching predicted and observed average values of the labor share, the consumption shares, or the trade-balance-to-output ratio) can reveal information about structural parameters that can be exploited in the calibration of the model. Second, the deterministic steady state is often used as a convenient point around which the equilibrium conditions of the stochastic economy are approximated.

For any variable we denote its steady-state value by removing the time subscript. Evaluating equilibrium condition (4.17) at the steady state yields

$$1 = \beta \left[1 + r^* + \psi_1 \left(e^{d - \bar{d}} - 1 \right) \right].$$

We assume that

$$\beta(1 + r^*) = 1.$$

In the context of the present model, this assumption is a normalization and is not necessary to ensure stationarity. Combining the above two restrictions, one obtains

$$d = \bar{d},$$

that is, the steady-state value of debt is the parameter $\bar{d}$. The steady-state version of (4.18) implies that

$$1 = \beta \left[\alpha \left(\frac{k}{h} \right)^{\alpha - 1} + 1 - \delta \right].$$

This expression delivers the steady-state capital-labor ratio, which we denote by κ. Formally,

$$\kappa \equiv \frac{k}{h} = \left(\frac{\beta^{-1} - 1 + \delta}{\alpha} \right)^{1/(\alpha - 1)}.$$

Using this expression to eliminate the capital-labor ratio from equilibrium condition (4.11) evaluated at the steady state, one obtains the following expression for the steady-state level of hours:

$$h = \left[(1 - \alpha) \kappa^{\alpha} \right]^{1/(\omega - 1)}.$$

Given the steady-state values of labor and the capital-labor ratio, the steady-state level of capital is simply given by

$$k = \kappa \, h.$$

Finally, the steady-state level of consumption can be obtained by evaluating equilibrium condition (4.16) at the steady state. This yields

$$c = -r^* \bar{d} + \kappa^{\alpha} h - \delta \, k.$$

This completes the characterization of the deterministic steady state of the present economy.

4.5 Calibration

An important intermediate step in computing the quantitative predictions of a business-cycle model is to assign values to its structural parameters. There are two main ways to accomplish this step. One is econometric estimation by such methods as the generalized method of moments (GMM), impulse response matching, maximum likelihood, or likelihood-based Bayesian methods. We will explain and apply several of these econometric techniques in later chapters. The second approach, which we study here, is calibration. Almost always, business-cycle studies employ a combination of calibration and econometric estimation.

In general, the calibration method assigns values to the parameters of the model in three different ways: (a) by using sources unrelated to the macro data the model aims to explain, (b) by matching first moments of the data that the model aims to explain, and (c) by matching second moments of the data that the model aims to explain.

To illustrate how calibration works, we adapt the calibration strategy adopted in Mendoza (1991) to the present model. His SOE-RBC model aims to explain the Canadian business cycle. The time unit in the model is meant to be 1 year. In the present model, there are 10 parameters that need to be calibrated: σ, δ, r^*, α, $\bar{d}$, ω, ϕ, ψ_1, ρ, and $\tilde{\eta}$. We separate these parameters into the three calibration categories described above.

Category A: Parameters calibrated using sources unrelated to the data that the model aims to explain

The parameters that fall into this category are the intertemporal elasticity of substitution, σ, the depreciation rate, δ, and the world interest rate, r^*. Based on parameter values widely used in related business-cycle studies, Mendoza sets σ equal to 2, δ equal to 0.1, and r^* equal to 4 percent per year.

Category B: Parameters set to match first moments of the data that the model aims to explain

In this category are the capital elasticity of the production function, α, and the parameter $\bar{d}$ pertaining to the country interest-rate premium. The parameter α is set to match the average labor share in Canada of 0.68. In the present model, the labor share, given by the ratio of labor income to output, or $w_t h_t / y_t$, equals $1 - \alpha$ at all times. To see this, note that in equilibrium, w_t equals the marginal product of labor, which, under the assumed Cobb-Douglas production function, is given by $(1 - \alpha) y_t / h_t$.

The parameter $\bar{d}$ is set to match the observed average trade-balance-to-output ratio in Canada of 2 percent. Combining the definition of the trade balance given in equation (4.20) with the resource constraint (4.16) implies that in the steady state,

$$tb = r^* \bar{d}.$$

This condition states that in the deterministic steady state, the country must generate a trade surplus sufficiently large to service its external debt. Dividing both sides by steady-state output and solving for $\bar{d}$ yields

$$\bar{d} = \frac{tb/y}{r^*} y.$$

At this point we know that $tb/y = 0.02$ and that $r^* = 0.04$, but y remains unknown. From the derivation of the steady state presented in Section 4.4, one can deduce that

$$y = \left[(1-\alpha)\kappa^{\alpha\omega}\right]^{\frac{1}{\omega-1}},$$

where $\kappa = [\alpha/(r^*+\delta)]^{1/(1-\alpha)}$. The only unknown parameter in this expression is ω. This means that if we knew ω, we could calculate y and then use this value to identify $\bar{d}$. Next, we discuss how the calibration strategy assigns values to ω and the remaining unknown structural parameters.

Category C: Parameters set to match second moments of the data that the model aims to explain

This category of parameters contains ω, which governs the wage elasticity of labor supply; ϕ, which defines the magnitude of capital adjustment costs; ψ_1, which determines the debt sensitivity of the interest rate; and ρ and $\tilde{\eta}$ defining, respectively, the persistence and volatility of the technology shock. The calibration strategy for these parameters is to match the following five second moments of the Canadian data at business-cycle frequency: a standard deviation of hours of 2.02 percent, a standard deviation of investment of 9.82 percent, a standard deviation of the trade-balance-to-output ratio of 1.87 percentage points, a serial correlation of output of 0.62, and a standard deviation of output of 2.81 percent.[3] These are natural targets, as their theoretical counterparts are directly linked to the parameters to be calibrated. In practice, this last step of the calibration procedure goes as follows: (i) Guess values for the five parameters in category (c). (This automatically determines a value for $\bar{d}$, pending from category (b).) (ii) Approximate the equilibrium dynamics of the model. (We will discuss how to accomplish this task shortly.) (iii) Calculate the implied five second moments to be matched in (c). (iv) If the match between actual and predicted second moments is judged satisfactory, the procedure has concluded. If not, try a new guess for the five parameters to be calibrated and return to (i).

There is a natural way to update the parameter guess. For instance, if the volatility of output predicted by the model is too low, raise the volatility of the innovation to the technology shock, $\tilde{\eta}$. Similarly, if the predicted volatility of investment is too high, increase the value of ϕ. And so on. In general, there are no guarantees that a set of parameter values will produce an exact match between the targeted empirical second moments and their theoretical counterparts. So some notion of distance and tolerance is in order. The parameter values that result from this calibration procedure are shown in Table 4.1.

Note that the calibration strategy presented here is just one of many possible ones. For instance, we could place δ in category (b) and add the average investment share as a first moment of the data to be matched. Similarly, we could take the parameter ω out of category (c) and place it instead in category (a). To assign a value to ω we could then use existing micro-econometric estimates of the Frisch elasticity of labor supply. Finally, a calibration approach that has been used extensively, especially in the early days of the RBC

---

3. The standard deviations of hours, investment, and output are measured as percentages because (the cyclical components of) hours, investment, and output are measured as percentage deviations of these indicators from trend.

Table 4.1   Calibration of the EDEIR SOE-RBC Model

Parameter	σ	δ	r^*	α	$\bar{d}$	ω	ϕ	ψ_1	ρ	$\tilde{\eta}$
Value	2	0.1	0.04	0.32	0.7442	1.455	0.028	0.000742	0.42	0.0129

literature, is to place ρ and $\tilde{\eta}$ into category (a) instead of (c). Under this approach, one uses Solow residuals as a proxy for the productivity shock A_t. Then one estimates a univariate representation of the Solow residual to obtain values for ρ and $\tilde{\eta}$.

4.6 Approximating Equilibrium Dynamics

The competitive equilibrium of the SOE-RBC model is described by a system of nonlinear stochastic difference equations. Closed-form solutions to this type of systems are typically unavailable. We therefore must resort to an approximate solution. Various techniques have been devised to solve such dynamic systems. The one we study in this section is based on a linear approximation of the equilibrium conditions. In Section 4.13 we study a global solution method based on value function iterations. In later chapters we discuss and apply other global solution methods as well as second-order approximation techniques.

It is important to choose carefully the base of the linearization. It is often appropriate to linearize the system with respect to the logarithm of some variables. This is known as log-linearization and is useful for variables whose empirical counterparts are expressed in log (or percent) deviations from trend. In the present model, this is the case with y_t, c_t, h_t, k_t, and A_t. For other variables, it is more natural to perform the linearization with respect to their levels rather than with respect to their logs. This is the case, for instance, with net interest rates, like r_t; or variables that can take negative values, such as tb_t, ca_t, and d_t.

Before performing the linearization of the equilibrium conditions of the open economy RBC model, we briefly explain how to linearize a function with respect to a mix of bases, the log for some variables and the level for others. As an illustration, consider the expression

$$s_t = E_t m(u_t, v_t, z_{t+1}).$$

We wish to linearize this expression with respect to the logs of s_t, u_t, and z_{t+1}, and with respect to the level of v_t. To this end, let $\hat{s}_t \equiv \ln(s_t/s)$, $\hat{u}_t \equiv \ln(u_t/u)$, and $\hat{z}_{t+1} \equiv \ln(z_{t+1}/z)$ denote the log-deviations of s_t, u_t, and z_{t+1} with respect to their respective deterministic steady-state values (denoted s, u, and z), and let $\hat{v}_t \equiv v_t - v$ denote the deviation of v_t from its steady-state value (denoted v). Then we can write the above expression as

$$s e^{\hat{s}_t} = E_t m \left(u e^{\hat{u}_t}, \hat{v}_t + v, z e^{\hat{z}_{t+1}} \right).$$

The linearization results from differentiating the above expression with respect to $\hat{s}_t$, $\hat{u}_t$, $\hat{v}_t$, and $\hat{z}_{t+1}$ around their respective deterministic steady-state values. Note that the deterministic steady-state values of all hatted variables is zero. When performing the differentiation, recall that the conditional expectations operator (E_t) is an integral and that the differentiation of an integral with respect to variables appearing in the integrand is the integral of the differentiated integrand. Then the desired linear approximation is given by

$$s\widehat{s}_t = m_u u \widehat{u}_t + m_v \widehat{v}_t + m_z z E_t \widehat{z}_{t+1},$$

where m_u, m_v, and m_z denote the partial derivatives of $m(\cdot, \cdot, \cdot)$ with respect to u_t, v_t, and z_{t+1}, respectively, evaluated at the steady state (u, v, z). Linearized expressions are often expressed in terms of elasticities. For example, dividing both sides of the above expression by s, we obtain

$$\widehat{s}_t = \epsilon_{mu} \widehat{u}_t + \epsilon_{mv} \widehat{v}_t + \epsilon_{mz} E_t \widehat{z}_{t+1},$$

where $\epsilon_{mu} \equiv m_u u / s$ and $\epsilon_{mz} \equiv m_z z / s$ denote the elasticities of m with respect to u and z, respectively, and $\epsilon_{mv} \equiv m_v / s$ denotes the semielasticity of m with respect to v, all evaluated at the steady state.

With this background, we now turn to the linearization of the equilibrium conditions of the SOE-RBC model.

We linearize the equilibrium conditions of the SOE-RBC model with respect to the logs of c_t, h_t, k_t, and A_t, and with respect to the level of d_t. Accordingly, let $\widehat{x}_t \equiv \ln(x_t / x)$, for $x_t = c_t$, h_t, k_t, A_t, and $\widehat{d}_t \equiv d_t - d$. Then the linearized version of equilibrium conditions (4.11), (4.13), and (4.16)–(4.18) is[4]

$$[\epsilon_{hh} - \epsilon_{ch}]\widehat{h}_t + [\epsilon_{hc} - \epsilon_{cc}]\widehat{c}_t = \widehat{A}_t + \alpha(\widehat{k}_t - \widehat{h}_t),$$

$$E_t \widehat{A}_{t+1} = \rho \widehat{A}_t,$$

$$\frac{1}{y}\widehat{d}_t = \frac{1}{y}[\psi_1 d + 1 + r^*]\widehat{d}_{t-1} + s_c \widehat{c}_t$$

$$+ \frac{s_i}{\delta}[\widehat{k}_{t+1} - (1 - \delta)\widehat{k}_t] - \widehat{A}_t - \alpha \widehat{k}_t - (1 - \alpha)\widehat{h}_t,$$

$$\epsilon_{ch}\widehat{h}_t + \epsilon_{cc}\widehat{c}_t = \psi_1 \beta \widehat{d}_t + \epsilon_{ch} E_t \widehat{h}_{t+1} + \epsilon_{cc} E_t \widehat{c}_{t+1},$$

and

$$\epsilon_{cc}\widehat{c}_t + \epsilon_{ch}\widehat{h}_t + \Phi''(0)k(\widehat{k}_{t+1} - \widehat{k}_t) = \epsilon_{cc} E_t \widehat{c}_{t+1} + \epsilon_{ch} E_t \widehat{h}_{t+1}$$

$$+ \frac{r^* + \delta}{1 + r^*} \left[E_t \widehat{A}_{t+1} + (\alpha - 1)(E_t \widehat{k}_{t+1} - E_t \widehat{h}_{t+1}) \right]$$

$$+ \frac{\Phi''(0)k}{1 + r^*}[E_t \widehat{k}_{t+2} - E_t \widehat{k}_{t+1}],$$

where $\epsilon_{hh} \equiv U_{hh}h/U_h$, $\epsilon_{ch} \equiv U_{ch}h/U_c$, $\epsilon_{hc} \equiv U_{hc}c/U_h$, $\epsilon_{cc} \equiv U_{cc}c/U_c$, $s_c \equiv c/F(k, h)$, $s_i \equiv \delta k/F(k, h)$, and $y \equiv F(k, h)$. The linearization uses the particular forms assumed for

---

4. The transversality condition (4.19) is not included in the linearized system, because it is always satisfied in the neighborhood of the deterministic steady state. Also, the linearized system includes equation (4.13) instead of (4.12).

the production function and the country premium function. Of course, we could have linearized an expanded version of the equilibrium conditions, including equations defining additional macro indicators of interest. For instance, the system could have included equations (4.3), (4.4), (4.20), and (4.21), jointly defining y_t, i_t, tb_t, and ca_t.

We now express the set of equilibrium conditions and its linearized version using a more compact notation, which applies to a large class of dynamic stochastic general equilibrium (DSGE) models, not just the SOE-RBC model. Let y_t be a vector collecting the control variables of the model. Control variables in period t are endogenous variables that are determined in period t. In the SOE-RBC model, as defined by equations (4.11), (4.13), and (4.16)–(4.18), the vector y_t contains $\ln c_t$ and $\ln h_t$. Let x_t^1 denote the vector of endogenous state variables. Endogenous state variables in period t are endogenous variables determined before period t. In the SOE-RBC model, x_t^1 includes $\ln k_t$ and d_{t-1}. Let x_t^2 denote the vector of exogenous state variables. Exogenous state variables in period t are exogenous variables that are determined in period t or earlier. In the SOE-RBC model, x_t^2 includes a single variable, $\ln A_t$. Let $x_t \equiv [x_t^{1\prime} \ x_t^{2\prime}]'$ denote the vector of state variables.

The equilibrium conditions of the model, given by equations (4.11), (4.13), and (4.16)–(4.18), can be written as

$$E_t f(y_{t+1}, y_t, x_{t+1}, x_t) = 0. \tag{4.31}$$

The law of motion of the exogenous state vector x_t^2 is given by

$$x_{t+1}^2 = \Lambda x_t^2 + \widetilde{\eta}\epsilon_{t+1}, \tag{4.32}$$

where, in general, ϵ_t is a vector of i.i.d. random variables with mean zero and unit variance, Λ is a square matrix with all eigenvalues inside the unit circle, and $\widetilde{\eta}$ is a matrix of parameters defining the variance-covariance matrix of innovations to the exogenous state vector. In the SOE-RBC model, ϵ_t, Λ, and $\widetilde{\eta}$ are all scalars (with $\Lambda = \rho$).

The deterministic steady state is a pair of constant vectors y and x that solves the system

$$f(y, y, x, x) = 0.$$

The steady-state vectors y and x are assumed to be known. In Section 4.4, we derived the steady state of the SOE-RBC model analytically.

We restrict attention to equilibria in which at every date t the economy is expected to converge to the nonstochastic steady state, that is, we impose

$$\lim_{j \to \infty} \begin{bmatrix} E_t y_{t+j} \\ E_t x_{t+j} \end{bmatrix} = \begin{bmatrix} y \\ x \end{bmatrix}. \tag{4.33}$$

This restriction implies that the transversality condition (4.19) is always satisfied.

As mentioned earlier, the representation of an equilibrium given by conditions (4.31)–(4.33) is quite general and applies to a large class of DSGE models. Thus, the solution technique discussed below is not restricted to the SOE-RBC model.

The first-order Taylor expansion of equation (4.31) is given by

$$f_{y'}E_t\widehat{y}_{t+1} + f_y\widehat{y}_t + f_{x'}E_t\widehat{x}_{t+1} + f_x\widehat{x}_t = 0, \tag{4.34}$$

where $\widehat{x}_t \equiv x_t - x$ and $\widehat{y}_t \equiv y_t - y$ denote, respectively, the deviations of x_t and y_t from their steady state values. The matrices $f_{y'}$, f_y, $f_{x'}$, and f_x denote, respectively, the partial derivatives of the function f with respect to y_{t+1}, y_t, x_{t+1}, and x_t evaluated at the non-stochastic steady state. These matrices are assumed to be known. Except for small models, like the SOE-RBC model studied here, these derivatives can be tedious to obtain by hand. The Matlab scripts indicated at the end of this section perform and evaluate these derivatives automatically.

The solution of the linear system (4.34), with the associated exogenous law of motion (4.32) and the terminal condition (4.33), is given by

$$\widehat{x}_{t+1} = h_x\widehat{x}_t + \eta\,\epsilon_{t+1}$$

and

$$\widehat{y}_t = g_x\widehat{x}_t.$$

The matrix η is given by

$$\eta = \begin{bmatrix} \emptyset \\ \widetilde{\eta} \end{bmatrix}.$$

The appendix to this chapter shows how to obtain the matrices h_x and g_x, given the matrices $f_{y'}$, f_y, $f_{x'}$, and f_x. The appendix also shows how to compute second moments and impulse response functions predicted by the model.

Matlab code for performing first-order accurate approximations to DSGE models and for computing second moments and impulse response functions is available on the book's Web site. Matlab code to solve the specific SOE-RBC EDEIR model studied here is also available on the book's Web site via http://press.princeton.edu/titles/11032.html.

4.7 The Performance of the Model

Having calibrated the SOE-RBC model and computed a first-order approximation to the equilibrium dynamics, we are ready to explore its quantitative predictions. As a point of reference, Table 4.2 displays empirical second moments of interest from the Canadian economy. The first three columns display the empirical second moments reported by Mendoza (1991). The table shows standard deviations, serial correlations, and contemporaneous correlations of output with output, consumption, investment, hours, and the trade-balance-to-output ratio. The data is annual, quadratically detrended, and covers the period 1946–1985. Although outdated, we choose to use the empirical moments reported in Mendoza (1991) to preserve coherence with the calibration strategy of Section 4.5. To gauge the stability of the empirical regularities and the out-of-sample performance of the SOE-RBC model, the middle three columns of Table 4.2 display empirical second moments

Table 4.2 Empirical and Theoretical Second Moments

Variable	Canadian Data						Model		
	1946–1985			1960–2011					
	σ_{x_t}	$\rho_{x_t,x_{t-1}}$	ρ_{x_t,GDP_t}	σ_{x_t}	$\rho_{x_t,x_{t-1}}$	ρ_{x_t,GDP_t}	σ_{x_t}	$\rho_{x_t,x_{t-1}}$	ρ_{x_t,GDP_t}
y	2.81	0.62	1	3.71	0.86	1	3.08	0.62	1
c	2.46	0.70	0.59	2.19	0.70	0.62	2.71	0.78	0.84
i	9.82	0.31	0.64	10.31	0.69	0.80	9.04	0.07	0.67
h	2.02	0.54	0.80	3.68	0.75	0.78	2.12	0.62	1
$\frac{tb}{y}$	1.87	0.66	−0.13	1.72	0.76	0.12	1.78	0.51	−0.04
$\frac{ca}{y}$							1.45	0.32	0.05

Sources: Empirical moments for the period 1946–1985 are taken from Mendoza (1991) and for the period 1960–2011 are based on the authors' calculations using data from WDI (GDP, consumption, investment, imports, and exports) and Statistics Canada (hours worked).
Notes: Empirical second moments are based on annual, per capita, and quadratically detrended data. Standard deviations are measured in percentage points. Theoretical moments are produced by running the Matlab code `edeir_run.m`.

computed using data from 1960 to 2011. Overall, the stylized facts displayed in the table appear to be quite stable across time. In particular, in both samples the ranking of volatilities is $i > y > c > tb/y$. All aggregates are positively serially correlated. However, investment has become much more persistent over time. The trade-balance-to-GDP ratio is slightly countercyclical in the early sample but slightly procyclical in the recent one. The Canadian economy appears to have become more volatile; in particular, the volatilities of output and hours worked have increased by 30 and 80 percent, respectively.

Table 4.2 also displays second moments predicted by the SOE-RBC EDEIR model. Comparing the early empirical second moments with their predicted counterparts, it should not come as a surprise that the model does very well at replicating the volatilities of output, hours, investment, and the trade-balance-to-output ratio, and the serial correlation of output. For we calibrated the parameters ω, ϕ, ψ_1, ρ, and $\tilde{\eta}$ to match these five moments. But the model performs relatively well along other dimensions. For instance, it correctly implies that consumption is less volatile than output and investment and is more volatile than hours and the trade-balance-to-output ratio. Also, the model correctly predicts that the trade-balance-to-output ratio is countercyclical. This prediction is of interest because the parameters ϕ and ρ governing the degree of capital adjustment costs and the persistence of the productivity shock (which, as we established in Chapter 3, are key determinants of the cyclicality of the trade-balance-to-output ratio) were set independently of the observed cyclical properties of the trade balance. The model does not perform equally well at explaining the comovement of the trade balance with output over the more recent sample. Exercise 4.10 asks you to use the empirical second moments associated with the 1960–2011 sample to recalibrate and reevaluate the SOE-RBC EDEIR model.

The model overpredicts the correlation of hours with output. The observed correlation is 0.8, whereas the predicted correlation is exactly unity. The prediction of a correlation of hours with output exactly equal to one is due to the assumed GHH form for the period

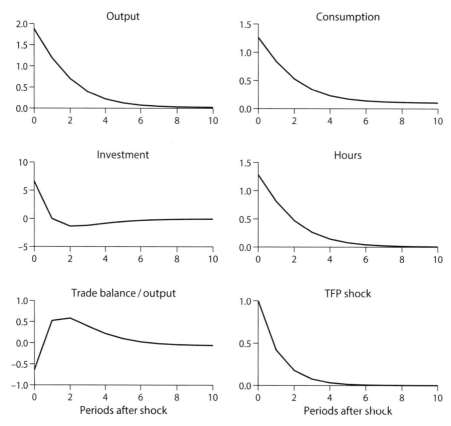

Figure 4.1   Responses to a 1-percent productivity shock.

Notes: To produce this figure, run the Matlab code `edeir_run.m`. The impulse responses of output, consumption, investment, hours, and TFP are expressed in percentage deviations from the deterministic steady state. The impulse response of the trade-balance-to-output ratio is expressed in percentage-point deviations from the steady state.

utility index. To see this, note that equilibrium condition (4.11), which equates the marginal product of labor to the marginal rate of substitution between consumption and leisure, can be written as $h_t^\omega = (1 - \alpha) y_t$. The log-linearized version of this condition is $\omega \widehat{h}_t = \widehat{y}_t$, which implies that $\widehat{h}_t$ and $\widehat{y}_t$ are perfectly correlated.

Figure 4.1 displays the impulse response functions of a number of variables of interest to a technology shock of size 1 percent in period 0. In response to this innovation, the model predicts an expansion in output, consumption, investment, and hours and a deterioration in the trade-balance-to-output ratio. The level of the trade balance, not shown, also falls on impact. This means that the initial increase in domestic absorption (i.e., the increase in $c_0 + i_0$) is larger than the increase in output. Further, the initial response of consumption is proportionally smaller than that of output, whereas the initial response of investment is about eight times as large as that of output. It follows that in the context of the present SOE-RBC model, investment plays a key role in generating a countercyclical initial response of the trade balance.

4.8 The Role of Persistence and Capital Adjustment Costs

In Chapter 3 we deduced that the negative response of the trade balance to a positive technology shock was not a general implication of the neoclassical model. In particular, we showed that two conditions must be met for the model to generate a deterioration in the trade balance in response to a positive productivity shock. First, capital adjustment costs must not be too stringent. Second, the productivity shock must be sufficiently persistent. To illustrate this conclusion, Figure 4.2 displays the impulse response function of the trade-balance-to-GDP ratio to a technology shock of unit size in period 0 under three alternative parameter specifications. The solid line reproduces the benchmark case from Figure 4.1. The dashed line depicts an economy where the persistence of the productivity shock is half as large as in the benchmark economy ($\rho = 0.21$). In this case, because the productivity shock is expected to die out quickly, the response of investment is relatively weak. In addition, the temporariness of the shock induces households to save most of the increase in income to smooth consumption over time. As a result, the expansion in aggregate domestic absorption is modest. At the same time, because the size of the productivity shock is the same as in the benchmark economy, the initial responses of output and hours are identical in both economies (recall that, by equation (4.30), h_t depends only on k_t and A_t, and that k_t is predetermined in period t). The combination of a weak response in domestic absorption and an initial response in output that is independent of the value of ρ results in an improvement in the trade balance when productivity shocks are not too persistent.

The bulleted line depicts the case of high capital adjustment costs. Here the parameter ϕ equals 0.084, a value three times as large as in the benchmark case. In this environment,

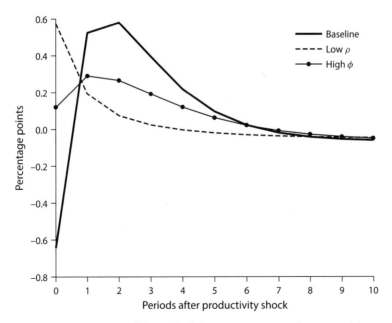

Figure 4.2 Response of the trade-balance-to-output ratio to a positive technology shock.

high adjustment costs discourage firms from increasing investment spending by as much as in the benchmark economy. As a result, the response of aggregate domestic demand is weaker, leading to an improvement in the trade-balance-to-output ratio.

4.9 The Complete Asset Markets (CAM) Model

The model economy considered thus far features incomplete asset markets. In that model, agents have access to a single financial asset that pays a non-state-contingent rate of return. What role does this severe form of market incompleteness play in amplifying business cycles? Would an economy in which agents have access to a richer set of assets that allow them to better hedge against risk display higher or lower aggregate volatility? How would the persistence and cyclicality of different macro indicators change if financial markets were assumed to be more complete? In this section, we address these questions by studying the polar case of complete asset markets. In the one-bond economy studied thus far, the financial market allows agents to smooth consumption over time by saving in a risk-free asset, but it does not allow them to smooth consumption across different states of nature. Under complete asset markets, agents are allowed to smooth consumption not only across time but also across different states of nature. The questions posed above can then be reformulated as follows: how does the predicted business cycle change as one allows agents to smooth consumption across both time and states of nature? As it will turn out, the answer to this question is that temporal smoothing through a single bond goes a long way, leaving little room for smoothing across states to make a difference for business cycles.

From a purely technical point of view, as we will see, the introduction of complete asset markets per se induces stationarity in the equilibrium dynamics, so there will be no need to introduce any ad hoc stationarity-inducing feature.

Preferences and technologies are as in the baseline model of Section 4.1. The period-by-period budget constraint of the household is given by

$$E_t q_{t,t+1} b_{t+1} = b_t + A_t F(k_t, h_t) - c_t - [k_{t+1} - (1-\delta)k_t] - \Phi(k_{t+1} - k_t), \quad (4.35)$$

where $q_{t,t+1}$ is a pricing kernel such that the period-t price of a random payment b_{t+1} in period $t + 1$ is given by $E_t q_{t,t+1} b_{t+1}$. To clarify the nature of the pricing kernel $q_{t,t+1}$, define the current state of nature as S^t. Let $p(S^{t+1}|S^t)$ denote the price of a contingent claim that pays one unit of consumption in a particular state S^{t+1} following the current state S^t. Then the current price of a portfolio paying $b(S^{t+1}|S^t)$ units of consumption goods in states S^{t+1} following S^t is given by $\sum_{S^{t+1}|S^t} p(S^{t+1}|S^t) b(S^{t+1}|S^t)$. Now let $\pi(S^{t+1}|S^t)$ denote the probability of occurrence of state S^{t+1}, given information available at the current state S^t. Multiplying and dividing the expression inside the summation sign by $\pi(S^{t+1}|S^t)$, we can write the price of the portfolio as $\sum_{S^{t+1}|S^t} \pi(S^{t+1}|S^t) \frac{p(S^{t+1}|S^t)}{\pi(S^{t+1}|S^t)} b(S^{t+1}|S^t)$. Now let $q_{t,t+1} \equiv p(S^{t+1}|S^t)/\pi(S^{t+1}|S^t)$ be the price of a contingent claim that pays one unit of good in state $S^{t+1}|S^t$ scaled by the inverse of the probability of occurrence of that state, given information available in S^t. Then we can write the price of the portfolio as

$\sum_{S^{t+1}|S^t} \pi(S^{t+1}|S^t)q_{t,t+1}b_{t+1}$, where b_{t+1} is short notation for $b(S^{t+1}|S^t)$. But this expression is simply the conditional expectation $E_t q_{t,t+1} b_{t+1}$.

Given the pricing kernel $q_{t,t+1}$, one can obtain the price of any asset. Of particular interest is the interest rate on a risk-free bond, which we denote r_t. To obtain r_t, note that $E_t q_{t,t+1}$ is the price in period t of an asset that pays 1 unit of the consumption good in every state of period $t+1$. Now an asset that pays the same amount in every future state is precisely a risk-free asset. It follows that

$$1 + r_t \equiv \frac{1}{E_t q_{t,t+1}} \tag{4.36}$$

represents the risk-free real interest rate in period t.

Households are assumed to be subject to a no-Ponzi-game constraint of the form

$$\lim_{j \to \infty} E_t q_{t,t+j} b_{t+j} \geq 0, \tag{4.37}$$

at all dates and under all contingencies, where the variable

$$q_{t,t+j} \equiv q_{t,t+1} q_{t+1,t+2} \cdots q_{t+j-1,t+j}$$

represents the pricing kernel such that $E_t q_{t,t+j} b_{t+j}$ is the period-t price of a stochastic payment b_{t+j} in period $t+j$. Clearly, $q_{t,t} = 1$.

To characterize the household's optimal plan, it is convenient to derive an intertemporal budget constraint. Begin by multiplying both sides of the sequential budget constraint (4.35) by $q_{0,t}$. Then apply the conditional expectations operator E_0 to obtain

$$E_0 q_{0,t} E_t q_{t,t+1} b_{t+1} = E_0 q_{0,t} \left[b_t + A_t F(k_t, h_t) - c_t - k_{t+1} + (1-\delta)k_t - \Phi(k_{t+1} - k_t) \right].$$

By the definition of the pricing kernel and the law of iterated expectations, we have that $E_0 q_{0,t} E_t q_{t,t+1} b_{t+1} = E_0 q_{0,t+1} b_{t+1}$. So we can write the above expression as

$$E_0 q_{0,t+1} b_{t+1} = E_0 q_{0,t} \left[b_t + A_t F(k_t, h_t) - c_t - k_{t+1} + (1-\delta)k_t - \Phi(k_{t+1} - k_t) \right].$$

Now sum this expression for $t = 0$ to $t = T > 0$. This yields

$$E_0 q_{0,T+1} b_{T+1} = b_0 + E_0 \sum_{t=0}^{T} q_{0,t} \left[A_t F(k_t, h_t) - c_t - k_{t+1} + (1-\delta)k_t - \Phi(k_{t+1} - k_t) \right].$$

Take the limit for $T \to \infty$ and use the no-Ponzi-game constraint (4.37) to obtain

$$b_0 \geq E_0 \sum_{t=0}^{\infty} q_{0,t} \left[c_t + k_{t+1} - (1-\delta)k_t + \Phi(k_{t+1} - k_t) - A_t F(k_t, h_t) \right]. \tag{4.38}$$

This expression states that the period-0 value of the stream of current and future trade deficits cannot exceed the value of the initial asset position b_0.

The household's problem consists of choosing contingent plans $\{c_t, h_t, k_{t+1}\}$ to maximize the lifetime utility function (4.1) subject to (4.38), given k_0, b_0, and exogenous processes $\{A_t, q_{0,t}\}$. The Lagrangian associated with this problem is

$$\mathcal{L} = E_0 \sum_{t=0}^{\infty} \left\{ \beta^t U(c_t, h_t) \right.$$

$$\left. + \xi_0 q_{0,t} \left[A_t F(k_t, h_t) - c_t - k_{t+1} + (1-\delta)k_t - \Phi(k_{t+1} - k_t) \right] \right\} + \xi_0 b_0,$$

where $\xi_0 > 0$ denotes the Lagrange multiplier on the time-0 present-value budget constraint (4.38). The first-order conditions associated with the household's maximization problem are (4.11), (4.18), (4.38) holding with equality, and

$$\beta^t U_c(c_t, h_t) = \xi_0 q_{0,t}. \tag{4.39}$$

Taking the ratio of this expression to itself evaluated at a particular state of period $t+1$ yields the Euler equation

$$\frac{\beta U_c(c_{t+1}, h_{t+1})}{U_c(c_t, h_t)} = q_{t,t+1},$$

which says that consumers equate their marginal rate of substitution of current consumption for consumption in a particular state next period to the probability-adjusted price of the corresponding state-contingent claim. In period t there is one Euler equation of this type for each state in period $t+1$ following the present state. In contrast, under incomplete asset markets, there is just one Euler equation in period t, equating the expected marginal rate of substitution between present and future consumption to the risk-free interest rate (see equation (4.7)). This difference reflects the fact that under complete markets, households have a richer set of financial instruments to diversify risk. As a result, under complete markets, households can smooth consumption across time and states, whereas under incomplete markets, they can only smooth consumption across time. In fact, the set of Euler equations faced by the household under complete markets implies the Euler equation under incomplete markets, since one of the assets available under complete markets is a risk-free bond. To see this, take expectations conditional on information available in period t on both sides of the complete-market Euler equation to obtain

$$\frac{\beta E_t U_c(c_{t+1}, h_{t+1})}{U_c(c_t, h_t)} = E_t q_{t,t+1}.$$

Now use (4.36) to eliminate $E_t q_{t,t+1}$ and rearrange to get

$$U_c(c_t, h_t) = \beta(1+r_t) E_t U_c(c_{t+1}, h_{t+1}),$$

which is identical to the Euler equation (4.7) associated with the incomplete-asset-market version of the model.

We assume that the economy is small and fully integrated to the international financial market. Let $q_{0,t}^*$ denote the pricing kernel prevailing in international financial markets. By the assumption of free capital mobility, we have that domestic asset prices must be equal to foreign asset prices, that is,

$$q_{0,t} = q_{0,t}^* \qquad (4.40)$$

at all dates and states. Foreign households are also assumed to have unrestricted access to international financial markets. Therefore, a condition like (4.39) must also hold abroad. Formally,

$$\beta^t U_{c^*}^*(c_t^*, h_t^*) = \xi_0^* q_{0,t}^*. \qquad (4.41)$$

Note that we are assuming that domestic and foreign households share the same subjective discount factor, β. Combining (4.39)–(4.41) yields

$$U_c(c_t, h_t) = \frac{\xi_0}{\xi_0^*} U_{c^*}^*(c_t^*, h_t^*) \qquad (4.42)$$

at all dates and states. This expression says that under complete asset markets, the marginal utility of consumption is perfectly correlated across countries. The constant $\frac{\xi_0}{\xi_0^*}$ reflects differences in per capita wealth between the domestic economy and the rest of the world. Because the present model is one of a small open economy, c_t^* and h_t^* are taken as exogenously given. We endogenize the determination of c_t^* and h_t^* in exercise 4.11. This exercise analyzes a two-country model with complete asset markets in which one country is large and the other is small.

A competitive equilibrium under complete asset markets is a set of processes $\{c_t, h_t, k_{t+1}, A_t\}$ satisfying

$$-\frac{U_h(c_t, h_t)}{U_c(c_t, h_t)} = A_t F_h(k_t, h_t), \qquad (4.11\ \mathrm{R})$$

$$\ln A_{t+1} = \rho \ln A_t + \tilde{\eta}\epsilon_{t+1}, \qquad (4.12\ \mathrm{R})$$

$$U_c(c_t, h_t)[1 + \Phi'(k_{t+1} - k_t)]$$
$$= \beta E_t U_c(c_{t+1}, h_{t+1}) \left[A_{t+1} F_k(k_{t+1}, h_{t+1}) + 1 - \delta + \Phi'(k_{t+2} - k_{t+1}) \right], \qquad (4.18\ \mathrm{R})$$

and

$$U_c(c_t, h_t) = \frac{\xi_0}{\xi_0^*} U_{c^*}^*(c_t^*, h_t^*), \qquad (4.42\ \mathrm{R})$$

given A_0, k_0, $\frac{\xi_0}{\xi_0^*}$, and the exogenous processes $\{\epsilon_t, c_t^*, h_t^*\}$. Equilibrium condition (4.42) reflects the fact that, because domestic consumers have access to a complete set of Arrow-Debreu contingent assets, they can fully diversify domestic risk. As a result, the marginal utility of consumption depends only on external uncertainty. Because the domestic economy is small, the domestic productivity shock A_t does not affect the foreign variables, which respond only to foreign shocks. The domestic economy, however, can be affected by foreign shocks via c_t^* and h_t^*. To be in line with the stochastic structure of the EDEIR model, we shut down all foreign shocks and focus attention only on the effects of innovations in domestic productivity. Therefore we assume that the foreign marginal utility of consumption is time invariant and given by $U_c^*(c^*, h^*)$, where c^* and h^* are constants. Let $\psi_{CAM} \equiv \frac{\xi_0}{\xi_0^*} U_{c^*}^*(c^*, h^*)$. Then, equilibrium condition (4.42) becomes

$$U_c(c_t, h_t) = \psi_{CAM} . \tag{4.43}$$

This expression says that in the absence of external risk, by appropriately choosing their asset portfolios, domestic consumers can attain a constant marginal utility of consumption at all times and under all contingencies. Exercise 4.5 studies a version of the present model in which ψ_{CAM} is stochastic, reflecting the presence of external shocks.

As shown in Schmitt-Grohé and Uribe (2003), the CAM model delivers stationary processes for all variables of interest. This means that replacing the assumption of incomplete asset markets with the assumption of complete asset markets eliminates the endogenous random walk problem that plagues the dynamics of the one-bond economy. The feature of the CAM model that is responsible for its stationarity property is equation (4.42) (or its counterpart (4.43) in the special case of no external uncertainty), which states that with complete asset markets the marginal utility of consumption is exogenous (constant). In contrast, in the one-bond model, in the absence of any ad hoc stationarity-inducing feature, the marginal utility of consumption follows a random walk. To see this, set $\beta(1 + r_t) = 1$ for all t in equation (4.7) to obtain $U_c(c_t, h_t) = E_t U_c(c_{t+1}, h_{t+1})$. This unit root is transmitted to other variables in the model, including consumption, debt, and the trade balance.

4.9.1 What Is the Current Account When Markets Are Complete?

We now wish to shed light on two questions that arise naturally in models with complete asset markets, but are not sufficiently studied in the context of small open economies: What is the current account when financial markets are complete? And how can one compute its equilibrium dynamics? In the one-bond economy the answer is simple: as discussed earlier, the current account equals the change in net bond holdings or, equivalently, the sum of the trade balance and interest on net bond holdings. Under complete asset markets, there is a large (possibly infinite) number of state-contingent financial assets, each with different returns. As a result, it is less clear how to keep track of the country's net foreign asset position or of its net investment income. It turns out that there is a simple way of characterizing and computing the equilibrium level of the current account under complete markets. Let us begin by addressing the simpler question of defining the trade balance. As in the one-bond model, the trade balance in the CAM model is simply given by equation (4.20). The current account can be defined as the change in the country's net foreign asset position. Let

$$s_t \equiv E_t q_{t,t+1} b_{t+1}$$

denote the net foreign asset position at the end of period t. Then the current account is given by

$$ca_t = s_t - s_{t-1}.$$

Alternatively, the current account can be expressed as the sum of the trade balance and net investment income. In turn, net investment income is given by the difference between the payoff in period t of assets acquired in $t - 1$, given by b_t, and the resources spent on contingent claims in $t - 1$, given by $E_{t-1}q_{t-1,t}b_t$. Thus the current account is given by

$$ca_t = tb_t + b_t - E_{t-1}q_{t-1,t}b_t.$$

To see that the above two definitions of the current account are identical, use the definition of the trade balance, equation (4.20), and the definition of the net foreign asset position s_t to write the sequential resource constraint (4.35) as

$$s_t = tb_t + b_t.$$

Subtracting s_{t-1} from both sides of this expression, we have

$$s_t - s_{t-1} = tb_t + b_t - E_{t-1}q_{t-1,t}b_t.$$

The left-hand side of this expression is our first definition of the current account and the right-hand side our second definition.

Summarizing, to obtain predictions for the current account, one must augment the set of equilibrium conditions (4.11), (4.12), (4.18), and (4.42) with the following four equations in the four unknowns tb_t, s_t, b_t, and ca_t:

$$s_t = E_t \beta \frac{U_c(c_{t+1}, h_{t+1})}{U_c(c_t, h_t)} b_{t+1},$$

$$ca_t = s_t - s_{t-1},$$

$$tb_t = A_t F(k_t, h_t) - c_t - [k_{t+1} - (1 - \delta)k_t] - \Phi(k_{t+1} - k_t),$$

and

$$s_t = b_t + tb_t.$$

The variables s_{t-1} and b_t are endogenous states (predetermined in period t), and tb_t and ca_t are control variables (determined in period t).

4.9.2 Quantitative Predictions of the CAM Model

To obtain quantitative predictions, we parameterize the functions U, F, and Φ as in the EDEIR model. Also as in the calibration of the EDEIR model, we assume that $\beta(1 + r^*) = 1$, where r^* is a parameter. The parameters σ, r^*, ω, α, ϕ, δ, ρ, and $\tilde{\eta}$ take the values displayed in Table 4.1. The parameter ψ_{CAM} is set so as to ensure that the steady-state levels of consumption in the CAM and EDEIR models are the same.

Table 4.3 displays unconditional second moments predicted by the CAM model. For comparison, the table also displays the predictions of the one-bond EDEIR model reproduced from Table 4.2. The predictions of the CAM model regarding output, consumption, investment, and the trade balance are qualitatively similar to those of the (EDEIR) incomplete-asset-market model. In particular, the model preserves the volatility ranking of

Table 4.3   The SOE-RBC Model with Complete Asset Markets: Predicted Second Moments

	σ_{x_t}		$\rho_{x_t, x_{t-1}}$		ρ_{x_t, GDP_t}	
Variable	CAM	EDEIR	CAM	EDEIR	CAM	EDEIR
y	3.1	3.1	0.61	0.62	1.00	1.00
c	1.9	2.71	0.61	0.78	1.00	0.84
i	9.1	9.0	0.07	0.07	0.66	0.67
h	2.1	2.1	0.61	0.62	1.00	1.00
$\frac{tb}{y}$	1.6	1.78	0.39	0.51	0.13	−0.04
$\frac{ca}{y}$	3.1	1.45	−0.07	0.32	−0.49	0.05

Notes: Standard deviations are measured in percentage points. The columns labeled CAM are produced with the Matlab program `cam_run.m`.

output, consumption, investment, and the trade balance. Also, the domestic components of aggregate demand are all positively serially correlated and procyclical. Note that the correlation of consumption with output is now unity. This prediction of the CAM model is a consequence of assuming complete markets and GHH preferences. Under complete asset markets the marginal utility of consumption, $U_c(c_t, h_t)$, is constant over time, so that up to first order consumption is linear in hours. In turn, with GHH preferences, as we deduced earlier in this chapter, hours are linearly related to output up to first order. A significant difference between the predictions of the complete- and incomplete-asset-market models is that the former implies a highly countercyclical current account, whereas the latter implies an acyclical current account.

4.10 Alternative Ways to Induce Stationarity

The open economy model analyzed in Section 4.1 features a debt-elastic country interest-rate premium. As mentioned earlier in this chapter, the inclusion of a debt-elastic premium responds to the need to obtain stationary dynamics up to first order. Had we assumed a constant interest rate, the linearized equilibrium dynamics would have contained an endogenous random walk component, and the steady state would have depended on initial conditions. Two problems emerge when the linear approximation possesses a unit root. First, one can no longer claim that when the support of the underlying shocks is sufficiently small, the linear system behaves like the original nonlinear system, which is ultimately the focus of interest. Second, when the variables of interest contain random walk elements, it is impossible to compute unconditional first and second moments (e.g., standard deviations, serial correlations, and correlations with output), which are the most common descriptive statistics of the business cycle.

Nonstationarity arises in the small open economy model from three features: an exogenous cost of borrowing in international financial markets (i.e., an exogenous country interest rate), an exogenous subjective discount factor, and incomplete asset markets. In Section 4.9 we relaxed the third feature and showed that the SOE-RBC model with complete asset markets is stationary. In this section and in Sections 4.11, 4.12, and 4.13, we study and evaluate stationarity-inducing devices that consist of altering the first two features (i.e., the exogeneity of the subjective discount factor and the exogeneity of the country interest rate) while maintaining the assumption of incomplete asset markets. Our analysis follows closely Schmitt-Grohé and Uribe (2003), but expands their analysis by including three additional approaches to inducing stationarity, a model with an internal interest-rate premium, a model with perpetually young consumers, and a model in which stationarity is induced by approximating the equilibrium using global methods and assuming that agents are impatient (achieved by making the subjective discount factor β smaller than the pecuniary discount factor $1/(1 + r^*)$).

One important question is whether the different stationarity-inducing devices affect the predicted business cycle of the small open economy. The answer is no, conditional on the stationarity-inducing device being calibrated to minimize the difference with the no-device formulation of the model. In this case, and given a common calibration, all models considered predict similar business-cycle fluctuations.

Before plunging into details, we note that the nature of the nonstationarity that is present in the small open economy model is different from the one that emerges from the introduction of nonstationary exogenous shocks. In the latter case, it is typically possible to find a transformation of variables that renders the model economy stationary in terms of the transformed variables. We will study an economy with nonstationary shocks and provide an example of a stationarity-inducing transformation in Section 5.2 of Chapter 5. In contrast, the nonstationarity that arises in the small open economy model with an exogenous cost of borrowing, an exogenous rate of time preference, and incomplete markets cannot be eliminated by any variable transformations.

4.10.1 The Internal Debt-Elastic Interest Rate (IDEIR) Model

The EDEIR model studied thus far assumes that the country interest-rate premium depends on the cross-sectional average of external debt. As a result, households take the country premium as exogenously given. The model with an internal debt-elastic interest rate assumes instead that the interest rate faced by domestic agents is increasing in the individual debt position, d_t. Consequently, households internalize the effect that their borrowing choices have on the interest rate they face. In all other aspects, the IDEIR and EDEIR models are identical.

Formally, in the IDEIR model the interest rate is given by

$$r_t = r^* + p(d_t),$$

where r^*, as before, denotes the world interest rate, but now $p(\cdot)$ is a household-specific interest-rate premium. Note that the argument of the interest-rate premium function is the household's own net debt position. This means that when deciding its optimal expenditure and savings plan, the household will take into account the fact that a change in its debt position alters the marginal cost of funds. The only optimality condition that changes relative to the EDEIR model is the Euler equation for debt accumulation, which now takes the form

$$U_c(c_t, h_t) = \beta[1 + r^* + p(d_t) + p'(d_t)d_t]E_t U_c(c_{t+1}, h_{t+1}). \tag{4.44}$$

This expression features the derivative of the premium with respect to debt, because households internalize the fact that as their net debt increases, so does the interest rate they face in financial markets. As a result, in the margin, the household cares about the marginal cost of borrowing, $1 + r^* + p(d_t) + p'(d_t)d_t$, and not about the average cost of borrowing, $1 + r^* + p(d_t)$.

The competitive equilibrium of the IDEIR economy is a set of processes $\{d_t, c_t, h_t, k_{t+1}, A_t\}$ satisfying (4.11), (4.12), (4.16), (4.18), (4.19), and (4.44), given A_0, d_{-1}, k_0, and the process $\{\epsilon_t\}$.

We assume the same functional forms and parameter values as in the EDEIR model (see Section 4.3). We note that in the model analyzed here the steady-state level of debt is no longer equal to $\bar{d}$. To see this, recall that $\beta(1 + r^*) = 1$ and note that the steady-state version of equation (4.44) imposes the following restriction on d:

$$(1 + d)e^{d - \bar{d}} = 1,$$

which does not admit the solution $d = \bar{d}$, except in the special case in which $\bar{d} = 0$. We set $\bar{d} = 0.7442$, which is the value imposed in the EDEIR model. The implied steady-state level of debt is then given by $d = 0.4045212$. Intuitively, households internalize that their own debt position drives up the interest rate, hence they choose to borrow less than households in the EDEIR economy, who fail to internalize the dependence of the interest rate on the stock of debt. In this sense, one can say that households in the EDEIR economy overborrow.[5] The fact that the steady-state debt is lower than $\bar{d}$ implies that the country premium is negative in the steady state. However, the marginal country premium, given by $p(d_t) + p'(d_t)d_t$, is nil in the steady state, as it is in the EDEIR economy. Recall that in the EDEIR economy, the marginal and average premia perceived by households are equal to each other and given by $p(\tilde{d}_t)$. An alternative calibration strategy is to impose $d = \bar{d}$, and to adjust β to ensure that equation (4.44) holds in the deterministic steady state. In this case, the country premium vanishes in the steady state, but the marginal premium is positive and equal to $\psi_1\bar{d}$.

4.10.2 The Portfolio Adjustment Cost (PAC) Model

In the portfolio adjustment cost (PAC) model, stationarity is induced by assuming that agents face convex costs of holding assets in quantities different from some long-run level. Preferences and technology are as in the EDEIR model. However, in contrast to what is assumed in that model, in the PAC model the interest rate at which domestic households can borrow from the rest of the world is assumed to be constant and equal to the world interest rate, r^*, that is, the country premium is nil at all times. The sequential budget constraint of the household is given by

$$d_t = (1 + r^*)d_{t-1} - A_t F(k_t, h_t) + c_t + k_{t+1} - (1 - \delta)k_t + \Phi(k_{t+1} - k_t) + \Psi(d_t), \quad (4.45)$$

---

5. Chapters 10, 11, and 12 study alternative models of overborrowing.

where $\Psi(\cdot)$ is a convex portfolio adjustment cost function satisfying $\Psi(\bar{d}) = \Psi'(\bar{d}) = 0$, for some $\bar{d}$. The first-order conditions associated with the household's maximization problem are identical to those associated with the EDEIR model, except that the Euler condition for debt, equation (4.17), now becomes

$$U_c(c_t, h_t) = \beta \frac{1 + r^*}{1 - \Psi'(d_t)} E_t U_c(c_{t+1}, h_{t+1}).$$ (4.46)

This optimality condition implies that the effective interest rate faced by the household, which we denote r_t, is debt elastic and is given by

$$1 + r_t = \frac{1 + r^*}{1 - \Psi'(d_t)}.$$ (4.47)

Because the portfolio adjustment cost function is convex, the effective interest rate is increasing in the stock of debt. In this regard, the PAC model is a close relative of the EDEIR model, as can be seen by comparing the above Euler equation with its counterpart in the EDEIR model, given by equation (4.17).

The specification adopted here assumes that households directly borrow from abroad. As shown in Uribe and Yue (2006), this setup can be decentralized as follows. Suppose that households face no portfolio adjustment costs and can borrow and lend at the interest rate r_t, which they take as exogenously given and, in particular, as independent of their own debt positions. Their sequential budget constraint is then given by

$$\tilde{d}_t = (1 + r_{t-1})\tilde{d}_{t-1} - A_t F(k_t, h_t) + c_t + k_{t+1} - (1 - \delta)k_t + \Phi(k_{t+1} - k_t) - \Pi_t,$$

where $\tilde{d}_t$ denotes household debt in period t, and Π_t denotes profit income in period t, which the household takes as exogenously given. The optimality conditions associated with the household problem are identical to those in the centralized version of the model, except that the Euler equation now becomes $U_c(c_t, h_t) = \beta(1 + r_t)E_t U_c(c_{t+1}, h_{t+1})$.

Assume that financial transactions between domestic and foreign residents are intermediated by domestic financial institutions, or banks. Suppose that there is a continuum of banks of measure one that behave competitively. They capture funds, d_t, from foreign investors at the world interest rate r^* and lend $\tilde{d}_t$ to domestic agents at the interest rate r_t. Banks face operational costs, $\Psi(d_t)$, that are increasing and convex in the volume of intermediation, d_t. Bank profits in period $t + 1$ are given by $\Pi_{t+1} \equiv (1 + r_t)\tilde{d}_t - (1 + r^*)d_t$. Banks are subject to the resource constraint $\tilde{d}_t = d_t - \Psi(d_t)$. The problem of domestic banks is then to choose $\tilde{d}_t$ and d_t to maximize profits subject to the resource constraint, taking r_t as given. The first-order condition associated with the bank's profit maximization problem is $1 + r_t = \frac{1 + r^*}{1 - \Psi'(d_t)}$, which is identical to equation (4.47). Each period, bank profits are distributed to domestic households in a lump-sum fashion. Replacing the expression for bank profits in the household's budget constraint and using the bank's resource constraint yields the budget constraint of the centralized economy, equation (4.45). It follows that the equilibrium allocations of the centralized and the decentralized economies are the same.

The competitive equilibrium of the PAC economy is a set of processes $\{d_t, c_t, h_t, k_{t+1}, A_t\}$ satisfying (4.11), (4.12), (4.18), (4.19), (4.45), and (4.46), given A_0, d_{-1}, k_0, and the process $\{\epsilon_t\}$.

The world interest rate is assumed to satisfy

$$\beta(1 + r^*) = 1.$$

This assumption implies that in the steady state, the Euler equation (4.46) becomes

$$\Psi'(d) = 0,$$

where d denotes the steady-state value of debt. The assumptions imposed on the portfolio adjustment cost $\Psi(\cdot)$ imply that the unique solution to the above expression is $d = \bar{d}$. It follows that the steady-state level of debt is independent of initial conditions.

We assume a quadratic form for $\Psi(\cdot)$,

$$\Psi(d_t) = \frac{\psi_2}{2}(d_t - \bar{d})^2,$$

where ψ_2 and $\bar{d}$ are constant parameters defining the portfolio adjustment cost function. The remaining functional forms and the calibration of common parameters are as in the EDEIR model. We calibrate $\bar{d}$ to 0.7442, which is the same value as in the EDEIR model. This means that the steady-state values of all endogenous variables are the same in the PAC and EDEIR models. We set ψ_2 at 0.00074, which ensures that the volatility of the current-account-to-output ratio is the same as in the EDEIR model.

At this point, it might be natural to expect the analysis of an external version of the PAC model, in which the portfolio adjustment cost depends on the aggregate level of debt, $\tilde{d}_t$, as opposed to the individual debt position d_t. However, this modification would fail to render the small open economy model stationary. The reason is that in this case, the optimality condition with respect to debt, given by equation (4.46) in the PAC model, would become $U_c(c_t, h_t) = \beta(1 + r^*)E_t U_c(c_{t+1}, h_{t+1})$, which, because $\beta(1 + r^*)$ equals one, implies that the marginal utility of consumption follows a random walk and is therefore nonstationary.

4.10.3 The External Discount Factor (EDF) Model

We next study an SOE-RBC model in which stationarity is induced by assuming that the subjective discount factor depends on endogenous variables. Specifically, we consider a preference specification in which the discount factor depends on endogenous variables that are taken as exogenous by individual households. We refer to this environment as the external discount factor (EDF) model.

Suppose that the discount factor depends on the average per capita levels of consumption and hours worked. Formally, preferences are described by

$$E_0 \sum_{t=0}^{\infty} \theta_t U(c_t, h_t), \tag{4.48}$$

with

$$\theta_{t+1} = \beta(\widetilde{c}_t, \widetilde{h}_t)\theta_t \quad t \geq 0, \quad \theta_0 = 1;$$

where $\widetilde{c}_t$ and $\widetilde{h}_t$ denote the cross-sectional averages of per capita consumption and hours, respectively, which the individual household takes as exogenously given.

In the EDF model, the interest rate is assumed to be constant and equal to r^*. The sequential budget constraint of the household therefore takes the form

$$d_t = (1+r^*)d_{t-1} - A_t F(k_t, h_t) + c_t + k_{t+1} - (1-\delta)k_t + \Phi(k_{t+1} - k_t), \quad (4.49)$$

and the no-Ponzi-game constraint simplifies to $\lim_{j \to \infty}(1+r^*)^{-j}E_t d_{t+j} \leq 0$.

The first-order conditions associated with the household's maximization problem are (4.11), (4.49), and

$$U_c(c_t, h_t) = \beta(\widetilde{c}_t, \widetilde{h}_t)(1+r^*)E_t U_c(c_{t+1}, h_{t+1}), \quad (4.50)$$

$$U_c(c_t, h_t)[1 + \Phi'(k_{t+1} - k_t)]$$
$$= \beta(\widetilde{c}_t, \widetilde{h}_t)E_t U_c(c_{t+1}, h_{t+1}) \left[A_{t+1}F_k(k_{t+1}, h_{t+1}) + 1 - \delta + \Phi'(k_{t+2} - k_{t+1}) \right], \quad (4.51)$$

and

$$\lim_{j \to \infty} E_t \frac{d_{t+j}}{(1+r^*)^j} = 0. \quad (4.52)$$

In equilibrium, individual and average per capita levels of consumption and effort are identical. That is,

$$c_t = \widetilde{c}_t, \quad (4.53)$$

and

$$h_t = \widetilde{h}_t. \quad (4.54)$$

A competitive equilibrium is a set of processes $\{d_t, c_t, h_t, \widetilde{c}_t, \widetilde{h}_t, k_{t+1}, A_t\}$ satisfying (4.11), (4.12), and (4.49)–(4.54), given A_0, d_{-1}, k_0, and the stochastic process $\{\epsilon_t\}$.

We evaluate the model using the same functional forms for the period utility function, the production function, and the capital adjustment cost function as in the EDEIR model. We assume that the subjective discount factor is of the form

$$\beta(c, h) = \left(1 + c - \frac{h^\omega}{\omega}\right)^{-\psi_3},$$

with $\psi_3 > 0$, so that increases in consumption or leisure make households more impatient.

To see that in the EDF model the steady-state level of debt is determined independently of initial conditions, start by noticing that in the steady state, equation (4.50) implies that

$$\beta(c, h)(1 + r^*) = 1,$$

where c and h denote the steady-state values of consumption and hours. Next, notice that, given this result, the steady-state values of hours, capital (k), and output ($k^\alpha h^{1-\alpha}$) can be found in exactly the same way as in the EDEIR model, with β replaced by $(1 + r^*)^{-1}$. Notice that k and h depend only on the deep structural parameters r^*, α, ω, and δ. With h in hand, the above expression delivers c, which depends only on the deep structural parameters defining h and on ψ_3. Finally, in the steady state, the resource constraint (4.49) implies that the steady-state level of debt, d, is given by $d = (c + \delta k - k^\alpha h^{1-\alpha})/r^*$, which depends only on structural parameters.

The EDF model features one new parameter relative to the EDEIR model, namely, the elasticity of the discount factor relative to the composite $1 + c_t - h_t^\omega/\omega$. We set ψ_3 to ensure that the steady-state trade-balance-to-output ratio equals 2 percent, in line with the calibration of the EDEIR model. The implied value of ψ_3 is 0.11.

Note that in our assumed specification of the endogenous discount factor, the parameter ψ_3 governs both the steady-state trade-balance-to-output ratio and the stationarity of the equilibrium dynamics. This dual role may create a conflict. On the one hand, one may want to set ψ_3 at a small value so as to ensure stationarity without affecting the predictions of the model at business-cycle frequency. On the other hand, matching the observed average trade-balance-to-output ratio might require a value of ψ_3 that does affect the behavior of the model at business-cycle frequency. For this reason, it might be useful to consider a two-parameter specification of the discount factor, such as $\beta(c_t, h_t) = (\tilde{\psi}_3 + c_t - \omega^{-1}h_t^\omega)^{-\psi_3}$, where $\tilde{\psi}_3 > 0$ is a parameter. With this specification, one can fix the parameter ψ_3 at a small value, just to ensure stationarity, and set the parameter $\tilde{\psi}_3$ to match the observed trade-balance-to-output ratio.

4.10.4 The Internal Discount Factor (IDF) Model

Consider now a variation of the EDF model in which the subjective discount factor depends on the individual levels of consumption and hours worked rather than on the aggregate levels. Specifically, suppose that preferences are given by equation (4.48), with the following law of motion for θ_t:

$$\theta_{t+1} = \beta(c_t, h_t)\theta_t; \quad t \geq 0, \quad \theta_0 = 1. \tag{4.55}$$

This preference specification was conceived by Uzawa (1968) and introduced in the small-open-economy literature by Mendoza (1991). Under these preferences, households internalize that their choices of consumption and leisure affect their valuations of future period utilities.

Households choose processes $\{c_t, h_t, k_{t+1}, d_t, \theta_{t+1}\}_{t=0}^\infty$ so as to maximize the utility function (4.48) subject to the sequential budget constraint (4.49), the law of motion of the discount factor (4.55), and the same no-Ponzi constraint as in the EDF economy. Let $\theta_t \lambda_t$ denote the Lagrange multiplier associated with (4.49) and $\theta_t \eta_t$ the Lagrange multiplier associated with (4.55). The first-order conditions associated with the household's maximization problem are (4.49), (4.52),

$$\lambda_t = \beta(c_t, h_t)(1 + r_t)E_t\lambda_{t+1}, \tag{4.56}$$

$$U_c(c_t, h_t) - \eta_t \beta_c(c_t, h_t) = \lambda_t, \tag{4.57}$$

$$- U_h(c_t, h_t) + \eta_t \beta_h(c_t, h_t) = \lambda_t A_t F_h(k_t, h_t), \tag{4.58}$$

$$\eta_t = -E_t U(c_{t+1}, h_{t+1}) + E_t \eta_{t+1} \beta(c_{t+1}, h_{t+1}), \tag{4.59}$$

and

$$\lambda_t [1 + \Phi'(k_{t+1} - k_t)]$$
$$= \beta(c_t, h_t) E_t \lambda_{t+1} \left[A_{t+1} F_k(k_{t+1}, h_{t+1}) + 1 - \delta + \Phi'(k_{t+2} - k_{t+1}) \right]. \tag{4.60}$$

These first-order conditions are fairly standard, except that the marginal utility of consumption is not given simply by $U_c(c_t, h_t)$ but rather by $U_c(c_t, h_t) - \beta_c(c_t, h_t)\eta_t$. The second term in this expression reflects the fact that an increase in current consumption lowers the discount factor ($\beta_c < 0$). In turn, a unit decline in the discount factor reduces utility in period t by η_t. Intuitively, $-\eta_t$ equals the expected present discounted value of utility from period $t + 1$ onward. To see this, iterate the first-order condition (4.59) forward to obtain $\eta_t = -E_t \sum_{j=1}^{\infty} \left(\frac{\theta_{t+j}}{\theta_{t+1}} \right) U(c_{t+j}, h_{t+j})$. Similarly, the marginal disutility of labor is not simply $U_h(c_t, h_t)$ but instead $U_h(c_t, h_t) - \beta_h(c_t, h_t)\eta_t$.

The competitive equilibrium of the IDF economy is a set of processes $\{d_t, c_t, h_t, k_{t+1}, \eta_t, \lambda_t, A_t\}$ satisfying (4.12), (4.49), (4.52), and (4.56)–(4.60), given the initial conditions A_0, d_{-1}, k_0, and the exogenous process $\{\epsilon_t\}$.

We pick the same functional forms as in the EDF model. The fact that both the period utility function and the discount factor have a GHH structure implies that, as in all versions of the SOE-RBC model considered thus far, the marginal rate of substitution between consumption and leisure depends only on hours worked and is independent of consumption. This yields the by-now familiar equilibrium condition $h_t^{\omega-1} = A_t F_h(k_t, h_t)$.

The steady state of the IDF economy is the same as that of the EDF economy. To see this, note that in the steady state, (4.56) implies that $\beta(c, h)(1 + r^*) = 1$, which also features in the EDF model. Also, in the steady state, equation (4.60) yields an expression for the capital-labor ratio that is the same as in all versions of the SOE-RBC model considered thus far. The fact that the labor supply schedule and the sequential budget constraint are identical in the EDF and IDF models implies that h, c, and d are also equal across the two models. This shows that the IDF model delivers a steady-state value of debt that is independent of initial conditions. Of course, the IDF model includes the variable η_t, which does not feature in the EDF model. The steady-state value of this variable is given by $-U(c, h)/r^*$.

We assign the same values to the structural parameters as in the EDF model.

4.10.5 The Model with No Stationarity-Inducing Features (NSIF)

For comparison with the models studied thus far, we now consider a version of the SOE-RBC model featuring no stationarity-inducing features (NSIF). In this model (i) the discount factor is constant; (ii) the interest rate at which domestic agents borrow from the rest of the world is constant (and equal to the subjective discount rate, $\beta(1 + r^*) = 1$); (iii) agents face no frictions in adjusting the size of their asset portfolios; and (iv) markets are incomplete, in the sense that domestic households have only access to a single risk-free international bond. Under this specification, the deterministic steady state of consumption depends on the assumed initial level of net foreign debt. Also, up to first order, the equilibrium dynamics contain a random walk component in such variables as consumption, the trade balance, and net external debt.

A competitive equilibrium in the nonstationary model is a set of processes $\{d_t, c_t, h_t, k_{t+1}, A_t\}$ satisfying (4.11), (4.12), (4.18), (4.49), (4.52), and the consumption Euler equation

$$U_c(c_t, h_t) = \beta(1 + r^*)E_t U_c(c_{t+1}, h_{t+1}),$$

given d_{-1}, k_0, A_0, and the exogenous process $\{\epsilon_t\}$.

It is clear from the above consumption Euler equation that in the NSIF model, the marginal utility of consumption follows a random walk (recall that $\beta(1 + r^*) = 1$). This property is transmitted to consumption, debt, and the trade balance. Also, because the above Euler equation imposes no restriction on the deterministic steady state, the steady-state values of consumption, debt, and the trade balance are all indeterminate. The model does deliver unique deterministic steady-state values for k_t and h_t. We calibrate the parameters $\sigma, r^*, \omega, \alpha, \phi, \delta, \rho$, and $\widetilde{\eta}$ using the values displayed in Table 4.1.

4.11 The Perpetual-Youth (PY) Model

In this section we present an additional way to induce stationarity in the SOE-RBC model. It is a discrete-time, stochastic, small open economy version of the perpetual-youth (PY) model due to Blanchard (1985). Cardia (1991) represents an early adoption of the PY model in the context of a small open economy. Our model differs from Cardia's in that we assume a preference specification that allows for an exact aggregation of this model. Our strategy avoids the need to resort to linear approximations prior to aggregation.

4.11.1 Basic Intuition

The basic intuition behind why the assumption of finite lives by itself helps eliminate the unit root in the aggregate net foreign asset position can be seen from the following simple example. Consider an economy in which debt holdings of individual agents follow a pure random walk of the form $d_{s,t} = d_{s,t-1} + \mu_t$. Here, $d_{s,t}$ denotes the net debt position at the end of period t of an agent born in period s, and μ_t is an exogenous shock common to all agents and potentially serially correlated. This is exactly the equilibrium evolution of debt we obtained in the quadratic-preference, representative-agent economy of Chapter 2 (see equation (2.21)). We now depart from the representative-agent assumption by introducing a constant and age-independent probability of death at the individual level. Specifically, assume that the population is constant over time and normalized to unity. Each period, individual agents face a probability $1 - \theta \in (0, 1)$ of dying. In addition, to keep the size of the population constant over time, we assume that $1 - \theta$ agents are born each period. Assume that those agents who die leave their outstanding debts unpaid and that newborns inherit no debts. Adding the left- and right-hand sides of the law of motion for debt over all agents alive in period t (i.e., applying the operator $(1 - \theta) \sum_{s=t}^{-\infty} \theta^{t-s}$ on both sides of the expression $d_{s,t} = d_{s,t-1} + \mu_t$) yields $d_t = \theta d_{t-1} + \mu_t$, where d_t denotes the aggregate debt position in period t. When performing the aggregation, recall that $d_{t,t-1} = 0$, because agents are born free of debts. Clearly, the resulting law of motion for the aggregate level of debt is mean reverting at the survival rate θ. The key difference with the representative agent model is that here, in each period a fraction $1 - \theta$ of the stock of debt simply disappears.

In what follows, we embed this basic stationarity result into the SOE-RBC model.

4.11.2 Perpetually Young Households

Each agent maximizes the utility function

$$-\frac{1}{2} E_0 \sum_{t=0}^{\infty} (\beta\theta)^t (x_{s,t} - \overline{x})^2$$

with

$$x_{s,t} = c_{s,t} - \frac{h_{s,t}^{\omega}}{\omega}, \tag{4.61}$$

where $c_{s,t}$ and $h_{s,t}$ denote, respectively, consumption and hours worked in period t by an agent born in period s. The parameter $\beta \in (0, 1)$ represents the subjective discount factor, and $\overline{x}$ is a parameter denoting a satiation point. The symbol E_t denotes the conditional expectations operator over aggregate states. Following the preference specification used in all the models studied in this chapter, we assume that agents derive utility from a quasi-difference between consumption and leisure. But we depart from the preference specifications used earlier in this chapter by assuming a quadratic period utility index. As will become clear shortly, this assumption is essential to achieve aggregation in the presence of aggregate uncertainty.

Financial markets are incomplete. Domestic consumers can borrow internationally by means of a bond paying a constant real interest rate. The debts of deceased domestic consumers are assumed to go unpaid. Foreign agents are assumed to lend to a large number of domestic consumers, so that the fraction of unpaid loans due to death is deterministic. To compensate foreign lenders for these losses, domestic consumers pay a constant premium over the world interest rate. Specifically, the gross interest rate at which domestic consumers borrow internationally is $(1 + r^*)/\theta$, where r^* denotes the world interest rate. Domestic agents can also lend internationally. The lending contract stipulates that if the domestic lender dies, then the foreign borrower is relieved of his debt obligations. Since foreign borrowers can perfectly diversify their loans across domestic agents, they pay a deterministic interest rate. To eliminate pure arbitrage opportunities, domestic consumers must lend at the rate $(1 + r^*)/\theta$. It follows that the gross interest rate on the domestic consumer's asset position (whether this position is positive or negative) is given by $(1 + r^*)/\theta$.

The budget constraint of a domestic consumer born in period $s \leq t$ is

$$d_{s,t} = \left(\frac{1 + r^*}{\theta}\right) d_{s,t-1} + c_{s,t} - \pi_t - w_t h_{s,t}, \tag{4.62}$$

where π_t and w_t denote, respectively, profits received from the ownership of stock shares and the real wage rate. To facilitate aggregation, we assume that agents do not trade shares and that the shares of the dead are passed to the newborn in an egalitarian fashion. Thus, share holdings are identical across agents. Agents are assumed to be subject to the following no-Ponzi-game constraint:

$$\lim_{j \to \infty} E_t \left(\frac{\theta}{1+r^*} \right)^j d_{s,t+j} \le 0. \tag{4.63}$$

The first-order conditions associated with the agent's maximization problem are (4.61), (4.62), (4.63) holding with equality, and

$$-(x_{s,t} - \overline{x}) = \lambda_{s,t}, \tag{4.64}$$

$$h_{s,t}^{\omega-1} = w_t, \tag{4.65}$$

and

$$\lambda_{s,t} = \beta(1+r^*)E_t\lambda_{s,t+1}. \tag{4.66}$$

Note that $h_{s,t}$ is independent of s (i.e., it is independent of the agent's birth date). This means that we can drop the subscript s from $h_{s,t}$ and write

$$h_t^{\omega-1} = w_t. \tag{4.67}$$

Use equations (4.61) and (4.65) to eliminate $c_{s,t}$ from the sequential budget constraint (4.62). This yields

$$d_{s,t} = \left(\frac{1+r^*}{\theta} \right) d_{s,t-1} - \pi_t - \left(1 - \frac{1}{\omega} \right) w_t h_t + \overline{x} + (x_{s,t} - \overline{x}).$$

To facilitate notation, we introduce the auxiliary variable

$$z_t \equiv \pi_t + \left(1 - \frac{1}{\omega} \right) w_t h_t - \overline{x}, \tag{4.68}$$

which is the same for all generations s, because both profits and hours worked are independent of the age of the cohort. Then the sequential budget constraint becomes

$$d_{s,t} = \left(\frac{1+r^*}{\theta} \right) d_{s,t-1} - z_t + (x_{s,t} - \overline{x}). \tag{4.69}$$

Now iterate this expression forward, apply the E_t operator, and use the transversality condition (i.e., equation (4.63) holding with equality), to obtain

$$\left(\frac{1+r^*}{\theta} \right) d_{s,t-1} = E_t \sum_{j=0}^{\infty} \left(\frac{\theta}{1+r^*} \right)^j \left[z_{t+j} - (x_{s,t+j} - \overline{x}) \right].$$

Using equations (4.64) and (4.66) to replace $E_t x_{s,t+j}$ yields

$$\left(\frac{1+r^*}{\theta}\right) d_{s,t-1} = E_t \sum_{j=0}^{\infty} \left(\frac{\theta}{1+r^*}\right)^j z_{t+j} - \frac{\beta(1+r^*)^2}{\beta(1+r^*)^2 - \theta} (x_{s,t} - \overline{x}).$$

Solve for $x_{s,t}$ to obtain

$$x_{s,t} = \overline{x} + \frac{\beta(1+r^*)^2 - \theta}{\beta\theta(1+r^*)} (\widetilde{z}_t - d_{s,t-1}), \tag{4.70}$$

where

$$\widetilde{z}_t \equiv \frac{\theta}{1+r^*} E_t \sum_{j=0}^{\infty} \left(\frac{\theta}{1+r^*}\right)^j z_{t+j}$$

denotes the weighted average of current and future expected values of z_t. It can be expressed recursively as

$$\widetilde{z}_t = \frac{\theta}{1+r^*} z_t + \frac{\theta}{1+r^*} E_t \widetilde{z}_{t+1}. \tag{4.71}$$

We now aggregate individual variables by summing over generations born at time $s \leq t$. Notice that at time t there are alive $1 - \theta$ people born in t, $(1 - \theta)\theta$ people born in $t - 1$, and, in general, $(1 - \theta)\theta^s$ people born in period $t - s$. Let

$$x_t \equiv (1 - \theta) \sum_{s=t}^{-\infty} \theta^{t-s} x_{s,t}$$

and

$$d_t \equiv (1 - \theta) \sum_{s=t}^{-\infty} \theta^{t-s} d_{s,t}$$

denote the aggregate levels of $x_{s,t}$ and $d_{s,t}$, respectively. Now multiply (4.70) by $(1 - \theta)\theta^{t-s}$ and then sum from $s = t$ to $s = -\infty$ to obtain the following expression for the aggregate version of equation (4.70):

$$x_t = \overline{x} + \frac{\beta(1+r^*)^2 - \theta}{\beta\theta(1+r^*)} (\widetilde{z}_t - \theta d_{t-1}). \tag{4.72}$$

When performing this step, keep in mind that $d_{t,t-1} = 0$. That is, consumers are born debt free.

Finally, aggregate the first-order condition (4.64) and the budget constraint (4.69) to obtain

$$-(x_t - \overline{x}) = \lambda_t \tag{4.73}$$

and

$$d_t = (1+r^*)d_{t-1} - z_t + x_t - \overline{x}, \tag{4.74}$$

where

$$\lambda_t \equiv (1 - \theta) \sum_{s=t}^{-\infty} \theta^{t-s} \lambda_{s,t}$$

denotes the cross-sectional average of marginal utilities of consumption.

4.11.3 Firms Producing Consumption Goods

We assume the existence of competitive firms that hire capital and labor services to produce consumption goods. These firms maximize profits, which are given by

$$A_t F(k_t, h_t) - w_t h_t - u_t k_t,$$

where the function F and the productivity factor A_t are as in the EDEIR model. The first-order conditions associated with the firm's profit-maximization problem are

$$A_t F_k(k_t, h_t) = u_t \tag{4.75}$$

and

$$A_t F_h(k_t, h_t) = w_t. \tag{4.76}$$

We assume perfect competition in product and factor markets. Because F is homogeneous of degree one, firms producing consumption goods make zero profits.

4.11.4 Firms Producing Capital Goods

We assume the existence of firms that buy consumption goods to transform them into investment goods, rent out capital, and pay dividends π_t. Formally, dividends in period t are given by

$$\pi_t = u_t k_t - i_t - \Phi(k_{t+1} - k_t). \tag{4.77}$$

The evolution of capital follows the law of motion given in (4.4), which we reproduce here for convenience:

$$k_{t+1} = (1 - \delta)k_t + i_t. \tag{4.78}$$

The optimization problem of the capital-producing firm is dynamic. This is because investment goods take one period to become productive capital and because of the presence of adjustment costs. The firm must maximize some present discounted value of current and future expected profits. A problem that emerges at this point is what discount factor the firm should use. This issue does not have a clear answer for two reasons: first, the owners of the firm change over time. Recall that the shares of the dead are distributed in equal parts among the newborn. It follows that the firm cannot use as its discount factor the intertemporal marginal rate of substitution of a "representative household," because the representative household does not exist. Second, the firm operates in a financial environment characterized by incomplete asset markets. For this reason, it cannot use the price of state-contingent claims to discount future profits, because there is no market for such claims.

One must therefore introduce assumptions regarding the firm's discounting behavior. These assumptions will in general not be innocuous with respect to the dynamics of capital accumulation. With this in mind, we will assume that the firm uses the discount factor $\beta^j \lambda_{t+j}/\lambda_t$ to calculate the period-t value of one unit of consumption delivered in a particular state of period $t + j$. Note that this discount factor uses the average marginal utility of consumption of agents alive in period $t + j$ relative to that of agents alive in period t. Note that we use as the subjective discount factor the parameter β and not $\beta\theta$. This is because the number of shareholders is constant over time (and equal to unity), unlike the size of a cohort born at a particular date, which declines at the mortality rate $1 - \theta$. The Lagrangian associated with the optimization problem of capital goods producers is then given by

$$\mathcal{L} = E_t \sum_{j=0}^{\infty} \beta^j \frac{\lambda_{t+j}}{\lambda_t} \left[u_{t+j}k_{t+j} - k_{t+j+1} + (1-\delta)k_{t+j} - \Phi(k_{t+j+1} - k_{t+j}) \right].$$

The first-order condition with respect to k_{t+1} is

$$\lambda_t[1 + \Phi'(k_{t+1} - k_t)] = \beta E_t \lambda_{t+1} \left[u_{t+1} + 1 - \delta + \Phi'(k_{t+2} - k_{t+1}) \right]. \qquad (4.79)$$

4.11.5 Equilibrium

Equations (4.67), (4.68), and (4.71)–(4.79) form a system of eleven equations in eleven unknowns: x_t, λ_t, h_t, w_t, u_t, π_t, i_t, k_t, d_t, z_t, and $\widetilde{z}_t$. Here we reproduce the system of equilibrium conditions for convenience:

$$h_t^{\omega-1} = w_t,$$

$$z_t \equiv \pi_t + \left(1 - \frac{1}{\omega}\right) w_t h_t - \overline{x},$$

$$\widetilde{z}_t = \frac{\theta}{1 + r^*} z_t + \frac{\theta}{1 + r^*} E_t \widetilde{z}_{t+1},$$

$$x_t = \overline{x} + \frac{\beta(1 + r^*)^2 - \theta}{\beta\theta(1 + r^*)} (\widetilde{z}_t - \theta d_{t-1}),$$

$$- (x_t - \overline{x}) = \lambda_t,$$

$$d_t = (1 + r^*)d_{t-1} - z_t + x_t - \overline{x},$$

$$A_t F_k(k_t, h_t) = u_t,$$

$$A_t F_h(k_t, h_t) = w_t,$$

$$\pi_t = u_t k_t - i_t - \Phi(k_{t+1} - k_t),$$

$$k_{t+1} = (1 - \delta)k_t + i_t,$$

and

$$\lambda_t[1 + \Phi'(k_{t+1} - k_t)] = \beta E_t \lambda_{t+1} \left[u_{t+1} + 1 - \delta + \Phi'(k_{t+2} - k_{t+1}) \right].$$

It is of interest to consider the special case in which $\beta(1 + r^*) = 1$. In this case, the evolution of external debt is given by

$$d_t = \theta d_{t-1} + \frac{1 + r^* - \theta}{\theta}\tilde{z}_t - z_t.$$

This expression shows that the stock of debt does not follow a random walk, as was the case in the representative-agent economy with quadratic preferences of Chapter 2. In fact, the (autoregressive) coefficient on past external debt is $\theta \in (0, 1)$. The mean-reverting property of aggregate external debt obtains in spite of the fact that individual debt positions follow a random walk. The reason that the aggregate level of external debt is trend reverting in equilibrium is because each period, a fraction $1 - \theta \in (0, 1)$ of the agents die and are replaced by newborns holding no financial assets. As a result, on average, the current aggregate level of debt is only a fraction θ of the previous period's level of debt. This intuition also holds when $\beta(1 + r^*) \neq 1$, although in this case individual levels of debt display a trend in the deterministic equilibrium.

In the deterministic steady state, the aggregate level of debt is given by

$$d = \frac{\theta(1 - \beta(1 + r^*))}{(1 + r^* - \theta)(\theta - \beta(1 + r^*))}y.$$

In the special case in which $\beta(1 + r^*)$ equals unity, the steady-state aggregate stock of debt is nil. This is because in this case agents, all of whom are born with no debts, wish to hold constant debt levels over time. In this case the steady state both of the aggregate and the individual levels of debt is zero. It can be shown that if $\beta(1 + r^*)$ is less than unity but larger than θ, the steady-state level of debt must be positive.

We adopt the same functional forms for F and Φ as in the EDEIR model. We calibrate ω, α, ϕ, δ, ρ, and $\tilde{\eta}$ at the values displayed in Table 4.1. We set $\beta = 1/1.04$ as in the EDEIR model. Consequently, the steady-state values of hours, capital, output, investment, consumption, and the trade balance are the same as in the EDEIR model. We set $\theta = 1 - 1/75$, which implies a life expectancy of 75 years. Finally, we calibrate r^* and $\bar{x}$ to ensure that in the steady state the trade-balance-to-output ratio is 2 percent and the degree of relative risk aversion, given by $-x/(x - \bar{x})$, is 2. This calibration results in an interest rate of 3.7451 percent and a satiation point of 0.6334.

4.12 Inducing Stationarity: Quantitative Comparison of Alternative Methods

Table 4.4 displays a number of unconditional second moments of interest implied by the IDF, EDF, EDEIR, IDEIR, PAC, CAM, and PY models. The NSIF model is nonstationary up to first order, and therefore does not have well-defined unconditional second moments. The second moments for all models other than the IDEIR and PY models are taken from Schmitt-Grohé and Uribe (2003). We compute the equilibrium dynamics by solving a log-linear approximation to the set of equilibrium conditions. The Matlab computer code used to compute the unconditional second moments and impulse response functions for all

Table 4.4   Second Moments across Models

	IDF	EDF	IDEIR	EDEIR	PAC	CAM	PY
Volatilities							
$\text{std}(y_t)$	3.1	3.1	3.1	3.1	3.1	3.1	3.1
$\text{std}(c_t)$	2.3	2.3	2.5	2.7	2.7	1.9	2.5
$\text{std}(i_t)$	9.1	9.1	9	9	9	9.1	8.7
$\text{std}(h_t)$	2.1	2.1	2.1	2.1	2.1	2.1	2.1
$\text{std}(\frac{tb_t}{y_t})$	1.5	1.5	1.6	1.8	1.8	1.6	1.5
$\text{std}(\frac{ca_t}{y_t})$	1.5	1.5	1.4	1.5	1.5	3.1	1.3
Serial Correlations							
$\text{corr}(y_t, y_{t-1})$	0.61	0.61	0.62	0.62	0.62	0.61	0.62
$\text{corr}(c_t, c_{t-1})$	0.7	0.7	0.76	0.78	0.78	0.61	0.74
$\text{corr}(i_t, i_{t-1})$	0.07	0.07	0.068	0.069	0.069	0.07	0.064
$\text{corr}(h_t, h_{t-1})$	0.61	0.61	0.62	0.62	0.62	0.61	0.62
$\text{corr}(\frac{tb_t}{y_t}, \frac{tb_{t-1}}{y_{t-1}})$	0.33	0.32	0.43	0.51	0.5	0.39	0.34
$\text{corr}(\frac{ca_t}{y_t}, \frac{ca_{t-1}}{y_{t-1}})$	0.3	0.3	0.31	0.32	0.32	−0.07	0.29
Correlations with Output							
$\text{corr}(c_t, y_t)$	0.94	0.94	0.89	0.84	0.85	1	0.94
$\text{corr}(i_t, y_t)$	0.66	0.66	0.68	0.67	0.67	0.66	0.69
$\text{corr}(h_t, y_t)$	1	1	1	1	1	1	1
$\text{corr}(\frac{tb_t}{y_t}, y_t)$	−0.012	−0.013	−0.036	−0.044	−0.043	0.13	−0.06
$\text{corr}(\frac{ca_t}{y_t}, y_t)$	0.026	0.025	0.041	0.05	0.051	−0.49	0.04

Notes: Standard deviations are measured in percent per year. IDF = internal discount factor; EDF = external discount factor; IDEIR = internal debt-elastic interest rate; EDEIR = external debt-elastic interest rate; PAC = portfolio adjustment costs; CAM = complete asset markets; PY = perpetual youth.
Source: Parts of the table are reproduced from Schmitt-Grohé and Uribe (2003).

models presented in this section is available on the book's Web site with the materials for this chapter.

Table 4.4 shows that regardless of how stationarity is induced, the models' predictions regarding second moments are virtually identical. One noticeable difference arises in the CAM model, which, as might be expected, predicts less volatile consumption. The low volatility of consumption in the complete markets model introduces a difference between the predictions of this model and those of the IDF, EDF, EDEIR, IDEIR, PAC, and PY models: because consumption is smoother in the CAM model, its role in determining the cyclicality of the trade balance is smaller. As a result, the CAM model predicts that the correlation between output and the trade balance is positive, whereas the models featuring incomplete asset markets all imply that this correlation is negative.

Figure 4.3 demonstrates that all the models being compared imply virtually identical impulse response functions to a technology shock. Each panel shows the impulse response of a particular variable in the eight models. For all variables, the impulse response functions

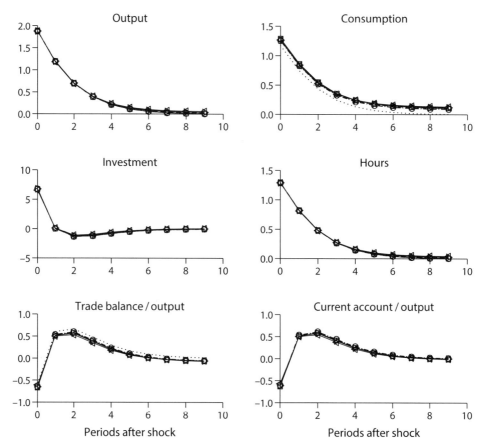

Figure 4.3   Impulse response to a unit technology shock across models.

Notes: Solid line, IDF model; squares, EDF model; dashed line, EDEIR model; dash-dotted line, PAC model; dotted line, CAM model; circles, NSIF model; right triangles, IDEIR model; left triangles, PY model. The impulse responses of output, consumption, investment, hours, and TFP are expressed in percentage deviations from the deterministic steady state. The impulse response of the trade-balance-to-output ratio is expressed in percentage-point deviations from the steady state.

are so similar that to the naked eye the graph appears to show just a single line. Again, the only small and barely noticeable difference is given by the responses of consumption and the trade-balance-to-GDP ratio in the complete markets model. In response to a positive technology shock, consumption increases less when markets are complete than when they are incomplete. This, in turn, leads to a smaller decline in the trade balance in the period in which the technology shock occurs.

4.13 Global Solution

Thus far, we have approximated the model using a first-order local approximation around the deterministic steady state. Here we approximate the equilibrium using a global method.

We assume that both the subjective and pecuniary discount factors are constant. To induce stationarity, we assume that households are more impatient than indicated by the pecuniary discount factor, that is, we assume that

$$\beta(1+r^*) < 1.$$

In all other respects, the model is identical to the baseline model of Section 4.1. The above restriction eliminates the random walk in debt and consumption. To understand why, assume first that the economy is deterministic. In such an environment, the condition $\beta(1+r^*) < 1$ induces households to accumulate debt in such a way that consumption approaches asymptotically its lowest possible level, given by the disutility of labor, h^ω/ω. Thus debt converges to a well-defined value given by the present discounted value of the stream of output, $AF(k, h)$, net of capital depreciation, δk, and consumption, h^ω/ω, that is, $d \rightarrow [AF(k, h) - \delta k - h^\omega/\omega]/r^*$, where all variables are evaluated at their asymptotic values. Of course, at the limit the household is infinitely unhappy. Thus when uncertainty is introduced in the form of stochastic variations in the technology shock A, *precautionary savings* create a well-defined debt distribution to the left of its asymptotic deterministic level. Since this precautionary savings motive cannot be captured by a first-order approximation, it follows that a higher-order approximation, like the global approximation pursued here, is needed to obtain a stationary solution.

The solution algorithm is based on value function iterations over a discretized state space. Specifically, we write the model as the solution to the Bellman equation

$$v(d, k, A) = \max_{\{d', k'\}} \left\{ U\left(AF(k, h) + (1-\delta)k - k' - \Phi(k' - k) + d' - (1+r^*)d - \frac{h^\omega}{\omega} \right) \right.$$

$$\left. + \beta E[v(d', k', A')|A] \right\},$$

subject to

$$d' \leq \bar{d},$$

where variables without a subscript or a superscript are dated in period t, and primed variables are dated in $t + 1$. The debt constraint places an upper limit on the level of net external debt, defined by the parameter $\bar{d}$. When $\bar{d}$ is set to a large number so that the debt constraint is never binding, the debt constraint serves only as a no-Ponzi-game restriction. But, as will become clear shortly, a more stringent debt limit is needed for the predictions of the model to be in line with the data. The online materials for this chapter provide replication files (`usg_soe_rbc_global.zip`).

We use the same functional forms for preferences, technologies, and adjustment costs as in previous sections and calibrate all parameters, except β and $\bar{d}$, as shown in Table 4.1. We discretize the state space with 9 equally spaced points for $\ln A$ from -0.04495 to 0.04495, 70 equally spaced points for d, and 30 equally spaced points for k. The ranges assigned to the two endogenous states, d and k, depend on the values assigned to β and $\bar{d}$, as explained below.

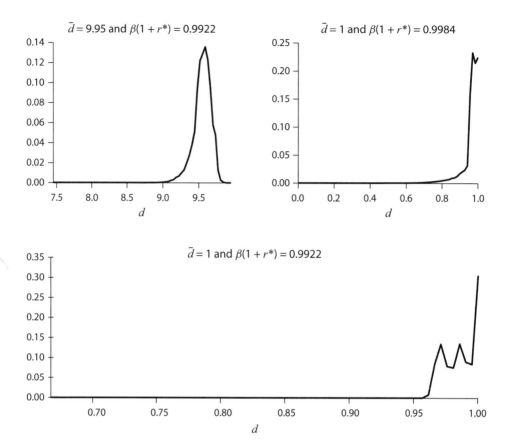

Figure 4.4 Probability distribution of debt under impatience and a global approximation.

Notes: The world interest rate is $r^* = 0.04$. The replication file `usg_plot_density.m` is in `usg_soe_rbc_global.zip`, available online.

Setting $\beta(1 + r^*)$ too close to unity results in a near random walk distribution of debt in equilibrium, which is difficult to approximate. We therefore set $\beta(1 + r^*)$ equal to 0.9922, which, recalling that $r^* = 0.04$, requires setting β equal to 0.954. This value of β introduces a significant difference of 82 basis points per year between the subjective and the pecuniary discount rates.

Consider first the case in which the debt limit $\bar{d}$ is set to a large number so that the borrowing constraint is never binding in equilibrium. Specifically, we set the range of d to be [7.45, 9.95]. The grid for k is [2.8, 3.8]. The top-left panel of Figure 4.4 displays the equilibrium probability distribution of d. The probability of debt being equal to its upper limit of 9.95 is zero, which implies that the debt limit is never binding in equilibrium. However, the implied average level of external debt, equal to 9.6, turns out to be excessive. Table 4.5 explains why. It shows that to support such a high level of debt, the economy must generate a trade balance surplus of 25.8 percent of GDP, more than 10 times larger than the one observed in Canada, the economy to which the model is calibrated. Under this calibration, the model is at odds with the data along other dimensions as well. For

Table 4.5   Calibration of the Discount Factor and the Debt Limit

Calibration	β	$\beta(1+r^*)$	$\bar{d}$	$E(tb/y)$	σ_i
Baseline	0.954	0.9922	1	2.9	8.7
Natural debt limit	0.954	0.9922	9.95	25.8	21.40
High patience	0.96	0.9984	1	2.6	9.9
Data				2.0	9.8

Notes: The world interest rate is $r^* = 0.04$. The replication file `usg_calibration_targets.m` is in `usg_soe_rbc_global.zip`, available online.

instance, the table shows that the predicted volatility of investment is 21.4 percent, more than twice what it is in the data. The intuition for why investment is so volatile is that at high levels of external debt, the intertemporal marginal rate of consumption substitution, $U'(c' - h'^\omega/\omega)/U'(c - h^\omega/\omega)$, becomes highly volatile. Recall that this variable represents the kernel households use to discount future returns to capital (see equations (4.8) and (4.10)). In turn, the reason the intertemporal marginal rate of consumption substitution is highly volatile is that consumption is close to its minimum possible level, given by the disutility of labor h^ω/ω. When $c - h^\omega/\omega$ is close to zero, the marginal utility of consumption becomes highly sensitive to changes in c or h.

It follows that a tighter limit on external debt is in order. Accordingly, we set $\bar{d}$ to 1. As shown in Table 4.5, this value is low enough to induce an average trade-balance-to-output ratio close to the observed value of 2 percent. The table also shows that with the tighter debt limit, the model improves significantly in explaining the observed volatility of investment (9.8 in the data versus 8.7 in the model). Indeed, the model does a pretty good job at explaining other second moments of interest as well. Table 4.6 displays the standard deviation, serial correlation, and correlation with output of output, consumption, investment, hours, the trade-balance-to-output ratio, and the current-account-to-output ratio. For comparison, the table reproduces from Table 4.2 the corresponding empirical moments and those implied by the EDEIR model.

Table 4.6   Model Predictions under a Global Approximation

Variable	Data			Global Solution			EDEIR		
	σ_{x_t}	$\rho_{x_t, x_{t-1}}$	ρ_{x_t, GDP_t}	σ_{x_t}	$\rho_{x_t, x_{t-1}}$	ρ_{x_t, GDP_t}	σ_{x_t}	$\rho_{x_t, x_{t-1}}$	ρ_{x_t, GDP_t}
y	2.81	0.62	1	3.56	0.68	1	3.08	0.62	1
c	2.46	0.70	0.59	2.96	0.77	0.98	2.71	0.78	0.84
i	9.82	0.31	0.64	8.70	0.09	0.69	9.04	0.07	0.67
h	2.02	0.54	0.80	2.44	0.68	1	2.12	0.62	1
$\frac{tb}{y}$	1.87	0.66	−0.13	1.23	−0.46	−0.04	1.78	0.51	−0.04
$\frac{ca}{y}$				1.21	−0.47	0.05	1.45	0.32	0.05

Notes: In the global solution, $\beta(1+r^*)$ takes the value 0.9922, and $\bar{d}$ is equal to 1. The replication file `usg_predictions.m` is in `usg_soe_rbc_global.zip`, available online. For second moments predicted by the EDEIR model and for empirical second moments, see the note to Table 4.2.

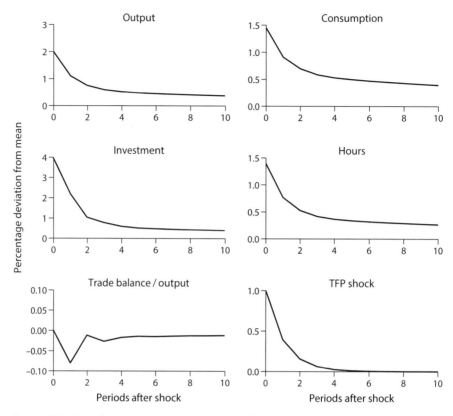

Figure 4.5   Impulse responses to a positive productivity shock under a global approximation.

Note: The replication file `usg_ir_rbc_global.m` is in `usg_soe_rbc_global.zip`, available online.

The main message of Table 4.6 is that the model with impatient agents solved using global methods performs as well as the EDEIR model solved with local approximation methods except for the serial correlation of the trade-balance-to-output ratio, which is better captured by the log-linearized EDEIR model. A similar result emerges from Figure 4.5, which displays impulse responses to a positive productivity shock. Comparing this figure with Figure 4.3 shows that the response of the model with impatient households obtained via a global approximation is similar to that obtained under local approximations and alternative stationarity-inducing mechanisms.

Finally, we note that the predictions implied by the global approximation are robust to a wide range of values of β. Table 4.5 shows that both the trade-balance-to-output ratio and the volatility of investment are little changed if β is raised to 0.96, a value quite close to $1/(1 + r^*) = 0.9615$. This value might be empirically appealing, because it implies a lower frequency of events in which the debt limit binds, 22 percent with $\beta = 0.96$ versus 31 percent at the baseline value of 0.954 (compare the top-right and the bottom panels of Figure 4.4).

4.14 Appendix

4.14.1 First-Order Accurate Approximations to Dynamic General Equilibrium Models

In this appendix we solve the system

$$f_{y'}E_t\widehat{y}_{t+1} + f_y\widehat{y}_t + f_{x'}E_t\widehat{x}_{t+1} + f_x\widehat{x}_t = 0, \qquad (4.34\text{ R})$$

reproduced from Section 4.6. The matrices $f_{y'}$, f_y, $f_{x'}$, and f_x are assumed to be known. Letting $A = [f_{x'}\ f_{y'}]$ and $B = -[f_x\ f_y]$, we can rewrite the system as

$$A\begin{bmatrix} E_t\widehat{x}_{t+1} \\ E_t\widehat{y}_{t+1} \end{bmatrix} = B\begin{bmatrix} \widehat{x}_t \\ \widehat{y}_t \end{bmatrix}.$$

Define the vector $\widehat{w}_t$ containing all control and state variables of the system. Formally, we have

$$\widehat{w}_{t+j} \equiv E_t\begin{bmatrix} \widehat{x}_{t+j} \\ \widehat{y}_{t+j} \end{bmatrix}$$

for $j \geq 0$. Note that this definition implies that

$$\widehat{w}_t \equiv \begin{bmatrix} \widehat{x}_t \\ \widehat{y}_t \end{bmatrix}.$$

We can then write the linear system as

$$A\widehat{w}_{t+1} = B\widehat{w}_t.$$

In accordance with (4.33), we seek solutions in which

$$\lim_{j\to\infty} \widehat{w}_{t+j} = 0.$$

This requirement means that at every point in time the vector w_t is expected to converge to its nonstochastic steady state, $w \equiv [x'\ y']'$.

The remainder of this section is based on Klein (2000) (see also Sims 2001). Consider the generalized Schur decomposition of A and B:

$$qAz = a$$

and

$$qBz = b,$$

where a and b are upper triangular matrices, and q and z are orthonormal matrices. Recall that a matrix a is said to be upper triangular if elements in row i and column j, denoted $a(i, j)$, are 0 for $i > j$. A matrix z is orthonormal if $z'z = zz' = I$.

Define

$$s_t \equiv z'\widehat{w}_t.$$

Then we have that

$$as_{t+1} = bs_t.$$

The ratio $b(i, i)/a(i, i)$ is known as the *generalized eigenvalue* of the matrices A and B. Assume, without loss of generality, that the ratios $|b(i, i)/a(i, i)|$ are increasing in i. Now partition $a, b, z, \widehat{w}_t$, and s_t as

$$a = \begin{bmatrix} a_{11} & a_{12} \\ \emptyset & a_{22} \end{bmatrix}, \quad b = \begin{bmatrix} b_{11} & b_{12} \\ \emptyset & b_{22} \end{bmatrix}; \quad z = \begin{bmatrix} z_{11} & z_{12} \\ z_{21} & z_{22} \end{bmatrix}; \quad \widehat{w}_t = \begin{bmatrix} \widehat{w}_t^1 \\ \widehat{w}_t^2 \end{bmatrix}, \quad s_t = \begin{bmatrix} s_t^1 \\ s_t^2 \end{bmatrix},$$

where a_{11} and b_{11} are square matrices whose diagonals generate the generalized eigenvalues of (A, B) with absolute values less than one, and a_{22} and b_{22} are square matrices whose diagonals generate the generalized eigenvalues of (A, B) with absolute values greater than one. The symbol $\emptyset$ denotes a matrix with elements 0. Then we have that

$$a_{22}s_{t+1}^2 = b_{22}s_t^2.$$

The partition of the matrix B guarantees that all diagonal elements of b_{22} are nonzero. In addition, recalling that a triangular matrix is invertible if the elements along its main diagonal are nonzero, it follows that b_{22} is invertible. So we can write

$$b_{22}^{-1}a_{22}s_{t+1}^2 = s_t^2.$$

By construction, the eigenvalues of $b_{22}^{-1}a_{22}$ are all less than unity in modulus. To arrive at this conclusion, we use three properties of upper triangular matrices: (i) the inverse of a nonsingular upper triangular matrix is upper triangular, (ii) the product of two upper triangular matrices is upper triangular, and (iii) the eigenvalues of an upper triangular matrix are the elements of its main diagonal. It follows that the only nonexplosive solution to the above difference equation is

$$s_t^2 = \emptyset,$$

for all t. This result and the definition of s_t^2 imply that

$$z_{12}'\widehat{w}_t^1 + z_{22}'\widehat{w}_t^2 = \emptyset.$$

Solving this expression for $\widehat{w}_t^2$ yields

$$\widehat{w}_t^2 = G\widehat{w}_t^1, \tag{4.80}$$

where

$$G \equiv -z_{22}'^{-1}z_{12}'. \tag{4.81}$$

The invertibility of z_{22}' follows from the fact that, being orthonormal, z' itself is invertible. The condition $s_t^2 = \emptyset$ for all t also implies that

$$a_{11}s_{t+1}^1 = b_{11}s_t^1.$$

The criteria used to partition A and B guarantee that the diagonal elements of the upper triangular matrix a_{11} are nonzero. Therefore, a_{11} is invertible, which allows us to write

$$s_{t+1}^1 = a_{11}^{-1} b_{11} s_t^1. \tag{4.82}$$

Now express s_t^1 as a linear transformation of $\widehat{w}_t^1$ as follows:

$$
\begin{aligned}
s_t^1 &= z_{11}' \widehat{w}_t^1 + z_{21}' \widehat{w}_t^2 \\
&= (z_{11}' + z_{21}' G) \widehat{w}_t^1 \\
&= (z_{11}' - z_{21}' z_{22}'^{-1} z_{12}') \widehat{w}_t^1 \\
&= z_{11}^{-1} \widehat{w}_t^1.
\end{aligned}
$$

The second and third equalities make use of equation (4.80) and identity (4.81), respectively. The last equality follows from the fact that z is orthonormal.[6]

Combining this expression with (4.82) yields

$$\widehat{w}_{t+1}^1 = H \widehat{w}_t^1,$$

where

$$H \equiv z_{11} a_{11}^{-1} b_{11} z_{11}^{-1}.$$

Finally, note that all eigenvalues of H are inside the unit circle. To see this, note that the eigenvalues of $z_{11} a_{11}^{-1} b_{11} z_{11}^{-1}$ must be the same as the eigenvalues of $a_{11}^{-1} b_{11}$. In turn, $a_{11}^{-1} b_{11}$ is upper triangular with diagonal elements less than one in modulus.

The analysis thus far has not delivered the matrices h_x and g_x that define the first-order accurate solution of the DSGE model. In the following section, we accomplish this task and derive conditions under which the equilibrium dynamics are locally unique.

4.14.2 Local Existence and Uniqueness of Equilibrium

Local Uniqueness of Equilibrium

Suppose that the number of generalized eigenvalues of the matrices A and B with absolute value less than unity is exactly equal to the number of states, n_x. That is, suppose that a_{11}

---

6. To see this, let $k \equiv z_{11}' - z_{21}' z_{22}'^{-1} z_{12}'$. We wish to show that $k = z_{11}^{-1}$. Note that the orthonormality of z implies that

$$
I = z'z = \begin{bmatrix} z_{11}' z_{11} + z_{21}' z_{21} & z_{11}' z_{12} + z_{21}' z_{22} \\ z_{12}' z_{11} + z_{22}' z_{21} & z_{12}' z_{12} + z_{22}' z_{22} \end{bmatrix}.
$$

Use element (2, 1) of $z'z$ to get $z_{12}' z_{11} = -z_{22}' z_{21}$. Premultiply by $z_{22}'^{-1}$ and postmultiply by z_{11}^{-1} to get $z_{22}'^{-1} z_{12}' = -z_{21} z_{11}^{-1}$. Use this expression to eliminate $z_{22}'^{-1} z_{12}'$ from the definition of k to obtain $k = [z_{11}' + z_{21}' z_{21} z_{11}^{-1}]$. Now use element (1, 1) of $z'z$ to write $z_{21}' z_{21} = I - z_{11}' z_{11}$. Using this equation to eliminate $z_{21}' z_{21}$ from the expression in square brackets, we get $k = [z_{11}' + (I - z_{11}' z_{11}) z_{11}^{-1}]$, which is simply z_{11}^{-1}. Finally, note that the invertibility of z_{11} follows from the invertibility of z.

and b_{11} are of size $n_x \times n_x$. In this case, the matrix H is also of size $n_x \times n_x$, and the matrix G is of size $n_y \times n_x$. Moreover, since $\widehat{w}_t^1$ must be conformable with H, we have that $\widehat{w}_t^1$ is given by the first n_x elements of $\widehat{w}_t$, which exactly coincide with $\widehat{x}_t$. In turn, this implies that $\widehat{w}_t^2$ must equal $\widehat{y}_t$. Defining

$$h_x \equiv H$$

and

$$g_x \equiv G,$$

we can then write

$$\widehat{x}_{t+1} = h_x \widehat{x}_t$$

and

$$\widehat{y}_t = g_x \widehat{x}_t,$$

which is the solution we were looking for. Notice that because $\widehat{x}_t$ is predetermined in period t, we have that $\widehat{y}_t$ and $\widehat{x}_{t+1}$ are uniquely determined in period t. The evolution of the linearized system is then unique and is given by

$$y_t - y = g_x(x_t - x)$$

and

$$x_{t+1} - x = h_x(x_t - x) + \eta \epsilon_{t+1}.$$

Summarizing, the condition for local uniqueness of the equilibrium is that the number of generalized eigenvalues of the matrices A and B is exactly equal to the number of states, n_x.

No Local Existence of Equilibrium

Now suppose that the number of generalized eigenvalues of the matrices A and B with absolute value less than one is smaller than the number of state variables, n_x. Specifically, suppose that a_{11} and b_{11} are of size $(n_x - m) \times (n_x - m)$, with $0 < m \leq n_x$. In this case, the matrix H is of order $(n_x - m) \times (n_x - m)$, and the matrix G is of order $(n_y + m) \times (n_x - m)$. Moreover, the vectors $\widehat{w}_t^1$ and $\widehat{w}_t^2$ no longer coincide with $\widehat{x}_t$ and $\widehat{y}_t$, respectively. Instead, $\widehat{w}_t^1$ and $\widehat{w}_t^2$ take the form

$$\widehat{w}_t^1 = \widehat{x}_t^a$$

and

$$\widehat{w}_t^2 = \begin{bmatrix} \widehat{x}_t^b \\ \widehat{y}_t \end{bmatrix},$$

where $\widehat{x}_t^a$ and $\widehat{x}_t^b$ are vectors of lengths $n_x - m$ and m, respectively, and they satisfy

$$\widehat{x}_t = \begin{bmatrix} \widehat{x}_t^a \\ \widehat{x}_t^b \end{bmatrix}.$$

The law of motion of $\widehat{x}_t$ and $\widehat{y}_t$ is then of the form

$$\widehat{x}_{t+1}^a = H\widehat{x}_t^a$$

and

$$\begin{bmatrix} \widehat{x}_t^b \\ \widehat{y}_t \end{bmatrix} = G\widehat{x}_t^a.$$

This expression states that $\widehat{x}_t^b$ is determined by $\widehat{x}_t^a$. But this is impossible, because $\widehat{x}_t^a$ and $\widehat{x}_t^b$ are predetermined independently of each other. We therefore say that locally there exists no equilibrium.

Summarizing, no local equilibrium exists if the number of generalized eigenvalues of the matrices A and B with absolute values less than one is smaller than the number of state variables, n_x.

Local Indeterminacy of Equilibrium
Finally, suppose that the number of generalized eigenvalues of the matrices A and B with absolute value less than one is larger than the number of state variables, n_x. Specifically, suppose that a_{11} and b_{11} are of size $(n_x + m) \times (n_x + m)$, with $0 < m \leq n_y$. In this case, the matrix H is of order $(n_x + m) \times (n_x + m)$, and the matrix G is of order $(n_y - m) \times (n_x + m)$. The vectors $\widehat{w}_t^1$ and $\widehat{w}_t^2$ take the form

$$\widehat{w}_t^1 = \begin{bmatrix} \widehat{x}_t \\ \widehat{y}_t^a \end{bmatrix}$$

and

$$\widehat{w}_t^2 = \widehat{y}_t^b,$$

where $\widehat{y}_t^a$ and $\widehat{y}_t^b$ are vectors of lengths m and $n^y - m$, respectively, and they satisfy

$$\widehat{y}_t = \begin{bmatrix} \widehat{y}_t^a \\ \widehat{y}_t^b \end{bmatrix}.$$

The law of motion of $\widehat{x}_t$ and $\widehat{y}_t$ is then of the form

$$\begin{bmatrix} \widehat{x}_{t+1} \\ \widehat{y}_{t+1}^a \end{bmatrix} = H \begin{bmatrix} \widehat{x}_t \\ \widehat{y}_t^a \end{bmatrix}$$

and

$$\widehat{y}_t^b = G \begin{bmatrix} \widehat{x}_t \\ \widehat{y}_t^a \end{bmatrix}.$$

These expressions state that one can freely pick $\widehat{y}_t^a$ in period t. Since $\widehat{y}_t^a$ is not pre-determined, the equilibrium is indeterminate. In this case, we say that the indeterminacy is of dimension m. The evolution of the system can then be written as

$$\begin{bmatrix} x_{t+1} - x \\ y_{t+1}^a - y^a \end{bmatrix} = H \begin{bmatrix} x_t - x \\ y_t^a - y^a \end{bmatrix} + \begin{bmatrix} \eta & \emptyset \\ v_\epsilon & v_\mu \end{bmatrix} \begin{bmatrix} \epsilon_{t+1} \\ \mu_{t+1} \end{bmatrix}$$

and

$$y_t^b - y^b = G \begin{bmatrix} x_t - x \\ y_t^a - y^a \end{bmatrix},$$

where y^a and y^b denote the steady-state values of y_t^a and y_t^b, respectively; the matrices v_ϵ and v_μ allow for nonfundamental uncertainty; and μ_t is an i.i.d. innovation with mean $\emptyset$ and variance-covariance matrix equal to the identity matrix.

Summarizing, the equilibrium displays *local indeterminacy* of dimension m if the number of generalized eigenvalues of the matrices A and B with absolute values less than one exceeds the number of state variables, n_x, by $0 < m \leq n_y$.

4.14.3 Computing Second Moments

Start with the equilibrium law of motion of the deviation of the state vector with respect to its steady-state value, which is given by

$$\widehat{x}_{t+1} = h_x \widehat{x}_t + \eta \epsilon_{t+1}.$$

Variance-Covariance Matrix of x_t

Let

$$\Sigma_x \equiv E \widehat{x}_t \widehat{x}_t'$$

denote the unconditional variance-covariance matrix of $\widehat{x}_t$ and let

$$\Sigma_\epsilon \equiv \eta \eta'.$$

Then we have that

$$\Sigma_x = h_x \Sigma_x h_x' + \Sigma_\epsilon.$$

We will describe two numerical methods to compute Σ_x.

Method 1

One way to obtain Σ_x is to make use of the following useful result. Let A, B, and C be matrices whose dimensions are such that the product ABC exists. Then

$$\text{vec}(ABC) = (C' \otimes A)\, \text{vec}(B),$$

where the vec operator transforms a matrix into a vector by stacking its columns, and the symbol $\otimes$ denotes the Kronecker product. Thus if the vec operator is applied to both sides of

$$\Sigma_x = h_x \Sigma_x h'_x + \Sigma_\epsilon,$$

the result is

$$\begin{aligned} \text{vec}(\Sigma_x) &= \text{vec}(h_x \Sigma_x h'_x) + \text{vec}(\Sigma_\epsilon) \\ &= \mathcal{F} \, \text{vec}(\Sigma_x) + \text{vec}(\Sigma_\epsilon), \end{aligned}$$

where

$$\mathcal{F} = h_x \otimes h_x.$$

Solving the above expression for $\text{vec}(\Sigma_x)$, we obtain

$$\text{vec}(\Sigma_x) = (I - \mathcal{F})^{-1} \text{vec}(\Sigma_\epsilon),$$

provided that the inverse of $(I - \mathcal{F})$ exists. The eigenvalues of $\mathcal{F}$ are products of the eigenvalues of the matrix h_x. Because all eigenvalues of the matrix h_x have by construction modulus less than one, it follows that all eigenvalues of $\mathcal{F}$ are less than one in modulus. This implies that $(I - \mathcal{F})$ is nonsingular and we can indeed solve for Σ_x. One possible drawback of this method is that one has to invert a matrix that has dimension $n_x^2 \times n_x^2$, which might be time consuming.

Method 2
The following iterative procedure, called the "doubling algorithm," may be faster than method 1 in cases in which the number of state variables, n_x, is large:

$$\Sigma_{x,t+1} = h_{x,t} \Sigma_{x,t} h'_{x,t} + \Sigma_{\epsilon,t},$$

$$h_{x,t+1} = h_{x,t} h_{x,t},$$

$$\Sigma_{\epsilon,t+1} = h_{x,t} \Sigma_{\epsilon,t} h'_{x,t} + \Sigma_{\epsilon,t},$$

with initial conditions

$$\Sigma_{x,0} = I,$$

$$h_{x,0} = h_x,$$

and

$$\Sigma_{\epsilon,0} = \Sigma_\epsilon.$$

Computing Other Second Moments
Once the variance-covariance matrix of the state vector, x_t, has been computed, it is easy to find other second moments of interest. For instance, consider the variance-covariance

matrix $E\widehat{x}_t\widehat{x}'_{t-j}$ for $j > 0$. Let $\mu_t = \eta\epsilon_t$. Then we have

$$E\widehat{x}_t\widehat{x}'_{t-j} = E\left[h_x^j\widehat{x}_{t-j} + \sum_{k=0}^{j-1} h_x^k\mu_{t-k}\right]\widehat{x}'_{t-j}$$

$$= h_x^j E\widehat{x}_{t-j}\widehat{x}'_{t-j}$$

$$= h_x^j\Sigma_x.$$

Similarly, consider the variance-covariance matrix of linear combinations of the state vector x_t. For instance, the co-state, or control vector y_t, is given by $y_t = y + g_x(x_t - x)$, which we can write as $\widehat{y}_t = g_x\widehat{x}_t$. Then

$$E\widehat{y}_t\widehat{y}'_t = Eg_x\widehat{x}_t\widehat{x}'_t g'_x$$

$$= g_x[E\widehat{x}_t\widehat{x}'_t]g'_x$$

$$= g_x\Sigma_x g'_x,$$

and, more generally,

$$E\widehat{y}_t\widehat{y}'_{t-j} = g_x[E\widehat{x}_t\widehat{x}'_{t-j}]g'_x$$

$$= g_x h_x^j\Sigma_x g'_x,$$

for $j \geq 0$.

4.14.4 Computing Impulse Response Functions

The impulse response of a variable—z_t in period $t + j$—to an impulse in period t is defined as

$$IR(z_{t+j}) \equiv E_t z_{t+j} - E_{t-1}z_{t+j}.$$

The impulse response function traces the expected behavior of the system from period t on given information available in period t, relative to what was expected at time $t - 1$. Using the law of motion $E_t\widehat{x}_{t+1} = h_x\widehat{x}_t$ for the state vector, letting x denote the innovation to the state vector in period 0 (i.e., $x = \eta\epsilon_0$), and applying the law of iterated expectations, we get that the impulse response of the state vector in period t is given by

$$IR(\widehat{x}_t) \equiv E_0\widehat{x}_t - E_{-1}\widehat{x}_t = h_x^t[x_0 - E_{-1}x_0] = h_x^t[\eta\epsilon_0] = h_x^t x; \quad t \geq 0.$$

The impulse response of the vector of controls $\widehat{y}_t$ is given by

$$IR(\widehat{y}_t) = g_x h_x^t x.$$

4.14.5 Matlab Code for Linear Perturbation Methods

The program `gx_hx.m` computes the matrices g_x and h_x using the Schur decomposition method. The program `mom.m` computes second moments. The program `ir.m` computes impulse response functions. These programs are available on the Web site for this book.

4.15 Exercises

4.1 (Dynamics of a Linear Economy) Consider an economy whose equilibrium dynamics has the reduced form

$$\widehat{c}_{t+1} = \gamma_{11}\widehat{c}_t$$

and

$$\widehat{d}_t = \gamma_{21}\widehat{c}_t + \gamma_{22}\widehat{d}_{t-1},$$

where c_t denotes consumption, and d_t denotes debt acquired in period t and maturing in period $t+1$. A hat denotes deviation from steady state. The variable d_{t-1} is an endogenous state and is predetermined in t, and the variable c_t is a control variable determined in t. The coefficients γ_{11}, γ_{21}, and γ_{22} are constant parameters. Suppose that $\gamma_{22} > 0$.

1. Find conditions on the parameters of the model under which
    1. the economy has a unique equilibrium converging to the steady state,
    2. debt converges monotonically to its steady-state value, and
    3. consumption is strictly decreasing in debt (i.e., c_t is a strictly decreasing function of d_{t-1}).

    Hint: Consult Appendix 4.14.2.

2. Find the policy functions for debt and consumption that are consistent with the three conditions imposed in the previous item.

4.2 (Variation of the PAC Model) This exercise aims to establish whether formulating portfolio adjustment costs as a function of the deviation of the household's debt position from an exogenous reference point, $d_t - \bar{d}$, or as a function of the change in its debt position, $d_t - d_{t-1}$, has consequences for the stationarity of the model.

Consider a small open economy populated by a large number of infinitely-lived households with preferences described by the utility function

$$E_0 \sum_{t=0}^{\infty} \beta^t \ln c_t,$$

where $\beta \in (0, 1)$ denotes the subjective discount factor, and c_t denotes consumption in period t. Each period, households receive an exogenous and stochastic endowment, y_t, and can borrow from (or lend to) international financial markets at the gross interest rate $1 + r$. Let d_t denote the stock of foreign debt held by households at the end of period t.

Households are subject to a portfolio adjustment cost of the form $\frac{\phi}{2}(d_t - d_{t-1})^2$, where ϕ is a positive constant. Assume that $\beta(1+r) = 1$.

1. State the household's period-by-period budget constraint.

2. State the household's utility maximization problem.

3. Write the Lagrangian of the household's problem.

4. Define a competitive equilibrium of this economy.

5. Suppose the endowment is nonstochastic and constant, $y_t = y$, for all t. Characterize the deterministic steady state. Does it exist? Is it unique? Hint: Consult Appendix 4.14.2.

6. Consider now a temporary endowment shock. Suppose $y_0 > y$ and $y_t = y$ for all $t > 0$ deterministically. Suppose that prior to period 0 the economy was in a deterministic steady state with $d_{-1} = d^*$. Is the economy stationary, that is, is d_t expected to return to d^*? Provide intuition.

4.3 (Variation of the EDF Model) This exercise analyzes the local stability of the equilibrium of the EDF model when the household's subjective discount factor is assumed to be increasing in aggregate consumption, $\theta'(c_t) > 0$, as opposed to decreasing, as is assumed in the baseline specification presented in Section 4.10.3. Consider a small open economy populated by infinitely-lived agents. Let c_t denote consumption in period t. Assume that the discount factor, denoted β_t, evolves over time according to $\beta_{t+1} = \theta(c_t)\beta_t$. Assume that the function θ is positive and bounded above by unity. Agents have access to international financial markets, where they can borrow or lend at the interest rate $r > 0$. Agents choose consumption and external debt, d_t, so as to maximize lifetime utility given by $\sum_{t=0}^{\infty} \beta_t U(c_t)$, where $U(\cdot)$ is an increasing and strictly concave function. Agents are endowed with $y > 0$ units of goods each period. Agents enter period 0 with a stock d_{-1} of net foreign debt. Assume that $\beta_0 = 1$. Assume that households are subject to some borrowing constraint that prevents them from engaging in Ponzi schemes. Assume that agents fail to internalize that their consumption choices affect their discount factor.

1. Characterize the competitive equilibrium of this economy.

2. Characterize the steady state of this economy. Consider the following two cases: (i) θ is strictly increasing in c and (ii) θ is strictly decreasing in c. What properties does the function $\theta(\cdot)$ need to have in each case to ensure existence of a steady state? What properties does the function $\theta(\cdot)$ need to have in each case to ensure that the steady state is unique? Provide an intuitive explanation for your results by comparing them to those you would obtain in an economy in which $\theta(\cdot)$ is independent of c_t. Which case, (i) or (ii), is more plausible to you and why?

3. Characterize the local stability of the economy in a small neighborhood around the steady state. Specifically, suppose that d_{-1} is not equal to the steady state. Under what conditions on the function $\theta(\cdot)$ does there exist a unique perfect foresight equilibrium converging back to the steady state?

4. Assume now, contrary to what was assumed above, that agents internalize that their own consumption choice in period t changes the discount factor, that is,

they internalize that θ depends on c_t. Characterize the competitive equilibrium of this economy. Give an intuitive explanation for the differences in equilibrium conditions in the economy with and without internalization.

5. Characterize the steady state of the economy described in question 4 above. Does it exist? Is it unique? Is it the same as in the economy without internalization?

6. Characterize the local stability of the steady state in the economy with internalization. Specifically, suppose that d_{-1} is not equal but is close to its steady state value. Under what conditions does there exist a unique perfect foresight equilibrium converging back to the steady state? Express your answer in terms of a condition involving the parameter r and the following four elasticities: $\epsilon_\theta \equiv \frac{\theta'(c)c}{\theta(c)}$, $\epsilon_{\theta\theta} \equiv \frac{\theta''(c)c}{\theta'(c)}$, $\epsilon_c \equiv \frac{U'(c)c}{U(c)}$, and $\epsilon_{cc} \equiv \frac{U''(c)c}{U'(c)}$, evaluated at the steady state value of c_t. Discuss how your result differs from that obtained in question 3 above.

4.4 (Complete Asset Markets and a Discrete Endowment Process) Consider an economy populated by a large number of identical consumers with preferences described by the utility function

$$E_0 \sum_{t=0}^{\infty} \beta^t U(c_t),$$

where c_t denotes consumption in period t, $\beta \in (0, 1)$ denotes the subjective discount factor, $U(\cdot)$ is a strictly increasing and differentiable function, and E_t denotes the mathematical expectations operator conditional on information available at time t. Suppose each consumer starts with an initial financial wealth equal to b_0 in period 0, measured in terms of consumption goods. Suppose that each period there are two possible states of nature, H and L, with transition probability matrix

$$\Pi = \begin{bmatrix} \pi_{HH} & \pi_{HL} \\ \pi_{LH} & \pi_{LL} \end{bmatrix},$$

where π_{ij}, for $i, j \in \{H, L\}$, denotes the probability that the state of nature in period $t + 1$ is j conditional on the state of nature in t being i, for all $t \geq 0$. The consumer is endowed with y_t units of consumption goods in period t, where y_t is a random variable taking the values y_H and y_L in states H and L, respectively, with $y_H > y_L > 0$. Consumers have access to the world financial market, which offers a complete set of state-contingent claims. Let p_{ij} be the price in units of consumption of period t of a state-contingent claim that pays 1 unit of consumption in $t + 1$ if the state of nature in period $t + 1$ is j conditional on the state of nature in period t being i, for $i, j \in \{H, L\}$ and $t \geq 0$. Suppose further that $p_{ij} = \beta\pi_{ij}$. Suppose that the state of nature in period 0 is H.

1. State the consumer's maximization problem.

2. Characterize the equilibrium process of consumption.

3. Characterize the equilibrium process of the trade balance.

4. Characterize the equilibrium process of the net foreign asset position (recall that in period 0 it is known and given by b_0).

5. Characterize the equilibrium process of the current account starting in period 1.

6. Compare the equilibrium processes of consumption, the trade balance, and the current account obtained above to those pertaining to another open economy that is identical to the one described above in all respects, except that its initial endowment is y^L.

4.5 (Complete Asset Markets and External Shocks) Consider the CAM model of Section 4.9. Suppose that the productivity factor A_t is constant and normalized to 1. Replace the equilibrium condition $U_c(c_t, h_t) = \psi_{CAM}$ with the expression

$$U_c(c_t, h_t) = x_t,$$

where x_t is an exogenous and stochastic random variable, which can be interpreted as an external shock. Assume that the external shock follows a process of the form

$$\widehat{x}_t = \rho \widehat{x}_{t-1} + \epsilon_t; \qquad \epsilon_t \sim N(0, \sigma_\epsilon^2),$$

where $\widehat{x}_t \equiv \ln(x_t/x)$, and x denotes the nonstochastic steady-state level of x_t. Let $\rho = 0.9$ and $\sigma_\epsilon = 0.02$. Calibrate all other parameters of the model following the calibration of the CAM model presented in Section 4.9. Finally, set the steady-state value of x_t in such a way that the steady-state level of consumption equals the level of steady-state consumption in the version of the CAM model studied in the main text.

1. Produce a table displaying the unconditional standard deviation, serial correlation, and correlation with output of $\widehat{y}_t, \widehat{c}_t, \widehat{i}_t, \widehat{h}_t$, and tb_t/y_t.

2. Produce a figure with five plots depicting the impulse responses to an external shock (a unit innovation in ϵ_t) of $\widehat{y}_t, \widehat{c}_t, \widehat{i}_t, \widehat{h}_t$, and tb_t/y_t.

3. Now replace the values of ρ and σ_ϵ given above with values such that the volatility and serial correlation of output implied by the model are the same as those reported for the Canadian economy in Table 4.2. Answer questions 1 and 2 above using these new parameter values.

4. Based on your answer to question 3, evaluate the ability of external shocks (as defined here) to explain business cycles in Canada.

4.6 (An AR(2) TFP Process and Excess Consumption Volatility) In this exercise you are asked to show that the SOE-RBC model can predict consumption to be more volatile than output when the productivity shock follows an AR(2) process displaying a hump-shaped impulse response. The theoretical model to be used is the EDEIR model presented in Section 4.1.1. Replace the AR(1) process with the following AR(2) specification:

$$\ln A_{t+1} = 1.42 \ln A_t - 0.43 \ln A_{t-1} + \epsilon_{t+1},$$

where ϵ_t is an i.i.d. random variable with mean zero and standard deviation $\sigma_\epsilon > 0$. Scale σ_ϵ to ensure that the predicted standard deviation of output is 3.08, the value predicted by the AR(1) version of this model. Otherwise use the same calibration and functional forms as presented in the chapter. Download the Matlab files for the EDEIR model from the book's Web site. Then modify them to accommodate the present specification.

1. Produce a table displaying the unconditional standard deviation, serial correlation, and correlation with output of output, consumption, investment, hours, the trade-balance-to-output ratio, and the current-account-to-output ratio.

2. Produce a 3 × 2 figure displaying the impulse responses of output, consumption, investment, hours, the trade-balance-to-output ratio, and TFP to a unit innovation in TFP.

3. Compare and contrast the predictions of the model under the AR(1) and the AR(2) TFP processes. Provide intuition.

4.7 (Durable Consumption, I) Consider an SOE model with nondurable and durable consumption goods. Let $c_{N,t}$ denote consumption of nondurables in period t, and let $c_{D,t}$ denote purchases of durables in period t. The stock of durable consumer goods, denoted s_t, is assumed to evolve over time as $s_t = (1 - \delta)s_{t-1} + c_{D,t}$, where $\delta \in (0, 1]$ denotes the depreciation rate of durable goods. Households have preferences over consumption, c_t, of the form $\sum_{t=0}^{\infty} \beta^t U(c_t)$, where U is increasing in consumption and concave. Consumption, c_t, is a composite of nondurable consumption and the service flow provided by the stock of consumer durables. Specifically, assume that

$$c_t = \left[(1 - \alpha)^{\frac{1}{\eta}} c_{N,t}^{1-\frac{1}{\eta}} + \alpha^{\frac{1}{\eta}} s_t^{1-\frac{1}{\eta}} \right]^{\frac{1}{1-\frac{1}{\eta}}},$$

where $\eta > 0$ and $\alpha \in (0, 1)$. Households have access to an internationally traded risk-free one-period bond, which pays the interest rate r_t when held between periods t and $t + 1$. The relative price of durables in terms of nondurables is one. The household is subject to a borrowing limit that prevents it from engaging in Ponzi schemes. Output, denoted y_t, is produced with capital according to a production function of the form $y_t = F(k_t)$, where k_t denotes physical capital. The capital stock evolves over time as $k_{t+1} = (1 - \delta_k)k_t + i_t$, where i_t denotes investment in period t, and δ_k is the depreciation rate on physical capital.

1. Describe the household's budget set.

2. State the optimization problem of the household.

3. Present the complete set of equilibrium conditions.

4. The interest rate is constant over time and equal to $r_t = r = \beta^{-1} - 1$. Assume that up to period -1, the economy was in a steady state equilibrium in which all variables were constant and $d = \bar{d} > 0$, where d denotes net external debt in the steady state. Find the share of expenditures on durables in total consumption expenditures in the steady state in terms of the parameters δ, r, α, and η. Suggest a strategy for calibrating those four parameters.

5. Assume that in period 0 the economy unexpectedly receives a positive income shock as a consequence of the rest of the world forgiving part of the country's net foreign debt. Assume that the positive income shock results in a 1 percent increase in the consumption of nondurables in period 0. Find the percentage increase in purchases of durables and in total consumption expenditures in period 0. Compare

your answer to the one you would have obtained if all consumption goods were nondurable.

6. Continuing to assume that consumption of nondurables has increased by 1 percent, find the change in the trade balance in period 0 expressed as a share of steady-state consumption expenditures. Is the response of the trade balance countercyclical? Compare your findings to those you would have obtained if all consumption goods were nondurable. How much amplification is there due to the presence of durables?

4.8 (Durable Consumption, II) Consider an economy populated by a large number of identical households with preferences described by the lifetime utility function

$$E_0 \sum_{t=0}^{\infty} \beta^t \frac{\left[\left(c_t^n - \frac{h_t^\omega}{\omega}\right) s_t^\gamma\right]^{1-\sigma} - 1}{1 - \sigma},$$

where c_t^n denotes consumption of nondurable goods, h_t denotes hours worked, and s_t denotes the stock of durable consumption goods. The parameter $\beta \in (0, 1)$ denotes the subjective discount factor; γ, $(\omega - 1)$, $(\sigma - 1) > 0$ are preference parameters; and E_t denotes the expectations operator conditional on information available in period t.

The law of motion of the stock of durables is assumed to be of the form

$$s_t = (1 - \delta)s_{t-1} + c_t^d,$$

where c_t^d denotes durable consumption in period t, and $\delta \in (0, 1)$ denotes the depreciation rate. The sequential budget constraint of the household is given by

$$d_t = (1 + r_{t-1})d_{t-1} + c_t^n + c_t^d + \frac{\phi^d}{2}(s_t - s_{t-1})^2 + i_t + \frac{\phi^k}{2}(k_{t+1} - k_t)^2 - A_t k_t^\alpha h_t^{1-\alpha},$$

where d_t denotes debt acquired in period t and maturing in period $t + 1$, r_t denotes the interest rate on assets held between periods t and $t + 1$, i_t denotes gross investment, k_t denotes the stock of physical capital, and A_t represents a technology factor assumed to be exogenous and stochastic. The parameters ϕ^d, $\phi^k > 0$ govern the degree of adjustment costs in the accumulation of durable consumption goods and physical capital, respectively. The parameter α resides in the interval $(0, 1)$. The capital stock evolves over time according to the law of motion

$$k_{t+1} = (1 - \delta)k_t + i_t.$$

Note that we assume that physical capital, k_t, is predetermined in period t and that investment, i_t, takes one period to become productive capital. In contrast, the stock of consumer durables, s_t, is nonpredetermined in period t, and expenditures in consumer durables in period t, c_t^d, become productive immediately. Finally, assume that the interest rate is debt elastic,

$$r_t = r^* + \psi \left[e^{\tilde{d}_t - \bar{d}} - 1\right],$$

where $\tilde{d}_t$ denotes the cross-sectional average level of debt per capita, and r^*, $\bar{d}$, and ψ are parameters. The productivity factor A_t evolves according to the expression

$$\ln A_{t+1} = \rho \ln A_t + \epsilon_{t+1},$$

where ϵ_t is a white noise process with mean zero and variance σ_ϵ^2, and $\rho \in (0, 1)$ is a parameter. Assume that $\beta(1 + r^*) = 1$.

1. Derive the complete set of equilibrium conditions.

2. Derive the deterministic steady state. Specifically, find analytical expressions for the steady-state values of c_t^n, h_t, s_t, k_{t+1}, d_t, r_t, i_t, tb_t, and ca_t in terms of the structural parameters of the model σ, β, δ, ω, α, γ, r^*, and $\bar{d}$. Here, tb_t and ca_t denote, respectively, the trade balance and the current account.

3. Assume the following parameter values: $\sigma = 2$, $\delta = 0.1$, $r^* = 0.04$, $\alpha = 0.3$, and $\omega = 1.455$. Calibrate $\bar{d}$ and γ so that in the steady state the debt-to-output ratio is 25 percent and the nondurable-consumption-to-output ratio is 68 percent. Report the implied numerical values of γ and $\bar{d}$. Also report the numerical steady-state values of r_t, d_t, h_t, k_t, c_t^n, s_t, c_t^d, i_t, tb_t, ca_t, and $y_t \equiv A_t k_t^\alpha h_t^{1-\alpha}$.

4. Approximate the equilibrium dynamics using a first-order perturbation technique. In performing this approximation, express all variables in logs, except for the stock of debt, the interest rate, the trade balance, the current account, the trade-balance-to-output ratio, and the current-account-to-output ratio. You are asked to complete the calibration of the model by setting values for ψ, ϕ^d, ϕ^k, ρ, and σ_ϵ to target key empirical regularities of medium-sized emerging countries documented in Chapter 1. Specifically, the targets are a standard deviation of output, σ_y, of 8.99 percent; a relative standard deviation of consumption, σ_c/σ_y, of 0.93; a relative standard deviation of gross investment, σ_i/σ_y, of 2.86; a serial correlation of output of 0.84; and a correlation between the trade-balance-to-output ratio and output of -0.24. In general, you will not be able to hit these targets exactly. Instead, you are required to define a distance between the targets and their corresponding theoretical counterparts and devise a numerical algorithm to minimize it. Define the distance as follows. Let $z(\psi, \phi^d, \phi^k, \rho, \sigma_\epsilon) \equiv x(\psi, \phi^d, \phi^k, \rho, \sigma_\epsilon) - x^*$, where x^* is the 5×1 vector of empirical targets (the five numbers given above), and $x(\psi, \phi^d, \phi^k, \rho, \sigma_\epsilon)$ is the 5×1 vector of theoretical counterparts as a function of the parameters. Let $D(\psi, \phi^d, \phi^k, \rho, \sigma_\epsilon) \equiv \sqrt{z(\psi, \phi^d, \phi^k, \rho, \sigma_\epsilon)'z(\psi, \phi^d, \phi^k, \rho, \sigma_\epsilon)}$ be the distance between the target and its theoretical counterpart.
   (i) Report the values of ψ, ϕ^d, ϕ^k, ρ, and σ_ϵ that you find.
   (ii) Complete the following table:

Statistic	Data	Prediction of the Model
σ_y	8.99	
σ_c/σ_y	0.93	
σ_i/σ_y	2.86	
$\text{corr}(y_t, y_{t-1})$	0.84	
$\text{corr}(tb_t/y_t, y_t)$	-0.24	

5. Produce a table displaying the model predictions. The table should contain the unconditional standard deviation; correlation with output; and the first-order

serial correlation of output, consumption, investment, consumption of durables, consumption of nondurables, the trade-balance-to-output ratio, and the current-account-to-output ratio. For consumption, consumption of durables, consumption of nondurables, and investment, report the standard deviation relative to output. Discuss how well the model is able to explain actual observed second moments that were not targeted in the calibration. Use the second moments reported in Table 1.2 to compare the model's predictions to actual data.

4.9 (Complete Markets and the Countercyclicality of the Trade Balance) Consider a small open economy with access to a complete array of internationally traded state contingent claims. There is a single good, which is freely traded internationally. Let $q_{t,t+1}$ denote the period-t price of a contingent claim that pays one good in a particular state of the world in period $t + 1$ divided by the probability of occurrence of that state. The small open economy takes the process for $q_{t,t+1}$ as exogenously given.

Households have preferences over consumption, c_t, and hours, h_t, given by

$$E_0 \sum_{t=0}^{\infty} \beta^t \left[\frac{\left(c_t - \frac{h_t^\omega}{\omega} \right)^{1-\sigma} - 1}{1 - \sigma} \right]; \quad \sigma, \omega > 1,$$

where E_0 denotes the expectations operator conditional on information available in period 0. Households produce goods according to the following production technology:

$$A_t k_t^\alpha h_t^{1-\alpha},$$

where A_t denotes an exogenous productivity factor, k_t denotes the capital stock in period t, and the parameter $\alpha \in (0, 1)$ denotes the elasticity of the production function with respect to capital. Domestic households are the owners of physical capital. The evolution of capital is given by

$$k_{t+1} = (1 - \delta)k_t + i_t,$$

where i_t denotes investment in physical capital in period t, and $\delta \in (0, 1)$ denotes the depreciation rate. In period 0, households are endowed with k_0 units of capital and hold contingent claims (acquired in period -1) that pay d_0 goods in period 0.

1. State the household's period-by-period budget constraint.
2. Specify a borrowing limit that prevents households from engaging in Ponzi schemes.
3. State the household's utility maximization problem. Indicate which variables and processes the household chooses and which ones it takes as given.
4. Derive the complete set of competitive equilibrium conditions.
5. Let $\widehat{x}_t \equiv \ln x_t/x$ denote the percentage deviation of a variable from its nonstochastic steady-state value. Assume that in the nonstochastic steady state, $q_{0,t} = \beta^t$ and

$A_t = 1$. Show that in response to a positive innovation in technology in period t, $\widehat{A}_t > 0$, the trade balance will respond countercyclically only if the response in investment in period t is positive. Then find the minimum percentage increase in investment in period t required for the trade balance to decline in period t in response to the technology shock. To answer this question, use a first-order accurate approximation to the solution of the model. Show that your answer is independent of the expected value of A_{t+1}.

6. Compare and contrast your findings in question 5 to the ones derived in Chapter 3 for a model with capital accumulation, no depreciation, no capital adjustment costs, inelastic labor supply, and incomplete markets. In particular, discuss how in that model the sign of the impulse response of the trade balance to a positive innovation in the technology shock, $\widehat{A}_t > 0$, depended on the persistence of the technology shock. Give an intuitive explanation for the similarities/differences that you identify.

7. Now find the size of $E_t \widehat{A}_{t+1}$ relative to the size of $\widehat{A}_t$ that guarantees that the trade balance deteriorates in period t in response to a positive innovation in A_t in period t. Your answer should be a condition of the form $\widehat{A}_t < M E_t \widehat{A}_{t+1}$, where M is a function of the structural parameters of the model. In particular, it is a function of α, β, δ, and ω. Find the value of M for $\alpha = 1/3$, $\delta = 0.08$, $\beta^{-1} = 1.02$, and $\omega = 1.5$.

8. Discuss to what extent your findings support or contradict principle I, derived in Chapter 3.

9. How would your answers to questions 5 and 7 change if the period utility function were separable in consumption, c_t, and hours, h_t?

4.10 (Calibrating the EDEIR Model Using Canadian Data over the Period 1960–2011) In Section 4.5, we calibrated the EDEIR model using second moments computed with Canadian data for the period 1946–1985. The middle panel of Table 4.2 updates the empirical second moments for the period 1960–2011. The present exercise uses these empirical regularities to calibrate and evaluate the SOE-RBC model.

1. Calibrate the EDEIR model as follows. Set $\beta = 1/1.04$, $\sigma = 2$, $\omega = 1.455$, $\alpha = 0.32$, $\delta = 0.10$, and $\bar{d} = 0.7442$. Set the remaining four parameters, ρ, $\widetilde{\eta}$, ϕ, and ψ_1, to match the observed standard deviations and serial correlations of output and the standard deviations of investment and the trade-balance-to-output ratio in Canada during 1960–2011. Approximate the equilibrium dynamics up to first order, and use a distance minimization procedure similar to the one used in exercise 4.8. Compare the resulting values for ρ, $\widetilde{\eta}$, ϕ, and ψ_1 with those reported in Table 4.1.

2. Compute theoretical second moments and present your findings as in the third panel of Table 4.2.

3. Comment on the ability of the model to explain observed business cycles in Canada during 1960–2011.

4. Compute the unconditional standard deviation of the productivity shock, $\ln A_t$, under the present calibration. Compare this number to the one corresponding to the 1946–1985 calibration presented in Section 4.5. Now do the same with the standard deviation of output. Discuss and interpret your findings.

4.11 (A Model of the U.S.-Canadian Business Cycle) Consider a world with two economies, Canada and the United States, indexed by $i = Can, US$, respectively. Suppose that both economies are populated by a large number of identical households with preferences given by

$$E_0 \sum_{t=0}^{\infty} \beta^t \frac{\left[c_t^i - \frac{(h_t^i)^\omega}{\omega} \right]^{1-\sigma} - 1}{1 - \sigma},$$

where c_t^i and h_t^i denote, respectively, consumption and hours worked in country i in period t. In both countries, households operate a technology that produces output, denoted y_t^i, using labor and capital, denoted k_t^i. The production technology is Cobb-Douglas and is given by

$$y_t^i = A_t^i (k_t^i)^\alpha (h_t^i)^{1-\alpha},$$

where A_t^i denotes a productivity shock in country i, which evolves according to the following AR(1) process:

$$\ln A_{t+1}^i = \rho^i \ln A_t^i + \eta^i \epsilon_{t+1}^i,$$

where ϵ_t^i is an i.i.d. innovation with mean zero and variance one, and ρ^i and η^i are country-specific parameters. Both countries produce the same good. The evolution of capital obeys the following law of motion:

$$k_{t+1}^i = k_t^i + \frac{1}{\phi^i} \left[\left(\frac{i_t^i}{\delta k_t^i} \right)^{\phi^i} - 1 \right] \delta k_t^i,$$

where i_t^i denotes investment in country i, and ϕ^i is a country-specific parameter.

Assume that asset markets are complete and that there exists free mobility of goods and financial assets between the United States and Canada, but that labor and installed capital are immobile across countries. Finally, assume that Canada has measure zero relative to the United States, so that the latter can be modeled as a closed economy.

Consider the business-cycle regularities for Canada for the period 1960–2011 shown in exercise 4.10. The following table displays observed standard deviations, serial correlations, and correlations with output for the United States for 1960–2011. The data are annual and are expressed in per capita terms. The series y, c, and i are in logs, and the series tb/y is in levels. All series were quadratically detrended. Standard deviations are measured in percentage points.

	U.S. Data 1960–2011		
Variable	σ_{x_t}	$\rho_{x_t, x_{t-1}}$	ρ_{x_t, GDP_t}
y	2.94	0.75	1.00
c	3.00	0.82	0.90
i	10.36	0.67	0.80
tb/y	0.94	0.79	−0.51

Source: Own calculations based on data from World Development Indicators.

1. Calibrate the model as follows. Assume that the deterministic steady-state levels of consumption per capita are the same in Canada and the United States. Set $\beta = 1/1.04$, $\sigma = 2$, $\omega = 1.455$, $\alpha = 0.32$, and $\delta = 0.10$. Set the remaining six parameters, ρ^i, η^i, and ϕ^i, for $i = Can, US$, to match the observed standard deviations and serial correlations of output and the standard deviations of investment in Canada and the United States. Use a distance minimization procedure as in exercise 4.8.

2. Approximate the equilibrium dynamics up to first order. Produce the theoretical counterparts of the two tables showing Canadian and U.S. business-cycle regularities.

3. Comment on the ability of the model to explain observed business cycles in Canada and the United States.

4. Plot the response of Canadian output, consumption, investment, hours, and the trade-balance-to-output ratio to a unit innovation in the Canadian productivity shock. On the same plot, show the response of the Canadian variables to a unit innovation to the U.S. productivity shock. Discuss the differences in the responses to a domestic and a foreign technology shock and provide intuition.

5. Compare, by means of a graph and a discussion, the predicted responses of Canada and the United States to a unit innovation in the U.S. productivity shock. The graph should include the same variables as the one for question 4.

6. Compute the fraction of the volatilities of Canadian output and the trade-balance-to-output ratio explained by the U.S. productivity shock according to the present model. To this end, set $\eta^{Can} = 0$, and compute the two standard deviations of interest. Then take the ratio of these standard deviations to their respective counterparts when both shocks are active.

7. This question aims to quantify the importance of common shocks as drivers of the U.S.-Canadian business cycle. Replace the process for the Canadian productivity shock with the following one:

$$\ln A_{t+1}^{Can} = \rho^{Can} \ln A_t^{Can} + \eta^{Can} \epsilon_{t+1}^{Can} + \nu \epsilon_{t+1}^{US}.$$

All other aspects of the model are as before. Recalibrate the model using an augmented version of the strategy described above that includes an additional parameter, ν, and an additional target, the cross-country correlation of output, which in the sample used here is 0.64. Report the new set of calibrated parameters. Compute the variance of Canadian output. Now set $\nu = 0$, keeping all other parameter values unchanged, and recalculate the variance of Canadian output. Explain.

4.12 (GHH Preferences and No Capital) Consider a small open economy populated by an infinite number of identical households with preferences of the form

$$(1 - \sigma)^{-1} \sum_{t=0}^{\infty} \beta^t \left(c_t - \frac{h_t^\omega}{\omega} \right)^{1-\sigma},$$

where c_t denotes consumption of a perishable good in period t; h_t denotes labor effort in period t; and $\beta \in (0, 1)$, $\sigma > 1$, and $\omega > 1$ are parameters. Each household operates a technology that produces consumption goods according to the relationship

$$y_t = h_t^\alpha,$$

where y_t denotes output, and $\alpha \in (0, 1)$ is a parameter. The household can borrow or lend in international financial markets at the interest rate $r_t = r^* + \rho(\tilde{d}_t)$, where r^* denotes the world interest rate and satisfies $\beta(1 + r^*) = 1$. The function $\rho(\tilde{d}_t)$ is a country interest-rate premium in period t, satisfying $\rho(0) = 0$, and $\rho(x) \neq 0$ for $x \neq 0$, where $\tilde{d}_t$ denotes the cross-sectional average debt holdings in period t and is taken as given by the individual household. Let d_t denote the household's debt holdings in period t maturing in $t + 1$. Households cannot play Ponzi games.

1. Write down the household's optimization problem.
2. Derive the first-order conditions associated with the household's optimization problem.
3. Display the complete set of equilibrium conditions.
4. Derive the steady state of the economy. In particular, compute the steady-state values of consumption, hours, output, the trade balance, the current account, and external debt, denoted, respectively, c, h, y, tb, ca, and d.
5. Derive analytically a first-order linear approximation of the equilibrium conditions. Express it as a first-order difference equation in the vector $[\hat{d}_{t-1} \ \hat{c}_t]'$, where $\hat{d}_{t-1} \equiv d_{t-1} - d$, and $\hat{c}_t \equiv \ln(c_t/c)$.
6. Derive conditions under which the perfect-foresight equilibrium is locally unique.

4.13 (An SOE-RBC Model with Cobb-Douglas Preferences) Modify the period utility function of the EDEIR model of Section 4.1 as follows:

$$U(c, h) = \frac{\left[c^{1-\omega}(1 - h)^\omega \right]^{1-\sigma} - 1}{1 - \sigma}.$$

All other features of the model are unchanged.

1. Derive analytically the steady state of the model.
2. Set all parameters of the model as in Table 4.1, except for ω. Calibrate ω to ensure that in the deterministic steady state, hours equal 1/3 (i.e., ensure that in the steady state, households spend one-third of their time working). Calculate the implied value of ω.
3. Produce a table of predicted second moments similar to Table 4.2. When performing this step, you might find it convenient to use as a starting point the Matlab programs for the EDEIR SOE-RBC model posted on the book's Web site.
4. Compare the predictions of the present model with those of its GHH-preference counterpart.

Business Cycles in Emerging Countries: Productivity Shocks versus Financial Frictions

In Chapter 1, we documented that the most striking difference between business cycles in the group of rich countries and business cycles in the group of emerging or poor countries is that the latter are twice as volatile as the former (see fact 8 in Chapter 1). In principle, the open economy RBC model studied in Chapter 4 can account for this difference. All that is needed is to increase the volatility of the productivity shock. After all, the calibration strategy adopted in Chapter 4, which is representative of much of the existing related literature, was to set the standard deviation of the exogenous productivity shock to match the observed variance of output. Since not only output but also all components of aggregate demand are more volatile in emerging and poor countries than in rich countries, increasing the volatility of the productivity shock will help in more than one dimension. However, not all volatilities increase by the same proportions as one moves from rich to emerging or poor economies.

In particular, a second important difference between the group of rich countries and the group of emerging and poor countries is that in the former consumption is less volatile than output, whereas in the latter consumption is at least as volatile as output (see fact 9 in Chapter 1). The open economy RBC model of Chapter 4 predicts that consumption is less volatile than output. This prediction is in line with the observed relative volatility of consumption in Canada, a rich economy to which the model was calibrated. A natural question is whether there exist calibrations of the open economy model of Chapter 4 that can account for the excess volatility of consumption observed in emerging countries.

5.1 Can the Open Economy RBC Model Generate Excess Consumption Volatility?

The answer to this question is "yes." We note, however, that simply jacking up the volatility of the productivity shock in the open economy RBC model will not do the job. The reason is

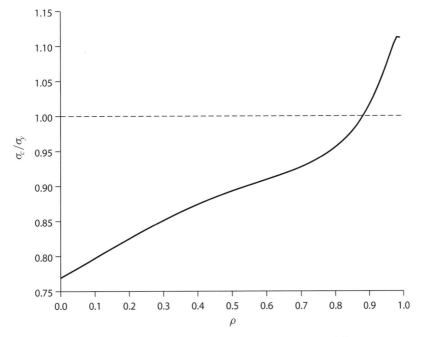

Figure 5.1 The relative volatility of consumption as a function of the persistence of the stationary technology shock.

that up to first order in models with a single exogenous shock, the ratio of any two standard deviations is independent of the standard deviation of the exogenous shock.

The analysis of a small open economy with capital of Chapter 3 provides the insight that the response of consumption relative to that of output to a productivity shock depends significantly on the persistence of the productivity shock. The more persistent the productivity shock is, the stronger the response of consumption will be. Building on this insight, it is natural to explore whether increasing the persistence of the productivity shock will allow the open economy model of Chapter 4 to explain the observed excess volatility of consumption in emerging and poor countries. Figure 5.1 displays the ratio of the volatility of consumption to the volatility of output, σ_c/σ_y, as a function of the persistence of the stationary productivity shock, ρ, predicted by the open economy RBC model of Chapter 4, Section 4.1.1. For values of ρ larger than 0.88 the volatility of consumption exceeds that of output.

Figure 5.2 helps build the intuition behind this result. It displays the impulse response of output to a 1 percent increase in productivity for two values of ρ, 0.42 (the value used in Chapter 4) and 0.99. For the lower value of ρ, the impulse response of output to a positive productivity shock is positive on impact and monotonically decreasing. This means that in the period the shock occurs, future output is expected to be lower than current output. Because consumption depends not on current output alone but also on the present discounted value of output, we have that the impact response of consumption is smaller than that of output. In contrast, when the technology shock is highly persistent, the response of

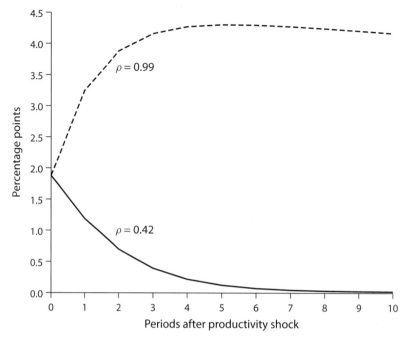

Figure 5.2   Impulse response of output to a 1 percent increase in productivity for high and low persistence of the stationary productivity shock.

output is hump shaped (see the dashed line in Figure 5.2). In this case, on impact, output may be smaller than the average of current and future values of output. Consequently the impact response of consumption may exceed that of output, suggesting a higher volatility of consumption relative to output. In turn, the reason that the response of output is hump shaped has to do with the behavior of investment. If the serial correlation of the technology shock is small, investment does not react much to innovations in productivity, since they are expected to die out quickly. Thus the response of output mimics that of technology. However, if the productivity shock is highly persistent, then firms will have an incentive to increase the stock of physical capital, to take advantage of the fact that capital will be highly productive for a number of periods. As a result, output may continue to increase even as productivity falls monotonically to its steady-state level.

It follows that capital accumulation is crucial for the open economy RBC model of Chapter 4 to capture the excess volatility of consumption characteristic of emerging economies. However, increasing the serial correlation of the stationary productivity shock may come at a cost. Recall, for instance, that in Chapter 4, the strategy for calibrating the parameter ρ was to match the observed serial correlation of output. Thus, in principle, a trade-off occurs between matching the excess volatility of consumption and matching the serial correlation of output.

A possible solution to this trade-off is to add an additional shock to the open economy RBC model. In Chapter 2, Section 2.4, we suggested that a possible way to induce excess volatility of consumption is to introduce nonstationary shocks. Aguiar and Gopinath (2007) pursue this strategy. Specifically, they adapt the closed economy RBC model with permanent and temporary TFP shocks due to King, Plosser, and Rebelo (1988) to an open economy setting. They argue that the open economy RBC model is an adequate framework for understanding aggregate fluctuations in emerging countries, provided it is augmented to allow for both stationary and nonstationary productivity shocks. We present this model next.

5.2 An Open Economy RBC Model with Stationary and Nonstationary Technology Shocks

Consider a small open economy populated by a large number of identical households seeking to maximize the utility function

$$E_0 \sum_{t=0}^{\infty} \beta^t \frac{[C_t^\gamma (1-h_t)^{1-\gamma}]^{1-\sigma} - 1}{1-\sigma}$$

subject to

$$\frac{D_{t+1}}{1+r_t} = D_t + C_t + K_{t+1} - (1-\delta)K_t + \frac{\phi}{2}\left(\frac{K_{t+1}}{K_t} - g\right)^2 K_t - Y_t,$$

and to a no-Ponzi-game constraint of the form

$$\lim_{j\to\infty} E_t \frac{D_{t+j+1}}{\Pi_{s=0}^{j}(1+r_{t+s})} \le 0,$$

where

$$Y_t = a_t K_t^\alpha (X_t h_t)^{1-\alpha}.$$

In the above expressions, C_t denotes consumption, h_t denotes hours worked, Y_t denotes output, K_t denotes the stock of physical capital, D_t denotes one-period debt acquired in $t-1$, r_t denotes the interest rate charged by the rest of the world, and a_t and X_t denote exogenous and stochastic productivity shocks. The parameters α, β, and δ lie in the interval $(0, 1)$, and the parameters γ, σ, ϕ, and g are positive. As before, the parameter ϕ introduces capital adjustment costs. Debt takes the form of one-period discount bonds. The household receives $D_{t+1}/(1+r_t)$ units of goods in period t in exchange for the promise to pay D_{t+1} units of goods in period $t+1$. From the point of view of the household, there is no difference between this formulation and the one assumed in Chapter 4.[1] Another difference with the model of Chapter 4 is that the period utility function takes a Cobb-Douglas form instead of a GHH form. The results reported in this chapter are unaffected by the aforementioned two differences with the model of Chapter 4.

---

1. To see this, introduce the change of variable $D_t' = D_t/(1 + r_{t-1})$.

The optimality conditions associated with the household's problem are

$$\frac{1-\gamma}{\gamma} \frac{C_t}{1-h_t} = (1-\alpha)a_t X_t \left(\frac{K_t}{X_t h_t}\right)^\alpha,$$

$$\gamma C_t^{\gamma(1-\sigma)-1}(1-h_t)^{(1-\gamma)(1-\sigma)} = \Lambda_t,$$

$$\Lambda_t = \beta(1+r_t)E_t\Lambda_{t+1},$$

and

$$\Lambda_t \left[1 + \phi\left(\frac{K_{t+1}}{K_t} - g\right)\right] = \beta E_t \Lambda_{t+1}\left[1 - \delta + \alpha a_{t+1}\left(\frac{K_{t+1}}{X_{t+1}h_{t+1}}\right)^{\alpha-1}\right.$$

$$\left. + \phi\frac{K_{t+2}}{K_{t+1}}\left(\frac{K_{t+2}}{K_{t+1}} - g\right) - \frac{\phi}{2}\left(\frac{K_{t+2}}{K_{t+1}} - g\right)^2\right],$$

where Λ_t denotes the Lagrange multiplier associated with the sequential budget constraint of the household.

As in Chapter 4, Section 4.1.1, the interest rate is assumed to be debt elastic:

$$r_t = r^* + \psi\left[e^{\tilde{D}_{t+1}/X_t - \bar{d}} - 1\right],$$

where r^*, ψ, and $\bar{d}$ are parameters, and $\tilde{D}_t$ denotes the cross-sectional average level of external debt per capita in period t. In equilibrium, because all households are identical, we have that

$$\tilde{D}_t = D_t.$$

The main difference between the present model and the one studied in Chapter 4 is that one of the productivity shocks is nonstationary. Specifically, the present economy is driven by a stationary productivity shock a_t and a nonstationary productivity shock X_t. We assume that X_t and a_t are mutually independent random variables with laws of motion given by

$$\ln a_t = \rho_a \ln a_{t-1} + \sigma_a \epsilon_t^a$$

and

$$\ln(g_t/g) = \rho_g \ln(g_{t-1}/g) + \sigma_g \epsilon_t^g,$$

where

$$g_t \equiv \frac{X_t}{X_{t-1}}$$

denotes the gross growth rate of X_t. The parameters ρ_a and ρ_g lie in the interval $(-1, 1)$, and σ_a and σ_g are positive. The variables ϵ_t^a and ϵ_t^g are assumed to be exogenous, mutually independent white noise processes distributed $N(0, 1)$. The parameter $g > 0$ denotes the gross growth rate of productivity in a nonstochastic equilibrium path. The productivity factor X_t is nonstationary in the sense that it displays both secular growth, at an average rate g, and a random walk component. Innovations in g_t have a permanent effect on the level of X_t.

Let $TFP_t \equiv Y_t/(K_t^\alpha h_t^{1-\alpha})$ be total factor productivity. Under the present technology specification, we have that

$$TFP_t = a_t X_t^{1-\alpha}. \tag{5.1}$$

Because a_t is a stationary random variable independent of X_t, total factor productivity inherits the nonstationarity of X_t. And this property will be transmitted in equilibrium to other variables of the model, including consumption, investment, the capital stock, the marginal utility of wealth, and the stock of external debt. Because none of these variables exhibits a deterministic steady state, it is impossible to linearize the model around such a point. Fortunately, however, there exists a simple stationary transformation of the variables of the model whose equilibrium behavior is described by a system of equations very similar to the one that governs the joint determination of the original variables. Specifically, let $c_t \equiv C_t/X_{t-1}, k_t \equiv K_t/X_{t-1}, d_t \equiv D_t/X_{t-1}$, and $\lambda_t \equiv X_{t-1}^{1+(\sigma-1)\gamma}\Lambda_t$. Then we can write the system of equilibrium conditions in stationary form as

$$\frac{g_t d_{t+1}}{1+r_t} = d_t + c_t + g_t k_{t+1} - (1-\delta)k_t + \frac{\phi}{2}\left(\frac{g_t k_{t+1}}{k_t} - g\right)^2 k_t - a_t k_t^\alpha (g_t h_t)^{1-\alpha},$$

$$r_t = r^* + \psi\left[e^{d_{t+1}-\bar{d}} - 1\right],$$

$$\frac{1-\gamma}{\gamma}\frac{c_t}{1-h_t} = (1-\alpha)a_t g_t \left(\frac{k_t}{g_t h_t}\right)^\alpha,$$

$$\gamma c_t^{\gamma(1-\sigma)-1}(1-h_t)^{(1-\gamma)(1-\sigma)} = \lambda_t,$$

$$\lambda_t = \beta(1+r_t)g_t^{\gamma(1-\sigma)-1}E_t\lambda_{t+1},$$

and

$$\lambda_t\left[1+\phi\left(\frac{g_t k_{t+1}}{k_t} - g\right)\right] = \beta g_t^{\gamma(1-\sigma)-1}E_t\lambda_{t+1}\left[1 - \delta + \alpha a_{t+1}\left(\frac{k_{t+1}}{g_{t+1}h_{t+1}}\right)^{\alpha-1}\right.$$

$$\left. + \phi\frac{g_{t+1}k_{t+2}}{k_{t+1}}\left(\frac{g_{t+1}k_{t+2}}{k_{t+1}} - g\right) - \frac{\phi}{2}\left(\frac{g_{t+1}k_{t+2}}{k_{t+1}} - g\right)^2\right].$$

This is a system of six stochastic difference equations in the endogenous variables $d_{t+1}, c_t, k_{t+1}, h_t, \lambda_t$, and r_t. This system, together with the laws of motion of g_t and a_t, possesses two properties that are useful for approximating equilibrium dynamics. First, it has a

Table 5.1   The Open Economy RBC Model with Stationary and Nonstationary Productivity Shocks

Calibrated Parameters						
β	γ	ψ	α	σ	δ	$\bar{d}$
0.98	0.36	0.001	0.32	2	0.05	0.1

Estimated Parameters					
σ_g	σ_a	ρ_g	ρ_a	g	ϕ
0.0213	0.0053	0.00	0.95	1.0066	1.37

Source: Aguiar and Gopinath (2007).
Note: The time unit is one quarter.

deterministic steady state that is independent of initial conditions. Second, the rational expectations dynamics of all variables are, up to first order, mean reverting (i.e., stationary).

Recalling that the variable transformations involve scaling by the nonstationary productivity factor, it follows that in this model consumption, output, the capital stock, investment, and net external debt all share the same stochastic trend, X_t. For instance, consumption satisfies $C_t = c_t X_{t-1}$. Since c_t is stationary, it follows directly that C_t carries the same random walk component as X_t. The existence of a common stochastic trend implies that in equilibrium, the shares of consumption, investment, capital, and external debt in GDP are all stationary variables. This property of the model is known as the *balanced-growth property*.

Aguiar and Gopinath (2007) econometrically estimate the parameters defining the laws of motion of the two productivity shocks, σ_a, σ_g, ρ_a, and ρ_g; the steady-state growth rate of productivity, g; and the parameter governing the strength of capital adjustment costs, ϕ. They calibrate the other parameters of the model. The six parameters listed in Table 5.1 are estimated on quarterly Mexican data over the period 1980:Q1 to 2003:Q1. Table 5.2 displays a number of second moments implied by these data. The econometric estimation consists in picking values for the six parameters so as to match these second moments as well as the observed average growth rate of GDP. Because the number of estimated parameters (six) is smaller than the number of moments matched (eleven), the estimation procedure uses a weighting matrix following the GMM technique. Table 5.1 displays the calibrated and estimated parameter values.

Table 5.2 displays ten empirical and predicted second moments for Mexico. The estimated model does a good job at matching all moments shown in the table. Of particular relevance is the ability of the model to match the fact that in Mexico, as in most other emerging countries, consumption is more volatile than output. As explained in detail in Chapter 2, Section 2.4, in the context of a model with nonstationary endowment shocks, the presence of nonstationary productivity shocks plays a key role in making this prediction possible. It is therefore of interest to calculate the importance of the nonstationary component of productivity in driving movements in total factor productivity implied by the econometrically estimated parameters. To this end, consider the growth rate of total factor productivity, which, from equation (5.1), can be written as

Table 5.2   Model Fit

Statistic	Data	Model
$\sigma(y)$	2.40	2.13
$\sigma(\Delta y)$	1.52	1.42
$\sigma(c)/\sigma(y)$	1.26	1.10
$\sigma(i)/\sigma(y)$	4.15	3.83
$\sigma(nx)/\sigma(y)$	0.80	0.95
$\rho(y)$	0.83	0.82
$\rho(\Delta y)$	0.27	0.18
$\rho(y, nx)$	-0.75	-0.50
$\rho(y, c)$	0.82	0.91
$\rho(y, i)$	0.91	0.80

Source: Aguiar and Gopinath (2007).
Notes: Variables in levels were Hodrick-Prescott (HP) filtered using a parameter of 1,600. Growth rates are unfiltered.

$$\Delta \ln TFP_t = \Delta \ln a_t + (1 - \alpha) g_t.$$

Because the two terms on the right-hand side of this expression are mutually independent, we can ask what fraction of the variance of $\Delta \ln TFP_t$ is explained by g_t. It is straightforward to deduce that the variance of $\Delta \ln a_t$ is given by $2\sigma_a^2/(1 + \rho_a)$. At the same time, the variance of g_t is given by $\sigma_g^2/(1 - \rho_g^2)$. Therefore, we have that

$$\frac{\text{var}((1 - \alpha) g_t)}{\text{var}(\Delta \ln TFP_t)} = \frac{(1 - \alpha)^2 \sigma_g^2/(1 - \rho_g^2)}{2\sigma_a^2/(1 + \rho_a) + (1 - \alpha)^2 \sigma_g^2/(1 - \rho_g^2)} \tag{5.2}$$

$$= \frac{(1 - 0.32)^2 \times 0.0213^2/(1 - 0.00^2)}{2 \times 0.0053^2/(1 + 0.95) + (1 - 0.32)^2 \times 0.0213^2/(1 - 0.00^2)}$$

$$= 0.8793.$$

That is, the estimated parameters imply that the nonstationary component of productivity explains 88 percent of the variance of the growth rate of total factor productivity. This is an indication that this model can fit the Mexican data best when nonstationary technology shocks play a significant role in moving total factor productivity at business-cycle frequency.

Aguiar and Gopinath (2007) also estimate the present model on quarterly Canadian data from 1981:Q1 to 2003:Q2 and find that the nonstationary component explains only 40 percent of movements in total factor productivity. Taken together, the Mexican and Canadian estimates suggest that, according to the present model, nonstationary productivity shocks are more relevant in emerging economies than in developed ones.

How should we interpret these results? Three aspects of the econometric estimation deserve special comments. One is that the data sample, 1980:Q1 to 2003:Q1, is relatively short. Recall that the main purpose of the estimation is to distinguish the stationary and

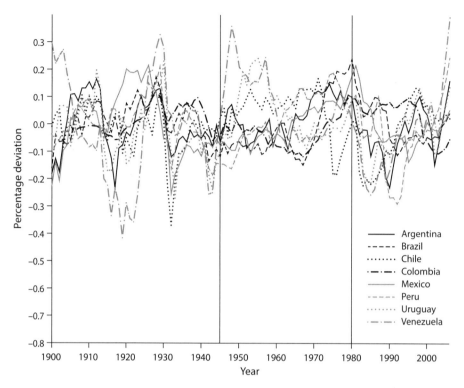

Figure 5.3   Business cycles in Latin America: 1900–2005.

Source: García-Cicco, Pancrazi, and Uribe (2010).
Note: Percent deviations of real GDP per capita from a cubic trend.

nonstationary components of the productivity shock. It is well known that the only reliable way to disentangle these two components is to use long samples. Short samples can lead to spurious results. In fact, Aguiar and Gopinath (2007) analyze direct evidence on Solow residuals, which in the present model coincide with total factor productivity, for Mexico and Canada over the period 1980–2000. They conclude that it is not possible in that short sample to determine reliably whether the nonstationary component is more important in Mexico than in Canada (see their figure 2).

Figure 5.3 shows why using short samples for estimation may be problematic. It displays the cyclical component of the log of real GDP per capita for eight Latin American countries over the period 1900–2005. In the figure, the cycle is computed as percent deviations of GDP from a cubic trend. The period 1980–2005 contains only between one and a half and two cycles for most of the Latin American economies included in the figure. Any econometric technique applied to so few cycles is likely to have a hard time telling apart stationary from nonstationary productivity shocks.

The second difficulty with the econometric strategy pursued by Aguiar and Gopinath is that it only allows for productivity shocks. This would not be a big problem if no other candidate shocks could be identified as potentially important in driving business cycles in emerging economies. But this is not the case. For example, a growing number of studies show that world interest-rate shocks and country-spread shocks play an important role in driving business cycles in emerging countries (see, e.g., Neumeyer and Perri 2005; Uribe and Yue 2006). Omitting these and other relevant shocks in the econometric estimation necessarily induces a bias in favor of the shocks that are included.

The third and final difficulty is that the present model limits attention to a frictionless neoclassical framework. This might also be an oversimplification, for a large body of work points to financial frictions, including default risk and balance-sheet effects, as important propagation mechanisms of business cycles in emerging economies (see Chapters 12 and 13). Omitting these sources of friction might cause a spurious increase in the estimated variance and persistence of the exogenous driving processes.

We address these concerns in the next section. Specifically, we will estimate an open economy model in which stationary and nonstationary productivity shocks compete with interest-rate and country-spread shocks. To obtain a reliable measure of the nonstationary component of productivity, we will estimate the model on long data samples spanning more than 100 years. And to capture the presence of financial frictions, we will let the data determine the size of the elasticity of the country interest rate. As it will turn out, once financial shocks and frictions are taken explicitly into account, the data assign a small role to nonstationary technology shocks as drivers of the business cycle.

5.3 Letting Technology Shocks Compete with Other Shocks and Frictions

In the model of Section 5.2, technology shocks monopolize the explanation of the business cycle in emerging countries. In this section, we make technology shocks compete with interest-rate shocks, preference shocks (random shifts in the marginal rate of intertemporal substitution), and public spending shocks (random changes in aggregate spending). The model studied here also generalizes the frictionless formulation of Section 5.2 by incorporating financial frictions in a structure that nests the frictionless environment as a special case. The purpose is to allow the data to choose how much importance to assign to each shock and friction. The presentation draws from García-Cicco, Pancrazi, and Uribe (2010), hereafter GPU.

5.3.1 Households

Consider an economy populated by a large number of identical households with preferences described by the utility function

$$E_0 \sum_{t=0}^{\infty} v_t \beta^t \frac{\left[C_t - \omega^{-1} X_{t-1} h_t^{\omega} \right]^{1-\gamma} - 1}{1 - \gamma}, \tag{5.3}$$

where C_t denotes consumption, h_t denotes hours supplied to the labor market, v_t denotes a preference shock, and X_t denotes a stochastic trend. This preference specification follows Schmitt-Grohé (1998). One might wonder why a stochastic trend appears in the utility function. The technical reason is that, as we will show shortly, this formulation makes it possible for a model with GHH preferences to exhibit balanced growth—that is, an equilibrium in which output, consumption, investment, and the capital stock all grow on average at the same rate and in which hours do not grow in the long run. From an economic point of view, X_t may reflect the impact of technological progress on household production, such as the successive inventions of the wood stove, the gas stove, and the microwave oven.

As in Section 5.2, we use uppercase letters to denote variables that contain a trend in equilibrium and lowercase letters to denote variables that do not. The laws of motion of v_t and X_t are assumed to be

$$\ln v_{t+1} = \rho_v \ln v_t + \epsilon_{t+1}^v,$$

and

$$\ln(g_{t+1}/g) = \rho_g \ln(g_t/g) + \epsilon_{t+1}^g,$$

where

$$g_t \equiv \frac{X_t}{X_{t-1}}$$

denotes the gross growth rate of X_t. The innovations ϵ_t^v and ϵ_t^g are assumed to be mutually independent i.i.d. processes with mean zero and variances σ_v^2 and σ_g^2, respectively. The parameter g measures the deterministic gross growth rate of the stochastic trend X_t. The parameters ρ_v, $\rho_g \in (-1, 1)$ govern the persistence of v_t and g_t, respectively.

Households face the period-by-period budget constraint

$$\frac{D_{t+1}^h}{1 + r_t} = D_t^h - W_t h_t - u_t K_t + C_t + S_t + I_t + \frac{\phi}{2}\left(\frac{K_{t+1}}{K_t} - g\right)^2 K_t - \Pi_t, \quad (5.4)$$

where D_{t+1}^h denotes the stock of one-period debt acquired by the household in period t and due in period $t + 1$, r_t denotes the country-specific interest rate on debt held between periods t and $t + 1$, I_t denotes gross investment, K_t denotes the stock of physical capital owned by the household, u_t denotes the rental rate of capital, and W_t denotes the real wage rate. The variable S_t is meant to capture aggregate shifts in domestic absorption, possibly stemming from unproductive government consumption, and is assumed to be exogenous and stochastic. The variable Π_t denotes profit receipts, which the household regards as exogenous. We assume that the detrended component of S_t, denoted

$$s_t \equiv \frac{S_t}{X_{t-1}}, \quad (5.5)$$

obeys the AR(1) process

$$\ln(s_{t+1}/\bar{s}) = \rho_s \ln(s_t/\bar{s}) + \epsilon_{t+1}^s,$$

where $\bar{s}$ is a parameter. The innovation ϵ_t^s is assumed to be white noise with mean zero and variance σ_s^2, and the parameter $\rho_s \in (-1, 1)$ governs the persistence of s_t.

The parameter ϕ introduces quadratic capital adjustment costs. The capital stock evolves according to the following law of motion:

$$K_{t+1} = (1 - \delta)K_t + I_t, \tag{5.6}$$

where $\delta \in [0, 1)$ denotes the depreciation rate of capital. Consumers are assumed to be subject to a no-Ponzi-scheme constraint of the form $\lim_{j \to \infty} E_t \dfrac{D^h_{t+j+1}}{\prod_{s=0}^{j}(1+r_{t+s})} \leq 0$.

The optimization problem of the household consists of choosing processes $\{C_t, h_t, D^h_{t+1}, K_{t+1}, I_t\}$ to maximize the utility function (5.3) subject to (5.4), (5.6), and the no-Ponzi-game constraint, taking as given the processes $\{W_t, u_t, X_t, r_t, v_t, s_t\}$, Π_t, and the initial conditions K_0 and D^h_0. Letting $\beta^t \lambda_t X_{t-1}^{-\gamma}$ denote the Lagrange multiplier associated with the sequential budget constraint, the optimality conditions associated with this problem are (5.4), (5.6), the no-Ponzi-game constraint holding with equality, and

$$v_t \left[C_t / X_{t-1} - \omega^{-1} h_t^\omega \right]^{-\gamma} = \lambda_t,$$

$$v_t \left[C_t / X_{t-1} - \omega^{-1} h_t^\omega \right]^{-\gamma} h_t^{\omega-1} = \frac{W_t}{X_{t-1}} \lambda_t,$$

$$\lambda_t = \beta \frac{1 + r_t}{g_t^\gamma} E_t \lambda_{t+1},$$

and

$$\left[1 + \phi \left(\frac{K_{t+1}}{K_t} - g \right) \right] \lambda_t = \frac{\beta}{g_t^\gamma} E_t \lambda_{t+1} \left[1 - \delta + u_{t+1} \right.$$

$$\left. + \phi \left(\frac{K_{t+2}}{K_{t+1}} \right) \left(\frac{K_{t+2}}{K_{t+1}} - g \right) - \frac{\phi}{2} \left(\frac{K_{t+2}}{K_{t+1}} - g \right)^2 \right].$$

5.3.2 Firms with Working-Capital Constraints

Firms are assumed to operate in perfectly competitive product and factor markets. They produce a single good with a Cobb-Douglas production function that uses capital and labor as inputs and is buffeted by stationary and nonstationary productivity shocks. Formally,

$$Y_t = a_t K_t^\alpha (X_t h_t)^{1-\alpha}, \tag{5.7}$$

where Y_t denotes output in period t, $\alpha \in (0, 1)$ is a parameter, and a_t represents a stationary productivity shock following an AR(1) process of the form

$$\ln a_{t+1} = \rho_a \ln a_t + \epsilon^a_{t+1}.$$

The innovation ϵ^a_t is assumed to be a white noise process with mean zero and variance σ_a^2, and the parameter $\rho_a \in [0, 1)$ governs the persistence of a_t.

Following Neumeyer and Perri (2005), Uribe and Yue (2006), and Chang and Fernández (2013), we assume that firms face a working-capital constraint. The formulation presented here is a variation of the one developed in Uribe and Yue (2006). Specifically, the firm must hold at least a fraction η of the payroll in the form of a noninterest-bearing asset, denoted M_t. Formally, the working-capital constraint takes the form

$$M_t \geq \eta W_t h_t,$$

where M_t is the amount of working capital held by the firm in period t. Firms can borrow or lend at the rate r_t. The evolution of the firm's debt is then given by[2]

$$\frac{D_{t+1}^f}{1+r_t} = D_t^f + (M_t - M_{t-1}) + \Pi_t^f + u_t K_t + W_t h_t - a_t K_t^\alpha \left(X_t h_t\right)^{1-\alpha}, \quad (5.8)$$

where D_{t+1}^f denotes the amount of discount debt acquired by the firm in period t maturing in period $t+1$, and Π_t^f denotes distributed profits. The firm chooses K_t, h_t, M_t, and D_{t+1}^f to maximize the present discounted value of distributed dividends,

$$E_0 \sum_{t=0}^\infty \beta^t X_{t-1}^{-\gamma} \lambda_t \Pi_t^f.$$

This expression uses the household's marginal utility of wealth to discount profits. This is reasonable, because the firm, and therefore also its profit stream, is assumed to belong to households. The firm is subject to a no-Ponzi-game constraint of the form

$$\lim_{j \to \infty} E_t \frac{D_{t+j+1}^f - M_{t+j+1}}{\prod_{s=0}^j (1+r_{t+s})} \leq 0.$$

The Lagrangian associated with the firm's profit maximization problem is given by

$$\mathcal{L} = E_0 \sum_{t=0}^\infty \beta^t X_{t-1}^{-\gamma} \lambda_t \left[a_t K_t^\alpha \left(X_t h_t\right)^{1-\alpha} - u_t K_t - W_t h_t - M_t + M_{t-1} \right.$$
$$\left. + \frac{D_{t+1}^f}{1+r_t} - D_t^f + \xi_t(M_t - \eta W_t h_t) \right],$$

where $\xi_t \lambda_t \beta^t X_{t-1}^{-\gamma}$ denotes the Lagrange multiplier on the working-capital constraint. The firm's optimality conditions with respect to D_{t+1}^f, K_t, h_t, and M_t are, respectively,

---

2. In periods in which $r_t < 0$, the presence of this noninterest-bearing asset gives rise to a pure arbitrage opportunity. Thus, the present analysis assumes that $r_t \geq 0$. An alternative way to eliminate this type of arbitrage opportunity is to assume that the rate of return on M_t is the minimum between 0 and r_t. Under this alternative, the term M_{t-1} in the definition of firm profits must be replaced by $M_{t-1}(1 + \min\{0, r_{t-1}\})$.

$$\lambda_t = \beta g_t^{-\gamma}(1 + r_t) E_t \lambda_{t+1},$$

$$\alpha a_t \left(\frac{X_t h_t}{K_t}\right)^{1-\alpha} = u_t,$$

$$(1 - \alpha)a_t X_t \left(\frac{K_t}{X_t h_t}\right)^{\alpha} = W_t(1 + \eta \xi_t),$$

and

$$\lambda_t(1 - \xi_t) = \beta E_t \lambda_{t+1} g_t^{-\gamma}.$$

Combining the first and the last optimality conditions yields

$$\xi_t = \frac{r_t}{1 + r_t},$$

which states that as long as the opportunity cost of funds is positive ($r_t > 0$), the working-capital constraint introduces a distortion that elevates the effective cost of labor. Now combining this expression with the first-order condition with respect to h_t yields

$$(1 - \alpha)a_t X_t \left(\frac{K_t}{X_t h_t}\right)^{\alpha} = W_t \left[1 + \frac{\eta r_t}{1 + r_t}\right].$$

This expression says that in the presence of a working-capital constraint, the total labor cost includes the standard wage component, given by $W_t h_t$, and a financial component, given by $\eta W_t h_t r_t/(1 + r_t)$. Note that an increase in the interest rate acts like an increase in the real wage, thereby inducing firms to reduce employment. This effect is of interest because it introduces a supply-side channel through which changes in the interest rate can affect production. In this way, interest-rate shocks are allowed to directly compete with technology shocks in determining movements in employment and output.

5.3.3 Interest-Rate Shocks

We augment the interest-rate specification of Section 5.2 by introducing interest-rate shocks. Specifically, the domestic interest rate is assumed to be given by

$$r_t = r^* + \psi \left(e^{\frac{\widetilde{D}_{t+1}/X_t - \bar{d}}{\bar{y}}} - 1\right) + e^{\mu_t - 1} - 1, \tag{5.9}$$

where $\widetilde{D}_{t+1}$ denotes the aggregate level of external debt in period t, and $\bar{d}$ and $\bar{y}$ are parameters. The variable μ_t is assumed to be exogenous and stochastic. It is meant to reflect exogenous, random variations in the world interest rate and the country spread. The law of motion of μ_t is given by

$$\ln \mu_{t+1} = \rho_\mu \ln \mu_t + \epsilon_{t+1}^\mu.$$

The innovation ϵ_t^μ is assumed to be a white noise process with mean zero and variance σ_μ^2, and the parameter $\rho_\mu \in [0, 1)$ governs the persistence of μ_t.

5.3.4 Equilibrium

Assume that there is a continuum of identical and perfectly competitive domestic financial intermediaries, or banks, that borrow funds in international financial markets and lend them to domestic households and firms. Also, the financial intermediaries accept noninterest-bearing (sight) deposits from firms. The balance sheet of the representative financial intermediary is

$$\frac{D_{t+1}^h + D_{t+1}^f}{1 + r_t} = \frac{D_{t+1}}{1 + r_t} + M_t, \tag{5.10}$$

where D_{t+1} denotes the amount of discount debt acquired by the bank in period t maturing in period $t + 1$. The left-hand side of this expression is the bank's asset portfolio, and the right-hand side represents its liabilities. The bank's profit in period t, denoted Π_t^b, is given by

$$\Pi_t^b = D_t^h + D_t^f - D_t - M_{t-1}. \tag{5.11}$$

Total profits received by households are given by

$$\Pi_t = \Pi^f + \Pi_t^b. \tag{5.12}$$

Combining (5.4), (5.7), (5.8), and (5.10)–(5.12) yields the economy's resource constraint:

$$\frac{D_{t+1}}{1 + r_t} = D_t + C_t + S_t + I_t + \frac{\phi}{2}\left(\frac{K_{t+1}}{K_t} - g\right)^2 K_t - Y_t.$$

Because all banks are identical, the aggregate level of external debt in period t equals D_t, that is,

$$\widetilde{D}_t = D_t$$

for all t.

As in Section 5.2, we perform a stationarity-inducing transformation by scaling trending variables by X_{t-1}. Specifically, define $y_t = Y_t/X_{t-1}$, $c_t = C_t/X_{t-1}$, $s_t = S_t/X_{t-1}$, $d_t = D_t/X_{t-1}$, and $k_t = K_t/X_{t-1}$. Then a stationary competitive equilibrium is given by a set of processes $\{c_t, h_t, \lambda_t, k_{t+1}, d_{t+1}, i_t, r_t, y_t\}$ satisfying

$$v_t[c_t - \omega^{-1}h_t^\omega]^{-\gamma} = \lambda_t,$$

$$h_t^{\omega - 1} = (1 - \alpha)a_t g_t^{1-\alpha}\left(\frac{k_t}{h_t}\right)^\alpha \left[1 + \frac{\eta r_t}{1 + r_t}\right]^{-1},$$

$$\lambda_t = \frac{\beta}{g_t^\gamma}(1 + r_t)E_t\lambda_{t+1},$$

$$\left[1 + \phi\left(\frac{k_{t+1}}{k_t}g_t - g\right)\right]\lambda_t = \frac{\beta}{g_t^\gamma}E_t\lambda_{t+1}\left[1 - \delta + \alpha a_{t+1}\left(\frac{g_{t+1}h_{t+1}}{k_{t+1}}\right)^{1-\alpha}\right.$$

$$\left. + \phi\frac{k_{t+2}}{k_{t+1}}g_{t+1}\left(\frac{k_{t+2}}{k_{t+1}}g_{t+1} - g\right) - \frac{\phi}{2}\left(\frac{k_{t+2}}{k_{t+1}}g_{t+1} - g\right)^2\right],$$

$$\frac{d_{t+1}}{1+r_t} g_t = d_t - y_t + c_t + s_t + i_t + \frac{\phi}{2} \left(\frac{k_{t+1}}{k_t} g_t - g \right)^2 k_t,$$

$$r_t = r^* + \psi \left(e^{\frac{d_{t+1} - \bar{d}}{\bar{y}}} - 1 \right) + e^{\mu_t - 1} - 1,$$

$$k_{t+1} g_t = (1 - \delta) k_t + i_t,$$

and

$$y_t = a_t k_t^\alpha (g_t h_t)^{1-\alpha},$$

given exogenous processes a_t, g_t, v_t, μ_t, and s_t and initial conditions k_0 and d_0.

5.4 Bayesian Estimation on a Century of Data

The econometric estimation uses annual per capita data from Argentina on output growth, consumption growth, investment growth, and the trade-balance-to-output ratio for the period 1900 to 2005. All four of these observable variables are assumed to be measured with error. Specifically, let the theoretical counterparts of the four observables be the vector

$$O_t^* = \begin{bmatrix} \Delta \ln Y_t \\ \Delta \ln C_t \\ \Delta \ln I_t \\ TB_t / Y_t \end{bmatrix},$$

where

$$TB_t \equiv Y_t - C_t - I_t - S_t - \frac{\phi}{2} \left(\frac{K_{t+1}}{K_t} - g \right)^2 K_t$$

denotes the trade balance.[3] Then the vector of observables, denoted O_t, is given by

$$O_t = O_t^* + \begin{bmatrix} \sigma_{g^Y}^{me} \epsilon_t^{me, g^Y} \\ \sigma_{g^C}^{me} \epsilon_t^{me, g^C} \\ \sigma_{g^I}^{me} \epsilon_t^{me, g^I} \\ \sigma_{TB/Y}^{me} \epsilon_t^{me, TB/Y} \end{bmatrix},$$

where $\sigma_{g^Y}^{me}$, $\sigma_{g^C}^{me}$, $\sigma_{g^I}^{me}$, $\sigma_{TB/Y}^{me}$ are positive parameters, and $\epsilon_t^{me,i}$ is an exogenous i.i.d. disturbance with mean zero and unit variance for $i = g^Y, g^C, g^I, TB/Y$.

The values assigned to the structural parameters are based on a combination of calibration and econometric estimation. The calibrated parameters are g, $\bar{d}/\bar{y}$, δ, r^*, α, γ, ω, and $\bar{s}/\bar{y}$ and are set to match long-run data relations from Argentina or in accordance with related business-cycle studies. Table 5.3 presents the calibrated parameter

---

3. Note that in the theoretical model, the definition of gross investment does not include investment adjustment costs. An alternative definition could include them. This distinction is immaterial in the present context, because up to first order adjustment costs are nil.

Table 5.3   Calibrated Parameters

Parameter	Value
g	1.0107
$\overline{d}/\overline{y}$	0.037
δ	0.1255
r^*	0.10
α	0.32
γ	2
ω	1.6
$\overline{s}/\overline{y}$	0.10

Note: The time unit is 1 year.

values. The parameter g is set to match the average growth rate of per capita GDP in Argentina over the period 1900 to 2005 of 1.0107 percent per year. We impose a steady-state trade-balance-to-output ratio of 0.3 percent, as observed on average in Argentina over the period 1900–2005. We set r^* to 10 percent per year, and impose the restriction $1 + r^* = \beta^{-1}g^\gamma$. This implies a steady-state interest rate of 10 percent (a value that is empirically plausible for an emerging market economy like Argentina) and a subjective discount factor, β, of 0.9286. A further implication of these restrictions is that the steady state of d_t equals $\overline{d}$. We restrict $\overline{y}$ to equal the steady-state value of detrended output, y_t. This restriction and the assumed target for the steady state of the trade-balance-to-output ratio implies a value of $\overline{d}/\overline{y}$ of 0.037, which coincides with the steady-state debt-to-output ratio. This value appears small when compared with the average debt-to-output ratio of 0.27 observed in Argentina post 1970 (Lane and Milesi-Ferretti 2007). But it is consistent with the low trade-balance-to-output ratio of 0.3 percent of GDP observed over the period 1900–2005. The value assigned to the depreciation rate δ implies an average investment share in GDP of 19 percent, which is in line with the average value observed in Argentina over the calibration period. There is no reliable data on factor income shares for Argentina. We therefore set the parameter α, which determines the average capital income share, to 0.32, a value commonly used in the related literature. The parameter γ, defining the curvature of the period utility function, takes the value 2, which is standard in related business-cycle studies. The parameter ω is calibrated at 1.6, which implies a labor-supply elasticity of $1/(\omega - 1) = 1.7$. Finally, the share of exogenous spending to GDP, s/y, is set at 10 percent, which implies that $\overline{s}/\overline{y}$ equals 0.10.

The remaining parameters are estimated using likelihood-based Bayesian techniques on a log-linear approximation of the equilibrium dynamics. The log-linear approximation is computed using the techniques and Matlab code introduced in Chapter 4. The estimated parameters consist of thirteen structural parameters and the standard deviations of the four measurement errors. The thirteen structural parameters are the ten parameters defining the stochastic processes of the shocks driving the model economy (σ_i and ρ_i, for $i = a, g, \nu, \mu, s$), the parameter ϕ (governing the strength of capital adjustment costs), the

Table 5.4 Bayesian Estimation

	Prior Distributions			Posterior Distributions			
Parameter	Min	Max	Mean	Mean	Median	5%	95%
σ_g	0	0.2	0.1	0.0082	0.0067	0.00058	0.021
ρ_g	−0.99	0.99	0	0.15	0.21	−0.69	0.81
σ_a	0	0.2	0.1	0.032	0.032	0.027	0.036
ρ_a	−0.99	0.99	0	0.84	0.84	0.75	0.91
σ_v	0	1	0.5	0.53	0.51	0.39	0.77
ρ_v	−0.99	0.99	0	0.85	0.85	0.76	0.93
σ_s	0	0.2	0.1	0.062	0.064	0.0059	0.12
ρ_s	−0.99	0.99	0	0.46	0.56	−0.42	0.92
σ_μ	0	0.2	0.1	0.12	0.11	0.067	0.18
ρ_μ	−0.99	0.99	0	0.91	0.92	0.83	0.98
ϕ	0	8	4	5.6	5.6	3.9	7.5
ψ	0	10	5	1.4	1.3	0.55	2.4
η	0	5	2.5	0.42	0.4	0.18	0.7
$\sigma_{g^Y}^{me}$	0.0001	0.013	0.0067	0.0045	0.0042	0.00051	0.0096
$\sigma_{g^C}^{me}$	0.0001	0.019	0.0095	0.0075	0.0076	0.00097	0.014
$\sigma_{g^I}^{me}$	0.0001	0.051	0.025	0.041	0.044	0.022	0.05
$\sigma_{TB/Y}^{me}$	0.0001	0.013	0.0065	0.0033	0.0031	0.00041	0.0068

Notes: All prior distributions are taken to be uniform. Moments of the posterior distribution are based on a 1-million-long MCMC chain. The symbol σ_i^{me} denotes the standard deviation of the measurement error associated with the observable i, for $i = g^Y$, g^C, g^I, and TB/Y, where g^i denotes the growth rate of variable i, for $i = Y, C, I$; and TB/Y denotes the trade-balance-to-output ratio. The data and Matlab code to reproduce this table are available on the book's Web site.

parameter ψ (determining the debt elasticity of the country-specific interest rate), and the parameter η (defining the size of the working-capital constraint).

Table 5.4 displays salient characteristics of the prior and posterior distributions of the estimated parameters. All prior distributions are assumed to be uniform. For the structural parameters, the supports of the uniform prior distributions are relatively wide. For example, for serial correlations, we allow for the maximum possible range that the parameter can take. Thus, the estimation results can be interpreted as maximum likelihood estimates. For the prior uniform distributions of the standard deviations of the four measurement errors, we impose upper bounds that imply that measurement errors can account for no more than 6.25 percent of the variance of the corresponding observable.

The statistics pertaining to the posterior distributions were computed using a Markov Chain Monte Carlo (MCMC) chain of length 1 million. The data and Matlab code to replicate the estimation are available online with the materials for this chapter on the book's Web site via http://press.princeton.edu/titles/11032.html.

Table 5.5 shows that the estimated model does a good job at matching a number of second moments typically used to characterize business cycles in emerging countries. In particular, the model replicates the excess volatility of consumption relative to output, the

Table 5.5   Empirical and Theoretical Second Moments

Statistic	g^Y	g^C	g^I	TB/Y
Standard Deviation				
Model	6.2	8.9	18.6	4.9
Data	5.3	7.5	20.4	5.2
	(0.43)	(0.6)	(1.8)	(0.57)
Correlation with g^Y				
Model		0.80	0.53	−0.18
Data		0.72	0.67	−0.035
		(0.07)	(0.09)	(0.09)
Correlation with TB/Y				
Model		−0.37	−0.31	
Data		−0.27	−0.19	
		(0.07)	(0.08)	
Serial Correlation				
Model	0.04	−0.06	−0.098	0.51
Data	0.11	−0.0047	0.32	0.58
	(0.09)	(0.08)	(0.10)	(0.07)

Notes: Empirical moments are computed using data from Argentina for the period 1900–2005. Standard deviations of empirical moments (given in parentheses) are computed using GMM. Theoretical moments are unconditional moments computed by evaluating the model at the posterior median of the estimated parameters. Replication files are available on the book's Web site.

high volatility of investment, and a volatility of the trade-balance-to-output ratio comparable to that of output growth. The estimated model also captures the procyclicality of consumption and investment and the slight countercyclicality of the trade-balance-to-output ratio.

5.5 How Important Are Trend Shocks?

An important result that emerges from Table 5.4 is that the parameters defining the stochastic process of the nonstationary productivity shock are estimated with significant uncertainty. Specifically, the posterior distribution of the standard deviation of innovations to the nonstationary productivity shock, σ_g, has a median of 0.67 percent but a 95 percent probability interval that ranges from 0 to 2.1 percent. Similarly, the posterior distribution of the serial correlation of the nonstationary productivity shock, ρ_g, has a median of 0.21, but a 95 percent probability interval that ranges from −0.69 to +0.81. In contrast, the parameters defining the process of the stationary productivity shock are estimated much more tightly. The parameter σ_a has a posterior median of 0.032 and a 95 percent probability interval of 0.027 to 0.036, and the parameter ρ_a has a posterior median of 0.84 and a 95 percent probability interval ranging from 0.75 to 0.91.

Consider now computing the share of the variance of the growth rate of total factor productivity explained by nonstationary productivity shocks. That is, consider computing the fraction of the variance of $\Delta \ln TFP_t \equiv \Delta \ln(a_t X_t^{1-\alpha})$ explained by $\Delta \ln(X_t^{1-\alpha})$. Recall from Section 5.2 that when only technology shocks are allowed in the model, nonstationary productivity shocks explain 88 percent of movements in total factor productivity, implying that trend shocks are a major driver of the business cycle in emerging countries. How does this share change when productivity shocks compete with other shocks and frictions? Evaluating the formula given in (5.2) using the MCMC chain for the posterior estimates of the relevant structural parameters, one can derive an MCMC chain of posterior draws of the share of the variance of TFP explained by nonstationary productivity shocks. Using this chain yields

$$\text{posterior median}\left(\frac{\text{var}(\Delta \ln(X_t^{1-\alpha}))}{\text{var}(\Delta \ln TFP_t)}\right)$$

$$= \text{posterior median}\left(\frac{(1-\alpha)^2\sigma_g^2/(1-\rho_g^2)}{2\sigma_a^2/(1+\rho_a) + (1-\alpha)^2\sigma_g^2/(1-\rho_g^2)}\right) = 0.024. \quad (5.13)$$

That is, nonstationary productivity shocks explain only 2.4 percent of movements in total factor productivity. This result suggests that the long data sample used for the estimation of the model plus the inclusion of additional shocks and financial frictions results in the data favoring stationary productivity shocks over nonstationary productivity shocks as drivers of total factor productivity.

Table 5.6 presents the predicted contribution of each shock to explaining the variances of output growth, consumption growth, investment growth, and the trade-balance-to-output ratio. Three key results emerge from this variance decomposition. First, nonstationary productivity shocks play a negligible role in explaining aggregate fluctuations. They account for less than 5 percent of the variances of all variables considered in the table. Output growth is driven primarily by stationary productivity shocks, which explain 82 percent of its unconditional variance. Second, variations in investment growth and the trade-balance-to-output ratio are mostly accounted for by interest-rate shocks. This source of uncertainty explains 52 percent of the variance of investment growth and 92 percent of the variance of the trade-balance-to-output ratio. Third, consumption growth is driven in roughly equal parts by stationary productivity shocks, interest-rate shocks, and preference shocks, with a slightly larger weight on the first shock.

This means that the data favor an explanation of the excess volatility of consumption relative to output based on disturbances other than nonstationary technology shocks. In Section 5.1, we showed that a sufficiently persistent stationary technology shock process can give rise to excess volatility of consumption relative to output. The present estimation delivers this channel by assigning a high posterior value to the serial correlation of the stationary productivity shock of 0.84. This value is about twice as large as the one needed to

Table 5.6   Variance Decomposition

Shock	g^Y	g^C	g^I	TB/Y
Nonstationary technology	2.6	1.1	0.2	0.1
Stationary technology	81.8	42.4	12.7	0.5
Preference	6.8	27.7	29.1	6.2
Interest rate	6.1	25.8	52.0	92.1
Spending	0.0	0.3	0.3	0.1
Measurement error	0.4	0.7	5.2	0.4

Note: Median of 1 million draws from the posterior distribution of the unconditional variance decomposition.

explain business cycles in Canada, the developed small open economy studied in Chapter 4, which does not display excess volatility of consumption. The intuition for why interest-rate and preference shocks are also important for delivering excess consumption volatility is that the former change the relative price of present consumption in terms of future consumption, and the latter alter the subjective valuation of present consumption relative to future consumption.

5.6 The Role of Financial Frictions

In the present quantitative analysis, financial frictions are introduced in two ways. First, we allow the data to choose a value for the debt elasticity of the country interest rate by estimating the parameter ψ. Second, we also estimate the parameter η defining the magnitude of the working-capital constraint on firms. How important are these financial frictions for the transmission of aggregate disturbances?

Consider first the importance of the parameter ψ. The assumed debt elasticity of the country premium captures, in a reduced-form fashion, a variety of financial frictions. For instance, models with imperfect enforcement of international loan contracts à la Eaton and Gersovitz (1981), which we study in detail in Chapter 13, predict that the country premium increases with the level of external debt. Similarly, models in which international borrowing is limited by collateral constraints, like those studied later in Chapter 12, imply a shadow interest premium that is increasing in the level of net external debt. By estimating the parameter ψ, we let the data determine the importance of this type of financial friction.

The posterior median estimate of ψ, shown in Table 5.4, is 1.3. How big a financial friction does this value represent? Consider a partial differentiation of equation (5.9) with respect to r_t and $\tilde{D}_{t+1}$:

$$\Delta r_t = \psi e^{(\tilde{D}_{t+1}/X_t - \bar{d})/\bar{y}} \frac{\Delta \tilde{D}_{t+1}}{X_t \bar{y}}.$$

Assume that debt is at its deterministic steady-state level. That is, set $\tilde{D}_{t+1}/X_t = \bar{d}$. We then have that

$$\Delta r_t = \psi \frac{\Delta \tilde{D}_{t+1}/X_t}{\bar{y}}.$$

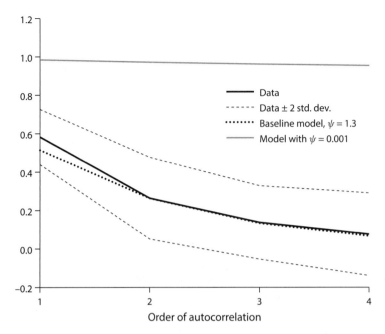

Figure 5.4   The autocorrelation function of the trade-balance-to-output ratio.

Now setting $\psi = 1.3$ (its posterior median estimate) yields

$$\Delta r_t = 1.3 \frac{\Delta \tilde{D}_{t+1}/X_t}{\overline{y}}.$$

This expression indicates that an increase in debt of 1 percent of GDP ($\Delta \tilde{D}_{t+1}/(\overline{y}X_t) = 0.01$) causes an increase of 1.3 percentage points in the interest rate ($\Delta r_t = 0.013$).

This nontrivial debt-elasticity of the interest rate plays an important role in explaining the cyclical behavior of the trade balance. Figure 5.4 displays the empirical and theoretical autocorrelation functions of the trade-balance-to-output ratio. The empirical autocorrelation function, shown as a dark solid line, is estimated using annual data from Argentina for the period 1900–2005. Dashed lines indicate the two-standard-deviation confidence interval. The point estimate of the autocorrelation function starts at about 0.6 and falls gradually toward 0. This pattern is observed more generally in emerging countries (see García-Cicco, Pancrazi, and Uribe 2010; Miyamoto and Nguyen 2013). The theoretical model captures the empirical pattern quite well. The predicted autocorrelation function, shown with a dotted line, lies close to its empirical counterpart and is entirely within the two-standard-error confidence band.

What role does the parameter ψ play in generating this result? To address this question, we fix ψ at 0.001 and then re-estimate the model. Figure 5.4 displays, with a gray solid line, the autocorrelation function of the trade-balance-to-output ratio predicted by the re-estimated model. In sharp contrast with the predictions of the baseline model, the model without the financial friction predicts an autocorrelation function that is flat, close to unity, and entirely outside the confidence band. Furthermore, the estimated model without the financial friction grossly overpredicts the volatility of the trade balance. Specifically, the model featuring $\psi = 0.001$ implies a standard deviation of the trade-balance-to-output ratio of 32.5 percentage points, six times larger than the observed standard deviation of 5.2 percentage points.

The intuition behind why a small value of the debt elasticity of the interest rate causes the trade-balance-to-output ratio to have an autocorrelation function that is flat and near unity and a standard deviation that is excessively large is as follows. In the absence of this financial friction, external debt follows a highly persistent process (a quasi-random walk). This is because as $\psi \to 0$, the linearized equilibrium dynamics are governed by an eigenvalue that approaches unity in modulus. If the stock of external debt is extremely persistent, then so is the trade balance, which is determined to a large extent by the need to service external interest obligations. In contrast, when ψ is sufficiently large (as in the baseline model), the stock of external debt follows a less persistent stationary process. In this case, movements in the level of debt cause endogenous, self-stabilizing changes in the country interest-rate premium. For example, if the level of external debt rises too far above its steady-state level, the country premium increases, inducing households to cut spending, thereby bringing debt closer to its steady-state level.

The following general result can be established regarding the role of ψ in generating a downward-sloping autocorrelation function of the trade-balance-to-output ratio. Holding all other parameters of the model constant, one can always find a positive but sufficiently small value of ψ such that the equilibrium dynamics are stationary up to first order and the autocorrelation function of the trade-balance-to-output ratio is flat and close to unity. This result implies that, if a particular calibration of an open economy model does not deliver a flat and near-unit autocorrelation function of the trade-balance-to-output ratio, it is because ψ has not been set to a small enough value, given the values assigned to all other parameters of the model. For example, in the SOE-RBC model of Chapter 4, Section 4.1, the parameter ψ takes the value 0.0011,[4] which is about the same as the value considered here, and nevertheless the predicted first-order serial correlation of the trade-balance-to-output ratio is 0.51, significantly below unity (see Table 4.2).

The above discussion motivates the question of what parameters other than the debt elasticity of the country interest rate affect the height and slope of the autocorrelation function of the trade-balance-to-output ratio. In general, given the value of ψ, several structural parameters play a role in determining the shape of the autocorrelation function of the trade-balance-to-output ratio. One such parameter is the one governing the degree of capital adjustment costs. Consider again the SOE-RBC model analyzed in Chapter 4, Section 4.1.1, which we will refer to here as the SGU model. The calibration of this model, shown in Table 4.1, is of particular interest for the present discussion, because it features

---

4. Notice that the specification of the country interest-rate premium in Chapter 4, Section 4.1, makes the interest rate a function of the level of debt as opposed to the level of debt relative to trend output. Therefore, to make the comparison possible, the value of ψ of 0.000742 used in Chapter 4 must be multiplied by the level of steady-state output in that model, which equals 1.4865.

a value of ψ of 0.000742 (see footnote 4 for an explanation of why this value has to be adjusted upward to 0.0011 to make it comparable with the GPU model) and predicts an autocorrelation of the trade-balance-to-output ratio of 0.51, significantly below unity. As we have just shown, the GPU model delivers a near unity serial correlation of the trade-balance-to-output ratio for $\psi = 0.001$. It follows that it cannot simply be the size of ψ that determines the persistence of the trade balance.

We argue here that the calibration of the SGU model in Chapter 4 features a capital adjustment cost coefficient that is about 20 times smaller than the one estimated for the GPU model. Let ϕ^{SGU} and ϕ^{GPU} be the values of this coefficient in the SGU and GPU models, respectively. From Table 4.1, we have that $\phi^{SGU} = 0.028$ and from the re-estimation of the GPU model with a fixed value of $\psi = 0.001$ (not shown), we find that $\phi^{GPU} = 2.0$. The comparison of the degree of capital adjustment costs is more complicated than simply comparing these two numbers, however, because the SGU and GPU models assume different specifications for the capital adjustment cost function. In the SGU model the capital adjustment cost function takes the form $\frac{\phi}{2}(k_{t+1} - k_t)^2$, whereas in the GPU model it takes the form $\frac{\phi}{2}K_t(K_{t+1}/K_t - g)^2$. In general, using the same value of ϕ in both models introduces different degrees of capital adjustment costs. One can show that in the absence of long-run growth, $g = 1$, and holding all other parameters equal across models, both specifications give rise to identical equilibrium dynamics up to first order as long as $k^{SGU}\phi^{SGU} = \phi^{GPU}$, where k^{SGU} denotes the steady-state level of capital in the SGU model. Thus if one wished to introduce in the SGU model the same degree of adjustment costs as in the GPU model, one must set $\phi^{SGU} = \frac{1}{k^{SGU}}\phi^{GPU}$. The calibration of Table 4.1 implies that $k^{SGU} = 3.4$. Thus, the value of ϕ^{SGU} that makes both models comparable is 0.59. This value is about 20 times larger than the value of 0.028 used to calibrate the SGU model in Chapter 4. We conclude that the GPU model estimated with a fixed ψ of 0.001 features a degree of capital adjustment cost that is about 20 times as large as the one used in the calibration of the SGU model in Chapter 4. Moreover, one can show that for values of ϕ^{SGU} ranging from 0.028 to 0.59, the SGU model implies serial correlations of the trade-balance-to-output ratio between 0.51 and 0.97, although the relationship is not monotone. Intuitively, the higher is the size of the adjustment costs, the more persistent investment will be. Since the trade-balance-to-output ratio is governed by the sum of the consumption share and the investment share, the persistence of investment is partially transmitted to the trade balance.

Finally, consider the role of the second financial friction contained in the model, namely, the working-capital constraint on wage payments. This friction turns out not to play a central role in the estimated model. This is reflected by the fact that interest-rate shocks explain a modest fraction of the variance of output growth, 6.1 percent. Indeed the parameter η, defining the magnitude of the working-capital friction, is estimated with significant uncertainty. Specifically, the median value of η is 0.4, which means that firms hold about 5 months of the wage bill as working capital, but the 95 percent posterior probability interval ranges from 0.18 to 0.70 (or 2–8 months). Moreover, the predictions of the model are virtually unchanged if the model is estimated under the constraint $\eta = 0$ (see García-Cicco, Pancrazi, and Uribe 2010). Chang and Fernández (2013) find a similar result using quarterly data from Mexico.

5.7 Imperfect Information and Noise Shocks

Thus far we have assumed that agents have the ability to distinguish what part of an innovation in total factor productivity comes from its nonstationary component and what part from its stationary component. Specifically, consider again the technology

$$Y_t = K_t^\alpha \left(A_t h_t\right)^{1-\alpha}, \tag{5.14}$$

where, as before, Y_t denotes output, K_t denotes the stock of physical capital, h_t denotes hours worked, and $\alpha \in (0, 1)$ is a parameter. Here the variable A_t denotes an exogenous and stochastic productivity factor. It is reasonable to assume that agents know the production technology (i.e., that it has a Cobb-Douglas form and the value taken by α). It is also reasonable to assume that agents observe K_t, h_t, and Y_t. This means that it is equally reasonable to assume that agents know A_t. But the model we have been studying thus far presumes much more information on the part of the individual agents, as it requires that they observe separately the different stochastic components of TFP. Specifically, we have been assuming that total factor productivity, A_t, is driven jointly by a stationary shock, z_t, and a nonstationary shock, X_t, as follows:

$$A_t = e^{z_t} X_t,$$

where the productivity components z_t and X_t are assumed to be mutually independent random variables. Agents are assumed to observe not only A_t but also separately X_t and z_t. This is a strong assumption, and it is therefore natural to ask how the predictions of the model change when one relaxes it.

Accordingly, in this section, we entertain the idea that although agents observe A_t, they cannot see either z_t or X_t. This informational imperfection can be consequential, because a given innovation in A_t implies different future paths of this variable, depending on whether the current movement originated in its stationary component z_t or in its nonstationary component X_t. Agents must form an expectation of z_t and X_t. In general, this expectation will be different, depending on whether they can or cannot observe separately the two productivity components z_t and X_t. This means that the assumption of imperfect information alters the transmission mechanism of the model.

In addition to the assumption of *imperfect information*, we assume that agents receive a *noisy signal* about the state of the nonstationary component of technology, X_t. This assumption adds a new source of uncertainty, which, although nonfundamental in nature, can affect investment, employment, and consumption decisions. Every period, agents observe present and past realizations of A_t and of a noisy signal, and they solve a *signal extraction problem* to disentangle the permanent and temporary components of A_t.

The role of imperfect information and noisy signals in explaining aggregate fluctuations has received some attention in the past few years. Erceg and Levin (2003), for example, use a neo-Keynesian model in which agents cannot observe separately persistent and transitory shifts in the monetary policy rule to explain the observed persistence of price inflation in the United States. Boz, Daude, and Durdu (2011) estimate an open economy model of an emerging economy much like the one we presented in Section 5.2 augmented with imperfect information and noisy signals about total factor productivity. Blanchard, L'Huillier, and Lorenzoni (2013) estimate a small-scale closed economy model in which aggregate activity is driven by a combination of fundamental and noise shocks that agents cannot observe separately. These papers find that informational frictions play an important role in determining short-run fluctuations. The analysis of this section is most closely related to Boz, Daude, and Durdu (2011).

To make this section self-contained and at the risk of being repetitious, we lay out the model from scratch. The stationary and nonstationary components of A_t obey the laws of motion

$$z_t = \rho_z z_{t-1} + \sigma_z \epsilon_t^z,$$

and

$$\hat{g}_t^x = \rho_x \hat{g}_{t-1}^x + \sigma_x \epsilon_t^x,$$

where

$$\hat{g}_t^x \equiv \ln\left(\frac{X_t}{X_{t-1}}\right) - g.$$

The parameter g represents the deterministic steady-state growth rate of X_t, the parameters ρ_z and ρ_x lie in the interval $(-1, 1)$, and the parameters σ_x and σ_z are positive. The variables ϵ_t^z and ϵ_t^x are assumed to be exogenous, mutually independent white noise processes distributed $N(0, 1)$.

Letting

$$\hat{g}_t + g \equiv \ln\left(\frac{A_t}{A_{t-1}}\right)$$

denote the growth rate of A_t, we have that

$$\hat{g}_t = z_t - z_{t-1} + \hat{g}_t^x. \tag{5.15}$$

As mentioned above, the key novelty of the present SOE model relative to those studied thus far is the assumption of imperfect information. Specifically, agents are assumed to observe current and past values of $\hat{g}_t$, but not values of its individual components z_t, z_{t-1}, and $\hat{g}_t^x$. The incompleteness of the representative agent's information set can in principle have real consequences, because current decisions regarding consumption, hours worked, and investment depend on the future expected growth rates of $\hat{g}_t$, which in turn depend distinctly on the current values of z_t, z_{t-1}, and $\hat{g}_t^x$. It is assumed that agents know the AR(1) structure of the stochastic processes z_t and $\hat{g}_t^x$ as well as the values taken by the parameters $\rho_z, \rho_x, \sigma_z, \sigma_x$, and g.

In addition, it is assumed that each period the representative agent receives a noisy signal s_t about the current state of $\hat{g}_t^x$. The signal takes the form

$$s_t = \hat{g}_t^x + n_t,$$

where the unobserved noise n_t is assumed to obey the law of motion

$$n_t = \rho_n n_{t-1} + \sigma_n \epsilon_t^n,$$

where ϵ_t^n is an i.i.d. random variable with mean 0 and variance 1, and $\rho_n \in (-1, 1)$ and $\sigma_n > 0$ are observed parameters. In the present model, therefore, agents will form expectations about future values of $\hat{g}_t$ using information on present and past realizations of $\hat{g}_t$ and s_t and on the parameters defining the stochastic processes z_t, $\hat{g}_t^x$, and n_t.

The representative household seeks to maximize the utility function

$$E_0 \sum_{t=0}^{\infty} \beta^t \frac{[C_t^{\gamma}(1-h_t)^{1-\gamma}]^{1-\sigma} - 1}{1-\sigma}$$

subject to the production technology (5.14), the sequential budget constraint

$$\frac{D_{t+1}}{1+r_t} = D_t + C_t + K_{t+1} - (1-\delta)K_t + \frac{\phi}{2}\left(\frac{K_{t+1}}{K_t} - e^g\right)^2 K_t - Y_t,$$

and a no-Ponzi-game constraint of the form

$$\lim_{j \to \infty} E_t \frac{D_{t+j+1}}{\Pi_{s=0}^{j}(1+r_{t+s})} \leq 0,$$

where C_t denotes consumption, D_t denotes net external debt due in period t, and r_t denotes the interest rate charged by the rest of the world on one-period debt acquired in period t. The parameters β and δ lie in the interval $(0, 1)$, and the parameters γ, σ, and ϕ are positive. According to the budget constraint, the stock of capital depreciates at the rate δ and is subject to quadratic adjustment costs governed by the parameter ϕ. The household takes the interest rate r_t as given.

Letting $\beta^t \Lambda_t$ denote the Lagrange multiplier attached to the sequential budget constraint, the optimality conditions associated with the household's problem are the no-Ponzi-game constraint holding with equality and

$$\frac{D_{t+1}}{1+r_t} = D_t + C_t + K_{t+1} - (1-\delta)K_t + \frac{\phi}{2}\left(\frac{K_{t+1}}{K_t} - e^g\right)^2 K_t - Y_t,$$

$$Y_t = A_t^{1-\alpha} K_t^{\alpha} h_t^{1-\alpha},$$

$$\frac{1-\gamma}{\gamma}\frac{C_t}{1-h_t} = (1-\alpha)A_t^{1-\alpha}\left(\frac{K_t}{h_t}\right)^{\alpha},$$

$$\gamma C_t^{\gamma(1-\sigma)-1}(1-h_t)^{(1-\gamma)(1-\sigma)} = \Lambda_t,$$

$$\Lambda_t = \beta(1+r_t)E_t\Lambda_{t+1},$$

and

$$\Lambda_t\left[1+\phi\left(\frac{K_{t+1}}{K_t} - e^g\right)\right] = \beta E_t \Lambda_{t+1}\left[1 - \delta + \alpha\left(\frac{K_{t+1}}{A_{t+1}h_{t+1}}\right)^{\alpha-1}\right.$$

$$\left. + \phi\frac{K_{t+2}}{K_{t+1}}\left(\frac{K_{t+2}}{K_{t+1}} - e^g\right) - \frac{\phi}{2}\left(\frac{K_{t+2}}{K_{t+1}} - e^g\right)^2\right].$$

To induce stationarity, we resort to the by-now familiar assumption that the interest rate is debt elastic,

$$r_t = r^* + \psi \left[e^{\tilde{D}_{t+1}/A_t - \overline{d}} - 1 \right],$$

where r^*, ψ, and $\overline{d}$ are parameters, and $\tilde{D}_t$ denotes the cross-sectional average level of external debt per capita due in period t. In equilibrium, because all households are identical, we have that

$$\tilde{D}_t = D_t.$$

Also, with the purpose of inducing stationarity, a familiar variable transformation is introduced involving scaling all trending variables by A_{t-1} or an appropriate function thereof. Specifically, let $y_t \equiv Y_t/A_{t-1}$, $c_t \equiv C_t/A_{t-1}$, $k_t \equiv K_t/A_{t-1}$, $d_t \equiv D_t/A_{t-1}$, and $\lambda_t \equiv \Lambda_t/A_{t-1}^{\gamma(1-\sigma)-1}$. Then the transformed version of the equilibrium conditions is

$$\frac{e^{g+\hat{g}_t} d_{t+1}}{1+r_t} = d_t + c_t + e^{g+\hat{g}_t} k_{t+1} - (1-\delta)k_t + \frac{\phi}{2} \left(\frac{e^{g+\hat{g}_t} k_{t+1}}{k_t} - e^g \right)^2 k_t - y_t, \quad (5.16)$$

$$y_t = e^{(1-\alpha)(g+\hat{g}_t)} k_t^\alpha h_t^{1-\alpha}, \quad (5.17)$$

$$\frac{1-\gamma}{\gamma} \frac{c_t}{1-h_t} = (1-\alpha)e^{(1-\alpha)(g+\hat{g}_t)} \left(\frac{k_t}{h_t} \right)^\alpha, \quad (5.18)$$

$$\gamma c_t^{\gamma(1-\sigma)-1}(1-h_t)^{(1-\gamma)(1-\sigma)} = \lambda_t, \quad (5.19)$$

$$\lambda_t = \beta(1+r_t)e^{(g+\hat{g}_t)[\gamma(1-\sigma)-1]} E_t \lambda_{t+1}, \quad (5.20)$$

$$\lambda_t \left[1 + \phi \left(\frac{e^{g+\hat{g}_t} k_{t+1}}{k_t} - e^g \right) \right]$$

$$= \beta e^{(g+\hat{g}_t)[\gamma(1-\sigma)-1]} E_t \lambda_{t+1} \left[1 - \delta + \alpha e^{(1-\alpha)(g+\hat{g}_{t+1})} \left(\frac{k_{t+1}}{h_{t+1}} \right)^{\alpha-1} \right. \quad (5.21)$$

$$\left. + \phi \frac{e^{g+\hat{g}_{t+1}} k_{t+2}}{k_{t+1}} \left(\frac{e^{g+\hat{g}_{t+1}} k_{t+2}}{k_{t+1}} - e^g \right) - \frac{\phi}{2} \left(\frac{e^{g+\hat{g}_{t+1}} k_{t+2}}{k_{t+1}} - e^g \right)^2 \right],$$

and

$$r_t = r^* + \psi \left[e^{d_{t+1} - \overline{d}} - 1 \right]. \quad (5.22)$$

The right-hand side of (5.21) shows that the agent must form expectations not about the future value of $\hat{g}_{t+1}$ but about a nonlinear object involving $\hat{g}_t$ and other variables of the model. This makes the problem analytically and computationally impractical. Up to first order, however, by construction, the right-hand side of (5.21) becomes linear in $E_t \hat{g}_{t+1}$.

Linearization simplifies the problem significantly, since it essentially reduces it to determining the conditional expectation of a single exogenous variable given the informational constraints faced by households. For this reason, the analysis that follows focuses on the linearized version of the model.

The linearized version of equations (5.16)–(5.22) is

$$
\frac{e^g}{1+r}\left(\frac{d}{y}\right)\left[\hat{g}_t + \hat{d}_{t+1} - \frac{1}{1+r}\hat{r}_t\right]
$$

$$
= \left(\frac{d}{y}\right)\hat{d}_t + \left(\frac{c}{y}\right)\hat{c}_t + e^g\left(\frac{k}{y}\right)(\hat{g}_t + \hat{k}_{t+1}) - (1-\delta)\left(\frac{k}{y}\right)\hat{k}_t - \hat{y}_t, \tag{5.23}
$$

$$
\hat{y}_t = (1-\alpha)\hat{g}_t + \alpha\hat{k}_t + (1-\alpha)\hat{h}_t, \tag{5.24}
$$

$$
\hat{c}_t + \left(\frac{h}{1-h}\right)\hat{h}_t = (1-\alpha)\hat{g}_t + \alpha(\hat{k}_t - \hat{h}_t), \tag{5.25}
$$

$$
[\gamma(1-\sigma)-1]\hat{c}_t - (1-\gamma)(1-\sigma)\left(\frac{h}{1-h}\right)\hat{h}_t = \hat{\lambda}_t, \tag{5.26}
$$

$$
\hat{\lambda}_t = \frac{1}{1+r}\hat{r}_t + [\gamma(1-\sigma)-1]\hat{g}_t + E_t\hat{\lambda}_{t+1}, \tag{5.27}
$$

$$
\hat{\lambda}_t + e^g\phi(\hat{g}_t + \hat{k}_{t+1} - \hat{k}_t) = [\gamma(1-\sigma)-1]\hat{g}_t + E_t\hat{\lambda}_{t+1}
$$

$$
+ \tilde{\beta}(\tilde{\beta}^{-1}+\delta-1)(1-\alpha)(E_t\hat{g}_{t+1} + E_t\hat{h}_{t+1} - \hat{k}_{t+1})
$$

$$
+ \tilde{\beta}\phi e^{2g}(E_t\hat{g}_{t+1} + E_t\hat{k}_{t+2} - \hat{k}_{t+1}), \tag{5.28}
$$

and

$$
\hat{r}_t = \psi d\hat{d}_{t+1}, \tag{5.29}
$$

where $\hat{x}_t \equiv \ln x_t - \ln x$ denotes the log-deviation of x_t from its deterministic steady-state value x, for $x_t = c_t, h_t, k_t, y_t, \lambda_t, d_t$, and $\hat{r}_t \equiv r_t - r$ denotes the deviation of r_t from its deterministic steady-state value, r. The parameter $\tilde{\beta} \equiv \beta e^{g[\gamma(1-\sigma)-1]}$ is assumed to satisfy $\tilde{\beta}(1+r^*) = 1$.

To underline the difference between the present model and its full-information counterpart, studied in Section 5.2, it is of interest to recall how $E_t\hat{g}_{t+1}$ is determined under full information. Applying the conditional expectations operator E_t to equation (5.15) yields $E_t\hat{g}_{t+1} = E_t z_{t+1} - E_t z_t + E_t\hat{g}_{t+1}^x$. Under full information, we can use the AR(1) processes assumed for z_t and $\hat{g}_t^x$ to obtain $E_t z_{t+1} = \rho_z z_t$, $E_t z_t = z_t$, and $E_t\hat{g}_{t+1}^x = \rho_x\hat{g}_t^x$. Using these expressions to eliminate $E_t z_{t+1}$, $E_t z_t$, and $E_t\hat{g}_{t+1}^x$ from the above expression yields $E_t\hat{g}_{t+1} = (\rho_z - 1)z_t + \rho_x\hat{g}_t^x$. That is, under full information, the expected value of $\hat{g}_{t+1}$ given information available in t depends on z_t and $\hat{g}_t^x$. But these are precisely the variables that households cannot observe under the information structure assumed in the model. Accordingly, the analysis that follows is concerned with the issue of how to extract information about $\hat{g}_{t+1}$ using information on its present and past realizations as well as on current and past realizations of the noisy signal s_t.

5.7.1 Using the Kalman Filter to Compute Future Expected TFP Growth

The *Kalman filter* is an iterative algorithm to compute optimal (or minimum mean-square-error) forecasts of stochastic variables obeying linear dynamic laws of motion with un-observed states. If the innovations driving the system are normally distributed, then these forecasts are indeed conditional expectations. These properties make the Kalman filter ideal for extracting information about $\hat{g}_{t+1}$, since $\hat{g}_t$ and the observed signal s_t are linearly related to the unobserved states z_t, z_{t-1}, and n_t, which, in turn, follow linear stochastic processes with normal disturbances. We note, incidentally, that the linear nature of these relationships is a primitive of the model and not a result of the linear approximation.

Let's begin by expressing the joint law of motion of z_t, $\hat{g}_t^x$, n_t, $\hat{g}_t$, and s_t in matrix form. To this end, define

$$\xi_t = \begin{bmatrix} z_t \\ z_{t-1} \\ \hat{g}_t^x \\ n_t \end{bmatrix} \quad \text{and} \quad o_t = \begin{bmatrix} \hat{g}_t \\ s_t \end{bmatrix}.$$

We refer to ξ_t as the *state vector* and to o_t as the *vector of observables*. Then the laws of motion of ξ_t and o_t are described by the following two equations, known, respectively, as the *state equation* and the *observation equation*:

$$\xi_{t+1} = F\xi_t + B\epsilon_{t+1} \tag{5.30}$$

and

$$o_t = H'\xi_t \tag{5.31}$$

where

$$F = \begin{bmatrix} \rho_z & 0 & 0 & 0 \\ 1 & 0 & 0 & 0 \\ 0 & 0 & \rho_x & 0 \\ 0 & 0 & 0 & \rho_n \end{bmatrix}, \quad B = \begin{bmatrix} \sigma_z & 0 & 0 \\ 0 & 0 & 0 \\ 0 & \sigma_x & 0 \\ 0 & 0 & \sigma_n \end{bmatrix}, \quad \epsilon_t = \begin{bmatrix} \epsilon_t^z \\ \epsilon_t^x \\ \epsilon_t^n \end{bmatrix}, \quad H' = \begin{bmatrix} 1 & -1 & 1 & 0 \\ 0 & 0 & 1 & 1 \end{bmatrix}.$$

The variance-covariance matrix of the innovation $B\epsilon_t$, given by BB', is denoted Q and is given by

$$Q = \begin{bmatrix} \sigma_z^2 & 0 & 0 & 0 \\ 0 & 0 & 0 & 0 \\ 0 & 0 & \sigma_x^2 & 0 \\ 0 & 0 & 0 & \sigma_n^2 \end{bmatrix}.$$

Then the Kalman filter yields:[5]

$$E_t o_{t+1} = H' E_t \xi_{t+1}$$

and

$$E_t \xi_{t+1} = F E_{t-1} \xi_t + K(o_t - H' E_{t-1} \xi_t),$$

where

$$K \equiv FPH(H'PH)^{-1}$$

is known as the gain matrix, and P is implicitly given by the Riccati equation,

$$P = F[P - PH(H'PH)^{-1} H'P]F' + Q, \tag{5.32}$$

and represents the steady-state mean square error of the forecast of ξ_{t+1}, that is, $P = E[(\xi_{t+1} - E_t \xi_{t+1})(\xi_{t+1} - E_t \xi_{t+1})']$.

5.7.2 Computation and Estimation

Technically, the model can be solved in two stages. In the first stage, the variables $\hat{g}_t$ and s_t are treated as states, and expectations in period t are taken, given the agent's information in period t, which does not include z_t, z_{t-1}, $\hat{g}_t^x$, or n_t.

Specifically, this entails creating a state vector, in this case of order 4 by 1, denoted $[\,\eta_{1t} \quad \eta_{2t} \quad \eta_{3t} \quad \eta_{4t}\,]'$ representing, respectively, $E_{t-1} z_t$, $E_{t-1} z_{t-1}$, $E_{t-1} \hat{g}_t^x$, and $E_{t-1} n_t$. Using the predictions of the Kalman filter presented above, the law of motion of the state vector is

$$\begin{bmatrix} \eta_{1t+1} \\ \eta_{2t+1} \\ \eta_{3t+1} \\ \eta_{4t+1} \end{bmatrix} = (F - KH') \begin{bmatrix} \eta_{1t} \\ \eta_{2t} \\ \eta_{3t} \\ \eta_{4t} \end{bmatrix} + K \begin{bmatrix} \hat{g}_t \\ s_t \end{bmatrix}. \tag{5.33}$$

And the conditional expectations of $\hat{g}_{t+1}$ and s_{t+1} are

$$\begin{bmatrix} E_t \hat{g}_{t+1} \\ E_t s_{t+1} \end{bmatrix} = H' \begin{bmatrix} \eta_{1t+1} \\ \eta_{2t+1} \\ \eta_{3t+1} \\ \eta_{4t+1} \end{bmatrix}. \tag{5.34}$$

The complete set of first-stage linearized equilibrium conditions is then given by equations (5.23)–(5.29), (5.33), and (5.34). This system contains 13 equations and 13 variables, given by six endogenous state variables (η_{1t}, η_{2t}, η_{3t}, η_{4t}, $\hat{k}_t$, $\hat{d}_t$), two exogenous state vari-

---

5. See, for example, Hamilton (1994), chapter 13.

ables ($\hat{g}_t$, s_t), and five endogenous control variables ($\hat{c}_t$, $\hat{h}_t$, $\hat{y}_t$, $\hat{r}_t$, $\hat{\lambda}_t$). Let us write the solution to the first-stage system as[6]

$$\mathbf{x}_{t+1} = h_x \mathbf{x}_t,$$

and

$$\mathbf{y}_t = g_x \mathbf{x}_t,$$

where

$$\mathbf{x}_t = \begin{bmatrix} \hat{k}_t \\ \hat{d}_t \\ \eta_{1t} \\ \eta_{2t} \\ \eta_{3t} \\ \eta_{4t} \\ \hat{g}_t \\ s_t \end{bmatrix}, \quad \mathbf{x}_{t+1} = \begin{bmatrix} \hat{k}_{t+1} \\ \hat{d}_{t+1} \\ \eta_{1t+1} \\ \eta_{2t+1} \\ \eta_{3t+1} \\ \eta_{4t+1} \\ E_t \hat{g}_{t+1} \\ E_t s_{t+1} \end{bmatrix}, \quad \text{and} \quad \mathbf{y}_t = \begin{bmatrix} c_t \\ h_t \\ y_t \\ r_t \\ \lambda_t \end{bmatrix}.$$

This is not the end of the computation algorithm, however, because in equilibrium, the variables $\hat{g}_t$ and s_t are not primitive exogenous states but control variables determined by the truly exogenous states z_t, z_{t-1}, $\hat{g}_t^x$, and n_t. Accordingly, next we express the system in terms of these primitive sources of uncertainty. We do this by appending equations (5.30) and (5.31) to the system as follows. Eliminate the last two elements of $\mathbf{x}_{t+1}$ and the last two rows of h_x. Let's denote the resulting objects, respectively, by $\mathbf{x}_{t+1}^1 \equiv [\ \hat{k}_{t+1}\ \ \hat{d}_{t+1}\ \ \eta_{1t+1}\ \ \eta_{2t+1}\ \ \eta_{3t+1}\ \ \eta_{4t+1}\ ]'$ and h_x^1. We can then write

$$\mathbf{x}_{t+1}^1 = h_x^1 \mathbf{x}_t.$$

Noting that the last two elements of $\mathbf{x}_t$ form the vector $o_t \equiv [\hat{g}_t\ \ s_t]$, we can write

$$\mathbf{x}_{t+1}^1 = h_x^{11} \mathbf{x}_t^1 + h_x^{12} o_t,$$

where h_x^{11} is the matrix that results from eliminating the last two columns of h_x^1, and h_x^{12} is the matrix formed by the last two columns of h_x^1. Now combine the above expression with (5.30) and (5.31) to obtain the equilibrium law of motion of the states of the model:

$$\mathbf{X}_{t+1} = H_x \mathbf{X}_t + \begin{bmatrix} \varnothing \\ I \end{bmatrix} B\epsilon_{t+1}$$

---

6. The solution of this system can be obtained using standard packages for computing the policy functions of linear dynamic stochastic general equilibrium (DSGE) models. Moreover, one need not linearize the model by hand. Programs that perform the linearization automatically can be utilized. The program `usg_noise_model.m` in the online file `usg_noise.zip` accomplishes this task.

where

$$
\mathbf{X}_t \equiv
\begin{bmatrix}
\hat{k}_t \\
\hat{d}_t \\
\eta_{1t} \\
\eta_{2t} \\
\eta_{3t} \\
\eta_{4t} \\
z_t \\
z_{t-1} \\
\hat{g}_t^x \\
n_t
\end{bmatrix},
\quad \text{and} \quad
H_x \equiv
\begin{bmatrix}
h_x^{11} & h_x^{12} H' \\
\emptyset & F
\end{bmatrix}.
$$

Finally, the evolution of the vector of controls is given by

$$
\mathbf{y}_t = G_x \mathbf{X}_t,
$$

where

$$
G_x \equiv [\, g_x^1 \quad g_x^2 H' \,],
$$

and where g_x^1 denotes the matrix that results from eliminating the last two columns of g_x, and g_x^2 denotes the matrix formed by the last two columns of g_x. The material for this chapter on the book's Web site contains Matlab code to solve the present model.

Given values for the parameters σ_z, σ_x, σ_n, ρ_z, ρ_x, and ρ_n, the computation of the matrices F, H, and Q is immediate. Computing P requires solving the Riccati equation given in (5.32). This is a simple iterative task. Starting with an initial guess P_0, successive approximations of P, denoted P_j, for $j = 1, 2, \ldots$, are obtained as $P_{j+1} = F[P_j - P_j H (H' P_j H)^{-1} H' P_j] F' + Q$. The approximation ends when P_j is sufficiently close to P_{j+1} according to a given metric and a given tolerance. Given P, the computation of K is immediate. The computation of P may introduce some time cost to the econometric estimation of the model if any of the parameters that define the matrices F, H, or Q belong to the vector of estimated parameters. This is because most existing methods for estimating DSGE models involve numerous evaluations of the coefficients of the model at different values of the vector of estimated parameters. In principle, each of these evaluations requires solving the Riccati equation defining the matrix P.

5.7.3 Incomplete Information Versus Noisy Information

The present model incorporates two types of informational imperfections. First, information is incomplete, since agents cannot observe separately the stationary and nonstationary components of total factor productivity. Second, information is noisy, since the signal s_t provides only a distorted image of the growth rate of the nonstationary component of total factor productivity.

Alternatively, one could have considered the case of incomplete information separately from the case of noisy information and then added noisy information to isolate its con-

Table 5.7   Calibrated Parameters

β	γ	ψ	α	σ	δ	$\bar{d}$	g
0.98	0.36	0.001	0.32	2	0.05	0.1	0.0018

Note: The time unit is one quarter.

tribution to the model's performance. Computing the case with incomplete information alone turns out to be quite simple. One must simply eliminate n_t from ξ_t, s_t from o_t, and ϵ_t^n from ϵ_t, and make the matrices F, H', and B conformable.

5.7.4 Estimation and Model Fit

In this section, we apply the concepts derived above to estimate the empirical importance of noise shocks. As usual, we estimate some parameters and calibrate others. The calibrated parameters appear in Table 5.7. The time unit is one quarter. The values assigned to all calibrated parameters are the same as those used by Boz, Daude, and Durdu (2011), except for the value assigned to g, which is set at the average growth rate of output per capita in the sample.

The remaining parameters of the model are estimated using quarterly Mexican data and Bayesian techniques. The estimation departs from the one conducted by Boz, Daude, and Durdu (2011) in three aspects. First, we use Bayesian techniques instead of GMM methods. Second, we allow the noise shock to be serially correlated. And third, we use a longer sample that includes 9 more years of data. The data consist of four variables: the growth rates of output, consumption, and investment per capita, and the trade-balance-to-GDP ratio. The sample covers the period 1980:Q2 to 2012:Q4.[7] Before estimation, we remove the mean of all four variables.

The estimated parameters are the standard deviations and serial correlations of the three exogenous driving processes (σ_z, σ_x, σ_n, ρ_z, ρ_x, and ρ_n) and the parameter ϕ defining capital adjustment costs. In addition, we allow for i.i.d. measurement errors in all four observables and estimate their standard deviations (σ_Y^{me}, σ_C^{me}, σ_I^{me}, and $\sigma_{TB/Y}^{me}$). We assume uniform priors for all estimated parameters. Table 5.8 displays the boundaries of the corresponding prior distributions. Because the model now contains a shock that we have not estimated before, we adopt loose priors for all estimated structural parameters. Adopting loose priors for the parameters other than those defining the noise process makes sense, because the inclusion of a new shock can alter the estimated importance of other sources of uncertainty.

Table 5.8 also displays salient features of the posterior distributions of the estimated parameters. These summary statistics are computed using an MCMC chain of length 1 million. The data appear to be informative about the estimated parameters, as indicated by the fact that the posterior distributions are tightly estimated in spite of loose uniform priors. The nonstationary productivity shock is estimated to be highly persistent, with a posterior

---

7. The data were extracted from the file `usg_data_quarterly.xls`, which is available on the Web site for the book with the materials for Chapter 1. In preparing the data, the growth rate of x_t was defined as $\Delta \ln x_t$.

Table 5.8   Bayesian Estimation of Imperfect-Information Model with Noise Shocks

Parameter	*Prior Distributions*			*Posterior Distributions*			
	Min	Max	Mean	Mean	Median	5%	95%
σ_x	0	0.2	0.1	0.0014	0.0013	0.0011	0.0016
ρ_x	−0.99	0.99	0	0.97	0.97	0.96	0.98
σ_z	0	0.2	0.1	0.022	0.022	0.02	0.024
ρ_z	−0.99	0.99	0	0.67	0.67	0.62	0.71
σ_n	0	0.2	0.1	0.002	0.002	0.0015	0.0027
ρ_n	−0.99	0.99	0	0.98	0.98	0.96	0.99
ϕ	0	8	4	0.54	0.54	0.42	0.67
$\sigma_{g^Y}^{me}$	0.0001	0.0034	0.0017	0.0034	0.0034	0.0034	0.0034
$\sigma_{g^C}^{me}$	0.0001	0.0057	0.0029	0.0056	0.0057	0.0055	0.0057
$\sigma_{g^I}^{me}$	0.0001	0.015	0.0073	0.014	0.014	0.014	0.014
$\sigma_{TB/Y}^{me}$	0.0001	0.0099	0.005	0.0096	0.0097	0.0091	0.0099

Notes: All prior distributions are taken to be uniform. Moments of the posterior distribution are based on a 1 million MCMC chain. The symbol σ_i^{me} denotes the standard deviation of the measurement error associated with the observable i, for $i = g^Y$, g^C, g^I, and TB/Y, where g^i denotes the growth rate of variable i, for $i = Y$, C, I, and TB/Y denotes the trade-balance-to-output ratio. The replication file `usg_noise_param_estim.m` is in `usg_noise.zip` on the book's Web site.

median of ρ_x of 0.97. This is counterintuitive, because the observed growth rates of output and other macroeconomic indicators display low serial correlations (see Table 5.9). However, the innovation to the nonstationary productivity shock is estimated to have a small standard deviation. The posterior median of σ_x is 0.0013, or slightly above one tenth of 1 percent. As a result, as we will see shortly, the estimated high serial correlation of the trend shock does not translate into unrealistically high serial correlations in macroeconomic variables of interest. This is an early indication that the estimated model does not assign a major role to nonstationary productivity shocks.

The standard deviation of the innovation of the noise component of the signal, σ_n, is estimated to be about 50 percent higher than the standard deviation of the innovation to the nonstationary component, σ_x (with posterior medians of 0.002 versus 0.0013, respectively). This means that the productivity signal that agents receive is quite noisy. In addition, the noise component of productivity growth is estimated to be highly persistent, with a posterior mean of ρ_n of 0.98. This is a significant departure from the parameterization adopted by Boz, Daude, and Durdu (2011), which imposes the noise shock to be serially uncorrelated ($\rho_n = 0$). The data do appear to favor serially correlated noise.

Table 5.9 presents empirical and predicted unconditional second moments of output growth, consumption growth, investment growth, and the trade-balance-to-output ratio. In general, the estimated model fits the data moderately well. It captures fairly well the standard deviations of output, consumption, and investment growth, as well as the correlations of consumption and investment growth with output growth. In particular, it predicts that

Table 5.9 Empirical and Theoretical Second Moments Implied by the Imperfect-Information Model with Noise Shocks

Statistic	g^Y	g^C	g^I	TB/Y
Standard Deviation				
Model	1.62	2.19	5.74	12.74
Data	1.36	2.30	5.82	3.95
Correlation with g^Y				
Model	1.00	0.65	0.91	−0.07
Data	1.00	0.61	0.60	−0.21
Serial Correlation				
Model	0.08	−0.00	−0.17	0.99
Data	0.32	−0.02	0.12	0.95

Notes: Empirical moments are computed using data from Mexico for the period 1980:Q2 to 2012:Q4. Theoretical moments are unconditional moments computed by evaluating the model at the posterior median of the estimated parameters. The replication file usg_noise_table_second_moments.m is online in usg_noise.zip.

consumption growth is more volatile than output growth, which is a prominent feature of the emerging-country business cycle. The model also captures the countercyclicality of the trade-balance-to-output ratio observed at business-cycle frequency. However, the predicted volatility of the trade balance share is three times as large as that observed in the data. The model also has a hard time replicating the observed serial correlations of output and investment growth. In particular, the model underpredicts the positive autocorrelations of output growth and counterfactually implies a negative serial correlation of investment growth.

5.7.5 The Importance of Noise Shocks

To measure the information content of the signal s_t, we compute the noise-to-signal ratio, which is defined as the fraction of the signal's unconditional variance explained by its noise component, n_t. Formally, we are interested in the ratio

$$\text{noise-to-signal ratio} \equiv \frac{\text{var}(n_t)}{\text{var}(s_t)}$$

$$= \frac{\sigma_n^2/(1-\rho_n^2)}{\sigma_n^2/(1-\rho_n^2) + \sigma_x^2/(1-\rho_x^2)}.$$

Evaluating the right-hand side of this expression at the posterior median of the corresponding parameters yields

$$\text{noise-to-signal ratio} = 0.78.$$

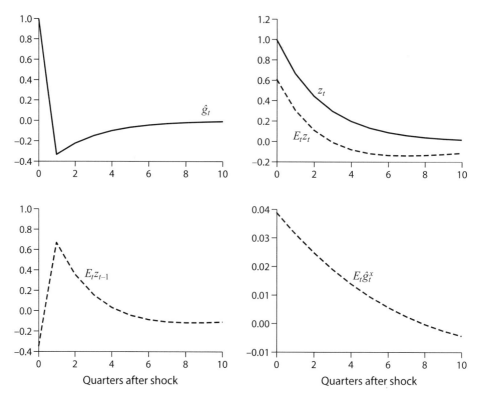

Figure 5.5   Response of TFP growth to a stationary technology shock (z_t) and perceived decomposition.

Note: The replication file `usg_noise_impulse_responses.m` is online in `usg_noise.zip`.

That is, 78 percent of the variance of the signal is explained by noise. According to this result, the signal that households receive conveys relatively little information about the state of the permanent component of TFP growth.

How does the presence of a weak signal affect agents' expectations about the current and future levels of the permanent and transitory components of productivity? The top left panel of Figure 5.5 displays the response of TFP growth, $\hat{g}_t$, to a 1 percent increase in the stationary component of TFP, z_t. Because z_t is an AR(1) process, its level increases by 1 percent on impact and then converges monotonically to the steady state from above (see the solid line in the top right panel). This implies that the response of $\hat{g}_t$, which in this case is equal to the response of $z_t - z_{t-1}$, increases by 1 percent on impact, then falls below zero in period 1, and then converges monotonically to zero from below (top left panel). Agents observe $\hat{g}_t$ and know that $\hat{g}_t = z_t - z_{t-1} + \hat{g}_t^x$, but they cannot observe z_t, z_{t-1}, or $\hat{g}_t^x$ individually. So they must form expectations about the current value of these objects on the basis of the observed values of $\hat{g}_t$ and s_t. The dashed lines depict the current expectations $E_t z_t$, $E_t z_{t-1}$, and $E_t \hat{g}_t^x$. On impact, agents estimate that z_t increased by about 0.6 percent, z_{t-1} by -0.3 percent, and $\hat{g}_t^x$ by 0.04 percent. This means that only 60 percent of the increase in TFP is attributed to its true cause z_t. Curiously, the observed increase in

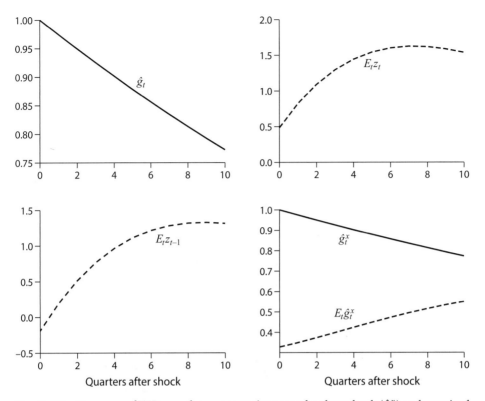

Figure 5.6 Response of TFP growth to a nonstationary technology shock ($\hat{g}_t^x$) and perceived decomposition.

Note: The replication file `usg_noise_impulse_responses.m` is online in `usg_noise.zip`.

productivity induces agents to revise down their previous period's expectation about z_{t-1}. This makes sense, because the smaller z_{t-1} is, the larger $\hat{g}_t$ will be. Agents have a hard time extracting information about the true state of the stationary component of productivity, as indicated by the fact that the difference between the corresponding actual and observed values of this object, $z_t - E_t z_t$, converges only gradually to zero.

Figure 5.6 displays the response of TFP growth and its true and perceived components to a nonstationary productivity shock, $\hat{g}_t^x$. As in the case of a shock to z_t, agents initially attribute the increase in TFP to changes in the current and past stationary components as well as to the nonstationary component. This time, however, the nonstationary shock receives a larger share than in the case of a stationary TFP shock (0.3 versus 0.04 percent). The reason is that agents now see both s_t and $\hat{g}_t$ increase by 1 percent, whereas in the case of a z_t shock, they see $\hat{g}_t$ increase by 1 percent and no change in s_t. The fact that s_t increases by 1 percent gives agents an indication that the impulse could have stemmed from the nonstationary component. However, this indication is quite unreliable, which causes agents' expectations to adjust slowly and nonmonotonically toward the true values of $\hat{g}_t^x$ and z_t. Indeed, the gap between z_t and $E_t z_t$ widens for the first eight quarters after the innovation in $\hat{g}_t^x$. The reason is that, because the signal is so noisy, agents attribute the

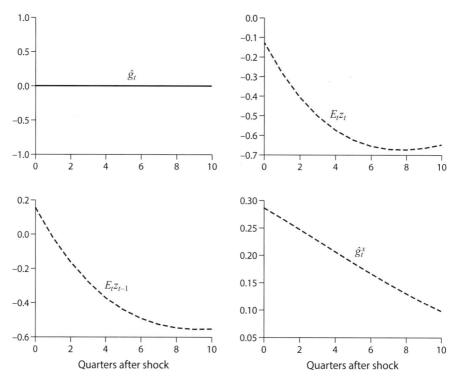

Figure 5.7   Response of TFP growth to a noise shock (n_t) and perceived decomposition.

Note: The replication file usg_noise_impulse_responses.m is online in usg_noise.zip.

observed increase in the level of productivity (A_t) mainly to the stationary component. Because z_t is mean reverting (and is therefore expected to fall over time), the continuous increase in A_t implies that initially agents must revise upward their expectation about the current state of z_t.

Finally, Figure 5.7 displays the response of TFP growth and its perceived decomposition to a noise shock (n_t). Clearly, TFP is not affected by this shock, so its response is mute. However, when agents see the signal increase by 1 percent, they place some weight on the possibility that it may be caused by an increase in the nonstationary component of productivity, $\hat{g}_t^x$. But since $\hat{g}_t$ does not move, for the perception of an increase in $\hat{g}_t^x$ to be consistent, it is necessary that agents perceive either a fall in z_t, an increase in z_{t-1}, or both. The last appears to be the case. After period 0, the perceived movements in z_t, z_{t-1}, and $\hat{g}_t^x$ must be consistent with no change in $\hat{g}_t$. So as $E_t\hat{g}_t^x$ falls gradually toward zero, $E_t(z_t - z_{t-1})$ increases gradually. This case is of interest, because it shows that a shock that is nonfundamental in nature (i.e., does not directly affect technology, preferences, or the availability of resources) can nevertheless have real consequences, because it affects the expected future path of fundamentals.

5.7.6 How Important Are Nonstationary Productivity Shocks?

The impulse-response analysis of the previous subsection demonstrates that the assumption of incomplete information has the potential to alter the model's transmission mechanism, because it affects agents' perception about future movements in fundamentals. The added assumption of informational noise incorporates a nonfundamental source of uncertainty with the potential to have real consequences. It is then natural to ask whether the present model with incomplete information and noise shocks predicts, like its perfect-information counterpart, that nonstationary productivity shocks are the main drivers of TFP.

To this end, we evaluate the ratio of the unconditional variance of the nonstationary component of TFP to the unconditional variance of TFP itself:

$$\frac{\text{var}(\hat{g}_t^x)}{\text{var}(\hat{g}_t)} = \frac{\sigma_x^2/(1-\rho_x^2)}{\sigma_x^2/(1-\rho_x^2) + 2\sigma_z^2/(1+\rho_z)}$$

$$= 0.06.$$

This computation says that the nonstationary component of TFP explains only 6 percent of the variance of TFP. The rest, 94 percent, is accounted for by stationary productivity shocks. This result is remarkable because the perfect-information environment, which, as we have shown earlier in this chapter, attributes a large role to the nonstationary component, is nested in the present model as a special case ($\sigma_n = 0$), and therefore could have been chosen by the econometric estimation. Indeed, restricting σ_n to be zero and re-estimating the model, one obtains that nonstationary productivity shocks account for 99 percent, or virtually all, of the variance of TFP growth. We conclude that the data favor a noisy environment in which productivity is driven mostly by stationary shocks over a highly informative environment in which productivity is driven primarily by nonstationary productivity shocks.

Consider now the contribution of each of the three driving forces (stationary productivity shocks, nonstationary productivity shocks, and noise shocks) to explaining movements in key macroeconomic indicators. Table 5.10 displays the unconditional variance decomposition of output growth, consumption growth, investment growth, the trade-balance-to-output ratio, and hours. The main message conveyed by the table is that once informational frictions are allowed for, nonstationary productivity shocks play a relatively minor role in explaining movements in output, consumption, and investment. However, nonstationary productivity shocks continue to be important drivers of the trade-balance-to-output ratio and of hours worked. A superficial reading of Table 5.10 may lead to the conclusion that overall, noise shocks play a minor role in explaining business cycles. This

Table 5.10 Variance Decomposition in the Imperfect-Information Model with Noise Shocks

Shock	g^Y	g^C	g^I	TB/Y	h
Stationary technology	67.0	81.4	69.5	4.2	2.8
Nonstationary technology	22.2	10.4	10.5	91.2	92.1
Noise	10.8	8.3	20.0	4.6	5.0

Notes: Calculated using the posterior median of the estimated parameters. The replication file `usg_noise_var_decomp.m` is online in `usg_noise.zip`.

conclusion would be mistaken, because the importance of noise shocks does not stem primarily from their direct impact on real variables but from the way they shape the transmission mechanism of other shocks.

5.8 Exercises

5.1 (Explaining the Serial Correlation of Investment Growth) The version of the GPU model estimated in this chapter predicts a negative first-order serial correlation of investment growth of -0.098 (see Table 5.5). In contrast, the empirical counterpart is positive and significant, with a point estimate of 0.32. This empirical fact is also observed in other emerging countries over long horizons. For example, Miyamoto and Nguyen (2013) report serial correlations of investment growth greater than or equal to 0.2 for Brazil, Mexico, Peru, Turkey, and Venezuela using annual data covering the period 1900–2006.

1. Think of a possible modification of the theoretical model that would result in an improvement of the model's prediction along this dimension. Provide intuition.
2. Implement your suggestion. Show the complete set of equilibrium conditions.
3. Re-estimate your model using the data set for Argentina, on which the GPU model of this chapter was estimated.
4. Summarize your results by expanding Table 5.5 with appropriate rows containing the predictions of your model.
5. Compare the performance of your model with the data and with the predictions of the version of the GPU model analyzed in this chapter.

5.2 (The Effect of Nonstationary Productivity Shocks on the Trade Balance in the Presence of Nontraded Goods) This exercise introduces nontradable goods, a subject we will take up in detail in Chapter 8. You may choose to postpone working on this exercise until you have read that chapter. However, the tools developed in the current chapter should be sufficient to do this exercise. Consider an economy populated by a large number of identical households with preferences described by the utility function

$$E_0 \sum_{t=0}^{\infty} \beta^t \frac{[C_t^{\gamma}(1 - h_t)^{1-\gamma}]^{1-\sigma} - 1}{1 - \sigma},$$

where C_t denotes consumption, and h_t denotes hours worked.

Let A_t denote domestic absorption. That is, A_t satisfies the identity

$$A_t = C_t + I_t,$$

where I_t denotes gross domestic investment. Assume that A_t is a composite of tradable and nontradable goods produced via the following aggregator function:

$$A_t = \left[\eta(A_t^T)^{1-1/\mu} + (1 - \eta)(A_t^N)^{1-1/\mu}\right]^{1/(1-1/\mu)},$$

where A_t^T and A_t^N denote, respectively, domestic absorptions of tradable and nontradable goods. Tradable and nontradable goods, denoted, respectively, Y_t^T and Y_t^N, are produced under constant returns to scale using capital and labor as inputs:

$$Y_t^T = z_t (K_t^T)^{1-\alpha_T} (X_t h_t^T)^{\alpha_T}$$

and

$$Y_t^N = z_t (K_t^N)^{1-\alpha_N} (X_t h_t^N)^{\alpha_N},$$

where K_t^i and h_t^i denote, respectively, capital and labor services employed in sector i, for $i = T, N$. The variable z_t represents an exogenous, stationary, stochastic productivity shock, and X_t represents an exogenous, stochastic, nonstationary productivity shock. The capital stocks evolve according to the following laws of motion:

$$K_{t+1}^T = (1-\delta) K_t^T + I_t^T - \frac{\phi}{2} \left(\frac{K_{t+1}^T}{K_t^T} - g \right)^2 K_t^T$$

and

$$K_{t+1}^N = (1-\delta) K_t^N + I_t^N - \frac{\phi}{2} \left(\frac{K_{t+1}^N}{K_t^N} - g \right)^2 K_t^N,$$

where I_t^i denotes investment in sector $i = T, N$ and satisfies

$$I_t = I_t^T + I_t^N.$$

Market clearing in the nontraded sector requires that domestic absorption equal production:

$$Y_t^N = A_t^N.$$

Also, market clearing in the labor market requires that

$$h_t = h_t^T + h_t^N.$$

Assume that the country has access to a single, one-period, internationally traded bond that pays the debt-elastic gross interest rate R_t when held between periods t and $t + 1$. The evolution of the household's net foreign debt position, D_t, is given by

$$\frac{D_{t+1}}{R_t} = D_t + A_t^T - Y_t^T,$$

with

$$R_t = R^* + \psi \left[e^{\tilde{D}_{t+1}/X_t - \bar{d}} - 1 \right],$$

where $\tilde{D}_t$ denotes average external debt per capita due in period t. Because households are homogeneous, we have that in equilibrium the following condition must hold:

$$\tilde{D}_t = D_t.$$

Finally, assume that the stationary productivity shock z_t follows an AR(1) process of the form

$$\ln z_t = \rho_z \ln z_{t-1} + \sigma_z \epsilon_t^z.$$

And the nonstationary productivity shock evolves according to

$$\ln(g_t/g) = \rho_g \ln(g_{t-1}/g) + \sigma_g \epsilon_t^g,$$

where

$$g_t \equiv \frac{X_t}{X_{t-1}},$$

$\rho_z, \rho_g \in (-1, 1)$, $\sigma_z, \sigma_g > 0$, and ϵ_t^z and ϵ_t^g are independent white noise processes distributed $N(0, 1)$.

Assume that the time unit is one quarter. Use the following table to calibrate the model:

β	γ	$\bar{d}$	ψ	α_T	α_N	σ	δ	σ_g	σ_z	ρ_g	ρ_z	g	ϕ	μ
0.98	0.36	0.10	0.001	0.40	0.80	2	0.05	0.0213	0.0053	0.00	0.95	1.0066	1.37	0.44

Guidelines for calibrating the parameter η are given below.

When addressing the numerical portions of the following questions, write your answers to four decimal places.

1. Write down the complete set of equilibrium conditions. Count the number of variables and equations.

2. Let p_t^N and p_t be the (shadow) relative prices of the nontradable good and the composite good in terms of tradable goods, respectively. Write down expressions for p_t^N and p_t in terms of A_t^T and A_t^N. Are p_t^N and p_t stationary variables? Why?

3. Write down the complete set of equilibrium conditions in stationary form along a balanced-growth path.

4. Derive a restriction on R^* that guarantees that the steady-state value of $d_{t+1} \equiv D_{t+1}/X_t$ along the balanced-growth path equals $\bar{d}$. Compute the steady state of the model. Set η to ensure that the share of nontraded output in total output, defined as $p_t^N Y_t^N/(p_t^N Y_t^N + Y_t^T)$, equals 0.65 in the steady state. Report the numerical value of η and the steady-state values of all endogenous variables of the model.

5. Report the numerical values of the eigenvalues of the matrix h_x defining the linearized equilibrium law of motion of the state vector.

6. Define GDP as $Y_t = (Y_t^T + p_t^N Y_t^N)/p_t$. Define the trade balance, TB_t, as $TB_t = Y_t - C_t - I_t$. Compute the unconditional standard deviations of the growth rates of consumption and output, defined, respectively, as $\Delta C_t \equiv \log(C_t/C_{t-1})$ and $\Delta Y_t \equiv \log(Y_t/Y_{t-1})$. Compute the correlation between ΔY_t and the trade-balance-to-output ratio, defined as $tby_t \equiv TB_t/Y_t$.

7. Compute other second moments of your choice and discuss whether they are in line with empirical regularities in emerging economies.

8. Explain how you would reparameterize the model to make it coincide with the one-sector model studied in Section 5.2. Answer the previous two questions under your proposed parameterization.

9. Based on your answers to the previous three questions, evaluate the ability of the present traded-nontraded model to explain key stylized facts in emerging countries. Provide intuition, making sure to emphasize the differences you can identify between the dynamics implied by the one-good SOE-RBC model and the present two-good SOE-RBC model.

5.3 (Slow Diffusion of Technology Shocks to the Country Premium, Household Production, and Government Spending) The model presented in Section 5.3 assumes that permanent productivity shocks affect not only the productivity of labor and capital in producing market goods but also the country premium, home production, and government spending. For instance, the assumption that the country interest rate depends on $\widetilde{D}_{t+1}/X_t$ implies that a positive innovation in X_t in period t causes, all other things equal, a fall in the country premium. In this exercise, we attenuate this type of effect by reformulating the model. Let

$$\widetilde{X}_t = \widetilde{X}_{t-1}^\zeta X_t^{1-\zeta},$$

with $\zeta \in [0, 1)$. Note that the original formulation obtains when $\zeta = 0$. Replace equations (5.3), (5.5), and (5.9), respectively, with

$$E_0 \sum_{t=0}^\infty v_t \beta^t \frac{\left[C_t - \omega^{-1} \widetilde{X}_{t-1} h_t^\omega\right]^{1-\gamma} - 1}{1-\gamma},$$

$$s_t = \frac{S_t}{\widetilde{X}_{t-1}},$$

and

$$r_t = r^* + \psi \left(e^{(\widetilde{D}_{t+1}/\widetilde{X}_t - \bar{d})/\bar{y}} - 1 \right) + e^{\mu_t - 1} - 1.$$

Keep all other features of the model as presented in Section 5.3.

1. Present the equilibrium conditions of the model in stationary form.

2. Using Bayesian techniques, re-estimate the model, adding ζ to the vector of estimated parameters. Assume a uniform prior distribution for ζ with support $[0, 0.99]$ and produce 1 million draws from the posterior distribution of the parameter vector. Present the estimation results in the form of a table like Table 5.4. Discuss your findings.

3. Characterize numerically the predictions of the model. In particular, produce tables similar to Tables 5.5 and 5.6. Discuss your results and provide intuition.

4. Compute the impulse responses of output, consumption, investment, the trade-balance-to-output ratio, and the country interest rate to a 1 percent innovation in g_t for three values of ζ, namely, 0, its posterior median, and 0.99.

5.4 (The Importance of Nonstationary Productivity Shocks in the GPU Model) The model of Section 5.3 introduces three modifications to the SOE-RBC model with stationary and nonstationary technology shocks of Section 5.2, namely, a longer sample, additional shocks, and financial frictions. A result of the Section 5.3 model is that once these modifications are put in place, nonstationary productivity shocks cease to play a central role in explaining business cycles. The goal of this exercise is to disentangle which of the three aforementioned modifications is responsible for this result. To this end, use Bayesian methods to estimate, one at a time, the following three variants of the model:

1. Shorter sample: Use data from 1975–2005.

2. Only technology shocks: Set to zero the standard deviations of the preference shock, the country interest-rate shock, and the spending shock.

3. No financial frictions: Set $\psi = 0.001$ and $\eta = 0$.

Use the same priors as in the body of the chapter, and produce MCMC chains of 1 million draws with an acceptance rate of 25 percent. In each case, report the implied variance decomposition of TFP, output growth, consumption growth, investment growth, and the trade-balance-to-output ratio and measures of model fit, using the formats of Tables 5.4, 5.5, and 5.6 and equation (5.13). Discuss your results.

5.5 (Letting Productivity, Noise, and Interest-Rate Shocks Compete) Augment the open economy model with imperfect information of Section 5.7 to allow for an interest-rate shock as in the GPU model of Section 5.3. To this end proceed as follows.

1. Re-estimate the model using Bayesian techniques. Use the Mexican data and prior distributions used in Section 5.7. Enlarge the vector of estimated parameters to include the parameter ψ governing the debt elasticity of the interest rate, and the standard deviation and serial correlation of the interest-rate shock. For these additional parameters, use the priors of Section 5.3.

2. Produce a table displaying the lower and upper bounds of the prior distributions along with the posterior mean, median, standard deviation, and the 5–95 percent probability interval.

For the remaining questions, evaluate the model at the posterior median of the estimated parameters.

3. Report the share of the variance of the signal s_t accounted for by noise shock n_t (i.e., the noise-to-signal ratio). Comment.

4. Report the share of the variance of TFP growth explained by the nonstationary productivity shock and contrast it to the case without interest-rate shocks and financial frictions.

5. Produce a table displaying the actual and predicted standard deviation; correlation with output growth; and serial correlation of output growth, consumption growth, investment growth, and the trade-balance-to-output ratio. Comment especially on the model's ability to explain the predicted volatility of the trade-balance-to-output ratio and the serial correlations of output and investment growth, which are the second moments that the version of the model without interest-rate shocks or financial frictions has the hardest time explaining.

6. Add one more line per moment to the table you produced in question 5, displaying the predicted second moment under perfect information. For this step, set $\sigma_n = 0$ and re-estimate the model. Discuss your findings.

5.6 (The Meaning of Variance Decomposition under Imperfect Information) Following the notation introduced in the body of this chapter, the first-order approximation to the equilibrium laws of motion of the state and control vectors, respectively, are given by $Y_t = G_x Y_t$ and $X_{t+1} = G_x X_t + [\emptyset; B]\epsilon_{t+1}$. One aspect that distinguishes models with imperfect information from models with perfect information is that in the former the standard deviations of the exogenous disturbances, which define the matrix B, also appear in the matrices H_x and G_x, whereas in the latter class of models G_x and H_x are independent of B. That is, the relative volatility of the underlying shocks affects the transmission mechanism under imperfect information but not under full information. In light of this fact, propose meaningful ways to evaluate the contribution of different shocks (in the context of the model laid out in Section 5.7, noise shocks, productivity shocks, etc.) under imperfect information. Discuss the concept of "variance decomposition" in this context. Apply your proposal to evaluating the contribution of different shocks in the model estimated in Section 5.7.

6

Interest-Rate Shocks

Business cycles in emerging market economies are correlated with the interest rate that these countries face in international financial markets. This observation is illustrated in Figure 6.1, which depicts detrended output and the country interest rate for seven developing economies between 1994:Q1 and 2001:Q4. Periods of low interest rates are typically associated with economic expansions, and periods of high interest rates are often characterized by depressed levels of aggregate activity.[1]

Data like those shown in Figure 6.1 have motivated researchers to ask what fraction of observed business-cycle fluctuations in emerging markets is due to movements in country interest rates. This question is complicated by the fact that the country interest rate is unlikely to be completely exogenous to the country's domestic conditions.[2] To clarify ideas, let R_t denote the gross interest rate at which the emerging country borrows in international markets, or the country interest rate. This interest rate can be expressed as $R_t = R_t^{us} S_t$. Here, R_t^{us} denotes the gross world interest rate, or the interest rate at which developed countries, like the United States, borrow and lend from one another, and S_t denotes the gross country interest-rate spread, or country interest-rate premium. Because the interest-rate premium is country specific, in the data we find an Argentine spread, a Colombian spread, and so forth. If the country in question is a small player in international financial markets, as many emerging economies are, it is reasonable to assume that the world interest rate, R_t^{us}, is exogenous to the emerging country's domestic conditions. We cannot say the same, however, about the country spread S_t. An increase in domestic output, for instance, may induce foreign lenders to lower spreads on beliefs that the country's ability to repay its debts has improved.

Interpreting the country interest-rate premium as an exogenous variable when in reality it has an endogenous component is likely to result in an overstatement of the importance of interest rates in explaining business cycles. To see why, consider the following example. Suppose that the interest-rate premium S_t is purely endogenous. Thus, its contribution to generating business cycles is nil. Assume, furthermore, that S_t is countercyclical (i.e.,

---

1. The estimated correlations (*p*-values) are: Argentina −0.67 (0.00), Brazil −0.51 (0.00), Ecuador −0.80 (0.00), Mexico −0.58 (0.00), Peru −0.37 (0.12), the Philippines −0.02 (0.95), and South Africa −0.07 (0.71).
2. A large literature argues that domestic variables affect the interest rate at which emerging markets borrow externally. See, for example, Edwards (1984), Cline (1995), and Cline and Barnes (1997).

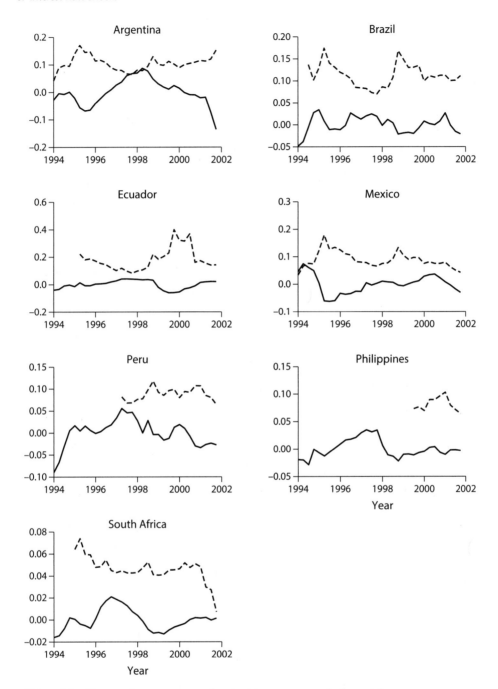

Figure 6.1 Country interest rates and output in seven emerging countries.

Source: Uribe and Yue (2006).

Notes: Output is seasonally adjusted and detrended using a log-linear trend. Country interest rates are real yields on dollar-denominated bonds of emerging countries issued in international financial markets. Country interest rates are from J.P. Morgan's Emerging Markets Bond Index (EMBI+); output data are from International Financial Statistics (IFS). The sample period is 1994:Q1 to 2001:Q4.

foreign lenders reduce the country spread in response to expansions in domestic aggregate activity). The researcher, however, wrongly assumes that the interest-rate premium is purely exogenous. Suppose now that a domestic productivity shock causes an expansion in output. In response to this output increase, the country interest-rate premium falls. The researcher erroneously attributes part of the increase in output to the decline in S_t. The right conclusion, of course, is that all of the increase in output is due to the productivity shock.

It follows that to quantify the macroeconomic effects of interest-rate shocks, the first step is to identify the exogenous components of country spreads. The identification process must combine statistical methods and economic theory. The particular combination adopted in this chapter is taken from Uribe and Yue (2006). A difference between the approaches adopted in this chapter and in Chapter 5 is that in the latter, inference about the importance of interest-rate shocks in driving business cycles is conducted without using observations on interest rates. There, this choice was motivated by a desire to let interest-rate shocks compete with other shocks that were treated as latent variables. In such a context, making interest rates observable would have put this source of uncertainty at a disadvantage. In contrast, in the current chapter observations on interest rates take center stage.

6.1 An Empirical Model

Consider the first-order VAR system

$$
A \begin{bmatrix} \widehat{y}_t \\ \widehat{\imath}_t \\ tby_t \\ \widehat{R}_t^{us} \\ \widehat{R}_t \end{bmatrix} = B \begin{bmatrix} \widehat{y}_{t-1} \\ \widehat{\imath}_{t-1} \\ tby_{t-1} \\ \widehat{R}_{t-1}^{us} \\ \widehat{R}_{t-1} \end{bmatrix} + \begin{bmatrix} \epsilon_t^y \\ \epsilon_t^i \\ \epsilon_t^{tby} \\ \epsilon_t^{rus} \\ \epsilon_t^r \end{bmatrix}, \tag{6.1}
$$

where y_t denotes real gross domestic output, i_t denotes real gross domestic investment, tby_t denotes the trade-balance-to-output ratio, R_t^{us} denotes the gross real U.S. interest rate, and R_t denotes the gross real (emerging) country interest rate. A hat on y_t and i_t denotes log-deviations from a linear trend. A hat on R_t^{us} and R_t denotes simply the log. We measure R_t^{us} as the 3-month gross Treasury bill rate divided by the average gross U.S. inflation over the previous four quarters and the country interest rate R_t as the sum of J.P. Morgan's EMBI+ stripped spread and the U.S. real interest rate. Output, investment, and the trade balance are seasonally adjusted.

To identify the shocks in the empirical model, Uribe and Yue (2006) impose the restriction that the matrix A be lower triangular with unit diagonal elements. Because R_t^{us} and R_t appear at the bottom of the system, this identification strategy presupposes that innovations in world interest rates (ϵ_t^{rus}) and innovations in country interest rates (ϵ_t^r) percolate into domestic real variables with a one-period lag. At the same time, the identification scheme implies that domestic shocks (ϵ_t^y, ϵ_t^i, and ϵ_t^{tby}) affect financial markets contemporaneously. This identification strategy is a natural one, because, conceivably, such decisions as employment and spending on durable consumption goods and investment goods take time to plan and implement. Also, it seems reasonable to assume that financial markets are able to react quickly to news about the state of the business cycle. Uribe and Yue (2006) discuss an alternative identification strategy that allows U.S. interest-rate shocks and country-spread shocks to affect real variables contemporaneously. They find that under this identification an increase in the U.S. interest rate leads to an expansion in domestic economic activity. Because it is difficult to rationalize this result on theoretical grounds, we conclude that it is unlikely that this identification strategy successfully uncovers the true transmission mechanism of interest-rate shocks, making the baseline identification preferable.

An additional restriction imposed on the VAR system is that the world interest rate R_t^{us} follows a univariate AR(1) process (i.e., $A_{4i} = B_{4i} = 0$, for all $i \neq 4$). Uribe and Yue (2006) adopt this restriction because it is reasonable to assume that disturbances in a particular (small) emerging country will not affect the real interest rate of a large country like the United States.

The country interest-rate shock, ϵ_t^r, can equivalently be interpreted as a country spread shock. To see this, consider substituting in equation (6.1) the country interest rate $\widehat{R}_t$ using the definition of country spread, $\widehat{S}_t \equiv \widehat{R}_t - \widehat{R}_t^{us}$. Clearly, because $\widehat{R}_t^{us}$ appears as a regressor in the bottom equation of the VAR system, the estimated residual of the newly defined bottom equation (call it ϵ_t^s) is identical to ϵ_t^r. Moreover, the impulse response functions of $\widehat{y}_t$, $\widehat{\iota}_t$, and tby_t associated with ϵ_t^s are identical to those associated with ϵ_t^r. Therefore, we interchangeably refer to ϵ_t^r as either a country interest rate shock or as a country spread shock.

The restrictions imposed on the matrices A and B identify the U.S. interest-rate shock ϵ_t^{rus} and the country interest-rate shock ϵ_t^r. The resulting VAR system is known as a structural vector autoregressive (SVAR) system. Uribe and Yue estimate the SVAR system (6.1) equation by equation with an intercept and country fixed effects on panel data from Argentina, Brazil, Ecuador, Mexico, Peru, the Philippines, and South Africa, over the period 1994:Q1–2001:Q4. The $\widehat{R}_t^{us}$ equation is estimated by OLS over the period 1987:Q1–2002:Q4. Table 6.1 presents the results of the estimation.

The estimated SVAR system can be used to address a number of questions central to disentangling the effects of country-spread shocks and world interest-rate shocks on aggregate activity in emerging markets: First, how do U.S. interest-rate shocks and country-spread shocks affect real domestic variables, such as output, investment, and the trade balance? Second, how do country spreads respond to innovations in U.S. interest rates? Third, how and by how much do country spreads move in response to innovations in emerging-country fundamentals? Fourth, how important are U.S. interest-rate shocks and country-spread shocks in explaining movements in aggregate activity in emerging countries? Fifth, how important are U.S. interest-rate shocks and country-spread shocks in accounting for movements in country spreads? The next section answers these questions with the help of impulse response functions and variance decompositions.

6.2 Impulse Response Functions

The solid lines in Figure 6.2 display the impulse response function implied by the estimated SVAR system (6.1) to a 1 percentage point increase in the country spread shock, ϵ_t^r. Dashed lines depict two-standard-deviation bands. In response to an unanticipated country-spread

Table 6.1   Parameter Estimates of the VAR System (6.1)

Independent Variable	Dependent Variable				
	$\widehat{y}_t$	$\widehat{\iota}_t$	tby_t	$\widehat{R}^{us}_t$	$\widehat{R}_t$
$\widehat{y}_t$	—	2.739 (10.28)	0.295 (2.18)	—	−0.791 (−3.72)
$\widehat{y}_{t-1}$	0.282 (2.28)	−1.425 (−4.03)	−0.032 (−0.25)	—	0.617 (2.89)
$\widehat{\iota}_t$	—	—	−0.228 (−6.89)	—	0.114 (1.74)
$\widehat{\iota}_{t-1}$	0.162 (4.56)	0.537 (3.64)	0.040 (0.77)	—	−0.122 (−1.72)
tby_t	—	—	—	—	0.288 (1.86)
tby_{t-1}	0.267 (4.45)	−0.308 (−1.30)	0.317 (2.46)	—	−0.190 (−1.29)
$\widehat{R}^{us}_t$	—	—	—	—	0.501 (1.55)
$\widehat{R}^{us}_{t-1}$	0.0002 (0.00)	−0.269 (−0.47)	−0.063 (−0.28)	0.830 (10.89)	0.355 (0.73)
$\widehat{R}_{t-1}$	−0.170 (−3.93)	−0.026 (−0.21)	0.191 (3.54)	—	0.635 (4.25)
R^2	0.724	0.842	0.765	0.664	0.619
Standard error	0.018	0.043	0.019	0.007	0.031
Number of observations	165	165	165	62	160

Source: Uribe and Yue (2006).

Notes: t-statistics are shown in parentheses. The system was estimated equation by equation with an intercept and country fixed effects (not shown). All equations except for the $\widehat{R}^{us}_t$ equation were estimated using instrumental variables with panel data from Argentina, Brazil, Ecuador, Mexico, Peru, the Philippines, and South Africa over the period 1994:Q1–2001:Q4. The $\widehat{R}^{us}_t$ equation was estimated by OLS over the period 1987:Q1–2002:Q4.

shock, the country spread itself increases and then quickly falls toward its long-run level. The half-life of the country spread response is about 1 year. Output, investment, and the trade-balance-to-output ratio respond as one would expect. They are unchanged in the period of impact, because of our assumption that external financial shocks take one quarter to affect production and absorption. In the two periods following the country-spread shock, output and investment fall and subsequently recover gradually until they reach their respective trend levels. The adverse spread shock produces a relatively larger contraction in aggregate absorption than in aggregate output. This is reflected in the fact that the trade-balance-to-output ratio improves in the two periods following the shock.

Figure 6.3 displays the response to a 1 percentage point increase in the U.S. interest-rate shock, ϵ^{rus}_t. The effects of U.S. interest-rate shocks on domestic variables and country spreads are measured with significant uncertainty, as indicated by the width of the two-standard-deviation error bands. The point estimates of the impulse response functions

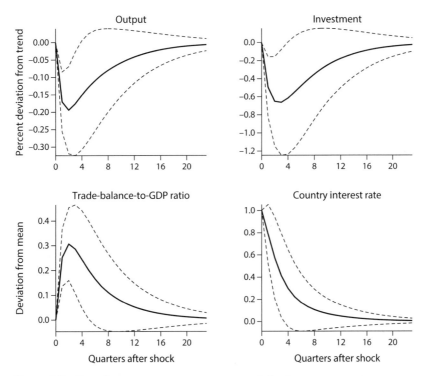

Figure 6.2   Impulse response to a country-spread shock.

Source: Uribe and Yue (2006).
Notes: Solid lines depict point estimates of impulse responses, and dashed lines depict two-standard-deviation error bands. The responses of output and investment are expressed as percentage deviations from their respective log-linear trends. The responses of the trade-balance-to-GDP ratio and the country interest rate are expressed as percentage point deviations from their respective means. The two-standard-error bands are computed using the delta method.

of output, investment, and the trade balance, however, are qualitatively similar to those associated with an innovation in the country spread. That is, aggregate activity and gross domestic investment contract, while net exports improve. However, the quantitative effects of an innovation in the U.S. interest rate are much more pronounced than those caused by a country-spread disturbance of equal magnitude. For instance, the trough in the output response is twice as large under a U.S. interest-rate shock than under a country-spread shock.

It is remarkable that the impulse response function of the country spread to a U.S. interest-rate shock displays a delayed overshooting. In effect, in the period of impact the country interest rate increases but by less than the jump in the U.S. interest rate. As a result, the country spread initially falls. However, the country spread recovers quickly, and after a couple of quarters it is more than 1 percentage point above its pre-shock level. Thus, country spreads increase significantly in response to innovations in the U.S. interest rate but with a short delay. The negative impact is in line with the findings of Eichengreen and Mody (1998) and Kamin and Kleist (1999). We note, however, that because the models estimated

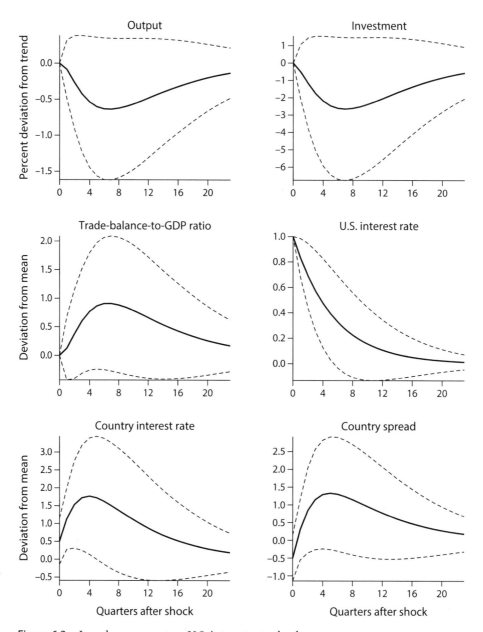

Figure 6.3   Impulse response to a U.S. interest-rate shock.

Source: Uribe and Yue (2006).

Notes: Solid lines depict point estimates of impulse responses, and dashed lines depict two-standard-deviation error bands. The responses of output and investment are expressed as percentage deviations from their respective log-linear trends. The responses of the trade-balance-to-GDP ratio, the country interest rate, and the U.S. interest rate are expressed as percentage point deviations from their respective means.

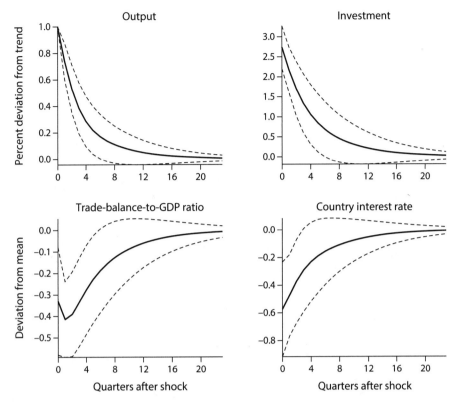

Figure 6.4 Impulse response to an output shock.

Source: Uribe and Yue (2006).
Notes: Solid lines depict point estimates of impulse response functions, and dashed lines depict two-standard-deviation error bands. The responses of output and investment are expressed as percentage deviations from their respective log-linear trends. The responses of the trade-balance-to-GDP ratio and the country interest rate are expressed as percentage point deviations from their respective means.

by these authors are static by construction, they are unable to capture the rich dynamic relation linking these two variables. The overshooting of country spreads is responsible for the much larger response of domestic variables to an innovation in the U.S. interest rate than to an innovation in the country spread of equal magnitude.

We now ask how innovations in output, ϵ_t^y, impinge on the variables of our empirical model. The model is vague about the precise nature of output shocks. They can reflect variations in total factor productivity, the terms of trade, etc. Figure 6.4 depicts the impulse response function to a 1 percent increase in the output shock. The response of output, investment, and the trade balance is very much in line with the impulse response to a positive productivity shock implied by the SOE-RBC model (see Figure 4.1 in Chapter 4). The response of investment is about three times as large as that of output. At the same time, the trade balance deteriorates significantly by about 0.4 percent and after two quarters starts to improve, converging gradually to its long-run level. More interestingly, the increase in

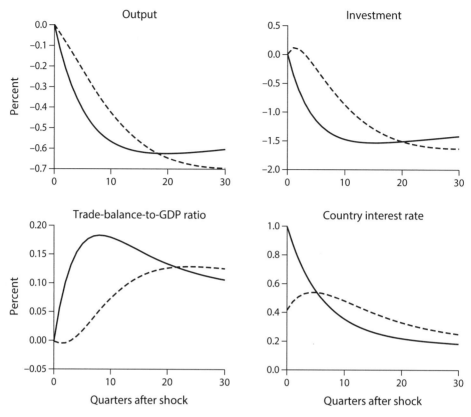

Figure 6.5   Responses to country-spread and U.S. interest-rate shocks (1994:Q1–2012:Q4 sample).

Notes: Solid lines depict responses to a 1 percent country-spread shock, and dashed lines depict responses to a 1 percent U.S. interest-rate shock. The responses of output and investment are expressed as percentage deviations from their respective log-linear trends. The responses of the trade-balance-to-GDP ratio and the country interest rate are expressed as percentage point deviations from their respective means. The countries included in the estimation are Argentina, Brazil, Bulgaria, Chile, Colombia, Ecuador, Hungary, Malaysia, Mexico, Peru, South Africa, South Korea, Thailand, Turkey, and Uruguay.

output produces a significant reduction in the country spread of about 0.6 percentage points (or 60 basis points). The half-life of the country-spread response is about five quarters. The countercyclical behavior of the country spread in response to output shocks suggests that country interest rates behave in ways that amplify the business-cycle effects of output shocks.

Robustness to Expanding the Time and Country Dimensions of the Data
Figures 6.5 and 6.6 display impulse responses to interest-rate, country-spread, and output shocks implied by the empirical model given in equation (6.1) estimated on an expanded data panel. Specifically, the data set now includes eleven additional years of quarterly data

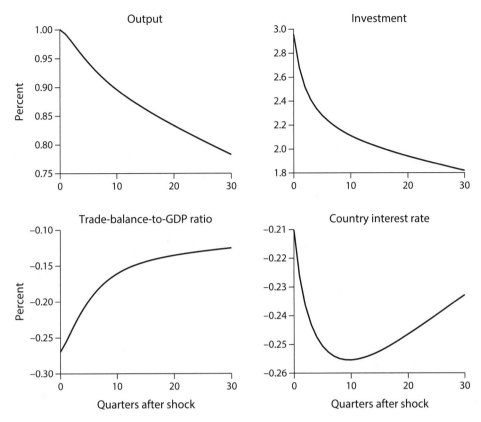

Figure 6.6 Response to an output shock (1994–2012 sample).

Notes: The responses of output and investment are expressed as percentage deviations from their respective log-linear trends. The responses of the trade-balance-to-GDP ratio and the country interest rate are expressed as percentage point deviations from their respective means. The countries included in the estimation are Argentina, Brazil, Bulgaria, Chile, Colombia, Ecuador, Hungary, Malaysia, Mexico, Peru, South Africa, South Korea, Thailand, Turkey, and Uruguay.

(the period 2002:Q1–2012:Q4) and nine additional countries (Bulgaria, Chile, Colombia, Hungary, Malaysia, South Korea, Thailand, Turkey, and Uruguay).[3]

The two figures suggest that the results reported by Uribe and Yue (2006) are robust to extending the temporal and geographic coverage of the data. In particular, both country-spread and U.S. interest-rate shocks cause sizable contractions in output and investment and an improvement in the trade-balance-to-GDP ratio. Also, increases in the U.S. interest rate are incorporated into country interest rates with a delay. Furthermore, a positive output shock causes an expansion in investment; a deterioration of the trade-balance-to-GDP ratio; and more importantly, a fall in the country interest rate. A difference between

---

3. The new data set is available on the book's Web site via http://press.princeton.edu/titles/11032.html, in the file `irs_data_update.mat`.

the baseline and expanded data sets is that the latter induces significantly more persistent responses.

6.3 Variance Decompositions

How important are world interest-rate shocks and country0spread shocks in explaining movements in output, investment, the trade balance, and the country interest rate itself? And how does the importance of these two shocks vary over forecast horizons? A common way to ascertain the contribution of different driving forces to movements of variables of interest at business-cycle frequency is to compute the variance of the forecast errors attributable to each shock at different horizons.

Forecast errors are computed as follows. In the VAR system (6.1), let

$$x_t \equiv [\hat{y}_t \ \hat{\imath}_t \ tby_t \ \widehat{R}_t^{us} \ \widehat{R}_t]'$$

be the vector of variables and $\epsilon_t \equiv [\epsilon_t^y \ \epsilon_t^i \ \epsilon_t^{tby} \ \epsilon_t^{rus} \ \epsilon_t^r]'$ the vector of orthogonal disturbances.[4] Then one can write the infinite-order moving average MA(∞) representation of x_{t+h} as

$$x_{t+h} = \sum_{j=0}^{\infty} C_j \epsilon_{t+h-j},$$

where

$$C_j \equiv (A^{-1}B)^j A^{-1}.$$

The h-period-ahead forecast of x_t at time t is given by the expected value of x_{t+h} conditional on information available at time t, that is,

$$E_t x_{t+h} = \sum_{j=h}^{\infty} C_j \epsilon_{t+h-j}.$$

The corresponding forecast error, denoted FE_t^h, is the difference between the actual value of x_{t+h} and its forecasted value:

$$FE_t^h \equiv x_{t+h} - E_t x_{t+h}$$

$$= \sum_{j=0}^{h-1} C_j \epsilon_{t+h-j}.$$

---

4. We note that the estimates of ϵ_t^y, ϵ_t^i, ϵ_t^{tby}, and ϵ_t^r (i.e., the sample residuals of the first, second, third, and fifth equations of the VAR system) are orthogonal to each other by construction. But because $\hat{y}_t$, $\hat{\imath}_t$, and tby_t are excluded from the R_t^{us} equation, we have that in any finite sample, the estimates of ϵ_t^{rus} will in general not be orthogonal to the estimates of ϵ_t^y, ϵ_t^i, or ϵ_t^{tby}. However, under our assumption that ϵ_t^{rus} is independent of ϵ_t^y, ϵ_t^i, and ϵ_t^{tby}, if the model is well specified, this lack of orthogonality should disappear as the sample size increases.

The variance-covariance matrix of the h-period-ahead forecast error is given by

$$FEV^h \equiv \sum_{j=0}^{h-1} C_j \Sigma_\epsilon C_j',$$

where Σ_ϵ is the variance-covariance matrix of ϵ_t. Thus, the variance of the h-period-ahead forecast error of x_t is simply the vector containing the diagonal elements of FEV^h. In turn, the variance-covariance matrix of the h-period-ahead forecasting error of x_t due to a particular shock, say, the ith shock, ϵ_t^i, is given by

$$FEV^{h,i} \equiv \sum_{j=0}^{h-1} (C_j \Lambda_i) \Sigma_\epsilon (C_j \Lambda_i)',$$

where Λ_i is a 5×5 matrix with all elements equal to zero except element (i, i), which takes the value one. The matrix $FEV^{h,i}$ is the ith component of the orthogonal decomposition of the forecast error variance for x_t. This decomposition satisfies the condition $FEV^h = \sum_{i=1}^{5} FEV^{h,i}$. Then for any variable of the VAR, say, the kth variable, the share of the h-period-ahead forecast-error variance attributable to ϵ_t^i, denoted $SFEV_k^{h,i}$, is given by the ratio of the kth diagonal element of $FEV^{h,i}$ to the kth diagonal element of FEV^h, that is,

$$SFEV_k^{h,i} = \frac{FEV_{kk}^{h,i}}{FEV_{kk}^h},$$

where the subscript kk denotes element (k, k). As the forecast horizon h approaches infinity, the decomposition of the variance of the forecast error coincides with the decomposition of the unconditional variance of the variable in question.

Figure 6.7 displays the share of the forecast-error variance of the variables contained in the SVAR system (6.1) at horizons 1 to 24 quarters ($h = 1, 2, \ldots, 24$), $SFEV_k^{h,i}$ for $h = 1, \ldots, 24$, $i = 4, 5$, and $k = 1, \ldots, 5$. Solid lines show the fraction of the variance of the forecast error explained jointly by U.S. interest-rate shocks and country-spread shocks (ϵ_t^{rus} and ϵ_t^r), given by $SFEV_k^{h,4} + SFEV_k^{h,5}$. Dashed lines depict the fraction of the variance of the forecast error explained by U.S. interest-rate shocks (ϵ_t^{rus}), given by $SFEV_k^{h,4}$. Because ϵ_t^{rus} and ϵ_t^r are orthogonal disturbances, the vertical distance between the solid line and the dashed line represents the variance of the forecast error explained by country-spread shocks, given by $SFEV_k^{h,5}$. For the purpose of the present discussion, we associate business-cycle fluctuations with the variance of the forecast error at a horizon of about 20 quarters, or 5 years. Researchers typically define business cycles as movements in time series at frequencies ranging from 6 quarters to 32 quarters (see, e.g., Stock and Watson 1999). Our choice of horizon falls in the middle of this window.

The estimated SVAR system (6.1) implies that innovations in the U.S. interest rate, ϵ_t^{rus}, explain about 20 percent of movements in aggregate activity (output and investment) in emerging countries at the business-cycle frequency. At the same time, country-spread shocks, ϵ_t^r, account for 12 percent of aggregate fluctuations in these countries. Thus, around

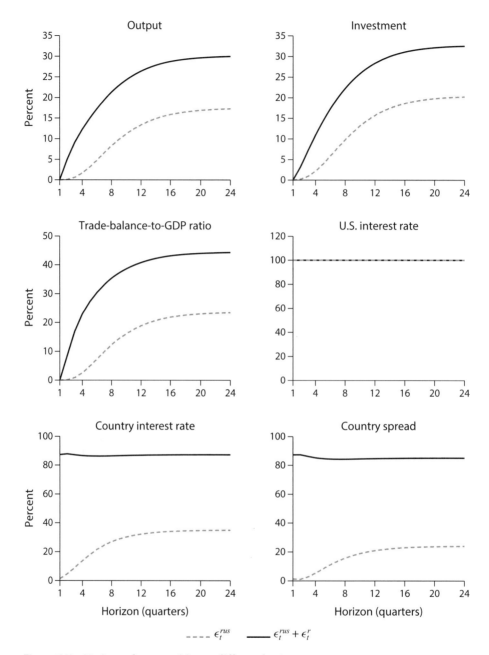

Figure 6.7   Variance decomposition at different horizons.

Source: Uribe and Yue (2006).

Notes: Solid lines depict the share of the variance of the h-quarter-ahead forecasting error explained jointly by ϵ_t^{rus} and ϵ_t^r for values of h between 1 and 24 quarters. Dashed lines depict the share of the variance of the h-quarter-ahead forecasting error explained by ϵ_t^{rus}.

Table 6.2 Forecast-Error Variance Decomposition

Variable	h = 20			h = ∞		
	ϵ_t^{rus}	ϵ_t^{r}	$\epsilon_t^{rus} + \epsilon_t^{r}$	ϵ_t^{rus}	ϵ_t^{r}	$\epsilon_t^{rus} + \epsilon_t^{r}$
$\widehat{y}_t$	17	13	30	17	13	30
$\widehat{\imath}_t$	20	12	32	20	12	32
tby_t	23	21	44	24	21	45
$\widehat{R}_t^{us}$	100	0	100	100	0	100
$\widehat{R}_t$	35	53	88	35	52	87
$\widehat{R}_t - \widehat{R}_t^{us}$	24	61	85	24	61	85

Notes: The table displays the share of the forecast-error variance of each variable in the first column explained by ϵ_t^{rus} and ϵ_t^{r} at horizons $h = 20, \infty$ quarters. All shares are expressed as percentages and are computed using the estimate of the SVAR system (6.1) given in Table 6.1. The decomposition at horizon ∞ corresponds to the unconditional variance decomposition.

30 percent of business-cycle fluctuations in emerging economies is explained by disturbances in external financial variables. These disturbances play an even stronger role in explaining movements in international transactions. In effect, U.S. interest-rate shocks and country-spread shocks are responsible for 44 percent of movements in the trade-balance-to-output ratio in the countries included in the panel.

Variations in country spreads are largely explained by innovations in U.S. interest rates and innovations in the country spreads themselves. Jointly, these two sources of uncertainty account for 85 percent of fluctuations in country spreads. Most of this fraction, about 60 percentage points, is attributed to country-spread shocks. This last result concurs with Eichengreen and Mody (1998), who interpret it as suggesting that arbitrary revisions in investor sentiments play a significant role in explaining the behavior of country spreads.

Table 6.2 extends the forecast-error variance decomposition to horizon-∞ quarters, which, as explained earlier, corresponds to the unconditional variance decomposition. It shows that in the present empirical model, the variance decomposition at forecast horizon-20 quarters is virtually identical to the unconditional variance decomposition.

6.4 An Open Economy Subject to Interest-Rate Shocks

The process of identifying country-spread shocks and U.S. interest-rate shocks involves a number of restrictions on the matrices defining the VAR system (6.1). To assess the plausibility of these restrictions, it is necessary to use the predictions of some theory of the business cycle as a metric. If the estimated shocks imply similar business-cycle fluctuations in the empirical as in theoretical models, we conclude that according to the proposed theory, the identified shocks are plausible.

Accordingly, we assess the plausibility of the identified shocks in four steps. First, we develop a standard model of the business cycle in small open economies. Second, we estimate the deep structural parameters of the model. Third, we feed into the model the estimated version of the fourth and fifth equations of the VAR system (6.1), describing the stochastic laws of motion of the U.S. interest rate and the country spread. Finally, we compare estimated impulse responses (i.e., those shown in Figures 6.2 and 6.3) with those implied by the proposed theoretical framework.

The basis of the theoretical model presented here is a standard small open economy like the one studied in Chapter 4. The results of this section were first obtained in contributions by Neumeyer and Perri (2005) and Uribe and Yue (2006). The exposition follows closely the latter authors.

The model departs from the canonical version of the SOE-RBC model along four dimensions. To be compatible with the assumption that it takes one period for financial shocks to affect output, investment and the trade balance, households make consumption and labor supply decisions prior to the realization of that period's world interest-rate shock and country-spread shock. Thus, innovations in the world interest rate or the country spread are assumed to have allocative effects with a one-period lag. Second, preferences are assumed to feature external habit formation, or "catching up with the Joneses," as in Abel (1990). This feature improves the predictions of the standard model by preventing an excessive contraction in private nonbusiness absorption in response to external financial shocks. Habit formation has been shown to help explain asset prices and business fluctuations in both developed economies (e.g., Boldrin, Christiano, and Fisher 2001) and emerging countries (e.g., Uribe 2002). Third, the process of capital accumulation is assumed to be subject to gestation lags and convex adjustment costs. In combination, these two frictions prevent excessive investment volatility, induce persistence, and allow for the observed nonmonotonic (hump-shaped) response of investment in response to a variety of shocks (Uribe 1997). Fourth, firms are assumed to be subject to a working-capital constraint of the type introduced in Section 5.3.2 of Chapter 5. This constraint introduces a direct supply-side effect of changes in the cost of borrowing in international financial markets and allows the model to predict a more realistic response of domestic output to external financial shocks.

6.4.1 Firms and Working-Capital Constraints

Output, denoted y_t, is produced by means of a production function that takes labor services, h_t, and physical capital, k_t, as inputs:

$$y_t = F(k_t, h_t), \tag{6.2}$$

where the function $F(\cdot, \cdot)$ is assumed to be homogeneous of degree one, increasing in both arguments, and concave. Firms hire labor and capital services from perfectly competitive markets.

The production process is subject to a working-capital constraint that requires firms to hold noninterest-bearing assets to finance a fraction of the wage bill each period. Formally, the working-capital constraint takes the form

$$m_t \geq \eta w_t h_t; \quad \eta \geq 0,$$

where m_t denotes the amount of working capital held by the representative firm in period t, and w_t denotes the wage rate in period t. As shown in Section 5.3.2 of Chapter 5, a working-capital constraint of this type results in the following factor demands by the firm:

$$F_h(k_t, h_t) = w_t \left[1 + \eta \left(\frac{R_t^d - 1}{R_t^d} \right) \right] \tag{6.3}$$

and

$$F_k(k_t, h_t) = u_t, \tag{6.4}$$

where R_t^d denotes the gross interest rate at which the firm can borrow in period t, and u_t denotes the rental rate of capital in period t.

It is clear from the first of these two efficiency conditions that the working-capital constraint distorts the labor market by introducing a wedge between the marginal product of labor and the real wage rate. This distortion is larger the larger the opportunity cost of holding working capital becomes, $(R_t^d - 1)/R_t^d$, and the higher the intensity of the working-capital constraint, η, becomes.

6.4.2 Capital Accumulation and Gestation Lags

The process of capital accumulation displays adjustment costs in the form of gestation lags and convex costs as in Uribe (1997). Producing 1 unit of capital good requires investing 1/4 units of goods for four consecutive periods. Let s_{it} denote the number of investment projects started in $t - i$ for $i = 0, 1, 2, 3$. Then gross investment in period t, denoted i_t, is given by

$$i_t = \frac{1}{4} \sum_{i=0}^{3} s_{it}. \tag{6.5}$$

In turn, the evolution of s_{it} is given by

$$s_{i+1t+1} = s_{it}, \tag{6.6}$$

for $i = 0, 1, 2$. The stock of capital obeys the law of motion

$$k_{t+1} = (1 - \delta)k_t + k_t \Phi \left(\frac{s_{3t}}{k_t} \right), \tag{6.7}$$

where $\delta \in (0, 1)$ denotes the rate of depreciation of physical capital. The process of capital accumulation is assumed to be subject to adjustment costs, as defined by the function Φ, which is assumed to be strictly increasing, concave, and to satisfy $\Phi(\delta) = \delta$ and $\Phi'(\delta) = 1$. These last two assumptions ensure the absence of adjustment costs in the steady state and that the steady-state level of investment is independent of Φ. The introduction of capital adjustment costs is commonplace in models of the small open economy. As discussed in Chapters 3 and 4, adjustment costs are a convenient and plausible way to avoid excessive investment volatility in response to changes in the interest rate faced by the country in international markets.

6.4.3 Households and Habit Formation

The economy is populated by a large number of infinitely-lived households with preferences described by the lifetime utility function

$$E_0 \sum_{t=0}^{\infty} \beta^t U(c_t - \mu \tilde{c}_{t-1}, h_t), \tag{6.8}$$

where c_t denotes consumption in period t, $\tilde{c}_{t-1}$ denotes the cross-sectional average level of consumption in period $t - 1$, and h_t denotes the fraction of time devoted to work in period t. Households take as given the process for $\tilde{c}_t$. The single-period utility index $U(\cdot, \cdot)$ is assumed to be increasing in its first argument, decreasing in its second argument, and concave. The parameter $\beta \in (0, 1)$ denotes a subjective discount factor, and the parameter μ measures the intensity of external habit formation.

Households have access to two types of asset, physical capital and a one-period bond. The capital stock is assumed to be owned entirely by domestic residents. Households have four sources of income: wages, capital rents, profits, and interest income from bond holdings. Each period, households allocate their wealth to purchases of consumption goods, investment goods, and financial assets. The household's period-by-period budget constraint is given by

$$d_t = R_{t-1}d_{t-1} + \Psi(d_t) + c_t + i_t - w_t h_t - u_t k_t - \pi_t, \tag{6.9}$$

where d_t denotes the household's debt position in period t; R_t denotes the gross interest rate; and π_t denotes profit income, which the household takes as given. We assume that households face costs of adjusting their foreign asset position as in Section 4.10.2 of Chapter 4. As discussed there, these adjustment costs represent one way to eliminate the familiar unit root present in SOE models. The portfolio-adjustment cost function $\Psi(\cdot)$ is assumed to be convex and to satisfy $\Psi(\bar{d}) = \Psi'(\bar{d}) = 0$, for some $\bar{d} > 0$.

Households choose consumption, labor supply, and investment one period in advance. Therefore, in period t the variables c_t, h_t, and $s_{i,t}$ ($i = 0, 1, 2, 3$) are predetermined. In period t, the household chooses c_{t+1}, h_{t+1}, $s_{i,t+1}$ ($i = 0, 1, 2, 3$), d_t, and k_{t+1} to maximize the utility function (6.8) subject to the budget constraint (6.9), the laws of motion of investment projects and capital (equations (6.5)–(6.7)), and a borrowing constraint of the form

$$\lim_{j \to \infty} E_t \frac{d_{t+j+1}}{\prod_{s=0}^{j} R_{t+s}} \leq 0 \tag{6.10}$$

that prevents Ponzi schemes. The Lagrangian associated with the household's optimization problem can be written as

$$\mathcal{L} = E_0 \sum_{t=0}^{\infty} \beta^t \left\{ U(c_t - \mu\tilde{c}_{t-1}, h_t) \right.$$

$$+ \lambda_t \left[d_t - R_{t-1}d_{t-1} - \Psi(d_t) + w_t h_t + u_t k_t + \pi_t - \frac{1}{4}\sum_{i=0}^{3} s_{it} - c_t \right]$$

$$+ \lambda_t q_t \left[(1-\delta)k_t + k_t \Phi\left(\frac{s_{3t}}{k_t}\right) - k_{t+1} \right] + \lambda_t \sum_{i=0}^{2} v_{it}(s_{it} - s_{i+1t+1}) \right\},$$

where $\beta^t\lambda_t$, $\beta^t\lambda_t v_{it}$, and $\beta^t\lambda_t q_t$ are the Lagrange multipliers associated with constraints (6.9), (6.6), and (6.7), respectively. The optimality conditions associated with the household's problem are (6.6), (6.7), (6.9), (6.10) holding with equality, and

$$E_t\lambda_{t+1} = U_c(c_{t+1} - \mu\tilde{c}_t, h_{t+1}), \tag{6.11}$$

$$E_t[w_{t+1}\lambda_{t+1}] = -U_h(c_{t+1} - \mu\tilde{c}_t, h_{t+1}), \tag{6.12}$$

$$\lambda_t\left[1 - \Psi'(d_t)\right] = \beta R_t E_t\lambda_{t+1}, \tag{6.13}$$

$$E_t\lambda_{t+1}v_{0t+1} = \frac{1}{4}E_t\lambda_{t+1}, \tag{6.14}$$

$$\beta E_t\lambda_{t+1}v_{1t+1} = \frac{\beta}{4}E_t\lambda_{t+1} + \lambda_t v_{0t}, \tag{6.15}$$

$$\beta E_t\lambda_{t+1}v_{2t+1} = \frac{\beta}{4}E_t\lambda_{t+1} + \lambda_t v_{1t}, \tag{6.16}$$

$$\beta E_t\left[\lambda_{t+1}q_{t+1}\Phi'\left(\frac{s_{3t+1}}{k_{t+1}}\right)\right] = \frac{\beta}{4}E_t\lambda_{t+1} + \lambda_t v_{2t}, \tag{6.17}$$

and

$$\lambda_t q_t = \beta E_t\left\{\lambda_{t+1}q_{t+1}\left[1 - \delta + \Phi\left(\frac{s_{3t+1}}{k_{t+1}}\right) - \frac{s_{3t+1}}{k_{t+1}}\Phi'\left(\frac{s_{3t+1}}{k_{t+1}}\right)\right] + \lambda_{t+1}u_{t+1}\right\}. \tag{6.18}$$

It is important to recall that, because of the assumed information structure, the variables c_{t+1}, h_{t+1}, and s_{0t+1} all reside in the information set of period t. Equation (6.11) states that in period t, households choose consumption and leisure for period $t + 1$ in such a way as to equate the marginal utility of consumption in period $t + 1$ to the expected marginal utility of wealth in that period, $E_t\lambda_{t+1}$. In general, the marginal utility of wealth will differ from the marginal utility of consumption ($\lambda_t \neq U_c(c_t - \mu\tilde{c}_{t-1}, h_t)$), because current consumption cannot react to unanticipated changes in wealth. Because of the presence of external habit formation, when households observe that their neighbors (the Joneses) increase current consumption, $\tilde{c}_t$, they wake up hungrier in period $t + 1$, which is reflected in a higher marginal utility of consumption. Equation (6.12) defines the household's labor supply schedule, by equating the marginal disutility of effort in period $t + 1$ to the expected utility value of the wage rate in that period.

Equation (6.13) is an asset pricing relation equating the intertemporal marginal rate of substitution in consumption to the rate of return on financial assets. As discussed in Section 4.10.2 of Chapter 4, because of the presence of frictions to adjust bond holdings, the relevant rate of return on this type of asset is not simply the market rate R_t but rather the shadow rate of return:

$$R_t^d \equiv \frac{R_t}{1 - \Psi'(d_t)}. \tag{6.19}$$

Intuitively, when the household's debt position is, say, above its steady-state level $\bar{d}$, we have that $\Psi'(d_t) > 0$, so that the shadow rate of return is higher than the market rate of return, providing further incentives for households to save, thereby reducing their debt positions.

Equations (6.14)–(6.16) show how to price investment projects at different stages of completion. The price of an investment project in its ith quarter of gestation equals the price of a project in the $(i-1)$th quarter of gestation plus 1/4 units of goods. Equation (6.17) links the cost of producing a unit of capital to the shadow price of installed capital, or Tobin's Q, q_t. Finally, equation (6.18) is a pricing condition for physical capital. It equates the revenue from selling one unit of capital today, q_t, to the discounted value of renting the unit of capital for one period and then selling it, $u_{t+1} + q_{t+1}$, net of depreciation and adjustment costs.

6.4.4 Driving Forces

One advantage of limited information methods like the one used by Uribe and Yue (2006) to assess the plausibility of the identified U.S. interest-rate shocks and country-spread shocks is that one need not feed into the model shocks other than those whose effects are of interest. Accordingly, all that is needed to close the model is to add a law of motion for the country interest rate R_t. We use the estimate of the bottom equation of the VAR system (6.1) presented in Table 6.1, which we reproduce here for convenience:

$$\widehat{R}_t = 0.635\widehat{R}_{t-1} + 0.501\widehat{R}_t^{us} + 0.355\widehat{R}_{t-1}^{us} - 0.791\widehat{y}_t + 0.617\widehat{y}_{t-1}$$

$$+ 0.114\widehat{\imath}_t - 0.122\widehat{\imath}_{t-1} + 0.288tby_t - 0.190tby_{t-1} + \epsilon_t^r, \tag{6.20}$$

where ϵ_t^r is an i.i.d. disturbance with mean zero and standard deviation 0.031. As indicated earlier, the variable tby_t stands for the trade-balance-to-GDP ratio and is given by:[5]

$$tby_t = \frac{y_t - c_t - i_t - \Psi(d_t)}{y_t}. \tag{6.21}$$

Because the process for the country interest rate defined by equation (6.20) involves the world interest rate, R_t^{us}, which is assumed to be an exogenous random variable, we

---

5. Because the portfolio-adjustment cost $\Psi(d_t)$ is incurred by households, the national income and product accounts would measure private consumption as $c_t + \Psi(d_t)$ and not simply as c_t. However, because of our assumption that $\Psi(\bar{d}) = \Psi'(\bar{d}) = 0$, it follows that $c_t + \Psi(d_t) = c_t$ up to first order.

must also include this variable's law of motion as part of the set of equations defining the equilibrium behavior of the theoretical model. Accordingly, the model includes the equation

$$\widehat{R}_t^{us} = 0.830\widehat{R}_{t-1}^{us} + \epsilon_t^{rus},\tag{6.22}$$

where ϵ_t^{rus} is an i.i.d. innovation with mean zero and standard deviation 0.007.

6.4.5 Equilibrium

In equilibrium all households consume identical quantities. Thus, individual consumption equals average consumption across households, or

$$c_t = \tilde{c}_t,\tag{6.23}$$

for $t \geq 0$. The resource constraint of the economy is given by

$$d_t = R_{t-1}d_{t-1} + \Psi(d_t) + c_t + i_t - y_t.\tag{6.24}$$

The derivation of this constraint combines the steps described in Section 4.10.2 of Chapter 4 and in Section 5.3.2 of Chapter 5.

An equilibrium is a set of processes $c_{t+1}, \tilde{c}_t, h_{t+1}, d_t, i_t, k_{t+1}, s_{it+1}$ ($i = 0, 1, 2, 3$), R_t, $R_t^d, R_t^{us}, w_t, u_t, y_t, tby_t, \lambda_t, q_t$, and v_{it} ($i = 0, 1, 2$), for $t \geq 0$, satisfying conditions (6.2)–(6.7) and (6.11)–(6.24), given $c_0, y_{-1}, i_{-1}, h_0, k_0, d_{-1}, tby_{-1}, R_{-1}$, and R_{-1}^{us}, and the processes for the exogenous innovations ϵ_t^{rus} and ϵ_t^r. An equilibrium also requires the satisfaction of the no-Ponzi-game constraint (6.10) with equality. The analysis that follows restricts attention to equilibria in which all variables remain in a small neighborhood of their respective deterministic steady states, which guarantees that this condition is met.

6.4.6 Estimation by Limited Information Methods

The parameterization of the model combines calibration and econometric estimation. We adopt the following standard functional forms for preferences, technology, capital adjustment costs, and portfolio adjustment costs:

$$U(c - \mu\tilde{c}, h) = \frac{\left[c - \mu\tilde{c} - \omega^{-1}h^\omega\right]^{1-\gamma} - 1}{1 - \gamma},$$

$$F(k, h) = k^\alpha h^{1-\alpha},$$

$$\Phi(x) = x - \frac{\phi}{2}(x - \delta)^2; \quad \phi > 0,$$

and

$$\Psi(d) = \frac{\psi}{2}(d - \bar{d})^2.$$

The parameterization of the model follows Uribe and Yue (2006). The model has ten parameters, six of which are calibrated, and the remaining four are econometrically estimated. The time unit is meant to be one quarter. We set $\gamma = 2$, $\omega = 1.455$, and $\alpha = 0.32$. The steady-state real interest rate faced by the small economy in international financial markets is set to 11 percent per year. This value is consistent with an average U.S. interest rate of about 4 percent and an average country premium of 7 percent, both of which are in line with actual data. The depreciation rate is set to 0.025, or 10 percent per year, which is a standard value in business-cycle studies. We impose the restriction $\beta R = 1$. Finally, the steady-state trade-balance-to-GDP ratio, tby, is set to 2 percent, which together with the other parameter values implies a value of $\overline{d}$ of 0.1881.

There remain four parameters to assign values to: ψ, ϕ, η, and μ. Because there exist no available estimates for those parameters for emerging economies, Uribe and Yue (2006) estimate them using a limited information approach. The estimation procedure consists of choosing values for these four parameters to minimize the distance between the estimated impulse response functions shown in Figures 6.2 and 6.3 and the corresponding theoretical impulse response functions implied by the model. The procedure matches the first 24 quarters of the impulse response functions of four variables (output, investment, the trade balance, and the country interest rate) to two shocks (the U.S. interest-rate shock and the country-spread shock). Thus, four parameter values are picked to match $185 (= 4 \times 2 \times 24 - 7)$ points. Seven degrees of freedom are lost, because the impact effects of both U.S. interest-rate shocks and country-spread shocks on output, investment, and the trade balance are by construction zero, and the impact effect of a unit country-spread shock on the country spread itself is unity. Formally, let IR^e denote the 185×1 vector of estimated impulse response functions, and $IR^m(\psi, \phi, \eta, \mu)$ denote the corresponding vector of impulse response functions implied by the theoretical model, which are functions of the four parameters to be estimated. Then (ψ, ϕ, η, μ) are estimated as

$$\arg \min_{\{\psi, \phi, \eta, \mu\}} [IR^e - IR^m(\psi, \phi, \eta, \mu)]' \Sigma_{IR^e}^{-1} [IR^e - IR^m(\psi, \phi, \eta, \mu)],$$

where Σ_{IR^e} is a diagonal matrix containing the variance of the empirical impulse response functions along the diagonal. This matrix penalizes those elements of the estimated impulse response functions associated with large error intervals. The resulting parameter estimates are $\psi = 0.00042$, $\phi = 72.8$, $\eta = 1.2$, and $\mu = 0.20$. The implied portfolio adjustment costs are small. For example, a 10 percent increase in d_t over its steady-state value $\overline{d}$ maintained over 1 year has a resource cost of 4×10^{-6} percent of annual GDP. In contrast, capital adjustment costs are more significant. For instance, starting in a steady-state situation, a 10 percent increase in investment for 1 year produces an increase in the capital stock of 0.88 percent. In the absence of capital adjustment costs, the capital stock would increase by 0.96 percent. The estimated value of η implies that firms maintain a level of working capital equivalent to about 3.6 months of wage payments. The estimated value of η is in line with the 0.4 value estimated on annual data in Chapter 5, which implies that firms hold on average 4.8 months of the payroll in working capital. Finally, the estimated degree of habit formation is modest compared to the values typically used to explain asset-price regularities in closed economies (e.g., Constantinides 1990). Table 6.3 gathers all parameter values.

Table 6.3   Parameter Values

Symbol	Value	Description
Calibrated parameters		
$R - 1 = \beta^{-1} - 1$	2.77%	Steady-state real country interest rate (quarterly)
γ	2	Inverse of intertemporal elasticity of substitution
ω	1.455	$1/(\omega - 1) =$ Labor supply elasticity
α	0.32	Capital elasticity of output
δ	0.025	Depreciation rate (quarterly)
$\bar{d}$	0.1881	Steady-state debt
Estimated parameters		
ϕ	72.8	Capital adjustment cost parameter
ψ	0.00042	Portfolio adjustment cost parameter
η	1.20	Fraction of wage bill subject to working-capital constraint
μ	0.20	Habit formation parameter

6.5 Theoretical and Estimated Impulse Responses

Figure 6.8 depicts impulse response functions for output, investment, the trade-balance-to-GDP ratio, and the country interest rate. The left column shows impulse responses to a U.S. interest-rate shock (ϵ_t^{rus}), and the right column shows impulse responses to a country-spread shock (ϵ_t^r). Dark solid lines display empirical impulse response functions, and dashed lines depict the associated two-standard-error bands. This information is reproduced from Figures 6.2 and 6.3. Gray solid lines depict theoretical impulse response functions.

The model replicates three key qualitative features of the estimated impulse response functions. First, output and investment contract in response to both a U.S. interest-rate shock and a country-spread shock. Second, the trade balance improves in response to both shocks. Third, the country interest rate displays a hump-shaped response to an innovation in the U.S. interest rate. These findings suggest that the scheme used to identify the parameters of the VAR system (6.1) is successful in isolating country-spread shocks and U.S. interest-rate shocks from the data.

6.6 Theoretical and Estimated Conditional Volatilities

Another way to ascertain whether the U.S. interest-rate shocks and country-spread shocks identified via the VAR analysis are plausible is to gauge the ability of the theoretical model to match the conditional standard deviations of the endogenous variables due to these two structural shocks implied by the VAR. This approach is related to the impulse response analysis of Section 6.5, because the conditional variance of any variable is given by the sum of its squared impulse response to the shock in question scaled by the variance of the shock itself.

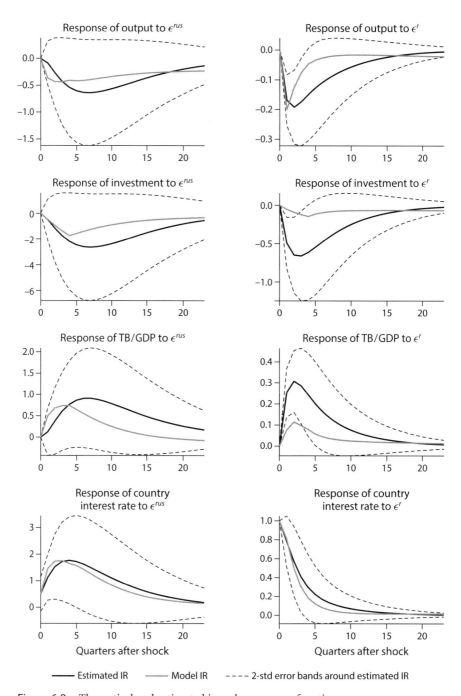

Figure 6.8   Theoretical and estimated impulse response functions.

Source: Uribe and Yue (2006).
Nots: The first column displays impulse responses to a U.S. interest-rate shock (ϵ^{rus}), and the second column displays impulse responses to a country-spread shock (ϵ^{r}). The Matlab replication program for the theoretical impulse response functions is `uribe_yue_run.m`.

Table 6.4 Conditional Volatilities Implied by the SVAR and Theoretical Models

| | ϵ_t^{rus} | | ϵ_t^{r} | | Unconditional |
Variable	SVAR	Theory	SVAR	Theory	SVAR
$\widehat{y}$	1.5	1.6	1.3	1.3	3.7
$\widehat{\imath}$	6.4	3.6	5.0	2.0	14.2
tby	2.1	1.6	2.0	0.9	4.4
$\widehat{R}^{us}$	1.3	1.3	0	0	1.3
$\widehat{R}$	3.8	3.5	4.7	4.4	6.5

Notes: The first two columns display standard deviations conditional on U.S. interest-rate shocks (ϵ_t^{rus}), and the next two columns display standard deviations conditional on country-spread shocks (ϵ_t^{r}). The fifth column displays unconditional standard deviations implied by the SVAR model. The variables $\widehat{y}_t$ and $\widehat{\imath}_t$ are measured in percentage deviations from steady state; tby_t, $\widehat{R}_t^{us}$, and $\widehat{R}_t$ are measured in percentage point deviations from their respective steady states. Interest rates are annualized.

Table 6.4 displays standard deviations conditional on U.S. interest-rate shocks (ϵ_t^{rus}) and country-spread shocks (ϵ_t^{r}) implied by the empirical SVAR model and the theoretical SOE model. The SOE model does well at capturing the importance of U.S. interest-rate and country-spread shocks in explaining movements in output and country interest rates. The model also does a satisfactory job accounting for variations in the trade balance due to U.S. interest-rate shocks. But the SOE model systematically underpredicts the volatilities of investment and the trade balance caused by country-spread shocks.

The last column of the table shows unconditional volatilities implied by the SVAR model. Comparing these volatilities with the conditional volatilities predicted by the SOE model (columns 2 and 4) shows that the two identified shocks jointly explain 30 percent of fluctuations in output (($(1.6^2 + 1.3^2)/3.7^2 = 0.31$). This number is close to the one implied by the SVAR model (($(1.5^2 + 1.3^2)/3.7^2 = 0.29$). However, the SOE model assigns less importance to the two interest-rate shocks in accounting for variations in investment and the trade balance than does the SVAR model (17% versus 33% and 8% versus 43%, respectively).

Overall, the results of this analysis suggest that the two interest-rate shocks (ϵ_t^{rus} and ϵ_t^{r}) identified by the SVAR model are sensible and economically important.

6.7 Global Risk Factors and Business Cycles in Emerging Economies

Thus far, we have studied how movements of a risk-free measure of global financial conditions (the real Treasury bill rate) and a measure of country-specific risk (embodied in country spreads) affect business cycles in emerging markets.[6] The analysis has abstracted from other global financial factors that are potentially important for understanding aggregate fluctuations in the developing world. One such factor is given by variations in global risk premia.

Akinci (2013) fills in this gap by expanding the SVAR model of Uribe and Yue (2006) to include the spread between the U.S. Baa corporate borrowing rate and the 20-year U.S. Treasury bond yield. Baa bonds are debt obligations issued by U.S. corporations with a medium degree of risk. To form an idea of the relative risk involved in this type of security, we note that the rating agency Moody's rates corporate bonds on a letter scale ranging from Aaa to C. Historically, the cumulative default rate over 20 years is less than 1 percent for Aaa rated bonds, more than 70 percent for C rated bonds, and 13 percent for Baa rated bonds (Fons, Cantor, and Mahoney 2002). Thus, the Baa corporate bond spread is the difference between the return on securities with medium default risk and securities with negligible default risk (Treasury bonds). An increase in the Baa corporate bond spread may reflect an elevated risk of default in the U.S. corporate sector or changes in market participants' attitudes toward this type of risk. The present analysis asks how variations in this global risk premium transmit to the real and financial sectors of emerging economies.

The expanded SVAR specification is

$$
A \begin{bmatrix} \widehat{y}_t \\ \widehat{\imath}_t \\ tby_t \\ \widehat{R}_t^{us} \\ \widehat{S}_t^{us} \\ \widehat{R}_t \end{bmatrix} = B(L) \begin{bmatrix} \widehat{y}_{t-1} \\ \widehat{\imath}_{t-1} \\ tby_{t-1} \\ \widehat{R}_{t-1}^{us} \\ \widehat{S}_{t-1}^{us} \\ \widehat{R}_{t-1} \end{bmatrix} + \begin{bmatrix} \epsilon_t^y \\ \epsilon_t^i \\ \epsilon_t^{tby} \\ \epsilon_t^{rus} \\ \epsilon_t^{sus} \\ \epsilon_t^r \end{bmatrix},
$$

where S_t^{us} denotes the U.S. risk premium as measured by the Baa corporate bond spread, and ϵ_t^{sus} denotes an innovation to the U.S. risk premium. The SVAR is of order 2, that is, $B(L) \equiv B_1 + B_2 L$, where B_1 and B_2 are 6×6 matrices of coefficients, and L denotes the lag operator. The identification scheme follows Uribe and Yue (2006) by imposing the condition that the matrix A be lower triangular. In addition, the block $[R_t^{us} \ S_t^{us}]'$ is assumed to follow a bivariate system. Akinci estimates the SVAR using a panel containing six countries (Argentina, Brazil, Mexico, Peru, South Africa, and Turkey) using quarterly data from 1994:Q1 to 2011:Q3.

The main result stemming from this estimation is that financial shocks—that is, the triplet $[\epsilon_t^{rus} \ \epsilon_t^{sus} \ \epsilon_t^r]$—play an even larger role than before in explaining business cycles in emerging countries. Jointly, these three shocks explain 42 percent of the variance of output, compared to 30 percent under the specification that omits global risk-premium shocks. This result reinforces the findings of Uribe and Yue (2006) reported earlier in this chapter.

---

6. Strictly speaking, the real Treasury bill rate is not risk free. The nominal rate of return on Treasury bills can be considered risk free, because the probability that the U.S. government will default on this type of obligation is perceived to be nil. The realized real rate of return on Treasury bills is the difference between the nominal rate of return and realized inflation. Because inflation has an unpredictable component, so does the real rate.

The main difference that emerges when global risk-premium shocks are taken explicitly into account is that they absorb much of the role that was previously assigned to the U.S. interest-rate shock. In particular, under the present SVAR specification, ϵ_t^{sus} explains 18 percent of the variance of output, whereas ϵ_t^{rus} explains only 6 percent, down from 17 percent in the specification without global risk-premium shocks.

The global risk factor also takes over the role previously played by the U.S. interest rate in driving country spreads. Under the present formulation, ϵ_t^{sus} explains 18 percent of movements in country spreads, whereas ϵ_t^{rus} explains only 5 percent, about 20 percentage points less than under the specification without global risk-premium shocks. One channel through which global risk-premium shocks affect real activity is through movements in country spreads. A 1 percentage point increase in the global risk premium leads to an increase in the country spread of 1.3 percentage points.

———

This chapter documents the importance of interest-rate shocks as drivers of business cycles in emerging markets. This source of uncertainty—whether stemming from movements in the risk-free U.S. interest rate, from elevated risk premia in the U.S. corporate sector, or from innovations in emerging-country spreads—accounts for more than one-third of the variance of output. In Chapters 9–13 we analyze how nominal and financial frictions propagate and amplify interest-rate shocks.

6.8 Exercises

6.1 (Countercyclical Interest-Rate Shocks) Consider a two-period small open endowment economy. Household preferences are given by

$$\log c_1 + \log c_2,$$

where c_1 and c_2 denote consumption in periods 1 and 2, respectively. Let y_1 and y_2 denote the endowments in periods 1 and 2, respectively. Households enter period 1 with zero net foreign assets, $d_0 = 0$. Assume free international capital mobility. The world interest rate is r^*, and households are subject to a no-Ponzi-game constraint of the form $d_2 \leq 0$, where d_t for $t = 1, 2$ denotes one-period debt assumed in period t and due in $t + 1$.

1. Write down the household's budget constraints in periods 1 and 2.
2. Derive the household's intertemporal budget constraint.
3. Write down the household's utility maximization problem.
4. Characterize the equilibrium allocation of consumption and the trade balance in periods 1 and 2.
5. Now assume that in period 1 the economy is hit by a negative (and purely temporary) endowment shock. Find the change in consumption and the trade balance in period 1. Is the response of the trade balance in period 1 pro- or countercyclical? Explain your findings.
6. As documented earlier in this chapter, in emerging economies the country interest rate tends to be countercyclical. To reflect this regularity, assume now that when y_1

falls, r^* increases. Let $\eta \equiv -d \ln(1 + r^*)/(d \ln y_1)$ denote the elasticity of the gross interest rate with respect to the period-1 endowment. Find conditions, in terms of η, y_1, y_2, and r^*, that guarantee that consumption moves procyclically and the trade balance moves countercyclically in period 1 in response to a period-1 endowment shock. Provide intuitive explanations for your findings.

6.2 (Interest-Rate Shocks, Investment, and the Trade Balance) Consider a two-period small open economy populated by a large number of households with preferences given by

$$\ln c_1 + \ln c_2,$$

where c_1 and c_2 denote consumption in periods 1 and 2, respectively, and as usual, ln denotes the natural logarithm. Households start period 1 with a zero net asset position. They have no endowments in either period but can produce goods in period 2 by operating the technology

$$y_2 = A\sqrt{i_1},$$

where y_2 denotes output in period 2, $A > 0$ is a productivity factor, and i_1 denotes investment in period 1. In period 1, households can participate in the international financial market, where the interest rate is r. They are subject to a no-Ponzi-game constraint of the form $d_2 \leq 0$, where d_t, for $t = 1, 2$, denotes one-period debt assumed in period t and maturing in period $t + 1$.

1. Write down the household's budget constraints in periods 1 and 2.
2. Derive the household's intertemporal budget constraint.
3. State the household's maximization problem.
4. Compute the equilibrium values of consumption, investment, the trade balance, the current account, and external debt in periods 1 and 2.
5. Suppose now that the interest rate increases to $r' > r$. Characterize the effect of this shock on investment and the trade balance in period 1. Is it qualitatively in line with the related SVAR evidence examined in this chapter? Explain.
6. Suppose that in period 1 agents learn that a positive productivity shock elevates A to $A' > A$. Analyze the effect of this innovation on the equilibrium levels of investment and the trade balance in period 1. How does this effect relate to the SVAR evidence studied in this chapter?

6.3 (An Economy with Periodic Interest-Rate Shocks) A perfect-foresight small open economy is inhabited by identical consumers with preferences of the form

$$\sum_{t=0}^{\infty} \beta^t \ln c_t,$$

where c_t denotes consumption of a perishable good, and $\beta \in (0, 1)$ denotes the discount factor. Households are subject to the budget constraint

$$d_t = (1 + r_{t-1})d_{t-1} + c_t - y$$

for $t \geq 0$, where d_t denotes one-period debt acquired in period t and maturing in $t + 1$, r_t denotes the interest paid on d_t, and y denotes a constant endowment of consumption goods received each period. Households are subject to the no-Ponzi-game constraint

$$\lim_{t \to \infty} \frac{d_t}{\prod_{s=0}^{t}(1 + r_s)} \leq 0.$$

The initial stock of debt, d_{-1}, is nil. The interest rate is time varying and given by

$$r_t = \begin{cases} r^H & \text{for } t = 0, 2, 4, \ldots \\ r^L & \text{for } t = 1, 3, 5, \ldots, \end{cases}$$

where r^L and r^H are parameters satisfying $0 < r^L < r^H$, and

$$\beta\sqrt{(1 + r^H)(1 + r^L)} = 1.$$

1. Derive the equilibrium path of consumption as a function of the structural parameters of the model: y, r^H, r^L, and β. Discuss its cyclical properties.
2. Characterize the equilibrium behavior of the trade balance, the current account, and external debt.
3. Discuss the macroeconomic effects of the assumed interest-rate variations.

6.4 (Interest-Rate Uncertainty) Consider a two-period economy inhabited by a large number of identical households with preferences described by the utility function

$$\ln C_1 + \ln C_2,$$

where C_1 and C_2 denote consumption in periods 1 and 2, respectively. Households are endowed with $Q > 0$ units of consumption goods each period, and start period 1 with no assets or debt carried over from the past. In period 1, households can borrow or lend by means of a bond, denoted B, that pays the world interest rate, denoted r^*. Assume that $r^* = 0$. The household is subject to a no-Ponzi-game constraint that prevents it from holding any debt at the end of period 2.

1. Write down the budget constraint of the household in periods 1 and 2.
2. Derive the household's intertemporal budget constraint.
3. Use the intertemporal budget constraint to eliminate C_2 from the utility function.
4. Derive the optimal levels of consumption in periods 1 and 2 as functions of exogenous parameters only. Derive the equilibrium levels of the trade balance and the current account.
5. Provide intuition.

Now assume that the world interest rate is not known with certainty in period 1; that is, the one-period bond carries a floating rate. Specifically, assume that r^* is given by

$$r^* = \begin{cases} \sigma & \text{with probability } 1/2 \\ -\sigma & \text{with probability } 1/2, \end{cases}$$

where $\sigma \in (0, 1)$ is a parameter. In this economy, financial markets are incomplete, because agents have access to a single bond in period 1. Preferences are described by the utility function

$$\ln C_1 + E_1 \ln C_2,$$

where E_1 denotes the mathematical expectations operator conditional on information available in period 1. The present economy nests the no-uncertainty economy described above as a special case in which $\sigma = 0$.

6. Write down the household's budget constraint in periods 1 and 2. To this end, let C_2^1 and C_2^2 denote consumption in period 2 when the world interest rate is σ and $-\sigma$, respectively. Note that the budget constraint in period 2 is state contingent.

7. Write down the household's intertemporal budget constraint. This is also a state-contingent object.

8. Derive the optimality conditions associated with the household's problem.

9. Show whether the equilibrium level of consumption in period 1 is greater than, less than, or equal to the one that arises when $\sigma = 0$.

10. Find the sign of the trade balance in equilibrium. Compare your answer to the one for the case $\sigma = 0$ and provide intuition. In particular, discuss why a mean-preserving increase in interest-rate uncertainty affects the trade balance in period 1 the way it does.

11. Are the results obtained above due to the particular (logarithmic) preference specification considered? To address this question, show that all the results obtained above continue to hold under a more general class of preferences, namely, the class of CRRA preferences

$$\frac{C_1^{1-\gamma} - 1}{1 - \gamma} + E_1 \frac{C_2^{1-\gamma} - 1}{1 - \gamma},$$

for $\gamma > 0$, which encompasses the log specification as a special case when $\gamma \to 1$.

12. Finally, show that interest-rate uncertainty does have real effects when the desired asset position in the absence of uncertainty is nonzero. To this end, return to the log preference specification and assume that the endowment in period 1 is zero and that the endowment in period 2 is $Q > 0$. How does the trade balance in period 1 compare under no uncertainty ($\sigma = 0$) and under uncertainty ($\sigma > 0$)?

6.5 (Inducing Stationarity and Interest-Rate Shocks) Chapter 4 shows that the business cycle implied by the SOE-RBC model is not affected by the method used to induce stationarity.

This result, however, was derived in the context of a model driven by technology shocks. The present exercise aims to establish whether this finding is robust to assuming that business cycles are driven by world interest-rate shocks.

1. Consider the external debt-elastic interest-rate (EDEIR) model of Section 4.1.1 of Chapter 4. Shut down the productivity shock by setting $\widetilde{\eta} = 0$. Replace equation (4.14) with

$$r_t = r_t^* + p(\widetilde{d}_t),$$

and

$$r_t^* = r^* + \xi(r_{t-1}^* - r^*) + \mu_t,$$

where $\mu_t \sim N(0, \sigma_\mu^2)$. Set $\xi = 0.8$ and $\sigma_\mu = 0.012$. Calibrate all other parameters of the model using the values given in Table 4.1. Using this version of the EDEIR model, compute the statistics considered in Table 4.4 and make a table. Make a figure showing impulse responses of output, consumption, hours, investment, the trade-balance-to-output ratio, and the current-account-to-output ratio implied by the EDEIR model driven by interest-rate shocks. Provide intuition for these results.

2. Now consider the internal discount factor (IDF) model of Section 4.10.4. Again, set $\widetilde{\eta} = 0$. Replace the assumption that $r_t = r^*$ with

$$r_t = r^* + \xi(r_{t-1} - r^*) + \mu_t.$$

Calibrate ξ, σ_μ, and all common parameters as in the previous question. Calibrate ψ_3 as in Section 4.10.4. Use the resulting calibrated model to compute unconditional second moments and impulse responses. Provide intuition for your results. To facilitate comparison, place the information generated here in the same table and figure produced in the previous question.

3. Compare the predictions of the EDEIR and IDF models driven by interest rate shocks. Does the stationarity-inducing mechanism make any difference for the business cycles implied by the SOE model driven by interest-rate shocks?

7

Importable Goods, Exportable Goods, and the Terms of Trade

Thus far we have studied models with a single traded good. This good is produced, consumed, sometimes imported, and sometimes exported. In reality, however, countries produce, consume, and trade in different goods. For example, Chile's exports are dominated by copper, but copper represents a small fraction of Chile's consumption or imports. Similarly, Norway's exports consist primarily of petroleum, whereas its imports are mostly manufactured goods. Thus for most countries it makes sense to think separately about importable and exportable goods. An *importable good* is either an imported good or a good that is produced domestically but is highly substitutable with a good that can be imported. An *exportable good* is either an exported good or a good that is sold domestically but is highly substitutable with a good that can be exported.

And there is a third category of goods, known as *nontradables,* that are neither imported nor exported. Nontradables are exclusively produced and consumed domestically. Personal services, utilities, and local transportation are classic examples of nontradable goods. Transportation costs are an important factor in determining the tradability of goods and services. For example, Engel and Rogers (1996) show empirically that distance is a key · determinant of price differences across cities. Few New Yorkers would travel to New Delhi just to get (import) a haircut because it is much cheaper there. Other factors causing goods to become nontradable include trade barriers, such as tariffs and quotas. In this regard, Engel and Rogers (1996) show that after controlling for distance, the existence of a national border between two cities greatly increases price differences.

The above three categories of goods give rise to important relative prices. The relative price of exportables in terms of importables is known as the *terms of trade.* And the relative price of a domestic consumption basket in terms of a foreign consumption basket is known as the *real exchange rate.* Movements in these relative prices are often considered important determinants of production, consumption, and employment. For example, a drop in the world price of copper can have significant negative consequences for domestic consumption and sectoral employment in Chile. Similarly, a country that suffers a contraction in aggregate demand due, for example, to an increase in the world interest rate, may experience a fall in the real exchange rate as weak domestic demand

216

depresses the relative price of nontradables. For this reason, movements in the terms of trade and the real exchange rate have been the subject of much empirical and theoretical investigation.

In the present chapter, we analyze the macroeconomic effects of movements in the terms of trade in the context of an economy with importable and exportable goods. In Chapter 8, we add nontraded goods to the picture and analyze the equilibrium determination of the real exchange rate.

7.1 A Simple Empirical Model of the Terms of Trade

The terms of trade are defined as the relative price of exports in terms of imports. Letting P_t^x and P_t^m denote, respectively, indices of world prices of exports and imports for a particular country, the terms of trade for that country are given by

$$tot_t \equiv \frac{P_t^x}{P_t^m}.$$

The typical emerging country is a small player in the world markets for the goods it exports and imports. It therefore makes sense to assume that the emerging country takes the terms of trade as exogenously given.[1] Thus variations in the terms of trade can be regarded as an exogenous source of aggregate fluctuations. Accordingly, we postulate that the terms of trade follow a univariate autoregressive process of the form

$$\widehat{tot}_t = \rho \, \widehat{tot}_{t-1} + \pi \epsilon_t^{tot}, \tag{7.1}$$

where $\widehat{tot}_t$ denotes the log-deviation of the terms of trade from trend, ϵ_t^{tot} is an i.i.d. innovation with mean zero and unit standard deviation, $\rho \in (-1, 1)$ denotes the serial correlation of the cyclical component of the terms of trade, and π denotes the standard deviation of the innovation in the terms-of-trade process.

We estimate equation (7.1) by OLS using annual data from 51 poor and emerging countries over the period 1980–2011.[2] The cyclical component of the terms of trade, $\widehat{tot}_t$, is obtained by removing a log-quadratic time trend.[3] The estimation is performed by OLS country by country, including an intercept (not shown). Table 7.1 displays country-by-country estimates of ρ and π and the associated R-squares. The cross-country

---

1. Exercise 7.1 asks you to econometrically test this hypothesis.
2. The data come from the World Bank's World Development Indicators database and is available in the file `data_annual.xls` posted with the materials for Chapter 1 on the book's Web site via http://press.princeton .edu/titles/11032.html. The series name is "net barter terms of trade index (2000=100)," and the series code is TT.PRI.MRCH.XD.WD. The time and cross-sectional dimensions of the sample are dictated by the requirement of at least 30 consecutive years of data. The countries included in the sample are Algeria, Argentina, Bolivia, Botswana, Brazil, Burundi, Cameroon, Central African Republic, Chile, China, Colombia, Comoros, Congo, Costa Rica, Côte d'Ivoire, Dominican Republic, Ecuador, Egypt, El Salvador, Ghana, Guatemala, Honduras, India, Indonesia, Jordan, Kenya, Madagascar, Malaysia, Mauritania, Mauritius, Mexico, Morocco, Mozambique, Namibia, Pakistan, Paraguay, Peru, Philippines, Rwanda, Senegal, South Africa, South Korea, Sudan, Thailand, Tunisia, Turkey, Uganda, Uruguay, Venezuela, Zambia, and Zimbabwe. The sample excludes Bangladesh, Gabon, Gambia, Lesotho, Panama, and Swaziland, countries for which the terms-of-trade data appear to be faulty.
3. Exercise 7.2 investigates detrending the terms of trade by HP filtering.

Table 7.1   Terms-of-Trade Process: Country-by-Country Estimates

Country	ρ	π	R^2
Algeria	0.43	0.20	0.18
Argentina	0.41	0.08	0.19
Bolivia	0.52	0.08	0.29
Botswana	0.52	0.06	0.33
Brazil	0.53	0.08	0.31
Burundi	0.59	0.17	0.34
Cameroon	−0.05	0.13	0.00
Central African Republic	0.86	0.09	0.71
Chile	0.61	0.09	0.38
China	0.75	0.05	0.61
Colombia	0.29	0.08	0.08
Comoros	0.33	0.15	0.11
Congo, Dem. Rep.	0.41	0.14	0.17
Costa Rica	0.53	0.07	0.30
Côte d'Ivoire	0.46	0.16	0.22
Dominican Republic	0.44	0.09	0.19
Ecuador	0.26	0.09	0.07
Egypt, Arab Rep.	0.70	0.09	0.50
El Salvador	0.32	0.13	0.12
Ghana	0.17	0.09	0.03
Guatemala	−0.43	0.11	0.19
Honduras	0.55	0.10	0.32
India	0.63	0.09	0.38
Indonesia	0.55	0.11	0.30
Jordan	0.48	0.08	0.22
Kenya	0.66	0.07	0.52
Madagascar	0.65	0.09	0.43
Malaysia	0.51	0.05	0.27
Mauritania	0.61	0.08	0.39
Mauritius	0.57	0.05	0.40
Mexico	0.78	0.09	0.60
Morocco	0.41	0.06	0.17
Mozambique	0.54	0.08	0.32
Namibia	0.53	0.08	0.26
Pakistan	0.61	0.08	0.39
Paraguay	0.40	0.12	0.15
Peru	0.52	0.08	0.27
Philippines	0.53	0.08	0.35
Rwanda	0.43	0.22	0.19
Senegal	0.75	0.09	0.50
South Africa	0.74	0.04	0.53
South Korea	0.69	0.05	0.41
Sudan	0.61	0.09	0.40
Thailand	0.55	0.04	0.34
Tunisia	0.74	0.03	0.55
Turkey	0.32	0.05	0.11
Uganda	0.52	0.14	0.35
Uruguay	0.39	0.07	0.19
Venezuela	0.29	0.16	0.08
Zambia	0.69	0.20	0.47
Zimbabwe	0.57	0.05	0.31
Mean	0.50	0.10	0.30
Median	0.53	0.09	0.31
Interquartile range	$\begin{bmatrix} 0.41 \\ 0.61 \end{bmatrix}$	$\begin{bmatrix} 0.07 \\ 0.11 \end{bmatrix}$	$\begin{bmatrix} 0.19 \\ 0.39 \end{bmatrix}$

Notes: Country-specific estimates of the equation $\widehat{tot}_t = \rho \, \widehat{tot}_{t-1} + \pi \epsilon_t^{tot}$; with $\epsilon_t^{tot} \sim (0, 1)$. The estimation uses annual data over the period 1980–2011 and includes an intercept. $\widehat{tot}_t$ denotes the log-deviation of the terms of trade from a quadratic time trend. See footnote 2 for the data source. Replication file `table_ar1_cbc.m` is available online in `usg_tot_svar.zip`.

means of ρ and π are 0.50 and 0.10, respectively. The parameter estimates display significant variation across countries. The cross-country interquartile range for ρ is $[0.41, 0.61]$, and for π it is $[0.07, 0.11]$. Also, the fit of the AR(1) process is modest, with a mean R-square of 0.30.

The terms-of-trade process evaluated at the mean parameter estimates is

$$\widehat{tot}_t = 0.50 \, \widehat{tot}_{t-1} + 0.10 \, \epsilon_t^{tot}.$$

This terms-of-trade process implies an unconditional standard deviation of $\widehat{tot}_t$ of 0.1155 (i.e., $\pi/\sqrt{1-\rho^2} = 0.1/\sqrt{1-0.50^2} = 0.1155$), which means that a one-standard-error deviation in the terms of trade places tot_t 11.55 percent away from its trend value. Terms-of-trade shocks vanish relatively quickly. Their half-life, defined as the value t such that $\rho^t = 1/2$, is just 1 year.

7.2 The Terms of Trade and the Trade Balance: Empirics

The effects of terms-of-trade shocks on the trade balance is an old subject of investigation. Does the trade balance improve or worsen when the terms of trade appreciate? Theoretically, the answer to this question is not unambiguous. Holding constant the quantities of goods imported and exported, an increase in the relative price of exports should improve the trade balance measured in terms of imports or exports. If, in addition, the higher relative price of exports induces domestic firms to produce more exportables, holding demands and production of importables constant, the improvement in the trade balance would be reinforced. However, there can be consumption substitution and income effects that go in the opposite direction. For example, if consumers substitute importable goods for exportable goods as the latter become more expensive, all other things equal, the trade balance would tend to deteriorate. Also, if the increase in the terms of trade makes households feel richer, the demand for consumption goods will go up. If consumption is mostly concentrated on importable goods, the income effect will tend to deteriorate the trade balance. There may also be intertemporal effects. If an improvement in the terms of trade is perceived as the beginning of further future improvements, aggregate demand may experience a strong expansion, causing the trade balance to deteriorate. But if the terms-of-trade improvement is expected to die out quickly, households may choose to save much of the increased income it generates, causing the trade balance to improve. Finally, the improvement in the terms of trade could trigger a surge in investment in physical capital, which would also tend to deteriorate the trade balance in the short run. The size of the investment surge will in general depend on the perceived persistence of the terms-of-trade improvement.

Which of these effects dominate? We begin by approaching this question empirically. Consider expanding the univariate autoregressive process (7.1) to include the trade balance. We continue to assume that the terms of trade follow a univariate autoregressive process

$$\widehat{tot}_t = \rho_1 \widehat{tot}_{t-1} + u_t^1, \tag{7.2}$$

where u_t^1 is a mean-zero i.i.d. innovation. The trade balance is assumed to evolve according to the following law of motion:

$$\widehat{tb}_t = \alpha_0 \widehat{tot}_t + \alpha_1 \widehat{tot}_{t-1} + \rho_2 \widehat{tb}_{t-1} + u_t^2, \tag{7.3}$$

where $\widehat{tb}_t$ denotes a detrended measure of the trade balance; α_0, α_1, and ρ_2 are parameters; and u_t^2 is a mean-zero i.i.d. innovation. Let $u_t \equiv [u_t^1 \ u_t^2]'$, and let the 2×2 matrix Σ be the variance-covariance matrix of u_t. We estimate equations (7.2) and (7.3) by OLS equation by equation and country by country, including a constant, which we omit for expositional convenience. The trade balance data come from Chapter 1. The trade balance is given by the difference between exports and imports and is expressed in units of GDP. As in that chapter, we construct a detrended measure of the trade balance by first dividing its level by the quadratic trend of output and then removing a quadratic trend from the resulting ratio. As in the estimation of equation (7.1), we use annual data from 51 poor and emerging countries over the period 1980–2011 (see footnote 2). The estimation delivers values for ρ_1, α_0, α_1, ρ_2, and Σ for each of the 51 countries in the panel. The estimates of ρ_1 are identical to those obtained under the one-equation model,

$$\rho_1 = \rho,$$

and are presented in Table 7.1.

The fact that equation (7.3) contains $\widehat{tot}_t$ as a regressor implies that u_t^1 and u_t^2 are orthogonal:

$$E u_t^1 u_t^2 = 0,$$

which implies that Σ is a diagonal matrix. This restriction identifies the structural terms-of-trade shock. Specifically, assume that the nonstructural innovation u_t is a linear combination of two structural orthogonal innovations

$$u_t = \Gamma \begin{bmatrix} \epsilon_t^1 \\ \epsilon_t^2 \end{bmatrix},$$

where Γ is a 2×2 matrix of coefficients, $\epsilon_t \equiv [\epsilon_t^1 \ \epsilon_t^2]'$ is a 2×1 i.i.d. random disturbance with mean zero and identity variance-covariance matrix. It follows that

$$\Sigma = \Gamma \Gamma'. \tag{7.4}$$

We have in hand an estimate of Σ, given by the variance-covariance matrix of the regression residual u_t. But we do not know Γ. Since, being a variance-covariance matrix, Σ is symmetric, equation (7.4) provides only 3 restrictions, which is insufficient to identify the 4 elements of Γ. We therefore must introduce one identification assumption. Specifically, we assume that $\gamma_{12} = 0$, where γ_{ij} denotes element (i, j) of Γ. This assumption makes ϵ_t^1 the only innovation that affects the terms of trade contemporaneously, and hence it identifies ϵ_t^1 as the terms-of-trade shock. It then follows from equation (7.4) that $\gamma_{11} = \sqrt{\sigma_{11}}$, where σ_{ij} denotes element (i, j) of Σ. Equation (7.4) and the fact that Σ is diagonal then imply that $\gamma_{21} = 0$ and that $\gamma_{22} = \sqrt{\sigma_{22}}$.

The estimate of γ_{11} is identical to the estimate of π from the one-equation model (7.1),

$$\gamma_{11} = \pi,$$

presented in Table 7.1. Rearranging terms in equations (7.2) and (7.3), we obtain the following structural vector autoregression (SVAR) system

$$\begin{bmatrix} \widehat{tot}_t \\ \widehat{tb}_t \end{bmatrix} = h_x \begin{bmatrix} \widehat{tot}_{t-1} \\ \widehat{tb}_{t-1} \end{bmatrix} + \Pi\epsilon_t, \tag{7.5}$$

where

$$h_x \equiv \begin{bmatrix} \rho & 0 \\ \alpha_0\rho + \alpha_1 & \rho_2 \end{bmatrix}, \quad \text{and} \quad \Pi \equiv \begin{bmatrix} \pi & 0 \\ \alpha_0\pi & \sqrt{\sigma_{22}} \end{bmatrix}.$$

We provide country-by-country estimates of h_x and Π on the book's Web site via http://press.princeton.edu/titles/11032.html, in the file `tot_svar_2eqn.mat`.

The cross-country mean of the estimated SVAR system is

$$\begin{bmatrix} \widehat{tot}_t \\ \widehat{tb}_t \end{bmatrix} = \begin{bmatrix} 0.50 & 0 \\ -0.02 & 0.57 \end{bmatrix} \begin{bmatrix} \widehat{tot}_{t-1} \\ \widehat{tb}_{t-1} \end{bmatrix} + \begin{bmatrix} 0.10 & 0 \\ 0.008 & 0.032 \end{bmatrix} \begin{bmatrix} \epsilon_t^{tot} \\ \epsilon_t^{tb} \end{bmatrix}.$$

The impact effect of a terms-of-trade shock on the trade balance is given by

$$\frac{\partial \widehat{tb}_t}{\partial \epsilon_t^{tot}} = \pi_{21}, \tag{7.6}$$

where π_{ij} denotes element (i, j) of the matrix Π. It follows that the sign of π_{21} determines whether a terms-of-trade shock improves or worsens the trade balance on impact. The dynamic effects (i.e., the effects in the periods following a terms-of-trade shock) depend, in addition, on the values taken by the elements of h_x.

The fact that the mean estimate of π_{21} is positive implies that the impact effect of a terms-of-trade shock on the trade balance is positive on average:

$$\frac{\partial \widehat{tb}_t}{\partial \epsilon_t^{tot}} = 0.008.$$

This expression says that an unexpected increase in the terms of trade equal in magnitude to one standard deviation of ϵ_t^{tot}—that is, an unexpected improvement in the terms of trade of 10 percent $(= \pi \times 100)$—improves the trade balance by 0.8 percent of (trend) GDP (or $\pi_{21} \times 100$ percent). The country-by-country estimates of the SVAR system yield 38 out of 51 cases in which π_{21} is positive, implying a positive impact response of the trade balance to an increase in the terms of trade in 75 percent of the countries in the panel. Otto (2003), using data from 40 developing countries spanning the period 1960–1996, estimates a positive response of the trade balance to an improvement in the terms of trade in 36 out of the 40 countries in his sample.

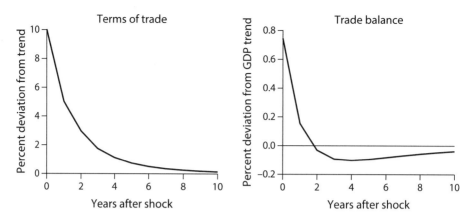

Figure 7.1   Response of the terms of trade and the trade balance to a positive innovation in the terms of trade: SVAR evidence.

Notes: Average of country-specific impulse responses estimated on annual data from 51 emerging and poor countries over the period 1980–2011. For country coverage, see footnote 2. Replication file `tot_ir_cbc.m` is available online in `usg_tot_svar.zip`.

Figure 7.1 displays the cross-country average impulse responses of the terms of trade and the trade balance to a 10 percent increase in the terms of trade. For each country, the impulse responses are constructed by setting $\epsilon_0^{tot} = 10/\pi_{11}$ and then tracing the dynamics of $\widehat{tot}_t$ and $\widehat{tb}_t$ implied by equation (7.5) for years $t = 0, \ldots, 10$. The figure displays the average of these impulse responses across the 51 countries in the sample. On impact, the trade balance improves by 0.77 percent of trend GDP. But the improvement is short-lived. Just two years after the shock, the trade balance is no longer above trend. Thus, according to the data analyzed here, the answer to the question posed at the beginning of this section is yes, the trade balance improves when the terms of trade appreciate, but only briefly.

7.3 Terms of Trade and the Trade Balance: Simple Explanations, Old and New

More than half a century ago, Harberger (1950) and Laursen and Metzler (1950) formalized, in the context of a Keynesian model, the argument that rising terms of trade should be associated with an improving trade balance. This conclusion became known as the Harberger-Laursen-Metzler (HLM) effect. This view remained more or less unchallenged until the early 1980s, when Obstfeld (1982) and Svensson and Razin (1983), using dynamic optimizing models of the current account, concluded that the effect of terms-of-trade shocks on the trade balance should depend crucially on the perceived persistence of the terms of trade. In their models a positive relation between terms of trade and the trade balance (i.e., the HLM effect) weakens as the terms of trade become more persistent and may even be overturned if the terms of trade are of a permanent nature. This view became known as the Obstfeld-Razin-Svensson (ORS) effect. Let us look at the HLM and ORS effects in some more detail.

7.3.1 The Harberger-Laursen-Metzler Effect

A simple way to obtain a positive relation between the terms of trade and the trade balance in the context of a Keynesian model is to start with the national accounting identity,

$$y_t = c_t + g_t + i_t + x_t - m_t,$$

where y_t denotes output, c_t denotes private consumption, g_t denotes public consumption, i_t denotes private investment, x_t denotes exports, and m_t denotes imports. Consider the following behavioral equations defining the dynamics of each component of aggregate demand. Public consumption and private investment are assumed to be independent of output. For simplicity, we assume that these two variables are constant over time and are given by

$$g_t = \bar{g}$$

and

$$i_t = \bar{i},$$

respectively, where $\bar{g}$ and $\bar{i}$ are positive parameters. Consumption is assumed to be an increasing linear function of output,

$$c_t = \bar{c} + \alpha y_t,$$

where $\alpha \in (0, 1)$ and $\bar{c} > 0$ are parameters. Imports are assumed to be proportional to output,

$$m_t = \mu y_t,$$

with $\mu \in (0, 1)$. In the jargon of the 1950s, the parameters α and μ are referred to as the marginal propensities to consume and import, respectively, whereas the term $\bar{c} + \bar{g} + \bar{i}$ is referred to as the autonomous component of domestic absorption. Output and all components of aggregate demand are expressed in terms of import goods. The quantity of goods exported in period t is denoted by q_t. Thus the value of exports in terms of importables, x_t, is given by

$$x_t = tot_t q_t,$$

where tot_t denotes the terms of trade. The terms of trade are assumed to evolve exogenously, and the quantity of goods exported, q_t, is assumed to be constant and given by

$$q_t = \bar{q},$$

where $\bar{q}$ is a positive parameter. Using the behavioral equations to eliminate c_t, i_t, g_t, x_t, and m_t from the national income identity, and solving for output yields

$$y_t = \frac{\bar{c} + \bar{g} + \bar{i} + tot_t \bar{q}}{1 + \mu - \alpha}.$$

The object $1/(1 + \mu - \alpha)$ is known as the *expenditure multiplier*. Letting $tb_t \equiv x_t - m_t$ denote the trade balance, we can write

$$tb_t = \frac{1 - \alpha}{1 + \mu - \alpha} tot_t \bar{q} - \frac{\mu(\bar{c} + \bar{g} + \bar{\imath})}{1 + \mu - \alpha},$$

which implies that

$$\frac{\partial tb_t}{\partial tot_t} = \frac{1 - \alpha}{1 + \mu - \alpha} \bar{q}.$$

According to this expression, an improvement in the terms of trade gives rise to an improvement in the trade balance. This result is known as the HLM effect. The HLM effect is stronger the larger is the volume of exports ($\bar{q}$), the smaller is the marginal propensity to import (μ), and the smaller is the marginal propensity to consume (α). The reason the sensitivity of the trade balance with respect to the terms of trade is decreasing in μ is that a higher value of μ weakens the endogenous expansion in aggregate demand to an exogenous increase in exports, as a larger fraction of income is used to buy foreign goods. Similarly, a larger value of α reduces the sensitivity of the trade balance to the terms of trade, because it exacerbates the endogenous response of aggregate demand to a terms-of-trade shock through private consumption.

The positive relation between the terms of trade and the trade balance predicted by the present model is qualitatively in line with the empirical estimates of the impact effect of a terms-of-trade shock on the trade balance obtained in Section 7.2 (see Figure 7.1). Thus the data appear to lend support to the HLM effect.

In the context of this model, the magnitude of the effect of a terms-of-trade shock on the trade balance is independent of whether terms-of-trade shocks are permanent or temporary in nature. The feature of the model driving this result is the assumption that the marginal propensity to consume, α, is independent of the persistence of terms-of-trade shocks. In contrast, suppose that the marginal propensity to consume is increasing in the persistence of the terms-of-trade shock. That is, assume that the marginal propensity to consume is given by $\alpha(\rho)$, with $\alpha'(\rho) > 0$, where, as before, ρ denotes the persistence of the terms of trade. This assumption is intuitively sound. It makes sense that households save a large fraction of temporary income shocks to smooth consumption over time and a small fraction of persistent income shocks. In this case, we have that

$$\frac{\partial tb_t}{\partial tot_t} = \frac{1 - \alpha(\rho)}{1 + \mu - \alpha(\rho)} \bar{q},$$

which implies that the sensitivity of the trade balance to terms-of-trade shocks is smaller when the persistence of the latter is higher. This is the channel stressed by Obstfeld (1982) and Svensson and Razin (1983). The main difference between the Harberger-Laursen-Metzler and the Obstfeld-Razin-Svensson approaches is that in the latter the marginal propensity to consume is endogenously determined by utility-maximizing agents and turns out to be increasing in ρ. We turn to this approach next.

7.3.2 *The Obstfeld-Razin-Svensson Effect*

The ORS effect is cast within a dynamic optimizing theoretical framework that differs fundamentally from the reduced-form Keynesian model we used to derive the HLM effect. Consider the small open endowment economy studied in Chapter 2. This is an economy inhabited by an infinitely-lived representative household with preferences described by the intertemporal utility function

$$-\frac{1}{2}E_0\sum_{t=0}^{\infty}\beta^t(c_t-\bar{c})^2,$$

where c_t denotes consumption, $\beta \in (0, 1)$ is a subjective discount factor, and $\bar{c}$ is a positive parameter defining the satiation point. Assume that the consumption good, c_t, is imported, and that each period the household is endowed with 1 unit of exportable goods, from which it derives no utility. As before, let tot_t denote the international relative price of exportable goods in terms of importable goods (i.e., the terms of trade). Then the household's unit endowment expressed in terms of importable goods is simply given by tot_t. The household faces the sequential budget constraint

$$d_t = (1+r)d_{t-1} + c_t - tot_t,$$

where d_t denotes the debt position assumed in period t and due in period $t+1$ expressed in terms of import goods, and $r > 0$ denotes a constant world interest rate and is assumed to satisfy $\beta(1+r) = 1$. Finally, the household is subject to the no-Ponzi-game constraint $\lim_{j\to\infty}(1+r)^{-j}E_t d_{t+j} \leq 0$. The economy is small in world product markets, so it takes the evolution of tot_t as exogenous. Assume that tot_t follows the AR(1) process

$$tot_t = \rho\, tot_{t-1} + \epsilon_t^{tot},$$

with $\rho \in (0, 1)$. The model is therefore identical to the stochastic-endowment economy studied in Chapter 2, with tot_t taking the place of y_t. We can then use the following result derived in Chapter 2 relating the equilibrium trade balance to past debt and the current terms of trade:

$$tb_t = rd_{t-1} + \frac{1-\rho}{1+r-\rho}\, tot_t,$$

which implies that

$$\frac{\partial tb_t}{\partial tot_t} = \frac{1-\rho}{1+r-\rho}. \tag{7.7}$$

According to this expression, an increase in the terms of trade in period t produces an improvement in the trade balance in period t. The intuition behind this result is that in response to a mean-reverting increase in export income stemming from an improvement in the terms of trade, households consume only part of the additional income and save the rest to smooth consumption over time. As a result, consumption increases by less than income, leading to an improvement in the trade balance.

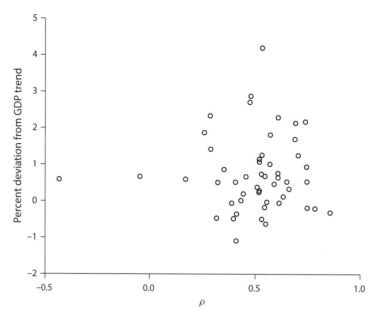

Figure 7.2   Testing for the ORS effect: Impact response of the trade balance to a terms-of-trade shock and the persistence of the terms of trade.

Notes: Each circle corresponds to a pair $(\rho, \pi_{21}/\pi_{11} \times 10)$ for a particular country, where the parameters ρ, π_{21}, and π_{11} are obtained by estimating the SVAR system (7.5). The list of countries and data information appear in footnote 2. Replication file `ors_test.m` is available online in `usg_tot_svar.zip`.

Importantly, equation (7.7) implies that the effect of terms-of-trade shocks on the trade balance is decreasing in ρ. This prediction is known as the ORS effect. Intuitively, consumption-smoothing households have more incentives to save in response to temporary shocks than in response to persistent shocks.

7.3.3 Testing for the ORS Effect

Is the ORS effect borne out in the data? If so, we should observe that countries experiencing more persistent terms-of-trade shocks display a weaker response of the trade balance to innovations in the terms of trade. Figure 7.2 plots the impact effect of a 10 percent terms-of-trade improvement on the trade balance as a function of the estimated persistence of the terms-of-trade shock, ρ, for the panel of 51 emerging and poor countries used in this chapter. Each circle in the figure corresponds to the pair $(\rho, \pi_{21}/\pi_{11} \times 10)$ for a particular country. Recall that according to the SVAR model, $\frac{\partial tb_t}{\partial \epsilon_t^{tot}} = \pi_{21}$ (see equation (7.6)). We scale by $10/\pi_{11}$ to capture the impact response of the trade balance to a 10 percent improvement in the terms of trade in each country. The cloud of circles displays no discernible decreasing pattern, suggesting that the data do not lend strong support to the ORS effect.

7.3.4 The ORS Effect in the SOE-RBC Model

The ORS effect is also present in models with endogenous labor supply and capital accumulation. A simple way to show this is to modify the SOE-RBC model of Chapter 4 by

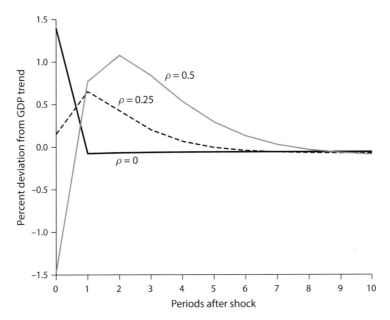

Figure 7.3 Impulse response of the trade balance to a terms-of-trade shock implied by the SOE-RBC model.

Notes: Response to a 1 percent increase in the terms of trade is shown. The calibration of the model is as in Table 4.1. Replication file `edeir_ir.m` is available online in `usg_tot_svar.zip`.

assuming again that households do not consume the good they produce. In this case, the productivity shock A_t can be interpreted as a terms-of-trade shock. The trade balance is then given by

$$tb_t = tot_t F(k_t, h_t) - c_t - i_t - \Phi(k_{t+1} - k_t),$$

which is equation (4.20) with tot_t taking the place of A_t in $y_t = A_t F(k_t, h_t)$. The main difference between this framework and the endowment economy analyzed in the previous section for the purpose of understanding the effect of terms-of-trade shocks on the trade balance is the presence of investment in physical capital. Because in the present model economy terms-of-trade shocks are identical to productivity shocks, a persistent increase in the terms of trade induces firms to increase the stock of capital to take advantage of the persistent expected increase in the value of the marginal product of capital (i.e., the marginal product of capital expressed in terms of imports, $tot_{t+j} F_k(k_{t+j}, h_{t+j})$ for $j > 0$). The increase in the desired stock of capital induces a surge in the demand for (imported) investment goods, which tends to deteriorate the trade balance. This effect is stronger when the terms-of-trade shock is perceived to be more persistent. Thus the introduction of capital accumulation into the model strengthens the ORS effect.

One way to visualize the presence of the ORS effect in the SOE-RBC model of Chapter 4 is to look at impulse responses. Figure 7.3 displays the impulse responses of the trade balance to a 1 percent increase in the terms of trade for three values of ρ: 0, 0.25, and 0.5. In constructing the figure, the logarithm of the terms of trade is assumed to follow the univariate AR(1) process given in equation (7.1), and all parameters of the model other

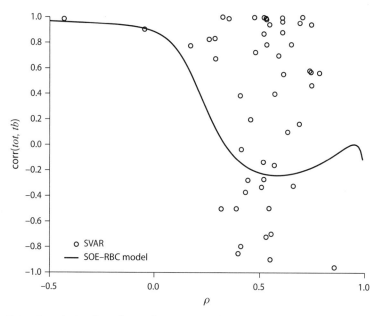

Figure 7.4   Correlation-based test of the ORS effect: Conditional correlation of the trade balance with the terms of trade and persistence of terms-of-trade shocks.

Notes: Each circle corresponds to one country. Replication file `tot_corr_tb_tot_rho.m` is available online in `usg_tot_svar.zip`.

than ρ are calibrated using the values shown in Table 4.1. The figure shows that the impact response of the trade balance decreases with ρ, implying that the more persistent the terms-of-trade shock is, the smaller the response of the trade balance will be. Actually, the initial response of the trade balance is negative for the largest value of ρ considered (0.5). In this case, the surge in investment caused by the improvement in the terms of trade is so strong that the trade balance deteriorates. After period 0, the response of the trade balance ceases to be decreasing in ρ. In fact, contrary to what the ORS effect states, the largest response is observed for the most persistent specification of the terms of trade.

The different picture that emerges from analyzing the impact response versus the response one or more periods later suggests that a better way to test for the ORS effect is to look at conditional correlations between the terms of trade and the trade balance. Accordingly, Figure 7.4 plots with a solid line the predicted conditional correlation of the trade balance with the terms of trade as a function of ρ. It shows that this correlation is positive and close to unity for negative values of ρ and falls as this parameter increases, turning negative as ρ approaches unity. Thus the impact effect of a terms-of-trade shock, shown in Figure 7.3, dominates and determines the sign of the conditional correlation. It follows that in the SOE-RBC model, the ORS effect is present not only in the impact effect of a terms-of-trade shock but more generally in the conditional comovement between the trade balance and the terms of trade.

To see whether the conditional correlation between the trade balance and the terms of trade also displays an ORS effect in the data, Figure 7.4 plots (with circles) country-by-country estimates of the correlation of the trade balance with the terms of trade as a function of the persistence of the terms-of-trade shock. Comparing model and data, the first thing to notice is that the model is driven by a single shock, namely, terms-of-trade shocks. Thus the empirical correlations must be computed conditional on terms-of-trade shocks only. To this end, we use country-by-country estimates of the SVAR (7.5) and, after shutting off the innovation ϵ_t^{tb} (by setting $\pi_{22} = 0$), compute the correlation between the trade balance and the terms of trade. Figure 7.4 shows that the cloud of circles does not resemble the declining pattern predicted by the SOE-RBC model. We therefore conclude that the ORS effect is not strongly supported by the data regardless of whether it is measured by the impact effect of a terms-of-trade shock on the trade balance or by the conditional correlation between the terms of trade and the trade balance.

7.4 How Important Are Terms-of-Trade Shocks?

Movements in terms of trade are generally believed to be an important source of business cycles. But how important? This section addresses this question by providing an empirical measure of the contribution of terms-of-trade shocks to aggregate fluctuations based on an SVAR model. Section 7.8 addresses the same question in the context of a dynamic stochastic general equilibrium (DSGE) model. As we will see, the two approaches arrive at somewhat different conclusions.

Consider expanding the SVAR system (7.5) to allow for other macroeconomic indicators of interest. Specifically, in addition to the terms of trade and the trade balance, let us include real GDP per capita (y_t), real private consumption per capita (c_t), and real gross investment per capita (i_t). Let

$$x_t = \begin{bmatrix} x_t^1 \\ x_t^2 \end{bmatrix}, \quad \text{with } x_t^1 = \widehat{tot}_t \text{ and } x_t^2 = \begin{bmatrix} \widehat{tb}_t \\ \widehat{y}_t \\ \widehat{c}_t \\ \widehat{i}_t \end{bmatrix}.$$

A hat on tot_t, y_t, c_t, and i_t denotes log-deviations from a quadratic time trend. As before, we construct $\widehat{tb}_t$ by first dividing the trade balance by the trend of output and then removing a quadratic trend from this ratio. The proposed SVAR structure is the natural extension of the bivariate SVAR presented in Section 7.2. Accordingly, we continue to assume that the terms of trade follow a univariate autoregressive process of order one,

$$x_t^1 = \rho_1 x_{t-1}^1 + u_t^1, \tag{7.8}$$

where u_t^1 is an i.i.d. random variable with mean zero. Let the law of motion of x_t^2 be

$$x_t^2 = \alpha_0 x_t^1 + \alpha_1 x_{t-1}^1 + \rho_2 x_{t-1}^2 + u_t^2, \tag{7.9}$$

where α_0 and α_1 are 4×1 vectors of coefficients, and ρ_2 is a 4×4 matrix of coefficients. The variable u_t^2 is a 4×1 random vector with mean zero and full-rank variance-covariance matrix Σ. Let nonstructural shocks u_t^1 and u_t^2 be related to structural innovations as follows:

$$\begin{bmatrix} u_t^1 \\ u_t^2 \end{bmatrix} = \begin{bmatrix} \gamma_{11} & \gamma_{12} \\ \gamma_{21} & \gamma_{22} \end{bmatrix} \begin{bmatrix} \epsilon_t^1 \\ \epsilon_t^2 \end{bmatrix}.$$

The vector

$$\epsilon_t \equiv \begin{bmatrix} \epsilon_t^1 \\ \epsilon_t^2 \end{bmatrix}$$

is assumed to be i.i.d. with mean zero and identity variance-covariance matrix.

We impose the identification assumption that ϵ_t^1 is the terms-of-trade shock. By this we mean that $\gamma_{11} > 0$ and that $\gamma_{12} = \emptyset$. In words, ϵ_t^1 is the only structural shock that affects the terms of trade contemporaneously. The fact that x_t^1 appears as a regressor in equation (7.9) implies that u_t^1 and u_t^2 are orthogonal. Thus we have

$$\emptyset = E[u_t^1 u_t^{2'}] = \gamma_{11}\gamma_{21}' + \gamma_{12}\gamma_{22}'.$$

By our identification assumption that $\gamma_{12} = \emptyset$, the second term on the right-hand side of this expression is zero. This means that the first term on the right-hand side must also be zero. Given our identification assumption that $\gamma_{11} > 0$, this term is zero only if $\gamma_{21} = \emptyset$. Summarizing, we have

$$u_t^1 = \gamma_{11}\epsilon_t^1,$$

and

$$u_t^2 = \gamma_{22}\epsilon_t^2.$$

It follows that equation (7.8) is identical to equation (7.1), so that $\rho_1 = \rho$ and $\gamma_{11} = \pi$. We have already obtained estimates of ρ and π for each of the 51 countries in the data panel used in this chapter (see Table 7.1). We obtain estimates of α_0, α_1, and ρ_2 by OLS equation by equation and country by country. These regressions also deliver an estimate of the matrix Σ for each country. Because the focus of the present analysis is to identify terms-of-trade shocks, the estimate of γ_{22} can be taken to be any matrix such that $\gamma_{22}\gamma_{22}' = \Sigma$. Without loss of generality, we set γ_{22} equal to the lower-triangular Cholesky decomposition of Σ.

Rearranging terms in (7.8) and (7.9), we can then write the SVAR system as

$$x_t = h_x x_{t-1} + \Pi\epsilon_t, \tag{7.10}$$

where

$$h_x \equiv \begin{bmatrix} \rho & \emptyset \\ \alpha_0\rho + \alpha_1 & \rho_2 \end{bmatrix}, \quad \text{and} \quad \Pi \equiv \begin{bmatrix} \pi & \emptyset \\ \alpha_0\pi & \gamma_{22} \end{bmatrix}.$$

Country-by-country estimates of h_x and Π are available on the book's Web site in the file `tot_svar_5eqn.mat`. These estimates vary substantially across countries, which makes it inadvisable to derive predictions from either the cross-country average of the matrices h_x and Π or from a panel estimate of the SVAR imposing cross-country constancy of h_x and Π. Shortly we will argue that both such approaches introduce severe bias in the estimated variance decomposition. Thus the approach adopted here, as in Section 7.3, is to first compute predictions of the SVAR model at the country level and then average them across countries.

Figure 7.5 displays the impulse responses of the five variables included in the SVAR system (7.10) to a 10 percent increase in the terms of trade. Impulse responses are computed as averages across countries point by point. The top-left panel displays the response of the terms of trade themselves (which is identical to that shown in the left panel of Figure 7.1) and the top-right panel the response of the trade balance (which is similar, but need not be identical to that shown in the right panel of Figure 7.1). The novelty of the figure is in the remaining panels. The improvement in the terms of trade causes an expansion in aggregate activity. Specifically, the 10 percent increase in the terms of trade causes an increase of 0.34 percent in GDP. Investment displays a somewhat larger expansion, albeit with a 1-year delay. Private consumption contracts on impact and then swiftly returns to its trend path.

A common way to gauge the importance of a particular shock in driving business cycles is to compute the fraction of the variances of indicators of interest explained by it. The variances of the variables included in the SVAR conditional on terms-of-trade shocks are computed as the variances resulting from shutting off all shocks other than the terms-of-trade shock by setting the 4×4 matrix $\pi_{22} = \emptyset$. Then each of these conditional variances is divided by the corresponding unconditional variance as implied by the SVAR model to obtain a share.

Table 7.2 displays the share of the variances of the five variables in the SVAR explained by terms-of-trade shocks for each of the 51 countries in the sample. The estimates reported in the table indicate that the median share of the variances of output, consumption, investment, and the trade balance explained by terms-of-trade shocks are small, ranging from 10 to 12 percent. This result obtains under three alternative ways of estimating the variance shares: (i) estimating country-specific variance shares and then taking averages across countries (the baseline approach); (ii) computing an average of the country-level SVAR coefficients (i.e., averages of the matrices h_x and Π) and using them to compute variance shares; and (iii) estimating an SVAR on a pooled data set (i.e., restricting h_x and Π to be the same across countries) and using it to derive the implied variance shares. And the contribution of terms-of-trade shocks might be even smaller due to a small sample bias. Fernández, Schmitt-Grohé, and Uribe (forthcoming) show, using a panel of 138 countries with 38 annual observations per country, that correcting for small sample bias lowers the median share of the variance of output explained by terms-of-trade shocks from 11 to 6 percent.

Table 7.2 also shows that there is significant cross-country dispersion in the estimated variance shares. The cross-country median absolute deviation[4] is almost as large as the median itself and, similarly, the cross-country standard deviations of the estimated variance shares are about as high as the cross-country medians.

The results reported in Table 7.2 are in line with earlier empirical studies. For example, Aguirre (2011) estimates that terms-of-trade shocks explain no more than 5 percent of movements in output at a quarterly frequency over the period 1994:Q1-2009:Q2 in a panel of 15 emerging countries. Broda (2004) uses annual data from 75 developing countries over

---

4. The median absolute deviation of a variable x is defined as median($|x - \text{median}(x)|$).

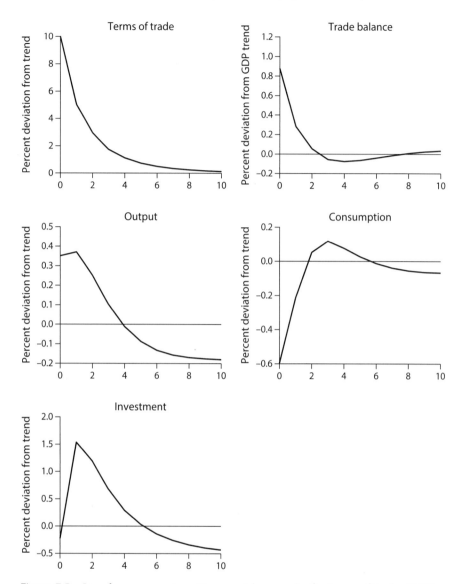

Figure 7.5 Impulse response to a 10-percent increase in the terms of trade: SVAR evidence.

Notes: For each variable, its impulse response is computed as the average impulse response across countries period by period. Replication file `tot_ir_cbc.m` is available online in `usg_tot_svar.zip`.

the period 1973-1996 to study the importance of terms-of-trade shocks conditional on the exchange-rate regime. For floaters, he finds that terms-of-trade shocks explain less than 3 percent of the variance of output, whereas for peggers, this fraction rises to 21 percent.[5]

---

5. Chapter 9 develops an open economy model with downward nominal wage rigidity that captures Broda's finding of a larger output effect of terms-of-trade shocks under currency pegs than under (optimal) floats.

Table 7.2 Share of Variance Explained by Terms-of-Trade Shocks: Country-Level SVAR Evidence

Country	tot	tb	y	c	i
Algeria	100	74	10	53	13
Argentina	100	25	31	17	26
Bolivia	100	2	3	11	8
Botswana	100	28	49	37	39
Brazil	100	43	11	4	16
Burundi	100	7	6	7	4
Cameroon	100	10	2	3	2
Central African Republic	100	27	4	8	10
Chile	100	31	17	12	21
China	100	11	10	9	33
Colombia	100	16	33	22	21
Comoros	100	18	6	10	21
Congo, Dem. Rep.	100	4	3	4	4
Costa Rica	100	19	1	2	2
Côte d'Ivoire	100	20	42	39	46
Dominican Republic	100	16	18	17	26
Ecuador	100	42	2	14	8
Egypt	100	22	1	1	13
El Salvador	100	11	10	10	11
Ghana	100	3	1	2	1
Guatemala	100	5	3	3	5
Honduras	100	3	1	1	3
India	100	3	12	18	3
Indonesia	100	5	10	6	14
Jordan	100	30	14	31	3
Kenya	100	8	0	12	3
Madagascar	100	8	4	2	2
Malaysia	100	17	8	12	10
Mauritania	100	41	13	18	13
Mauritius	100	12	2	10	1
Mexico	100	11	19	12	11
Morocco	100	2	3	1	4
Mozambique	100	10	2	6	5
Namibia	100	30	14	23	3
Pakistan	100	11	27	12	10
Paraguay	100	9	11	11	10
Peru	100	12	2	5	11
Philippines	100	22	11	14	9
Rwanda	100	4	1	0	0
Senegal	100	3	0	0	2
South Africa	100	6	13	9	10
South Korea	100	21	6	11	27
Sudan	100	19	39	10	21
Thailand	100	1	4	2	3
Tunisia	100	22	22	18	29
Turkey	100	3	15	20	31
Uganda	100	42	9	5	22
Uruguay	100	17	34	33	14
Venezuela	100	42	24	34	11
Zambia	100	42	1	33	9
Zimbabwe	100	7	10	34	17
Mean	100	18	12	13	13
Median	100	12	10	11	10
Median absolute deviation	0	11	9	9	8
Standard deviation	0	15	12	12	11
Using cross-country mean of h_x and Π	100	7	3	1	2
Panel estimation	100	4	1	1	1

Notes: Shares are expressed as percentages. Replication file `table_v_share_cbc.m` is available online in `usg_tot_svar.zip`.

Taken together, the available empirical evidence stemming from SVAR models suggests that the contribution of terms-of-trade shocks to business-cycle fluctuations in emerging and poor economies is modest and exhibits large cross-sectional variation. What do theoretical models have to say about this? This is the subject of the following sections.

7.5 The MX Model

In Section 7.3.2 we argued that one can use the SOE-RBC model of Chapter 4 to provide a story of the contribution of the terms of trade to aggregate fluctuations. We did so by interpreting the productivity shock as a terms-of-trade shock. One unrealistic implication of this way of modeling terms-of-trade shocks is the implicit assumption of an extreme degree of production and absorption specialization, whereby the entire GDP is exported and the totality of domestic absorption (the sum of consumption and investment) is imported. In reality, most countries export only a fraction of GDP and import only a fraction of domestic absorption. Table 1.1 in Chapter 1 documents that the average trade share in emerging and poor countries is about 40 percent. In this section, we capture this fact by expanding the SOE-RBC model of Chapter 4 to allow for two sectors of production, one producing importable goods and the other producing exportable goods, and by allowing both importable and exportable goods to be useful in the production of final consumption and investment goods. We refer to this model as the importable-exportable model or simply as the MX model.

We continue to assume that the country is small in the sense that it takes international prices of goods and financial assets as exogenously given. In particular, the terms of trade continue to be an exogenous variable for the small open economy.

7.5.1 Households

Consider an economy populated by a large number of households with preferences defined over streams of consumption and labor and described by the utility function

$$E_0 \sum_{t=0}^{\infty} \beta^t U(c_t, h_t^m, h_t^x),$$

where c_t denotes consumption, h_t^m denotes hours worked in the importable sector, and h_t^x hours worked in the exportable sector. Households maximize their lifetime utility subject to the sequential budget constraint

$$c_t + i_t^m + i_t^x + \Phi_m(k_{t+1}^m - k_t^m) + \Phi_x(k_{t+1}^x - k_t^x) + d_t$$

$$= \frac{d_{t+1}}{1 + r_t} + w_t^m h_t^m + w_t^x h_t^x + u_t^m k_t^m + u_t^x k_t^x,$$

where i_t^j, k_t^j, w_t^j, and u_t^j denote (respectively) gross investment, the capital stock, the real wage, and the rental rate of capital in sector j, for $j = m, x$, with the superscript m (x) denoting the sector producing importable (exportable) goods. The variable d_t denotes the stock of debt due in period t, and r_t denotes the interest rate on debt held from period t to

$t + 1$. The function $\Phi_i(\cdot)$ for $i = m, x$ introduces capital adjustment costs and is assumed to be nonnegative, convex, and satisfy $\Phi_i(0) = \Phi_i'(0) = 0$. Consumption, investment, wages, rental rates, debt, and capital adjustment costs are all expressed in units of consumption. The capital stocks obey the familiar laws of motion

$$k_{t+1}^m = (1 - \delta)k_t^m + i_t^m, \tag{7.11}$$

and

$$k_{t+1}^x = (1 - \delta)k_t^x + i_t^x. \tag{7.12}$$

Two features of this economy aim at slowing down the speed of sectoral reallocation of factors of production. First, the fact that sector-specific hours worked enter as separate arguments in the utility function allows for imperfect substitutability of labor across different activities. Second, the introduction of two capital adjustment cost functions, one for each sectoral capital stock, implies costs of moving capital from one sector to the other. These assumptions capture the fact that both labor and capital might be sector specific, and that moving these factors of production across sectors might entail costs (e.g., retooling in the case of labor and reconditioning in the case of capital). For example, a tractor used to produce soybeans on a farm cannot be instantaneously flipped to the city to produce sweaters.

Use the laws of motion for capital (7.11) and (7.12) to eliminate i_t^m and i_t^x from the sequential budget constraint. Then, letting $\lambda_t \beta^t$ denote the Lagrange multiplier associated with the household's budget constraint, we have that the first-order optimality conditions with respect to $c_t, h_t^m, h_t^x, d_{t+1}, k_{t+1}^m$, and k_{t+1}^x are, respectively,

$$U_1(c_t, h_t^m, h_t^x) = \lambda_t, \tag{7.13}$$

$$-U_2(c_t, h_t^m, h_t^x) = \lambda_t w_t^m, \tag{7.14}$$

$$-U_3(c_t, h_t^m, h_t^x) = \lambda_t w_t^x, \tag{7.15}$$

$$\lambda_t = \beta(1 + r_t)E_t\lambda_{t+1}, \tag{7.16}$$

$$\lambda_t \left[1 + \Phi_m'(k_{t+1}^m - k_t^m)\right] = \beta E_t \lambda_{t+1} \left[u_{t+1}^m + 1 - \delta + \Phi_m'(k_{t+2}^m - k_{t+1}^m)\right], \tag{7.17}$$

and

$$\lambda_t \left[1 + \Phi_x'(k_{t+1}^x - k_t^x)\right] = \beta E_t \lambda_{t+1} \left[u_{t+1}^x + 1 - \delta + \Phi_x'(k_{t+2}^x - k_{t+1}^x)\right]. \tag{7.18}$$

These optimality conditions are similar to those pertaining to the one-sector SOE-RBC model of Chapter 4 (see equations (4.7), (4.8), (4.23), and (4.28)), except that now there are sector-specific conditions for capital and labor. It is clear from equations (7.17) and (7.18) that in the steady state the rental rates of capital are the same in both sectors. This is because of the assumption of no marginal capital adjustment costs at constant levels of capital, $\Phi_i'(0) = 0$ for $i = m, x$, and a common depreciation rate. This is not the case with labor. In general the model will feature sectoral wage differentials that persist even in the steady state.

7.5.2 Production of Final Goods

The production of final goods can be modeled as taking place within the household or by firms operating in perfectly competitive markets. We adopt the latter, decentralized, approach, because it delivers, as a byproduct, the relative prices of importables and exportable goods in terms of final goods. The final good is produced using importable and exportable goods as intermediate inputs. Firm profits are given by

$$A(a_t^m, a_t^x) - p_t^m a_t^m - p_t^x a_t^x,$$

where $A(a_t^m, a_t^x)$ denotes the quantity of final goods produced; a_t^m and a_t^x denote, respectively, the domestic absorptions of importable and exportable goods; and p_t^m and p_t^x denote the relative prices of importables and exportables in terms of units of the final good, which is taken to be the numeraire. The function $A(a^m, a^x)$ denotes an aggregation technology and is often referred to as the *Armington aggregator* after the work of Armington (1969). We assume that the Armington aggregator is increasing, concave, and homogeneous of degree one. Firms in this sector are assumed to behave competitively in intermediate and final goods markets. Then profit maximization implies that

$$A_1(a_t^m, a_t^x) = p_t^m \tag{7.19}$$

and

$$A_2(a_t^m, a_t^x) = p_t^x. \tag{7.20}$$

These two optimality conditions, together with the assumption of linear homogeneity of the aggregator function, imply that firms make zero profits every period.

7.5.3 Production of Importable and Exportable Goods

Importable and exportable goods are produced with capital and labor via the technologies

$$y_t^m = F^m(k_t^m, h_t^m) \tag{7.21}$$

and

$$y_t^x = F^x(k_t^x, h_t^x), \tag{7.22}$$

where y_t^j denotes output in sector $j = m, x$. The production functions F^j, $j = m, x$, are assumed to be increasing, concave, and homogeneous of degree one. Profits of firms producing exportable and importable goods are given by

$$p_t^j F^j(k_t^j, h_t^j) - w_t^j h_t^j - u_t^j k_t^j,$$

for $j = m, x$. Firms are assumed to behave competitively in product and factor markets. Then the first-order profit maximization conditions are

$$p_t^m F_1^m(k_t^m, h_t^m) = u_t^m, \tag{7.23}$$

$$p_t^m F_2^m(k_t^m, h_t^m) = w_t^m, \tag{7.24}$$

$$p_t^x F_1^x(k_t^x, h_t^x) = u_t^x, \tag{7.25}$$

and

$$p_t^x F_2^x(k_t^x, h_t^x) = w_t^x. \tag{7.26}$$

These efficiency conditions and the assumption of linear homogeneity of the production technologies imply that firms in both sectors make zero profits at all times.

7.5.4 Equilibrium

In equilibrium the demand for final goods must equal the supply of this type of good:

$$c_t + i_t^m + i_t^x + \Phi_m(k_{t+1}^m - k_t^m) + \Phi_x(k_{t+1}^x - k_t^x) = A(a_t^m, a_t^x). \tag{7.27}$$

Imports, denoted m_t, are defined as the difference between the domestic absorption of importables and output in the importable sector:

$$m_t = p_t^m(a_t^m - y_t^m). \tag{7.28}$$

The price of importables appears on the right-hand side of this definition, because m_t is expressed in units of final goods, whereas y_t^m and a_t^m are expressed in units of importable goods. Similarly, exports, denoted x_t, are given by the difference between output in the exportable sector and the domestic absorption of exportables:

$$x_t = p_t^x(y_t^x - a_t^x). \tag{7.29}$$

Like imports, exports are measured in terms of final goods. Combining these two definitions, the household's budget constraint, and the definitions of profits in the final- and intermediate-good markets, and taking into account that firms make zero profits at all times, yields the following expression linking the growth rate of external debt to interest payments and the trade balance:

$$\frac{d_{t+1}}{1 + r_t} = d_t + m_t - x_t. \tag{7.30}$$

To ensure a stationary equilibrium process for external debt up to first order, we assume that the country interest-rate premium is debt elastic, as in Section 4.1.1 of Chapter 4:

$$r_t - r^* = p(d_{t+1}), \tag{7.31}$$

where r^* denotes the world interest rate, assumed to be constant. The country premium, $p(d)$, is assumed to be increasing.

The terms of trade are defined as the relative price of exportable goods in terms of importable goods:

$$tot_t = \frac{p_t^x}{p_t^m}. \tag{7.32}$$

As in the empirical analysis conducted earlier in this chapter, we assume that the country is small in international product markets and therefore takes the evolution of the terms of trade as given. Also in line with that empirical analysis, we assume an AR(1) structure for the law of motion of the logarithm of the terms of trade:

$$\ln\left(\frac{tot_t}{tot}\right) = \rho \ln\left(\frac{tot_{t-1}}{tot}\right) + \pi \epsilon_t^{tot}, \tag{7.33}$$

where tot denotes the steady-state value of tot_t, ϵ_t^{tot} is a white noise process with mean zero and unit variance, and $\rho \in (-1, 1)$ and $\pi > 0$ are parameters.

A competitive equilibrium is then a set of processes c_t, h_t^m, h_t^x, d_{t+1}, i_t^m, i_t^x, k_{t+1}^m, k_{t+1}^x, a_t^m, a_t^x, p_t^x, y_t^m, y_t^x, p_t^m, r_t, w_t^m, w_t^x, u_t^x, u_t^m, λ_t, m_t, x_t, and tot_t satisfying equations (7.11)–(7.33), given initial conditions k_0^m, k_0^x, d_0, and tot_{-1}, and the stochastic process ϵ_t^{tot}.

7.5.5 Observables

A meaningful comparison of the model predictions with data requires expressing theoretical and empirical variables in the same units. This is not much of an issue in one-good models like the ones studied in previous chapters. But it can get tricky in models with multiple goods. The present model economy, for instance, produces two types of goods, importables and exportables. How do we aggregate these two outputs into a single measure of GDP? And how does this measure compare to the one used in the empirical analysis?

The data used to describe business cycles in emerging and poor countries in Chapter 1 are taken from the World Development Indicators (WDI) database. Real GDP, real consumption, real investment, and the real trade balance are obtained by deflating the corresponding variables measured in current prices by the GDP deflator. In terms of the notation of this section, GDP at current prices is given by $P_t^m y_t^m + P_t^x y_t^x$, where P_t^i denotes the nominal price of good i in period t, for $i = m, x$. The WDI uses a Paasche index for the GDP deflator, defined as the ratio of current-price to constant-price GDP. In the model, GDP at constant prices is given by $P_0^m y_t^m + P_0^x y_t^x$, where $t = 0$ is taken to be the base year. Thus, the GDP deflator in period t, denoted P_t, is given by

$$P_t = \frac{P_t^m y_t^m + P_t^x y_t^x}{P_0^m y_t^m + P_0^x y_t^x}.$$

Real GDP in period t is then equal to nominal GDP in period t divided by the GDP deflator in period t, $(P_t^m y_t^m + P_t^x y_t^x)/P_t$, or $P_0^m y_t^m + P_0^x y_t^x$. Now the definition of equilibrium given in subsection 7.5.4 does not include the nominal prices P_0^m and P_0^x. However, we can scale the entire path of GDP by the constant P_0^c, the nominal price of consumption in period 0. Then, real GDP in any period t equals $p_0^m y_t^m + p_0^x y_t^x$, where, as before, $p_0^m \equiv P_0^m/P_0^c$ and $p_0^x \equiv P_0^x/P_0^c$ denote, respectively, the relative prices of importable and exportable goods in terms of consumption goods, variables for which the model has precise predictions. We arbitrarily associate the state of the economy in the base period with the deterministic steady state, so that $p_0^m = p^m$ and $p_0^x = p^x$. Then the theoretical counterpart of the observed measure of real GDP, denoted y_t^o (o for observable), is given by[6]

$$y_t^o = p^m y_t^m + p^x y_t^x.$$

Similarly, the theoretical counterpart of observed consumption is the ratio of nominal consumption, $P_t^c c_t$, to the GDP deflator, or

---

6. In the model, there is no population growth, so real GDP and real GDP per capita are the same.

$$c_t^o \equiv \frac{P_t^c c_t}{P_t} = c_t \frac{p^m y_t^m + p^x y_t^x}{p_t^m y_t^m + p_t^x y_t^x}.$$

The theoretical counterpart of observed investment and the trade balance are obtained in a similar fashion.

7.6 Parameterization of the MX Model

In this section we introduce functional forms for preferences and technologies and present a strategy to parameterize the MX model. An innovation of the approach taken here is the use of data on trade in value added and on sectoral GDP to calibrate the share parameter of the Armington aggregator and sectoral relative productivities.

7.6.1 Preferences and Technologies in the MX Model

We assume that the utility function takes a CRRA form in a quasi-linear composite of consumption, effort allocated to the importable sector, and effort allocated to the exportable sector:

$$U(c, h^m, h^x) = \frac{[c - G(h^m, h^x)]^{1-\sigma} - 1}{1 - \sigma},$$

where $\sigma > 0$ is a parameter. In turn, the composite $G(h^m, h^x)$ is assumed to be separable in sectoral employment:

$$G(h^m, h^x) = \frac{(h^m)^{\omega_m}}{\omega_m} + \frac{(h^x)^{\omega_x}}{\omega_x},$$

where $\omega_m, \omega_x > 0$ are parameters. This preference specification belongs to the GHH family studied in Chapter 4. As such, it implies that the income elasticity of the labor supply is zero for both types of labor and that the wage elasticities of labor supply are $1/(\omega_m - 1)$ and $1/(\omega_x - 1)$ in the importable and exportable sectors, respectively.

We assume Cobb-Douglas technologies for the production of importable and exportable goods:

$$F^m(k^m, h^m) = A^m \left(k^m\right)^{\alpha_m} \left(h^m\right)^{1-\alpha_m},$$

and

$$F^x(k^x, h^x) = A^x \left(k^x\right)^{\alpha_x} \left(h^x\right)^{1-\alpha_x},$$

where $A^m, A^x > 0$ and $\alpha_m, \alpha_x \in (0, 1)$ are parameters.

As in the baseline SOE-RBC model of Chapter 4, the debt-elastic interest-rate premium and the capital adjustment cost functions take the forms

$$p(d) = \bar{p} + \psi \left(e^{d-\bar{d}} - 1\right),$$

and

$$\Phi_i(x) = \frac{\phi_i}{2} x^2, \quad i = m, x,$$

where ψ, $\phi_i \geq 0$, $\bar{p} > 0$, and $\bar{d}$ are parameters. The parameter $\bar{p}$ is new and captures the fact that on average emerging and poor countries pay a positive interest-rate premium. In Chapter 4, this parameter is set to 0, because Canada is assumed to be able to borrow at the world interest rate.

We assume that the Armington aggregator takes a constant-elasticity-of-substitution (CES) form

$$A(a_t^m, a_t^x) = \left[\chi \left(a_t^m \right)^{1-\frac{1}{\mu}} + (1 - \chi) \left(a_t^x \right)^{1-\frac{1}{\mu}} \right]^{\frac{1}{1-\frac{1}{\mu}}},$$

with $\mu > 0$ and $\chi \in (0, 1)$. The parameter μ represents the intratemporal elasticity of substitution between exportable and importable absorption and is often referred to as the trade elasticity. To see why μ can be interpreted as an elasticity of substitution, combine the efficiency conditions (7.19) and (7.20) and evaluate the result using the assumed CES functional form of the aggregator function to obtain

$$\frac{a_t^x}{a_t^m} = \left(\frac{1 - \chi}{\chi} \right)^{\mu} \left(\frac{p_t^x}{p_t^m} \right)^{-\mu}. \tag{7.34}$$

From this expression, it follows that

$$\frac{\partial \ln(a_t^x / a_t^m)}{\partial \ln(p_t^x / p_t^m)} = -\mu.$$

According to this expression, a 1 percent increase in the relative price of exportables (i.e., a 1 percent increase in the terms of trade) induces a μ percent fall in the relative absorption of exportables, as agents substitute importables for exportables in total absorption. As the trade elasticity converges to unity ($\mu \to 1$), the CES Armington aggregator converges to a Cobb-Douglas form with share parameter χ, that is,

$$\lim_{\mu \to 1} A(a^m, a^x) = (a^m)^\chi (a^x)^{1-\chi}.$$

As the trade elasticity converges to zero, the CES Armington aggregator adopts a Leontief form:

$$\lim_{\mu \to 0} A(a^m, a^x) = \min\{a^m, a^x\}.$$

And as the trade elasticity becomes infinite, the CES Armington aggregator becomes linear:

$$\lim_{\mu \to \infty} A(a^m, a^x) = \chi a^m + (1 - \chi)a^x.$$

Exercise 7.3 asks you to prove these properties.

The parameter χ is known as the share parameter. The reason is that in the special case in which $\mu = 1$, condition (7.34) implies that

$$\mu \to 1 \Rightarrow \chi = \frac{p_t^m a_t^m}{p_t^m a_t^m + p_t^x a_t^x}.$$

The right-hand side of this expression is the share of expenditure on importable goods in total expenditure. When $\mu \neq 1$, the parameter χ does not have the interpretation of an expenditure share.

The model has 20 structural parameters: β, δ, r^*, tot, ρ, π, σ, ω_m, ω_x, α_m, α_x, A^m, A^x, ψ, $\overline{d}$, $\overline{p}$, ϕ_m, ϕ_x, μ, and χ. We set $\sigma = 2$, $\omega_m = \omega_x = 1.455$, $\alpha_m = \alpha_x = 0.32$, $\delta = 0.1$, and $r^* = 0.04$, as in the calibration of the SOE-RBC model of Chapter 4. We assume that emerging and poor countries pay an interest-rate premium of 7 percent on average as in the calibration of the emerging-country model of Chapter 6. This implies that $\overline{p} = 0.07$. We set $\beta = 1/(1 + r^* + \overline{p})$. We set tot and A^m equal to unity. The calibration of ρ and π defining the stochastic process for the terms of trade uses the country-specific estimates presented in Table 7.1. Thus there is one value of ρ and one value of π for each country. Seven parameters remain to be assigned values: μ, χ, $\overline{d}$, A^x, ψ, ϕ_m, and ϕ_x. We calibrate the first four and estimate the last three.

7.6.2 Calibration of the Elasticity of Substitution between Importables and Exportables, μ

A vast literature deals with estimating the elasticity of substitution between exportable and importable goods, μ. One branch of this literature uses aggregate data at quarterly frequency and estimates μ in the context of open economy DSGE models. This body of work typically estimates μ to be below unity. For instance, Corsetti, Dedola, and Leduc (2008); Gust, Leduc, and Sheets (2009); and Justiniano and Preston (2010) all estimate μ to lie between 0.8 and 0.86. Miyamoto and Nguyen (2014) estimate μ to be 0.4. A second branch of the literature infers the value of μ from trade liberalization episodes using average changes in quantities and prices observed over periods of 5–10 years. This approach typically yields values of μ greater than one, in the neighborhood of 1.5 (see, e.g., Whalley 1985).

It is intuitive that studies based on low-frequency data deliver values of μ higher than studies based on quarterly data: it is natural to expect that agents can adjust more fully to relative price changes in the long run than in the short run. Because our empirical study of the effects of terms-of-trade shocks uses annual data, it is sensible to adopt a value of μ in between those stemming from the two aforementioned bodies of work. Accordingly, we set μ equal to 1.

7.6.3 Calibration of the Share Parameter, χ

We set $\chi = 0.74$. This number, along with the values assigned to A^x and $\overline{d}$, are inferred from three observable macroeconomic relationships. The first one is the average share of exports in GDP, denoted s_x, and defined as

$$s_x = \frac{x}{p^x y^x + p^m y^m},$$

where variables without a subscript denote deterministic steady-state values. The second observable relationship is the average share of exportable output in GDP, denoted s_{yx}, and defined as

$$s_{yx} = \frac{p^x y^x}{p^x y^x + p^m y^m}.$$

And the third observable relationship is the average share of the trade balance in GDP, denoted s_{tb}, and given by

$$s_{tb} = \frac{x - m}{p^x y^x + p^m y^m}.$$

To see how χ is related to s_x, s_{yx}, and s_{tb}, start by writing equation (7.34) in steady-state form:

$$\frac{a^x}{a^m} = \left(\frac{1 - \chi}{\chi}\right)^\mu \left(\frac{p^x}{p^m}\right)^{-\mu}. \tag{7.35}$$

Let $\Upsilon \equiv p^x a^x / (p^m a^m)$ be the steady-state exportable-to-importable absorption ratio. Then we can solve the above expression for χ to obtain

$$\chi = \frac{(\Upsilon tot^{\mu-1})^{-1/\mu}}{1 + (\Upsilon tot^{\mu-1})^{-1/\mu}}.$$

In turn, we have that

$$\Upsilon = \frac{p^x a^x}{p^m a^m}$$

$$= \frac{p^x y^x - x}{p^m y^m + m}$$

$$= \frac{s_{yx} - s_x}{1 - s_{yx} + s_x - s_{tb}}.$$

It follows from the above two expressions that knowing μ, tot, s_x, s_{yx}, and s_{tb} yields a value for χ. At this point, we have values for μ and tot. We set s_{tb} equal to 1 percent. This value, together with the average interest rate of 11 percent, yields an average debt-to-output ratio of 10 percent, which is consistent with the average level of net external asset holdings of emerging and developing countries estimated by Lane and Milesi-Ferretti (2007). We now turn to the calibration of s_x and s_{yx}.

7.6.4 Calibration of the Share of Exports of Value-Added in GDP, s_x

We set s_x equal to 0.21. Obtaining a value for this share parameter is not straightforward. In the MX model, the country exports and imports only value added. In reality, exports and imports consist not only of value added but also of intermediate goods. To illustrate the difference between gross and value-added exports, consider the example of maquiladoras in Mexico. The Mexican maquiladoras are manufacturing firms that import raw materials and intermediate goods, assemble them, and then export these assembled goods. The value of the export includes the value added in Mexico but also the value of the imported raw materials and the imported intermediate goods. Thus gross exports are larger than exports of value added. As a second example, consider iPhone assemblers in China. According to

Table 7.3   Gross and Value-Added Export Shares in 13 Poor and Emerging Countries, 1995 and 2008

Country	1995			2008		
	$\frac{x^g}{y}$	$\frac{x}{y}$	$\frac{x}{x^g}$	$\frac{x^g}{y}$	$\frac{x}{y}$	$\frac{x}{x^g}$
Argentina	9	8	91	24	20	86
Brazil	7	6	90	14	12	88
Chile	28	24	85	43	34	79
China	19	16	87	34	22	65
India	10	9	90	23	17	76
Indonesia	24	21	85	29	23	82
Malaysia	87	51	59	100	61	61
Mexico	27	19	73	27	18	68
Philippines	29	20	69	35	20	58
South Africa	22	19	88	34	27	79
South Korea	27	21	76	51	28	56
Thailand	40	28	70	73	45	62
Turkey	17	15	89	23	17	73
Mean	27	20	81	39	27	72

Sources: Data are from OECD and the TiVA data set.
Notes: x^g = gross exports, x = exports of value added, and y = value added. Trade shares are in percentages. Series codes are EXGR_GDP and FDDVA_GDP, available online at www.oecd.org/trade/valueadded.

the OECD (2012), the sale of 10 iPhones by China to the United States generates gross exports of $1,875. Of this gross export, only $65, or 3.5 percent, is value added for China, corresponding to the assembly of the smart phones. The remaining 96.5 percent are exports of previously imported goods, including $229 in components from the United States (audio codec, connectivity, GPS, memory, and touchscreen controller), $207 from Taiwan (touch screen and camera), $161 from Germany (baseband, power management, and transceiver components), $800 from South Korea (DRAM memory), and $413 from other countries.

While in the model all exports and imports are value added, national income and product accounts data provides only information on gross exports. Fortunately, the Organisation for Economic Co-operation and Development (OECD) in collaboration with the World Trade Organization (WTO) collects data on trade in value added. This trade share data is available (for selected years) in the Trade in Value-Added (TiVA) database. Letting x^g denote gross exports and $y \equiv p^x y^x + p^m y^m$ denote gross domestic product (i.e., total value added), the gross export share is given by x^g/y, and the value-added export share by x/y. Table 7.3 presents gross and value-added trade shares for 13 poor and emerging countries in 1995 (the earliest date for which data is available) and in 2008. The 13 countries included in the table represent the intersection of the set of countries in the OECD-TiVA data set and the set of 51 countries in the sample we used to estimate the SVAR model of Section 7.4 (see footnote 2 for the complete list of countries). In 1995, gross exports exceeded exports of value added on average by 7 percent of GDP. For example, in Mexico gross exports exceeded value-added exports by 8 percentage points of GDP, reflecting the fact that gross exports contained previously imported raw materials and intermediate inputs. The country with the largest difference between gross exports and value-added exports is Malaysia, where in 1995 the gross export share was 87 percent of GDP but the value-added export share was only 51 percent of GDP.

The table also reports gross and value-added trade shares for the year 2008. Comparing trade shares in 2008 with trade shares in 1995 reveals that the gap between gross export shares and value-added export shares has widened significantly. In 2008, on average gross exports exceeded value-added exports by 12 percent of GDP, almost twice the difference observed in 1995. For example, in South Korea only 56 percent of gross exports represent value-added exports in 2008, whereas in 1995 the value-added component of gross exports was 76 percent.

The cross-country average share of value added in gross exports was 81 percent in 1995. This figure is computed as the cross-country arithmetic mean of the ratio x/x^g. We use this number to calibrate the value-added export share, s_x. We pick the year 1995 instead of 2008, because the former falls in the middle of the sample period used to estimate the SVAR model of Section 7.4. In that data sample, the average gross export share across time and countries is 26 percent of GDP, or $x^g/y = 0.26$. Thus we set

$$s_x = \frac{x}{y}$$

$$= \frac{x}{x^g} \frac{x^g}{y}$$

$$= 0.81 \times 0.26$$

$$= 0.21.$$

7.6.5 Calibration of the Share of Exportable Output in GDP, s_{yx}

We set the relative size of the sector producing exportable goods, $s_{yx} \equiv p^x y^x / y$, to 0.47. To calibrate this share, we use data on sectoral GDP. Specifically, the UNCTAD *Handbook of Statistics* reports panel data on GDP shares for three kinds of activity: agriculture ($s_{i,t}^{agr}$), industry ($s_{i,t}^{mfg}$), and services ($s_{i,t}^{ser}$), where i denotes country and t denotes year.[7] From this source, we extract a data set in which t ranges from 1995 to 2012 and i includes all 51 poor and emerging countries used in the estimation of the SVAR system of Section 7.4.[8] The next step is to determine what fraction of these three shares belongs to the exportable sector and what to the importable. This task is not straightforward. In reality, no single sector can be viewed as purely exportable or purely importable. For example, in every year, every country imports and exports agricultural goods. So the agricultural sector cannot be categorized as fully importable or fully exportable. To address this issue, we adopt the convention that

---

7. The data are available online at unctadstat.unctad.org.
8. The beginning of the sample period is dictated by data availability.

a fraction $s_{x,i,t}^{agr}$ of the share of agricultural GDP in country i and year t belongs to the exportable sector, where $s_{x,i,t}^{agr} \equiv x_{i,t}^{agr}/(x_{i,t}^{agr} + m_{i,t}^{agr})$ denotes the ratio of exports in the agricultural sector to the sum of agricultural exports and agricultural imports in country i in year t. We adopt the same convention for the other two sectors, manufacturing and services. Thus the share of exportable GDP in total GDP in country i and year t, $s_{yx,i,t}$, is given by

$$s_{yx,i,t} = s_{i,t}^{agr} s_{x,i,t}^{agr} + s_{i,t}^{mfg} s_{x,i,t}^{mfg} + s_{i,t}^{ser} s_{x,i,t}^{ser}.$$

The export share, $s_{x,i,t}^{k}$, for $k = agr, mfg, ser$, is calculated as follows. Table 3.1 of the UNCTAD *Handbook of Statistics* reports gross exports and gross imports by main SITC Revision 3 product group for the following five groups: (1) all food items, (2) agricultural raw materials, (3) fuels, (4) ores, metals, precious stones and nonmonetary gold, and (5) manufactured goods. We allocate exports and imports of groups (1) and (2) to agricultural activity, and exports and imports of groups (3)–(5) to industry activity. Table 5.1 of the UNCTAD *Handbook of Statistics* reports exports and imports of services. Then, s_{yx} is given by the average of $s_{yx,i,t}$ across countries $i = 1, \ldots, 51$ and years $t = 1995, \ldots, 2011$.

7.6.6 Estimation of the Capital Adjustment Cost Parameters, ϕ_m and ϕ_x, and the Debt Elasticity of the Interest Rate, ψ

The parameters ϕ_m, ϕ_x, and ψ are estimated country by country by a method-of-moments technique consisting of matching two volatility ratios predicted by the empirical SVAR model of Section 7.4.[9] The two targeted volatility ratios are the ratio of the standard deviation of investment to the standard deviation of output and the ratio of the standard deviation of the trade-balance-to-trend-output ratio to the standard deviation of output. All standard deviations, empirical and theoretical, are conditional on terms-of-trade shocks. This procedure yields one triplet (ϕ_m, ϕ_x, ψ) per country. The estimated triplets vary across countries not only because of cross-country variations in the relative conditional volatilities of investment and the trade-balance-to-output ratio, but also because of cross-country variations in the persistence of terms-of-trade shocks, ρ. Table 7.4 displays the estimates of ϕ_m, ϕ_x, and ψ along with the observed and theoretical conditional volatility ratios. The cross-country medians of the estimated values of ϕ_m, ϕ_x, and ψ are 1.82, 1.56, and 0.18, respectively. There is sizable variation in the estimates across countries. The cross-country median absolute deviations of ϕ_m, ϕ_x, and ψ are, respectively, 1.46, 1.51, and 0.17.[10]

Table 7.5 summarizes the calibration of the MX model.

---

9. Even though the number of parameters to be estimated (three) exceeds the number of targeted moments (two), there is no under-identification problem, because, in general, no subset of parameters can exactly match the targeted moments.

10. It might seem strange that the median absolute deviations of ϕ_x and ψ are almost identical to their respective medians. The reason is that the individual estimates display clusters at zero or near zero. To see this, take, for example, the five numbers 0, 0, 0.7, 0.8, and 2. Because of the two zeroes, both the median and the median absolute deviation equal 0.7.

Table 7.4   Country-Specific Estimates of the Capital Adjustment Cost Parameters and the Debt Elasticity of the Interest Rate

| | Estimated Parameters | | | Targets | | | |
| | | | | σ_i/σ_y | | σ_{tb}/σ_y | |
Country	ϕ_m	ϕ_x	ψ	Data	Model	Data	Model
Algeria	2.26	3.19	0.01	2.93	3.04	2.12	2.18
Argentina	2.00	3.27	0.44	2.16	2.35	0.26	0.26
Bolivia	1.44	1.83	0.27	3.46	3.71	0.48	0.47
Botswana	1.97	1.26	0.01	7.09	6.44	2.09	2.11
Brazil	0.20	2.23	0.20	2.91	2.71	0.55	0.55
Burundi	0.53	1.37	0.07	4.21	4.02	0.77	0.80
Cameroon	0.18	0.42	1.34	2.24	2.26	0.29	0.31
Central African Republic	1.03	0.00	0.01	8.17	7.72	1.56	1.61
Chile	2.53	3.65	0.19	2.83	2.83	0.42	0.44
China	8.02	8.83	0.34	1.88	2.02	0.26	0.26
Colombia	0.77	1.37	0.25	2.83	2.92	0.41	0.41
Comoros	0.40	0.00	0.00	18.17	13.03	3.88	3.90
Congo, Dem. Rep.	0.00	0.48	1.02	2.72	2.96	0.19	0.19
Costa Rica	0.15	0.82	0.01	4.73	4.84	2.43	2.60
Côte d'Ivoire	7.33	0.55	8.36	3.52	3.17	0.22	0.22
Dominican Republic	2.72	3.26	0.31	2.56	2.75	0.34	0.34
Ecuador	0.35	0.78	0.01	4.20	4.00	2.24	2.15
Egypt	0.28	0.00	0.00	18.56	9.98	4.63	4.58
El Salvador	1.70	2.33	0.40	2.43	2.60	0.30	0.29
Ghana	0.13	0.04	0.04	7.96	8.08	1.30	1.40
Guatemala	0.08	1.27	0.20	5.73	5.36	0.83	0.83
Honduras	0.02	0.17	0.04	7.54	7.77	1.33	1.35
India	1.50	2.24	1.10	2.36	2.58	0.22	0.22
Indonesia	27.55	0.00	9.49	4.90	3.23	0.27	0.27
Jordan	20.12	20.11	0.05	0.81	0.82	1.12	1.18
Kenya	0.27	0.05	0.00	12.04	9.83	3.48	3.53
Madagascar	2.97	4.56	0.02	2.92	2.90	1.34	1.39
Malaysia	0.06	1.69	0.02	4.40	4.26	1.76	1.78
Mauritania	2.06	1.74	0.00	5.14	5.39	3.11	3.12
Mauritius	1.10	1.90	0.01	4.01	4.33	2.75	2.70
Mexico	14.38	15.92	0.18	1.54	1.65	0.38	0.37
Morocco	18.58	0.00	4.28	5.26	4.67	0.51	0.51
Mozambique	1.16	0.79	0.01	7.77	7.30	2.30	2.25
Namibia	11.64	5.02	0.00	3.84	3.80	3.50	3.64
Pakistan	0.12	0.57	0.04	5.55	5.39	1.06	1.05
Paraguay	0.88	5.65	0.54	1.79	1.82	0.44	0.45
Peru	0.05	0.17	0.88	4.03	4.12	0.46	0.48
Philippines	4.94	6.00	0.14	2.09	2.27	0.54	0.53
Rwanda	29.98	27.81	0.31	0.78	1.08	0.55	0.55
Senegal	0.95	0.03	0.00	19.12	9.67	3.17	3.20
South Africa	2.78	1.12	5.08	2.50	2.26	0.19	0.19
South Korea	2.90	4.23	0.08	2.84	2.87	0.75	0.69
Sudan	3.81	0.00	4.56	4.06	3.70	0.43	0.43
Thailand	2.97	3.98	0.28	2.51	2.63	0.34	0.34
Tunisia	12.80	5.77	0.18	2.85	3.02	0.47	0.48
Turkey	28.32	0.00	7.88	6.17	3.79	0.28	0.28
Uganda	2.05	2.28	0.03	4.12	4.35	1.27	1.22
Uruguay	2.42	5.55	0.72	1.75	1.82	0.26	0.25
Venezuela	0.67	1.56	0.07	2.24	2.45	0.81	0.82
Zambia	1.82	1.56	0.00	5.67	5.26	2.78	2.75
Zimbabwe	26.13	0.05	5.77	7.11	3.82	0.41	0.41
Median	1.82	1.56	0.18	3.84	3.70	0.55	0.55
Median absolute deviation	1.47	1.51	0.17	1.42	1.12	0.30	0.30

Notes: σ_i, σ_y, and σ_{tb} denote, respectively, the standard deviations of investment, output, and the trade-balance-to-trend-output ratio conditional on terms-of-trade shocks implied by the SVAR model. In the estimation the parameter space was bounded by ϕ^m, ϕ^x, $\psi \in (10^{-5}, 30)$.

Table 7.5   Calibration of the MX Model

Calibrated Structural Parameters

σ	δ	r^*	$\bar{p}$	α_m, α_x	ω_m, ω_x	μ	tot	A^m	β	π	ρ
2	0.1	0.04	0.07	0.32	1.455	1	1	1	$(1+r^*+\bar{p})^{-1}$	*	*

Moment Restrictions

s_x	s_{tb}	s_{yx}	σ_i/σ_y	σ_{tb}/σ_y
0.21	0.01	0.47	**	**

Implied Structural Parameter Values

χ	$\bar{d}$	A^x	β	ϕ_m	ϕ_x	ψ
0.7399	0.0103	0.9732	0.9009	**	**	**

* Country-specific values are given in Table 7.1.
** Country-specific values are given in Table 7.4.

7.7 Response of the MX Model to Terms-of-Trade Shocks

How does the MX model adjust to an innovation in the terms of trade? Figure 7.6 displays cross-country median impulse responses to a 10 percent increase in the terms of trade. Because the calibration of the model features country-specific values for ρ, ϕ_m, ϕ_x, and ψ, the impulse response of the model is computed country by country. Then cross-country medians of impulse responses are computed point by point.

Intuitively, the increase in the terms of trade (i.e., the increase in the relative price of exports in terms of imports) induces a substitution in production away from importable goods and toward exportable goods. As a result, employment, investment, and output increase in the export sector and decline in the import sector. There is also a substitution effect on domestic absorption in favor of importable goods. The elevated demand for importables, together with the decline in the production of importables, drives up imports. Similarly, the decline in the domestic absorption of exportables, together with the increase in the domestic production of exportables, results in an increase in exports.

Because the improvement in the terms of trade causes both imports and exports to rise, the response of the trade balance is ambiguous. As shown in the left panel of row 2 in the figure, the trade balance deteriorates on impact. Thus, the model fails to capture the HLM effect present in the data (see the discussion in Section 7.2).

In the MX model, the appreciation of the terms of trade leads to a boom in aggregate output, consumption, and investment; see the left panels of rows 4, 5, and 3, respectively, in Figure 7.6. This prediction of the model is only partially supported by the empirical SVAR model of Section 7.4. Figure 7.5 shows that according to the SVAR model, on impact the improvement in the terms of trade causes output to increase but consumption and investment to decline. It follows that the impact response of consumption and investment predicted by the MX model, although quite intuitive, is at odds with the predictions of the empirical SVAR model.

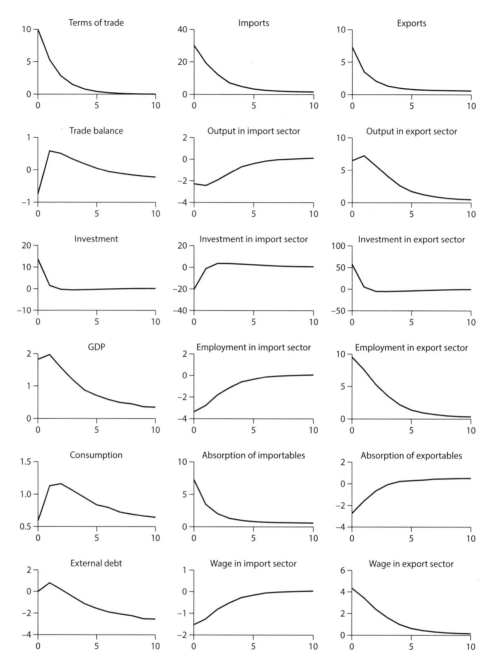

Figure 7.6 Impulse responses to a terms-of-trade shock in the MX model.

Notes: All variables except for the trade balance and external debt are expressed as percentage deviations from steady state. The trade balance and external debt are expressed in level deviations from steady state as a percentage of steady-state output. Impulse responses are cross-country medians. For each country, impulse responses are produced using the country-specific calibrations of ϕ_m, ϕ_x, ψ, and ρ. Replication file `plot_mx_ir.m` is available online in `usg_mx.zip`.

Table 7.6 Share of Variances Explained by Terms-of-Trade Shocks: The MX Model Versus the Empirical SVAR Model

Variable	(1) MX Model	(2) Empirical SVAR Model
Terms of trade	100	100
Trade balance	27	12
Output	18	10
Consumption	24	11
Investment	20	10

Notes: Each entry is the cross-country median of the fraction of the variance of the corresponding indicator explained by terms-of-trade shocks in percentages. In column (1) the numerator of the fraction is the variance conditional on terms-of-trade shocks predicted by the MX model for country-specific calibrations of ϕ_m, ϕ_x, ψ, ρ, and π. It is computed by running the Matlab script `tot_mx_var.cbc.m` in `usg_mx.zip`. The denominator is the unconditional variance implied by the empirical country-specific SVAR model. Column (2) reproduces the row labeled "Median" from Table 7.2.

7.8 Terms-of-Trade Shocks: Less Important in Data Than in Theory

How important are terms-of-trade shocks in the MX model? And how does this prediction square with that of the empirical SVAR model? To address these questions we first compute the variance of macroeconomic indicators of interest predicted by the MX model. These variances are conditional on terms-of-trade shocks, since terms-of-trade shocks are the only source of uncertainty included. Next we divide these theoretical conditional variances by the corresponding empirical unconditional variances implied by the SVAR model. We perform these two steps country by country and then compute the cross-country medians.

Table 7.6 shows that according to the MX model, terms-of-trade shocks explain on average around 20 percent of the variance of output, consumption, investment, and the trade balance, making them an important source of business cycles in emerging and poor countries.

However, the implied role assigned to terms-of-trade shocks by the MX model is smaller than that reported by Mendoza (1995) and Kose (2002). Mendoza (1995) finds, in the context of a three-sector SOE-RBC model, that the terms of trade explain 31 percent of the variance of output in developing countries.[11] In the context of a multisector SOE-RBC model, Kose (2002) finds that over 80 percent of the variance of output in developing countries is due to variations in world prices. A potential explanation for why the predictions of the MX model are more in line with the SVAR evidence is that the approach adopted here is

---

11. Mendoza reports that the ratio of the standard deviation of output conditional on terms-of-trade shocks to the unconditional standard deviation of output is 0.56. The square of this number, 0.31, is the share of the variance of output explained by terms-of-trade shocks.

more flexible, as it estimates key parameters of the model—namely, ϕ_m, ϕ_x, ψ, ρ, and π—at the country level. A further reason is that the estimation of these parameters is based on matching observed second moments conditional on terms-of-trade shocks.

How do the model-based predictions compare with those stemming from the empirical SVAR model? To address this question, column (2) of Table 7.6 reproduces from Table 7.2 the cross-country median of the share of variances explained by terms-of-trade shocks according to the empirical SVAR model. The SVAR model predicts that terms-of-trade shocks explain about 10 percent of the variance of output, consumption, investment, and the trade balance. That is, the contribution of terms-of-trade shocks to business-cycle fluctuations is about twice as large in the MX model as it is in the empirical SVAR model. We conclude that the theoretical model overpredicts the importance of terms-of-trade shocks as a source of business cycles. Table 7.7 presents predictions for each of the 51 countries in the panel.

What could explain the gap between the predictions of the theoretical and empirical models? In Chapter 8 we introduce nontradable goods. These goods are neither exportable nor importable. Nontradable goods are often estimated to represent a large portion of GDP. Since the nontraded sector is not directly affected by terms-of-trade shocks, the introduction of nontraded goods might create a buffer that mitigates the effects of terms-of-trade shocks on aggregate volatility. But this need not be the case: even in an economy with a large nontraded sector, movements in the terms of trade might generate sizable fluctuations in aggregate activity through income and substitution effects.

Exercises 7.4–7.6 provide some additional ideas in the context of the MX model. Exercise 7.4 leaves the theoretical model as is and tries to bring the data closer to the model. Specifically, it entertains the hypothesis that commodity prices might be a better measure of the terms of trade than export and import prices (the measure used here), especially for countries whose exports are concentrated in a small number of commodities. For example, for a country like Chile, the world copper price might be a more important source of fluctuations than an index of all Chilean export prices. Shousha (2015); Fernández, González, and Rodríguez (2015); and Fernández, Schmitt-Grohé, and Uribe (forthcoming) fall in this line of research. Exercises 7.5 and 7.6 aim to bring the predictions of the MX model closer to the predictions of the empirical SVAR model. Specifically, exercise 7.5 introduces delays in the reaction of investment to changes in the terms of trade, and exercise 7.6 considers the possibility that the government uses tax policy to isolate the country from fluctuations in world prices. The latter modification could be interpreted as a metaphor for nominal rigidities in prices of traded goods and imperfect exchange-rate pass-through.

7.8.1 Sensitivity Analysis

Table 7.8 presents some robustness checks. It displays the share of the variance of the trade balance, output, consumption, and investment explained by terms-of-trade shocks in the MX model for several variations in the parameter configuration. The parameters being modified are those that are new in the MX model relative to the one-good SOE-RBC model analyzed earlier in this chapter, namely, the elasticity of substitution between exportables and importables, μ, and the share parameter χ. We change one parameter value at a time, keeping all other structural parameters at their baseline values, shown in Table 7.5.

Table 7.7   Share of Variance Explained by Terms-of-Trade Shocks: Country-Level Predictions

Country	tot MX	tot SVAR	tb MX	tb SVAR	y MX	y SVAR	c MX	c SVAR	i MX	i SVAR
Algeria	100	100	302	74	39	10	325	53	55	13
Argentina	100	100	4	25	5	31	5	17	5	26
Bolivia	100	100	13	2	18	3	60	11	45	8
Botswana	100	100	10	28	17	49	6	37	11	39
Brazil	100	100	60	43	15	11	14	4	20	16
Burundi	100	100	42	7	29	6	45	7	18	4
Cameroon	100	100	9	10	2	2	2	3	2	2
Central African Republic	100	100	3,758	27	551	4	511	8	1,142	10
Chile	100	100	16	31	8	17	9	12	10	21
China	100	100	19	11	18	10	7	9	65	33
Colombia	100	100	6	16	13	33	24	22	9	21
Comoros	100	100	1,223	18	377	6	7,171	10	732	21
Congo, Dem. Rep.	100	100	2	4	2	3	2	4	2	4
Costa Rica	100	100	387	19	25	1	221	2	42	2
Côte d'Ivoire	100	100	12	20	26	42	26	39	23	46
Dominican Republic	100	100	5	16	6	18	6	17	10	26
Ecuador	100	100	108	42	6	2	62	14	20	8
Egypt	100	100	6,460	22	291	1	6,517	1	1,114	13
El Salvador	100	100	20	11	20	10	22	10	24	11
Ghana	100	100	32	3	13	1	16	2	8	1
Guatemala	100	100	39	5	18	3	12	3	30	5
Honduras	100	100	225	3	106	1	42	1	250	3
India	100	100	115	3	473	12	280	18	139	3
Indonesia	100	100	24	5	49	10	23	6	30	14
Jordan	100	100	7	30	3	14	6	31	1	3
Kenya	100	100	2,041	8	38	0	606	12	480	3
Madagascar	100	100	108	8	49	4	255	2	19	2
Malaysia	100	100	13	17	6	8	32	12	7	10
Mauritania	100	100	68	41	21	13	72	18	24	13
Mauritius	100	100	137	12	21	2	304	10	20	1
Mexico	100	100	51	11	93	19	219	12	59	11
Morocco	100	100	8	2	14	3	8	1	18	4
Mozambique	100	100	148	10	23	2	86	6	60	5
Namibia	100	100	189	30	80	14	93	23	18	3
Pakistan	100	100	48	11	120	27	72	12	42	10
Paraguay	100	100	17	9	22	11	18	11	20	10
Peru	100	100	29	12	5	2	9	5	25	11
Philippines	100	100	19	22	10	11	23	14	10	9
Rwanda	100	100	61	4	14	1	46	0	4	0
Senegal	100	100	2,652	3	488	0	5,162	0	536	2
South Africa	100	100	5	6	11	13	24	9	7	10
South Korea	100	100	15	21	5	6	8	11	24	27
Sudan	100	100	27	19	53	39	23	10	24	21
Thailand	100	100	1	1	3	4	5	2	3	3
Tunisia	100	100	8	22	7	22	9	18	11	29
Turkey	100	100	3	3	14	15	6	20	11	31
Uganda	100	100	749	42	179	9	372	5	473	22
Uruguay	100	100	4	17	8	34	6	33	4	14
Venezuela	100	100	27	42	15	24	9	34	8	11
Zambia	100	100	2,071	42	39	1	1,346	33	375	9
Zimbabwe	100	100	3	7	5	10	7	34	2	17
Median	100	100	27	12	18	10	24	11	20	10
Median absolute deviation	0	0	628	11	81	9	724	9	163	8

Notes: Shares are expressed as percentages. See note to Table 7.6. The replication file is `tot_mx_var_cbc.m` online in `usg_mx.zip`.

Table 7.8   Share of Variances Explained by Terms-of-Trade Shocks in the MX Model: Sensitivity Analysis

Parameterization	*Variance Share*					
	tot	tb	y	c	i	$s_m + s_x$
MX model						
Baseline	100	27	18	24	20	0.41
$\mu = 1.5$	100	44	36	48	35	0.59
$\mu = 0.75$	100	20	10	13	14	0.31
$\chi = 0.5$	100	9	1	1	5	0.06
SVAR model	100	12	10	11	10	0.41

Notes: Variance shares are expressed as percentages. See note to Table 7.6. The baseline calibration is $\mu = 1$ and $\chi = 0.7399$. The sum $s_m + s_x \equiv (m + x)/y$ denotes the trade share.

Increasing the elasticity of substitution, μ, from its baseline value of 1 to 1.5 drives model and data further apart. Under this parameterization, the MX model attributes 44 percent of variations in output to terms-of-trade shocks, more than 4 times the share implied by the empirical SVAR model. The reason the MX economy is now more sensitive to variations in the terms of trade is that, as μ increases, the economy becomes more open. Table 7.8 shows that the trade share, $s_m + s_x$, increases from 41 to 59 percent. To see why the economy becomes more open to international trade, note that in a steady-state with $tot = 1$, as μ increases, the marginal productivity of a^m increases relative to that of a^x in the production of the final good $A(a^m, a^x)$. In turn, this increase in relative productivity is because the weight on a^m in the Armington aggregator, given by $\chi = 0.7399$, is higher than the weight on a^x, which is given by $1 - \chi = 0.2601$. Technically, equation (7.35) implies that a^m/a^x increases with μ. Now if a^m increases relative to a^x, the economy imports more and exports more, raising the trade share and hence increasing its exposure to terms-of-trade shocks.

When the elasticity of substitution, μ, falls from 1 to 0.75, the share of variance of output attributed to terms-of-trade shocks—according to the MX model—falls from 18 percent to 10 percent, which is the value predicted by the empirical model. One might be tempted to conclude that all it takes to bring the MX model close to the data is a reduction in μ from 1 to 0.75. However, lowering μ results in a reduction in the predicted trade openness from 41 percent to 31 percent. Thus setting $\mu = 0.75$ results in an economy that is more closed to international trade than the typical economy contained in our 51-country panel.

Finally, Table 7.8 shows that reducing the weight on importables in the Armington aggregator, χ, from its baseline value of 0.7399 to 0.5 leads to a drastic reduction in the share of the variance of output accounted for by terms-of-trade shocks from 18 percent to 1 percent. Again, one might be tempted to conclude that all it takes to bring data and model closer together is an appropriate adjustment of the share parameter, χ. Yet, as in the case of varying μ, this would be the wrong conclusion. For, as shown in the table, lowering the value of χ comes at the expense of a reduction in trade openness from 41 percent to 6 percent. The intuition for this result is that lessening the productivity of importable goods in the production of final goods by reducing χ induces agents to import less. In fact, the considered reduction in χ is so large that it causes a reversal in the tradability of goods. The good that used to be exported is now imported and vice versa. It follows that lowering χ does not represent an empirically compelling route to bring the predictions of the MX model and the empirical SVAR model closer together.

The next chapter investigates whether the shortcomings of the MX model identified here could be due to the model's empirically unrealistic assumption that all goods are tradable.

7.9 Exercises

7.1 (Testing the Univariate Specification for the Terms of Trade) Throughout the chapter we have assumed that the typical poor or emerging country is too small to affect its terms of trade. This exercise scrutinizes this assumption. For each of the 51 countries in the panel underlying the empirical analysis of Section 7.4, test the null hypothesis that the terms of trade follow a univariate process against the alternative hypothesis that they also depend on one-period lagged values of output, consumption, investment, and the trade balance. Always include a constant in your regressions. Report the countries for which the null hypothesis can be rejected at the 95 percent confidence level. In completing this exercise, you might find it useful to consult an econometrics textbook, such as Hamilton (1994, section 11.2).

7.2 (HP-Filtered Terms-of-Trade Process) Use the HP filter with smoothing parameter $\lambda = 100$ to obtain the cyclical component of the terms of trade for the 51 countries considered in Section 7.1. See Section 1.5 of Chapter 1 for a discussion of the HP filter. Then estimate equation (7.1) country by country. Report your findings in a format similar to Table 7.1. Compare the estimated process under quadratic and HP detrending.

7.3 (Special Cases of the CES Armington Aggregator) Consider the CES Armington aggregator

$$A(a^m, a^x) = \left[\chi \left(a^m\right)^{1-\frac{1}{\mu}} + (1-\chi) \left(a^x\right)^{1-\frac{1}{\mu}} \right]^{\frac{1}{1-\frac{1}{\mu}}}.$$

Show that

$$\lim_{\mu \to 1} A(a^m, a^x) = (a^m)^\chi (a^x)^{1-\chi},$$

$$\lim_{\mu \to 0} A(a^m, a^x) = \min\{a^m, a^x\},$$

and

$$\lim_{\mu \to \infty} A(a^m, a^x) = \chi a^m + (1-\chi)a^x.$$

Note that the share parameter χ drops from the Armington aggregator as $\mu \to 0$. This may be an undesirable property for certain applications. Provide an alternative specification of the CES aggregator such that

$$\lim_{\mu \to 0} A(a^m, a^x) = \min\{\chi a^m, (1 - \chi)a^x\}.$$

7.4 (Export Commodity Prices) The SVAR evidence presented in Section 7.4 suggests that the terms of trade play a small role in explaining business cycles in emerging and poor countries. Some experts have argued that for commodity-exporting countries, world commodity prices can be an important driver of aggregate activity. To test this hypothesis, consider the case of Chile, a country for which about half of its exports are concentrated in a single commodity, namely, copper. The present exercise consists of replacing the terms of trade with the real price of copper in the SVAR analysis of Section 7.4. To this end, download the time series of the spot price of copper in dollars at the London Market at an annual frequency from the IMF-IFS data set, available on the book's Web site. Deflate this series using the U.S. consumer price index. Remove a quadratic time trend from the natural logarithm of the real copper price. Use the raw data corresponding to Chile contained in the file `data_annual.xls` (posted online with the materials for Chapter 1) for the remaining four variables of the SVAR. Apply the same detrending and transformations of the variables as in the body of the chapter. Then estimate the SVAR system, equations (7.8) and (7.9), for Chile with your commodity price index taking the place of tot_t. The sample should be from 1980 to 2011. Plot impulse responses of all variables in the SVAR to a 10 percent copper price increase. Finally, estimate the share of the variance of each variable in the SVAR system explained by copper price shocks. Discuss your findings, and compare them to those reported in Section 7.4 (especially Table 7.2) for the case of Chile. Is the price of copper a more important driver of Chilean business cycles than the Chilean terms of trade?

7.5 (Time-to-Build and the Effects of Terms-of-Trade Shocks) An important problem of the MX model of Section 7.5 is that it exaggerates the role of the terms of trade relative to the predictions of the empirical SVAR model. Consider the possibility of bringing model and data closer together by introducing delays in the process of capital accumulation. Here, the hope is that if building capital takes time, terms-of-trade shocks may not induce large increases in investment because by the time investment becomes capital, much of the shock might have faded away (recall that the cross-country median value of ρ—implying a half-life of terms-of-trade shocks—is only 1 year). Specifically, assume that investment goods take i years rather than 1 year to become productive capital, that is, model the law of motion of the capital stocks as

$$k_{t+1}^j = (1 - \delta)k_t^j + i_{t-i}^j,$$

for $j = m, x$. Calibrate the model using the parameter values given in Table 7.5 and the cross-country medians of ρ, π, ϕ, and ψ, given in Tables 7.1 and 7.4. Consider three specifications, $i = 1, 2$, and 3. Plot the associated impulse responses of all variables of interest to a 1 percent increase in the terms of trade. Explain the results. Then for each value of i, compute the predicted variances of output, consumption, investment, and the trade balance due to terms-of-trade shocks. Discuss your answer, emphasizing the potential of the proposed channel.

7.6 (Tariffs and the Effects of Terms-of-Trade Shocks) Continuing with the theme of the previous two exercises, one possible explanation for the mismatch between the predictions of the theoretical and empirical models regarding the importance of terms-of-trade shocks is the presence of trade tariffs. To the extent that trade taxes move systematically in the opposite direction as the terms of trade, the domestic relative price of exportables and importables will be insensitive to movements in their world counterparts, which, in turn, may attenuate the effects of terms-of-trade shocks on domestic activity. Continue to assume that p_t^x and p_t^m denote the domestic prices of exportables and importables, respectively, in terms of final goods, and that $tot_t \equiv p_t^x/p_t^m$ denotes the domestic terms of trade. The novelty in the present setting is that there is a tax that introduces a wedge, denoted γ_t, between the domestic and the foreign terms of trade. Specifically, assume that

$$tot_t = tot_t^* \gamma_t,$$

where tot_t^* denotes the foreign terms of trade. The wedge γ_t is one minus a proportional trade barrier, which might take the form of a combination of import and export taxes. As before, the country takes the evolution of the foreign terms of trade as given. Assume that tot_t^* follows the AR(1) process

$$\ln\left(\frac{tot_t^*}{tot^*}\right) = \rho \ln\left(\frac{tot_{t-1}^*}{tot^*}\right) + \pi \epsilon_t^{tot*},$$

where tot^* denotes the steady-state value of tot_t^*. Assume that the government increases taxes on exports (or reduces taxes on imports) when the foreign terms of trade improve. Specifically, assume that

$$\gamma_t = \left(\frac{tot_t^*}{tot^*}\right)^{-\eta},$$

with $\eta > 0$. Finally, assume that the government rebates the proceeds of trade taxes to households in a lump-sum fashion. Calibrate the model using the values for the structural parameters given in Table 7.5 and the cross-country medians of ρ, π, ϕ, and ψ, given in Tables 7.1 and 7.4. Consider different values of η ranging from 0 to 1. For each value of η compute the variances of output, consumption, investment, and the trade balance due to terms-of-trade shocks. Discuss your results.

Nontradable Goods and the Real Exchange Rate

The MX model of Chapter 7 overstates the importance of terms-of-trade shocks as drivers of business cycles by a factor of two. Specifically, we showed that a plausible calibration of the MX model implies that terms-of-trade shocks explain about 20 percent of the observed variances of output, consumption, investment, and the trade balance, while an estimated SVAR model assigns only 10 percent of the observed variance of these variables to variations in the terms of trade (see Table 7.6).

One unrealistic feature of the MX model is that all goods in the economy are internationally traded. Goods are either importable or exportable. Therefore, it is natural that in this environment the terms of trade, being the relative price of exportables in terms of importables, play a significant role in the allocation of resources and expenditures across sectors and time. The assumption that all goods are tradable would be an acceptable modeling abstraction if it were empirically compelling (i.e., if most goods could be categorized as either importable or exportable). However, in reality the bulk of goods fall into a third category, known as nontradables. Nontradables are goods whose prices are not equalized across countries, because, for various reasons (e.g., transportation costs and trade barriers) trading them across borders is economically unviable.

In this chapter we explore the role of nontradable goods with an emphasis on how they affect the transmission of aggregate disturbances, including terms-of-trade shocks. The introduction of new features into any model increases the chances of explaining facts that the original model was unable to address. At first glance, this looks like a win-win proposition. However, because a richer model makes predictions for a larger set of variables, the number of dimensions along which it can be confronted with data also increases. This is the case, for example, with the introduction of nontradables into the MX model. The resulting three-sector model could bring data and model closer together with regard to the importance of terms-of-trade shocks as a source of fluctuations, but it will also make predictions for new variables, such as the relative price of nontradables in terms of tradables, which will have to be confronted with the data.

8.1 The Real Exchange Rate

The relative price of nontradables in terms of tradables is an important macroeconomic variable. One reason is that it plays a role in determining price-level differences across countries. The relative price of final consumption across countries is known as the *real exchange rate*. Specifically, the real exchange rate, denoted RER_t, is defined as the ratio of the foreign consumer price index to the domestic consumer price index expressed in a common currency,

$$RER_t \equiv \frac{\mathcal{E}_t P_t^*}{P_t},\tag{8.1}$$

where P_t^* denotes the nominal price of consumption in the foreign country in units of foreign currency, P_t denotes the nominal price of consumption in the domestic country in units of domestic currency, and $\mathcal{E}_t$ denotes the nominal exchange rate, defined as the price of one unit of foreign currency in terms of domestic currency. When RER_t increases, the domestic economy becomes relatively cheaper than the foreign economy. In this case, we say that the real exchange rate depreciates. Conversely, when RER_t decreases, the domestic economy becomes relatively more expensive than the foreign economy, and we say that the real exchange rate appreciates.

The presence of nontradable goods introduces price differences across countries. As a result, variations in the relative price of nontradables lead to variations in the real exchange rate. Movements in the real exchange rate have been the subject of much study in open economy macroeconomics and will feature prominently in the remainder of this chapter as well as in chapters to come.

8.2 The TNT Model

To understand the precise way in which the relative price of nontradables affects the real exchange rate, we begin by studying the workings of a simple perfect-foresight endowment economy with tradable and nontradable goods known as the tradable-nontradable (TNT) model. The TNT model is of interest, because it allows for an analytical characterization of the equilibrium response of the real exchange rate, the relative price of nontradables, and aggregate activity to various shocks, and because its main predictions extend to more complex economic environments.

Consider an economy populated by identical households with preferences described by the utility function

$$\sum_{t=0}^{\infty} \beta^t U(c_t),$$

where the consumption good, c_t, is a composite of importable goods and nontradable goods, obtained via the following aggregation technology:

$$c_t = A(c_t^m, c_t^n),$$

where c_t^m and c_t^n denote consumption of importables and nontradables, respectively. Assume that the Armington aggregator $A(\cdot, \cdot)$ is increasing in both arguments, concave, homogeneous of degree one, and differentiable. The period budget constraint of the household is given by

$$c_t^m + p_t^n c_t^n + d_t = \frac{d_{t+1}}{1+r} + tot_t y^x + p_t^n y^n,$$

where p_t^n denotes the relative price of nontradables in terms of importables; d_t denotes external debt maturing in t expressed in terms of importables; d_{t+1} denotes external debt assumed in t and maturing in $t+1$; $r > 0$ denotes the interest rate; tot_t denotes the terms of trade (defined as the relative price of exportables in terms of importables); and y^x and y^n denote constant endowments of exportables and nontradable goods, respectively. Households derive no utility from consuming exportable goods; therefore the entire endowment of exportables is exported. The economy is not endowed with importable goods, so all the consumption of importable goods is imported.

Households choose sequences $\{c_t^m, c_t^n, d_{t+1}\}_{t=0}^{\infty}$ to maximize their lifetime utility subject to the period budget constraint presented above and a no-Ponzi-game constraint of the form

$$\lim_{j \to \infty} (1+r)^{-j} d_{t+j} \leq 0,$$

taking as given the price sequences $\{p_t^n, tot_t\}_{t=0}^{\infty}$ and the initial debt position d_0.

Letting $\beta^t \lambda_t$ denote the Lagrange multiplier associated with the period budget constraint, the first-order optimality conditions of the household's problem are the period budget constraint itself, and

$$U'(c_t) A_1(c_t^m, c_t^n) = \lambda_t, \tag{8.2}$$

$$\lambda_t = \beta(1+r)\lambda_{t+1}, \tag{8.3}$$

$$p_t^n = \frac{A_2(c_t^m, c_t^n)}{A_1(c_t^m, c_t^n)}, \tag{8.4}$$

and

$$\lim_{j \to \infty} (1+r)^{-j} d_{t+j} = 0. \tag{8.5}$$

Using the fact that the aggregator function A is increasing, homogeneous of degree one, and concave, we can rewrite the optimality condition (8.4) as

$$p_t^n = P\left(\frac{c_t^m}{c_t^n}\right), \tag{8.6}$$

where the function $P(\cdot)$ is increasing:

$$P'(\cdot) > 0.$$

Exercise 8.1 asks you to establish this result.

8.2.1 The Real Exchange Rate and the Relative Price of Nontradables

In the present model there is a one-to-one relationship between the relative price of non-tradables in terms of importables, p_t^n, and the real exchange rate, RER_t. To see this, begin by dividing the numerator and denominator of the right-hand side of equation (8.1) by the domestic nominal price of the importable good, denoted P_t^m, to obtain

$$RER_t = \frac{\mathcal{E}_t P_t^* / P_t^m}{P_t / P_t^m}.$$

The denominator is the domestic relative price of the final consumption good in terms of importables, which we denote by p_t^c. Assume that the *law of one price* holds for importable goods. This means that when expressed in the same currency, the domestic and foreign prices of importables are equal to each other, that is,

$$P_t^m = \mathcal{E}_t P_t^{m*}.$$

Then the numerator of the previous equation becomes P_t^* / P_t^{m*}. This is the foreign relative price of the final consumption good in terms of importables, which we denote p_t^{c*}. This relative price is taken as given by the small open economy. Further, we assume that p_t^{c*} is constant and normalized to unity. Then we can express the real exchange rate as

$$RER_t = \frac{1}{p_t^c}. \tag{8.7}$$

We now wish to link the relative price of final consumption goods, p_t^c, to the relative price of nontradables, p_t^n. To this end, it is useful to decentralize the production of final consumption goods. This step leaves the equilibrium of the model unchanged. It simply allows us to obtain a market price for the final consumption good. Imagine that the production of final consumption goods is not performed in the household, as assumed thus far, but by firms acting in perfectly competitive markets. Profits of these firms are given by

$$p_t^c A(c_t^m, c_t^n) - c_t^m - p_t^n c_t^n.$$

Firms choose c_t^m and c_t^n to maximize profits, taking p_t^c and p_t^n as given. The first-order optimality condition with respect to c_t^m is

$$p_t^c A_1(c_t^m, c_t^n) = 1.$$

Combining this expression with (8.6) and (8.7) and taking into account that $A_1(\cdot, \cdot)$ is homogeneous of degree zero, we can write the real exchange rate as

$$RER_t = A_1\left(P^{-1}(p_t^n), 1\right)$$

$$\equiv e(p_t^n).$$

Because $A_1(\cdot, \cdot)$ is decreasing in its first argument and $P(\cdot)$ is increasing, we have that $e(\cdot)$ is decreasing:

$$e'(\cdot) < 0.$$

This means that the real exchange rate is a decreasing function of the relative price of nontradables. The real exchange rate appreciates if and only if the relative price of non-tradables increases, and the real exchange rate depreciates if and only if the relative price of nontradables decreases. This relationship between the real exchange rate and the relative price of nontradables is intuitive. Recall that in the present model the law of one price holds for importables, so that importables have the same price domestically and abroad when expressed in the same currency. Therefore, if in the domestic economy nontradables become more expensive in terms of importables, then the domestic consumption basket becomes more expensive relative to the foreign consumption basket. Because of this one-to-one relationship, the relative price of nontradables itself is often referred to as the (inverse of the) real exchange rate. We follow this tradition and use the terms "real-exchange-rate appreciation" and "increases in the relative price of nontradables" interchangeably. Similarly, we use interchangeably the terms "real-exchange-rate depreciation" and "decrease in the relative price of nontradables."

8.2.2 The Equilibrium Real Exchange Rate

The defining property of nontradable goods is that their domestic demand must equal their domestic supply, since they can be neither imported nor exported. Therefore, we have that in equilibrium,

$$c_t^n = y^n. \tag{8.8}$$

Combining this market-clearing condition with the period budget constraint yields the following resource constraint in the tradable sector:

$$c_t^m + d_t = \frac{d_{t+1}}{1+r} + tot_t y^x. \tag{8.9}$$

To avoid inessential debt dynamics, assume that the subjective and pecuniary discount factors are equal to each other, that is,

$$\beta = \frac{1}{1+r}.$$

This condition together with the Euler equation (8.3) implies that the marginal utility of wealth is constant over time:

$$\lambda_t = \lambda,$$

for all $t \geq 0$. In turn, the facts that c_t^n and λ_t are both constant over time imply, by optimality condition (8.2), that consumption of importable goods is constant over time:

$$c_t^m = c^m,$$

for all $t \geq 0$. Then iterating the resource constraint (8.9) forward $j \geq 1$ times yields

$$d_t = \frac{d_{t+j}}{(1+r)^j} + \sum_{s=0}^{j-1} \frac{tot_{t+s} y^x - c^m}{(1+r)^s}.$$

Taking the limit as $j \to \infty$, using the transversality condition (8.5), and solving for c^m yields the following expression for the equilibrium level of consumption of importables:

$$c^m = -\frac{r}{1+r} d_0 + \frac{r}{1+r} \sum_{t=0}^{\infty} \frac{tot_t y^x}{(1+r)^t}. \qquad (8.10)$$

Intuitively, households consume the annuity value of the lifetime endowment of exportable goods net of interest obligations on their initial external debt. Accordingly, consumption of importables is increasing in the terms of trade and in the endowment of exportables, and it is decreasing in the initial stock of external debt.

Evaluating optimality condition (8.6) at the equilibrium values of c_t^m and c_t^n implies that the relative price of nontradables is constant over time,

$$p_t^n = p^n,$$

where

$$p^n = P\left(\frac{c^m}{y^n}\right). \qquad (8.11)$$

According to this expression, the relative price of nontradables is increasing in the desired demand for importable goods, c^m, and decreasing in the endowment of nontradables, y^n.

8.2.3 Adjustment of the Real Exchange Rate to Terms-of-Trade Shocks

We are now ready to determine the effect of terms-of-trade shocks on the relative price of nontradables and the real exchange rate. Suppose that the terms of trade experience a temporary increase in period 0. Specifically, assume that tot_0 increases, but tot_t remains unchanged for all $t > 0$. From (8.10) and (8.11) we have that

$$\left.\frac{d\, p^n}{d\, tot}\right|_{\text{temporary}} = \frac{r}{1+r} \frac{y^x}{y^n} P'\left(\frac{c^m}{y^n}\right) > 0.$$

Intuitively, the increase in the relative price of the exportable endowment creates a positive income effect. As a result, households increase their demand for all consumption goods—importables and nontradables. Because the supply of nontradables is fixed at y^n, the increase in the demand for nontradables requires an increase in the relative price of nontradables to eliminate the excess demand. Because the relative price of nontradables increases, the real exchange rate, RER_t, appreciates in response to the temporary improvement in the terms of trade (i.e., the domestic economy becomes more expensive relative to the rest of the world).

Consider now a permanent increase in the terms of trade, so that tot_t increases for all $t \geq 0$. In this case, equilibrium condition (8.10) implies that

$$\left. \frac{d\, c^m}{d\, tot} \right|_{\text{permanent}} = y^x.$$

In turn, this result and equation (8.11) yield

$$\left. \frac{d\, p^n}{d\, tot} \right|_{\text{permanent}} = \frac{y^x}{y^n} P'\left(\frac{c^m}{y^n} \right) > 0.$$

Clearly, the last two expressions imply that permanent changes in the terms of trade have a larger effect on the relative price of nontradables than do temporary changes in the terms of trade:

$$\left. \frac{d\, p^n}{d\, tot} \right|_{\text{permanent}} > \left. \frac{d\, p^n}{d\, tot} \right|_{\text{temporary}} > 0.$$

This result is intuitive. The more permanent is the increase in the terms of trade, the larger the income effect it generates will be, and therefore the larger the increase will be in the desired demand for nontradables, which in turn requires a larger increase in the relative price of nontradables to clear the market.

8.2.4 Adjustment of the Real Exchange Rate to Interest-Rate Shocks

How do interest-rate shocks affect the relative price of nontradables and the real exchange rate? To answer this question, assume that the interest rate experiences a one-time increase in period 0. Specifically, assume that the interest rate equals $r_0 > r$ in period 0 and r for all $t > 0$. Assume further, for simplicity, that the terms of trade are constant over time, $tot_t = tot$, for all $t \geq 0$. Because the interest rate is constant starting in period 1, we know from the previous analysis that beginning in period 1 consumption is also constant over time. Specifically,

$$c_t^m = c_1^m,$$

for all $t \geq 1$, where

$$c_1^m = -\frac{r}{1+r} d_1 + tot\, y^x. \tag{8.12}$$

The resource constraint (8.9) evaluated at $t = 0$ implies that

$$c_0^m + d_0 = \frac{d_1}{1+r_0} + tot\, y^x. \tag{8.13}$$

Combining (8.2) with the Euler equation (8.3) evaluated at $t = 0$ yields

$$U'(A(c_0^m, y^n)) A_1(c_0^m, y^n) = \beta(1+r_0) U'(A(c_1^m, y^n)) A_1(c_1^m, y^n). \tag{8.14}$$

The three-equation system (8.12)–(8.14) is in three unknowns, c_0^m, c_1^m, and d_1. All other variables and parameters in this system are known. Equation (8.14) and the fact that $\beta(1 + r_0) > 1$ imply that $c_1^m > c_0^m$. This is intuitive. A higher interest rate induces households to save more by substituting future consumption for present consumption. We now wish to show that c_0^m falls. We do so by contradiction. Suppose that, contrary to what we wish to show, c_0^m increases. Then, by (8.13), d_1 must increase. But if d_1 increases, then, by (8.12), c_1^m must fall, which contradicts the finding that $c_1^m > c_0^m$. This establishes that c_0^m falls, that is,

$$\frac{d\,c_0^m}{d\,r_0} < 0.$$

Now this expression together with (8.6) and (8.8) implies that

$$\frac{d\,p_0^n}{d\,r_0} = P'\left(\frac{c_0^m}{y^n}\right)\frac{1}{y^n}\frac{d\,c_0^m}{d\,r_0} < 0.$$

This expression says that the real exchange rate depreciates in response to a temporary increase in the interest rate. Intuitively, the increase in the interest rate dampens consumption demand for all goods in period 0 as households' desired savings increases. Because the supply of nontradables is fixed, the price of nontradables must fall to clear the market.

8.2.5 Adjustment of Output to Terms-of-Trade Shocks in the TNT Model

In Chapter 7 we argued that an important shortcoming of the MX model is that it assigns too large a role to the terms of trade as a driver of the business cycle relative to the predictions stemming from estimated SVAR models. Could this difficulty in part stem from the fact that all goods are tradable in that theoretical environment? To answer this question in the context of the present environment, consider characterizing how the effect of a terms-of-trade shock on output changes as the share of nontradables in the production of final goods changes. Does this effect become smaller the larger the share of nontradables is?

Aggregate output, denoted y_t, is the sum of tradable output and nontradable output expressed in terms of final goods:

$$y_t = \frac{P_t^x y^x + P_t^n y^n}{P_t},$$

where P_t^x, P_t^n, and P_t denote, respectively, the nominal prices of exportable, nontradable, and final goods. Dividing the numerator and denominator by the nominal price of importables gives

$$y_t = \frac{tot_t y^x + p_t^n y^n}{p_t^c}.$$

Recalling that $p_t^c = 1/A_1(c_t^m, y^n)$ and that $p_t^n = A_2(c_t^m, y^n)/A_1(c_t^m, y^n)$, we can write

$$y_t = A_1(c_t^m, y^n)tot_t y^x + A_2(c_t^m, y^n)y^n.$$

Adding and subtracting $A_1(c_t^m, y^n)c_t^m$ to the right-hand side, and taking into account that $A(\cdot, \cdot)$ is homogeneous of degree one, we can write output as

$$y_t = A(c_t^m, y^n) + A_1(c_t^m, y^n)(tot_t y^x - c_t^m). \tag{8.15}$$

The first term on the right-hand side is final consumption, c_t. The second term is the trade balance expressed in terms of final consumption goods (recall that $A_1(c_t^m, y^n) = 1/p_t^c$). Therefore, equation (8.15) says that output equals consumption plus the trade balance, or

$$y_t = c_t + tb_t,$$

where $tb_t \equiv (tot_t y^x - c_t^m)/p_t^c$ denotes the trade balance expressed in terms of final goods.

Now assume that there is an unexpected permanent increase in the terms of trade in period 0. Equilibrium conditions (8.10) and (8.15) imply that

$$\frac{d\,y_0}{d\,tot} = \frac{y^x}{p_t^c} + A_{11}(c^m, y^n)(tot\,y^x - c^m)y^x.$$

This expression is intuitive. If the trade balance is small, we can forget about the second term on the right-hand side. In this case, a unit increase in the terms of trade increases output by the size of exportable output measured in terms of final goods.

Does the presence of nontradables dampen the output effect of a terms-of-trade shock? In particular, how does the output effect of a terms-of-trade shock change with the share of nontradables in total consumption? Assume, for simplicity, that the aggregator function takes the Cobb-Douglas form

$$A(c^m, y^n) = (c^m)^\alpha (y^n)^{1-\alpha},$$

with $\alpha \in (0, 1)$. The parameter $1 - \alpha$ determines the share of domestic expenditure devoted to nontradable goods. To see this, note that under the Cobb-Douglas specification for $A(\cdot, \cdot)$, the household's optimality condition (8.4) implies that $1 - \alpha = \frac{p_t^n c_t^n}{c_t^m + p_t^n c_t^n}$. Now notice that condition (8.10) implies that in equilibrium, consumption of importables, c^m, is independent of α. It follows immediately that $A_1(c^m, y^n) = \alpha(c^m/y^n)^{\alpha-1}$ takes the value 1 when $1 - \alpha = 0$ and the value 0 when $1 - \alpha = 1$. Also, $A_{11}(c^m, y^n) = \alpha(\alpha - 1)(c^m/y^n)^{\alpha-2}$ equals 0 when $1 - \alpha = 0$ and also when $1 - \alpha = 1$. We then have that

$$\left.\frac{d\,y_0}{d\,tot}\right|_{1-\alpha=0} = y^x > 0 \quad \text{and} \quad \left.\frac{d\,y_0}{d\,tot}\right|_{1-\alpha=1} = 0.$$

This expression states that as the share of nontradables in total expenditure increases from zero to 100 percent, the output effect of an improvement in the terms of trade falls from a positive value to zero. The relationship between the share of nontradables in consumption and the effect of the terms of trade on output is in general nonmonotonic.

This result, however, applies to a measure of output in terms of units of final consumption goods. That is, the measure of output here results from dividing nominal output by the consumer price index. The quantitative analysis of the MX model in Chapter 7 (see in particular Section 7.5.5) is based on a measure of output that results from dividing nominal output by a Paasche GDP deflator. We argued there that this measure of output is the one that is comparable with the data on real GDP used in the empirical analysis. Under this definition, real GDP in period t in the present model is given by $P^x y_t^x + P^N y_t^n$, where P^x and P^n are two constants denoting the base-year prices of exportable and nontradable goods. Noting that the present model assumes that both y_t^x and y_t^n are exogenous and constant endowments, we obtain that output at constant GDP prices is constant and independent of the terms of trade, regardless of the size of the nontraded sector. Thus a meaningful discussion of the effects of the terms of trade on movements in real GDP requires laying out a more complex production structure, in which the quantities of different goods produced in the economy are endogenous. We take up this issue in Section 8.4.

8.3 Empirical Evidence on the Effects of Terms-of-Trade Shocks on the Real Exchange Rate and Aggregate Activity

The TNT model of Section 8.2 predicts that a positive innovation in the terms of trade should be accompanied by an appreciation of the real exchange rate. That is, improvements in the terms of trade are predicted to make the country more expensive. Is this prediction consistent with the data?

To address this question, we expand the SVAR model of Section 7.4 in Chapter 7 to include the real exchange rate.[1] Specifically, the empirical model is

$$x_t = h_x x_{t-1} + \Pi \epsilon_t.$$

Assume that the vector x_t is given by

$$x_t \equiv \begin{bmatrix} \widehat{tot}_t \\ \widehat{tb}_t \\ \widehat{y}_t \\ \widehat{c}_t \\ \widehat{i}_t \\ \widehat{RER}_t \end{bmatrix},$$

where $\widehat{tot}_t$, $\widehat{y}_t$, $\widehat{c}_t$, $\widehat{i}_t$, and $\widehat{RER}_t$ denote log-deviations of the terms of trade, real output per capita, real private consumption per capita, real gross investment per capita, and the real exchange rate from their respective quadratic time trends. The variable $\widehat{tb}_t$ is constructed by dividing the trade balance by the trend component of output and then removing a quadratic time trend. As the empirical measure of RER_t we use the bilateral U.S. dollar real exchange rate, defined as

$$RER_t = \frac{\mathcal{E}_t P_t^{US}}{P_t},$$

---

1. The material in this and the following sections draws on Schmitt-Grohé and Uribe (forthcoming).

where $\mathcal{E}_t$ denotes the dollar nominal exchange rate, given by the domestic-currency price of one U.S. dollar, P_t^{US} denotes the U.S. consumer price index, and P_t denotes the domestic consumer price index.[2] The sample period is 1980 to 2011. Only countries for which at least 30 consecutive years of data for all components of x_t is available were included in the estimation. The resulting sample contains 38 countries.[3] We continue to impose the identification assumptions that the off-diagonal elements of the first rows of the matrices h_x and Π are nil. The second of these restrictions identifies the terms-of-trade shock as the first element of the vector ϵ_t.

Figure 8.1 displays the response of the variables included in the vector x_t to a 10 percent improvement in the terms of trade. The responses of variables other than the real exchange rate are similar to those implied by the five-variable SVAR presented in Section 7.4 of Chapter 7. Specifically, the SVAR implies that a terms-of-trade appreciation improves the trade balance (the HLM effect) and leads to an expansion in aggregate activity. The novelty of the figure is the response of the real exchange rate. The improvement in the terms of trade causes a real-exchange-rate appreciation, that is, the country becomes more expensive vis-à-vis the rest of the world. On impact, the 10 percent improvement in the terms of trade leads to a 1.6 percent real-exchange-rate appreciation with a half-life of about 2 years. The estimated response of the real exchange rate is qualitatively in line with the predictions of the TNT model studied in Section 8.2.

The present empirical model implies that terms-of-trade shocks explain a modest fraction of cyclical fluctuations in emerging and poor countries. Table 8.1 displays the share of the variances of output, consumption, investment, the real exchange rate, and the trade balance explained by terms-of-trade shocks for each of the 38 countries included in our panel. Terms-of-trade shocks explain on average between 9 and 14 percent of the variances of all variables included in the SVAR. The estimated importance of terms-of-trade shocks is close to that obtained in the five-variable SVAR that excludes the real exchange rate studied in Section 7.4 of Chapter 7 with the exception of Egypt.

---

2. An alternative measure of RER_t is the real effective exchange rate, which is based on the value of a currency against a trade-weighted average of foreign currencies. We do not use this measure because of insufficient data availability. In the WDI database, our requirement of at least 30 years of data is satisfied by only 26 of the 51 countries in our panel.

3. The data come from the World Bank's World Development Indicators database and, except for the real exchange rate, are available in the file `usg_data_annual.xls` posted with the online materials for Chapter 1 on the book's Web site via http://press.princeton.edu/titles/11032.html. In the construction of the empirical measure of RER_t, the series used for the consumer price index is FP.CPI.TOTL and for the nominal exchange rate is PA.NUS.FCRF, both from the WDI database. The WDI does not provide CPI data for Argentina. The Argentine CPI index was taken from INDEC until 2006, and from IPC-7-Provincias from 2007 to 2011 due to systematic underreporting by INDEC during this period. The file `wdi_cpi.xls`, available in the online materials for Chapter 8 on the book's Web site, contains data on nominal exchange rates and consumer price indices. The file `cpi_arg.xls` contains the consumer price data for Argentina. The countries included in the sample are Algeria, Argentina, Bolivia, Botswana, Brazil, Burundi, Cameroon, Central African Republic, Colombia, Congo, Costa Rica, Côte d'Ivoire, Dominican Republic, Egypt, El Salvador, Ghana, Guatemala, Honduras, India, Indonesia, Jordan, Kenya, Madagascar, Malaysia, Mauritius, Mexico, Morocco, Pakistan, Paraguay, Peru, Philippines, Senegal, South Africa, South Korea, Sudan, Thailand, Turkey, and Uruguay.

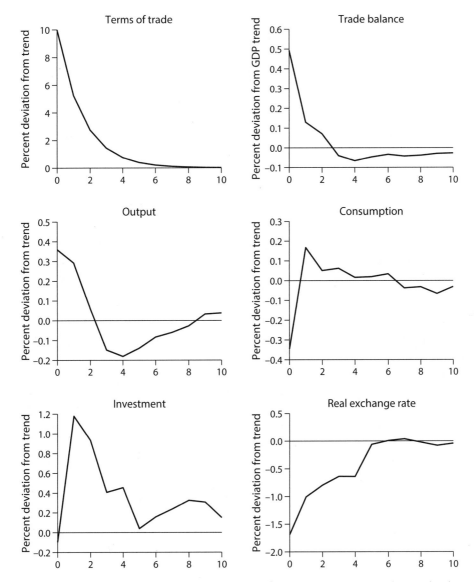

Figure 8.1 Response of the real exchange rate and aggregate activity to an innovation in the terms of trade: SVAR evidence.

Note: Replication file `rer_ir.m` is available online in `usg_rer_svar.zip`.

There is significant cross-country dispersion of the estimated importance of terms-of-trade shocks. The median absolute deviations of the contribution of terms-of-trade shocks to the variances of the variables included in the SVAR is about two-thirds as large as the median. The associated standard deviations (not shown) are about twice as large as the median absolute deviations.

Table 8.1　Share of Variance Explained by Terms-of-Trade Shocks: Country-Level SVAR Evidence

Country	*tot*	*tb*	*y*	*c*	*i*	*RER*
Algeria	100	67	7	58	8	24
Argentina	100	28	22	14	16	33
Bolivia	100	6	6	8	12	7
Botswana	100	20	50	32	32	8
Brazil	100	47	16	4	28	57
Burundi	100	4	2	4	1	9
Cameroon	100	9	14	13	13	16
Central African Republic	100	37	6	14	13	53
Colombia	100	7	18	7	13	13
Congo, Dem. Rep.	100	3	1	1	7	12
Costa Rica	100	17	3	1	2	2
Côte d'Ivoire	100	30	43	36	43	70
Dominican Republic	100	20	17	16	28	14
Egypt	100	62	58	46	65	48
El Salvador	100	8	2	4	4	22
Ghana	100	4	4	3	3	4
Guatemala	100	5	1	2	2	13
Honduras	100	7	5	1	7	15
India	100	4	13	19	1	1
Indonesia	100	13	22	17	23	14
Jordan	100	31	13	32	4	5
Kenya	100	6	4	9	12	2
Madagascar	100	7	8	1	3	6
Malaysia	100	6	5	3	5	1
Mauritius	100	9	2	6	2	4
Mexico	100	12	17	12	10	28
Morocco	100	2	2	2	3	10
Pakistan	100	3	10	2	2	3
Paraguay	100	12	7	8	10	1
Peru	100	16	19	14	23	15
Philippines	100	19	13	17	8	38
Senegal	100	4	8	3	19	57
South Africa	100	12	11	9	8	23
South Korea	100	17	2	3	28	36
Sudan	100	20	38	10	21	18
Thailand	100	14	13	15	2	25
Turkey	100	4	14	19	31	3
Uruguay	100	20	36	37	15	30
Median	100	12	10	9	10	14
Median absolute deviation	0	7	6	6	7	10

Notes: Shares are expressed as percentages. Replication file `table_v_share_cbc.m` is available online in `usg_rer_svar.zip`.

8.4 The MXN Model

In Chapter 7 we argued that a model with only importable and exportable goods (the MX model) exaggerates the importance of terms-of-trade shocks, as it predicts that their contribution to business-cycle fluctuations is about twice as large as observed in the data. In this section we expand the MX model to include a nontraded sector and ask whether the addition of this sector can reduce the predicted importance of terms-of-trade shocks to values that concur with the empirical evidence reported here.

The model includes three sectors, an importable sector (M), an exportable sector (X), and a nontradable sector (N). We refer to this model as the MXN model. Because the nontraded sector is not directly affected by movements in the relative price of exportables in terms of importables and because the nontraded sector is large, it should act as a buffer that dampens the aggregate effects of terms-of-trade shocks.

8.4.1 Households

The model economy is populated by a large number of identical households with preferences described by the utility function

$$E_0 \sum_{t=0}^{\infty} \beta^t U(c_t, h_t^m, h_t^x, h_t^n),$$

where c_t denotes consumption, h_t^m denotes hours worked in the importable sector, h_t^x hours worked in the exportable sector, and h_t^n hours worked in the nontradable sector. Households maximize their lifetime utility subject to the sequential budget constraint:

$$c_t + i_t^m + i_t^x + i_t^n + \Phi_m(k_{t+1}^m - k_t^m) + \Phi_x(k_{t+1}^x - k_t^x) + \Phi_n(k_{t+1}^n - k_t^n) + p_t^\tau d_t$$

$$= \frac{p_t^\tau d_{t+1}}{1 + r_t} + w_t^m h_t^m + w_t^x h_t^x + w_t^n h_t^n + u_t^m k_t^m + u_t^x k_t^x + u_t^n k_t^n,$$

where i_t^j, k_t^j, w_t^j, and u_t^j denote, respectively, gross investment, the capital stock, the real wage, and the rental rate of capital in sector j, for $j = m, x, n$ with the superscripts m, x, and n denoting the sector producing, respectively, importable, exportable, and nontraded goods. The functions $\Phi_j(\cdot)$, $j = m, x, n$, introduce capital adjustment costs and are assumed to be increasing and convex and to satisfy $\Phi_j(0) = \Phi_j'(0) = 0$. The variable p_t^τ denotes the relative price of the tradable composite good in terms of final goods (to be formally defined below), d_t denotes the stock of debt in period t, denominated in units of the tradable composite good, and r_t denotes the interest rate on debt held from period t to $t + 1$. Consumption, investment, wages, rental rates, debt, and capital adjustment costs are all expressed in units of final goods.

The capital stocks obey the familiar laws of motion:

$$k^m_{t+1} = (1 - \delta)k^m_t + i^m_t, \tag{8.16}$$

$$k^x_{t+1} = (1 - \delta)k^x_t + i^x_t, \tag{8.17}$$

and

$$k^n_{t+1} = (1 - \delta)k^n_t + i^n_t. \tag{8.18}$$

Using these laws of motion to eliminate i^m_t, i^x_t, and i^n_t from the household's budget constraint and letting $\lambda_t \beta^t$ denote the Lagrange multiplier associated with the resulting budget constraint, we have that the first-order optimality conditions with respect to c_t, h^m_t, h^x_t, h^n_t, d_{t+1}, k^m_{t+1}, k^x_{t+1}, and k^n_{t+1} are, respectively,

$$U_1(c_t, h^m_t, h^x_t, h^n_t) = \lambda_t, \tag{8.19}$$

$$- U_2(c_t, h^m_t, h^x_t, h^n_t) = \lambda_t w^m_t, \tag{8.20}$$

$$- U_3(c_t, h^m_t, h^x_t, h^n_t) = \lambda_t w^x_t, \tag{8.21}$$

$$- U_4(c_t, h^m_t, h^x_t, h^n_t) = \lambda_t w^n_t, \tag{8.22}$$

$$\lambda_t p^\tau_t = \beta(1 + r_t) E_t \lambda_{t+1} p^\tau_{t+1}, \tag{8.23}$$

$$\lambda_t \left[1 + \Phi'_m(k^m_{t+1} - k^m_t) \right] = \beta E_t \lambda_{t+1} \left[u^m_{t+1} + 1 - \delta + \Phi'_m(k^m_{t+2} - k^m_{t+1}) \right], \tag{8.24}$$

$$\lambda_t \left[1 + \Phi'_x(k^x_{t+1} - k^x_t) \right] = \beta E_t \lambda_{t+1} \left[u^x_{t+1} + 1 - \delta + \Phi'_x(k^x_{t+2} - k^x_{t+1}) \right], \tag{8.25}$$

and

$$\lambda_t \left[1 + \Phi'_n(k^n_{t+1} - k^n_t) \right] = \beta E_t \lambda_{t+1} \left[u^n_{t+1} + 1 - \delta + \Phi'_n(k^n_{t+2} - k^n_{t+1}) \right]. \tag{8.26}$$

These optimality conditions are identical to those associated with the MX model, except for three of them. One is equation (8.22), which equates the marginal disutility of working in the nontraded sector, $-U_4(c_t, h^m_t, h^x_t, h^n_t)$, to the real wage in that sector expressed in units of utility, $\lambda_t w^n_t$. The second is the Euler equation for bonds, equation (8.23), which now features the relative price of the tradable composite good in terms of final goods, p^τ_t. To see why this price appears in the Euler equation for bonds, note first that in both the MX and MXN models, debt is denominated in units of the tradable composite good, whereas the household's budget constraint is expressed in units of the final good. In the MX model, the tradable composite good is the final good, so its relative price is identically equal to one. In the MXN model, however, the tradable composite good is not the final good. The third difference is the Euler equation (8.26), governing the optimal accumulation of capital in the nontraded sector.

8.4.2 Firms Producing Final Goods

Final goods are produced using nontradable goods and a composite of tradable goods via the technology $B(a_t^\tau, a_t^n)$, where a_t^τ denotes the tradable composite good, and a_t^n denotes the nontraded good. The aggregator function $B(\cdot, \cdot)$ is assumed to be increasing, concave, and homogeneous of degree one. Final goods are sold to households, which then allocate them to consumption or investment purposes. Producers of final goods behave competitively. Their profits are given by

$$B(a_t^\tau, a_t^n) - p_t^\tau a_t^\tau - p_t^n a_t^n,$$

where p_t^n denotes the relative price of nontradable goods in terms of final goods. The firm's profit maximization conditions are

$$B_1(a_t^\tau, a_t^n) = p_t^\tau \tag{8.27}$$

and

$$B_2(a_t^\tau, a_t^n) = p_t^n. \tag{8.28}$$

These expressions define the domestic demand functions for the tradable composite good and the nontraded good.

8.4.3 Firms Producing the Tradable Composite Good

The tradable composite good is produced using importable and exportable goods as intermediate inputs via the technology

$$a_t^\tau = A(a_t^m, a_t^x), \tag{8.29}$$

where a_t^m and a_t^x denote the domestic absorptions of importable and exportable goods, respectively. The aggregator function $A(\cdot, \cdot)$ is increasing, concave, and linearly homogeneous. Profits are given by

$$p_t^\tau A(a_t^m, a_t^x) - p_t^m a_t^m - p_t^x a_t^x,$$

where p_t^m denotes the relative price of importable goods in terms of final goods, and p_t^x denotes the relative price of exportable goods in terms of final goods. Firms in this sector are assumed to behave competitively in intermediate and final goods markets. Then profit maximization implies that

$$p_t^\tau A_1(a_t^m, a_t^x) = p_t^m, \tag{8.30}$$

and

$$p_t^\tau A_2(a_t^m, a_t^x) = p_t^x. \tag{8.31}$$

These two expressions represent the domestic demand functions for importable and exportable goods, respectively.

8.4.4 Firms Producing Importable, Exportable, and Nontradable Goods

Importable, exportable, and nontradable goods are produced with capital and labor via the technologies

$$y_t^m = A^m F^m(k_t^m, h_t^m), \tag{8.32}$$

$$y_t^x = A^x F^x(k_t^x, h_t^x), \tag{8.33}$$

and

$$y_t^n = A^n F^n(k_t^n, h_t^n), \tag{8.34}$$

where y_t^j and A^j denote, respectively, output and a productivity factor in sector $j = m, x, n$. The production functions $F^j(\cdot, \cdot)$, $j = m, x, n$, are assumed to be increasing in both arguments, concave, and homogeneous of degree one. Profits of firms producing importable, exportable, or nontraded goods are given by

$$p_t^j A^j F^j(k_t^j, h_t^j) - w_t^j h_t^j - u_t^j k_t^j,$$

for $j = m, x, n$. Firms are assumed to behave competitively in product and factor markets. Then the first-order profit maximization conditions are

$$p_t^m A^m F_1^m(k_t^m, h_t^m) = u_t^m, \tag{8.35}$$

$$p_t^m A^m F_2^m(k_t^m, h_t^m) = w_t^m, \tag{8.36}$$

$$p_t^x A^x F_1^x(k_t^x, h_t^x) = u_t^x, \tag{8.37}$$

$$p_t^x A^x F_2^x(k_t^x, h_t^x) = w_t^x, \tag{8.38}$$

$$p_t^n A^n F_1^n(k_t^n, h_t^n) = u_t^n, \tag{8.39}$$

and

$$p_t^n A^n F_2^n(k_t^n, h_t^n) = w_t^n. \tag{8.40}$$

These efficiency conditions represent the sectoral demand functions for capital and labor. Together with the assumption of linear homogeneity of the production technologies, they imply that firms make zero profits at all times.

8.4.5 Market Clearing

In equilibrium the demand for final goods must equal the supply of this type of goods:

$$c_t + i_t^m + i_t^x + i_t^n + \Phi_m(k_{t+1}^m - k_t^m)$$
$$+ \Phi_x(k_{t+1}^x - k_t^x) + \Phi_n(k_{t+1}^n - k_t^n) = B(a_t^\tau, a_t^n). \tag{8.41}$$

Also, the demand for nontradables must equal the production of nontradables:

$$a_t^n = y_t^n. \tag{8.42}$$

Imports, denoted m_t, are defined as the difference between the domestic absorption of importables, a_t^m, and importable output, y_t^m, or

$$m_t = p_t^m(a_t^m - y_t^m). \tag{8.43}$$

The price of importables appears on the right-hand side of this definition, because m_t is expressed in units of final goods, whereas y_t^m and a_t^m are expressed in units of importable goods. Similarly, exports, denoted x_t, are given by the difference between exportable output, y_t^x, and the domestic absorption of exportables, a_t^x:

$$x_t = p_t^x(y_t^x - a_t^x). \tag{8.44}$$

Like imports, exports are measured in terms of final goods.

Combining the above two definitions, the household's budget constraint, and the definitions of profits in the final- and intermediate-good markets, and taking into account that firms make zero profits at all times, yields the following economy-wide resource constraint:

$$p_t^\tau \frac{d_{t+1}}{1+r_t} = p_t^\tau d_t + m_t - x_t. \tag{8.45}$$

To ensure a stationary equilibrium process for external debt, we assume, as in the MX model, that the country interest-rate premium is debt elastic:

$$r_t = r^* + p(d_{t+1}), \tag{8.46}$$

where r^* denotes the sum of world interest rate and the constant component of the interest-rate premium, and $p(d)$ denotes the debt-elastic component of the country interest-rate premium. We assume that $p(\bar{d}) = 0$ and $p'(\bar{d}) > 0$, for some constant $\bar{d}$.

The terms of trade, denoted tot_t, are defined as the relative price of exportable goods in terms of importable goods, that is,

$$tot_t = \frac{p_t^x}{p_t^m}. \tag{8.47}$$

As in the empirical analysis conducted earlier in this chapter, we assume that the country is small in international product markets and therefore takes the evolution of the terms of trade as given. Also in line with the empirical analysis, we assume an AR(1) structure for the law of motion of the logarithm of the terms of trade:

$$\ln\left(\frac{tot_t}{\overline{tot}}\right) = \rho \ln\left(\frac{tot_{t-1}}{\overline{tot}}\right) + \pi \epsilon_t^{tot}, \tag{8.48}$$

where ϵ_t^{tot} is a white noise process with mean zero and unit variance, and $\overline{tot} > 0$, $\rho \in (-1, 1)$, and $\pi > 0$ are parameters.

8.4.6 Competitive Equilibrium

A competitive equilibrium is then a set of 33 processes k_{t+1}^m, i_t^m, k_{t+1}^x, i_t^x, k_{t+1}^n, i_t^n, c_t, h_t^m, h_t^x, h_t^n, λ_t, w_t^m, w_t^x, w_t^n, p_t^τ, r_t, u_t^m, u_t^x, u_t^n, a_t^m, a_t^x, a_t^τ, p_t^m, p_t^x, a_t^n, p_t^n, y_t^m, y_t^x, y_t^n, m_t, x_t,

d_{t+1}, and tot_t satisfying equations (8.16)–(8.48), given initial conditions k_0^m, k_0^x, k_0^n, d_0, and tot_{-1}, and the stochastic process ϵ_t^{tot}.

8.4.7 Observables

As discussed in Chapter 7, for the quantitative analysis that follows we must express output, consumption, investment, and the trade balance at constant GDP prices, using a Paasche GDP deflator. For this is the way in which the data used in the empirical analysis are expressed. In the present model, this measure of real GDP, which we refer to as observable GDP and denote by y_t^o, is given by

$$y_t^o = p^m y_t^m + p^x y_t^x + p^n y_t^n,$$

where p^i for $i = m, x, n$ denotes the steady-state value of the relative price of good i in terms of final consumption goods. Real consumption at constant GDP prices, denoted c_t^o, is given by

$$c_t^o = \frac{p^m y_t^m + p^x y_t^x + p^n y_t^n}{p_t^m y_t^m + p_t^x y_t^x + p_t^n y_t^n} c_t.$$

Similar expressions apply to investment and the trade balance. For a more detailed discussion of this issue, see Section 7.5.5 of Chapter 7.

8.4.8 Functional Forms

As in the MX model, we assume that the period utility function is CRRA in a quasi-linear composite of consumption and labor:

$$U(c, h^m, h^x, h^n) = \frac{[c - G(h^m, h^x, h^n)]^{1-\sigma} - 1}{1 - \sigma},$$

where

$$G(h^m, h^x, h^n) = \frac{(h^m)^{\omega_m}}{\omega_m} + \frac{(h^x)^{\omega_x}}{\omega_x} + \frac{(h^n)^{\omega_n}}{\omega_n},$$

with $\sigma, \omega_m, \omega_x, \omega_n > 0$. This specification implies that sectoral labor supplies are wealth inelastic.

The technologies for producing importables, exportables, and nontradables are all assumed to be Cobb-Douglas:

$$F^m(k^m, h^m) = \left(k^m\right)^{\alpha_m} \left(h^m\right)^{1-\alpha_m},$$

$$F^x(k^x, h^x) = \left(k^x\right)^{\alpha_x} \left(h^x\right)^{1-\alpha_x},$$

and

$$F^n(k^n, h^n) = \left(k^n\right)^{\alpha_n} \left(h^n\right)^{1-\alpha_n},$$

where $\alpha_m, \alpha_x, \alpha_n \in (0, 1)$. We assume that the Armington aggregators used in the production of the tradable composite good and the final good take CES forms, that is,

$$A(a_t^m, a_t^x) = \left[\chi_m \left(a_t^m \right)^{1 - \frac{1}{\mu_{mx}}} + (1 - \chi_m) \left(a_t^x \right)^{1 - \frac{1}{\mu_{mx}}} \right]^{\frac{1}{1 - \frac{1}{\mu_{mx}}}}$$

$$B(a_t^\tau, a_t^n) = \left[\chi_\tau \left(a_t^\tau \right)^{1 - \frac{1}{\mu_{\tau n}}} + (1 - \chi_\tau) \left(a_t^n \right)^{1 - \frac{1}{\mu_{\tau n}}} \right]^{\frac{1}{1 - \frac{1}{\mu_{\tau n}}}},$$

with $\chi_m, \chi_\tau \in (0, 1)$, and $\mu_{mx}, \mu_{\tau n} > 0$. The specification of the interest-rate premium and the capital adjustment costs are as in the MX model of Chapter 7:

$$p(d) = \psi \left(e^{d - \bar{d}} - 1 \right),$$

and

$$\Phi_j(x) = \frac{\phi_j}{2} x^2,$$

with $\psi, \phi_j > 0$, for $j = m, x, n$.

8.4.9 Calibration of the MXN Model

The present model is medium scale in size and lies at the intersection of trade and business-cycle analysis. The characterization of the steady state is complex—even numerically. The calibration of the model inherits this complexity.

Tables 8.2 and 8.3 summarize the calibration of the MXN model. As usual, we denote the steady-state value of a variable by dropping the time subscript. The equilibrium conditions (8.16)–(8.48) evaluated at the steady state and adopting the assumed functional forms represent a system of 33 equations in 52 unknowns: the 33 endogenous variables listed in the definition of equilibrium given in Section 8.4.6 and 19 structural parameters, namely, $A^m, A^x, A^n, \delta, \omega_m, \omega_x, \omega_n, \beta, \chi_m, \mu_{mx}, \chi_\tau, \mu_{\tau n}, \alpha_m, \alpha_x, \alpha_n, r^*, \bar{d}, \overline{tot}$, and σ. Therefore, we must add 19 calibration restrictions. The structural parameters ψ, ρ, π, and ϕ_j, $j = m, x, n$ do not appear in the steady-state system. We will address the calibration of these parameters shortly.

We enumerate the required 19 restrictions in parentheses. In line with the calibration of the MX model of Chapter 7, we assume that the time unit is 1 year and set

1. $\sigma = 2$,

2–4. $\omega_m = \omega_x = \omega_n = 1.455$,

5. $\delta = 0.1$,

6. $r^* = 0.11$,[4]

---

[4]. This value is high because it is the sum of the world interest rate, 0.04, and the invariant component of the country premium, 0.07 (Uribe and Yue 2006).

Table 8.2   Calibration of the MXN Model

Calibrated Structural Parameters

σ	δ	r^*	α_m, α_x	α_n	$\omega_m, \omega_x, \omega_n$	μ_{mx}	$\mu_{\tau n}$	$\overline{tot}$	A^m, A^n	β	π	ρ
2	0.1	0.11	0.35	0.25	1.455	1	0.5	1	1	$1/(1+r^*)$	$*$	$*$

Moment Restrictions

s_n	s_x	s_{tb}	$\dfrac{p^m y^m}{p^x y^x}$	$\dfrac{\sigma_{i_m + i_x}}{\sigma_{i_n}}$	$\dfrac{\sigma_i}{\sigma_y}$	$\dfrac{\sigma_{tb}}{\sigma_y}$
0.5	0.2	0.01	1	1.5	$**$	$**$

Implied Structural Parameter Values

χ_m	χ_τ	$\overline{d}$	A^x	β	ϕ_m	ϕ_x	ϕ_n	ψ
0.8980	0.4360	0.0078	1	0.9009	$**$	$**$	$**$	$**$

Notes: $s_n \equiv p^n y^n / y$, $s_x \equiv x/y$, and $s_{tb} \equiv (x-m)/y$, where $y \equiv p^m y^m + p^x y^x + p^n y^n$.
$*$ Country-specific values are given in Table 7.1.
$**$ Country-specific values are given in Table 8.3.

    7. $\mu_{mx} = 1$,

    8. $\overline{tot} = 1$,

    9. $A^m = 1$,

    10. $\beta = 1/(1+r^*)$.

In our sample, the average export share in GDP is 20 percent. So we impose

    11. $x/(p^m y^m + p^x y^x + p^n y^n) = 0.2$.

And the average trade-balance-to-GDP ratio is 1 percent, or

    12. $(x-m)/(p^m y^m + p^x y^x + p^n y^n) = 0.01$.

This adds 12 restrictions, which means that we are still 7 restrictions short. We normalize the productivity factor A^n to unity, which adds the restriction

    13. $A^n = 1$.

Na (2015) estimates an average labor share for emerging countries of 70 percent, so we impose

    14. $(w^m h^m + w^x h^x + w^n h^n)/(p^m y^m + p^x y^x + p^n y^n) = 0.7$.

It is generally assumed that in emerging and poor countries the nontraded sector is more labor intensive than the export- or import-producing sectors. For instance, based on Argentine data, Uribe (1997) calculates the labor share in the nontraded sector to be 0.75. We follow this calibration and impose the restriction

    15. $w^n h^n / (p^n y^n) = 0.75$.

Table 8.3 Country-Specific Estimates of the Capital Adjustment Cost Parameters and the Debt Elasticity of the Interest Rate

Country	ϕ_m	ϕ_x	ϕ_n	ψ	σ_i/σ_y Data	σ_i/σ_y Model	σ_{tb}/σ_y Data	σ_{tb}/σ_y Model
Algeria	32.0	0.2	35.1	0.0	2.8	2.7	2.2	2.2
Argentina	0.2	3.2	39.8	7.0	2.0	2.0	0.4	0.4
Bolivia	0.0	39.9	5.3	0.9	4.4	3.2	0.8	0.8
Botswana	0.0	37.9	1.1	0.1	5.9	4.4	1.6	1.6
Brazil	38.9	0.1	14.3	1.0	3.2	1.9	0.5	0.5
Burundi	35.5	0.9	5.5	0.3	2.5	2.5	0.9	0.9
Cameroon	2.0	29.1	26.3	20.0	2.1	2.3	0.1	0.5
Central African Republic	32.4	2.6	0.0	0.0	7.8	2.3	1.7	1.6
Colombia	0.0	12.6	0.0	14.6	3.1	2.5	0.4	0.4
Congo, Dem. Rep.	39.7	0.0	38.8	4.0	8.2	1.7	0.3	0.3
Costa Rica	38.1	0.7	10.2	0.1	3.0	3.0	1.5	1.5
Côte d'Ivoire	20.0	0.0	20.0	3.2	3.4	1.7	0.3	0.3
Dominican Republic	20.0	0.0	20.0	1.7	2.9	1.6	0.4	0.5
Egypt	34.5	0.0	0.2	0.2	5.7	3.0	1.0	1.0
El Salvador	0.0	39.1	40.0	3.3	3.4	2.9	0.6	0.7
Ghana	0.0	19.1	8.9	3.2	9.6	3.4	0.9	0.9
Guatemala	37.1	0.0	3.7	4.4	9.3	9.2	1.8	2.0
Honduras	0.0	35.3	2.5	0.3	6.0	3.6	1.1	1.1
India	20.0	3.6	20.0	1.5	1.5	1.6	0.3	0.3
Indonesia	37.7	0.0	17.3	1.9	4.3	1.9	0.3	0.3
Jordan	20.0	11.2	20.0	0.1	1.0	1.9	1.3	1.5
Kenya	34.5	0.0	1.9	0.4	5.2	2.7	0.7	0.7
Madagascar	22.5	0.3	3.0	0.3	2.6	2.6	0.9	0.9
Malaysia	0.0	35.3	0.4	0.1	4.4	4.5	1.7	1.7
Mauritius	39.6	0.1	6.0	0.0	4.3	3.9	2.3	2.3
Mexico	32.1	6.0	39.9	0.4	1.6	1.8	0.4	0.4
Morocco	0.0	35.8	38.4	2.6	5.0	2.9	0.7	0.7
Pakistan	0.0	33.7	3.3	0.2	8.1	3.3	1.1	1.1
Paraguay	0.0	3.8	36.7	2.6	2.1	2.3	0.6	0.6
Peru	20.0	0.0	40.0	3.7	2.2	1.8	0.2	0.2
Philippines	26.4	0.2	27.8	1.1	1.8	1.8	0.4	0.4
Senegal	38.9	10.1	12.4	0.2	14.2	1.7	0.9	0.9
South Africa	30.3	0.0	1.0	1.1	2.5	2.1	0.3	0.3
South Korea	30.8	0.1	0.8	0.2	4.9	2.9	1.0	1.0
Sudan	34.0	0.0	6.1	0.9	4.1	2.2	0.4	0.4
Thailand	20.0	9.1	20.0	0.6	0.7	1.2	0.6	0.6
Turkey	20.0	0.0	20.0	6.7	6.3	1.8	0.3	0.3
Uruguay	34.2	0.8	20.0	5.7	1.7	1.8	0.3	0.3
Median	21.2	0.8	13.4	0.9	3.4	2.3	0.6	0.7
Median absolute deviation	15.1	0.8	10.6	0.8	1.4	0.6	0.3	0.3

We assume that the importable and exportable sectors are equally labor intensive, that is, we impose

16. $w^m h^m / (p^m y^m) = w^x h^x / (p^x y^x).$

We follow the usual practice of proxying the share of nontraded output in total output by the observed share of the service sector in GDP. Using data from UNCTAD's *Handbook of Statistics* on sectoral GDP for 51 poor and emerging countries over the period 1995–2012, we obtain an average share of services in GDP of slightly above 50 percent (for details on the data, see Section 7.6.5 of Chapter 7). Thus we impose the restriction

17. $p^n y^n / (p^m y^m + p^x y^x + p^n y^n) = 0.5.$

In Chapter 7, we also document that in emerging and poor countries the exportable and importable sectors are of about the same size. Therefore we impose the restriction

18. $p^x y^x = p^m y^m.$

Finally, Akinci (2011) surveys the literature on estimates of the elasticity of substitution between tradables and nontradables in emerging and poor countries and arrives at a value close to 0.5. Thus we set

19. $\mu_{\tau n} = 0.5.$

This completes the calibration strategy of all parameters appearing in the set of steady-state equilibrium conditions.

The parameters π, ρ, ψ, and ϕ_j, for $j = m, x, n$ do not appear in the steady-state equilibrium conditions, but they do play a role in the equilibrium dynamics. We calibrate π and ρ country by country using the econometric estimates presented in Table 7.1 of Chapter 7. We use a method of moments to estimate the capital adjustment cost parameters, ϕ_m, ϕ_x, ϕ_n, and the parameter ψ governing the debt elasticity of the country premium. To this end, we impose three moment restrictions.[5] First, McIntyre (2003) estimates, using OECD data over the period 1970–1992, that the standard deviation of investment in the traded sector is 1.5 times as large as its counterpart in the nontraded sector. We assume that this relationship also holds for emerging and poor countries and conditional on terms-of-trade shocks. Thus one of the moment restrictions we impose is $\sigma_{i_m + i_x} / \sigma_{i_n} = 1.5$ conditional on terms-of-trade shocks. The other two moment restrictions are the country-by-country empirical estimates of the investment-to-output-volatility ratio and the trade-balance-to-output-volatility ratio conditional on terms-of-trade shocks. The empirical estimates of these volatility ratios are those implied by the country-by-country estimates of the SVAR presented in Section 8.3. Thus this estimation procedure delivers one set of parameters ϕ_m, ϕ_x, ϕ_n, and ψ for each country.

---

5. As in the estimation of the MX model in Chapter 7, the number of parameters to be estimated (four) exceeds the number of targeted moments (three). However, there is no under-identification problem, because no subset of parameters can exactly match the targeted moments. In Schmitt-Grohé and Uribe (forthcoming) we employ an impulse-response-matching estimation strategy, which allows for a large number of overidentifying restrictions.

Table 8.3 shows that the parameter estimation yields a satisfactory match of the observed and predicted volatility of the trade balance relative to output conditional on terms-of-trade shocks, with a cross-country median of 0.6 in the data versus 0.7 in the model. The match is less satisfactory for the relative volatility of investment, with cross-country medians of 3.4 in the data and 2.3 in the model. One may wonder why the estimated values of ϕ_j, for $j = m, x, n$, are not lower, given that the model underpredicts the relative volatility of investment. The reason is that, although reducing the ϕ_j values raises all sectoral investment volatilities, it need not result in higher aggregate investment volatility. For as the ϕ_j values go down, sectoral investments become increasingly negatively correlated, conspiring against the volatility of aggregate investment. This negative correlation among sectoral investments is intuitive, because when the relative price of exportables in terms of importables rises (i.e., when the terms of trade appreciate), the value of the marginal product of capital increases in the exportable sector and declines in the importable sector. Thus an improvement in the terms of trade acts like a positive productivity shock in the exportable sector and a negative productivity shock in the importable sector.

Table 8.3 strongly suggests that there is no such thing as a representative emerging or poor country. It shows that the estimated parameters display significant cross-country variations. The median absolute deviations of all four estimated parameters are about as large as the corresponding medians themselves.[6] For this reason, in the analysis that follows, we adopt the approach of deriving model implications country by country as opposed to deriving implications for a model economy calibrated to the average parameter estimate.

8.5 Response of the Real Exchange Rate and Real Activity to Terms-of-Trade Shocks in the MXN Model

As explained earlier, the real exchange rate is defined as the ratio of the foreign consumer price index to the domestic consumer price index. Formally,

$$RER_t = \frac{\mathcal{E}_t P_t^*}{P_t},$$

where $\mathcal{E}_t$ denotes the nominal exchange rate, defined as the domestic currency price of one unit of foreign currency, P_t^* denotes the foreign price of consumption, and P_t denotes the domestic price of consumption. Divide the numerator and denominator by the domestic currency price of the tradable composite good, denoted P_t^τ, to get $RER_t = (\mathcal{E}_t P_t^*/P_t^\tau)/(P_t/P_t^\tau)$. We assume that the law of one price holds for importable and exportable goods and that the technology for aggregating importables and exportables into the tradable composite good, $A(\cdot, \cdot)$, is common across countries. Then the law of one price must also hold for the tradable composite good, that is, $\mathcal{E}_t P_t^{\tau*} = P_t^\tau$, where $P_t^{\tau*}$ denotes the foreign price of the tradable composite good. This yields $RER_t = (P_t^*/P_t^{\tau*})/(P_t/P_t^\tau)$. We assume that the terms-of-trade shocks that are relevant to our

---

6. As mentioned in Section 7.6.6, it might seem strange that the median absolute deviations of ϕ_x and ψ are almost identical to their respective medians. The reason is that the individual estimates display clusters at zero or near zero. To see this, take, for example, the five numbers 0, 0, 0.7, 0.8, and 2. Because of the two zeroes, both the median and the median absolute deviation equal 0.7.

small open economy do not affect the relative price of the tradable composite good in terms of consumption goods in the rest of the world. We therefore assume that $P_t^*/P_t^{\tau*}$ is constant. Without loss of generality, we normalize $P_t^*/P_t^{\tau*}$ to unity. Finally, noting that $p_t^\tau \equiv P_t^\tau/P_t$, we have

$$RER_t = p_t^\tau,$$

which says that the economy becomes more expensive relative to the rest of the world if and only if the tradable good becomes cheaper relative to the final consumption good. It can be shown (see exercise 8.4) that there is a one-to-one negative relationship between p_t^τ and p_t^n. That is, the tradable good becomes more expensive relative to the final consumption good if and only if the nontradable good becomes cheaper relative to the final consumption good. This means that we can express the real exchange rate as a decreasing function of the relative price of nontradables:

$$RER_t = G(p_t^n), \quad G' < 0.$$

Figure 8.2 displays the response of the MXN economy to a 10 percent increase in the terms of trade. The impulse responses shown in the figure are medians across the impulse responses implied by the country-specific calibrations. The model does a good job at capturing the response of the real exchange rate to a terms-of-trade shock. Comparing Figures 8.1 and 8.2 shows that in both the SVAR and the MXN models, an improvement in the terms of trade appreciates the real exchange rate. The explanation behind this result has to do with substitution and income effects. An increase in the relative price of exportables induces a substitution of importable and nontraded absorption for exportable absorption. At the same time, the increase in the price of exportables produces a positive income effect that boosts the domestic demand for all types of goods. Both effects drive up the price of nontradables, because the expansion in the demand for this type of goods must be met by domestic producers, who require a higher price to produce more. The top right panel of Figure 8.2 shows indeed that nontradables become more expensive after the positive terms-of-trade shock. In turn, the increase in the price of nontradables translates into an increase in the price of the final good relative to the price of the tradable composite good, that is, p_t^τ falls.

Intuitively, the increase in the terms of trade produces an expansion in exports. Imports also increase, because as these goods become cheaper relative to exportable goods, consumers increase demand and domestic producers cut back supply. The net effect on the trade balance turns out to be positive. Thus the MXN model is in line with the Harberger-Laursen-Metzler effect present in the SVAR model and discussed in detail in Chapter 7.

In line with the predictions of the SVAR model, the MXN model implies that output expands in response to an improvement in the terms of trade (left column in row 3 of Figure 8.2). This expansion is the result of increased activity in the export and the nontraded sectors, which is only partially offset by a contraction in the importable sector (row 4 of Figure 8.2). The similarity between model and data ends at the qualitative level, however: the increase in output predicted by the MXN model is about four times larger than that implied by the empirical SVAR model.

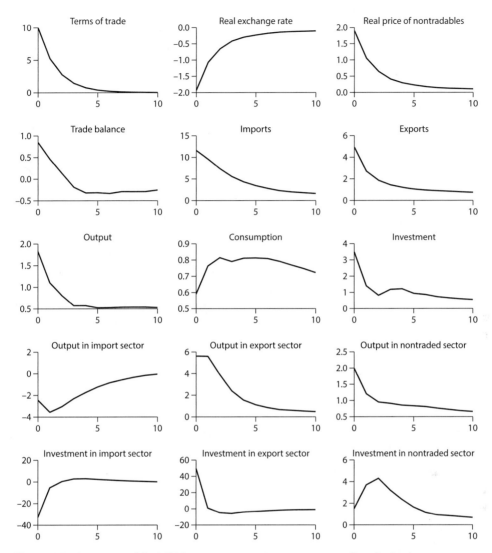

Figure 8.2   Response of the MXN economy to a 10 percent terms-of-trade shock.

Notes: All variables with the exception of the trade balance are expressed as percentage deviations from steady state. The trade balance is expressed in level deviations from steady state as a percentage deviation of steady-state output. Impulse responses are cross-country medians. For each country, impulse responses are produced using the country-specific calibrations of ϕ_m, ϕ_x, ϕ_n, ψ, and ρ. The replication file `plot_mxn_ir.m` is in `usg_mxn.zip`, available on the book's Web site.

The MXN model predicts that both consumption and investment increase in response to the improvement in the terms of trade. This prediction is partly supported by the data. The SVAR predicts that the expansion in consumption and investment is delayed by one period, whereas the MXN model predicts that both variables increase on impact. In addition, as in the case of output, the magnitudes of the theoretical responses are much larger than their empirical counterparts.

Finally, earlier we pointed out that in the MXN model, lowering the adjustment cost parameters ϕ_j, for $j = m, x, n$, does not necessarily result in an increase in aggregate investment volatility because of a negative cross-sectoral correlation of investment, which soaks up the volatility of each individual component. This effect is patently displayed in the bottom row of Figure 8.2. The 10 percent improvement in the terms of trade causes aggregate investment to increase by less than 4 percent. However, investment in the exportable sector increases by 50 percent, while in the importable sector it decreases by 30 percent. It would be of interest to see whether this prediction of the MXN model is borne out by the data.

8.6 The Terms-of-Trade Disconnect

In Chapter 7, we found that the MX model overestimates the importance of terms-of-trade shocks as a source of business cycles by a factor of two. The MX model assumes that all goods are internationally traded. We speculated that omitting the nontraded sector could in principle explain the exaggerated importance the MX model ascribes to terms-of-trade shocks.

Table 8.4 is in line with this conjecture. It shows that the MXN model predicts a more subdued role for terms-of-trade shocks than does the MX model, thereby getting closer to the data. However, concluding that the MXN model provides a satisfactory explanation of the importance of terms-of-trade shocks would be misplaced. The picture that emerges from a country-by-country analysis suggests a different conclusion.

Table 8.4   Share of Variances Explained by Terms-of-Trade Shocks: The MXN Model Versus the Empirical SVAR Model

Variable	MX Model	MXN Model	Empirical SVAR Model
Terms of trade	100	100	100
Trade balance	27	17	12
Output	18	14	10
Consumption	24	17	9
Investment	20	5	10
Real exchange rate	—	1	14

Notes: Each entry is the cross-country median of the fraction of the variance of the corresponding indicator explained by terms-of-trade shocks in percent. Column 1 reproduces from Table 7.6 the results for a model without nontraded goods (MX model). Column 2 corresponds to the MXN model. In columns 1 and 2 the numerator of the fraction is the variance conditional on terms-of-trade shocks predicted by the MX and MXN models, respectively, for country-specific calibrations of ϕ_m, ϕ_x, ϕ_n, ψ, ρ, and π. The denominator is the unconditional variance implied by the empirical country-specific SVAR model. Column 3 reproduces the row labeled "Median" from Table 8.1. The replication file `mxn_var.m` in `usg_mxn.zip` is available on the book's Web site.

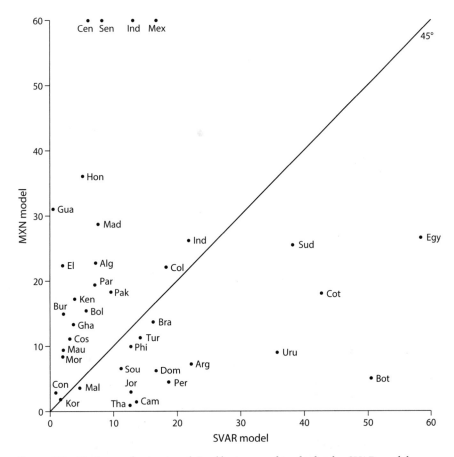

Figure 8.3 Variance of output explained by terms-of-trade shocks: SVAR model versus MXN model.

Notes: The variance of output explained by terms-of-trade shocks in the SVAR and MXN models is expressed as a percentage of the observed total variance of output. The replication file `mxn_versus_svar.m` is available online in `usg_mxn.zip`.

Figure 8.3 plots the share of the variance of output explained by the terms of trade according to the empirical SVAR model (horizontal axis) against the corresponding share according to the MXN model (vertical axis). Each point in the figure represents one of the 38 countries in our sample. If the predictions of the MXN model were in line with the data, all points would lie on the 45° line. The cloud of points not only fails to trace out the 45° line, it also does not even suggest a positive relation between the predictions of the empirical and theoretical models. A similar lack of correlation between theory and data is apparent for consumption, investment, the trade balance, and the real exchange rate, as shown by Figure 8.4. Table 8.5 shows the misalignment of model and data in numbers. It is in this precise sense that we say that there seems to be a disconnect between data and model when it comes to explaining the real effects of terms-of-trade shocks.

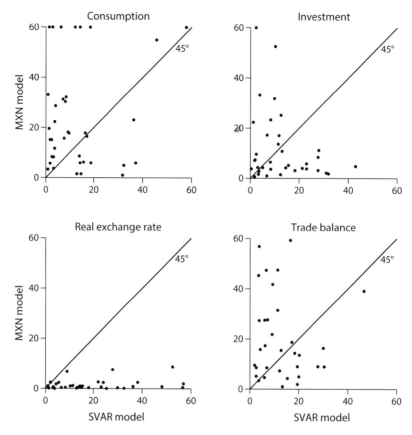

Figure 8.4 Variance of consumption, investment, the trade balance, and the real exchange rate explained by terms-of-trade shocks: SVAR model versus MXN model.

Notes: Variances explained by terms-of-trade shocks in the SVAR and MXN models are expressed as percentages of the respective observed total variances. The replication file `mxn_versus_svar.m` is available online in `usg_mxn.zip`.

We have argued that when one looks at the data through the lens of SVAR models, terms-of-trade shocks play a modest role in generating aggregate fluctuations in emerging and poor countries. A panel of 38 countries containing annual data from 1980 to 2011 yields a median contribution of terms of trade to the overall variance of output of about 10 percent. This result is at odds with the standard view, built on the predictions of calibrated microfounded dynamic business-cycle models, according to which terms-of-trade disturbances explain at least 30 percent of movements in aggregate activity. We formulated a more flexible specification of this framework and estimated key structural parameters using country-level data. We found that on average across countries this specification predicts that terms-of-trade shocks explain about 13 percent of movements in aggregate activity, which is broadly in line with the predictions of the SVAR model.

Table 8.5   Share of Variance Explained by Terms-of-Trade Shocks: Country-Level Predictions of the MXN Model

Country	tot MXN	tot SVAR	tb MXN	tb SVAR	y MXN	y SVAR	c MXN	c SVAR	i MXN	i SVAR	RER MXN	RER SVAR
Algeria	100	100	212	67	23	7	145	58	23	8	2	24
Argentina	100	100	9	28	7	22	6	14	5	16	0	33
Bolivia	100	100	17	6	15	6	30	8	17	12	0	7
Botswana	100	100	2	20	5	50	1	32	2	32	0	8
Brazil	100	100	39	47	14	16	12	4	8	28	1	57
Burundi	100	100	27	4	15	2	29	4	4	1	7	9
Cameroon	100	100	22	9	1	14	2	13	1	13	1	16
Central African Republic	100	100	837	37	136	6	293	14	25	13	9	53
Colombia	100	100	9	7	22	18	31	7	11	13	0	13
Congo, Dem. Rep.	100	100	9	3	3	1	3	1	1	7	1	12
Costa Rica	100	100	59	17	11	3	33	1	7	2	3	2
Côte d'Ivoire	100	100	16	30	18	43	23	36	5	43	2	70
Dominican Republic	100	100	9	20	6	17	6	16	3	28	0	14
Egypt	100	100	28	62	27	58	55	46	8	65	1	48
El Salvador	100	100	132	8	22	2	22	4	33	4	3	22
Ghana	100	100	16	4	13	4	8	3	2	3	0	4
Guatemala	100	100	358	5	31	1	15	2	144	2	0	13
Honduras	100	100	47	7	36	5	20	1	17	7	0	15
India	100	100	57	4	185	13	243	19	22	1	1	1
Indonesia	100	100	16	13	26	22	17	17	6	23	1	14
Jordan	100	100	9	31	3	13	5	32	3	4	2	5
Kenya	100	100	28	6	17	4	32	9	14	12	2	2
Madagascar	100	100	28	7	29	8	86	1	10	3	2	6
Malaysia	100	100	5	6	4	5	8	3	4	5	0	1
Mauritius	100	100	42	9	9	2	81	6	7	2	2	4
Mexico	100	100	48	12	69	17	186	12	53	10	8	28
Morocco	100	100	10	2	8	2	6	2	4	3	1	10
Pakistan	100	100	5	3	18	10	15	2	1	2	1	3
Paraguay	100	100	31	12	19	7	16	8	32	10	1	1
Peru	100	100	4	16	4	19	9	14	4	23	0	15
Philippines	100	100	14	19	10	13	18	17	6	8	3	38
Senegal	100	100	45	4	102	8	246	3	3	19	2	57
South Africa	100	100	7	12	7	11	18	9	4	8	1	23
South Korea	100	100	19	17	2	2	4	3	11	28	1	36
Sudan	100	100	14	20	25	38	18	10	4	21	0	18
Thailand	100	100	1	14	1	13	2	15	0	2	0	25
Turkey	100	100	3	4	11	14	6	19	2	31	0	3
Uruguay	100	100	5	20	9	36	6	37	4	15	0	30
Median	100	100	17	12	14	10	17	9	5	10	1	14
Median absolute deviation	0	0	11	7	8	6	12	6	4	7	0	10

Note: The replication file `mxn_var.m` is online in `usg_mxn.zip`.

Based on these results, one might arrive at two conclusions. First, terms-of-trade shocks play a small role in explaining business cycles in emerging and poor countries. Second, a more flexible specification of the model on which the conventional view is built can reconcile theory and data. However, the second conclusion would be misplaced. Even though on average the importance assigned to terms-of-trade shocks by the theoretical model is similar to that predicted by the empirical SVAR model, the predictions of the two models at the country level are far apart. We therefore conclude that there is a disconnect between the standard theoretical model and the data.

The resolution of the disconnect is likely to involve a combination of better empirical and theoretical models as means to interpret the data. Incorporating the ideas discussed in exercises 7.4–7.6 into the MXN model may represent a good starting point.

8.7 Exercises

8.1 (Properties of the Armington Aggregator) Assume that the Armington aggregator $A(x, y)$ is increasing in both arguments, homogeneous of degree one, and concave. Show that $A_2(x, y)/A_1(x, y)$ can be written as $P(x/y)$, with $P'(\cdot) > 0$.

8.2 (Secular Trend in the Real Exchange Rate) Modify the endowment economy of Section 8.2 by assuming that $\beta < 1/(1+r)$. Characterize the equilibrium dynamics. Provide intuition for the equilibrium behavior of the real exchange rate.

8.3 (A Two-Period TNT Economy with Production) Consider a two-period economy populated by identical households with preferences defined by the utility function

$$\ln c_1 + \ln c_2,$$

where c_1 and c_2 denote consumption in periods 1 and 2, respectively. Suppose that consumption is a composite of tradable and nontradable goods given by

$$c_t = \sqrt{c_t^T c_t^N},$$

for $t = 1, 2$, where c_t^T and c_t^N denote consumption of tradables and nontradables in period t, respectively. Let p_t denote the relative price of nontradables in terms of tradables. Households are endowed with 2 units of labor per period, which they supply to the market inelastically. Let w_t denote the wage rate in period t expressed in terms of tradables. Households are the owners of firms, from which they receive profits each period. Assume also that households start period 1 without any assets or liabilities and can borrow or lend in the international credit market at a zero interest rate.

Tradable and nontradable goods are produced using labor as the sole input via the technologies

$$y_t^T = \sqrt{h_t^T},$$

and

$$y_t^N = \sqrt{h_t^N},$$

where y_t^i and h_t^i denote output and employment in sector i in period t for $i = T, N$ and $t = 1, 2$. Firms in both sectors behave competitively. They pay the wage w_t per unit of labor and distribute profits to households.

1. Write down the household's utility maximization problem.
2. Derive the optimality conditions associated with the household's problem.
3. Write down the firms' profit maximization problems and derive the associated optimality conditions.
4. Write down the market-clearing conditions in this economy.
5. Calculate the equilibrium values of consumption of tradables, consumption of nontradables, the wage rate, the relative price of nontradables, the trade balance, and the current account in periods 1 and 2. The answer to this question consists of 12 numbers, but show your work. Provide intuition for the temporal behavior of the relative price of nontradables and the current account.

8.4 (The Real Exchange Rate and the Price of Nontradables in the MXN Model) Show that in the MXN model there is a one-to-one negative relationship between RER_t and p_t^n. Demonstrate that this negative relationship holds for any positive value of the intratemporal elasticity of substitution between tradables and nontradables, $\mu_{\tau n}$.

8.5 (An Economy with a Leontief Aggregator) Consider a small open economy inhabited by identical consumers with preferences described by the utility function

$$\sum_{t=0}^{\infty} \beta^t [\ln c_t - \gamma h_t],$$

where c_t denotes consumption, h_t denotes hours worked, and $\beta \in (0, 1)$ and $\gamma > 0$ are parameters. The consumption good is a composite made of tradable and nontradable consumption goods via a Leontief aggregator. Formally,

$$c_t = \min\{c_t^T, c_t^N\},$$

where c_t^T and c_t^N denote, respectively, domestic absorption of tradables and nontradables in period t. To produce his nontraded consumption, each consumer operates a linear technology that uses labor as the sole input:

$$c_t^N = Ah_t,$$

where $A > 0$ is a parameter. In addition, households can borrow or lend in the international financial market at the rate $r > 0$. Their sequential budget constraint is given by

$$d_t = (1 + r)d_{t-1} + c_t^T - y^T,$$

where d_t denotes the level of net external debt assumed in period t and maturing in period $t+1$, and $y^T > 0$ denotes a constant endowment of tradable goods. In period 0, households start with outstanding debt equal to $d_{-1} > 0$. Finally, households are subject to a no-Ponzi-game constraint of the form

$$\lim_{t \to \infty} (1+r)^{-t} d_t \le 0.$$

1. Characterize the equilibrium levels of consumption, consumption of nontradables, and hours worked.

2. Suppose that in period 0 and unexpectedly, foreign lenders decide to forgive an amount $\Delta^d > 0$ of the debt. Assuming that Δ^d is relatively small, characterize the effect of this debt forgiveness shock on consumption, consumption of nontradables, and hours worked.

3. Now suppose that $\Delta^d = 0$. Instead, assume that in period 0 the nontraded sector experiences a permanent increase in productivity. Specifically the productivity factor A increases by $\Delta^A > 0$. Characterize the effect of this positive productivity shock on consumption, consumption of nontradables, and hours worked.

8.6 (Dutch Disease and De-Industrialization) Consider a small open economy populated by a large number of identical households with preferences given by the utility function

$$\sum_{t=0}^{\infty} \beta^t [\ln c_t^T + \ln c_t^N],$$

where c_t^T and c_t^N denote consumption of tradable and nontradable goods, respectively, and $\beta \in (0, 1)$ is the subjective discount factor. Households start period 0 with debt obligations equal to d_0 units of tradable goods (assets if $d_0 < 0$). In any period t, households can issue discount debt. Specifically, the promise to pay d_{t+1} units of tradable goods in period $t+1$ provides $d_{t+1}/(1+r)$ units of tradables in period t, with r denoting a constant interest rate. Assume that the market and subjective discount factors are the same, that is, let

$$\beta(1+r) = 1.$$

Borrowing is limited by a no-Ponzi-game constraint of the form $\lim_{t \to \infty} d_{t+1}/(1+r)^t \le 0$. Each period, the household is endowed with one unit of labor, which it fully allocates to the production of tradable and nontradable goods using the technologies

$$y_t^T = A^T h_t^T$$

and

$$y_t^N = A^N h_t^N,$$

where y_t^T and y_t^N denote tradable and nontradable output, h_t^T and h_t^N denote the fraction of time allocated to tradable and nontradable production, and A^T and A^N are parameters defining sectoral productivity. For the purpose of this exercise, think of the traded sector as the industrial sector and of the nontraded sector as the service sector. Let p_t denote the relative price of nontradables in terms of tradables, which we will refer to as the real exchange rate.

1. Write down the household's utility maximization problem (i.e., objective function, choice variables, and budget constraints).

2. Derive the first-order optimality conditions associated with the household's optimization problem.

3. Assuming that both goods are produced in equilibrium, derive the equilibrium levels of consumption of tradable and nontradable goods, sectoral employment, and the real exchange rate. Hint: All of these equilibrium values are functions of the initial level of debt and of the structural parameters of the model.

4. Characterize the effect of an increase in the initial level of debt, d_0, on consumption of tradables and nontradables, sectoral employment, and the real exchange rate. Provide intuition.

5. We say that the economy de-industrializes when the share of employment allocated to the tradable sector falls permanently. Show that there exists a level of initial external debt, which we will denote by $\bar{d}_0$, below which the economy becomes completely de-industrialized (i.e., $h_t^T = 0$ for all t). Derive $\bar{d}_0$ as a function of the structural parameters of the model. The country's net debt position can be driven below $\bar{d}_0$ by a sequence of temporary shocks of any nature. When a sequence of possibly temporary shocks causes a permanent reduction in the size of a large productive sector of the economy we say that the economy suffered a case of Dutch disease. More specifically, economists refer to Dutch disease when the temporary shocks are linked to commodity prices and the sector that shrinks is the industrial or manufacturing sector.

6. Suppose now that d_0 is such that the economy is completely de-industrialized. Derive the equilibrium level of the real exchange rate. Discuss intuitively how d_0 affects the real exchange rate under these circumstances. Make a comparison with the case in which both goods are produced in equilibrium.

9

Nominal Rigidity, Exchange Rates, and Unemployment

In this chapter we build a theoretical framework in which the presence of nominal rigidities can induce an inefficient adjustment to aggregate disturbances. The analysis is guided by two objectives. One is to convey in an intuitive manner how nominal rigidities amplify the business cycle in open economies. The second is to develop a framework from which one can derive quantitative predictions useful for policy evaluation.

To motivate the type of theoretical environment we will study in this chapter, take a look at Figure 9.1. It displays the current account, nominal hourly wages, and the unemployment rate on the periphery of Europe between 2000 and 2011. The inception of the euro in 1999 was followed by massive capital inflows into the region, possibly driven by expectations of a quick convergence of peripheral and central Europe to core Europe (Germany and France). The boom lasted from 2000 to 2008 and was characterized by large current account deficits, spectacular nominal wage increases, and declining rates of unemployment. With the onset of the global crisis of 2008, capital inflows dried up abruptly (see the sharp reduction in the current account deficit), and the region suffered a severe *sudden stop*. At the same time, central banks were unable to change the course of monetary policy because the respective countries were either in the eurozone or pegging to the euro. In spite of the collapse in aggregate demand and the lack of a devaluation, nominal wages remained as high as during the boom. Meanwhile, massive unemployment affected all countries in the region. The data in Figure 9.1 do not provide any indication of causality. In this chapter we will interpret episodes of the type illustrated in the figure through the lens of a theoretical model in which, following a negative external shock, the combination of downward nominal wage rigidity and a fixed exchange rate can cause massive involuntary unemployment.

This chapter builds on Schmitt-Grohé and Uribe (2016a).

9.1 An Open Economy with Downward Nominal Wage Rigidity

We develop a model of a small open economy in which nominal wages are downwardly rigid. The model features two types of goods: tradables and nontradables. The economy is driven by two exogenous shocks, a country interest-rate shock and a terms-of-trade shock.

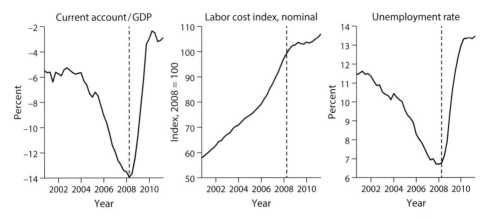

Figure 9.1   Boom-bust cycle in peripheral Europe: 2000–2011.

Source: Schmitt-Grohé and Uribe (2016a).
Note: Data represent arithmetic mean of Bulgaria, Cyprus, Estonia, Greece, Ireland, Lithuania, Latvia, Portugal, Spain, Slovenia, and Slovakia.

9.1.1 Households

Consider an economy populated by a large number of identical households with preferences described by the utility function

$$E_0 \sum_{t=0}^{\infty} \beta^t U(c_t),$$ (9.1)

where c_t denotes consumption. The period utility function U is assumed to be strictly increasing and strictly concave, and the parameter β, denoting the subjective discount factor, resides in the interval $(0, 1)$. The symbol E_t denotes the mathematical expectations operator conditional on information available in period t. The consumption good is a composite of tradable consumption, c_t^T, and nontradable consumption, c_t^N. The aggregation technology is of the form

$$c_t = A(c_t^T, c_t^N),$$ (9.2)

where A is an increasing, concave, and linearly homogeneous function.

We assume that all external liabilities of the household are denominated in foreign currency. This assumption is motivated by the empirical literature on the "original sin," which documents that virtually all debt issued by emerging countries is denominated in foreign currency (see, e.g., Eichengreen, Hausmann, and Panizza 2005). Specifically, households are assumed to have access to a one-period, internationally traded, state noncontingent bond denominated in tradables. We let d_t denote the level of debt assumed in period $t - 1$ and due in period t, and r_t is the interest rate on debt held between periods t and $t + 1$. The sequential budget constraint of the household is given by

$$P_t^T c_t^T + P_t^N c_t^N + \mathcal{E}_t d_t = P_t^T y_t^T + W_t h_t + \Phi_t + \frac{\mathcal{E}_t d_{t+1}}{1 + r_t},$$ (9.3)

where P_t^T denotes the nominal price of tradable goods, P_t^N the nominal price of non-tradable goods, $\mathcal{E}_t$ the nominal exchange rate (defined as the domestic currency price of one unit of foreign currency), y_t^T the endowment of traded goods, W_t the nominal wage rate, h_t hours worked, and Φ_t nominal profits from the ownership of firms. The variables r_t and y_t^T are assumed to be exogenous and stochastic. Movements in y_t^T can be interpreted either as shocks to the physical availability of tradable goods or as shocks to the country's terms of trade.

Households supply inelastically $\bar{h}$ hours to the labor market each period. Thus hours worked must satisfy $h_t \leq \bar{h}$. In Section 9.13 we study the case of an endogenous labor supply.

Households are assumed to be subject to a debt limit

$$d_{t+1} \leq \bar{d}, \tag{9.4}$$

which prevents them from engaging in Ponzi schemes, where $\bar{d}$ denotes the natural debt limit.

We assume that the law of one price holds for tradables. Specifically, letting P_t^{T*} denote the foreign currency price of tradables, the *law of one price* implies that

$$P_t^T = P_t^{T*}\mathcal{E}_t.$$

We further assume that the foreign currency price of tradables is constant and normalized to unity: $P_t^{T*} = 1$.[1] Thus we have that the nominal price of tradables equals the nominal exchange rate:

$$P_t^T = \mathcal{E}_t.$$

Households choose contingent plans $\{c_t, c_t^T, c_t^N, d_{t+1}\}$ to maximize (9.1) subject to (9.2)–(9.4), taking as given $P_t^T, P_t^N, \mathcal{E}_t, W_t, h_t, \Phi_t, r_t$, and y_t^T. Letting $p_t \equiv P_t^N/P_t^T$ denote the relative price of nontradables in terms of tradables and using the fact that $P_t^T = \mathcal{E}_t$, the optimality conditions associated with this problem are (9.2)–(9.4) plus

$$\frac{A_2(c_t^T, c_t^N)}{A_1(c_t^T, c_t^N)} = p_t, \tag{9.5}$$

$$\lambda_t = U'(c_t)A_1(c_t^T, c_t^N),$$

$$\frac{\lambda_t}{1+r_t} = \beta E_t \lambda_{t+1} + \mu_t,$$

$$\mu_t \geq 0,$$

and

$$\mu_t(d_{t+1} - \bar{d}) = 0,$$

---

1. Exercise 9.8 relaxes this assumption.

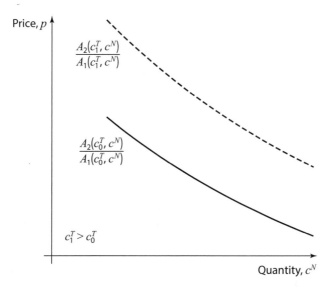

Figure 9.2   The demand for nontradables.

where $\beta^t \lambda_t / P_t^T$ and $\beta^t \mu_t$ denote the Lagrange multipliers associated with (9.3) and (9.4), respectively.

Equation (9.5) describes the household's demand for nontradables as a function of the relative price of nontradables, p_t, and the level of tradable absorption, c_t^T. Given c_t^T, the demand for nontradables is strictly decreasing in p_t. This property is a consequence of the assumptions made about the aggregator function A (see exercise 9.1). It reflects the fact that as the relative price of nontradables increases, households tend to consume relatively fewer nontradables. The demand function for nontradables is depicted in Figure 9.2 with a downward-sloping solid line. An increase in the absorption of tradables shifts the demand schedule up and to the right, reflecting normality. Such a shift is shown with a dashed downward sloping line in Figure 9.2 for an increase in traded consumption from c_0^T to $c_1^T > c_0^T$. It follows that absorption of tradables can be viewed as a shifter of the demand for nontradables. Of course, c_t^T is itself an endogenous variable that is determined simultaneously with all other endogenous variables of the model.

9.1.2 Firms

Nontraded output, denoted y_t^N, is produced by perfectly competitive firms. Each firm operates a production technology given by

$$y_t^N = F(h_t),$$

which uses labor services as the sole input. The function F is assumed to be strictly increasing and concave. Firms choose the amount of labor input to maximize profits, given by

$$\Phi_t \equiv P_t^N F(h_t) - W_t h_t.$$

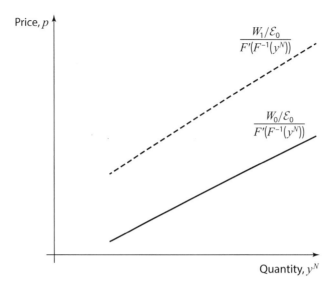

Figure 9.3   The supply of nontradables.

The optimality condition associated with this problem is $P_t^N F'(h_t) = W_t$. Dividing both sides by P_t^T and using the facts that $P_t^T = \mathcal{E}_t$ and that $h_t = F^{-1}(y_t^N)$ yields a supply schedule of nontradable goods of the form

$$p_t = \frac{W_t/\mathcal{E}_t}{F'(F^{-1}(y_t^N))}.$$

This supply schedule is depicted with a solid upward-sloping line in Figure 9.3. All other things equal, the higher is the relative price of the nontraded good, the larger is the supply of nontradable goods. Also, the higher is the labor cost, $W_t/\mathcal{E}_t$, the smaller is the supply of nontradables at each level of the relative price p_t. That is, an increase in the nominal wage rate, holding constant the nominal exchange rate, causes the supply schedule to shift up and to the left. Figure 9.3 displays (with a dashed upward-sloping line) the shift in the supply schedule that results from an increase in the nominal wage rate from W_0 to $W_1 > W_0$, holding the nominal exchange rate constant at $\mathcal{E}_0$.

A currency devaluation, holding the nominal wage constant, shifts the supply schedule down and to the right. Intuitively, a devaluation that is not accompanied by a change in nominal wages reduces the real labor cost, thereby inducing firms to increase the supply of nontradable goods for any given relative price. To illustrate this effect, assume that the nominal wage equals W_1 and the nominal exchange rate equals $\mathcal{E}_0$. The corresponding supply schedule is the upward-sloping dashed line in Figure 9.3. To keep the graph simple, suppose that the government devalues the currency to a level $\mathcal{E}_1 > \mathcal{E}_0$ such that $W_1/\mathcal{E}_1 = W_0/\mathcal{E}_0$. Such a devaluation shifts the supply schedule back to its original position (given by the solid line).

9.1.3 Downward Nominal Wage Rigidity and the Labor Market

The central friction emphasized in this chapter is downward nominal wage rigidity. Specifically, we impose:

$$W_t \geq \gamma W_{t-1}, \quad \gamma > 0. \tag{9.6}$$

The parameter γ governs the degree of downward nominal wage rigidity. The higher γ is, the more downwardly rigid nominal wages will be. This setup nests the cases of absolute downward rigidity (when $\gamma \geq 1$) and full wage flexibility (when $\gamma = 0$). In Section 9.4 we present empirical evidence suggesting that γ is close to unity when time is measured in quarters.

The presence of downwardly rigid nominal wages implies that the labor market will in general not clear. Instead, involuntary unemployment, given by $\bar{h} - h_t$, will be a regular feature of this economy. Actual employment must satisfy

$$h_t \leq \bar{h} \tag{9.7}$$

at all times. We postulate that at any point in time, wages and employment must satisfy the slackness condition

$$(\bar{h} - h_t)\left(W_t - \gamma W_{t-1}\right) = 0. \tag{9.8}$$

This condition states that in periods in which the economy suffers from involuntary unemployment ($h_t < \bar{h}$), the lower bound on nominal wages must be binding ($W_t = \gamma W_{t-1}$). It also states that in periods in which the lower bound on nominal wages is not binding ($W_t > \gamma W_{t-1}$), the economy must be operating at full employment ($h_t = \bar{h}$). Notice that the equilibrium level of employment is always given by the minimum of the demand for labor h_t and the supply of labor $\bar{h}$. Therefore, equilibrium employment is not always demand determined. For example, during booms, employment may be supply determined (at $\bar{h}$). In other words, households are never required to work more hours than they wish to at the going wage, and firms are never forced to hire more workers than they desire at the going wage.

9.1.4 Equilibrium

In equilibrium the market for nontraded goods must clear at all times. That is, the condition

$$c_t^N = y_t^N$$

must hold for all t. Combining this condition, the production technology for nontradables, the household's budget constraint, and the definition of firm's profits, we obtain the following market-clearing condition for traded goods:

$$c_t^T + d_t = y_t^T + \frac{d_{t+1}}{1 + r_t}.$$

Let

$$w_t \equiv \frac{W_t}{\mathcal{E}_t}$$

denote the real wage in terms of tradables and

$$\epsilon_t \equiv \frac{\mathcal{E}_t}{\mathcal{E}_{t-1}}$$

the gross devaluation rate of the domestic currency. Then the wage constraint (9.6) and the slackness condition (9.8) can be expressed in real terms as $w_t \geq \gamma w_{t-1}/\epsilon_t$ and $(\bar{h} - h_t)(w_t - \gamma w_{t-1}/\epsilon_t) = 0$, respectively.

A competitive equilibrium is a set of stochastic processes $\{c_t^T, h_t, w_t, d_{t+1}, p_t, \lambda_t, \mu_t\}_{t=0}^{\infty}$ satisfying

$$c_t^T + d_t = y_t^T + \frac{d_{t+1}}{1+r_t}, \tag{9.9}$$

$$d_{t+1} \leq \bar{d}, \tag{9.10}$$

$$\mu_t \geq 0, \tag{9.11}$$

$$\mu_t(d_{t+1} - \bar{d}) = 0, \tag{9.12}$$

$$\lambda_t = U'(A(c_t^T, F(h_t)))A_1(c_t^T, F(h_t)), \tag{9.13}$$

$$\frac{\lambda_t}{1+r_t} = \beta E_t \lambda_{t+1} + \mu_t, \tag{9.14}$$

$$p_t = \frac{A_2(c_t^T, F(h_t))}{A_1(c_t^T, F(h_t))}, \tag{9.15}$$

$$p_t = \frac{w_t}{F'(h_t)}, \tag{9.16}$$

$$w_t \geq \gamma \frac{w_{t-1}}{\epsilon_t}, \tag{9.17}$$

$$h_t \leq \bar{h}, \tag{9.18}$$

and

$$(\bar{h} - h_t)\left(w_t - \gamma \frac{w_{t-1}}{\epsilon_t}\right) = 0, \tag{9.19}$$

given an exchange rate policy $\{\epsilon_t\}_{t=0}^{\infty}$, initial conditions w_{-1} and d_0, and exogenous stochastic processes $\{r_t, y_t^T\}_{t=0}^{\infty}$.

Notice that all markets except the labor market are in equilibrium. One might therefore wonder whether this situation violates Walras' law, according to which, if all markets but one can be verified to be in equilibrium, then the remaining market must also be in equilibrium. The answer is that Walras' law is not applicable in the current environment, because the present model does not feature a Walrasian equilibrium. A Walrasian equilibrium is built using the assumption that at the price vector submitted by a fictitious auctioneer, all market participants submit notional demand and supplies of final goods and inputs of production. That is, supplies and demands computed under the assumption that at the given price vector (regardless of whether it happens to be the equilibrium price vector or not) the agent could buy or sell any desired quantities of final goods and inputs of production subject only to her budget constraints. But this is not the case in the present non-Walrasian equilibrium. In particular, at any given price vector the household's labor supply is not its desired supply of labor, $\bar{h}$, but its realized employment, h_t, reflecting the fact that households internalize the existence of rationing in the labor market. As a result, adding up the budget constraints of all households and using the fact that all markets but the labor market clear does not yield the result that the aggregate desired supply of labor equals the aggregate desired demand of labor, or $\bar{h} = h_t$, but rather the tautology that the desired demand for labor equals the desired demand for labor, $h_t = h_t$. In other words, in the present model, the fact that in equilibrium all but one market clear does not imply that the remaining market must also clear.

To characterize the competitive equilibrium, one must specify the exchange-rate regime. We will study a variety of empirically realistic exchange-rate policies. We begin with currency pegs, a policy that is frequently observed in the emerging-country world.

9.2 Currency Pegs

Countries can find themselves confined to a currency peg in a number of ways. For instance, a country could have adopted a currency peg as a way to stop high or hyperinflation in a swift and nontraumatic way. A classical example is the Argentine Convertibility Law of April 1991, which, by mandating a one-to-one exchange rate between the Argentine peso and the U.S. dollar, painlessly eliminated hyperinflation virtually overnight. Another route by which countries arrive at a currency peg is the joining of a monetary union. Recent examples include emerging countries in the periphery of the European Union, such as Ireland, Portugal, Greece, and a number of small eastern European countries that joined the eurozone. Most of these countries experienced an initial transition into the euro characterized by low inflation, low interest rates, and economic expansion.

However, history has shown time and again that fixed exchange-rate arrangements are easy to adopt but difficult to maintain. Continuing with the example of the Argentine peg of the 1990s, its initial success in stabilizing inflation and restoring growth turned into a nightmare by the end of the decade. Starting in 1998 Argentina was hit by a string of large negative external shocks, including depressed commodity prices and elevated country premia, which pushed the economy into a deep deflationary recession. Between 1998 and late 2001, the subemployment rate, which measures the fraction of the population that is either unemployed or involuntarily working part time, increased by 10 percentage points. At the same time, consumer prices were falling at a rate near 1 percent per year. Eventually, the crisis led to the demise of the peg in December 2001.

The Achilles' heel of currency pegs is that they hinder the efficient adjustment of the economy to negative external shocks, such as drops in the terms of trade (captured by the variable y_t^T in our model) or hikes in the country interest rate (captured by the variable r_t). The reason is that such shocks produce a contraction in aggregate demand that requires a decrease in the relative price of nontradables, that is, a real depreciation of the domestic currency, to bring about an expenditure switch away from tradables and toward nontradables. In turn, the required real depreciation may come about via a nominal devaluation of the domestic currency, a fall in nominal prices, or both. The currency peg rules out a devaluation. Thus the only way the necessary real depreciation can occur is through a decline in the nominal price of nontradables. However, when nominal wages are downwardly rigid, producers of nontradables are reluctant to lower prices, for doing so might render their enterprises no longer profitable. As a result, the necessary real depreciation takes place too slowly, causing recession and unemployment along the way.

This narrative goes back at least to Keynes (1925), who argued that Britain's 1925 decision to return to the gold standard at the 1913 parity despite the significant increase in the aggregate price level that took place during World War I would cause deflation in nominal wages with deleterious consequences for employment and economic activity. Similarly, Friedman's (1953) seminal essay points at downward nominal wage rigidity as the central argument against fixed exchange rates. This section formalizes this narrative in the context of the dynamic, stochastic, optimizing model developed in Section 9.1. Later sections use parameterized versions of this model to generate precise quantitative predictions for aggregate activity around external crises and for the welfare costs of currency pegs.

A currency peg is an exchange-rate policy in which the nominal exchange rate is fixed. The gross devaluation rate therefore satisfies

$$\epsilon_t = 1,$$

for all $t \geq 0$. Under a currency peg, the economy is subject to two nominal rigidities. One is policy induced: the nominal exchange rate, $\mathcal{E}_t$, is kept fixed by the monetary authority. The second is structural and is given by the downward rigidity of the nominal wage W_t. The combination of these two nominal rigidities results in a real rigidity. Specifically, under a currency peg, the real wage expressed in terms of tradables, $w_t \equiv W_t/\mathcal{E}_t$, is downwardly rigid. Formally, equation (9.17) becomes

$$w_t \geq \gamma w_{t-1}, \tag{9.20}$$

and the slackness condition (9.19) becomes

$$(\bar{h} - h_t)(w_t - \gamma w_{t-1}) = 0. \tag{9.21}$$

As a result of this real rigidity, in general the labor market is in disequilibrium and features involuntary unemployment. The magnitude of the labor market disequilibrium is a function of the amount by which the past real wage, w_{t-1}, exceeds the current full-employment real wage. It follows that under a currency peg w_{t-1} becomes a relevant state variable for the economy.

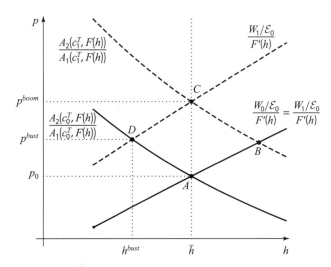

Figure 9.4 Currency pegs, downward wage rigidity, and unemployment.

A competitive equilibrium under a currency peg is a set of stochastic processes $\{c_t^T,$ $h_t, w_t, d_{t+1}, p_t, \lambda_t, \mu_t\}_{t=0}^{\infty}$ satisfying (9.9)–(9.15), (9.18), (9.20), and (9.21), given initial conditions w_{-1} and d_0 and exogenous stochastic processes $\{r_t, y_t^T\}_{t=0}^{\infty}$.

9.2.1 A Peg-Induced Externality

Figure 9.4 illustrates the adjustment of the economy to a boom-bust episode under a currency peg. Because in equilibrium $c_t^N = y_t^N = F(h_t)$, the figure plots the demand and supply schedules for nontraded goods in terms of employment in the nontraded sector, so that the horizontal axis measures h_t. The intersection of the demand and supply schedules therefore indicates the equilibrium demand for labor, given c_t^T and $W_t/\mathcal{E}_t$. The figure also shows the labor supply, $\bar{h}$ (dotted vertical line). Suppose that the initial position of the economy is at point A, where the labor market is operating at full employment, $h_t = \bar{h}$. Suppose that in response to a positive external shock, such as a decline in the country interest rate, traded absorption increases from c_0^T to $c_1^T > c_0^T$, causing the demand function to shift up and to the right. If nominal wages stayed unchanged, the new intersection of the demand and supply schedules would occur at point B. However, at point B the demand for labor would exceed the supply of labor $\bar{h}$. The excess demand for labor drives up the nominal wage from W_0 to $W_1 > W_0$, causing the supply schedule to shift up and to the left. The new intersection of the demand and supply schedules occurs at point C, where all hours of labor are employed and there is no excess demand for labor. Because nominal wages are upwardly flexible, the transition from point A to point C happens instantaneously.

Suppose now that the external shock fades away, and therefore that absorption of tradables goes back to its original level c_0^T. The decline in c_t^T shifts the demand schedule back to its original position, indicated by the downward-sloping solid line. However, the economy does not immediately return to point A. Due to downward nominal wage rigidity, the nominal wage stays at W_1, and because of the currency peg, the nominal exchange rate remains at $\mathcal{E}_0$. For simplicity, we draw Figure 9.4 assuming that γ is unity. As a result, the supply schedule does not move. The new intersection is at point D. There the economy suffers involuntary unemployment equal to $\bar{h} - h^{bust}$. Involuntary unemployment will persist over time unless the government does something to boost the economy. This is because, if γ is equal to unity, nominal wages will not fall and the economy will be stuck at point D, with permanent involuntary unemployment of $\bar{h} - h^{bust}$. If γ is less than unity, nominal wages will gradually return to their initial level W_0. In this case, the supply schedule shifts gradually down and to the right, until it eventually intersects the demand schedule at point A, where full employment is restored. This entire transition, however, is characterized by involuntary unemployment and a depressed level of activity in the nontraded sector.

The dynamics described above suggest that the combination of downward nominal wage rigidity and a currency peg creates a negative externality. The nature of this externality is that in periods of economic expansion, elevated demand for nontradables drives nominal (and real) wages up. Although this increase in wages occurs in the context of full employment and strong aggregate activity, it places the economy in a vulnerable situation, because in the contractionary phase of the cycle, downward nominal wage rigidity and the currency peg hinder the downward adjustment of real wages, causing unemployment. Individual agents understand this mechanism but are too small to internalize the fact that their own expenditure choices collectively exacerbate disruptions in the labor market.

9.2.2 Volatility and Average Unemployment

The present model implies an endogenous connection between the amplitude of the cycle and the average level of involuntary unemployment. The larger the degree of aggregate volatility is, the larger the average level of involuntary unemployment will be. This connection between a second moment (the volatility of the underlying shocks) and a first moment (average unemployment) opens the door to large welfare gains from optimal stabilization policy.

The predicted connection between the volatility of the underlying shocks and the mean level of involuntary unemployment is due to two maintained assumptions: (i) employment is determined as the minimum between the desired demand for labor and the desired supply of labor, and (ii) wages are more rigid downwardly than upwardly. The mechanism is as follows. The economy responds efficiently to positive external shocks, as nominal wages adjust upward to ensure that firms are on their labor demand schedules and households are on their labor supply schedules. In sharp contrast, the adjustment to negative external shocks is inefficient, as nominal wages fail to fall, forcing households off their labor supply schedules and generating involuntary unemployment. Thus over the business cycle, the economy fluctuates between periods of full employment (or zero unemployment) and periods of positive unemployment, implying positive unemployment on average. Further, the implied level of unemployment during recessions is larger the larger is the amplitude of the underlying shocks. This is for two reasons. First, the reduction in the demand for labor during contractions is naturally larger the larger is the amplitude of shocks buffeting the economy. Second, the larger is the amplitude of the underlying shocks, the larger the increase in nominal wages during booms will be, which exacerbates the negative effects of wage rigidity during contractions. It follows that mean unemployment is increasing in the variance of the underlying shocks.

This prediction represents an important difference with existing sticky-wage models à la Erceg, Henderson, and Levin (2000). In this class of models, assumption (i) does not hold. Instead, it is assumed that employment is always demand determined. As a result, increases in involuntary unemployment during recessions are roughly offset by reductions in unemployment during booms. Consequently the average level of unemployment does not depend in a quantitatively relevant way on the amplitude of the business cycle.

Interestingly, the direct connection between aggregate uncertainty and the average level of unemployment predicted by the present model does not require assumption (ii) (downward wage rigidity). It suffices to impose assumption (i), that is, employment is determined as the minimum of the demand and supply of labor. The following example illustrates this point. Consider an economy in which the nominal wage rate is absolutely rigid in both directions. Specifically, suppose that $W_t = \bar{W}$, for all t, where $\bar{W}$ is a parameter. Let the exchange-rate regime be a currency peg with $\mathcal{E}_t = \bar{\mathcal{E}}$ for all t, where $\bar{\mathcal{E}} > 0$ is a parameter. Suppose that agents have no access to international financial markets, $d_t = 0$ for all t. In this environment, consumption of tradables equals the endowment of tradables at all times, $c_t^T = y_t^T$ for all t. Suppose that preferences are logarithmic $U(A(c_t^T, c_t^N)) = \ln c_t^T + \ln c_t^N$. Assume that the endowment of tradables, y_t^T, can take on the values $\bar{y} + \sigma$ or $\bar{y} - \sigma$ each with probability 1/2, where $\bar{y} = 1$, and $0 < \sigma < 1$ is a parameter. According to this specification, $E(y_t^T) = 1$, and $\text{var}(y_t^T) = \sigma^2$. Assume that the technology for producing nontradables is $F(h_t) = h_t^\alpha$ and that households supply inelastically one unit of labor each period ($\bar{h} = 1$). Finally, let $\bar{w} \equiv \bar{W}/\bar{\mathcal{E}}$ denote the real wage rate expressed in terms of tradables, and suppose that $\bar{w} = \alpha$. This value of $\bar{w}$ is the flexible-wage real wage that would obtain if the endowment took its unconditional mean value, $E(y_t^T) = 1$. The equilibrium conditions associated with this economy are

$$\frac{c_t^T}{c_t^N} = p_t,$$

$$\alpha p_t (h_t^d)^{\alpha-1} = w_t,$$

$$c_t^T = y_t^T,$$

$$c_t^N = h_t^\alpha,$$

$$w_t = \bar{w},$$

and

$$h_t = \min\{\bar{h}, h_t^d\},$$

where h_t^d denotes the desired demand for labor by firms. The first equation is the demand for nontradables, the second is the supply of nontradables, the third and fourth are the market clearing conditions for tradables and nontradables, respectively. The last equation states that employment is determined as the minimum of the supply and demand for labor. It is straightforward to verify that the solution to the above system is

$$h_t = \begin{cases} 1 - \sigma & \text{if } y_t^T = 1 - \sigma \\ 1 & \text{if } y_t^T = 1 + \sigma. \end{cases}$$

Let $u_t \equiv \bar{h} - h_t$ denote the unemployment rate. It follows that the equilibrium distribution of u_t is given by

$$u_t = \begin{cases} \sigma & \text{with probability } \frac{1}{2} \\ 0 & \text{with probability } \frac{1}{2}. \end{cases}$$

The unconditional mean of the unemployment rate is then given by

$$E(u_t) = \frac{\sigma}{2}.$$

This expression shows that the average level of unemployment increases linearly with the volatility of tradable endowment, even though wage rigidity is symmetric.

The assumption that nominal wages are only downwardly inflexible amplifies the effect of volatility on average unemployment. To see this, replace the assumption $W_t = \bar{W}$ with the assumption $W_t \geq W_{t-1}$ and $W_{-1} = \alpha \bar{\mathcal{E}}$. In this case, nominal wages are absolutely inflexible downwardly, but perfectly flexible upwardly. Suppose that all other aspects of the economy are unchanged. In this environment, during booms (i.e., when $y_t^T = 1 + \sigma$) the economy is in full employment and the real wage equals $(1 + \sigma)\alpha$, which is larger than $\bar{w}$, the real wage that prevails during booms when wages are bidirectionally rigid. This makes the economy more vulnerable to negative shocks. Indeed, when $y_t^T = 1 - \sigma$, the real wage fails to fall, causing a contraction in employment to $(1 - \sigma)/(1 + \sigma)$, which is lower than $1 - \sigma$ (the level of employment during contractions in the economy with bidirectional wage rigidity). It follows that the average rate of unemployment is $E(u_t) = \sigma/(1 + \sigma)$, which is larger than $\sigma/2$, the average rate of unemployment in the economy with two-sided wage rigidity (recall that σ must be less than 1).

In sum, the above example illustrates that the connection between aggregate volatility and the mean level of unemployment does not require the assumption of one-sided (downward) wage rigidity but is a consequence of the assumption that employment is determined as the minimum between labor demand and labor supply. The example also reveals that downward nominal wage rigidity does exacerbate the increasing relation between the average unemployment rate and the variance of the underlying shocks.

9.2.3 Adjustment to a Temporary Fall in the Interest Rate

This section presents an analytical example showing that when the central bank pegs the domestic currency, a positive external shock can be the prelude to a slump with persistent unemployment. In this example, as in many observed boom-bust cycles in emerging countries, agents borrow internationally to take advantage of temporarily lower interest rates. The resulting capital inflow drives up domestic absorption of tradables and nominal wages.

When the interest rate returns to its long-run level, aggregate demand falls, and unemployment emerges as real wages—made rigid by the combination of nominal wage rigidity and a currency peg—are stuck at a level too high to be consistent with full employment.

Suppose that preferences are given by $U(A(c_t^T, c_t^N)) = \ln c_t^T + \ln c_t^N$ and that the technology for producing nontradable goods is $F(h_t) = h_t^\alpha$, with $\alpha \in (0, 1)$. Suppose that the endowment of tradables is constant over time and given by $y_t^T = y^T$; that $\bar{h} = 1$; and that $\beta(1 + r) = 1$, where $r > 0$ is a parameter. Assume that nominal wages are downwardly rigid and that $\gamma = 1$. Finally, suppose that prior to period 0, the economy had been at a full-employment equilibrium with $d_{t+1} = 0$, $c_t^T = y^T$, $h_t = 1$, $w_t = \alpha y^T$, and $c_t^N = 1$, for $t < 0$.

Consider the adjustment of this economy to a temporary decline in the interest rate. Specifically, suppose that

$$r_t = \begin{cases} r & t < 0 \\ \underline{r} < r & t = 0 \\ r & t > 0. \end{cases}$$

Suppose that the interest-rate shock in period 0 comes as a complete surprise, but that from this period on, agents enjoy perfect foresight, so they know the future paths of r_t and y_t^T with certainty.

To characterize the equilibrium dynamics induced by this positive external shock, we must find a set of deterministic sequences $\{c_t^T, h_t, w_t, d_{t+1}, p_t, \lambda_t, \mu_t\}_{t=0}^\infty$ satisfying conditions (9.9)–(9.19), with $\epsilon_t = 1$ for all t.

Begin by conjecturing that the debt limit (9.10) never binds (i.e., $d_t < \bar{d}$ for all t) and that external debt is constant from period 1 on (i.e., $d_t = d_1$, for all $t \geq 1$). Once we have found the equilibrium dynamics, we must verify that these two conjectures are satisfied. The first conjecture together with equilibrium condition (9.12) implies that

$$\mu_t = 0,$$

for all t. Then, by equilibrium conditions (9.13) and (9.14), we have that

$$c_1^T = \beta(1 + \underline{r})c_0^T,$$

and

$$c_t^T = c_1^T,$$

for all $t \geq 1$. Recalling that $d_0 = 0$, we have that the resource constraint (9.9) in period 0 is given by

$$c_0^T = y^T + \frac{d_1}{1 + \underline{r}}.$$

By the second conjecture, the resource constraint in period 1 is given by

$$c_1^T + d_1 = y^T + \frac{d_1}{1 + r}.$$

Solving the above four expressions yields

$$c_0^T = y^T \left[\frac{1}{1+\underline{r}} + \frac{r}{1+r} \right] > y^T,$$

$$c_t^T = y^T \left[\frac{1}{1+r} + \frac{r}{1+r} \frac{1+\underline{r}}{1+r} \right] < y^T,$$

and

$$d_t = y^T \left[1 - \frac{1+\underline{r}}{1+r} \right] > 0,$$

for $t \geq 1$. Notice that if $\underline{r} = r$, then $c_1^T = y^T$ and $d_t = 0$. However, because $\underline{r} < r$, the economy experiences a boom in traded consumption in period 0. This boom is financed with external debt, $d_1 > 0 = d_0$. That is, the country experiences a current account deficit, or capital inflows, in period 0. In period 1, consumption falls permanently to a level lower than the one observed prior to the interest-rate shock, and the trade balance switches permanently from a deficit to a surplus. This permanent trade-balance surplus is large enough to pay the interest on the external debt generated by the consumption boom of period 0.

The surge in capital inflows in period 0 is accompanied by full employment, that is, $h_0 = 1$. To see this, suppose on the contrary that $h_0 < 1$. Then by condition (9.16) we have that $\alpha c_0^T / h_0 = w_0$. But since $c_0^T > y^T$ and $h_0 < 1$, this expression implies that $w_0 > \alpha y^T = w_{-1}$, violating the slackness condition (9.19). It follows that $h_0 = 1$. The initial rise in capital inflows also elevates the period-0 real wage. Specifically, by (9.16) and the fact that $h_0 = 1$, we have that $w_0 = \alpha c_0^T > \alpha y^T = w_{-1}$. This increase in labor costs results in an increase in the relative price of nontradables, or a real-exchange-rate appreciation. This can be seen from equation (9.5), which implies that $p_0 = c_0^T > y^T = p_{-1}$. Graphically, the dynamics described here correspond to a movement from point A to point C in Figure 9.4.

The elevation in real wages that takes place in period 0 puts the economy in a vulnerable situation in period 1, when the interest rate increases permanently from $\underline{r}$ to r. In particular, in period 1, the economy enters into a situation of chronic involuntary unemployment. To see this note that by (9.15) and (9.16), the full-employment real wage in period 1 is αc_1^T, which is lower than $\alpha c_0^T = w_0$. As a result, the lower bound on wage growth must be binding in period 1, that is, condition (9.17) must hold with equality. Recalling that $\epsilon_t = 1$ for all t and that $\gamma = 1$, we then have that $w_1 = w_0$. Combining this expression with (9.15) and (9.16) yields the following expression for the equilibrium level of involuntary unemployment:

$$1 - h_1 = 1 - \frac{1+\underline{r}}{1+r} > 0.$$

This level of unemployment persists indefinitely. To see this, note that at the beginning of period 2, the state of the economy is $\{r_2, y_2^T, d_2, w_1\}$, which, as we have shown, equals $\{r, y^T, d_1, w_0\}$, which, in turn, is the state of the economy observed at the beginning of

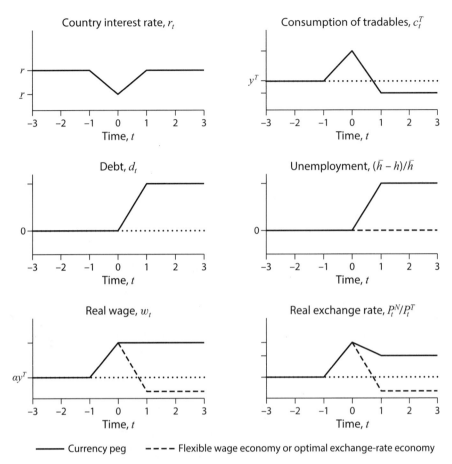

Figure 9.5 A temporary decline in the country interest rate.

period 1. A similar argument can be made for periods $t = 3, 4, \ldots$. It follows that for all $t \geq 1$, the unemployment rate is given by

$$1 - h_t = 1 - \frac{1 + \underline{r}}{1 + r} > 0.$$

Notice that the larger the decline in the interest rate is in period 0, the larger the unemployment rate will be in periods $t \geq 1$. Figure 9.5 presents a graphical summary of the adjustment process.

It is of interest to compare the dynamic adjustment of the present economy to the one that would take place under flexible wages ($\gamma = 0$). This adjustment is shown by the dashed lines in Figure 9.5. The responses of tradable consumption and external debt are identical whether wages are rigid or not. The reason is that in this example preferences are additively separable in consumption of tradables and nontradables. However, the behavior of the remaining variables of the model is quite different under flexible and sticky wages. Contrary to what happens under sticky wages, the flexible-wage equilibrium is characterized by full employment at all times. Full employment is supported by a permanent fall in nominal (and real) wages in period 1. This decline in labor costs allows firms to lower the relative price of nontradables permanently. In turn, lower relative prices for nontradables induce consumers to switch expenditures from tradables to nontradables.

9.3 Optimal Exchange-Rate Policy

In the example we just analyzed, the reason the economy experiences unemployment when the country interest rate increases is that real wages are too high to clear the labor market. This downward rigidity in real wages is the consequence of downwardly rigid nominal wages and a fixed exchange-rate regime. The example suggests that the unemployment problem could be addressed by any policy that results in lower real wages. One way to lower the real wage is to devalue the currency. By making the nominal price of tradables more expensive—recall that $P_t^T = \mathcal{E}_t$—a devaluation lowers the purchasing power of wages in terms of tradables. In turn, this erosion in the real value of wages induces firms to hire more workers. In this section, we formalize this intuition by characterizing the optimal exchange-rate policy. We begin by characterizing an exchange-rate policy that guarantees full employment at all times and then show that this policy is indeed Pareto optimal.

9.3.1 The Full-Employment Exchange-Rate Policy

Consider an exchange-rate policy in which each period the central bank sets the devaluation rate to ensure full employment in the labor market, that is, to ensure that

$$h_t = \bar{h},$$

for all $t \geq 0$. We refer to this exchange-rate arrangement as the full-employment exchange-rate policy.

The equilibrium dynamics associated with the full-employment exchange-rate policy are illustrated in Figure 9.4. Suppose that, after being hit by a negative external shock, the economy is stuck at point D with involuntary unemployment equal to $\bar{h} - h^{bust}$. At point D, the desired demand for tradables is c_0^T, the nominal wage is W_1, and the nominal exchange rate is $\mathcal{E}_0$. Suppose that the central bank devalues the domestic currency so as to deflate the purchasing power of nominal wages to a point consistent with full employment. Specifically, suppose that the central bank sets the exchange rate at the level $\mathcal{E}_1 > \mathcal{E}_0$, satisfying $(W_1/\mathcal{E}_1)/F'(\bar{h}) = A_2(c_0^T, F(\bar{h}))/A_1(c_0^T, F(\bar{h}))$. The devaluation causes the supply schedule to shift down and to the right, intersecting the demand schedule at point A, where unemployment is nil ($h = \bar{h}$). The devaluation lowers the real cost of labor, making it viable for firms to slash prices. The relative price of nontradables falls from p^{boom} at the peak of the cycle to p_0 after the negative external shock. This fall in the relative price of nontradables induces households to switch expenditure away from tradables and toward nontradables in a magnitude compatible with full employment.

The full-employment policy amounts to setting the devaluation rate to ensure that the real wage equals the full-employment real wage rate at all times. Formally, the full-employment exchange-rate policy ensures that

$$w_t = \omega(c_t^T), \tag{9.22}$$

where $\omega(c_t^T)$ denotes the full-employment real wage rate and is given by

$$\omega(c_t^T) \equiv \frac{A_2(c_t^T, F(\bar{h}))}{A_1(c_t^T, F(\bar{h}))} F'(\bar{h}). \tag{9.23}$$

The assumed properties of the aggregator function A ensure that the function $\omega(\cdot)$ is strictly increasing in the domestic absorption of tradables, c_t^T:[2]

$$\omega'(c_t^T) > 0.$$

There exists a whole family of full-employment exchange-rate policies. Specifically, combining conditions (9.17) and (9.22), we have that any exchange-rate policy satisfying

$$\epsilon_t \geq \gamma \frac{w_{t-1}}{\omega(c_t^T)} \tag{9.24}$$

ensures full employment at all times. To see this, suppose on the contrary that the above devaluation policy allows for h_t to be less than $\bar{h}$ for some $t \geq 0$. Then by the slackness condition (9.19) we have that

$$w_t = \frac{\gamma w_{t-1}}{\epsilon_t}.$$

Solve this expression for ϵ_t, and use the resulting expression to eliminate ϵ_t from (9.24) to obtain $w_t \leq \omega(c_t^T)$. Now using (9.15) and (9.16) to eliminate w_t and (9.23) to eliminate $\omega(c_t^T)$, we can rewrite this inequality as

$$\frac{A_2(c_t^T, F(h_t))}{A_1(c_t^T, F(h_t))} F'(h_t) \leq \frac{A_2(c_t^T, F(\bar{h}))}{A_1(c_t^T, F(\bar{h}))} F'(\bar{h}).$$

Because the left-hand side of this expression is strictly decreasing in h_t, we have that the only value of h_t that satisfies the above inequality is $\bar{h}$. But this is a contradiction, since we started by assuming that $h_t < \bar{h}$. We have therefore shown that under any exchange-rate policy belonging to the family defined by (9.24), unemployment is nil at all dates and states.

A natural question to ask is whether the full-employment exchange-rate policy is the most desirable policy from a social point of view. This question is nontrivial, because the welfare of households does not depend directly on the level of employment but rather on the level of consumption of final goods.

---

2. Exercise 9.4 asks you to prove this statement.

9.3.2 Pareto Optimality of the Full-Employment Exchange-Rate Policy

Consider a social planner who wishes to maximize the welfare of the representative household. Under what constraints does the social planner operate? The answer to this question depends on the issue the researcher is interested in. Here we consider the problem of a local policymaker who takes as given the international asset market structure. Specifically, we assume that the social planner has access to a single internationally traded state-noncontingent bond denominated in units of tradable goods that pays the exogenously given interest rate r_t. We also assume that external debt must be bounded above by $\bar{d}$. Further, we assume that the planner takes as given the endowment process y_t^T, the technology for producing nontradables $F(h_t)$, and the time endowment $\bar{h}$. Given these constraints, the social planner picks processes for consumption, hours worked, and net foreign debt to maximize the welfare of the representative household.

We refer to the solution of the social planner's problem as the Pareto optimal allocation. The key difference between the competitive equilibrium and the Pareto optimal allocation is that the social planner can circumvent the goods and labor markets and impose directly the number of hours each household must work and the quantities of tradables and nontradables it can consume each period. This implies, in particular, that the allocation problem faced by the planner is not affected by the presence of nominal rigidities.

Formally the social planner's problem is given by

$$\max_{\{c_t^T, h_t, d_{t+1}\}_{t=0}^{\infty}} E_0 \sum_{t=0}^{\infty} \beta^t U(A(c_t^T, F(h_t)))$$

subject to

$$h_t \leq \bar{h}, \tag{9.25}$$

$$c_t^T + d_t = y_t^T + \frac{d_{t+1}}{1 + r_t}, \tag{9.26}$$

and

$$d_{t+1} \leq \bar{d}. \tag{9.27}$$

Because the objective function is concave and the constraints define a convex set, the first-order conditions associated with this problem are necessary and sufficient for an optimum. Let $\beta^t \eta_t$, $\beta^t \lambda_t$, and $\beta^t \mu_t$ denote the Lagrange multipliers associated with (9.25), (9.26), and (9.27), respectively. The first-order conditions with respect to η_t and h_t are

$$h_t \leq \bar{h},$$

$$U'(A(c_t^T, F(h_t)))A_2(c_t^T, F(h_t))F'(h_t) = \eta_t,$$

and the associated slackness condition is

$$\eta_t(\bar{h} - h_t) = 0.$$

Because the functions U, A, and F are strictly increasing, the second optimality condition implies that η_t is positive. It then follows from the slackness condition that $h_t = \bar{h}$ for all t. In words, the Pareto optimal allocation features full employment at all times.

The first-order conditions of the social planner's problem with respect to λ_t, μ_t, c_t^T, and d_{t+1} are

$$c_t^T + d_t = y_t^T + \frac{d_{t+1}}{1 + r_t},$$

$$d_{t+1} \leq \bar{d},$$

$$\lambda_t = U'(A(c_t^T, F(h_t)))A_1(c_t^T, F(h_t)),$$

and

$$\frac{\lambda_t}{1 + r_t} = \beta E_t \lambda_{t+1} + \mu_t,$$

with

$$\mu_t \geq 0,$$

and

$$\mu_t(d_{t+1} - \bar{d}) = 0.$$

These conditions are identical to competitive equilibrium conditions (9.9)–(9.14). This means that the processes μ_t, λ_t, c_t^T, d_{t+1}, and h_t that satisfy the conditions for Pareto optimality also satisfy the competitive equilibrium conditions when the exchange-rate policy belongs to the class of full-employment exchange-rate policies defined by (9.24).

We have therefore established that the real allocation associated with the full-employment exchange-rate policy is Pareto optimal. In other words, any exchange-rate policy that does not induce full employment is welfare dominated by the full-employment exchange-rate policy.

9.3.3 When Is It Inevitable to Devalue?

Because under the optimal exchange policy the real wage is always equal to the full-employment real wage, $\omega(c_t^T)$, equation (9.24) implies that for all $t > 0$ the devaluation rate satisfies

$$\epsilon_t \geq \gamma \frac{\omega(c_{t-1}^T)}{\omega(c_t^T)}; \quad t > 0.$$

Recalling that $\omega(\cdot)$ is a strictly increasing function of c_t^T, this expression states that optimal devaluations occur in periods of contraction in aggregate expenditure in tradables. A nonstructural econometric analysis of data stemming from this model may lead to the erroneous conclusion that devaluations are contractionary (see, for instance, the empirical literature surveyed in section 3.4 of Frankel 2011). However, the role of optimal devaluations is precisely the opposite, namely, to prevent the contraction in the tradable sector from spilling over into the nontraded sector. It follows that under the full-employment exchange-rate policy, devaluations are indeed expansionary in the sense that should they not take place, aggregate contractions would be even larger. Thus under the full-employment exchange-rate regime, the present model turns the view that devaluations are contractionary on its head and instead predicts that contractions are devaluatory.

Consider, for example, the case of a temporary decline in the country interest rate studied in Section 9.2.3. The equilibrium dynamics under the optimal exchange-rate policy are shown by dashed lines in Figure 9.5. Recall that under a currency peg, the permanent contraction in tradable consumption that occurs in period 1 causes a permanent increase in involuntary unemployment. Under the optimal exchange-rate policy, the path of tradable consumption is identical, but the permanent contraction in period 1 does not spill over to the nontraded sector or the labor market, which continues to operate under full employment. The monetary authority is able to maintain full employment by devaluing the currency in period 1 (not shown in the figure), which reduces the real cost of labor and makes it optimal for firms not to fire workers.

The full-employment exchange-rate policy completely eliminates any real effect stemming from nominal wage rigidity. Indeed, one can show that the equilibrium under the full-employment exchange-rate policy is identical to the equilibrium of an economy with full wage flexibility ($\gamma = 0$).[3] Consider again the case of a temporary decline in the country interest rate studied in Section 9.2.3. The equilibrium dynamics under fully flexible wages are identical to those associated with the full-employment exchange-rate policy (shown with dashed lines in Figure 9.5), except that the decline in the real wage that occurs in period 1 is brought about by a decline in the nominal wage under flexible wages but by a devaluation of the currency under downward wage rigidity and the full-employment exchange-rate policy.

9.4 Empirical Evidence on Downward Nominal Wage Rigidity

The central friction in the model we have analyzed in this chapter is downward nominal wage rigidity. In this section, we review a body of empirical work suggesting that downward nominal wage rigidity is a widespread phenomenon. This type of nominal friction has been detected in micro and aggregated data stemming from developed, emerging, and poor regions of the world. It has also been found both in formal and informal labor markets. An important by-product of this review is an estimate of the parameter γ governing the degree of nominal wage rigidity in the theoretical model. We will need this parameter value to study the quantitative predictions of the model.

9.4.1 Evidence from Micro Data

Various studies have examined the rigidity of hourly wages using micro data. Gottschalk (2005), for example, uses panel data from the Survey of Income and Program Participation (SIPP) to estimate the frequency of wage declines, increases, and no changes for male and female hourly workers working for the same employer during 1986–1993 in the United

---

3. See exercise 9.5.

Table 9.1   Probability of Decline, Increase, or No
Change in Nominal Wages between Interviews

	Interviews 1 Year Apart	
	Males	Females
Decline	5.1	4.3
Constant	53.7	49.2
Increase	41.2	46.5

Source: Gottschalk (2005).
Notes: U.S. data, SIPP panel 1986–1993, within-job changes.
Data are expressed as percentages.

States.[4] Table 9.1 shows that over the course of 1 year only a small fraction of workers experiences a decline in nominal wages, while about half of workers experience no change. The large mass at no change suggests that nominal wages are rigid. The small mass to the left of zero suggests that nominal wages are downwardly rigid. It is worth noting that the sample period used by Gottschalk includes the 1990–1991 U.S. recession, because it implies that the observed scarcity of nominal wage cuts took place in the context of elevated unemployment.

Barattieri, Basu, and Gottschalk (2012) report similar findings using data from the 1996–1999 SIPP panel. Figure 9.6 shows that during this period the distribution of nominal wage changes was also truncated to the left of zero. The figure does not show the frequency corresponding to no wage changes. The reason for this omission is that the mass at zero changes is high, so that including it would make the rest of the figure less visible.

Gertler, Huckfeldt, and Trigari (2016) also use micro data from the SIPP to study wage rigidity. They investigate whether wages of new hires coming from unemployment are sticky, arguing that this is the margin relevant for determining involuntary unemployment due to wage rigidity. Using data for 1990–2012, they find that the wages of new hires coming from unemployment are no more cyclical than those of existing workers. This finding, taken together with the findings of earlier studies documenting wage stickiness for existing workers, is interpreted by these authors as suggesting that wages are sticky at the relevant margin. We note that Gertler, Huckfeldt, and Trigari document rigidity of real wages (and in fact of real earnings), as opposed to nominal hourly wages, the measure we have been focusing on here. Yet their findings are relevant, because they allow one to address the question of whether nominal wages of new hires are more flexible than nominal wages of existing hires. As documented by Barattieri, Basu, and Gottschalk (2012), using the same data set as Gertler, Huckfeldt, and Trigari, nominal wages of the latter group are downwardly rigid in nominal terms and hence the results of Gertler, Huckfeldt, and Trigari suggest that nominal wages of new hires are also downwardly rigid.

If nominal wages are downwardly flexible, then nominal wage cuts should most commonly be observed in recessions in which inflation is low. In this regard it is of interest that

---

4. The SIPP has been conducted by the Bureau of Labor Statistics since 1983. It is a stratified representative sample of the U.S. population. Individuals are interviewed every 4 months for a period of 24–48 months.

Figure 9.6   Distribution of nonzero U.S. nominal wage changes, 1996–1999.

Source: Barattieri, Basu, and Gottschalk (2012).

nominal wage cuts were rare in the United States during the Great Recession that started in 2007. Daly, Hobijn, and Lucking (2012) use micro panel data on wage changes of individual workers to construct the empirical distribution of wage changes in 2011.[5] Figure 9.7 displays the empirical distribution of annual nominal wage changes in 2011. The pattern is similar to that documented by Barattieri, Basu, and Gottschalk (2012): there is significant mass at no wage changes and more mass to the right of no changes than to the left. To emphasize the asymmetry in the distribution, Daly, Hobijn, and Lucking use a dashed line to show a (symmetric) normal distribution. Figure 9.7 suggests that during the Great Recession, even though unemployment was high and inflation was below its 2 percent target, nominal wage cuts were less frequent than increases.

A similar pattern of downward nominal wage rigidity based on microeconomic data is found in other developed countries. See, for example, Fortin (1996) for Canada; Kuroda and Yamamoto (2003) for Japan; and Fehr and Goette (2005) for Switzerland. Downward nominal wage rigidity is also found in industry-level wage data. See, for example, Holden and Wulfsberg (2008) for evidence from 19 OECD countries during 1973–1999.

9.4.2 Evidence from Informal Labor Markets

The evidence referenced above is based on data from formal labor markets in developed economies. However, a similar pattern of asymmetry in nominal wage adjustments emerges in informal labor markets located in poor areas of the world. Kaur (2012), for example,

---

5. The data come from the Current Population Survey, which, like the SIPP, is collected by the Bureau of Labor Statistics.

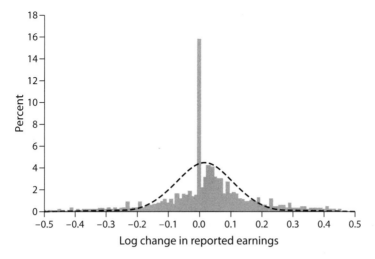

Figure 9.7   Distribution of U.S. nominal wage changes, 2011.

Source: Redrawn from Daly, Hobijn, and Lucking (2012).

studies the behavior of nominal wages in casual daily agricultural labor markets in ru-
ral India. Specifically, she examines market-level wage and employment responses to local
rainfall shocks in 500 Indian districts from 1956 to 2008. She finds that nominal wage
adjustment is asymmetric. In particular, nominal wages rise in response to positive rain
shocks but fail to fall during droughts. In addition, negative rain shocks cause labor rationing and unemployment. Importantly, inflation, which is uncorrelated with local rainfall
shocks, moderates these effects. During periods of relatively high inflation, local droughts
are more likely to result in lower real wages and less labor rationing. This effect suggests
that nominal rather than real wages are downwardly rigid.

9.4.3 Evidence from the Great Depression of 1929

According to the National Bureau of Economic Research, the Great Depression in the
United States started in August 1929 and ended in March 1933. By 1931, the economy had
experienced an enormous contraction. Employment in the manufacturing sector in 1931
stood 31 percent below its 1929 level. Figure 9.8 shows that in spite of a highly distressed
labor market, nominal wages remained remarkably firm.[6] Between August 1929 and August
1931, the nominal wage rate, shown by a solid line in the figure, fell by only 0.6 percent per
year. In contrast, consumer prices, shown by a dashed line, fell by 6.6 percent per year over
the same period. As a result, in the first 2 years of the Great Depression, real wages increased
by 12 percent in the midst of massive unemployment. In the second half of the depression,
nominal wages fell, but nominal prices fell even faster. As a result, by the end of the Great

---

6. The graph shows the nominal wage rate as opposed to average hourly earnings. The problem with the latter
series is that it includes compensation for overtime work. Contractions in overtime employment cause drops in
average hourly earnings that are not reflective of downward wage flexibility.

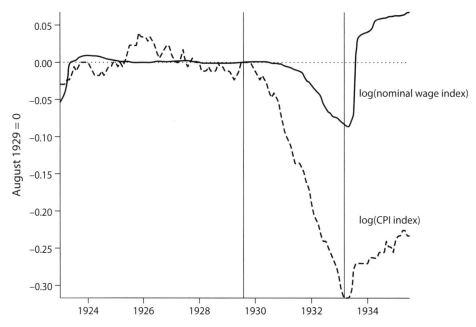

Figure 9.8 Nominal wage rate and consumer prices, United States, January 1923–July 1935.

Sources: Data are from the Bureau of Labor Statistics and the National Bureau of Economic Research. *Notes:* The solid line is the natural logarithm of an index of manufacturing money wage rates (NBER data series m08272b), August 1929 equal to zero. The dashed line is the logarithm of the consumer price index (Bureau of Labor Statistics series ID CUUR0000SA0), August 1929 equal to zero.

Depression the real wage rate was 26 percent above its 1929 level. The observed resilience of nominal wages in a context of extreme underutilization of the labor force is indicative of downward nominal wage rigidity.

9.4.4 Evidence from Emerging Countries and Inference on γ

The empirical literature surveyed thus far establishes that nominal wage rigidity is significant and asymmetric. However, because it uses data from developed and poor regions of the world, it does not provide evidence on the importance of downward nominal wage rigidity in emerging countries. In addition, this literature does not lend itself to calibrating the wage-rigidity parameter γ, because it does not provide information on the speed of downward adjustments of nominal wages. In Schmitt-Grohé and Uribe (2016a), we examine data from emerging countries and propose an empirical strategy for identifying γ. The approach consists of observing the behavior of nominal hourly wages during periods of rising unemployment. We focus on episodes in which an economy undergoing a severe recession keeps the nominal exchange rate fixed. Two prominent examples are Argentina during the second half of its Convertibility Plan (1996–2001) and the periphery of Europe during the Great Recession of 2008.

Figure 9.9 displays subemployment (defined as the sum of unemployment and underemployment) and nominal hourly wages expressed in pesos for Argentina during 1996–

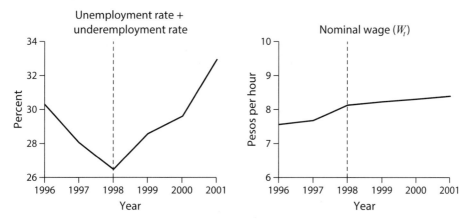

Figure 9.9 Unemployment and nominal wages in Argentina, 1996–2001.

Source: Schmitt-Grohé and Uribe (2016a).

2001. The Convertibility Plan was in effect from April 1991 to December 2001 and consisted of a peg of the Argentine peso to the U.S. dollar at a one-for-one rate with free convertibility.

The subperiod 1998–2001 is of particular interest, because during that time the Argentine central bank was holding on to the currency peg even though the economy was undergoing a severe contraction and both unemployment and underemployment were in a steep ascent. The contraction was caused by a combination of large adverse external disturbances, including a collapse in export commodity prices, a 100 percent devaluation in Brazil (Argentina's main trading partner) in 1999, and a deterioration in international borrowing conditions following the Southeast Asian and Russian financial crises of 1998.

In the context of a flexible-wage model, one would expect that the rise in unemployment would be associated with falling real wages. With the nominal exchange rate pegged, the fall in real wages must materialize through nominal wage deflation. However, during this period, the nominal hourly wage never fell. Indeed, it increased from 7.87 pesos in 1998 to 8.14 pesos in 2001. The model developed in this chapter predicts that with rising unemployment, the lower bound on nominal wages should be binding, and therefore γ should equal the gross growth rate of nominal wages. We wish to parameterize the model so that one period corresponds to one quarter. An estimate of the parameter γ can then be constructed as the average quarterly growth rate of nominal wages over the three-year period considered, that is, $\gamma = (W_{2001}/W_{1998})^{1/12}$. This yields a value of γ of 1.0028. This value means that, because of the presence of downward nominal wage rigidity, nominal wages must rise by at least 1.12 percent per year.

For this estimate of γ to represent an appropriate measure of wage rigidity in the context of the theoretical model, it must be adjusted to account for the fact that the model abstracts from foreign inflation and long-run productivity growth (see exercises 9.8 and 9.9). To carry out this adjustment, we use the growth rate of the U.S. GDP deflator as a proxy for foreign inflation. Between 1998 and 2001, the U.S. GDP deflator grew by 1.77 percent per year on average. We set the long-run growth rate in Argentina at 1.07 percent per year, to match the average growth rate of Argentine per capita real GDP during 1900–2005 reported in García-Cicco, Pancrazi, and Uribe (2010). The adjusted value of γ is then given by $1.0028/(1.0107 \times 1.0177)^{1/4} = 0.9958$.

Finally, we note that during the 1998–2001 Argentine contraction, consumer prices, unlike nominal wages, did fall. The CPI inflation rate was on average -0.86 percent per year during 1998–2001. It follows that real wages rose not only in dollar terms but also in terms of CPI units. Incidentally, this evidence provides some support for the assumption, implicit in the theoretical framework developed in this chapter, that downward nominal rigidities are less stringent for product prices than for factor prices.

The second episode from the emerging-market world that we use to document the presence of downward nominal wage rigidity and to infer the value of γ is the Great Recession of 2008 in the periphery of Europe. Table 9.2 presents an estimate of γ for 12 European economies that are either on the euro or pegged to the euro. The first two columns of the table show the unemployment rate in 2008:Q1 and 2011:Q2. The starting point of this period corresponds to the beginning of the Great Recession in Europe according to the Center for Economic and Policy Research's Euro Area Business Cycle Dating Committee. The 2008 crisis caused unemployment rates to rise sharply across all 12 countries. The table also displays the total growth of nominal hourly labor cost in manufacturing, construction, and services (including the public sector) over the 13-quarter period 2008:Q1–2011:Q2.[7] Despite the large surge in unemployment, nominal wages grew in most countries and in those in which they fell, the decline was modest. The implied value of γ, shown in the last column of Table 9.2, is given by the average growth rate of nominal wages over the period considered (that is, $\gamma = (W_{2011:Q2}/W_{2008:Q1})^{1/13}$). The estimated values of γ range from 0.996 for Lithuania to 1.028 for Bulgaria.

To adjust γ for foreign inflation, we proxy this variable with the inflation rate in Germany. During the 13-quarter sample period considered in Table 9.2, inflation in Germany was 3.6 percent, or about 0.3 percent per quarter. To adjust for long-run growth, we use the average growth rate of per capita output in the southern periphery of Europe of 1.2 percent per year or 0.3 percent per quarter.[8] Allowing for these effects suggests an adjusted estimate of γ in the interval [0.990, 1.022].

9.5 The Case of Equal Intra- and Intertemporal Elasticities of Substitution

For the remainder of this chapter, we assume a CRRA form for the period utility function, a CES form for the aggregator function, and an isoelastic form for the production function of nontradables:

$$U(c) = \frac{c^{1-\sigma} - 1}{1 - \sigma}, \tag{9.28}$$

$$A(c^T, c^N) = \left[a(c^T)^{1-\frac{1}{\xi}} + (1-a)(c^N)^{1-\frac{1}{\xi}}\right]^{\frac{1}{1-\frac{1}{\xi}}}, \tag{9.29}$$

---

7. The public sector is not included for Spain due to data limitations.
8. This figure corresponds to the average growth rate of per capita real GDP in Greece, Spain, Portugal, and Italy during 1990–2011 according to the World Development Indicators (WDI) database.

Table 9.2   Unemployment, Nominal Wages, and γ: Evidence from the Eurozone

Country	Unemployment Rate 2008:Q1 (%)	2011:Q2 (%)	Wage Growth $\frac{W_{2011:Q2}}{W_{2008:Q1}}$ (%)	Implied Value of γ
Bulgaria	6.1	11.3	43.3	1.028
Cyprus	3.8	6.9	10.7	1.008
Estonia	4.1	12.8	2.5	1.002
Greece	7.8	16.7	−2.3	0.9982
Ireland	4.9	14.3	0.5	1.0004
Italy	6.4	8.2	10.0	1.007
Lithuania	4.1	15.6	−5.1	0.996
Latvia	6.1	16.2	−0.6	0.9995
Portugal	8.3	12.5	1.91	1.001
Spain	9.2	20.8	8.0	1.006
Slovenia	4.7	7.9	12.5	1.009
Slovakia	10.2	13.3	13.4	1.010

Source: Schmitt-Grohé and Uribe (2016a).
Notes: W is an index of nominal average hourly labor cost in manufacturing, construction, and services. Unemployment is the economy-wide unemployment rate.

and

$$F(h) = h^{\alpha},$$

with σ, ξ, a, $\alpha > 0$. These functional forms are commonplace in the quantitative business-cycle literature.

A case that is of significant interest analytically, computationally, and empirically is one in which the intra- and intertemporal elasticities of consumption substitution are equal to each other, that is, the case in which

$$\xi = \frac{1}{\sigma}.$$

This restriction greatly facilitates the characterization of equilibrium, because it renders the equilibrium processes of external debt, d_t, and consumption of tradables, c_t^T, independent of the level of activity in the nontraded sector. This implication is also of interest because it means that any welfare differences across exchange-rate regimes must be attributable to the effects of exchange-rate policy on unemployment and not to transitional dynamics in external debt. Finally, we argue in Section 9.7 that the case of equal intra- and intertemporal elasticities of substitution is empirically plausible.

To see that setting $\xi = 1/\sigma$ renders the equilibrium levels of external debt and tradable consumption independent of the level of activity in the nontraded sector, note that under this restriction we have that

$$U(A(c_t^T, c_t^N)) = \frac{a c_t^{T\,1-\sigma} + (1-a)c_t^{N\,1-\sigma} - 1}{1 - \sigma},$$

which is additively separable in c_t^T and c_t^N. Therefore, equation (9.13) becomes

$$\lambda_t = ac_t^{T-\sigma},$$

which is independent of c_t^N. Thus, the equilibrium processes $\{c_t^T, d_{t+1}, \mu_t, \lambda_t\}_{t=0}^\infty$ can be obtained as the solution to the subsystem of equilibrium conditions (9.9)–(9.14). Clearly, this result holds for any exchange-rate policy and for any degree of wage rigidity. In particular, we have that when $\xi = 1/\sigma$, the equilibrium behavior of d_t and c_t^T is the same under a currency peg, under the optimal exchange-rate policy, and under full wage flexibility. We impose this parameter restriction in the quantitative analysis that follows. For an analysis of the case $\sigma \neq 1/\xi$, see Schmitt-Grohé and Uribe (2016a).

9.6 Approximating Equilibrium Dynamics

The equilibrium dynamics under the optimal exchange-rate policy can be characterized as the solution to the following value function problem:

$$v^{OPT}(y_t^T, r_t, d_t) = \max_{\{d_{t+1}, c_t^T\}} \left\{ U(A(c_t^T, F(\bar{h}))) + \beta E_t v^{OPT}(y_{t+1}^T, r_{t+1}, d_{t+1}) \right\} \quad (9.30)$$

subject to (9.9) and (9.10), where the function $v^{OPT}(y_t^T, r_t, d_t)$ represents the welfare level of the representative agent under the full-employment exchange-rate policy in state (y_t^T, r_t, d_t). To approximate the solution to this dynamic programming problem, we apply the method of value function iteration over a discretized version of the state space.

We assume that the exogenous driving forces y_t^T and r_t follow a joint discrete Markov process with 21 points for y_t^T and 11 points for r_t. In Section 9.7.1, we econometrically estimate the parameters defining this process.

We discretize the level of debt with 501 equally spaced points in the interval 1 to 8. The solution of the above dynamic programming problem yields the equilibrium processes for d_{t+1} and c_t^T for all possible states (y_t^T, r_t, d_t). Given these processes, the equilibrium processes of all other endogenous variables under the optimal exchange-rate policy can be readily obtained. The variable h_t equals $\bar{h}$ for all t, p_t can be obtained from (9.15), and w_t from (9.16). Finally, if a particular full-employment exchange-rate policy has been chosen from the family defined in equation (9.24), it can be readily backed out.

The maintained parameter restriction $\xi = 1/\sigma$ implies that the solution for d_{t+1} and c_t^T just described also applies to the fixed exchange-rate economy. Under a currency peg, however, the past real wage, w_{t-1}, becomes relevant for the determination of employment, current wages, nontradable output, and the relative price of nontradables. As a result, the fixed exchange-rate economy carries an additional endogenous state variable, w_{t-1}. To discretize the past real wage, we use 500 points between 0.25 and 6. Points are equally spaced on a logarithmic scale. Computing the equilibrium level of the real wage, w_t, given values for w_{t-1} and c_t^T, requires solving a static problem and involves no iterative procedure. Specifically, begin by assuming that $h_t = \bar{h}$. Then use (9.23) to obtain the full-employment real wage, $\omega(c_t^T)$ (given a value for c_t^T, this is just a number). Next, check whether the full-employment real wage satisfies the lower bound on nominal wages when $\epsilon_t = 1$, that is, whether $\omega(c_t^T) \geq \gamma w_{t-1}$. If so, then $w_t = \omega(c_t^T)$. Otherwise, the lower bound on nominal wages is binding and $w_t = \gamma w_{t-1}$. The resulting value of w_t will in general not coincide exactly with any point in the grid, so pick the closest grid point. Given w_t and c_t^T, all other endogenous variables can be easily obtained. For example, h_t and p_t are the solution to (9.15) and (9.16).

When $\xi \neq 1/\sigma$, approximating the dynamics of the model under a currency peg is computationally more demanding. The reason is that in this case the dynamics of debt and tradable consumption are affected by the level of activity in the nontraded sector. As a result, the equilibrium dynamics of d_{t+1} and c_t^T can no longer be obtained separately from the dynamics of variables pertaining to the nontraded sector. In addition, because of the distortions created by nominal rigidities, aggregate dynamics cannot be cast in terms of a Bellman equation without introducing additional state variables (such as the individual level of debt, which households perceive as distinct from its aggregate counterpart). In Schmitt-Grohé and Uribe (2016a), we show that one can approximate the solution by Euler equation iteration over a discretized version of the state space $(y_t^T, r_t, d_t, w_{t-1})$.

9.7 Parameterization of the Model

We calibrate the model at a quarterly frequency. The model contains two types of parameters: structural parameters pertaining to preferences, technologies, and nominal frictions, and parameters defining the stochastic process of the exogenous driving forces. We begin by estimating the latter set of parameters.

9.7.1 Estimation of the Exogenous Driving Process

We assume that the law of motion of tradable output and the country interest rate is given by the following autoregressive process:

$$
\begin{bmatrix} \ln y_t^T \\ \ln \frac{1+r_t}{1+r} \end{bmatrix} = A \begin{bmatrix} \ln y_{t-1}^T \\ \ln \frac{1+r_{t-1}}{1+r} \end{bmatrix} + \epsilon_t, \tag{9.31}
$$

where ϵ_t is a white noise process of order 2 by 1 distributed $N(\emptyset, \Sigma_\epsilon)$. The parameter r denotes the deterministic steady-state value of the country interest rate r_t. We estimate this system using Argentine data from 1983:Q1 to 2001:Q4.

Our empirical measure of y_t^T is the cyclical component of Argentine GDP in agriculture, forestry, fishing, mining, and manufacturing.[9] As in the empirical business-cycle analysis of Chapter 1, we obtain the cyclical component by removing a log-quadratic time trend. Panel (a) of Figure 9.10 displays the resulting time series. We measure the country interest rate as the sum of the EMBI+ spread for Argentina and the 90-day Treasury bill rate, deflated using a measure of expected dollar inflation.[10] Specifically, we construct the time

---

9. The data were downloaded from www.indec.mecon.ar.

10. EMBI+ stands for Emerging Markets Bond Index Plus. The EMBI+ tracks total returns for traded external debt instruments (external meaning foreign currency–denominated fixed income) in the emerging markets. Included in the EMBI+ are U.S.-dollar denominated Brady bonds, Eurobonds, and traded loans issued by sovereign entities. Instruments in the EMBI+ must have a minimum face value outstanding of $500 million, a remaining life of 2.5 years or more, and must meet strict criteria for secondary market trading liquidity. The EMBI+ is produced by J. P. Morgan. The time series starts in 1993 or later, depending on the country, and has a daily frequency. We convert the daily time series into a quarterly time series by taking the arithmetic average of daily observations in each quarter.

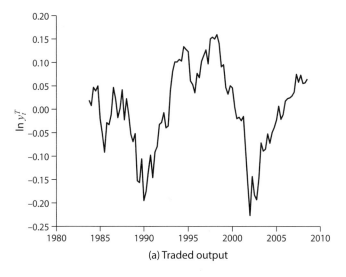

(a) Traded output

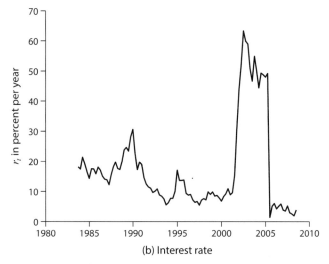

(b) Interest rate

Figure 9.10   Traded output and interest rate in Argentina, 1983:Q1–2008:Q3.

Note: Traded output is expressed in log deviations from a quadratic time trend.

series for the quarterly real Argentine interest rate, r_t, as $1 + r_t = (1 + i_t)E_t\frac{1}{1+\pi_{t+1}}$, where i_t denotes the dollar interest rate charged to Argentina in international financial markets, and π_t is U.S. CPI inflation. For 1983:Q1–1997:Q4, we take i_t to be the Argentine interest-rate series constructed by Neumeyer and Perri (2005).[11] For 1998:Q1–2001:Q4, we measure

---

11. The time series is available online at www.fperri.net/data/neuperri.xls. For 1983:Q1–1994:Q1, these authors compute the interest rate as the sum of the 90-day U.S. Treasury bill rate and their own calculation of a spread on Argentine bonds. For 1994:Q1–1997:Q4, they use the EMBI+ spread.

i_t as the sum of the EMBI+ spread and the 90-day Treasury bill rate, which is in line with the definition used in Neumeyer and Perri since 1994:Q2. We measure $E_t \frac{1}{1+\pi_{t+1}}$ by the fitted component of a regression of $\frac{1}{1+\pi_{t+1}}$ onto a constant and two lags. This regression uses quarterly data on the growth rate of the U.S. CPI index from 1947:Q1 to 2010:Q2.

Our OLS estimates of the matrices A and Σ_ϵ and of the scalar r are

$$A = \begin{bmatrix} 0.79 & -1.36 \\ -0.01 & 0.86 \end{bmatrix}; \qquad \Sigma_\epsilon = \begin{bmatrix} 0.00123 & -0.00008 \\ -0.00008 & 0.00004 \end{bmatrix}; \qquad r = 0.0316.$$

According to these estimates, both $\ln y_t^T$ and r_t are highly volatile, with unconditional standard deviations of 12.2 percent and 1.7 percent per quarter (6.8 percent per year), respectively. Also, the unconditional contemporaneous correlation between $\ln y_t^T$ and r_t is high and negative at -0.86. This means that periods of relatively low traded output are associated with high interest rates and vice versa. The estimated joint autoregressive process implies that both traded output and the real interest rate are highly persistent, with first-order autocorrelations of 0.95 and 0.93, respectively. Finally, we estimate a steady-state real interest rate of 3.16 percent per quarter, or 13.2 percent per year. This high average value reflects the fact that our sample covers a period in which Argentina underwent a great deal of economic turbulence.

We discretize the joint AR(1) process for y_t^T and r_t given in equation (9.31) using 21 equally spaced points for $\ln y_t^T$ and 11 equally spaced points for $\ln((1+r_t)/(1+r))$. The first and last values of the grids for $\ln y_t^T$ and $\ln((1+r_t)/(1+r))$ are set to $\pm\sqrt{10}$ times the respective standard deviations (± 0.3858 and ± 0.0539, respectively). We construct the transition probability matrix of the state $(\ln y_t^T, \ln((1+r_t)/(1+r)))$ using the simulation approach proposed in Schmitt-Grohé and Uribe (2009). This approach consists of simulating a time series of length 1,000,000 drawn from the system (9.31) and associating each observation in the time series with one of the 231 possible discrete states by distance minimization. The resulting discrete-valued time series is used to compute the probability of transitioning from a particular discrete state in one period to a particular discrete state in the next period. The resulting transition probability matrix captures well the covariance matrices of orders 0 and 1.[12]

9.7.2 Calibration of Preferences, Technologies, and Nominal Rigidities

The values assigned to the structural parameters are shown in Table 9.3. We set the parameter γ governing the degree of downward nominal wage rigidity to 0.99. This is a conservative value. The estimates of γ based on data from Argentina and the periphery of Europe presented in Section 9.4 suggest that γ, after correcting for foreign inflation and long-run growth, lies in the interval [0.99, 1.022]. We set γ to the lower bound of this interval, which represents the greatest degree of downward wage flexibility consistent with the data used in the estimation.

---

12. The transition probability matrix is available in the file tpm.mat and is produced by the Matlab script tpm.m. Both files are available in the online materials for this chapter, available on the book's Web site via http://press .princeton.edu/titles/11032.html.

Table 9.3   Calibration of the Model

Parameter	Value	Description
γ	0.99	Degree of downward nominal wage rigidity
σ	2	Inverse of intertemporal elasticity of consumption
y^T	1	Steady-state tradable output
r	0.0316	Steady-state interest rate (quarterly)
$\bar{h}$	1	Labor endowment
a	0.26	Share of tradables
ξ	0.5	Elasticity of substitution between tradables and nontradables
α	0.75	Labor share in nontraded sector
β	0.9635	Quarterly subjective discount factor

Note: The time unit is one quarter.

We normalize the steady-state levels of output of tradables and hours at unity. Then, if the steady-state trade-balance-to-output ratio is small, as is the case in Argentina (see Table 1.6 in Chapter 1), the parameter a is approximately equal to the share of traded output in total output. We set this parameter at 0.26, which is the share of traded output (as defined above) observed in Argentine data during 1980:Q1–2010:Q1. Uribe (1997) presents evidence suggesting that the labor share in the nontraded sector in Argentina is 0.75. Accordingly we set α equal to this value. As in the RBC models studied in Chapter 4, we set σ equal to 2. As mentioned there, this value is commonly used in business-cycle studies. Using time series data for Argentina during 1993:Q1–2001:Q3, González Rozada et al. (2004) estimate the elasticity of substitution between traded and nontraded consumption, ξ, to be 0.44. This estimate is consistent with the cross-country estimates of Stockman and Tesar (1995). These authors include in their estimation both developed and developing countries. Restricting the sample to include only developing countries yields a value of ξ of 0.43 (see Akinci 2011). We set ξ equal to 0.5. We pick this particular value for two reasons. First, it is close to the value suggested by existing empirical studies. Second, this value is the reciprocal of the one assigned to σ. As discussed in Section 9.5, the restriction $\xi = 1/\sigma$ implies that the dynamics of external debt and tradable consumption are independent of the exchange-rate policy or the degree of nominal wage rigidity. This implication greatly facilitates the numerical characterization of the equilibrium dynamics.[13]

We set $\bar{d}$ at the natural debt limit, which we define as the level of external debt that can be supported with zero tradable consumption when the household perpetually receives the lowest possible realization of tradable endowment, $y^{T\min}$, and faces the highest possible realization of the interest rate, $r^{\max}$. Formally, $\bar{d} \equiv y^{T\min}(1 + r^{\max})/r^{\max}$. Given our discretized estimate of the exogenous driving process, $\bar{d}$ equals 8.34.

---

13. In Schmitt-Grohé and Uribe (2016a), we consider the case in which $1/\sigma = 0.2$ and $\xi = 0.44$.

We calibrate the subjective discount factor β to match the average external-debt-to-output ratio of 23 percent per year observed in Argentina during 1983–2001 (Lane and Milesi-Ferretti 2007). We set β at 0.9635. This value yields an average debt-to-output ratio of 23.2 percent per year under the optimal exchange-rate policy and of 21.5 percent under a currency peg.

9.8 External Crises and Exchange-Rate Policy: A Quantitative Analysis

We are now ready to quantitatively characterize the response of the model economy to a large negative external shock. We have in mind extraordinary contractions like the 1989 or 2001 crises in Argentina, or the 2008 Great Recession in peripheral Europe. During the great Argentine crises of 1989 and 2001, for example, traded output fell by about two standard deviations in 2.5 years, and the country premium experienced equally large increases. We are particularly interested in contrasting the model economy's adjustment to this type of external shock under the two polar exchange-rate arrangements we have been considering thus far: a currency peg and the optimal exchange-rate policy.

9.8.1 Definition of an External Crisis

We define an external crisis that starts in period t as a situation in which tradable output is at or above trend in quarter t and at least two standard deviations below trend in quarter $t + 10$. To characterize the typical behavior of the economy during such episodes, we simulate the model for 20 million quarters and identify windows $(t - 10, t + 30)$ in which movements in traded output conform to the definition of an external crisis. Then for each variable of interest, we average all windows and subtract the respective mean taken over the entire sample of 20 million quarters. The beginning of the typical crisis is normalized at $t = 0$.

Figure 9.11 displays the predicted average behavior of the two exogenous variables, traded output and the country interest rate, during a crisis. The downturn in traded output can be interpreted either as a drastic fall in the quantity of tradables produced by the economy or as an exogenous collapse in the country's terms of trade. The figure shows that at the trough of the crisis (period 10), tradable output is 25 percent below trend. The contraction in tradable output is accompanied by a sharp increase in the interest rate that international financial markets charge to the emerging economy. The country interest rate peaks in quarter 10 at about 14 percentage points per year (about two standard deviations) above its average value. This behavior of the interest rate is dictated by the estimated high negative correlation between tradable output and country interest rates. Indeed, the typical crisis would look quite similar to the one shown in Figure 9.11 if we had defined a crisis episode as one in which the country interest rate is at or below its average level in period 0 and at least two standard deviations above its average level in period 10.

How do the endogenous variables of the model, such as unemployment, real wages, consumption, the trade balance, and inflation, respond to these large negative external shocks? As we will see next, the answer depends crucially on the exchange-rate policy put in place by the monetary authority.

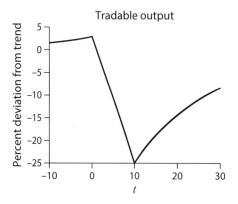 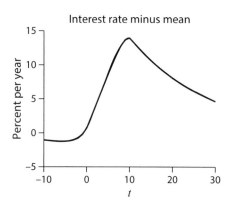

Figure 9.11   The source of a crisis.

9.8.2 Crisis Dynamics under a Currency Peg

Figure 9.12 depicts with solid lines the response of the endogenous variables to the external crisis defined in Section 9.8.1 when the exchange-rate policy takes the form of a currency peg.

The large exogenous increase in the country interest rate and the large fall in tradable endowment cause households to sharply reduce consumption of tradable goods. At the trough of the crisis, in quarter 10, tradable consumption is about 33 percent below trend. This adjustment is so pronounced that, even though the endowment of tradables falls significantly during the crisis, the trade balance actually improves. The bottom-left panel of Figure 9.12 shows that the trade-balance-to-output ratio rises by about 3 percentage points between the beginning and the trough of the crisis. The severity of the contraction in the absorption of tradables is driven primarily by the country interest-rate hike, which causes a substitution effect against current consumption and a negative wealth effect stemming from an increase in interest payments on the external debt. The elevated cost of debt service causes the country's external debt to increase during the crisis, in spite of the positive trade balance. The stock of external debt increases not only as a fraction of output (see the bottom-right panel of Figure 9.12), but also in levels (not shown in Figure 9.12).

The contraction in the traded sector spills over to the nontraded sector in ways that can be highly deleterious. The full-employment real wage, $\omega(c_t^T)$, shown by a dashed line in the top-right panel of Figure 9.12, falls by 66 percent between periods 0 and 10. In contrast, the real wage, w_t, shown by a solid line in the top-right panel of Figure 9.12, falls by only 10 percent. The reason for the insufficient downward adjustment in the real wage is, of course, the combination of downward nominal wage rigidity and a currency peg. Recall that the real wage, expressed in terms of tradables, equals the ratio of the nominal wage, W_t, and the nominal exchange rate, $\mathcal{E}_t$. Therefore, a fall in the real wage requires either a fall in nominal wages, a depreciation of the currency (i.e., an increase in $\mathcal{E}_t$), or a combination of both. Due to downward nominal wage rigidity, nominal wages can fall most by 1 percent per quarter (since γ equals 0.99). At the same time, because of the currency peg, the nominal exchange rate is constant over time. It follows that the real wage can fall by at most 1 percent

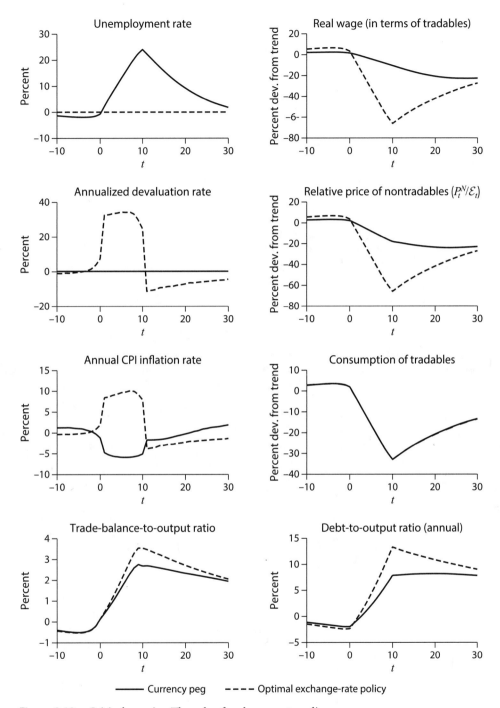

Figure 9.12 Crisis dynamics: The role of exchange-rate policy.

per quarter. Thus, real wages fall by only 10 percent between the beginning of the crisis in period 0 and the beginning of the recovery in period 10—more than 50 percentage points short of what would be necessary to ensure full employment.

The sluggish downward adjustment of the real wage causes massive disequilibrium in the labor market. The top-left panel of Figure 9.12 shows that the rate of involuntary unemployment increases to 25 percent at the trough of the crisis. Furthermore, unemployment is highly persistent. Five years after the trough of the crisis, the unemployment rate remains more than 7 percentage points above average. The persistence of unemployment is due to the slow downward adjustment of real wages.

In spite of the large contraction in aggregate demand, the relative price of nontradables in terms of tradables, $P_t^N/\mathcal{E}_t$, falls little during the crisis. This is because labor costs (the real wage) remain too high, making it unprofitable for firms to implement large price cuts. As a consequence of the insufficient fall in the relative price of nontradables, households do not face a strong enough incentive to switch expenditure away from tradables and toward nontradables. Put differently, the combination of downward nominal wage rigidity and a currency peg hinders the ability of the price system to signal to firms and consumers that during the crisis, there is a relative aggregate scarcity of tradable goods and a relative aggregate abundance of nontradable goods.

The predictions of our model suggest that a rigid exchange-rate policy whereby the necessary real depreciation is forced to occur via product-price and wage deflation is highly costly in terms of unemployment and forgone consumption of nontradables. As we will see next, the present economy requires large devaluations to bring about full employment.

9.8.3 Crisis Dynamics under Optimal Exchange-Rate Policy

We have seen in Section 9.3 that there exists a whole family of optimal exchange-rate policies, defined by condition (9.24). Each member of this family supports the Pareto optimal real allocation. However, different members of this family can deliver different outcomes for nominal variables, such as the devaluation rate, price inflation, and wage inflation. Here we consider the following specification for the optimal exchange-rate policy:

$$\epsilon_t = \frac{w_{t-1}}{\omega(c_t^T)}. \tag{9.32}$$

With $\gamma < 1$, this policy clearly belongs to the family defined in condition (9.24). According to this policy, the central bank devalues the domestic currency when the full employment wage falls below the past real wage and revalues the currency when the full employment wage exceeds the past real wage. This policy specification has three interesting properties. First, it ensures that nominal wages are constant at all times. To see this, note that in the Pareto optimal allocation, the real wage equals the full-employment real wage, that is, $w_t = \omega(c_t^T)$. Then using the fact that $w_t \equiv W_t/\mathcal{E}_t$ and that $\epsilon_t = \mathcal{E}_t/\mathcal{E}_{t-1}$, we can write the above exchange-rate policy as $\mathcal{E}_t/\mathcal{E}_{t-1} = (W_{t-1}/\mathcal{E}_{t-1})/(W_t/\mathcal{E}_t)$, which implies that $W_t = W_{t-1}$ for all $t \geq 0$. Thus the assumed exchange-rate policy stabilizes the nominal price that suffers from downward rigidity. A second property of the assumed optimal exchange-rate policy is that it implies that the nominal price of nontradables is also constant over time. This can be seen from equation (9.16), which states that $p_t F'(h_t) = w_t$. Noticing that under the Pareto optimal allocation, h_t is constant and equal to $\bar{h}$, and that $p_t = P_t^N/\mathcal{E}_t$, we have that in equilibrium $P_t^N F'(\bar{h}) = W_t$. Since W_t is constant, so is P_t^N. A third property of interest is that the assumed optimal exchange-rate policy implies zero inflation and zero devaluation on average. To see this note that the relative price of nontradables, p_t, is a stationary variable. That is, it may move over the business cycle, but does not have a trend. Since p_t equals $P_t^N/\mathcal{E}_t$ and P_t^N is constant, we have that the nominal exchange rate must also be stationary, that is, $\mathcal{E}_t$ does not have a trend. This means that the devaluation rate, $\epsilon_t - 1$, must be zero on average. Finally, because the nominal price of nontradables, P_t^N, is constant and the nominal price of tradables, $\mathcal{E}_t$, is stationary, it follows that the nominal price of the composite consumption good, P_t, must be stationary. This implies in turn that the CPI inflation, which is a combination of inflation in tradable and nontradable prices, must be zero on average.

Figure 9.12 displays with dashed lines the average response of the economy to the external crisis defined in Section 9.8.1 under the optimal exchange-rate policy. The central difference between the optimal exchange-rate policy and a currency peg is that under the optimal exchange-rate policy the external crisis does not spill over to the nontraded sector. Indeed, as we saw in Section 9.3, the unemployment rate is nil under the optimal exchange-rate policy. The government ensures full employment through a series of devaluations of the domestic currency, which are quite large under the present parameterization of the model. Figure 9.12 shows that the monetary authority devalues the currency at an annualized rate of about 35 percent each quarter for the duration of the contractionary phase of the crisis (quarters 0 to 10). These large devaluations drastically lower the real value of wages in terms of tradables, thereby reducing the labor cost faced by firms. The top-right panel of Figure 9.12 shows that the real wage, expressed in terms of tradables, falls by more than 60 percent over the first 10 quarters of the crisis. As we will see shortly, this sizable drop in the real value of wages is in line with the Argentine experience at the time of the large devaluation of December 2001 that ended the 10-year-long exchange-rate peg known as the Convertibility Plan (see Figure 9.14 later in the chapter). In turn, the decline in real labor costs allows firms to lower the relative price of nontradable goods in terms of tradable goods, which results in a large depreciation of the real exchange rate of over 60 percent (see the right panel in the second row of Figure 9.12). This sizable change in relative prices induces households to redirect their spending toward nontradable goods. The large nominal and real depreciation of the currency predicted by the model is in line with the empirical findings of Burstein, Eichenbaum, and Rebelo (2005), who report that the primary force behind the observed large drop in the real exchange rate that occurred after the large devaluations in Argentina (2002), Brazil (1999), Korea (1997), Mexico (1994), and Thailand (1997) was the slow adjustment in the nominal price of nontradable goods.

During the crisis, the optimal exchange-rate policy drives the CPI inflation rate to about 10 percent per year (see the left panel in row 3 of Figure 9.12). In contrast, under the exchange-rate peg the economy experiences deflation of about 6 percent per year. The model thus speaks strongly against allowing the economy to fall into deflation during a crisis.

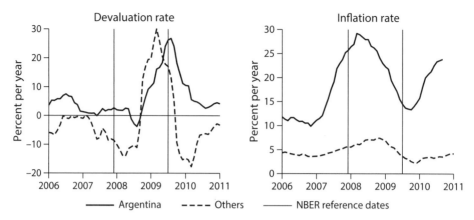

Figure 9.13   Devaluation and inflation in Latin America, 2006–2011.

9.8.4 Devaluations, Revaluations, and Inflation in Reality

The particular optimal exchange-rate policy given in equation (9.32) has the property of inducing zero devaluation and zero inflation on average. This means that the elevated rates of devaluation and inflation predicted during crisis must be followed by revaluations and low inflation in the recovery phase. The left panel in row 2 of Figure 9.12 shows that revaluations are predicted to begin as soon as the economy begins to recover. Is this prediction borne out in the data?

Figure 9.13 displays the CPI inflation rate and the devaluation rate against the U.S. dollar for Argentina and an average of Brazil, Chile, Colombia, Mexico, Peru, and Uruguay during the 2008 Great Recession. Vertical lines mark the beginning and end of the Great Recession in the United States according to the NBER. The crisis, which started in the United States in 2008, arrived in South America 1 year later. All countries in the sample responded to the crisis with sizable devaluations. This response is in line with the predictions of the model under the optimal exchange-rate policy. Both in Argentina and in the group of Latin American countries considered, CPI inflation picked up during the crisis. At the same time, all countries with the exception of Argentina revalued their currencies as soon as the recovery began. In contrast, Argentina continued to devalue its currency during the recovery. As predicted by the model, the countries that revalued experienced lower inflation than Argentina did.

9.9 Empirical Evidence on the Expansionary Effects of Devaluations

Are devaluations expansionary in the way suggested by the model? Here we examine two episodes pointing in this direction. Both involve countries that are hit by severe negative shocks during a currency peg. After some years of increasing unemployment and general economic duress, these countries decide to abandon the fixed exchange rate regime and to allow their currencies to depreciate. In both cases, the devaluations were followed by a reduction in real wages and an expansion of aggregate employment.

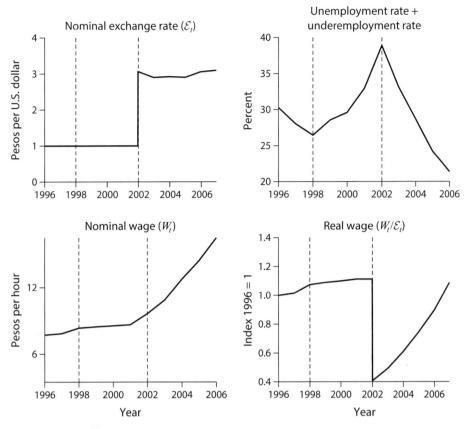

Figure 9.14 Nominal wages and unemployment in Argentina, 1996–2006.

Source: Schmitt-Grohé and Uribe (2016a).

9.9.1 *Exiting a Currency Peg: Argentina Post Convertibility*

Figure 9.14 displays the nominal exchange rate, subemployment, and nominal hourly wages expressed in pesos and in U.S. dollars for Argentina during 1996–2006. As discussed in Section 9.4.4, the Argentine peso was pegged to the U.S. dollar from April 1991 to December 2001. Since 1998 Argentina had been undergoing a severe contraction that had pushed the subemployment rate to 35 percent. In spite of widespread unemployment and a fixed exchange rate, nominal wages did not decline in this period. In December 2001 Argentina abandoned the peg, devaluing the peso by 250 percent (see the top-left panel of the figure). As shown in the bottom-right panel of the figure, the devaluation coincided with a vertical decline in the real wage by a magnitude proportional to the devaluation. Following the real wage decline, labor market conditions improved quickly. By 2005 the subemployment rate had fallen by 12 percentage points.

The sizable fall in real wages right after the devaluation of December 2001 suggests that the 1998–2001 period was one of censored wage deflation, which further strengthens the view that nominal wages suffer from downward inflexibility. The fact that nominal wages increased after the devaluation indicates that the size of the devaluation exceeded the one necessary to restore full employment. More importantly, it suggests that nominal wages are not upwardly rigid. Taken together the dynamics of nominal wages from 1998 to 2006 is consistent with the view that nominal wages are downwardly rigid but upwardly flexible.

9.9.2 Exiting the Gold Standard: Europe 1929–1935

Another piece of indirect historical evidence of the expansionary effects of devaluations is provided by the international effects of the Great Depression of 1929–1933. Friedman and Schwartz (1963) observe that countries that left the gold standard early enjoyed more rapid recoveries than those that stayed on gold longer. The first group of countries was known as the sterling bloc and consisted of the United Kingdom, Sweden, Finland, Norway, and Denmark, and the second group was known as the gold bloc and was formed by France, Belgium, the Netherlands, and Italy. The sterling bloc countries left gold beginning in 1931, whereas the gold block countries stayed on gold much longer, some until 1935.

One can think of the gold standard as a currency union in which members peg their currencies, not to the currency of another country member, but to gold. Thus abandoning the gold standard is akin to abandoning a currency peg. When the sterling bloc countries left the gold standard, they effectively devalued their currencies, as the price of their currencies in terms of gold went down.

The difference in economic performance was associated with earlier reflation of price levels in the countries leaving gold earlier. Importantly, as pointed out by Eichengreen and Sachs (1985), real wages behaved differently in countries that left the gold standard early and in countries that stuck to it longer. Figure 9.15 shows the change in real wages and in industrial production between 1929 and 1935 in the sterling and gold blocks. It shows that relative to their respective 1929 levels, real wages in the sterling bloc countries were lower than real wages in the gold bloc countries. And industrial production in the sterling bloc countries in 1935 exceeded their respective 1929 levels, whereas industrial production in the gold bloc countries was below their respective 1929 levels. This suggests two things. First, countries in which real wages increased less showed stronger growth in industrial production. Second, only the countries that devalued showed moderation in real wage growth. Taken together, these two facts suggest that in the Great Depression years, nominal wages were downwardly rigid in Europe and that abandoning a peg during a recession can be expansionary.

9.10 The Welfare Costs of Currency Pegs

Thus far we have used the theoretical model to compare the performance of currency pegs and the optimal exchange-rate policy during episodes of external crisis. We saw that currency pegs do a poor job at negotiating this type of situation. In this section we use the theoretical laboratory to compare the performances of currency pegs and the optimal exchange-rate policy not just during periods of economic duress but also along the infinite life of households. To this end, we calculate the level of welfare of individual households living in each of the two exchange-rate regimes.

The key variable to understand welfare differences across exchange-rate regimes in the model we are working with is the rate of involuntary unemployment. To see this, note

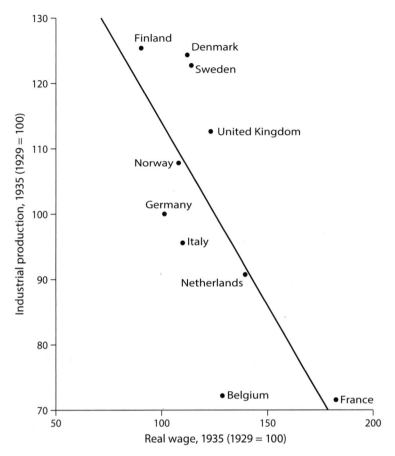

Figure 9.15   Changes in real wages and industrial production, 1929–1935.

Source: Redrawn from Eichengreen and Sachs (1985).

that because of our assumption that the intra- and intertemporal elasticities of substitution are equal to each other ($\sigma = 1/\xi$), the behavior of tradable consumption is identical across exchange-rate regimes (see Section 9.5 for a demonstration). Consequently any welfare differences across exchange-rate regimes must stem from the behavior of nontradable consumption. In turn, since nontradable goods are produced with labor only, all welfare differences must be explained by differences in the predicted dynamics of involuntary unemployment.

We define the welfare cost of a currency peg, denoted $\Lambda(y_t^T, r_t, d_t, w_{t-1})$, as the percentage increase in the consumption stream of a representative individual living in a currency-peg economy that would make him as happy as living in the optimal exchange-rate economy. Specifically, $\Lambda(y_t^T, r_t, d_t, w_{t-1})$ is implicitly given by

$$E_t \sum_{s=0}^{\infty} \beta^s \frac{\left[c_{t+s}^{PEG} \left(1 + \frac{\Lambda(y_t^T, r_t, d_t, w_{t-1})}{100} \right) \right]^{1-\sigma} - 1}{1 - \sigma} = v^{OPT}(y_t^T, r_t, d_t), \qquad (9.33)$$

where c_t^{PEG} denotes the equilibrium process of consumption in the currency-peg economy, and $v^{OPT}(y_t^T, r_t, d_t)$ denotes the value function associated with the optimal exchange-rate policy, defined in equation (9.30). Solving for $\Lambda(y_t^T, r_t, d_t, w_{t-1})$, we obtain

$$\Lambda(y_t^T, r_t, d_t, w_{t-1}) = 100 \left\{ \left[\frac{v^{OPT}(y_t^T, r_t, d_t)(1-\sigma) + (1-\beta)^{-1}}{v^{PEG}(y_t^T, r_t, d_t, w_{t-1})(1-\sigma) + (1-\beta)^{-1}} \right]^{1/(1-\sigma)} - 1 \right\},$$

where $v^{PEG}(y_t^T, r_t, d_t, w_{t-1})$ denotes the value function associated with the currency-peg economy and is given by

$$v^{PEG}(y_t^T, r_t, d_t, w_{t-1}) = E_t \sum_{s=0}^{\infty} \beta^s \frac{\left(c_{t+s}^{PEG} \right)^{1-\sigma} - 1}{1-\sigma}.$$

Table 9.4 reports the median and the mean of $\Lambda(y_t^T, r_t, d_t, w_{t-1})$ along with the average rate of unemployment induced by a currency peg. The distribution of $\Lambda(y_t^T, r_t, d_t, w_{t-1})$ is a function of the equilibrium distribution of the state $(y_t^T, r_t, d_t, w_{t-1})$. In turn the distribution of $(y_t^T, r_t, d_t, w_{t-1})$, and in particular that of w_{t-1}, depends on the exchange-rate regime in place.[14] Because we are interested in the welfare costs of living in a currency peg, we compute the mean and median of the welfare costs of pegs shown in Table 9.4 using the equilibrium distribution of the state $(y_t^T, r_t, d_t, w_{t-1})$ induced by the currency peg.

The mean welfare cost of a currency peg is 7.8 percent of the consumption stream. That is, households living in a currency-peg economy require on average 7.8 percent more consumption in every date and state to be indifferent between staying in the currency-peg regime and switching to the optimal exchange-rate regime. This is a big number as welfare costs go in monetary business-cycle theory. Even under the most favorable initial conditions, the welfare cost of a currency peg is large, 4.0 percent of consumption each period. (This figure corresponds to the lower bound of the support of the probability density of $\Lambda(y_t^T, r_t, d_t, w_{t-1})$.)

As mentioned earlier, the welfare cost of pegs is entirely explained by involuntary unemployment. Table 9.4 reports an average rate of unemployment of 11.7 percent under the currency peg. A back-of-the-envelope calculation can help show how unemployment translates into welfare costs. The average fall in nontradable consumption due to unemployment in the nontraded sector is approximately given by the product of the labor elasticity of nontradable output, α, times the average level of unemployment, or $0.75 \times 11.7 = 8.8$ percent per quarter. In turn, the total consumption loss is roughly given by the share of nontradables in total consumption. Under the present parameterization this is about 0.75 times the loss of nontradable consumption, or $0.75 \times 8.8 = 6.6$, which is close to the exact mean welfare cost.

---

14. When $\sigma \neq 1/\xi$, the distribution of d_t also depends on the exchange-rate regime in place. This case is treated in Schmitt-Grohé and Uribe (2016a).

Table 9.4 The Welfare Costs of Currency Pegs

Parameterization	Welfare Cost of Peg		Average Unemployment Rate under Peg
	Mean	Median	
Baseline			
$\gamma = 0.99$	7.8	7.2	11.7
Lower Downward Wage Rigidity			
$\gamma = 0.98$	5.7	5.3	8.9
$\gamma = 0.97$	3.5	3.3	5.6
$\gamma = 0.96$	2.8	2.7	4.6
Higher Downward Wage Rigidity			
$\gamma = 0.995$	14.3	13.0	19.5
Symmetric Wage Rigidity, $\frac{1}{\gamma} \geq \frac{W_t}{W_{t-1}} \geq \gamma$			
$\gamma = 0.99$	3.3	3.0	5.2
$\gamma = 0.98$	2.8	2.5	4.4

Notes: The welfare cost of a currency peg is expressed as a percentage of consumption per quarter (see equation (9.33)). The mean and median of the welfare cost of a peg is computed over the distribution of the state $(y_t^T, r_t, d_t, w_{t-1})$ induced by the peg economy.

Figure 9.16 displays the unconditional distribution of $\Lambda(y_t^T, r_t, d_t, w_{t-1})$. The distribution is skewed to the right, implying that the probability of very high welfare costs is nonnegligible. For instance, the probability of occurrence of a state associated with welfare costs larger than 10 percent of consumption per quarter is 15 percent, and the probability of occurrence of a state associated with welfare costs larger than 15 percent of consumption per quarter is 1.9 percent. Which states put the economy in such a vulnerable situation? Figure 9.17 sheds light on what these states are. It displays the welfare cost of currency pegs as a function of the four state variables. In each panel only one state variable is allowed to vary (along the horizontal axis), and the remaining three state variables are fixed at their respective unconditional means. The figure shows that currency pegs are more painful when the country is initially more indebted, when it inherits higher past real wages, when the tradable sector is undergoing a contraction (e.g., because of unfavorable terms of trade), or when the country interest-rate premium is high.

The fact that unemployment is the main source of welfare losses associated with currency pegs suggests that a key parameter determining the magnitude of these welfare losses should be γ, which governs the degree of downward nominal wage rigidity. The baseline calibration ($\gamma = 0.99$) implies that nominal wages can fall frictionlessly up to 4 percent per year. In Section 9.4, we argue that this is a conservative value in the sense that it allows for falls in nominal wages during crises that are much larger than those observed either in the 2001 Argentine crisis or in the ongoing crisis in peripheral Europe, even after correcting for foreign inflation and long-run growth. We now consider alternative values that allow for lower and higher degrees of downward nominal wage rigidity.

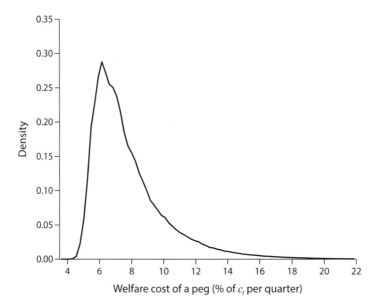

Figure 9.16 Probability density function of the welfare cost of currency pegs.

Notes: The welfare cost of a currency peg is defined in equation (9.33). The density function of welfare costs is computed over the distribution of the state $(y_t^T, r_t, d_t, w_{t-1})$ induced by the peg economy.

On the more flexible side, we consider values of γ that allow for nominal wage declines of up to 16 percent per year. Taking into account that the largest wage decline observed in Argentina in 2001 or in the periphery of Europe since the onset of the Great Recession was 1.6 percent per year (Lithuania; see Table 9.2), it follows that we are considering degrees of wage rigidity substantially lower than those implied by observed wage movements during large contractions. Table 9.4 shows that the mean welfare cost of a currency peg is strictly increasing in the degree of downward nominal wage rigidity. As γ falls from its baseline value of 0.99 to the smallest value considered, 0.96, the welfare cost of a peg falls from 7.8 to 2.8 percent of consumption per quarter. This welfare cost is still a large figure compared to existing results in monetary economics. The intuition explaining why currency pegs are less painful when wages are more downwardly flexible is straightforward. A negative aggregate demand shock reduces the demand for nontradables, which requires a fall in the real wage rate to avoid unemployment. Under a currency peg this downward adjustment must be brought about exclusively by a fall in nominal wages. The less downwardly rigid nominal wages are, the faster the downward adjustment in both the nominal and the real wage will be. Therefore the less downwardly rigid nominal wages are, the smaller the resulting level of unemployment will be. Table 9.4 confirms this intuition. The average rate of involuntary unemployment falls from 11.7 percent to 4.6 percent as γ falls from its baseline value of 0.99 to 0.96.

We also consider a higher degree downward nominal wage rigidity than the one used in the baseline parameterization. Specifically, Table 9.4 includes the case $\gamma = 0.995$. This value

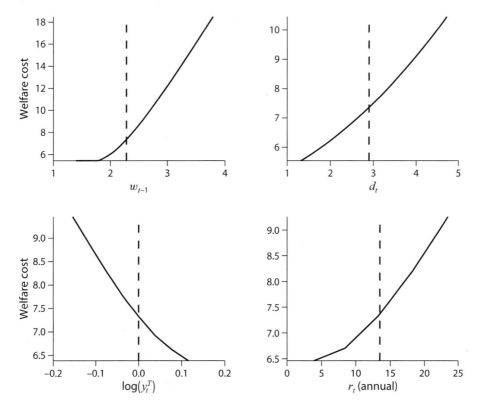

Figure 9.17 Welfare cost of currency pegs as a function of the state variables.

Notes: In each plot, all states except the one shown on the horizontal axis are fixed at their unconditional mean values. The dashed vertical lines indicate the unconditional mean of the state displayed on the horizontal axis (under a currency peg if the state is endogenous).

of γ is perhaps of greater empirical interest than the low values just considered, because unlike those, it lies in the range of estimates obtained in Section 9.4. This level of γ allows nominal wages to fall by up to 2 percent per year, half the fall permitted under the baseline parameterization. The associated welfare costs of pegs are extremely high: 14.3 percent of consumption on average, with an average rate of unemployment of 19.5 percent.

The finding of large welfare costs of currency pegs predicted by the present model economy stands in stark contrast to a large body of work, pioneered by Lucas (1987), suggesting that the costs of business cycles (not just of suboptimal monetary or exchange-rate policy) are minor. Lucas's approach to computing the welfare costs of business cycles consists of first removing a trend from a consumption time series and then evaluating a second-order approximation of welfare, using observed deviations of consumption from trend. Implicit in this methodology is the assumption that the trend is unaffected by policy. In the present model, however, suboptimal monetary or exchange-rate policy creates an endogenous connection between the amplitude of the business cycle and the average rate of unemployment (see the analysis in Section 9.2.2). In turn, through its effect on the average level of unemployment, suboptimal exchange-rate policy has a significant effect on the average level of consumption. And indeed, as we saw earlier in this section, lower average consumption is the main reason currency pegs are so costly in the present model. It follows that applying Lucas's methodology to data stemming from the present model would overlook the effects of policy on trend (or average) consumption and therefore would result in spuriously low welfare costs.

9.11 Symmetric Wage Rigidity

We have shown that the welfare cost of currency pegs is increasing in the degree of downward nominal wage rigidity governed by the parameter γ. We can think of this parameter as reflecting the intensive margin of wage rigidity. We now consider tightening the extensive margin of wage rigidity. We do so by imposing an upper bound on the rate at which nominal wages can increase from one period to the next. Specifically, we now assume the following constraint on nominal wage adjustments:

$$\gamma \leq \frac{W_t}{W_{t-1}} \leq \frac{1}{\gamma}.$$

Table 9.4 shows that for the baseline value of γ of 0.99, increasing nominal wage rigidity along the extensive margin reduces unemployment and is welfare improving. The rate of involuntary unemployment falls from 11.7 percent under downward nominal wage rigidity to less than half that value under symmetric wage rigidity. This result may seem surprising, for it suggests that less wage flexibility is desirable. However, this prediction of the model is quite intuitive.

As we saw analytically in Section 9.2.2, the imposition of upward rigidity in nominal wages alleviates the peg-induced externality. Upward wage rigidity curbs the increase of nominal wages during booms, thereby reducing the required magnitude of wage declines during the contractionary phase of the cycle. As a result, recessions bring about less unemployment when wages are bidirectionally rigid.

Consider now increasing wage flexibility along the intensive margin by lowering γ, but keeping a symmetric specification of wage rigidity. In the presence of symmetric wage rigidity, lowering γ creates a trade-off. On one hand, higher downward wage flexibility is desirable, because it allows for a more efficient adjustment of real wages during a downturn. On the other hand, higher upward wage flexibility is undesirable, because by allowing for larger wage increases during booms, it exacerbates the peg-induced externality. Table 9.4 shows that this trade-off is resolved in favor of higher wage flexibility along the intensive margin. Involuntary unemployment falls from 5.2 to 4.4 percent when γ is reduced from 0.99 to 0.98. With lower unemployment the welfare costs of a currency peg are also smaller, 2.8 percent of consumption instead of 3.3 percent.

We close this section by pointing out that the reason we consider the case of symmetric wage rigidity is for comparison with existing related frameworks—not because of its empirical relevance. The evidence presented in Section 9.4 speaks clearly in favor of asymmetric specifications. We conclude that of all the parameterizations shown in Table 9.4, the ones of greatest empirical relevance are those pertaining to the case in which wages are downwardly rigid and γ takes the value 0.99 or 0.995.

9.12 The Mussa Puzzle

In an influential empirical study, Mussa (1986) compares the behavior of nominal and real exchange rates under fixed and floating exchange-rate regimes. He analyzes data from 13 industrialized countries from 1957–1984.[15] During the subperiod 1957–1970, the countries in the sample pegged their currencies to the U.S. dollar by an exchange-rate agreement known as Bretton Woods. (Recall that prior to 2000, the Euro Area, or eurozone, did not yet exist, so each European country had its own currency.) During the second subperiod, 1973–1984, countries in the sample adopted flexible exchange-rate regimes as a consequence of the breakdown of the Bretton Woods agreement.

Mussa documents three important facts about nominal and real exchange rates across fixed and floating exchange-rate regimes. First, the variability of the real exchange rate is much higher under flexible exchange rates than under fixed exchange rates. Second, under flexible exchange rates, movements in real exchange rates mimic movements in nominal exchange rates. This fact essentially suggests that under floating exchange-rate regimes, observed changes in real exchange rates inherit the stochastic properties of observed changes in nominal exchange rates. Third, the volatility of national inflation rates is broadly the same under floating and fixed exchange-rate regimes.

The reason these facts are often referred to as a puzzle is that they suggest that relative prices depend on the behavior of nominal prices. At the time of Mussa's writing, the dominant paradigm for understanding short-run fluctuations was the flexible-price, neoclassical, real-business-cycle framework treated in Chapter 4 of this book. In a neoclassical world, real variables, including relative prices, are determined by real factors, such as technologies, preferences, and real disturbances. In this type of environment, nominal exchange regime neutrality holds, in the sense that the exchange-rate regime can have effects on other nominal variables but does not matter for real allocations. Stockman (1988), for example, shows the difficulties faced by flexible-price models to capture the Mussa facts.

Since the publication of Mussa's work in 1986, nominal rigidities have found their way into the standard paradigm, changing researchers' views on the ability of monetary policy in general, and exchange-rate policy in particular, to shape the course of real variables. An early analysis of the Mussa puzzle in the context of a sticky-price model is Monacelli (2004).

We wish to ascertain whether the predictions of the theoretical model analyzed in this chapter are consistent with the empirical regularities documented by Mussa. To this end, let's define the real depreciation rate, denoted ϵ_t^{RER}, as the gross growth rate of the real exchange rate. That is,

$$\epsilon_t^{RER} \equiv \frac{RER_t}{RER_{t-1}},$$

where RER_t denotes the real exchange rate as defined in equation (8.1) of Chapter 8, which we reproduce here for convenience:

$$RER_t \equiv \frac{\mathcal{E}_t P_t^*}{P_t}. \qquad (8.1\,\text{R})$$

---

15. The countries included in the sample are Austria, Belgium, Denmark, France, Italy, Japan, Luxembourg, Netherlands, Norway, Sweden, Switzerland, the United Kingdom, and West Germany.

Table 9.5   Real and Nominal Exchange Rates under Fixed and
Floating Exchange-Rate Regimes

Variable	Peg	Float	
		Optimal	Suboptimal
Standard deviation (ϵ_t^{RER})	12.0	32.5	5.2
Standard deviation (ϵ_t)	0	45.2	44.0
Correlation ($\epsilon_t^{RER}, \epsilon_{t-1}^{RER}$)	0.18	−0.04	0.04
Correlation ($\epsilon_t, \epsilon_{t-1}$)	—	−0.04	0.95
Correlation ($\epsilon_t^{RER}, \epsilon_t$)	—	0.99	−0.15
Standard deviation (π_t)	13.2	13.2	44.3

Notes: Standard deviations are expressed as percentages per year. The
optimal floating exchange-rate policy is given by $\epsilon_t = w_{t-1}/\omega(c_t^T)$, and
the suboptimal floating exchange-rate policy is given by $\epsilon_t = \omega(c_t^T)/w_{t-1}$.

Table 9.5 compares the behavior of ϵ_t^{RER} under a currency peg and under the optimal exchange-rate policy given in equation (9.32). The first of Mussa's facts means that the standard deviation of ϵ_t^{RER} is larger under flexible exchange rate regimes than under currency pegs. The first line of Table 9.5 shows that the predicted standard deviation of the real depreciation rate is much larger under the optimal floating exchange-rate policy than under the peg. This prediction of the model is consistent with Mussa's first fact. Rows 2–5 of the table show that under the optimal flexible exchange-rate regime, the nominal and real exchange rates have similar standard deviations and first-order serial correlations, and are highly positively contemporaneously correlated. This finding suggests that the model captures Mussa's second observation, namely, that under flexible exchange rates the real exchange rate shares, to a large extent, the stochastic properties of the nominal exchange rate. Finally, the last row of the table shows that the predicted volatility of CPI inflation, denoted $\pi_t \equiv P_t/P_{t-1}$, is the same under the peg and the optimal floating regime, which concurs with Mussa's third fact.

At this point, it is important to clarify a common misconception. Many empirical studies classify exchange-rate regimes into fixed or floating and then derive stylized facts associated with each regime. This practice is problematic because in reality there is not just one floating exchange-rate regime but an infinite family of them. And importantly, different floating exchange-rate regimes can induce different real allocations and, in particular, different nominal and real-exchange-rate dynamics. To illustrate this point, we consider an alternative floating exchange-rate policy that does not belong to the class of optimal exchange-rate policies given by (9.24). Specifically, assume that the central bank sets the devaluation rate according to the rule $\epsilon_t = \omega(c_t^T)/w_{t-1}$. This policy could be named the "anti-optimal" floating exchange-rate regime, as it revalues when the optimal rule, given in (9.32), calls for devaluations and vice versa. Table 9.5 shows that under this alternative floating exchange-rate policy, the model fails to capture all three of the Mussa facts. Seen through the lens of the present model, it follows that Mussa's facts can be interpreted as suggesting that during the early post–Bretton Woods period, overall, the countries in the sample adopted floating regimes that gave rise to exchange-rate and inflation dynamics that are consistent with the ones associated with optimal exchange-rate policy.

9.13 Endogenous Labor Supply

We now relax the assumption of an inelastic labor supply schedule. Specifically, we consider a period-utility specification of the form

$$U(c_t, \ell_t) = \frac{c_t^{1-\sigma} - 1}{1 - \sigma} + \varphi \frac{\ell_t^{1-\theta} - 1}{1 - \theta}, \tag{9.34}$$

where ℓ_t denotes leisure in period t, and φ and θ are positive parameters. Under this specification, the household's optimization problem features a new first-order condition determining the desired amount of leisure:

$$\varphi(\ell_t^v)^{-\theta} = w_t \lambda_t, \tag{9.35}$$

where ℓ_t^v denotes the desired or voluntary amount of leisure. Equation (9.35) is a notional labor supply. It is notional in the sense that the worker may not be able to work the desired number of hours. We assume that households are endowed with $\bar{h}$ hours per period. Let h_t^v denote the number of hours that households desire to work (the voluntary labor supply). The (voluntary) labor supply is the difference between the endowment of hours and voluntary leisure, that is,

$$h_t^v = \bar{h} - \ell_t^v. \tag{9.36}$$

As before, households may not be able to sell all of the hours they supply to the labor market. Let h_t denote the actual number of hours worked. Then we impose

$$h_t^v \geq h_t. \tag{9.37}$$

This expression states that nobody can be forced to work longer hours than they wish. We impose the following slackness condition:

$$(h_t^v - h_t) \left(w_t - \gamma \frac{w_{t-1}}{\epsilon_t} \right) = 0. \tag{9.38}$$

Expressions (9.35)–(9.38) are the counterparts of conditions (9.7) and (9.19) in the baseline economy. All other conditions describing aggregate dynamics are as before.

An important remaining issue is how to evaluate welfare in the present environment. This issue is not trivial, because now leisure has two components, voluntary leisure, ℓ_t^v, and involuntary leisure (or, synonymously, involuntary unemployment), which we denote by u_t. Involuntary leisure is given by the difference between the number of hours the household voluntarily supplies to the market, h_t^v, and the number of hours the household is actually employed, h_t, that is,

$$u_t = h_t^v - h_t.$$

How should voluntary and involuntary leisure enter in the utility function? One possibility is to assume that voluntary and involuntary leisure are perfect substitutes. In this case, the second argument of the period utility function is $\ell_t = \ell_t^v + u_t$. However, there exists an extensive empirical literature suggesting that voluntary and involuntary leisure are far from perfect substitutes. For instance, Krueger and Mueller (2012), using longitudinal data from a survey of unemployed workers in New Jersey, find that even though the unemployed spend relatively more time in leisure-related activities, they enjoy these activities to a lesser degree than their employed counterparts and thus, on an average day, report higher levels of sadness than the employed do. Similarly, Winkelmann and Winkelmann (1998), using longitudinal data of working-age men in Germany, find that, after controlling for individual fixed effects and income, unemployment has a large nonpecuniary detrimental effect on life satisfaction. Another source of nonsubstitutability between voluntary and involuntary leisure stems from the fact that the unemployed spend more time than the employed looking for work, an activity that they perceive as highly unsatisfying. Krueger and Mueller (2012), for example, report that the unemployed work 391 minutes less per day than the employed but spend 101 minutes more per day on job search. In addition, these authors find that job search generates the highest feeling of sadness after personal care out of 13 time-use categories.

Based on this evidence, it is important to consider specifications in which voluntary and involuntary leisure are imperfect substitutes in utility. Specifically, we model leisure as

$$\ell_t = \ell_t^v + \delta u_t.$$

The existing literature strongly suggests that δ is less than unity. However, estimates of this parameter are not available. For this reason, we consider three values of δ: 0.5, 0.75, and 1.

We calibrate the remaining new parameters of the model as follows. We assume that under full employment households spend a third of their time working. In addition, we adopt a Frisch wage elasticity of labor supply of 2, which is on the high end of available empirical estimates from micro and aggregate data (see, e.g., Blundell and MaCurdy 1999; Smets and Wouters 2007; and Justiniano, Primiceri, and Tambalotti 2010). Finally, we normalize the number of hours worked under full employment to unity so as to preserve the size of the nontraded sector relative to the traded sector as in the baseline economy. This calibration strategy yields $\varphi = 1.11$, $\bar{h} = 3$, and $\theta = 1$.

Table 9.6 shows that the average rate of involuntary unemployment rises from 11.7 to 30.9 percent as the labor supply elasticity increases from 0 to 2. The reason involuntary unemployment is much larger on average with an elastic labor supply specification is that during slumps, households experience a negative income effect, which induces them to increase their supply of labor. However, during slumps, employment is determined by the demand for labor and is not affected by the shift in labor supply. It follows that all of the increase in the labor supply contributes to increasing involuntary unemployment. During booms, regardless of the labor supply elasticity, employment is determined by the intersection of the labor supply and the labor demand schedules, and involuntary unemployment is nil. Thus, with an elastic labor supply, the unemployment problem becomes worse during contractions but stays the same during booms. On net, therefore, unemployment must be higher in the economy with an endogenous labor supply. It is important to note that

Table 9.6   Endogenous Labor Supply and the Welfare Costs of Currency Pegs

Parameterization	Welfare Cost of Peg		Average Unemployment Rate under Peg
	Mean	Median	
Baseline (inelastic labor supply)	7.8	7.2	11.7
Endogenous labor supply			
$\delta = 0.5$	16.5	15.2	30.9
$\delta = 0.75$	8.2	7.5	30.9
$\delta = 1$	1.7	1.5	30.9

Notes: The welfare cost of a currency peg is expressed as a percentage of consumption per quarter. Unemployment rates are expressed as percentages.

the behavior of unemployment is independent of the assumed value of δ, the parameter governing the relative valuation of voluntary and involuntary unemployment. Technically, this is because δ does not appear in any equilibrium condition of the model but affects only the welfare consequences of unemployment. Intuitively, the reason unemployment is independent of δ is that the household takes the number of hours worked as exogenously given. Then δ simply measures how differently households feel about voluntary and involuntary leisure.

Table 9.6 also shows the welfare cost of currency pegs relative to the optimal exchange-rate policy implied by the endogenous labor-supply model. The welfare cost of a currency peg depends significantly on the degree of substitutability between voluntary and involuntary leisure, measured by the parameter δ. The more substitutable voluntary and involuntary leisure are (i.e., the larger δ is), the lower the welfare cost of currency pegs will be. This result should be expected. Consider the case in which voluntary and involuntary unemployment are perfect substitutes ($\delta = 1$). In this case pegs reduce welfare, because involuntary unemployment reduces the production and hence consumption of nontradable goods. However, unemployment increases leisure one for one and in this way increases utility, greatly offsetting the negative welfare effect of lower nontradable consumption. As δ falls, the marginal contribution of involuntary unemployment to total leisure (and therefore welfare) also falls. For a value of δ of 0.75, for instance, the welfare cost of currency pegs is 8.2 percent per period, which is higher than in the case with inelastic labor supply. When δ equals 0.5, the welfare cost currency pegs rises to 16.5 percent of consumption per period.

It follows that allowing for endogenous labor supply increases the average rate of unemployment caused by the combination of a currency peg and downward nominal wage rigidity, and it may increase or decrease the welfare cost of currency pegs, depending on how enjoyable involuntary leisure is assumed to be.

9.14 Production in the Traded Sector

Thus far we have assumed that the supply of tradables, y_t^T, is exogenous. This section relaxes this assumption by considering a specification in which tradables are produced with labor. Specifically, suppose that

$$y_t^T = e^{z_t} \left(h_t^T \right)^{\alpha_T},$$

where y_t^T denotes production of tradable goods, h_t^T denotes labor employed in the traded sector, and $\alpha_T \in (0, 1)$ is a parameter. The variable z_t is assumed to be exogenous and stochastic. One can interpret z_t either as a productivity shock in the traded sector or as a disturbance in the country's terms of trade. As before, assume that firms are perfectly competitive in product and labor markets. Further, we assume that labor is perfectly mobile across sectors. We make this assumption to create a sharp contrast with the baseline formulation, in which labor is completely immobile across sectors. A more realistic formulation would be one in which, in the short run, labor does move across sectors, but sluggishly. The assumption of free labor mobility across sectors implies that wages are equalized across sectors.

Firms in the traded sector choose labor to maximize profits, which are given by

$$P_t^T e^{z_t} \left(h_t^T \right)^{\alpha_T} - W_t h_t^T .$$

The first-order condition associated with the firm's profit-maximization problem is

$$\alpha_T P_t^T e^{z_t} \left(h_t^T \right)^{\alpha_T - 1} = W_t.$$

Let h_t^N denote hours employed in the nontraded sector. Total hours worked, denoted by h_t, are then given by

$$h_t = h_t^T + h_t^N .$$

All other conditions of the model are as in the baseline formulation.

In Schmitt-Grohé and Uribe (2016a) we assume that z_t and r_t follow the joint stochastic process given in equation (9.31), with z_t taking the place of $\ln y_t^T$, and calibrate the parameter α_T at 0.5. We find that average unemployment under a currency peg continues to be high. This result might appear counterintuitive, because one might think that during contractions the unemployment created in the nontraded sector could be absorbed by the traded sector. However, because nominal wages are also downwardly rigid in the traded sector, firms there have no incentives to hire more workers during a contraction. At the same time, the model predicts that, although high, the unemployment rate under a currency peg is lower in the economy with production in the traded sector than in the economy with an exogenous tradable output. The reason is that employment in the traded sector acts as a stabilizer of the wage rate during booms, thereby attenuating the negative externality caused by the combination of downward nominal wage rigidity and a currency peg. To see this, consider a decline in the country interest rate that raises the desired absorption of tradable and nontradable goods. This shock causes the demand for labor to increase in the nontraded sector, driving up wages. This increase in wages induces firms in the traded sector to reduce employment. In turn, these freed-up hours dampen the increase in wages required to clear the labor market. This dampening effect is beneficial, because it means that once the boom is over the economy begins to trend down with lower real wages, making the downward wage rigidity less stringent.

9.15 Product Price Rigidity

Consider now the case of product price rigidity. We first analyze the case of downward rigidity and then introduce symmetric price rigidity. Throughout this section, we assume that nominal wages are fully flexible.

9.15.1 Downward Price Rigidity

Suppose that the nominal price of nontradables is subject to the following constraint:

$$P_t^N \geq \gamma_p P_{t-1}^N,$$

where γ_p is a parameter governing the degree of downward nominal price rigidity. Dividing both sides of this expression by the nominal exchange rate, $\mathcal{E}_t$, yields

$$p_t \geq \frac{\gamma_p}{\epsilon_t} p_{t-1}. \tag{9.39}$$

Expression (9.39) replaces condition (9.17) of the model with downward nominal wage rigidity.

Define the full-employment relative price of nontradables, denoted $\rho(c_t^T)$, as the value of p_t that induces households to voluntarily demand the full-employment level of nontradable output, $F(\bar{h})$, given their desired consumption of tradables, c_t^T. By equation (9.15), we have that $\rho(c_t^T)$ is given by

$$\rho(c_t^T) \equiv \frac{A_2(c_t^T, F(\bar{h}))}{A_1(c_t^T, F(\bar{h}))}.$$

Given the assumed properties of the aggregator function $A(\cdot, \cdot)$, we have that $\rho(c_t^T)$ is increasing in c_t^T. Intuitively, all other things equal, households have an incentive to consume more tradables when nontradables become more expensive. Also, since A_1 is increasing in its second argument and A_2 is decreasing in its second argument, equation (9.15) implies that p_t equals $\rho(c_t^T)$ if and only if h_t equals $\bar{h}$.

Therefore we can postulate the following slackness condition:

$$(\bar{h} - h_t)\left(p_t - \frac{\gamma_p}{\epsilon_t} p_{t-1}\right) = 0, \tag{9.40}$$

which replaces condition (9.19) of the economy with downward nominal wage rigidity. The new slackness condition states that if the economy experiences involuntary unemployment $(h_t < \bar{h})$, then the price of nontradables must be stuck at its lower bound. By the properties of $\rho(c_t^T)$, this means that in this situation p_t must exceed its full-employment level. Slackness condition (9.40) also states that should the lower bound on the price of nontradables not bind, then the economy must have full employment. This, in turn, means that in these circumstances p_t must equal its full-employment value, $\rho(c_t^T)$.

An equilibrium in the economy with downward nominal price rigidity is then a set of stochastic processes $\{c_t^T, h_t, d_{t+1}, p_t, \lambda_t, \mu_t\}_{t=0}^{\infty}$ satisfying (9.9)–(9.15), (9.18), (9.39), and

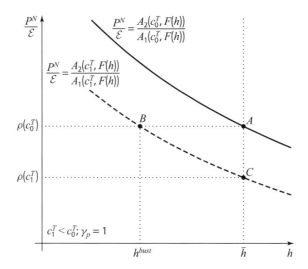

Figure 9.18 Adjustment to a negative external shock with downward price rigidity under a currency peg.

(9.40), given an exchange-rate policy $\{\epsilon_t\}_{t=0}^{\infty}$, initial conditions d_0 and p_{-1}, and exogenous stochastic processes $\{r_t, y_t^T\}_{t=0}^{\infty}$.[16]

Consider now the workings of this economy under a currency peg, $\epsilon_t = 1$ for all t. Figure 9.18 illustrates the economy's adjustment to a negative external shock, such as an increase in r_t or a fall in y_t^T, that reduces the desired consumption of tradables. Before the shock, the demand for traded consumption is equal to c_0^T, and the demand schedule for nontraded goods is given by the solid downward-sloping line. The economy is at point A and enjoys full employment. Suppose that the negative external shock lowers traded consumption from c_0^T to $c_1^T < c_0^T$. Consequently, the demand schedule shifts down and to the left, as depicted by the dashed downward-sloping line.

Under price flexibility, the new equilibrium would be at point C. In this equilibrium, the relative price of nontradables, p, falls from $\rho(c_0^T)$ to $\rho(c_1^T)$. All this adjustment occurs via a fall in the nominal price of nontradables, P^N, since the nominal exchange rate is constant. However, under downward nominal price rigidity, P^N cannot fall (for this illustration, we assume $\gamma_p = 1$). As a result, the relative price of nontradables is stuck at $\rho(c_0^T)$, and the equilibrium is at point B. At this point, the economy suffers from involuntary unemployment in the amount $\bar{h} - h^{bust}$. Also, firms are rationed in product markets in the sense that at the going price, they would like to sell more units than are demanded by consumers.

---

16. Note that the labor demand schedule, $p_t F'(h_t) = w_t$, is no longer part of the set of equilibrium conditions. This is because firms are off their labor demand schedule when the economy suffers from involuntary unemployment, as they are rationed in product markets and thus employment is indirectly determined by the demand for nontradable goods. In such periods the real wage falls to zero, and the value of the marginal product of labor exceeds the real wage: $p_t F'(h_t) > w_t$. In a model with an endogenous labor supply, the real wage is positive and equal to the value that ensures that households are on their labor supply schedule.

Notice that here a fall in wages would not solve the unemployment problem, since firms cannot sell more than $F(h^{bust})$ units of goods in the market. Note also that the unemployment problem is more severe under price rigidity than under wage rigidity for identical values of γ and γ_p. To see this, recall that under downward nominal wage rigidity, the equilibrium after the negative shock is somewhere between points B and C, implying less unemployment than under downward price rigidity.

The peg-induced externality—analyzed in Section 9.2.1 for the case of downward wage rigidity—is also present under downward price rigidity. To see this, consider a positive external shock that increases the desired consumption of tradables. This shock pushes the demand schedule for nontradables up and to the right. The new equilibrium features full employment, a higher nominal price of nontradables, and no rationing in the goods market. On the surface, no problems arise in the adjustment process. However, the increase in the nominal price of nontradables makes the economy weaker: once the positive external shock fades away, the nominal price of nontradables will have to fall to induce households to consume a quantity of nontradables compatible with full employment of the labor force. But this fall in the nominal price does not take place quickly enough if prices are rigid, and involuntary unemployment emerges. Collectively, households would be better off if they limited the initial expansion in the demand for nontradables. And they understand this. But each household is too small to reduce the price increase by curbing its individual expenditure. Here lies the peg-induced externality.

The optimal exchange-rate policy under price rigidity is quite similar to its counterpart under wage rigidity. Indeed, as exercise 9.12 asks you to demonstrate, under certain conditions, any exchange-rate policy that is optimal under downward nominal wage rigidity is also optimal under downward nominal price rigidity. In response to negative external shocks, the monetary authority can preserve full employment (point C in Figure 9.18) by devaluing the currency. In this way, the monetary authority can bring down the relative price of nontradables from $\rho(c_0^T)$ to $\rho(c_1^T)$. The required depreciation becomes larger as the contraction in the demand for tradable goods caused by the negative external shock increases. We then have that, as in the case of downward nominal wage rigidity, contractions are devaluatory.

To quantify the consequences of a currency peg for unemployment and welfare under downward price rigidity, we calibrate the model using the same parameter values as in the case of downward nominal wage rigidity (see Table 9.3), except that now $\gamma = 0$. For comparison with the case of wage rigidity, we set $\gamma_p = 0.99$. Table 9.7 shows that the mean unemployment rate under a currency peg is 14.1 percent, which is higher than the mean unemployment rate under wage rigidity. This finding confirms the intuition built on Figure 9.18. With higher average unemployment, the welfare costs of currency pegs under downward price rigidity are also larger, with a mean of 9.9 percent of consumption per period, compared to 7.8 percent of consumption under downward wage rigidity.

9.15.2 Symmetric Price Rigidity

Unlike the empirical literature on wage rigidity, the empirical literature on price rigidity has not drawn attention to asymmetries in product price adjustments (see, e.g., Nakamura and Steinsson 2008). This suggests that the case of greatest empirical relevance may be one in

Table 9.7   Price Rigidity and the Welfare Costs of Currency Pegs

Parameterization	Welfare Cost of Peg		Average Unemployment Rate under Peg
	Mean	Median	
Baseline wage rigidity ($\gamma = 0.99$ and $\gamma_p = 0$)	7.8	7.2	11.7
Nominal price rigidity ($\gamma = 0$, $\gamma_p = 0.99$)			
Downward price rigidity ($P_t^N / P_{t-1}^N \geq \gamma_p$)	9.9	9.0	14.1
Symmetric price rigidity ($1/\gamma_p \geq P_t^N / P_{t-1}^N \geq \gamma_p$)	4.4	3.9	6.6

Notes: The welfare cost of a currency peg is expressed as a percentage of consumption per quarter. Unemployment rates are expressed as percentages.

which price rigidity is symmetric. For this reason, we now consider an economy in which the nominal price of nontradables is subject to the constraint

$$\gamma_p \leq \frac{P_t^N}{P_{t-1}^N} \leq \frac{1}{\gamma_p}.$$

As in the case of nominal wage rigidity studied in Section 9.11, increasing the degree of price rigidity by adding upward price rigidity to an economy with downward price rigidity results in a paradoxical result: currency pegs are associated with lower unemployment and higher welfare. Table 9.7 shows that unemployment and the welfare costs of currency pegs fall by more than half as upward rigidity is added. The intuition behind this result is the same as in the case of wage rigidity. If price falls are costly, then preventing prices from increasing during booms may be a good thing. In other words, adding upward price rigidity to an economy with downward price rigidity ameliorates the peg-induced externality.

9.16 Staggered Price Setting: The Calvo Model

In this section we present an alternative way of modeling price rigidity known as staggered price setting. This model, which has become commonplace in monetary economics, was proposed by Calvo (1983) and Yun (1996). As in the model of Section 9.15.2, in the Calvo model price rigidity is bidirectional: the upward and downward adjustment of nominal prices is sluggish. An important difference between the sticky price model studied in Section 9.15.2 and the Calvo model is that in the former firms are allowed to choose how much to produce at the posted price, whereas in the latter they are forced to satisfy demand even if the price is below marginal cost. An implication of this difference is that in the Calvo model the labor supply must be wage elastic for price stickiness to have first-order effects. Another difference with the model studied in previous sections is that the Calvo model assumes imperfect competition in product markets. This assumption allows firms to satisfy demand without going out of business when their prices differ from those of their closest competitors.

9.16.1 Households

As in Section 9.13, preferences are defined over streams of consumption and labor effort. Specifically, the lifetime utility function of the representative household is given by

$$E_0 \sum_{t=0}^{\infty} \beta^t [U(c_t) - V(h_t)], \qquad (9.41)$$

where c_t denotes consumption, and h_t denotes hours worked. The period subutility function U is assumed to be strictly increasing and strictly concave, and the period subutility function V is assumed to be strictly increasing and strictly convex. We continue to assume that the consumption good is a composite of tradable consumption, c_t^T, and nontradable consumption, c_t^N, with the aggregation technology

$$c_t = A(c_t^T, c_t^N). \qquad (9.42)$$

The sequential budget constraint of the household is given by

$$P_t^T c_t^T + P_t^N c_t^N + \mathcal{E}_t d_t = P_t^T y_t^T + W_t h_t + \Phi_t + T_t + \frac{\mathcal{E}_t d_{t+1}}{1 + r_t}, \qquad (9.43)$$

which is identical to the one assumed earlier in this chapter, except for the variable T_t, which denotes lump-sum transfers received from the government. We continue to assume that the law of one price holds for tradables and that the foreign price of tradables is constant and equal to unity, so that $P_t^T = \mathcal{E}_t$. Also as before, we assume that borrowing is limited by the constraint

$$d_{t+1} \leq \bar{d}, \qquad (9.44)$$

which prevents agents from engaging in Ponzi schemes. Households choose contingent plans $\{c_t, c_t^T, c_t^N, h_t, d_{t+1}\}$ to maximize the lifetime utility function (9.41) subject to the aggregation technology (9.42), the sequential budget constraint (9.43), and the no-Ponzi-game constraint (9.44), taking as given P_t^T, P_t^N, $\mathcal{E}_t$, W_t, Φ_t, T_t, r_t, and y_t^T. The optimality conditions associated with this problem are (9.42)–(9.44) and

$$\frac{A_2(c_t^T, c_t^N)}{A_1(c_t^T, c_t^N)} = p_t,$$

$$\lambda_t = U'(c_t) A_1(c_t^T, c_t^N),$$

$$\frac{\lambda_t}{1 + r_t} = \beta E_t \lambda_{t+1} + \mu_t,$$

$$\mu_t \geq 0,$$

$$\mu_t(d_{t+1} - \bar{d}) = 0,$$

and

$$V'(h_t) = \lambda_t \frac{W_t}{P_t^T},$$

where $\beta^t \lambda_t / P_t^T$ and $\beta^t \mu_t$ denote the Lagrange multipliers associated with (9.43) and (9.44), respectively. These optimality conditions are identical to those associated with the model of Section 9.1, except for the last one, which represents a labor supply schedule. It states that the number of hours supplied to the market is increasing in the real wage, W_t / P_t^T, and in the marginal utility of wealth, λ_t.

9.16.2 Firms Producing Final Nontraded Goods

The nontraded good is produced with a continuum of varieties of intermediate nontraded inputs via the technology

$$
y_t^N = \left[\int_0^1 \left(a_{it}^N \right)^{1 - \frac{1}{\mu}} di \right]^{\frac{1}{1 - \frac{1}{\mu}}},
\tag{9.45}
$$

where y_t^N denotes output of the final nontraded good, a_{it}^N denotes the quantity of intermediate goods of type $i \in [0, 1]$ used in the production of the final nontraded good, and $\mu > 1$ denotes the elasticity of substitution across varieties. This functional form is known as a Dixit-Stiglitz aggregator. It is increasing and homogeneous of degree one in the intermediate inputs.

We assume that firms producing the final nontraded good operate in a perfectly competitive environment. Profits are given by

$$
P_t^N y_t^N - \int_0^1 P_{it}^N a_{it}^N di,
$$

where P_{it}^N denotes the nominal price of variety i in period t. The firm chooses y_t^N and a_{it}^N for all $i \in [0, 1]$ to maximize profits subject to the production technology (9.45), taking as given P_t^N and P_{it}^N. The first-order conditions associated with this problem are (9.45) and

$$
a_{it}^N = y_t^N \left(\frac{P_{it}^N}{P_t^N} \right)^{-\mu},
\tag{9.46}
$$

for $i \in [0, 1]$. According to this expression, the demand for the intermediate good of variety i is increasing in the level of final output and decreasing in the relative price of the variety in terms of the final good, with a price elasticity of $-\mu$. Using this expression to eliminate a_{it}^N from the Dixit-Stiglitz aggregator (9.45) yields the following expression for the price of the final nontraded good in terms of the prices of intermediate goods:

$$
P_t^N = \left[\int_0^1 (P_{it}^N)^{1-\mu} di \right]^{\frac{1}{1-\mu}},
\tag{9.47}
$$

which says that the price of the final nontraded good is increasing and homogeneous of degree one in the price of the intermediate goods.

9.16.3 Firms Producing Nontraded Intermediate Goods

Nontraded intermediate goods are produced by monopolistically competitive firms indexed by $i \in [0, 1]$ using labor, denoted h_{it}, as the sole factor input. Each firm operates a production technology given by

$$
y_{it}^N = h_{it}^\alpha,
\tag{9.48}
$$

where y_{it}^N denotes the quantity of intermediate good i produced in period t, and $\alpha \in (0, 1]$ is a parameter.

Firm i faces a demand for intermediate good i given by (9.46). Production is demand determined. This means that, given the posted price P_{it}^N, firms must set production to ensure that all customers are served, that is,

$$y_{it}^N = a_{it}^N. \tag{9.49}$$

This assumption represents a departure from the model studied earlier in this chapter, in which firms are not forced to satisfy demand at a loss.

Firms behave competitively in the labor market, and the government subsidizes employment at the proportional rate τ. Profits of firm i in period t, which we denote by Φ_{it}, are then given by

$$\Phi_{it} = P_{it}^N a_{it}^N - (1 - \tau) W_t h_{it}.$$

The labor subsidy is commonly assumed in Calvo models. It is meant to undo the distortion introduced by imperfect competition and facilitates the characterization of optimal monetary policy, as it results in a model with a single distortion, namely, the one stemming from price rigidity. Use equations (9.46), (9.48), and (9.49) to eliminate a_{it}^N, h_{it}, and y_{it}^N, respectively, from the above definition of profits to obtain

$$P_{it}^N y_t^N \left(\frac{P_{it}^N}{P_t^N} \right)^{-\mu} - (1 - \tau) W_t y_t^{N \frac{1}{\alpha}} \left(\frac{P_{it}^N}{P_t^N} \right)^{-\frac{\mu}{\alpha}}.$$

This representation of profits depends on a single variable endogenous to the firm, namely, the price of intermediate good i, P_{it}^N. Under price flexibility, the optimal pricing decision consists of choosing P_{it}^N to maximize the above expression. Under price stickiness, the pricing problem is quite different. The key assumption of the Calvo model is that firms cannot re-optimize prices every period. Specifically, with exogenous probability $\theta \in (0, 1)$ a firm cannot reset its price in period t and must charge the same price as in the previous period, and with probability $1 - \theta$ it can adjust the price freely. Consider the pricing decision of a firm that can re-optimize its price in period t. Let $\tilde{P}_{it}^N$ denote the price chosen in t. Then with probability θ, the price will continue to be $\tilde{P}_{it}^N$ in period $t + 1$. With probability θ^2, the price will continue to be $\tilde{P}_{it}^N$ in period $t + 2$, and so on. In general, with probability θ^s the price will continue to be $\tilde{P}_{it}^N$ in period $t + s$. The original Calvo (1983) formulation assumes that $\tilde{P}_{it}^N$ is set following an ad hoc rule of thumb. The innovation introduced by Yun (1996) is to assume that the firm picks $\tilde{P}_{it}^N$ in a profit-maximizing fashion. As in much of the modern new-Keynesian literature (e.g., Woodford 2003), we adopt Yun's approach. Specifically, the present discounted value of profits associated with $\tilde{P}_{it}^N$ is given by

$$E_t \sum_{s=0}^{\infty} Q_{t,t+s} \theta^s \left[\tilde{P}_{it}^N y_{t+s}^N \left(\frac{\tilde{P}_{it}^N}{P_{t+s}^N} \right)^{-\mu} - (1 - \tau) W_{t+s} y_{t+s}^{N \frac{1}{\alpha}} \left(\frac{\tilde{P}_{it}^N}{P_{t+s}^N} \right)^{-\frac{\mu}{\alpha}} \right],$$

where $Q_{t,t+s}$ is a state-contingent nominal discount factor that converts nominal payments in period $t + s$ into a nominal payment in period t. The firm takes $Q_{t,t+s}$ as given. We will discuss its equilibrium value below. The firm picks $\tilde{P}_{it}^N$ to maximize the above expression. The associated first-order condition is

$$
E_t \sum_{s=0}^{\infty} Q_{t,t+s} \theta^s y_{t+s}^N \left(\frac{\tilde{P}_{it}^N}{P_{t+s}^N} \right)^{-\mu} \left\{ \frac{\mu-1}{\mu} \tilde{P}_{it}^N - \frac{1}{\alpha}(1-\tau)W_{t+s} \left[y_{t+s}^N \left(\frac{\tilde{P}_{it}^N}{P_{t+s}^N} \right)^{-\mu} \right]^{\frac{1-\alpha}{\alpha}} \right\} = 0.
$$
(9.50)

The first term in the expression in squiggly brackets, $\frac{\mu-1}{\mu}\tilde{P}_{it}^N$, is the marginal revenue in period $t + s$, and the second term, $\frac{1}{\alpha}(1-\tau)W_{t+s} \left[y_{t+s}^N \left(\frac{\tilde{P}_{it}^N}{P_{t+s}^N} \right)^{-\mu} \right]^{\frac{1-\alpha}{\alpha}} = \frac{(1-\tau)W_{t+s}}{\alpha(h_{it+s}^N)^{\alpha-1}}$,

is the marginal cost. The factor $y_{t+s}^N \left(\frac{\tilde{P}_{it}^N}{P_{t+s}^N} \right)^{-\mu}$ in front of the squiggly brackets is the quantity sold in period $t + s$. All these objects are conditional on the price of good i not changing between periods t and $t + s$. It follows that the price set in period t equates the present discounted values of marginal revenues and marginal costs weighted by the level of production.

9.16.4 Aggregation and Equilibrium

The firm's first-order condition (9.50) has only one firm-specific variable, namely, $\tilde{P}_{it}^N$. Therefore, all firms that get to re-optimze their price in period t will choose the same price, regardless of idiosyncratic price histories. This means that we can drop the subscript i from $\tilde{P}_{it}^N$, which greatly facilitates aggregation. Using this fact and equation (9.47), we can write the price of the final nontradable good as

$$
(P_t^N)^{1-\mu} = \int_0^1 (P_{it}^N)^{1-\mu} di
$$

$$
= \theta P_{t-1}^{N}{}^{1-\mu} + (1-\theta) \left(\tilde{P}_t^N \right)^{1-\mu}.
$$

The first term in the second equality uses the fact that, because the firms that do not get to change their price in period t are picked randomly, the average of the prices charged by these θ firms equals the price of the final good in period $t - 1$. Dividing both sides of the above expression by $(P_t^N)^{1-\mu}$ yields

$$
1 = \theta(\pi_t^N)^{\mu-1} + (1-\theta)(\tilde{p}_t^N)^{1-\mu},
$$

where $\pi_t^N \equiv P_t^N/P_{t-1}^N$ denotes the gross rate of inflation of nontradables, and $\tilde{p}_t^N \equiv \tilde{P}_t^N/P_t^N$ denotes the relative price of re-optimized prices in terms of final nontraded goods.

We assume that firms are owned by domestic households. This means that the nominal discount factor used by firms, $Q_{t,t+s}$, must coincide with that of private households:

$$Q_{t,t+s} = \beta^s \frac{\lambda_{t+s} P_t^T}{\lambda_t P_{t+s}^T}.$$

Let $p_t \equiv P_t^N / P_t^T$ denote the relative price of nontradables in terms of tradables, and use the above expression for $Q_{t,t+s}$, to write the first-order condition (9.50) as

$$E_t \sum_{s=0}^{\infty} \beta^s \theta^s \frac{\lambda_{t+s}}{\lambda_t} y_{t+s}^N \left(\tilde{p}_t^N \prod_{k=1}^{s} \frac{1}{\pi_{t+k}^N} \right)^{-\mu} \tag{9.51}$$

$$\left\{ \frac{\mu-1}{\mu} \left(\tilde{p}_t^N \prod_{k=1}^{s} \frac{1}{\pi_{t+k}^N} \right) p_{t+s} - \frac{1-\tau}{\alpha} w_{t+s} \left[y_{t+s}^N \left(\tilde{p}_t^N \prod_{k=1}^{s} \frac{1}{\pi_{t+k}^N} \right)^{-\mu} \right]^{\frac{1-\alpha}{\alpha}} \right\} = 0,$$

where $w_t \equiv W_t / \mathcal{E}_t$ denotes the real wage expressed in terms of tradable goods. For the characterization of equilibrium it is convenient to write this equilibrium condition in recursive form. To this end, first define the present discounted values of marginal revenue and marginal cost as follows:

$$pvmc_t =$$

$$\frac{1-\tau}{\alpha} E_t \sum_{s=0}^{\infty} \beta^s \theta^s \frac{\lambda_{t+s}}{\lambda_t} y_{t+s}^N \left(\tilde{p}_t^N \prod_{k=1}^{s} \frac{1}{\pi_{t+k}^N} \right)^{-\mu} w_{t+s} \left[y_{t+s}^N \left(\tilde{p}_t^N \prod_{k=1}^{s} \frac{1}{\pi_{t+k}^N} \right)^{-\mu} \right]^{\frac{1-\alpha}{\alpha}}$$

and

$$pvmr_t = \frac{\mu-1}{\mu} E_t \sum_{s=0}^{\infty} \beta^s \theta^s \frac{\lambda_{t+s}}{\lambda_t} \left(\tilde{p}_t^N \prod_{k=1}^{s} \frac{1}{\pi_{t+k}^N} \right)^{1-\mu} p_{t+s} y_{t+s}^N.$$

Then we can rewrite equation (9.51) as

$$pvmr_t = pvmc_t.$$

Now applying some algebra, express $pvmc_t$ and $pvmr_t$ in recursive form as

$$pvmc_t = \frac{1-\tau}{\alpha} (y_t^N)^{\frac{1}{\alpha}} w_t (\tilde{p}_t^N)^{-\frac{\mu}{\alpha}} + \beta \theta E_t \frac{\lambda_{t+1}}{\lambda_t} \left(\frac{\tilde{p}_t^N}{\tilde{p}_{t+1}^N} \frac{1}{\pi_{t+1}^N} \right)^{-\frac{\mu}{\alpha}} pvmc_{t+1},$$

and

$$pvmr_t = \frac{\mu-1}{\mu} y_t^N p_t (\tilde{p}_t^N)^{1-\mu} + \beta \theta E_t \frac{\lambda_{t+1}}{\lambda_t} \left(\frac{\tilde{p}_t^N}{\tilde{p}_{t+1}^N} \frac{1}{\pi_{t+1}^N} \right)^{1-\mu} pvmr_{t+1}.$$

Total hours worked, denoted h_t, is the sum of hours worked across all intermediate goods producing firms, that is,

$$h_t = \int_0^1 h_{it}\, di.$$

To obtain a relationship between total hours worked and aggregate output of nontradables, use (9.48) to eliminate h_{it} from the above expression. Then we have that

$$h_t = \int_0^1 y_{it}^{1/\alpha}\, di = \int_0^1 \left[y_t^N \left(\frac{P_{it}^N}{P_t^N} \right)^{-\mu} \right]^{1/\alpha} di = y_t^{N\,1/\alpha} \int_0^1 \left(\frac{P_{it}^N}{P_t^N} \right)^{-\mu/\alpha} di.$$

Let

$$s_t \equiv \int_0^1 \left(\frac{P_{it}^N}{P_t^N} \right)^{-\mu/\alpha} di.$$

The variable s_t measures price dispersion. If all i varieties sell for the same price, then $s_t = 1$; otherwise, as will become clear shortly, $s_t \geq 1$. Using the definition of s_t in the above expression yields

$$y_t^N = s_t^{-\alpha} h_t^\alpha.$$

This expression shows that price dispersion acts as a negative productivity shock. The higher is price dispersion, the lower will be the aggregate level of output associated with a given level of employment. When prices are fully flexible, all firms charge the same price ($P_{it}^N = P_t^N$), so $s_t = 1$, and $y_t^N = h_t^\alpha$. It follows that s_t represents a measure of output loss due to the presence of price rigidity.

We now show that $s_t \geq 1$. To this end, let $v_{it} \equiv \left(\frac{P_{it}^N}{P_t^N} \right)^{1-\mu}$, so that

$$s_t = \int_0^1 v_{it}^{\frac{\mu}{(\mu-1)\alpha}}\, di.$$

The exponent on v_{it}, $\frac{\mu}{(\mu-1)\alpha}$, is greater than 1, because $\mu > 1$ and $0 < \alpha \leq 1$, making the right-hand side a convex function of v_{it}. Then by Jensen's inequality, we have

$$\int_0^1 v_{it}^{\frac{\mu}{(\mu-1)\alpha}}\, di \geq \left(\int_0^1 v_{it} di \right)^{\frac{\mu}{(\mu-1)\alpha}}.$$

By equation (9.47), the right-hand side of this equation is 1, and the left-hand side is s_t. Therefore we have shown that

$$s_t \geq 1.$$

Using the fact that all firms that cannot change their price in a given period then charge last period's price, and that all firms that can change their price choose the same price, namely, $\tilde{P}_t^N$, it follows that the measure of price dispersion, s_t, evolves over time as follows:

$$s_t = \int_0^1 \left(\frac{P_{it}^N}{P_t^N} \right)^{-\mu/\alpha} di$$

$$= \theta \int_0^1 \left(\frac{P_{it-1}^N}{P_t^N} \right)^{-\mu/\alpha} di + (1-\theta) \left(\frac{\tilde{P}_t^N}{P_t^N} \right)^{-\mu/\alpha}$$

$$= \theta s_{t-1} (\pi_t^N)^{\mu/\alpha} + (1-\theta)(\tilde{p}_t^N)^{-\mu/\alpha}.$$

In equilibrium the market for nontradable goods clears:

$$y_t^N = c_t^N.$$

Aggregate profit income is

$$\Phi_t = \int_0^1 \Phi_{it} di$$

$$= \int_0^1 \left(P_{it}^N y_{it}^N - (1-\tau)W_t h_{it} \right) di$$

$$= P_t^N y_t^N - (1-\tau)W_t h_t,$$

where the last equality follows from the fact that the producers of final nontraded goods make zero profits and from the definition of h_t. The government finances labor subsidies with lump-sum taxes. This implies that the period-by-period budget constraint of the government is

$$\tau W_t h_t = T_t.$$

Combining the above three expressions with the household's sequential budget constraint (9.43) yields the familiar resource constraint:

$$c_t^T + d_t = y_t^T + \frac{d_{t+1}}{1+r_t}.$$

Finally, we can write the gross growth rate of the relative price of nontradables in terms of tradables as the ratio of the inflation of nontradables to the depreciation rate:

$$\frac{p_t}{p_{t-1}} = \frac{\pi_t^N}{\epsilon_t},$$

where, as before, $\epsilon_t \equiv \mathcal{E}_t / \mathcal{E}_{t-1}$ denotes the gross rate of depreciation of the domestic currency.

Then a competitive equilibrium is a set of processes c_t^T, π_t^N, p_t, h_t, λ_t, w_t, $\tilde{p}_t^N$, y_t^N, s_t, d_{t+1}, μ_t, $pvmc_t$, and $pvmr_t$ satisfying

$$c_t^T + d_t = y_t^T + \frac{d_{t+1}}{1 + r_t}, \tag{9.52}$$

$$\lambda_t = U'(A(c_t^T, y_t^N))A_1(c_t^T, y_t^N), \tag{9.53}$$

$$\frac{\lambda_t}{1 + r_t} = \beta E_t \lambda_{t+1} + \mu_t, \tag{9.54}$$

$$d_{t+1} \leq \bar{d}, \tag{9.55}$$

$$\mu_t \geq 0,$$

$$\mu_t(d_{t+1} - \bar{d}) = 0,$$

$$\frac{A_2(c_t^T, y_t^N)}{A_1(c_t^T, y_t^N)} = p_t, \tag{9.56}$$

$$V'(h_t) = \lambda_t w_t, \tag{9.57}$$

$$y_t^N = s_t^{-\alpha} h_t^\alpha, \tag{9.58}$$

$$s_t = \theta s_{t-1}(\pi_t^N)^{\mu/\alpha} + (1 - \theta)(\tilde{p}_t^N)^{-\mu/\alpha}, \tag{9.59}$$

$$1 = \theta(\pi_t^N)^{\mu-1} + (1 - \theta)(\tilde{p}_t^N)^{1-\mu}, \tag{9.60}$$

$$pvmr_t = pvmc_t, \tag{9.61}$$

$$pvmc_t = \frac{1 - \tau}{\alpha}(y_t^N)^{\frac{1}{\alpha}} w_t(\tilde{p}_t^N)^{-\frac{\mu}{\alpha}} + \beta\theta E_t \frac{\lambda_{t+1}}{\lambda_t}\left(\frac{\tilde{p}_t^N}{\tilde{p}_{t+1}^N}\frac{1}{\pi_{t+1}^N}\right)^{-\frac{\mu}{\alpha}} pvmc_{t+1}, \tag{9.62}$$

$$pvmr_t = \frac{\mu - 1}{\mu} y_t^N p_t(\tilde{p}_t^N)^{1-\mu} + \beta\theta E_t \frac{\lambda_{t+1}}{\lambda_t}\left(\frac{\tilde{p}_t^N}{\tilde{p}_{t+1}^N}\frac{1}{\pi_{t+1}^N}\right)^{1-\mu} pvmr_{t+1}, \tag{9.63}$$

and

$$p_t = p_{t-1}\frac{\pi_t^N}{\epsilon_t}, \tag{9.64}$$

given exogenous processes y_t^T and r_t, initial conditions d_0 and s_{-1}, an exchange-rate policy ϵ_t, and a subsidy policy τ.

We assume that the government sets the labor subsidy so as to offset the distortion in the labor market created by the presence of imperfect competition in product markets:

$$\tau = \frac{1}{\mu}. \tag{9.65}$$

9.16.5 The Flexible-Price Equilibrium

Suppose all firms get the opportunity to set their price optimally every period, that is, $\theta = 0$. This is an environment in which all prices are fully flexible. In this environment, equilibrium condition (9.60) collapses to

$$\tilde{p}_t^N = 1.$$

It then follows from equilibrium condition (9.59) that

$$s_t = 1,$$

which says that there is no efficiency loss due to price dispersion. This means that a given level of employment yields the maximum level of final nontradable goods. Formally, equilibrium condition (9.58) now becomes

$$y_t^N = h_t^\alpha.$$

Finally, (9.61)–(9.63) collapse to the static condition

$$p_t = \frac{w_t}{\alpha h_t^{\alpha-1}},$$

which says that in equilibrium firms behave as if they operated in a perfectly competitive environment, in the sense that they equate price to marginal cost every period.

A flexible-price equilibrium is then a set of processes c_t^T, h_t, d_{t+1}, λ_t, and μ_t satisfying

$$c_t^T + d_t = y_t^T + \frac{d_{t+1}}{1 + r_t}, \tag{9.66}$$

$$\lambda_t = U'(A(c_t^T, h_t^\alpha))A_1(c_t^T, h_t^\alpha),$$

$$\frac{\lambda_t}{1 + r_t} = \beta E_t \lambda_{t+1} + \mu_t,$$

$$d_{t+1} \leq \bar{d}, \tag{9.67}$$

$$\mu_t \geq 0,$$

$$\mu_t(d_{t+1} - \bar{d}) = 0,$$

and

$$V'(h_t) = \alpha\lambda_t \frac{A_2(c_t^T, , h_t^\alpha)}{A_1(c_t^T, , h_t^\alpha)} h_t^{\alpha-1},$$

given exogenous processes y_t^T and r_t and the initial condition d_0. This is indeed the best possible equilibrium, in the sense that its associated allocation is the solution to the social planner's problem

$$\max_{\{c_t^T, h_t, d_{t+1}\}} E_0 \sum_{t=0}^{\infty} \beta^t [U(A(c_t^T, h_t^\alpha)) - V(h_t)],$$

subject to (9.66) and (9.67). As the following analysis shows, the flexible-price equilibrium provides a useful benchmark for the characterization of optimal exchange-rate policy.

9.16.6 Optimal Exchange-Rate Policy

Is there an exchange-rate policy that can support the flexible-price equilibrium? The answer to this question turns out to be yes. To see this, suppose for simplicity that $s_{-1} = 1$. (Exercise 9.14 considers the general case $s_{-1} > 1$.) Now imagine an exchange-rate policy that fully stabilizes the nominal price of nontradables, so that

$$\pi_t^N = 1,$$

for all t. We will show shortly that such an exchange-rate policy does exist. Combining the above equation with equilibrium condition (9.60), we obtain $\tilde{p}_t^N = 1$, for all t. This expression implies that firms that get to change their price in the current period choose the average price level P_t^N. The fact that $\pi_t^N = \tilde{p}_t^N = 1$ then implies, from equilibrium condition (9.59), that $s_t = 1$ for all t. That is, there is no output loss due to price dispersion, or $y_t^N = h_t^\alpha$. Finally, using the above results, we have that (9.61)–(9.63) become

$$p_t = \frac{w_t}{\alpha h_t^{\alpha-1}}, \tag{9.68}$$

for all t. This completes the proof that a policy that fully stabilizes the price of nontradables achieves the flexible-price equilibrium.

To obtain the optimal devaluation rate, use the flexible-price processes for c_t^T and y_t^N to construct the flexible-price real exchange rate, p_t, from equilibrium condition (9.56). Then use this process for p_t to evaluate equilibrium condition (9.64), which gives the optimal process ϵ_t:

$$\epsilon_t = \frac{p_{t-1}}{p_t}.$$

It follows that any shock that causes a real exchange rate depreciation (a fall in p_t) in the flexible-price equilibrium, such as a contraction in tradable output y_t^T or an increase in the interest rate r_t, must be accompanied by a devaluation. Thus the present model shares two important predictions with the models of downward nominal wage rigidity or downward nominal price rigidity studied earlier in this chapter. First, stabilization of the nominal price of nontradables is optimal. And second, contractions are devaluatory.

9.16.7 The Open Economy New-Keynesian Phillips Curve

At this point it is of interest to digress and derive a linearized version of the equilibrium price setting conditions (9.61)–(9.63), which gives rise to an open-economy version of the familiar new-Keynesian Phillips curve.

Define $\hat{x}_t = \ln(x_t/x)$, where x denotes the deterministic steady-state value of x_t. We perform the log-linearization around the deterministic steady state with $\pi^N = 1$. The log-linear version of (9.62) is

$$\widehat{pvmc}_t = -\frac{\mu}{\alpha}\widehat{p}_t^N + (1-\beta\theta)\left(\frac{1}{\alpha}\widehat{y}_t^N + \widehat{w}_t\right)$$

$$+ \beta\theta E_t\left[\widehat{\lambda}_{t+1} - \widehat{\lambda}_t + \frac{\mu}{\alpha}\left(\widehat{p}_{t+1}^N + \widehat{\pi}_{t+1}^N\right) + \widehat{pvmc}_{t+1}\right].$$

The log-linear version of (9.60) is

$$\widehat{p}_t^N = \frac{\theta}{1-\theta}\widehat{\pi}_t^N.$$

Combine the above two expressions to eliminate $\widehat{p}_t^N$, which yields

$$\widehat{pvmc}_t = -\frac{\mu}{\alpha}\frac{\theta}{1-\theta}\widehat{\pi}_t^N + (1-\beta\theta)\left(\frac{1}{\alpha}\widehat{y}_t^N + \widehat{w}_t\right)$$

$$+ \beta\theta E_t\left[\widehat{\lambda}_{t+1} - \widehat{\lambda}_t + \frac{\mu}{\alpha}\frac{1}{1-\theta}\widehat{\pi}_{t+1}^N + \widehat{pvmc}_{t+1}\right].$$

The log-linearization of (9.63) is

$$\widehat{pvmr}_t = (1-\mu)\frac{\theta}{1-\theta}\widehat{\pi}_t^N + (1-\beta\theta)\left(\widehat{y}_t^N + \widehat{p}_t\right)$$

$$+ \beta\theta E_t\left[\widehat{\lambda}_{t+1} - \widehat{\lambda}_t - (1-\mu)\frac{1}{1-\theta}\widehat{\pi}_{t+1}^N + \widehat{pvmr}_{t+1}\right].$$

And the log-linearization of (9.61) is

$$\widehat{pvmr}_t = \widehat{pvmc}_t.$$

Using this expression in the linearized versions of (9.63) and (9.62) yields

$$0 = \left(-\frac{\mu}{\alpha} - 1 + \mu\right)\frac{\theta}{1-\theta}\widehat{\pi}_t^N + (1-\beta\theta)\left[\left(\frac{1}{\alpha} - 1\right)\widehat{y}_t^N + \widehat{w}_t - \widehat{p}_t\right]$$

$$+ \beta E_t\left[\left(\frac{\mu}{\alpha} + 1 - \mu\right)\frac{\theta}{1-\theta}\widehat{\pi}_{t+1}^N\right].$$

Now define

$$\widehat{mc}_t \equiv \left(\frac{1}{\alpha} - 1\right)\widehat{y}_t^N + \widehat{w}_t - \widehat{p}_t$$

as the log-deviation of aggregate marginal cost in the nontraded sector from steady state. Combining this definition with the above expression yields

$$\widehat{\pi}_t^N = \beta E_t\widehat{\pi}_{t+1}^N + \kappa\widehat{mc}_t, \tag{9.69}$$

with $\kappa = \left[\frac{(1-\theta)(1-\beta\theta)}{\theta\left(\frac{\mu}{\alpha}+1-\mu\right)}\right] > 0$. This expression is known as the new-Keynesian Phillips curve. It relates current inflation to expected future inflation and marginal costs.

9.16.8 Crisis Dynamics in the Calvo Model

In this section we numerically characterize the equilibrium dynamics triggered by an external crisis. The exercise is identical to the one conducted in Section 9.8. As in that section, we compare two alternative exchange-rate policies: the optimal one and a currency peg.

To simulate equilibrium dynamics, we follow much of the new-Keynesian literature and employ perturbation methods.[17] Since the perturbation method cannot handle occasionally binding constraints, we must eliminate the borrowing limit (9.55). In its place, we assume an externally debt-elastic interest rate, following Schmitt-Grohé and Uribe (2003) (see also the exposition in Section 4.1.1 of Chapter 4). Specifically, we assume that

$$r_t = r_t^* + \psi \left[e^{d_{t+1} - \bar{d}} - 1 \right], \tag{9.70}$$

where r_t is now an endogenous variable, and r_t^* is an exogenous variable.

A competitive equilibrium is then a set of processes c_t^T, r_t, p_t, h_t, λ_t, w_t, $\tilde{p}_t^N$, y_t^N, s_t, d_{t+1}, π_t^N, $pvmc_t$, and $pcmr_t$ satisfying (9.52), (9.53), (9.56)–(9.64), (9.70), and

$$\frac{\lambda_t}{1 + r_t} = \beta E_t \lambda_{t+1},$$

given exogenous processes y_t^T and r_t^*, initial conditions d_0 and s_{-1}, an exchange-rate policy, ϵ_t, and the labor-subsidy policy (9.65).

Table 9.8 summarizes the calibration of the model. The time unit is one quarter. As in previous sections, we adopt the functional forms

$$U(c) = \frac{c^{1-\sigma} - 1}{1 - \sigma},$$

$$A(c^T, c^N) = \left[a(c^T)^{1-\frac{1}{\xi}} + (1-a)(c^N)^{1-\frac{1}{\xi}} \right]^{\frac{1}{1-\frac{1}{\xi}}},$$

and

$$F(h) = h^\alpha,$$

with $\sigma = 1/\xi = 2$, $a = 0.26$, and $\alpha = 0.75$. As in Section 9.13, we assume that the marginal disutility of labor takes the form

$$V'(h) = \varphi(\bar{h} - h)^{-\chi},$$

with $\varphi = 1.11$, $\bar{h} = 3$, and $\chi = 1$.[18] These parameter values ensure a Frisch wage elasticity of labor supply of 2, a share of time spent working of one third, and a steady-state value

---

17. Alternatively, one could apply global methods as we did earlier in this chapter. The present setup, however, is somewhat more complex, as it includes two forward-looking equations in addition to the consumption Euler equation, namely, equations (9.62) and (9.63). Both models have the same number of state variables. In the Calvo model the state variables are d_t and s_{t-1}, and in the model of the previous sections they are d_t and w_{t-1}.

18. In Section 9.13, the equivalent of the parameter χ is denoted θ.

Table 9.8 Calibration of the Calvo Model

Parameter	Value	Description
θ	0.7	Probability of no price change in nontraded sector
μ	6	Elasticity of substitution across intermediate nontradables
σ	2	Inverse of intertemporal elasticity of consumption
β	1.0316^{-1}	Quarterly subjective discount factor
φ	1.11	Preference parameter
χ	1	Preference parameter
$\bar{h}$	3	Labor endowment
a	0.26	Share of tradables
ξ	0.5	Elasticity of substitution between tradables and nontradables
α	0.75	Labor share in nontraded sector
ψ	0.0000335	Parameter of debt-elastic interest rate
$\bar{d}$	2.9014	Parameter of debt-elastic interest rate
y^T	1	Steady-state tradable output
r^*	0.0316	Steady-state interest rate (quarterly)

Notes: The time unit is a quarter. The values assigned to $\sigma, a, \xi, \alpha, y^T$, and r^* are taken from Table 9.3. The values assigned to φ, χ, and $\bar{h}$ are taken from Section 9.13.

of hours worked of unity. The bivariate driving forces (y_t^T, r_t^*) are assumed to follow the AR(1) process

$$\begin{bmatrix} \ln y_t^T \\ \ln \frac{1+r_t^*}{1+r^*} \end{bmatrix} = \begin{bmatrix} 0.79 & -1.36 \\ -0.01 & 0.86 \end{bmatrix} \begin{bmatrix} \ln y_{t-1}^T \\ \ln \frac{1+r_{t-1}^*}{1+r^*} \end{bmatrix} + \sigma_\epsilon \Gamma \, \epsilon_t,$$

with

$$\sigma_\epsilon = 1, \qquad \Gamma \Gamma' = \begin{bmatrix} 0.00123 & -0.00008 \\ -0.00008 & 0.00004 \end{bmatrix}, \qquad \text{and} \qquad r = 0.0316,$$

which is identical to the one given in equation (9.31), with r_t^* and r^* taking the places of r_t and r, respectively, and $\sigma_\epsilon^2 \Gamma \Gamma' = \Sigma_\epsilon$. As earlier in this chapter, our primary concern here is to characterize the cyclical behavior of the economy under alternative exchange-rate policies and not to ascertain the contribution of particular shocks to short-run fluctuations.[19] For this reason, the results presented below obtain under any matrix Γ satisfying the above restriction. We introduce the scalar σ_ϵ, because it facilitates the Taylor expansion of the equilibrium conditions around the deterministic steady state $\sigma_\epsilon = 0$. This will turn out to be particularly useful later in the section, when we approximate the model up to second order to compute welfare.

There are two new parameters in the present model: θ, the probability of not being able to change the price in a given period, and ψ, the parameter governing the debt elasticity

---

19. This issue is taken up in exercise 9.15.

of the interest rate. There is scanty empirical evidence on the frequency of nominal price changes in nontraded goods in emerging countries. A reason for this scarcity is likely given by the fact that for much of the postwar period, emerging countries experienced relatively high levels of inflation. An exception is Gagnon (2009), who, using Mexican micro consumer-price data, reports a monthly frequency of nominal price changes in nonregulated services in Mexico slightly below 10 percent over two low-inflation periods, one preceding and the other following the 1994 "Tequila" crisis. This evidence suggests a quarterly probability of no price change of nontradables of 70 percent. Accordingly, we set θ equal to 0.7. We calibrate ψ to match the unconditional standard deviation of (percentage deviations from trend of) tradable consumption of 18.5 percent implied by all models studied earlier in this chapter.[20] The implied value of ψ is 0.0000335.

We are now ready to quantitatively characterize the behavior of the model during a large external crisis. The definition of a large crisis follows the one given in Section 9.8.1. Specifically, an external crisis that starts in period t is a situation in which tradable output is at or above trend in quarter t and at least two standard deviations below trend in quarter $t + 10$. We simulate the model for 3 million quarters and identify windows $(t - 10, t + 30)$ in which movements in traded output conform to the definition of an external crisis. Then for each variable of interest, we average all windows and subtract the respective mean taken over the entire sample of 3 million periods. The beginning of the typical crisis is normalized at $t = 0$. The behavior of the exogenous variables y_t^T and r_t^* is displayed in Figure 9.11. The large decline in tradable output in the typical crisis is coupled with a large increase in the country interest rate due to the strong negative correlation between y_t^T and r_t^* present in the Argentine data.

Figure 9.19 displays the behavior of the endogenous variables of the model during the typical external crisis under two alternative exchange-rate policies: a currency peg (shown with solid lines) and the optimal exchange-rate policy (dashed lines). Comparing Figures 9.12 and 9.19 suggests that the dynamic response of the Calvo model is similar to that implied by the model with downward nominal wage rigidity. Because preferences are separable in tradable and nontradable consumption ($\sigma = 1/\xi$), the responses of consumption of tradables (row 3, right column), the level of external debt (not shown), and the level of the trade balance (not shown) are identical under the peg and the optimal exchange-rate policy. The crisis causes a contraction in tradable consumption of about 25 percent.

The primary role of the optimal exchange-rate policy is to prevent the external crisis from spreading to the nontraded sector. In fact, employment is unaffected by the crisis, as shown in the top left panel of the figure. To see this analytically, combine equilibrium conditions (9.53), (9.56), (9.57), and (9.68), and use the assumption $\sigma = 1/\xi$ to obtain

$$\alpha(1 - a)(\bar{h} - h_t) = \varphi h_t^{1-\alpha+\alpha/\xi},$$

which implies that h_t is constant over time under the optimal exchange-rate policy. This prediction is akin to the full-employment result obtained under optimal exchange-rate

---

20. Those models do not incorporate a debt-elastic interest rate. Instead, stationarity is induced by setting $\beta(1 + r) < 1$ and approximating the equilibrium with global methods (see Section 9.7).

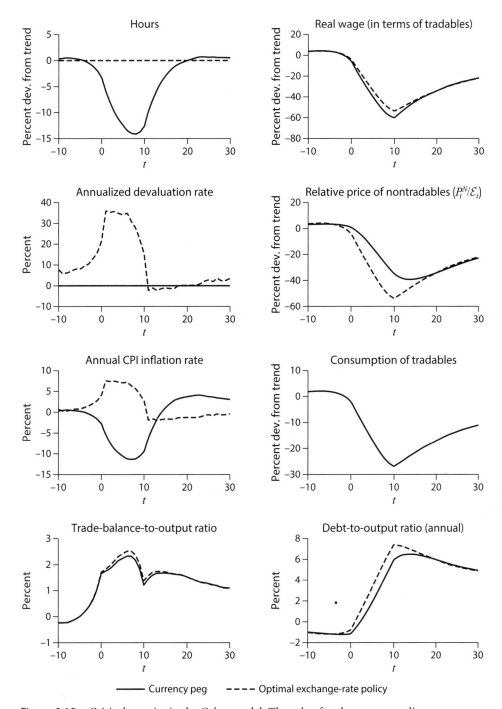

Figure 9.19 Crisis dynamics in the Calvo model: The role of exchange-rate policy.

Note: This graph is produced by the Matlab programs in `calvo.zip`, available online with the materials for this chapter on the book's Web site.

policy in the model with downward nominal wage rigidity expounded earlier in this chapter. The monetary authority manages to maintain full employment by implementing large devaluations throughout the crisis on the order of 30–40 percent per year. The devaluations allow the price of nontradables, which is rigid in nominal terms, to decline in real terms; that is, they allow the real exchange rate to depreciate. In turn the depreciation induces an expenditure switch away from tradables and toward nontradables, which is the optimal adjustment under flexible prices. In contrast, under the currency peg, employment falls by about 15 percent. The reason is that due to price stickiness, throughout the crisis the relative price of nontradables stays too high to be consistent with firms operating at full capacity.

Finally, like in the model with nominal price rigidity of Section 9.15, the real wage displays a significant downward adjustment during the crisis both under the optimal exchange-rate policy and under the peg. In fact, under the peg, the real wage falls by more than under the optimal policy. The reason is that wages are fully flexible, whereas firms are rationed by weak demand, which causes the market clearing real wage to plummet. This prediction of the sticky-price model is counterfactual. The lack of sizable downward wage adjustment in the private sector observed during crises in fixed-exchange-rate economies or in monetary unions (see, e.g., the cases of the periphery of Europe in 2008–2011 and Argentina during 1998–2001 shown in Figures 9.1 and 9.9, respectively) suggests that downward wage rigidity is a more plausible source of nominal rigidity for understanding the adjustment of emerging economies with fixed exchange rates.

9.16.9 Welfare Costs of Currency Pegs in the Calvo Model

We consider two welfare measures: an unconditional measure and a measure conditional on the initial state of the economy being the deterministic steady state. We define the unconditional welfare cost of a currency peg as the proportional increase in the stream of consumption in the currency-peg economy that makes households unconditionally indifferent between living in the currency-peg economy and living in the optimal exchange-rate economy. Formally, letting $\lambda^u(\sigma_\epsilon)$ be the unconditional welfare cost of a currency peg, we have

$$E \sum_{t=0}^{\infty} \beta^t \left[U\left(\left(1 + \frac{\lambda^u(\sigma_\epsilon)}{100}\right) c_t^p \right) - V(h_t^p) \right] = E \sum_{t=0}^{\infty} \beta^t [U(c_t^o) - V(h_t^o)],$$

where c_t^p and h_t^p denote consumption and hours worked in the currency-peg economy, respectively, and c_t^o and h_t^o denote consumption and hours worked in the optimal exchange-rate economy, respectively. The unconditional welfare cost of a currency peg depends on the level of uncertainty in the economy, captured by the scalar σ_ϵ. We wish to obtain a second-order accurate measure of $\lambda^u(\sigma_\epsilon)$. To this end, we begin by defining the welfare functions associated with each of the two exchange-rate arrangements considered. Let $v_t^o \equiv v^o(x_t^o, \sigma_\epsilon)$ denote welfare under the optimal exchange-rate policy, where $x_t^o \equiv (y_t^T, r_t^*, d_t)$ is the vector of exogenous and endogenous state variables in the optimal exchange-rate economy. Then v_t^o can be written recursively as

$$v_t^o = U(c_t^o) - V(h_t^o) + \beta E_t v_{t+1}^o. \tag{9.71}$$

Similarly, let $v_t^P \equiv v^P(x_t^P, \sigma_\epsilon)$ denote welfare under a currency peg, where $x_t^P \equiv (y_t^T, r_t^*, d_t, s_{t-1}, p_{t-1})$ denotes the state vector in the currency-peg economy. We can write v_t^P recursively as

$$v_t^P = U(c_t^P) - V(h_t^P) + \beta E_t v_{t+1}^P.$$

We also define subwelfare functions for consumption and hours worked in the currency-peg economy, $v_t^{pc} \equiv v^{pc}(x_t^P, \sigma_\epsilon)$ and $v_t^{ph} \equiv v^{ph}(x_t^P, \sigma_\epsilon)$, respectively, with recursive representations

$$v_t^{pc} = U(c_t^P) + \beta E_t v_{t+1}^{pc} \tag{9.72}$$

and

$$v_t^{ph} = V(h_t^P) + \beta E_t v_{t+1}^{ph}. \tag{9.73}$$

Using the CRRA form assumed for $U(\cdot)$, we can then write the unconditional welfare cost of a currency peg as

$$\lambda^u(\sigma_\epsilon) = \left\{ \left[\frac{(Ev^o(x_t^o, \sigma_\epsilon) + Ev^{ph}(x_t^P, \sigma_\epsilon))(1-\sigma)(1-\beta)+1}{Ev^{pc}(x_t^P, \sigma_\epsilon)(1-\sigma)(1-\beta)+1} \right]^{\frac{1}{1-\sigma}} - 1 \right\} \times 100.$$

The unconditional expectations on the right-hand side are independent of the state of the economy. Let $G^o(\sigma_\epsilon) \equiv Ev^o(x_t^o, \sigma_\epsilon)$ be the unconditional expectation of welfare under the optimal exchange-rate policy. Similarly, let $G^P(\sigma_\epsilon) \equiv Ev^P(x_t^P, \sigma_\epsilon)$, $G^{pc}(\sigma_\epsilon) \equiv Ev^{pc}(x_t^P, \sigma_\epsilon)$, and $G^{ph}(\sigma_\epsilon) \equiv Ev^{ph}(x_t^P, \sigma_\epsilon)$. Then we can write the above expression as

$$\lambda^u(\sigma_\epsilon) = \left\{ \left[\frac{(G^o(\sigma_\epsilon) + G^{ph}(\sigma_\epsilon))(1-\sigma)(1-\beta)+1}{G^{pc}(\sigma_\epsilon)(1-\sigma)(1-\beta)+1} \right]^{\frac{1}{1-\sigma}} - 1 \right\} \times 100.$$

After some algebra, we have that the second-order Taylor expansion of $\lambda^u(\sigma_\epsilon)$ around the zero-inflation nonstochastic steady state ($\sigma_\epsilon = 0$) is given by

$$\lambda^u(\sigma_\epsilon) \approx \left[\frac{G^o_{\sigma_\epsilon\sigma_\epsilon}(0) + G^{ph}_{\sigma_\epsilon\sigma_\epsilon}(0) - G^{pc}_{\sigma_\epsilon\sigma_\epsilon}(0)}{G^{pc}(0)(1-\sigma) + (1-\beta)^{-1}} \right] \frac{\sigma_\epsilon^2}{2} \times 100,$$

where $G^i_{\sigma_\epsilon\sigma_\epsilon}(0)$ denotes the second derivative of $G^i(\sigma_\epsilon)$ evaluated at $\sigma_\epsilon = 0$, for $i = o, pc, ph$. In deriving the above expression, keep in mind that $\lambda^u(0) = 0$ and $G^i_{\sigma_\epsilon}(0) = 0$ for $i = o, pc, ph$ (see Schmitt-Grohé and Uribe 2004).

Consider now the welfare cost of a currency peg conditional on a particular state of the economy, which we denote by $\lambda^c(x_0^P, \sigma_\epsilon)$. This conditional welfare cost is defined as

$$E_0 \sum_{t=0}^{\infty} \beta^t \left[U\left(\left(1 + \frac{\lambda^c(x_0^P, \sigma_\epsilon)}{100}\right) c_t^P \right) - V(h_t^P) \right] = E_0 \sum_{t=0}^{\infty} \beta^t [U(c_t^o) - V(h_t^o)].$$

By a logic similar to the one used to derive the unconditional welfare cost of a peg, we have that

$$\lambda^c(x_0^P, \sigma_\epsilon) = \left\{ \left[\frac{(v^o(x_0^o, \sigma_\epsilon) + v^{ph}(x_0^P, \sigma_\epsilon))(1 - \sigma)(1 - \beta) + 1}{v^{pc}(x^P, \sigma_\epsilon)(1 - \sigma)(1 - \beta) + 1} \right]^{\frac{1}{1-\sigma}} - 1 \right\} \times 100.$$

Let x^P denote the deterministic steady-state value of x_t^P. Notice that in the nonstochastic steady state by construction the elements of the state vector x_t^o that are also elements of the state vector x_t^P take the same values. The second-order Taylor expansion of $\lambda^c(x_0^P, \sigma_\epsilon)$ around $x_0^P = x^P$ and $\sigma_\epsilon = 0$ is

$$\lambda^c(x^P, \sigma_\epsilon) \approx \left[\frac{v^o_{\sigma_\epsilon \sigma_\epsilon}(x^o, 0) + v^{ph}_{\sigma_\epsilon \sigma_\epsilon}(x^P, 0) - v^{pc}_{\sigma_\epsilon \sigma_\epsilon}(x^P, 0)}{v^{pc}(x^P, 0)(1 - \sigma) + (1 - \beta)^{-1}} \right] \frac{\sigma_\epsilon^2}{2} \times 100.$$

To compute the second derivatives of the welfare and subwelfare functions evaluated at the steady state, that is, to compute the objects $v^o_{\sigma_\epsilon \sigma_\epsilon}(x^o, 0)$ and $v^i_{\sigma_\epsilon \sigma_\epsilon}(x^P, 0)$ for $i = ph, pc$, we follow the approach proposed by Schmitt-Grohé and Uribe (2007). This approach consists of adding equation (9.71) to the set of equilibrium conditions of the optimal exchange-rate-policy economy and equations (9.72) and (9.73) to the equilibrium conditions of the currency-peg economy. Then both sets of enlarged equilibrium conditions are approximated to second order. In performing this step, we use the Matlab code provided in Schmitt-Grohé and Uribe (2004). The file `calvo_welfare.zip`, available on the book's Web site with the materials for this chapter, contains the welfare calculations pertaining to the present model.

Table 9.9 displays the unconditional and conditional welfare costs of a currency peg for various degrees of price stickiness, as measured by price durations ranging from one

Table 9.9   The Welfare Cost of Currency Pegs in the Calvo Model

Price Duration $1/(1 - \theta)$ (quarters)	Price Stickiness θ (prob. no change)	Unconditional Cost $\lambda^u(1)$ (%)	Conditional Cost $\lambda^c(1)$ (%)
1	0.00	0.00	0.00
2	0.50	2.23	2.04
3.33 *	0.70	3.63	3.10
4	0.75	4.11	3.41
5	0.80	4.65	3.71
6	0.83	5.05	3.88
7	0.86	5.35	3.98
8	0.88	5.57	4.02

Notes: *, baseline. The welfare costs are expressed as percentages of consumption each period. Conditional welfare costs are computed at the initial state as equal to the deterministic steady state. Matlab scripts to replicate this table are contained in the file `welfare_calvo.zip`, available on the book's Web site.

(flexible prices) to eight quarters. Clearly, if prices are fully flexible, the welfare cost of a currency peg is nil, since in that case all firms set prices at marginal costs. At the baseline calibration of $\theta = 0.7$, which implies an average price duration of about three quarters, the welfare cost of a currency peg is substantial, around 3 percent of consumption per quarter. This is a large number in business-cycle studies and is driven by the combination of nominal rigidity and highly volatile shocks. It suggests, in line with the results obtained in the economy with downward nominal wage rigidity, that emerging countries—precisely because they are subject to large shocks—are particularly hurt by suboptimal monetary policy.

9.17 Exercises

9.1 (The Demand Schedule of Nontradables) In Section 9.1 we assume that the aggregator function, $A(c^T, c^N)$, given in (9.2), is increasing, concave, and linearly homogeneous.

1. Show that these assumptions are sufficient to ensure that the demand schedule of nontradables, given in equation (9.5) and depicted in Figure 9.2, is downward sloping in the space (c^N, p), holding c^T constant.

2. Show that the aforementioned assumptions about the aggregator $A(c^T, c^N)$ are sufficient to guarantee that increases (decreases) in c^T shift the demand schedule up and to the right (down and to the left).

3. Assume that the aggregator function takes the Cobb-Douglas form $A(c^T, c^N) = \sqrt{c^T c^N}$. Find the demand function of nontradables.

4. Now assume the CES form $A(c^T, c^N) = \left[a(c^T)^{1-\frac{1}{\xi}} + (1-a)(c^N)^{1-\frac{1}{\xi}}\right]^{\frac{1}{1-\frac{1}{\xi}}}$. Derive the demand function of nontradables. Interpret the parameter ξ.

9.2 (Unwanted Positive Shocks) Show that in the example of Section 9.2.3, the fall in the interest rate is welfare decreasing under downward nominal wage rigidity but is welfare increasing under flexible wages. How can this be?

9.3 (Is More Wage Rigidity Desirable?) Modify the example of Section 9.2.3 to allow for wage rigidity in both directions: downward and upward. Characterize the economy's response to a temporary decline in the interest rate. Show that welfare is higher under full wage rigidity than under downward wage rigidity. Provide intuition.

9.4 (Properties of the Full-Employment Real Wage) Show that $\omega'(c_t^T)$ is positive.

9.5 (Pareto Optimality of the Flexible-Wage Equilibrium) Demonstrate that when nominal wages are fully flexible, the competitive equilibrium is Pareto optimal for any exchange-rate policy.

9.6 (Optimality of Constant Nominal Interest Rates) Consider the devaluation rate rule

$$\epsilon_t = \frac{w_{t-1}}{\omega(c_t^T)}.$$

Suppose that all other features of the model are as in the body of the chapter. In particular, assume that the period utility function is given by equation (9.28), that the Armington aggregator is given by equation (9.29) with $\xi = 1/\sigma$, and that $P_t^{T*} = 1$ for all t.

1. Show that for $\gamma < 1$, this policy is optimal.
2. Show that under this policy the nominal wage, W_t, and the nominal price of nontradables, P_t^N, are constant in equilibrium.
3. Let R_t denote the gross nominal interest rate on a risk-free, one-period, nominal bond denominated in domestic currency held from period t to $t + 1$. In other words, one unit of domestic currency invested in this bond in period t always pays R_t units of domestic currency in period $t + 1$ in interest plus principal. Show that under the devaluation rule specified above, the equilibrium interest rate is constant and equal to $1/\beta$. Provide intuition.

9.7 (Optimality of Constant Nominal Interest Rates, Continued) Show that any constant interest-rate rule of the form $R_t = \delta$, where δ is a parameter, supports the full-employment equilibrium, provided that $\delta \geq \gamma/\beta$.

9.8 (Foreign Inflation) Assume that the foreign price of tradable goods, P_t^{T*}, grows at the deterministic gross rate, π^*, that is, $P_{t+1}^{T*}/P_t^{T*} = \pi^*$. How do the equilibrium conditions (9.9)–(9.19) change with the introduction of this assumption?

9.9 (Trend Growth) Continue to assume, as in exercise 9.8, that the foreign price of tradables grows at the rate π^*. In addition, assume that the production of nontradables is given by $Y_t^N = X_t F(h_t)$ and that the endowment of tradables is given by $Y_t^T = X_t y_t^T$, where X_t is a deterministic trend that grows at the gross rate g, that is, $X_{t+1}/X_t = g$. Again, show how equilibrium conditions (9.9)–(9.19) are modified by the imposition of this assumption. Hint: As in the model in Chapter 5, you will have to transform some variables appropriately to make them stationary. The equilibrium conditions should include only stationary variables.

9.10 (Exchange-Rate Policy and GDP in Terms of Tradables) Take a look at the two bottom panels of Figure 9.12 showing the behavior of the trade-balance-to-output ratio and the debt-to-output ratio predicted by the model of Section 9.1 during an external crisis under a currency peg and under the optimal exchange-rate policy. Note that these responses differ across the two exchange-rate regimes, even though the responses of the levels of the trade balance and the external debt are identical across exchange-rate policies, due to the assumption $\sigma = 1/\xi$. Of course, all differences must be due to the fact that output (measured in terms of tradables) behaves differently across exchange-rate regimes. Explain analytically the nature of these differences. Consider in particular the cases $\xi = 1$ and $\xi > 1$ under the maintained assumption $\sigma = 1/\xi$.

9.11 (The CPI Index) Show that if the technology for producing the composite consumption given in (9.2) is of the CES form, then the consumption price level, P_t, can be expressed as a CES function of the nominal prices of tradables and nontradables, $\mathcal{E}_t$ and P_t^N, respectively.

9.12 (Optimal Exchange-Rate Policy under Price or Wage Stickiness) Compare the optimal exchange-rate policies implied by the model with downward nominal wage rigidity developed in Section 9.1 and the model with downward product price rigidity developed in Section 9.15.

1. Show that the families of optimal exchange-rate policies are identical under downward price rigidity and downward wage rigidity provided that: $\gamma = \gamma_p$, the economy was in full employment in period -1, and the sources of uncertainty are stochastic disturbances in r_t and y_t^T.

2. Show that, in particular, it is optimal to fully stabilize the nominal wage or the nominal price of nontradables.

3. Show how these results would change in the presence of productivity shocks in the nontraded sector.

9.13 (Productivity Shocks in the Nontraded Sector) Consider an economy like the one developed in Section 9.1, in which the nontraded good is produced with the technology $y_t^N = e^{z_t} h_t^\alpha$, where z_t denotes an exogenous and stochastic productivity shock. Assume that z_t evolves according to the law of motion $z_t = \rho z_{t-1} + \mu_t$, where $\rho \in [0, 1)$ is a parameter, and μ_t is an i.i.d. disturbance with mean zero and standard deviation σ_μ. Suppose that the endowment of tradables is constant and equal to $y^T > 0$ and that the interest rate is constant and equal to r. Assume that r satisfies $\beta(1 + r) = 1$. Assume that the period utility function and the aggregator function are given by (9.28) and (9.29), respectively, with $\xi = 1/\sigma < 1$. Suppose that $d_0 = 0$ and that the economy was operating at full employment in $t = -1$.

1. Find the equilibrium process of consumption of tradables, c_t^T.

2. Derive the optimal devaluation rate, ϵ_t, as a function of present and past values of the productivity shock.

3. Provide a graphical analysis of the effect of an increase in productivity ($z_0 > z_{-1}$) under the optimal exchange-rate policy and under a currency peg. Provide intuition.

4. Suppose that the monetary authority follows the optimal exchange-rate policy that makes the domestic currency as strong as possible relative to the foreign currency at all times. Find the unconditional correlation between the net devaluation rate, $\ln \epsilon_t$, and the growth rate of productivity, z_t/z_{t-1}. Provide intuition.

5. How would the sign of the correlation obtained in question 4 and the intuition behind it change in the case $\xi = 1/\sigma > 1$?

9.14 (Optimal Policy with Initial Price Dispersion (Yun 2005)) Consider the staggered-price model of Section 9.16. Suppose that $s_{-1} < 1$. Show that there is an exchange-rate policy that supports the flexible-price equilibrium. Characterize the path of nontradable inflation induced by this (optimal) exchange-rate policy. Provide intuition.

9.15 (The Importance of Interest-Rate and Endowment Shocks) Consider the two-sector open economy with staggered price setting à la Calvo-Yun studied in Section 9.16. As an identification assumption, postulate that interest-rate shocks can affect r_t and y_t^T contemporaneously and that output shocks can affect y_t^T but not r_t contemporaneously.

1. Compute the matrix Γ under this identification scheme.

2. Compute the share of the variances of tradable output, y_t^T; hours, h_t; consumption, c_t; the real exchange rate, p_t; and the trade-balance-to-output ratio, $tb_t/(y_t^T + p_t y_t^N)$ explained by interest-rate shocks under the two alternative exchange-rate policies considered in Section 9.16, the optimal exchange-rate policy and a currency peg. Comment.

3. Produce two figures, similar to Figure 9.19, displaying the dynamics of a typical external crisis, conditional on each of the two shocks. Provide intuition.

4. What fraction of the welfare costs of currency pegs reported in Table 9.9 is attributable to interest-rate shocks?

5. Answer questions 1–4 under the alternative identification assumption that output shocks can affect the interest contemporaneously but not vice versa.

9.16 (Exchange-Rate Overshooting) Dornbusch's (1976) celebrated exchange-rate overshooting result states that an unanticipated monetary expansion causes a larger depreciation of the nominal exchange rate in the short run than in the long run. The present exercise aims to ascertain whether the neo-Keynesian model of Section 9.16 captures this effect. To this end, assume that monetary policy is neither a currency peg nor the optimal exchange-rate policy (the two polar cases analyzed in Section 9.16) but instead takes the form of the following Taylor-type interest-rate feedback rule:

$$\hat{i}_t = 1.5\hat{\pi}_t + 0.125\hat{y}_t + \eta_t,$$

where i_t denotes the gross domestic nominal interest rate, π_t denotes the gross consumer price inflation rate, and y_t denotes real output. As before, a hat over a variable denotes log-deviation from the deterministic steady state. The variable η_t denotes an exogenous monetary-policy shock and is assumed to be i.i.d. with mean zero and standard deviation σ_η. Note that the variables i_t, π_t, and y_t were not defined in the model of Section 9.16, so you have to properly define these variables and derive additional equilibrium conditions linking them to the variables of the original model. For example, for i_t assume that households have access to a nominally risk-free one-period bond and derive the household's first-order condition associated with holdings of this bond. Use a log-linearized version of the model calibrated as in Section 9.16. Plot the impulse response of the devaluation rate, ϵ_t, to a 1 percentage-point decline in η_t. We would say that the model captures the overshooting effect if $\hat{\epsilon}_t$ initially jumps up and later falls below zero and converges to its steady-state value from below. Provide intuition.

10

Exchange-Rate Policy
and Capital Controls

In Chapter 9 we studied a model with nominal rigidities in which the nominal exchange rate can be used to bring about the Pareto optimal allocation. We established that the optimal exchange-rate policy calls for devaluations when the economy is hit by negative external shocks. And when these shocks are large, so are the required devaluations. However, for many emerging countries, such as those that are members of a currency union, devaluations may not be an option. This chapter explores the potential of nonmonetary policies to address the distortions created by nominal rigidities when the exchange-rate regime is suboptimal. We begin by studying tax policies that can bring about the first-best (or Pareto optimal) allocation and then analyze optimal capital control policy.

We analyze these questions in the context of the model developed in Chapter 9, in which nominal frictions take the form of downwardly rigid nominal wages. We will assume that the nominal exchange rate is fixed. But the insights of this chapter apply more broadly to any suboptimal exchange-rate regime.

10.1 First-Best Fiscal Policy under Fixed Exchange Rates

Because wage rigidity creates a distortion in the labor market, and because nontradable goods are labor intensive (in the model as well as in the data), it is reasonable to begin by studying fiscal instruments directly targeting the labor market or the market for nontraded goods as vehicles to remedy this source of inefficiency.

We start by studying optimal labor subsidy schemes, which are perhaps the most direct way to address the distortions created by the combination of wage rigidity and suboptimal exchange-rate policy. Contributions in this area include Schmitt-Grohé and Uribe (2012a, 2016a) and Farhi, Gopinath, and Itskhoki (2014). The treatment here follows the former authors.

10.1.1 Labor Subsidies

In the model developed in Chapter 9, negative external shocks cause involuntary unemployment because the combination of downward nominal wage rigidity and a currency peg prevents the real wage from falling to the level compatible with full employment. In

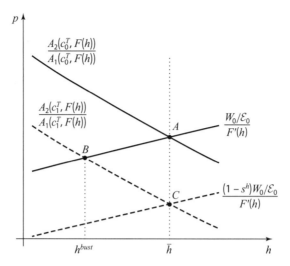

Figure 10.1   Adjustment under the optimal labor subsidy policy.

these circumstances, a labor subsidy would reduce the firm's perceived labor cost, thereby increasing the demand for labor. Specifically, suppose that the government subsidizes employment at the firm level at the proportional rate s_t^h. Profits expressed in terms of tradable goods are then given by

$$p_t F(h_t) - (1 - s_t^h) w_t h_t.$$

The firm's optimality condition becomes

$$p_t = (1 - s_t^h) \frac{w_t}{F'(h_t)}.$$

This expression states that for any given real wage, w_t, the larger the subsidy, s_t^h, is, the lower will be the marginal cost of labor perceived by the firm, $(1 - s_t^h) w_t$. Therefore, for any given relative price, p_t, the larger the subsidy is, the larger will be the number of hours the firm is willing to hire.

Figure 10.1 illustrates how labor subsidies of this form can bring about the efficient allocation. Consider a situation in which an external shock, such as an increase in the country interest rate, brings the economy from an initial situation with full employment (point A) to one with involuntary unemployment in the amount $\bar{h} - h_{bust}$ (point B). The labor subsidy causes the labor supply schedule to shift down and to the right, as shown by the dashed upward-sloping line. The new intersection of the demand and supply schedules is at point C, where full employment is restored. Unlike what happens under the optimal exchange-rate policy, under the optimal labor subsidy, the real wage does not fall during the crisis. Specifically, the real wage received by the household remains constant at $w_0 = W_0/\mathcal{E}_0$. Once the negative external shock dissipates (i.e., once the interest rate falls back to its original level), the fiscal authority can safely remove the subsidy without compromising its full-employment objective.

This graphical analysis suggests that a labor subsidy can support full employment at all times. Let's now establish this result more formally. A relevant question is how the government should finance this subsidy. It turns out that in the present model the government can tax any source of income in a nondistorting fashion. Suppose, for instance, that the government levies a proportional tax, τ_t, on all sources of household income, wage income, profits, and the tradable endowment. In this case, the government budget constraint takes the form

$$s_t^h w_t h_t = \tau_t \left(y_t^T + w_t h_t + \phi_t \right),$$

where ϕ_t denotes profits expressed in terms of tradables. Implicit in this budget constraint is the simplifying assumption that the government issues no debt (i.e., that it follows a balanced-budget rule). This assumption entails no loss of generality. The left-hand side of this expression represents the government's outlays, consisting of subsidies to firms. The right-hand side represents tax revenues. Given the level of labor subsidies, s_t^h, the income tax rate, τ_t, adjusts endogenously to guarantee the government's budget constraint holds period by period. To see that τ_t is nondistorting, consider the household's budget constraint, which now takes the form

$$c_t^T + p_t c_t^N + d_t = (1 - \tau_t)(y_t^T + w_t h_t + \phi_t) + \frac{d_{t+1}}{1 + r_t}.$$

Let's inspect each source of household income separately. Because the endowment of tradable goods, y_t^T, is assumed to be exogenous, it is not affected by taxation. Similarly, profit income from the ownership of firms, ϕ_t, is taken as given by individual households. Consequently, the imposition of profit taxes at the household level is nondistorting. Finally, notice that households either supply $\bar{h}$ hours of work inelastically (in periods of full employment) or are rationed in the labor market (in periods of unemployment). In any event, households take their employment status as given. As a result, taxes do not alter households' incentives to work. (Exercise 10.2 asks you to demonstrate that income taxes continue to be nondistorting even when the labor supply is endogenous.) It follows that the first-order conditions associated with the household's utility-maximization problem are the same as those given in Section 9.1 of Chapter 9 for an economy without taxation of household income.

Combining the government budget constraint; the household budget constraint; the definition of firm's profits; and the market clearing condition in the nontraded sector, $c_t^N = F(h_t)$, yields the resource constraint (9.9). An equilibrium under a currency peg ($\epsilon_t = 1$) with labor subsidies is then given by a set of processes $\{c_t^T, h_t, w_t, d_{t+1}, p_t, \lambda_t, \mu_t\}_{t=0}^{\infty}$ satisfying

$$c_t^T + d_t = y_t^T + \frac{d_{t+1}}{1 + r_t}, \tag{10.1}$$

$$d_{t+1} \leq \bar{d}, \tag{10.2}$$

$$\mu_t \geq 0, \tag{10.3}$$

$$\mu_t(d_{t+1} - \bar{d}) = 0, \tag{10.4}$$

$$\lambda_t = U'(A(c_t^T, F(h_t)))A_1(c_t^T, F(h_t)), \tag{10.5}$$

$$\frac{\lambda_t}{1 + r_t} = \beta E_t \lambda_{t+1} + \mu_t, \tag{10.6}$$

$$p_t = \frac{A_2(c_t^T, F(h_t))}{A_1(c_t^T, F(h_t))}, \tag{10.7}$$

$$p_t = (1 - s_t^h)\frac{w_t}{F'(h_t)}, \tag{10.8}$$

$$w_t \geq \gamma w_{t-1}, \tag{10.9}$$

$$h_t \leq \bar{h}, \tag{10.10}$$

and

$$(\bar{h} - h_t)(w_t - \gamma w_{t-1}) = 0, \tag{10.11}$$

given a labor-subsidy policy, $\{s_t^h\}_{t=0}^{\infty}$, initial conditions w_{-1} and d_0, and exogenous stochastic processes $\{r_t, y_t^T\}_{t=0}^{\infty}$. This set of equilibrium conditions is identical to that pertaining to an economy with a currency peg but without labor subsidies given in Section 9.2, except that here the labor subsidy s_t^h creates a wedge between the marginal cost of production of nontradables and the relative price of nontradables (equation (10.8)). The benevolent government will manipulate this wedge to undo the real wage rigidity created by the combination of downward nominal wage rigidity and a currency peg.

Consider a policymaker who wishes to set the labor subsidy s_t^h in a *Ramsey* optimal fashion. The optimization problem faced by this policymaker is to maximize

$$E_0 \sum_{t=0}^{\infty} U(A(c_t^T, F(h_t))), \tag{10.12}$$

subject to the complete set of equilibrium conditions (10.1)–(10.11). To see that the Ramsey optimal labor-subsidy policy supports the Pareto optimal allocation, consider the less restricted problem of maximizing (10.12) subject to only three constraints, namely, (10.1), (10.2), and (10.10). This less restricted optimization problem is the optimization problem of the Pareto planner and therefore yields the Pareto optimal allocation, which, among other things, is characterized by full employment at all times: $h_t = \bar{h}$ for all t (see Chapter 9, Section 9.3.2). To establish that this allocation is indeed the solution to the Ramsey optimization problem, we must show that the remaining constraints of the Ramsey problem, namely, (10.3)–(10.9) and (10.11), are also satisfied. To see this, notice that equations (10.3)–(10.6) are first-order conditions of the less restricted optimization problem, so they are always satisfied. Also, since the Pareto optimal allocation implies full employment at all times, the slackness condition (10.4) is always satisfied. Now set p_t to satisfy (10.7). Then for every $t \geq 0$, given w_{t-1}, set w_t at any arbitrary value satisfying (10.9). Finally, set the labor subsidy, s_t^h, to satisfy equation (10.8). This completes the proof that the Pareto optimal allocation solves the optimization of the Ramsey planner. In other words, the Ramsey optimal labor subsidy policy supports the Pareto optimal allocation.

10.1.2 Equivalence of Labor Subsidies and Devaluations

How does the optimal labor subsidy in the present economy compare to the optimal devaluation policy studied in Chapter 9? Combine equilibrium conditions (10.7) and (10.8) and evaluate the result at the optimal allocation to obtain

$$w_t(1 - s_t^h) = \frac{A_2(c_t^T, F(\bar{h}))}{A_1(c_t^T, F(\bar{h}))} F'(\bar{h}).$$

As in Chapter 9, define

$$\omega(c_t^T) \equiv \frac{A_2(c_t^T, F(\bar{h}))}{A_1(c_t^T, F(\bar{h}))} F'(\bar{h}).$$

Then we can write $w_t = \omega(c_t^T)/(1 - s_t^h)$. Finally, combine this expression with equilibrium condition (10.9) to get

$$\frac{1}{1 - s_t^h} \geq \frac{\gamma w_{t-1}}{\omega(c_t^T)}. \tag{10.13}$$

Any subsidy policy satisfying this condition is Ramsey and Pareto optimal. As in the case of optimal exchange-rate policy, there exists a whole family of labor-subsidy policies that supports the Pareto optimal allocation. Furthermore, comparing this expression with condition (9.24), we obtain the following equivalence result:

If the process for the devaluation policy ϵ_t is optimal in the economy with no labor subsidies, then the process $s_t^h \equiv (\epsilon_t - 1)/\epsilon_t$ is optimal in the economy with a fixed exchange rate.

This relationship between the optimal exchange-rate policy and the optimal labor-subsidy policy as alternative ways of achieving the first-best allocation is useful to gauge the magnitude of the labor subsidy necessary to preserve full employment during crises. In Chapter 9, we found that during a large crisis like the one observed in Argentina in 2001, the model predicts optimal devaluations of between 30 and 40 percent per year, or between 7 and 9 percent per quarter, for about 2.5 years (see Figure 9.12). Using the formula given above, the implied optimal labor subsidy required to prevent unemployment ranges from 6.5 to 8 percent. These are large numbers. Consider a labor share of 75 percent of GDP and a share of nontradables of 75 percent of GDP as well. Then the budgetary impact of a labor subsidy of 6.5–8 percent is 3.5 to 4.5 percent of GDP.

Finally, we note that a property of the optimal labor subsidies characterized here is that there is a sense in which they are good for only one crisis. Specifically, suppose the fiscal authority grants a labor subsidy during a crisis and keeps it in place once the crisis is over. When the next crisis comes, the old subsidy does not help at all to avoid unemployment. The reason is that the recovery after the first crisis causes nominal wages to increase, placing the economy in a vulnerable situation to face the next downturn. The new crisis would then require another increase in labor subsidies. This logic leads to a process for labor subsidies converging to 100 percent. To avoid this situation, the policymaker must remove the subsidy as soon as the crisis is over. In this way, the recoveries occur in the context of nominal wage stability, and the optimal subsidy policy is stationary. Formally, the stationary optimal labor-subsidy policy takes the form

$$\frac{1}{1 - s_t^h} = \max\left\{1, \frac{\gamma w_{t-1}}{\omega(c_t^T)}\right\},$$

which clearly belongs to the family of optimal labor-subsidy policies given in equation (10.13).

10.1.3 Sales Subsidies

Another fiscal alternative to achieve the Pareto optimal allocation under a currency peg is to subsidize sales in the nontraded sector. Let s_t^{yN} be a proportional subsidy on sales in the nontraded sector. Then profits of a representative firm in the nontraded sector are given by

$$(1 + s_t^{yN}) p_t F(h_t) - \frac{W_t}{\mathcal{E}_t} h_t.$$

The profit-maximization condition of the firm becomes

$$p_t = \frac{1}{1 + s_t^{yN}} \frac{W_t / \mathcal{E}_t}{F'(h_t)}.$$

According to this expression, an increase in the sales subsidy increases the marginal revenue of the firm. Like a wage subsidy, a sales subsidy shifts the supply schedule down and to the right. The graphical analysis is therefore qualitatively identical to that used to explain the workings of the optimal wage subsidy shown in Figure 10.1. Clearly the following equivalence result obtains: if the labor-subsidy process s_t^h is Pareto optimal under a currency peg without sales taxes, then the sales tax process $s_t^{yN} = s_t^h / (1 - s_t^h)$ is Pareto optimal under a currency peg without labor subsidies.

10.1.4 Consumption Subsidies

A third fiscal instrument that can be used to ensure full employment at all times in a pegging economy with downward nominal wage rigidity is a proportional subsidy to the consumption of nontradables. Specifically, assume that the after-subsidy price of nontradable goods faced by consumers is $(1 - s_t^{cN}) p_t$. The subsidy on nontraded consumption makes nontradables less expensive relative to tradables. It can therefore be used by the government during a crisis to facilitate an expenditure switch toward nontraded consumption and away from tradable consumption. With subsidies on nontraded consumption, the demand schedule is given by

$$(1 - s_t^{cN}) p_t = \frac{A_2(c_t^T, F(h_t))}{A_1(c_t^T, F(h_t))}.$$

Figure 10.2 illustrates how the consumption subsidy can be used to ensure the efficient functioning of the labor market. Suppose a negative external shock reduces the desired demand for tradable goods, shifting the demand schedule for nontradables down and to the left as indicated by the downward-sloping dashed line in the figure. As discussed before, in the absence of any intervention, the pegging economy would be stuck at the inefficient point B, with involuntary unemployment. The introduction of the subsidy to nontraded consumption shifts the demand schedule back up and to the right. If the magnitude of the subsidy is chosen appropriately, the demand schedule will cross the supply schedule exactly at point A, where the labor market returns to full employment. Note that the real exchange rate does not adjust to the external shock. However, the after-tax real exchange rate experiences a depreciation when the consumption subsidy is implemented. This perceived depreciation boosts the demand for nontradables, thereby preventing a spillover to the nontraded sector of a contraction originating in the traded sector.

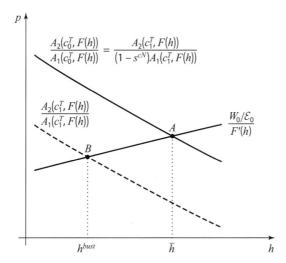

Figure 10.2   Adjustment under optimal taxation of nontradable consumption.

This fiscal instrument is equivalent to a labor subsidy in the following sense. If the labor subsidy s_t^h implements the Pareto optimal allocation under a currency peg, then so does the consumption tax $s_t^{cN} = s_t^h$. Taken together the results of this section show that the optimal devaluation policy is equivalent to a currency peg with optimal labor subsidies or optimal sales subsidies in the nontraded sector or optimal subsidies for the consumption of nontradables.

A criticism that can be raised against all three fiscal stabilization schemes considered here is that the implied tax policies inherit the stochastic properties of the underlying sources of uncertainty (i.e., r_t and y_t^T). This means that tax rates must change at business-cycle frequencies. To the extent that changes to the tax code are subject to legislative approval, the long and uncertain lags involved in this process might render the implementation of the optimal tax policy impractical.

10.2 Capital Controls

Fixed exchange-rate arrangements are often part of broader economic reform programs that include liberalization of international capital flows. For small emerging economies, such a policy combination has been a mixed blessing. A case in point is the periphery of the European Union. Figure 10.3 displays the current-account-to-GDP ratio, an index of nominal hourly wages in euros, and the rate of unemployment for 11 peripheral members of the European Union from 2000 to 2011. As members of the European Union these countries enjoy free capital mobility with other member countries. In addition, all 11 countries were either on the euro (Cyprus, Greece, Ireland, Portugal, Slovakia, Slovenia, and Spain) or were pegging to the euro (Bulgaria, Estonia, Lithuania, and Latvia) during the Great Recession. In the early 2000s, these countries enjoyed large capital inflows, which, through their expansionary effect on domestic absorption, led to sizable appreciations in hourly wages. With the onset of the global recession in 2008, however, capital inflows dried

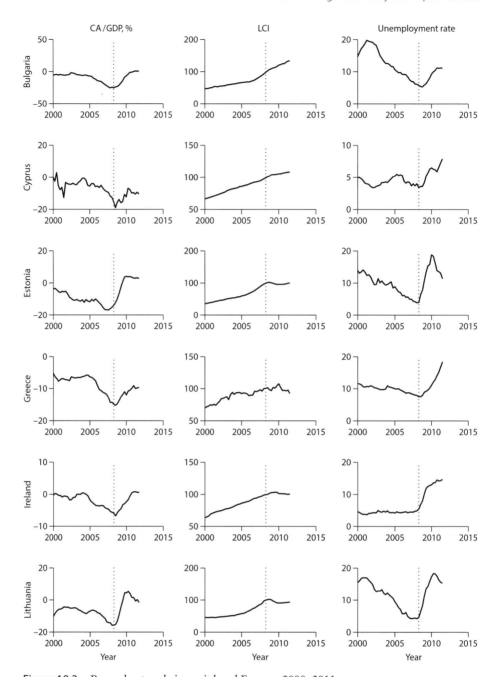

Figure 10.3   Boom-bust cycle in peripheral Europe, 2000–2011.

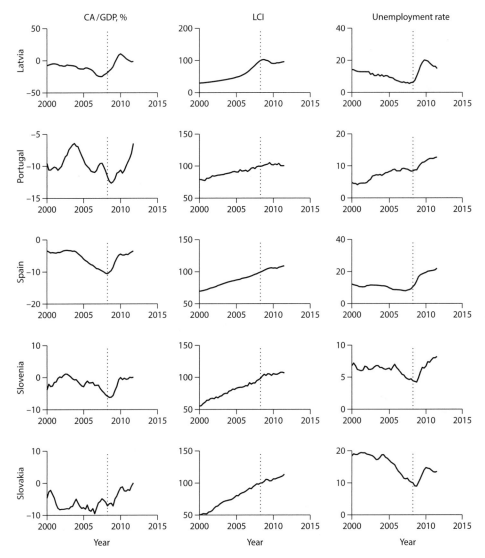

Figure 10.3 *(continued)*

Notes: CA/GDP, current-account-to-GDP ratio (percent); LCI, nominal labor cost index (2008 = 100). The vertical dotted line indicates 2008:Q2, the onset of the Great Recession in Europe. The sample period is 2000:Q4 to 2011:Q3. All data are from Eurostat: http://epp.eurostat.ec.europa.eu/portal/page/portal/statistics/search_database.

up, and aggregate demand collapsed. At the same time nominal wages remained at the level they had achieved at the peak of the boom. The combination of depressed levels of aggregate demand and high nominal wages was associated with a massive increase in involuntary unemployment. In turn, local monetary authorities were unable to reduce real wages via a devaluation because of their commitment to the currency union.

Viewed through the lens of the model with nominal rigidities studied earlier in this chapter and in Chapter 9, the type of empirical evidence presented above suggests the possibility that countries might benefit from adopting prudential capital controls (i.e., from taxing net capital inflows during booms and subsidizing them during contractions). Capital controls essentially represent a wedge between the interest rate at which the rest of the world is willing to lend to domestic residents and the interest rate effectively paid by these agents. In other words, by using capital controls, the government can control the interest rate. Therefore, raising capital controls during booms can curb the expansion in aggregate demand and in this way slow nominal wage growth. In turn, this would allow the economy to enter the contractionary phase of the cycle with a lower level of wages, which would result in less unemployment. Unemployment could be even further reduced if during the contraction, the policy authority subsidized net capital inflows. Thus capital controls can be viewed as one way out of Mundell's (1963) trilemma of international finance, according to which a country cannot simultaneously have a fixed exchange rate, free capital mobility, and an independent interest-rate policy. For, by stifling free capital mobility, capital controls allow a country to pursue an independent interest-rate policy.

Imposing capital controls, however, comes at a cost. The reason is that capital controls distort the real interest rate perceived by private domestic agents, thereby introducing inefficiencies in the intertemporal allocation of consumption of tradable goods. Thus the government contemplating the imposition of capital controls faces a trade-off between intertemporal distortions, caused by capital controls themselves, and static distortions, caused by the combination of downward nominal wage rigidity and suboptimal exchange-rate policy. The remainder of this chapter is devoted to analyzing this trade-off from a Ramsey perspective. The analysis follows Schmitt-Grohé and Uribe (2012a, 2016a). See also Farhi and Werning (2012).

10.2.1 Capital Controls as a Distortion of the Interest Rate

We embed capital controls in the small open economy with downward nominal wage rigidity developed in Chapter 9. Throughout the analysis, we assume that the nominal exchange rate is constant.

Let τ_t^d denote a tax on net foreign debt in period t. Then the household's sequential budget constraint is given by

$$c_t^T + p_t c_t^N + d_t = (1 - \tau_t)(y_t^T + w_t h_t + \phi_t) + \frac{(1 - \tau_t^d)d_{t+1}}{1 + r_t}.$$

The government intervention in the international financial market through the capital control variable τ_t^d alters the effective gross interest rate paid by the household from $1 + r_t$ to $(1 + r_t)/(1 - \tau_t^d)$. The rate τ_t^d can take positive or negative values. When it is positive, the government discourages external borrowing by raising the effective interest rate. In this case, we say that the government imposes capital controls. When τ_t^d is negative, the government subsidizes international borrowing by lowering the effective interest rate. As we will see shortly, a benevolent government will make heavy use of cyclical adjustments in capital controls to stabilize consumption and employment.

The variable τ_t denotes a proportional tax rate (or subsidy rate if negative) on personal income. In Section 10.1.1, we showed that τ_t is a nondistorting tax instrument in the present economy. The government is assumed to set τ_t so as to balance its budget period by period. Specifically, τ_t is used to rebate or finance any revenue or deficit generated by capital controls. Assuming that the government starts out with no public debt outstanding, its balanced-budget rule implies that, given τ_t^d, the income tax rate τ_t is set residually to satisfy

$$\tau_t^d \frac{d_{t+1}}{1+r_t} + \tau_t(y_t^T + w_t h_t + \phi_t) = 0.$$

10.2.2 Equilibrium under Capital Controls and a Currency Peg

The introduction of capital controls alters only one of the equilibrium conditions of the economy with a currency peg given in Section 9.2: the Euler equation (9.14) stemming from the household's choice of foreign debt. This optimality condition now becomes

$$\frac{\lambda_t}{\frac{1+r_t}{1-\tau_t^d}} = \beta E_t \lambda_{t+1} + \mu_t.$$

It is clear from this expression that the gross interest rate that is relevant for the household is not $1 + r_t$ but $(1 + r_t)/(1 - \tau_t^d)$.

A competitive equilibrium under a fixed exchange-rate regime with capital controls is then a set of processes $\{c_t^T, d_{t+1}, h_t, w_t, \lambda_t, \mu_t\}_{t=0}^{\infty}$ satisfying

$$c_t^T + d_t = y_t^T + \frac{d_{t+1}}{1+r_t}, \tag{10.14}$$

$$\frac{A_2(c_t^T, F(h_t))}{A_1(c_t^T, F(h_t))} F'(h_t) = w_t, \tag{10.15}$$

$$h_t \leq \bar{h}, \tag{10.16}$$

$$w_t \geq \gamma w_{t-1}, \tag{10.17}$$

$$d_{t+1} \leq \bar{d}, \tag{10.18}$$

$$\lambda_t = U'(A(c_t^T, F(h_t)))A_1(c_t^T, F(h_t)), \tag{10.19}$$

$$\frac{\lambda_t(1 - \tau_t^d)}{1+r_t} = \beta E_t \lambda_{t+1} + \mu_t, \tag{10.20}$$

$$\mu_t \geq 0, \tag{10.21}$$

$$\mu_t(d_{t+1} - \bar{d}) = 0, \tag{10.22}$$

and

$$(h_t - \bar{h})(w_t - \gamma w_{t-1}) = 0, \tag{10.23}$$

given exogenous stochastic processes $\{y_t^T, r_t\}_{t=0}^{\infty}$, initial conditions d_0 and w_{-1}, and a capital-control policy $\{\tau_t^d\}_{t=0}^{\infty}$.

10.3 Optimal Capital Controls under Fixed Exchange Rates

Assume that the government is benevolent in the sense that it chooses the capital control policy to maximize the lifetime welfare of the representative household subject to the complete set of equilibrium conditions given by (10.14)–(10.23). This type of optimization problem is known as the *Ramsey problem,* its solution as the *Ramsey optimal equilibrium,* and the resulting policy as the *Ramsey optimal policy.* As will become clear shortly, in the present model the Ramsey optimal capital control policy turns out to be time consistent: in any given period and taking the fixed exchange rate as given, the government has no incentive to deviate from the Ramsey optimal capital control policy.

The Ramsey planner's optimization problem consists of choosing processes $\{\tau_t^d, c_t^T, d_{t+1}, h_t, w_t, \lambda_t, \mu_t\}_{t=0}^\infty$ to maximize (10.12) subject to conditions (10.14)–(10.23).

The strategy we adopt to characterize the Ramsey equilibrium is to first solve a simplified Ramsey optimization problem and then show that the solution to this problem also solves the original Ramsey optimization problem. Specifically, we first drop conditions (10.19)–(10.23) from the set of constraints of the Ramsey planner's problem and then show that the solution to the resulting less constrained Ramsey problem satisfies the omitted constraints. This second step ensures that the solution to the less constrained Ramsey planner's problem is indeed the Ramsey optimal equilibrium.

To see that the solution to the less constrained Ramsey problem also satisfies the constraints omitted from the original Ramsey problem, suppose that the processes $\{c_t^T, h_t, w_t\}$ solve the less constrained problem. Now pick λ_t to satisfy (10.19). Next set $\mu_t = 0$ for all t.[1] This implies that (10.21) and (10.22) are satisfied. Then pick τ_t^d to satisfy (10.20). It remains to show that the slackness condition (10.23) is satisfied when evaluated at the allocation that solves the less-constrained Ramsey problem. To see that this is the case, consider the following proof by contradiction. Suppose, contrary to what we wish to show, that the allocation solving the less constrained Ramsey problem is such that $h_{t'} < \bar{h}$ and $w_{t'} > \gamma w_{t'-1}$ at some date $t' \geq 0$. Consider now a small increase in hours only at date t' from $h_{t'}$ to $\tilde{h} \leq \bar{h}$, holding the processes $\{c_t^T, d_{t+1}\}_{t=0}^\infty$ unchanged. Clearly this perturbation in hours does not violate the resource constraint (10.14), because h_t does not appear in this equation. From (10.15) we have that the real wage in period t' falls to

$$\tilde{w} \equiv \frac{A_2(c_{t'}^T, F(\tilde{h}))}{A_1(c_{t'}^T, F(\tilde{h}))} F'(\tilde{h}) < w_{t'}.$$

Because A_1, A_2, and F' are continuous functions, the wage lower bound (10.17) is satisfied provided the increase in hours is sufficiently small (recall that we are assuming that prior to the perturbation, this lower bound holds with strict inequality). In period $t' + 1$, the wage lower bound (10.17) is also satisfied because $\tilde{w} < w_{t'}$. We have therefore established that

---

1. Note that in states in which the Ramsey allocation calls for setting $d_{t+1} < \bar{d}$, μ_t must be chosen to be zero. However, in states in which the Ramsey allocation yields $d_{t+1} = \bar{d}$, μ_t need not be chosen to be zero. In these states, any positive value of μ_t could be supported in the decentralization of the Ramsey equilibrium. Of course, in this case, τ_t^d will depend on the chosen value of μ_t. In particular, τ_t^d will be strictly decreasing in the arbitrarily chosen value of μ_t.

the perturbation is feasible. Finally, the perturbation is clearly welfare increasing, because it raises the consumption of nontradables in period t' without affecting the consumption of tradables in any period or the consumption of nontradables in any period other than t'. It follows that an allocation that does not satisfy the slackness condition (10.23) cannot be a solution to the less constrained Ramsey problem. This completes the proof that the solution to the less constrained problem is indeed the Ramsey optimal equilibrium.

One can write the Ramsey optimal allocation recursively as the solution to the following *Bellman equation* problem:

$$v(y_t^T, r_t, d_t, w_{t-1}) = \max \left[U(A(c_t^T, F(h_t))) + \beta E_t v(y_{t+1}^T, r_{t+1}, d_{t+1}, w_t) \right], \quad (10.24)$$

subject to (10.14)–(10.18), where $v(y_t^T, r_t, d_t, w_{t-1})$ denotes the value function of the representative household. This representation is quite useful for computational purposes, and we will exploit it in the quantitative analysis presented later in the chapter.

Note that the capital control rate τ_t^d does not appear in this problem. However, from the arguments presented above, we have that it is readily backed out as

$$\tau_t^d = 1 - \beta(1 + r_t) \frac{E_t U'(A(c_{t+1}^T, F(h_{t+1}))) A_1(c_{t+1}^T, F(h_{t+1}))}{U'(A(c_t^T, F(h_t))) A_1(c_t^T, F(h_t))}, \quad (10.25)$$

where c_t^T and h_t are evaluated at the solution of the above Bellman equation problem.

10.4 The Optimality of Prudential Capital Control Policy

We now present an analytical example showing the prudential nature of optimal capital controls. In this example, following a temporary decline in the interest rate, the Ramsey government introduces capital controls to discourage capital inflows. It does so to attenuate the impact on future unemployment once the interest rate goes back up to its long-run level.

The example is a continuation of the one analyzed in Chapter 9, Section 9.2.3. There we studied the response to a temporary decline in the interest rate under a currency peg and under the optimal exchange-rate policy, assuming free capital mobility in both cases. Here we characterize the response of the economy under a currency peg and Ramsey optimal capital controls.[2]

Preferences are given by $U(c_t) = 2 \ln(c_t)$ and $A(c_t^T, c_t^N) = \sqrt{c_t^T c_t^N}$. The technology for producing nontradable goods is $F(h_t) = h_t^\alpha$, with $\alpha \in (0, 1)$. The economy starts period 0 with no outstanding debt, $d_0 = 0$. The endowment of tradables, $y^T > 0$, is constant over time. The real wage in period -1 equals αy^T. The economy is subject to a temporary interest rate decline in period 0. Specifically, $r_t = r$ for all $t \neq 0$, and $r_0 = \underline{r} < r$. This interest-rate shock is assumed to be unanticipated. Assume that $\beta(1 + r) = 1$, $\gamma = 1$, $\bar{h} = 1$,

---

2. In the context of the present model, capital controls would be superfluous under the optimal exchange-rate policy, since the latter achieves the first-best allocation even under free capital mobility. In Chapter 13, Section 13.12, we will study a version of the present model with imperfect enforcement of international debt contracts. In that environment, both the exchange rate and capital controls play nontrivial roles in the Ramsey equilibrium.

and $\alpha > r$.[3] Finally, assume that the economy was at a full-employment equilibrium in periods $t < 0$, with $d_t = 0$, $c_t^T = y^T$, $c_t^N = 1$, and $h_t = 1$.

Recall that aggregate dynamics under free capital mobility and a currency peg are given by

$$c_0^T = y^T \left[\frac{1}{1 + \underline{r}} + \frac{r}{1 + r} \right] > y^T,$$

$$c_t^T = y^T \left[\frac{1}{1 + r} + \frac{r}{1 + r} \frac{1 + \underline{r}}{1 + r} \right] < y^T; \quad t \geq 1,$$

$$d_t = y^T \left[1 - \frac{1 + \underline{r}}{1 + r} \right] > 0; \quad t \geq 1,$$

$$h_0 = 1,$$

and

$$h_t = \frac{1 + \underline{r}}{1 + r} < 1; \quad t \geq 1.$$

Figure 10.4 depicts these equilibrium dynamics with solid lines. Under free capital mobility and a fixed exchange rate, the fall in the interest rate in period 0 causes an expansion in the consumption of tradables financed by external debt and an increase in real wages and the relative price of nontradables (not shown). In period 1, the country interest rate rises to its long-run value, and consumption of tradables falls permanently to a level below the endowment. The resulting trade surplus is used to pay the interest on the debt incurred in period 0. The fall in aggregate demand in period 1 puts downward pressure on real wages. However, because nominal wages are downwardly rigid and the nominal exchange rate is fixed, the real wage cannot fall, causing disequilibrium in the labor market and the emergence of permanent involuntary unemployment.

We conjecture that under Ramsey optimal capital controls and a currency peg, the equilibrium allocation is given by

$$c_t^T = y^T; \quad t \geq 0,$$

$$h_t = 1; \quad t \geq 0,$$

$$d_{t+1} = 0; \quad t \geq 0,$$

and

$$\tau_t^d = \begin{cases} 1 - \frac{1 + \underline{r}}{1 + r} > 0 & \text{for } t = 0 \\ 0 & \text{for } t \geq 1. \end{cases}$$

Figure 10.4 displays these equilibrium dynamics with dotted lines. The Ramsey optimal capital control policy taxes capital inflows in period 0 by setting $\tau_0^d > 0$, which raises the

---

3. Exercise 10.5 deals with the case $\alpha < r$.

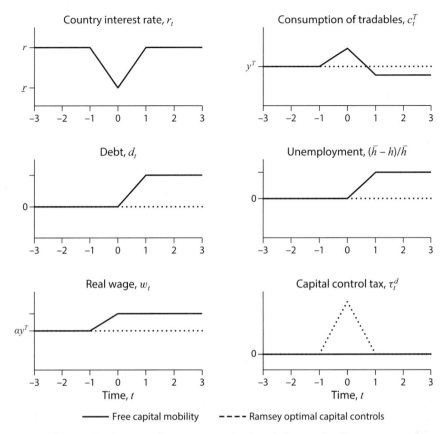

Figure 10.4 Adjustment under Ramsey optimal capital control policy to a temporary interest rate decline.

cost of external borrowing above $\underline{r}$. Indeed, the Ramsey planner finds it optimal to fully undo the temporary decline in the world interest rate. The effective interest rate faced by domestic households, $(1 + r_t)/(1 - \tau_t^d) - 1$, equals r even in period 0. In this way, the Ramsey planner curbs the boom in aggregate demand and limits the appreciation of real wages in period 0. Consumption is fully smoothed over time, and as a result the labor market is unaffected by the temporary decline in the interest rate.

In the absence of downward nominal wage rigidity, it would be optimal for the economy to take advantage of the temporary fall in the interest rate and expand the absorption of tradables in period 0. Thus by imposing capital controls at $t = 0$, the planner distorts the intertemporal allocation of consumption of tradables. This distortion is of course welfare decreasing in isolation. However, the gains stemming from avoiding unemployment in periods $t \geq 1$ more than offset these welfare losses. In fact in the present example, the trade-off between distortions in the allocation of tradable consumption and unemployment is resolved entirely in favor of the latter. In general the resolution of the trade-off will involve some unemployment and some increase in the absorption of tradables (see exercise 10.5).

We now show formally the validity of the conjectured Ramsey optimal equilibrium. The optimal capital control policy is the solution to the problem of maximizing the value function (10.24) subject to (10.14)–(10.18). The appendix to this chapter shows that under Ramsey optimal capital controls, beginning in period $t = 1$ all variables are constant—that is, $c_t^T = c_1^T$, $h_t = h_1$, $d_{t+1} = d_1$, and $w_t = w_1$ for all $t \geq 1$. Because $c_t^T = y^T$ for all t, welfare in the conjectured Ramsey optimal equilibrium is

$$v^{opt} = \frac{1}{1-\beta} \ln y^T.$$

To see that the conjecture is correct, consider first an alternative solution in which $c_0^T > y^T$. In this case, $d_1 > 0$ and therefore $c_1^T < y^T$. The surplus $y^T - c_1^T$ is necessary to service the debt. The full-employment wage in period 0 is $\alpha c_0^T > \alpha y^T \equiv w_{-1}$. It follows that $h_0 = 1$, and $w_0 = \alpha c_0^T$. In period 1, the full-employment wage rate is αc_1^T, which is clearly less than w_0. As a result, we have that in period 1 the lower bound on wages binds, that is, $w_1 = w_0$. Equation (10.15) then implies that $h_t = c_t^T / c_0^T < 1$ and that $\ln c_t^N = \alpha(\ln c_1^T - \ln c_0^T)$ for all $t \geq 1$. Lifetime utility is then given by

$$\tilde{v} = \frac{1 - \frac{1+\alpha}{1+r}}{1-\beta} \ln c_0^T + \frac{\frac{1+\alpha}{1+r}}{1-\beta} \ln c_1^T.$$

Because, by assumption, $\alpha > r$, the coefficient on $\ln c_0^T$ is negative and the coefficient on $\ln c_1^T$ is positive. This means that moving from $c_0^T = c_1^T = y^T$ to $c_0^T > y^T > c_1^T$ must be welfare decreasing. It follows that $v^{opt} > \tilde{v}$. Therefore we have established that $c_0^T > y^T$ is not Ramsey optimal. The intuition for why the parameter α, governing labor productivity, is relevant for establishing this result is that if labor productivity is too low, then it would not pay for the planner to avoid unemployment by raising capital controls, because the additional output of nontradables resulting from higher employment is too little. In this case, the planner prefers to preserve intertemporal efficiency in the allocation of tradables at the expense of some unemployment in the nontraded sector (see exercise 10.5).

We must now check that $c_0^T < y^T$ is not Ramsey optimal. To this end, begin by noticing that if $c_0^T < y^T$, then $d_1 < 0$, and therefore $c_t^T > y^T$ for all $t \geq 1$. In this case the full-employment real wage in period 0 is $\alpha c_0^T < \alpha y^T = w_{-1}$, which implies the existence of involuntary unemployment in period 0. Equation (10.15) then implies that $h_0 = c_0^T / y^T < 1$. By a similar logic, there is full employment starting in period 1: $h_t = 1$ for $t \geq 1$. Lifetime welfare is then given by

$$\hat{v} = (1 + \alpha) \ln c_0^T + \frac{\beta}{1-\beta} \ln c_1^T - \alpha \ln y^T.$$

Now combine the sequential budget constraint (10.14) evaluated at $t = 0$ and $t = 1$, given, respectively, by $c_0^T = y^T + d_1/(1+\underline{r})$ and $c_1^T = y^T - \frac{r}{1+r} d_1$, to obtain

$$c_1^T = \left(1 + r\frac{1+r}{1+r}\right) y^T - \frac{r(1+r)}{(1+r)} c_0^T.$$

Using this expression to eliminate c_1^T from lifetime welfare, we obtain

$$\hat{v} = (1+\alpha)\ln c_0^T + \frac{\beta}{1-\beta}\ln\left[\left(1+r\frac{1+\underline{r}}{1+r}\right)y^T - \frac{r(1+\underline{r})}{(1+r)}c_0^T\right] - \alpha\ln y^T.$$

Notice that $\hat{v} = v^{opt}$ when $c_0^T = y^T$. Moreover, the derivative of $\hat{v}$ with respect to c_0^T is positive for any $c_0^T \leq y^T$. This implies that $\hat{v} < v^{opt}$ for any $c_0^T < y^T$. We have therefore established the validity of the conjectured Ramsey optimal equilibrium.

Finally, the capital control policy that supports the Ramsey equilibrium can be read off the household's Euler equation (10.25) evaluated at $c_0^T = c_1^T = y^T$, which yields

$$\tau_0^d = 1 - \frac{1+\underline{r}}{1+r} > 0,$$

for $t = 0$ and

$$\tau_t^d = 0,$$

for $t \geq 1$. These two expressions underline the prudential nature of optimal capital controls under fixed exchange rates. The government imposes restrictions on international capital inflows in period 0, when the country faces particularly favorable borrowing conditions from the rest of the world and relaxes them as soon as the cost of foreign funds goes up.

10.5 Optimal Capital Controls during a Boom-Bust Episode

To gauge the role of optimal capital controls in a more realistic economy, we now characterize the Ramsey optimal equilibrium in the calibrated economy of Chapter 9 (Section 9.7). This is a stochastic environment characterized by random disturbances to the country interest rate, r_t, and to the endowment of tradables, y_t^T. We estimated the joint law of motion of these two exogenous driving forces using data from Argentina for 1983:Q1–2001:Q4. The functional forms for preferences and technologies are as in Chapter 9, Section 9.5, and the calibration of the structural parameters of the model is taken from Table 9.3 in that chapter. Under this more realistic stochastic structure, no closed form solution exists to the Ramsey optimal capital control problem. Therefore we resort to numerical methods to approximate the solution to the value-function problem of maximizing (10.24) subject to (10.14)–(10.18). We apply a value-function iteration procedure over a discretized state space. The discretization of the exogenous state space is the same as that described in Chapter 9, Section 9.6. For the discretization of the endogenous state variables, d_t and w_{t-1}, we use 501 equally spaced points in the interval $[\underline{d}, \overline{d}] = [-7, 8]$ for d_t and 500 equally spaced points for the natural logarithm of w_{t-1} in the interval $[\underline{w}, \overline{w}] = [0.25, 6]$. The Matlab program vfi_ramsey.m computes the equilibrium policy function, and simu.m produces simulated time series of variables of interest. These programs are available online with the materials for this chapter on the book's Web site via http://press.princeton.edu/titles/11032.html.

We define a boom-bust episode as a situation in which tradable output, y_t^T, is at or below trend in period 0, at least one standard deviation above trend in period 10, and at least one standard deviation below trend in period 20. To characterize the typical boom-bust cycle, we simulate the model economy for 20 million periods and select all subperiods that satisfy the definition of a boom-bust episode. We then average across these episodes.

Figure 10.5 depicts the model's predictions during a boom-bust cycle. Solid lines correspond to the economy with free capital mobility (i.e., no capital controls) and dashed lines to the economy with optimal capital controls. The two top panels of the figure display the dynamics of the two exogenous driving forces, tradable output and the country interest rate. By construction, y_t^T and r_t are unaffected by capital controls.

The middle-left panel of the figure shows that the Ramsey government uses capital controls in a prudential fashion during boom-bust episodes. It increases them from about half a percent at the beginning of the episode to almost 3 percent at the peak of the cycle and then relaxes them drastically during the contraction to such a degree that at the bottom of the crisis, it actually subsidizes capital inflows at a rate of about 2 percent.

The increase in capital controls during the expansionary phase of the cycle puts sand in the wheels of capital inflows, thereby curbing the boom in tradable consumption (see the middle-right panel of Figure 10.5). In the contractionary phase, the fall in capital controls fosters tradable absorption, thereby inducing a soft landing. Thus the main effect of optimal capital controls is to produce a much smoother path of tradable consumption than in the economy with free capital mobility. Recall that under the maintained assumption of equality of the intratemporal and intertemporal elasticities of substitution, $\sigma = 1/\xi$, the behavior of traded consumption in the peg economy with free capital mobility is the same as in the first-best allocation. As is evident from the figure, the Ramsey planner finds it optimal to deviate sharply from the first-best path of tradable consumption. This deviation is welfare reducing by itself. However, because unemployment depends directly on variations in the level of tradable absorption through the latter's role as a shifter of the demand schedule for nontradables, and because optimal capital controls stabilize the absorption of tradables, unemployment is low over the boom-bust cycle. Specifically, as can be seen from the bottom-left panel of Figure 10.5, in the absence of capital controls unemployment increases sharply by about 20 percentage points during the recession. In contrast, under optimal capital controls the rate of unemployment is virtually zero. It follows that the Ramsey planner's trade-off between distorting the intertemporal allocation of tradable consumption and reducing unemployment is overwhelmingly resolved in favor of the latter.

10.6 Level and Volatility Effects of Optimal Capital Controls under a Currency Peg

Under fixed exchange rates, Ramsey optimal capital controls are prudential not only during boom-bust episodes but also unconditionally over the business cycle. Table 10.1 displays unconditional first and second moments of macroeconomic indicators of interest for the economies with free capital mobility (FCM) and optimal capital controls (OCC). The correlation between τ_t^d and y_t^T is 0.7, and the correlation between τ_t^d and r_t is -0.9. This means that the government tends to restrict (facilitate) capital inflows when the country is hit by positive (negative) shocks. This prudential implementation of capital controls is reflected in an implied correlation between the capital control tax rate and output of 0.7.

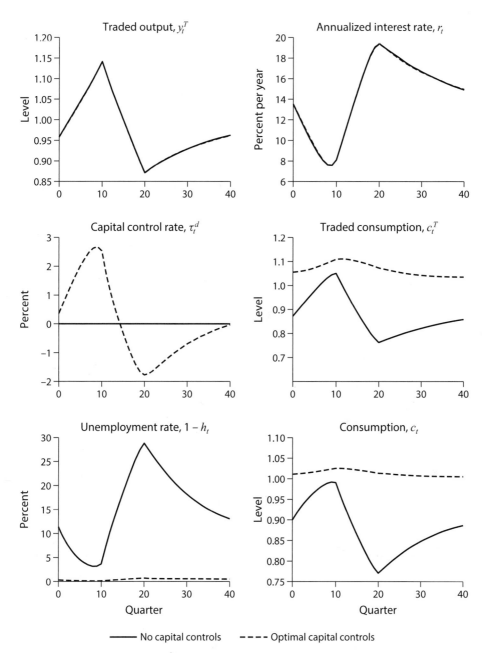

Figure 10.5 Prudential policy for peggers: Boom-bust dynamics with and without capital controls.

Note: This figure is produced with the Matlab program `plot_bb_level.m`, available on the book's Web site.

Table 10.1   Optimal Capital Controls and Currency Pegs: Level and Volatility Effects

	Capital Control Tax Rate	Country Interest Rate	Effective Interest Rate	Unemployment Rate	Growth in Traded Consumption
	$100 \times \tau_t^d$	$400 \times r_t$	$400 \times \left(\frac{1+r_t}{1-\tau_t^d} - 1 \right)$	$100 \times \left(\frac{\bar{h}-h_t}{\bar{h}} \right)$	$400 \times \ln(c_t^T/c_{t-1}^T)$
Mean					
FCM	0	12.7	12.7	11.8	0.0
OCC	0.6	12.6	15.1	0.4	0.0
Standard Deviation					
FCM	0	7.1	7.1	10.4	23.2
OCC	2.4	7.1	5.0	1.5	4.9
Correlation with y_t^T					
FCM	—	−0.8	−0.8	−0.6	0.1
OCC	0.7	−0.8	0.3	−0.2	0.2
Correlation with r_t					
FCM	—	1.0	1.0	0.7	−0.2
OCC	−0.9	1.0	−0.3	0.2	−0.3
Correlation with GDP					
FCM	—	−0.8	−0.8	−1.0	0.3
OCC	0.7	−0.8	0.2	−0.5	0.3

Notes: FCM, free capital mobility ($\tau_t^d = 0$ for all t); OCC, optimal capital controls. GDP is expressed in terms of units of the composite good.

The optimal capital control policy is highly effective in reducing involuntary unemployment. The average unemployment rate falls from 11.8 percent under free capital mobility to 0.4 percent under optimal capital controls. The virtually complete eradication of unemployment is achieved through a drastic reduction in the volatility of the shifter of the demand for nontradables, namely, the domestic absorption of tradables. The standard deviation of the growth rate of consumption of tradables falls from 23.2 percent under free capital mobility to only 4.9 percent under optimal capital controls. In turn, this smoothing of tradable consumption is engineered via a time-varying wedge between the country interest rate, r_t, and the effective interest rate perceived by households, $(1+r_t)/(1-\tau_t^d) - 1$. The size of the wedge is governed by the size of the capital control tax rate, τ_t^d. Indeed, capital controls are so strongly prudential that even though the country interest rate is markedly countercyclical (with a correlation of −0.8 with output), the effective interest rate under optimal capital controls is procyclical (with a correlation of 0.2 with output).

The strong interference of the Ramsey planner with the intertemporal allocation of tradable consumption represents a large deviation from the first-best allocation. Recall that given the assumption of equality of the inter- and intratemporal elasticities of substitution ($1/\sigma = \xi$), the path of traded consumption under a peg with free capital mobility coincides with the path associated with the first-best allocation. Thus, as in the simple analytical example of Section 10.4, in the present economy the trade-off between an inefficient intertemporal allocation of tradable consumption and unemployment is resolved in favor of eliminating unemployment.

10.7 Overborrowing under Fixed Exchange Rates

The present model predicts that economies with free capital mobility and a fixed exchange rate overborrow in international financial markets. This prediction is evident from Figure 10.6, which shows the unconditional distribution of external debt in the calibrated fixed exchange-rate economy of the previous section under free capital mobility (solid line) and under optimal capital controls (dashed line). The average level of external debt is 22.4 percent of output under free capital mobility and -14.0 percent of output under optimal capital controls. The Ramsey planner induces a lower average level of external debt by taxing borrowing at a positive rate. Table 10.1 shows that the effective interest rate (i.e., the after-tax interest rate) is 2.5 percentage points higher than the pre-tax interest rate. It follows that pegging economies with free capital mobility accumulate inefficiently large amounts of external debt.

The reason the average external debt is lower under optimal capital controls than under free capital mobility has to do with the higher variance of external debt under optimal

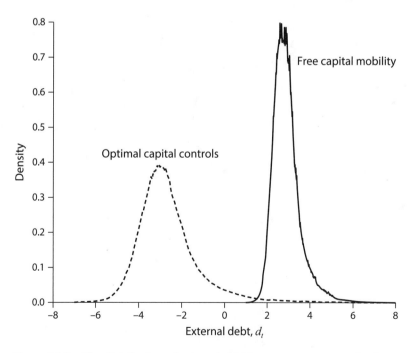

Figure 10.6 The distribution of external debt in a peg economy under free capital mobility and under optimal capital controls.

capital controls (1.6^2 versus 0.65^2). A more volatile process for external debt requires centering the debt distribution further away from the natural debt limit for precautionary reasons (see Figure 10.6). But why does the Ramsey planner like wide swings in the external debt position? The answer is that such variations are necessary to insulate the domestic absorption of tradable goods from exogenous disturbances buffeting the economy (recall that the main role of capital controls in a peg economy is to smooth the consumption of tradables). If c_t^T does not move much over the business cycle, the resource constraint of the economy dictates that disturbances in y_t^T or r_t must be met by compensating movements in d_{t+1}. In the peg economy with free capital mobility, c_t^T is more responsive to variations in y_t^T or r_t, so d_{t+1} need not adjust so much. Put differently, in the peg economy with optimal capital controls, external debt plays the role of a shock absorber to a much larger extent than it does in the peg economy with free capital mobility.

We close this section by commenting on the commonly held view that imposing capital controls amounts to making the current account more closed. This need not be the case. Indeed, in the present model, optimal capital controls play the opposite role. Under optimal capital controls, the economy makes more heavy use of the current account to smooth consumption than it does under free capital mobility. The volatility of the current account, given by the standard deviation of $d_t/(1 + r_{t-1}) - d_{t+1}/(1 + r_t)$, is 50 percent higher under optimal capital controls than under free capital mobility. It follows that, far from insulating the economy from world financial markets, optimal capital controls foster international asset transactions over the business cycle.

10.8 The Welfare Cost of Free Capital Mobility in Fixed Exchange-Rate Economies

The model studied in this chapter predicts that the combination of a fixed exchange rate and free capital mobility entails excessive external debt and unemployment. Both these factors tend to depress consumption and therefore reduce welfare. In this section we put a number to these welfare losses.

The welfare cost of free capital mobility in a fixed exchange-rate economy conditional on a particular state $\{y_t^T, r_t, d_t, w_{t-1}\}$, denoted $\Lambda^{FCM}(y_t^T, r_t, d_t, w_{t-1})$, is defined as the permanent percentage increase in the lifetime consumption stream required by an individual living in a fixed exchange-rate economy with free capital mobility to be as well off as an individual living in a fixed exchange-rate economy with optimal capital controls. Formally, $\Lambda^{FCM}(y_t^T, r_t, d_t, w_{t-1})$ is implicitly given by

$$E_t \sum_{s=0}^{\infty} \beta^s \frac{\left[c_{t+s}^{FCM} \left(1 + \frac{\Lambda^{FCM}(y_t^T, r_t, d_t, w_{t-1})}{100} \right) \right]^{1-\sigma} - 1}{1-\sigma} = v^{OCC}(y_t^T, r_t, d_t, w_{t-1}), \quad (10.26)$$

where c_t^{FCM} denotes the equilibrium process of consumption in the currency-peg economy with free capital mobility (and is identical to c_t^{PEG} in the notation of Section 9.10 in Chapter 9) and $v^{OCC}(y_t^T, r_t, d_t, w_{t-1})$ denotes the value function associated with the optimal capital control policy in the fixed exchange-rate economy and is given by

$$v^{OCC}(y_t^T, r_t, d_t, w_{t-1}) \equiv E_t \sum_{s=0}^{\infty} \beta^s \frac{\left(c_{t+s}^{OCC}\right)^{1-\sigma} - 1}{1 - \sigma},$$

where c_t^{OCC} denotes the equilibrium process of consumption in the fixed exchange-rate economy with optimal capital controls. Solving for $\Lambda^{FCM}(y_t^T, r_t, d_t, w_{t-1})$ yields

$$\Lambda^{FCM}(y_t^T, r_t, d_t, w_{t-1})$$

$$= 100 \left\{ \left[\frac{v^{OCC}(y_t^T, r_t, d_t, w_{t-1})(1 - \sigma) + (1 - \beta)^{-1}}{v^{FCM}(y_t^T, r_t, d_t, w_{t-1})(1 - \sigma) + (1 - \beta)^{-1}} \right]^{1/(1-\sigma)} - 1 \right\},$$

where $v^{FCM}(y_t^T, r_t, d_t, w_{t-1})$ denotes the value function associated with free capital mobility and a fixed exchange rate and is given by

$$v^{FCM}(y_t^T, r_t, d_t, w_{t-1}) \equiv E_t \sum_{s=0}^{\infty} \beta^s \frac{\left(c_{t+s}^{FCM}\right)^{1-\sigma} - 1}{1 - \sigma}.$$

This value function is identical to $v^{PEG}(y_t^T, r_t, d_t, w_{t-1})$ introduced in Section 9.10 in Chapter 9. Because the state vector is stochastic, the conditional welfare cost measure, $\Lambda^{FCM}(y_t^T, r_t, d_t, w_{t-1})$, is itself stochastic. We wish to compute the unconditional mean of $\Lambda^{FCM}(y_t^T, r_t, d_t, w_{t-1})$. This requires knowledge of the unconditional probability distribution of the state vector $(y_t^T, r_t, d_t, w_{t-1})$. The distribution of the endogenous elements of the state vector—namely, d_t and w_{t-1}—depends on the exchange-rate policy (a currency peg) and on the capital control regime. Because we are analyzing the welfare gains of switching from a peg with free capital mobility to a peg with optimal capital controls, the relevant probability distribution is the one associated with the peg economy under free capital mobility. Let λ^{FCM} denote the unconditional mean of $\Lambda^{FCM}(y_t^T, r_t, d_t, w_{t-1})$ and $\pi^{FCM}(y_t^T, r_t, d_t, w_{t-1})$ the unconditional probability of the state vector $(y_t^T, r_t, d_t, w_{t-1})$ under a peg with free capital mobility. Then λ^{FCM} is given by

$$\lambda^{FCM} = \sum_{\{y_t^T, r_t, d_t, w_{t-1}\}} \pi^{FCM}(y_t^T, r_t, d_t, w_{t-1}) \Lambda^{FCM}(y_t^T, r_t, d_t, w_{t-1}),$$

where the sum is over all points in the discretized four-dimensional state space. The calibrated economy yields

$$\lambda^{FCM} = 3.65.$$

This number means that for an economy with a fixed exchange rate, the average welfare gains of switching from free capital mobility to optimal capital controls are large. The representative household living in a peg economy with free capital mobility requires an increase of 3.65 percent in its entire consumption stream to be indifferent between continuing to live in that economy and switching to a peg economy with optimal capital controls.

An important fraction of the welfare cost of free capital mobility is accounted for by the transitional dynamics put in motion as policy switches from free capital mobility to Ramsey optimal capital controls. Recall that the peg economy with free capital mobility is on average substantially more indebted than the peg economy with optimal capital controls. Therefore, the transition from a free capital mobility regime to the optimal capital control regime requires a significant amount of deleveraging. In turn, deleveraging requires households to temporarily cut consumption of traded goods, making it less enticing to switch from free capital mobility to optimal capital controls. To quantify the welfare impact of these transitional dynamics, one can compute the unconditional welfare cost of free capital mobility in a peg economy. Formally, this welfare measure, which we denote λ^{FCMU}, is given by

$$E \sum_{t=0}^{\infty} \beta^t U \left(c_t^{FCM} \left(1 + \frac{\lambda^{FCMU}}{100} \right) \right) = E \sum_{t=0}^{\infty} \beta^t U(c_t^{OCC}),$$

where the unconditional expectation on the left-hand side is computed by using the distribution of the state vector $\{y_t^T, r_t, d_t, w_{t-1}\}$ under free capital mobility and the expectation on the right-hand side by using the distribution under optimal capital controls. Solving for λ^{FCMU} gives

$$\lambda^{FCMU} = 100 \left\{ \left[\frac{E c^{OCC^{1-\sigma}}}{E c^{FCM^{1-\sigma}}} \right]^{\frac{1}{1-\sigma}} - 1 \right\}.$$

This welfare measure is useful for answering the following question. Suppose there are two countries, A and B. Both countries have a fixed exchange-rate regime in place. Country A operates under free capital mobility, whereas country B applies optimal capital controls. Not knowing the state of either economy, by how much would the consumption stream in country A have to be increased for individuals to be indifferent between being born in countries A or B? The calibrated economy implies that

$$\lambda^{FCMU} = 13.0.$$

This number suggests that unconditionally the welfare gains of optimal capital controls are enormous. Much of these gains are explained by the fact that unemployment is much higher in the peg economy with free capital mobility than in the peg economy with optimal capital controls (see Table 10.1).

10.9 Are Observed Capital Controls Prudential?

Until recently, capital controls were generally considered a bad idea. It was argued that they hinder the efficient allocation of capital across countries, thereby reducing growth potential. However, the fact that many of the external crises that occurred in the past two decades began with large waves of capital inflows (e.g., the crises in Southeast Asia, Russia, and Latin America in the late 1990s and early 2000s, and more recently in the periphery of Europe) has made many in academia and policy circles look at capital controls with more benign eyes. The most salient indication of this change of sentiment is given by the IMF, which, after holding a longstanding negative view on capital controls, now accepts them as one more tool for macroeconomic stabilization (see International Monetary Fund 2011).

This change of mind has spurred theoretical work on the cyclical properties of optimal capital controls. The present chapter, for example, has been devoted to showing that the combination of a nominal rigidity and suboptimal monetary policy (e.g., a currency peg) gives rise to an externality that can be dealt with through optimal capital control policy. Another strand of the literature, which we will study in Chapter 12, motivates the use of capital controls in the context of models with financial frictions. In this class of model, international borrowing is limited by collateral constraints. In turn, the value of collateral is assumed to depend on some price (e.g., the relative price of real estate) that individual households take as given. During booms, this price goes up, expanding the value of collateral and inducing households to borrow and spend excessively. Similarly, during recessions the price that determines the value of collateral falls, causing deleveraging and an excessive contraction in aggregate spending. Thus the model features a pecuniary externality that exacerbates booms and busts. In this context, capital controls can be useful as a means to induce households to internalize the pecuniary externality. In both theories summarized above, optimal capital controls are prudential in nature. The policy authority should impose restrictions on international capital flows during booms and relax them during contractions, rather than passively waiting until the crisis occurs to pick up the broken pieces.

A natural question is whether in reality capital controls are procyclical, or prudential, as suggested by theory. Fernández, Rebucci, and Uribe (2015) address this empirical question. Their starting point is a data set of capital control indices constructed by Schindler (2009) covering 91 countries during 1995–2005. The Schindler index is based on information on capital controls provided by the IMF's *Annual Report on Exchange Arrangements and Exchange Restrictions* (AREAER). The index covers six asset categories (equity, bonds, money markets, mutual funds, financial credit, and foreign direct investment) and distinguishes between controls on capital inflows and controls on capital outflows. The index takes on 13 equally spaced values between 0 (no restrictions) and 1 (restrictions on all types of transactions).

Fernández, Rebucci, and Uribe (2015) extend the Schindler data set to cover 1995–2011. They find that capital controls are remarkably stable. The average standard deviation of the capital control index across all countries is 0.07 for inflows and 0.06 for outflows. These standard deviations are tiny. Recall that the index ranges from 0 to 1 in steps of 0.083. The second main finding reported in Fernández, Rebucci, and Uribe is that, contrary to what the recent theories of macro prudential policy suggest, capital controls are virtually acyclical. Specifically, the average correlation between the capital control index and output is -0.01 for inflows and -0.03 for outflows.

Because the second moments reported above are unconditional, they may not fully represent the prudential content of observed capital control policy. The reason is that policymakers may be willing to put the capital control machinery to work only in response to large deviations of aggregate activity from trend. Under this conjecture, unconditional moments may be dominated by normal, relatively small, fluctuations that do not trigger movements in international capital restrictions. Motivated by this possibility, Fernández,

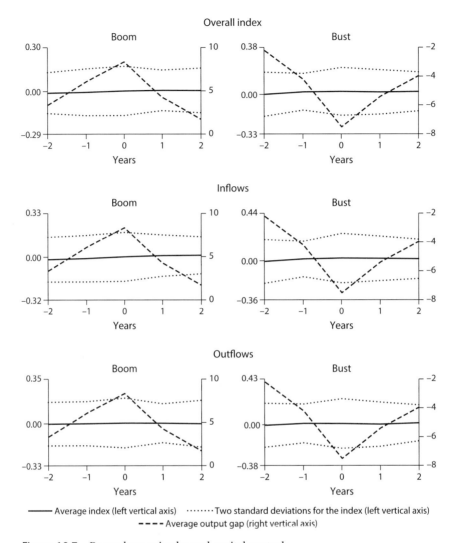

Figure 10.7   Boom-bust episodes and capital controls.

Source: Fernández, Rebucci, and Uribe (2015).
Notes: Booms (busts) are defined as periods longer than or equal to 3 years in which the output gap is always positive (negative). Capital controls and the output gap are expressed in deviations from trend and averaged across episodes. Output gaps are in percent.

Rebucci, and Uribe (2015) examine the behavior of capital controls conditional on the economy experiencing a boom or a bust in aggregate activity. They define a boom (bust) as a situation in which output is above (below) trend for at least 3 consecutive years.

Figure 10.7 displays the average deviation of output (dashed lines) and capital controls (solid lines) from their respective trends across all booms (left column) and busts (right column) in the sample. It also shows (dotted lines) a two-standard-deviation band around the average behavior of capital controls. The main message of the figure is that capital controls are virtually flat during booms or busts in aggregate activity. On average, policymakers do not seem to use capital controls in a consistent fashion (either prudentially or nonprudentially). Fernández, Rebucci, and Uribe (2015) show that this result is robust to disaggregating the data by level of economic development, exchange-rate regime, level of external indebtedness, or asset category. They also find that the result holds if one defines booms and busts not in terms of output but in terms of the current account or the real exchange rate.

Fernández, Rebucci, and Uribe (2015) offer two explanations for the lack of cyclicality observed in actual capital control policy. One possible explanation is that theory is ahead of actual policymaking. Capital controls should be procyclical, but policymakers are not yet aware or fully convinced of the benefits of applying capital controls in a prudential fashion. Under this interpretation, one should expect that as time goes by and the new theories penetrate policymaking spheres, observed capital controls will become more procyclical. The second explanation offered by Fernández, Rebucci, and Uribe is that policymaking may be running ahead of theory. Policy authorities may have information about effects of capital controls that are not incorporated in existing theories. These theoretically unaccounted-for effects may call for the optimal capital control policy to be unresponsive over the business cycle, in line with the empirical evidence. Under this interpretation, one should expect that over time, as academic research assimilates the feedback received from economic practitioners, new models will begin to play down the convenience of applying capital controls in a prudential fashion. Time will tell which, if either, of these two explanations ends up being vindicated.

10.10 Appendix: Equilibrium for $t \geq 1$ in Section 10.4

We wish to show that in the economy analyzed in Section 10.4, in which the nominal exchange rate is constant and capital controls are set in a Ramsey optimal fashion, the equilibrium allocation features constant values for consumption, debt, hours, and wages for $t \geq 1$.

The optimal capital control problem for $t \geq 1$ can be written as:

$$\max_{\{c_t^T, h_t, w_t, d_{t+1}\}_{t=1}^{\infty}} \sum_{t=1}^{\infty} \beta^t [\ln c_t^T + \alpha \ln h_t], \tag{10.27}$$

subject to

$$c_t^T + d_t = y^T + \frac{d_{t+1}}{1+r}, \tag{10.28}$$

$$\alpha \frac{c_t^T}{h_t} = w_t, \tag{10.29}$$

$$h_t \leq 1, \tag{10.30}$$

$$w_t \geq w_{t-1}, \tag{10.31}$$

and

$$d_{t+1} \leq \bar{d}, \tag{10.32}$$

given d_1 and w_0.

Consider next the less restrictive problem of maximizing (10.27) subject to (10.28), (10.30), and (10.32), given d_1. It is straightforward to see that the solution of this problem is $c_t^T = c^{T*} \equiv y^T - \frac{r}{1+r}d_1$, $d_{t+1} = d_1$, and $h_t = 1$ for all $t \geq 1$. For this solution to comply with equilibrium condition (10.29), the wage rate must satisfy $w_t = \alpha c^{T*}$ for all $t \geq 1$. In turn, for equilibrium condition (10.31) to hold, we need

$$\alpha c^{T*} \geq w_0. \tag{10.33}$$

Therefore if this condition holds, the solution to the less constrained problem is also the solution to the original Ramsey problem, and the Ramsey optimal allocation implies constant paths for consumption, debt, hours, and wages, which is what we set out to show.

Now assume that condition (10.33) is not satisfied, that is, assume that

$$\alpha c^{T*} < w_0. \tag{10.34}$$

Use equation (10.29) to eliminate h_t from the utility function and from (10.30). Then we can rewrite the Ramsey problem as

$$\max_{\{c_t^T, w_t, d_{t+1}\}_{t=1}^{\infty}} \sum_{t=1}^{\infty} \beta^t [(1+\alpha) \ln c_t^T + \alpha \ln \alpha - \alpha \ln w_t], \tag{10.35}$$

subject to (10.28), (10.31), (10.32), and

$$w_t \geq \alpha c_t^T, \tag{10.36}$$

given d_1 and w_0. Constraint (10.36) guarantees that h_t is always less than or equal to 1.

Consider the less restrictive problem consisting of dropping (10.36) from the above maximization problem. Since the indirect utility function (10.35) is separable in consumption of tradables and wages and since the only constraint in the less restrictive problem that features wages (i.e., equation (10.31)) contains neither consumption of tradables nor debt, we can separate the less restricted problem into two independent problems. One is

$$\max_{\{c_t^T, d_{t+1}\}_{t=1}^{\infty}} \sum_{t=1}^{\infty} \beta^t [(1+\alpha) \ln c_t^T + \alpha \ln \alpha], \tag{10.37}$$

subject to (10.28) and (10.32). The solution of this problem is $c_t^T = c^{T*}$ and $d_{t+1} = d_1$ for all $t \geq 1$.

The second problem is

$$\max_{\{w_t\}_{t=1}^{\infty}} \sum_{t=1}^{\infty} \beta^t [-\alpha \ln w_t],$$

subject to (10.31), given w_0. The solution to this problem is $w_t = w_0$ for all $t \geq 1$.

It remains to show that the solutions to these two problems satisfy the omitted constraint (10.36). To see that this is indeed the case, note that $w_t = w_0 > \alpha c^{T*} = \alpha c_t^T$, where the inequality follows from (10.34).

We have therefore shown that in the Ramsey equilibrium all variables are constant for $t \geq 1$.

10.11 Exercises

10.1 (Sudden Stops) Consider an open economy that lasts for only two periods, denoted 1 and 2. Households are endowed with 10 units of tradables in period 1 and 13.2 units in period 2 ($y_1^T = 10$ and $y_2^T = 13.2$). The country interest rate is 10 percent, or $r = 0.1$, and the nominal exchange rate, defined as the price of foreign currency in terms of domestic currency, is fixed and equal to 1 in both periods ($\mathcal{E}_1 = \mathcal{E}_2 = 1$). Suppose that the foreign-currency price of tradable goods is constant and equal to one in both periods, and that the law of one price holds for tradable goods in both periods. Nominal wages are downwardly rigid. Specifically, assume that the nominal wage, measured in terms of domestic currency, is subject to the constraint

$$W_t \geq W_{t-1},$$

for $t = 1, 2$, with $W_0 = 8.25$. Suppose the economy starts period 1 with no assets or debts carried over from the past ($d_1 = 0$). Households are subject to the no-Ponzi-game constraint $d_3 \leq 0$.

Suppose that the household's preferences are defined over consumption of tradable and nontradable goods in periods 1 and 2, and are described by the following utility function:

$$\ln C_1^T + \ln C_1^N + \ln C_2^T + \ln C_2^N,$$

where C_i^T and C_i^N denote, respectively, consumption of tradables and nontradables in period $i = 1, 2$. Let p_1 and p_2 denote the relative prices of nontradables in terms of tradables in periods 1 and 2, respectively. Households supply inelastically $\bar{h} = 1$ units of labor to the market each period. Finally, firms produce nontradable goods using labor as the sole input. The production technology is given by

$$y_t^N = h_t^\alpha$$

for $t = 1, 2$ where y_t^N and h_t denote, respectively, nontradable output and hours employed in period $t = 1, 2$. The parameter α is equal to 0.75.

1. Compute the equilibrium levels of consumption of tradables and the trade balance in periods 1 and 2.

2. Compute the equilibrium levels of employment, nontradable output, and the relative price of nontradables in periods 1 and 2.

3. Suppose now that the country interest rate increases to 32 percent. Calculate the equilibrium levels of consumption of tradables, the trade balance, consumption of nontradables, the level of unemployment, and the relative price of nontradables in periods 1 and 2. Provide intuition.

4. Given the situation in the previous question, calculate the minimum devaluation rates in periods 1 and 2 consistent with full employment in both periods. To answer this question, assume that the nominal exchange rate in period 0 was also fixed at unity. Explain.

5. Continue to assume that $W_0 = 8.25$ and that the interest rate is 32 percent. Assume also that the government is not willing to devalue the domestic currency, so that $\mathcal{E}_1 = \mathcal{E}_2 = 1$. Instead, the government chooses to apply capital controls in period 1. Specifically, let $d_2/(1 + r_1)$ denote the amount of funds borrowed in period 1, which generate the obligation to pay d_2 in period 2. Suppose that in period 1 the government imposes a proportional tax/subsidy τ_1 on borrowed funds, so that the amount received by the household is $(1 - \tau_1)d_2/(1 + r_1)$. Suppose that this tax/subsidy is rebated/financed in a lump-sum fashion. Calculate the Ramsey optimal level of τ_1.

10.2 (Labor Subsidies) Modify the model of Section 10.1.1 by assuming that households have preferences of the type given in equation (9.34) in Chapter 9. Show that a labor subsidy at the firm level financed by a proportional income tax at the household level (i.e., the fiscal scheme studied in Section 10.1.1) can support the Pareto optimal allocation.

10.3 (Optimal Lump-Sum Transfers and Hand-to-Mouth Consumers) Consider an economy in which the government can participate in the international financial market but households cannot. Assume further that the only fiscal policy instruments available to the government are lump-sum taxes or transfers. The exchange-rate regime is a currency peg. The government sets the level of external debt and lump-sum taxes or transfers in a Ramsey optimal fashion. All other aspects of the model are as in Section 9.1. Show that the equilibrium real allocation is identical to the one obtained in Section 10.3 under Ramsey optimal capital control policy.

10.4 (Equivalence between Capital Controls and Consumption Taxes) Show that the allocation under Ramsey optimal capital controls characterized in Section 10.3 can be replicated with a Ramsey optimal consumption tax scheme in which the tax rate on next period's consumption is determined in the current period.

10.5 (Interest-Rate Shocks, Capital Controls, and Unemployment) Consider the analytical example of Section 10.4. In that example, in response to a temporary decline in the interest rate from r to $\underline{r}$, the Ramsey optimal capital control policy induces a constant path for tradable consumption and ensures full employment at all times. The Ramsey planners achieve this allocation by imposing capital controls in period 0 to make the effective interest rate perceived by domestic households, $(1 + \underline{r})/(1 - \tau_0^d)$, insensitive to the change in the world interest rate. These results hinge on the assumption $\alpha > r$. Redo the analysis of Section 10.4 assuming that $\alpha < r$. Provide intuition.

11

Policy Credibility and Balance-of-Payments Crises

An overarching theme of the empirical analysis conducted in Chapter 1 is that business cycles in emerging countries are characterized by booms and contractions that are larger in amplitude than those observed in developed countries. One possible explanation for this phenomenon is simply that emerging countries are subject to larger shocks. Chapters 5–8 are devoted to evaluating this hypothesis. A second explanation argues that emerging countries suffer from more pronounced nominal and financial frictions than do advanced economies. This is the subject of Chapters 9 and 10, as well as Chapters 12 and 13. A third explanation is that emerging countries suffer from more severe economic and political distortions than do developed countries. The lack-of-credibility literature, which is the focus of this chapter, pertains to this explanation. It argues that policies that in principle are beneficial to the economy can have unintended consequences if the policymaker who is in charge of implementing them lacks credibility.

The *imperfect-credibility hypothesis* is due to Calvo (1986, 1987a,b). Its basic premise is disarmingly simple. Suppose that the government, possibly with good intentions, announces the permanent removal of a consumption tax. The public, however, interprets the policy as temporary, and therefore believes that it will be abandoned after a certain period. As a result, the public, taking advantage of what it perceives to be a temporarily lower consumption tax, increases spending. In the aggregate, the spending boom is financed by current account deficits. At some point, the expansion ends, either because the tax cut is abandoned or because the public becomes convinced that it is indeed permanent. At this point, spending collapses, and the current account experiences a (possibly sharp) reversal.

The imperfect-credibility theory can be applied to a variety of policy environments. For instance, Calvo (1986) and Calvo and Végh (1993) study the consequences of noncredible inflation-stabilization programs. In this case, the consumption tax takes the form of an *inflation tax*. We study this application in Section 11.4. Calvo (1987a) applies the imperfect-credibility hypothesis to shed light on the dynamics of balance-of-payment crises. In this application, the consumption tax also takes the form of inflation, but the model is explicit about the source of lack of credibility, namely, agents' disbelief in the government's ability to cut the fiscal deficit to a level consistent with low inflation in the long run. Calvo (1987b) applies the lack-of-credibility hypothesis to explain the large current account deficits observed in the aftermath of trade liberalizations in emerging countries. We begin this chapter by studying a consumption tax reform that lacks credibility.

11.1 The Model

The model economy is small and open to international trade in goods and financial assets. There is no uncertainty, and households are endowed with constant quantities of tradable and nontradable goods each period. The government imposes a proportional consumption tax and rebates its proceeds to households in a lump-sum fashion.

11.1.1 Households

The economy is populated by a large number of identical infinitely-lived households with preferences described by the utility function

$$\sum_{t=0}^{\infty} \beta^t [U(c_t^T) + V(c_t^N)], \tag{11.1}$$

where c_t^T denotes consumption of tradable goods in period t, c_t^N denotes consumption of nontraded goods in period t, $\beta \in (0, 1)$ denotes a subjective discount factor, and $U(\cdot)$ and $V(\cdot)$ denote period subutility functions assumed to be increasing and strictly concave. Each period, households receive constant endowments of exportable and nontraded goods, denoted by y^T and y^N, respectively.

Households start period t with a stock of debt, d_{t-1}^h, carried over from the previous period. Debt is denominated in units of tradable goods and carries a constant interest rate $r > 0$. In addition, households receive a lump-sum transfer of s_t units of tradable goods from the government each period. Consumption is subject to a proportional tax at the rate τ_t. The household's sequential budget constraint is then given by

$$d_t^h - (1+r)d_{t-1}^h - y^T - p_t y^N - s_t + (1+\tau_t)(c_t^T + p_t c_t^N), \tag{11.2}$$

where p_t denotes the relative price of nontradables in terms of tradables, or the real exchange rate. To prevent Ponzi games, households are subject to the following borrowing constraint:

$$\lim_{j \to \infty} \frac{d_{t+j}^h}{(1+r)^j} \leq 0.$$

The fact that the period utility function is increasing implies that in the optimal plan the no-Ponzi-game constraint must hold with equality. Then combining the sequential budget constraint and the no-Ponzi-game constraint holding with equality yields the following intertemporal budget constraint:

$$(1+r)d_{-1}^h = \sum_{t=0}^{\infty} \left(\frac{1}{1+r}\right)^t [y^T + p_t y^N + s_t - (1+\tau_t)(c_t^T + p_t c_t^N)].$$

To avoid inessential long-run dynamics, assume that the subjective and market discount rates are identical, that is,

$$\beta = \frac{1}{1+r}.$$

The consumer's problem consists of choosing sequences $\{c_t^T, c_t^N\}_{t=0}^{\infty}$ to maximize her lifetime utility function subject to the above intertemporal budget constraint. Letting λ_0 denote the Lagrange multiplier associated with the intertemporal budget constraint, the optimality conditions associated with this problem are the intertemporal budget constraint itself,

$$U'(c_t^T) = \lambda_0(1 + \tau_t), \tag{11.3}$$

and

$$p_t = \frac{V'(c_t^N)}{U'(c_t^T)}. \tag{11.4}$$

The first efficiency condition states that the consumption tax rate introduces a wedge between the marginal utility of wealth, λ_0, and the marginal utility of consumption, $U'(c_t^T)$. This implies that anticipated time variations in the consumption tax distort the intertemporal allocation of consumption. In particular, periods with high expected tax rates are associated with relatively low consumption, and periods with low expected tax rates are associated with relatively high consumption. The second efficiency condition shows that the tax rate does not distort the intratemporal allocation of consumption of tradables and nontradables. This is because both types of expenditures are taxed at the same rate each period. The multiplier λ_0 is determined in period 0 and is constant from that period on, as long as households are not surprised by new information.

11.1.2 The Government

Like households, the government can borrow or lend in the international financial market at the interest rate r. The government's sources of income are tax revenues, $\tau_t(c_t^T + p_t c_t^N)$, and the issuance of new public debt, $d_t^g - d_{t-1}^g$. Government spending consists of interest payments, rd_{t-1}^g, and lump-sum transfers to households, s_t. The sequential budget constraint of the government is then given by

$$d_t^g = (1+r)d_{t-1}^g - \tau_t(c_t^T + p_t c_t^N) + s_t. \tag{11.5}$$

The expression $s_t - \tau_t(c_t^T + p_t c_t^N)$ represents the primary fiscal deficit in period t, and $s_t + rd_{t-1}^g - \tau_t(c_t^T + p_t c_t^N)$ represents the secondary fiscal deficit. We assume that fiscal policy is such that in the long run, the government's debt position does not grow in absolute value at a rate larger than the interest rate. That is, we assume that the fiscal policy ensures that

$$\lim_{t \to \infty} \frac{d_t^g}{(1+r)^t} = 0.$$

This condition together with the government's sequential budget constraint implies the intertemporal government budget constraint:

$$(1+r)d_{-1}^g = \sum_{t=0}^{\infty} \left(\frac{1}{1+r}\right)^t [\tau_t(c_t^T + p_t c_t^N) - s_t].$$

This constraint states that the present discounted value of current and future primary fiscal surpluses must be large enough to cover the government's initial debt position.

11.1.3 Equilibrium

In equilibrium, the market for nontradable goods must clear, that is,

$$y^N = c_t^N,$$

which implies that consumption of nontradables is constant in equilibrium. Using this market-clearing condition to eliminate c_t^N from efficiency condition (11.4) yields

$$p_t = \frac{V'(y^N)}{U'(c_t^T)}. \tag{11.6}$$

This expression says that the relative price of nontradables mimics the behavior of the equilibrium consumption of tradables. The intuition behind this result is familiar from Chapter 8. Given the relative price p_t, an increase in the desired consumption of tradables, c_t^T, will always be accompanied by a corresponding desired increase in the consumption of nontradables, since both goods are normal. Because the supply of nontradables is fixed, the relative price of nontradables must increase to prevent excess demand for this type of good.

Let $d_t \equiv d_t^h + d_t^g$ denote the country's consolidated net foreign debt position. Then combining the sequential budget constraints of the household and the government (equations (11.2) and (11.5), respectively) and the market clearing condition in the nontraded sector ($y^N = c_t^N$) yields the following sequential resource constraint of the economy:

$$d_t = (1+r)d_{t-1} - y^T + c_t^T. \tag{11.7}$$

Similarly, combining the intertemporal budget constraints of the household and the government with the market-clearing condition in the nontraded sector yields the intertemporal economy-wide resource constraint:

$$(1+r)d_{-1} = \sum_{t=0}^{\infty} \left(\frac{1}{1+r}\right)^t (y^T - c_t^T). \tag{11.8}$$

According to this expression, the present discounted value of the stream of current and future trade surpluses must equal the country's initial net debt position.

A competitive equilibrium is a scalar λ_0 and sequences $\{c_t^T, p_t, d_t\}_{t=0}^{\infty}$ satisfying (11.3) and (11.6)–(11.8), given the initial debt position d_{-1} and a sequence of tax rates $\{\tau_t\}_{t=0}^{\infty}$ specified by the government.

The focus of our analysis is to compare the economic effects of tax reforms under different degrees of credibility. We begin with the analysis of a credible tax reform.

11.2 A Credible Tax Reform

Suppose that prior to period 0, the consumption tax rate was equal to τ^H and was expected to remain at that value forever. Further, assume that the economy was in a steady state, with a constant level of debt. That is, $d_t = d_{-1}$, for $t < 0$. Then the sequential resource constraint (11.7) implies that

$$c^T_{-1} = y^T - rd_{-1}. \tag{11.9}$$

Suppose that in period 0 the government unexpectedly implements a permanent tax reform consisting of lowering τ_t from its past level, τ^H, to a lower level, $\tau^L < \tau^H$. Formally the time path of τ_t is given by

$$\tau_t = \tau^L, \quad \text{for } t \geq 0.$$

It follows directly from the efficiency condition (11.3) that in this case consumption of tradables is constant from period 0 on (recall that λ_0 is constant for $t \geq 0$). The intuition behind this result is that because consumption of tradables is taxed at the same rate in all periods, households have no incentive to substitute expenditure intertemporally.

Taking into account that consumption of tradables is constant from period 0 on, the intertemporal resource constraint (11.8) implies that

$$c^T_t = y^T - rd_{-1} = c^T_{-1},$$

for $t \geq 0$. This means that the credible tax reform does not affect the time path of tradable consumption even between periods -1 and 0.

Importantly, the equilibrium level of consumption is independent of the level at which the government sets the tax rate. Any credible, permanent tax cut implemented unexpectedly at time 0 has no effect on equilibrium consumption.

The fact that consumption of tradables is unaffected by the tax reform along with the sequential resource constraint (11.7) implies that debt is also unaffected by the credible tax reform, that is,

$$d_t = d_{-1},$$

for all $t \geq 0$. Similarly, the trade balance, $tb_t \equiv y^T - c^T_t$; the current account, $ca_t \equiv tb_t - rd_{t-1}$; and the real exchange rate, p_t, are all unaffected by the permanent and credible tax reform.

We conclude that in the present economy, an unexpected credible tax reform is neutral in the sense that it leaves the real allocation unchanged.

11.3 A Noncredible Tax Reform

The type of noncredible tax reform we have in mind is one in which in period 0 the government announces a permanent tax cut from τ^H to τ^L, but the public (correctly or incorrectly) believes that the tax reform will be abandoned in period $T > 0$ and the tax rate will return to τ^H.

As a stepping stone, we begin by characterizing equilibrium under a credible but temporary tax reform. We will then show that the resulting equilibrium is identical to the one associated with a noncredible tax reform. Accordingly, assume that in period 0 the government unexpectedly announces and implements a temporary tax cut. The announcement specifies that the consumption tax rate is reduced from τ^H to τ^L between periods 0 and $T - 1$, and is permanently increased back to τ^H in period T. Formally, the announced path of τ_t is given by

$$\tau_t = \begin{cases} \tau^L & \text{for } 0 \leq t \leq T - 1 \\ \tau^H & \text{for } t \geq T, \end{cases} \tag{11.10}$$

with $\tau^L < \tau^H$. Here $T > 0$ denotes the duration of the tax reform.

It is clear from equation (11.3) that consumption of tradables is constant over the periods $0 \leq t \leq T - 1$ and $t \geq T$. We can therefore write

$$c_t^T = \begin{cases} c^1 & \text{for } 0 \leq t \leq T - 1 \\ c^2 & \text{for } t \geq T, \end{cases} \tag{11.11}$$

where c^1 and c^2 are two scalars determined endogenously. Because the period subutility function $U(\cdot)$ is concave, it follows from the efficiency condition (11.3) that c^1 is greater than c^2. Intuitively, households substitute consumption in the low-tax period for consumption in the high-tax period. We can then write

$$c^1 = (1 + \kappa)c^2,$$

where κ is a positive scalar determined endogenously. In particular, κ is an increasing function of the intertemporal tax distortion $(1 + \tau^H)/(1 + \tau^L)$. For example, if the period subutility function $U(\cdot)$ is of the CRRA form, $U(c) = c^{1-\sigma}/(1 - \sigma)$, then from equation (11.3) we have that $1 + \kappa = \left(\frac{1+\tau^H}{1+\tau^L}\right)^{1/\sigma}$. Of course, the traded consumption stream must respect the intertemporal resource constraint (11.8). This restriction implies the following relationship between c^1 and c^2:

$$y^T - rd_{-1} = (1 - \beta^T)c^1 + \beta^T c^2, \tag{11.12}$$

where we have used the assumption that $1/(1 + r) = \beta$. By equation (11.9), the left-hand side of equation (11.12) is equal to c_{-1}^T, which is also equal to the level of traded consumption that results under the credible permanent tax reform discussed in Section 11.2. We can then write equation (11.12) as

$$c_{-1}^T = (1 - \beta^T)c^1 + \beta^T c^2.$$

Because $\beta^T \in (0, 1)$, it follows from this expression that c_{-1}^T is a weighted average of c^1 and c^2. We therefore have that

$$c^1 > c_{-1}^T > c^2.$$

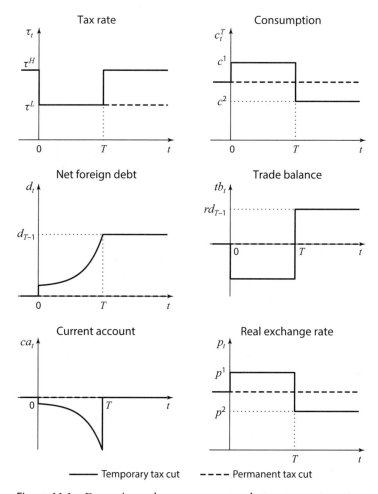

Figure 11.1 Dynamics under a permanent and a temporary tax cut.

This means that the announcement of the temporary tax reform causes tradable consumption to rise to c^1 at time 0, stay at that elevated level until period $T - 1$, and then fall in period T to a new long-run level c^2, which is lower than the pre-reform level of consumption. The top-right panel of Figure 11.1 depicts with a solid line the dynamics of tradable consumption under the temporary tax cut and with a dashed line the dynamics under a permanent tax cut. The temporary tax cut generates a boom in aggregate spending that ends in a contraction larger than the boom itself. This is because the boom is financed with external debt, which results in higher interest payments from period T on.

Figure 11.1 depicts the behavior of the trade balance, the current account, the net foreign debt position, and the real exchange rate induced by the temporary tax cut. The figure assumes, without loss of generality, that the initial net debt position is nil ($d_{-1} = 0$). In the pre-reform equilibrium, $t < 0$, agents expect the tax rate to be constant forever. Thus we have that before the tax reform, traded consumption equals the traded endowment,

$c^T_{-1} = y^T$, the trade balance is zero, $tb_{-1} = y^T - c^T_{-1} = 0$, and so is the current account, $ca_{-1} = y^T - c^T_{-1} - rd_{-2} = 0$ (since $d_{-2} = d_{-1} = 0$). Recalling that $c^1 > c^T_{-1} = y^T > c^2$, we have that for $t \geq 0$, the path of the trade balance is given by

$$tb_t = \begin{cases} y^T - c^1 < 0 & \text{for } 0 \leq t < T \\ y^T - c^2 > 0 & \text{for } t \geq T. \end{cases}$$

Thus the initial consumption boom causes a trade balance deficit that lasts for the duration of the tax cut. When the policy is abandoned, consumption falls, and the trade balance displays a sharp reversal from deficit to surplus. This trade surplus equals rd_{T-1} and is large enough to service the external debt.

The evolution of external debt is given by $d_t = (1 + r)d_{t-1} + c^1 - y^T$, for $0 \leq t < T$. Since d_{-1} is assumed to be zero, we have that

$$d_t = (c^1 - y^T) \sum_{j=0}^{t} (1 + r)^j > 0,$$

for $0 \leq t < T$. This expression states that the foreign debt position is positive and increasing over time at an increasing rate until period T. Recalling that the current account equals the change in debt, $ca_t = -(d_t - d_{t-1})$, we have that the equilibrium path of the current account, while the tax cut lasts, is given by

$$ca_t = (y^T - c^1)(1 + r)^t < 0,$$

for $0 \leq t < T$. According to this expression, the current account is negative and deteriorates exponentially between periods 0 and T. The paths of the current account and the debt position are unsustainable in the long run. Therefore, in period T the household cuts traded consumption to a point at which external debt stops growing and the current account experiences a sudden improvement to a balanced position. Formally, we have

$$d_t = d_{T-1}; \quad t \geq T,$$

and

$$ca_t = 0; \quad t \geq T.$$

During the boom, the real exchange rate appreciates (p_t increases). This effect is evident from equilibrium condition (11.6) and the fact that tradable consumption booms during the tax cut. This real exchange-rate appreciation is necessary to fend off the increased demand for nontradables triggered by the temporary tax cut. In period T, aggregate demand collapses and so does the relative price of nontradables.

11.3.1 Lack of Credibility and Overborrowing

The present model is one of overborrowing in the sense that it delivers an initial phase ($0 \leq t < T$) in which households embark in a socially inefficient spending spree, with external debt growing at an increasing rate and the current account displaying widening imbalances. Overborrowing ends in a sudden stop in period T, with a reversal of the current account and a sharp contraction in domestic absorption.

To see that the consumption boom induced by the temporary tax cut is socially inefficient, note that the path of traded consumption must have the same present discounted value whether the tax cut is temporary or permanent. However, the former is less smooth. Because the utility function of households is concave, it must be the case that the temporary tax cut results in lower welfare than the permanent one. To show this more formally, consider the problem of a benevolent social planner trying to design a tax policy that maximizes welfare subject to the constraint that the policy must belong to the family of temporary policies defined in (11.10). The planner's objective function is to choose scalars c^1 and c^2 to maximize the household's lifetime utility function evaluated at the consumption path given in (11.11), subject to the lifetime resource constraint (11.12). That is, the planner's problem is[1]

$$\max_{c^1, c^2} \left[(1 - \beta^T)U(c^1) + \beta^T U(c^2) \right]$$

subject to

$$y^T - rd_{-1} = (1 - \beta^T)c^1 + \beta^T c^2,$$

given T and d_{-1}. Because the period subutility function $U(\cdot)$ is assumed to be strictly concave, the objective function is strictly concave in c^1 and c^2. Also, because the constraint is linear in c^1 and c^2, it describes a convex set of feasible pairs (c^1, c^2). It follows that the first-order conditions of this problem are necessary and sufficient for a maximum. These conditions are

$$U'(c^1) = \mu,$$

and

$$U'(c^2) = \mu,$$

where μ denotes the Lagrange multiplier on the constraint. Clearly the solution to this problem is $c^1 = c^2$. It then follows immediately from (11.3) that the set of taxes that supports the solution to the planner's problem satisfies $\tau^L = \tau^H$. Consequently, any temporary tax cut ($\tau^L < \tau^H$) is welfare dominated by a permanent tax change. It is in this precise sense that we say that the increase in external debt that finances the consumption boom after a temporary tax cut represents overborrowing.

11.3.2 Equivalence of Imperfect Credibility and Temporariness

In the present model, the terms *temporariness* and *imperfect credibility* are equivalent in a specific sense. To illustrate this idea, suppose that instead of announcing a temporary

---

1. We omit the multiplicative factor $(1 - \beta)^{-1}$ from the objective function because it is a constant and therefore does not affect the solution. The same goes for the term $V(y^N)$.

tax cut, in period 0 the government announces a permanent tax cut but that the public disbelieves the announcement. Specifically, the government announces a permanent tax reduction from τ^H to τ^L, but the public believes that the tax rate will return to τ^H in period T. The dynamics between periods 0 and $T - 1$ are identical to the ones associated with the temporary tax reform. This is because consumption decisions during the period $0 \leq t < T$ are based on expectations of a future tax increase regardless of whether the government explicitly announces the increase or the public believes it will take place. Suppose now that in period T, contrary to the public's expectations, the government maintains the tax reform ($\tau_t = \tau^L$ for $t \geq T$), and moreover that the policy becomes credible to the public. From the point of view of period T, the situation is one in which the tax policy is constant forever and fully credible. It follows from our analysis of a credible permanent tax cut in Section 11.2 that tradable consumption must be constant from $t = T$ on. A constant level of tradable consumption can only be sustained by a constant level of debt. To see this, note that the difference equation $d_t = (1 + r)d_{t-1} - y^T + c^T$, for $t \geq T$, implies a path of d_t that converges $\pm\infty$ at a rate larger than r (implying a violation of the no-Ponzi-game constraint in the first case and a suboptimal accumulation of wealth in the second) unless c^T is such that $(1 + r)d_{T-1} - y^T + c^T$ equals d_{T-1}. That is, a constant path of traded consumption is sustainable over time only if the external debt position is also constant over time. Thus traded consumption must satisfy $d_{T-1} = (1 + r)d_{T-1} - y^T + c^T$, where c^T is the level of consumption prevailing for $t \geq T$. Comparing this expression with equation (11.12), it follows that c^T must equal c^2, the equilibrium level of tradable consumption associated with a credible but temporary tax cut over the period $t \geq T$. This result establishes that the equilibrium path of tradable consumption is identical whether the tax reform is credible but temporary or permanent but noncredible.

11.4 Lack of Credibility and Exchange-Rate Policy

Thus far we have studied the macroeconomic effects of noncredible policy in the context of a fiscal reform. However, the same principles apply in the context of monetary policy. Credibility of monetary policy is of particular relevance for high-inflation countries trying to stabilize price growth. For example, a central element of successful inflation stabilization policies is fiscal sustainability. Doubts on the part of the public regarding the ability of the government to reduce fiscal deficits can give rise to expectations that the disinflation program is doomed to be abandoned.

Calvo (1986) uses this idea to interpret a curious property of exchange-rate-based inflation-stabilization programs in emerging countries (e.g., those implemented through-out Latin America in the 1980s and 1990s). Specifically, these disinflation episodes appear to violate the conventional wisdom according to which quick and sharp reductions in the rate of inflation come at the cost of reduced economic activity. Indeed, an empirical reg-ularity associated with exchange-rate-based inflation-stabilization programs is that their initial phase is characterized by a boom in aggregate activity, trade balance deficits, real exchange-rate appreciation, and a surge in capital inflows. Figure 11.2 illustrates these em-pirical regularities for the case of the Argentine disinflation program of 1991. This program,

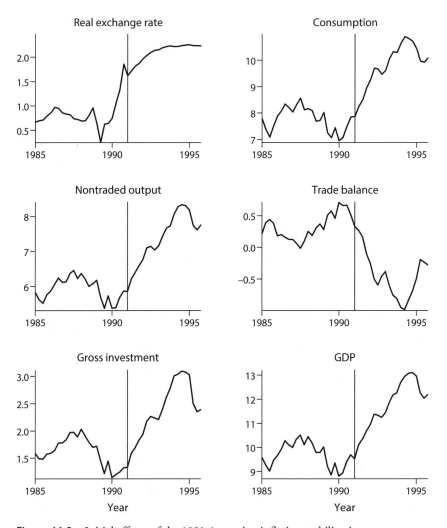

Figure 11.2 Initial effects of the 1991 Argentine inflation stabilization program.

Source: Uribe (2002).

Notes: All variables except for the real exchange rate are expressed in millions of Argentine pesos of 1986 and are seasonally adjusted. Nontraded output is defined as value added in the services sector. The real exchange rate is defined as the CPI-adjusted exchange rate between the Argentine peso and the U.S. dollar. An increase in this variable corresponds to a real appreciation (Argentina becoming more expensive relative to the United States).

known as the Convertibility Plan, swiftly eliminated high inflation by pegging the Argentine peso to the U.S. dollar.

According to the lack-of-credibility hypothesis, the boom following the implementation of an inflation stabilization plan is due to the public's expectation that low inflation is only temporary and that high inflation will eventually resume. Because money is used in transactions, inflation plays the role of a tax on consumption purchases. A temporary reduction in inflation therefore induces agents to substitute current consumption for future consumption, generating a boom in domestic absorption. Next we spell out this intuition more formally.

11.4.1 A Cash-in-Advance Economy

Consider a model economy like the one analyzed thus far. Suppose for simplicity that the consumption tax is nil ($\tau_t = 0$ for all t). Instead assume that consumption expenditure is subject to a *cash-in-advance constraint* of the form

$$M_t \geq \alpha (P_t^T c_t^T + P_t^N c_t^N),$$

where M_t denotes nominal money holdings, P_t^T is the nominal price of tradables, P_t^N is the nominal price of nontradables, and $\alpha > 0$ is a scalar. According to this expression, households must hold at least a fraction α of their nominal spending in the form of domestic money (pesos, say). This model of the demand for money stresses its role as a medium of exchange. The model was first introduced by Clower (1967) and later popularized by Lucas (1980).

The sequential budget constraint of the household is given by

$$P_t^T d_t^h = P_t^T (1+r) d_{t-1}^h - P_t^T y^T - P_t^N y^N - P_t^T s_t$$
$$+ P_t^T c_t^T + P_t^N c_t^N + M_t - M_{t-1}. \qquad (11.13)$$

Suppose that the law of one price holds for tradable goods. That is, assume that $P_t^T = \mathcal{E}_t P_t^{T*}$, where $\mathcal{E}_t$ denotes the nominal exchange rate defined as the domestic-currency price of one unit of foreign currency (pesos per dollar), and P_t^{T*} denotes the foreign price of the tradable good denominated in foreign currency. Assume for simplicity that P_t^{T*} is constant and normalized to unity. Then $P_t^T = \mathcal{E}_t$. Let $m_t \equiv M_t / P_t^T$ denote real money balances measured in units of tradable goods and $p_t \equiv P_t^N / P_t^T$ denote, as before, the relative price of nontradables in terms of tradables. Then the sequential budget constraint and cash-in-advance constraint can be written, respectively, as

$$d_t^h = (1+r) d_{t-1}^h - y^T - p_t y^N - s_t + c_t^T + p_t c_t^N + m_t - \frac{m_{t-1}}{\epsilon_t}, \qquad (11.14)$$

and

$$m_t \geq \alpha (c_t^T + p_t c_t^N), \qquad (11.15)$$

where

$$\epsilon_t \equiv \frac{\mathcal{E}_t}{\mathcal{E}_{t-1}}$$

denotes the gross nominal devaluation rate in period t. The household maximizes the lifetime utility function (11.1) subject to the above two constraints and to a no-Ponzi-game constraint. Let $\beta^t \lambda_t$ and $\beta^t \lambda_t \eta_t$ denote the Lagrange multipliers associated with the sequential budget constraint (11.14) and the cash-in-advance constraint (11.15), respectively. Then the first-order conditions with respect to d_t^h, c_t^T, c_t^N, and m_t are, respectively,

$$\lambda_t = \beta(1+r)\lambda_{t+1}, \tag{11.16}$$

$$U'(c_t^T) = \lambda_t(1+\alpha\eta_t), \tag{11.17}$$

$$V'(c_t^N) = \lambda_t p_t(1+\alpha\eta_t), \tag{11.18}$$

and

$$\lambda_t = \beta\frac{\lambda_{t+1}}{\epsilon_{t+1}} + \eta_t\lambda_t, \tag{11.19}$$

with

$$\eta_t \geq 0, \quad \text{and} \quad \eta_t\left[m_t - \alpha(c_t^T + p_t c_t^N)\right] = 0. \tag{11.20}$$

As before, we assume that $\beta(1+r) = 1$. Then, optimality condition (11.16) implies that λ_t is constant over time, or $\lambda_t = \lambda_0 > 0$ for all $t \geq 0$. The Lagrange multiplier η_t reflects the shadow price of real money balances. Optimality condition (11.17) shows that the need to use money for consumption purchases introduces a wedge between the marginal utility of consumption, $U'(c_t^T)$, and the marginal utility of wealth, λ_t. The higher is the shadow price of liquidity, the larger this wedge will be.

The shadow price η_t also appears in the first-order condition with respect to m_t, equation (11.19). The left-hand side of this expression says that holding one additional unit of real balances requires sacrificing one unit of tradable consumption, which reduces utility by λ_t. The right-hand side has two terms. The first term says that the extra unit of money held from t to $t+1$ is worth $1/\epsilon_{t+1}$ units of tradable consumption in period $t+1$, or $\beta\lambda_{t+1}/\epsilon_{t+1}$ utils. The second term, $\lambda_t\eta_t$, is the value of the liquidity services provided by the additional unit of real money. At the optimum, the cost shown on the left-hand side must equal the benefits shown on the right-hand side.

The ratio ϵ_{t+1}/β represents the gross interest rate between periods t and $t+1$ on domestic-currency denominated bonds. That is, if we let i_t denote the nominal interest rate, we have that $1 + i_t = \epsilon_{t+1}/\beta$.[2] The higher is the expected rate of depreciation of the domestic currency, the higher the nominal interest rate will be. We assume that the path of ϵ_t is such that the nominal interest rate is always strictly positive. Then equation (11.19) implies that η_t is strictly positive. With $\eta_t > 0$, it follows from condition (11.20) that the cash-in-advance constraint holds with equality. This is intuitive, because i_t represents the opportunity cost of holding money and if it is positive, then households will hold the minimum amount of money necessary to carry out consumption purchases.

---

2. To show this formally, assume that, in addition to foreign bonds, the household has access to domestic currency bonds that pay the nominal interest rate i_t when held from t to $t+1$. Modify the sequential budget constraint, equation (11.13), accordingly and derive the optimality condition associated with this type of bond.

We can then reduce the first-order conditions (11.16)–(11.20) to

$$U'(c_t^T) = \lambda_0 \left[1 + \alpha \left(1 - \frac{\beta}{\epsilon_{t+1}} \right) \right], \tag{11.21}$$

and

$$p_t = \frac{V'(c_t^N)}{U'(c_t^T)}.$$

These conditions are identical to (11.3) and (11.4) of the tax-reform economy, with $\alpha(1 - \beta/\epsilon_{t+1})$ taking the place of τ_t. In other words, the expected devaluation rate plays the role of a consumption tax. This is because ϵ_{t+1} is the rate at which real money holdings in period t lose value between periods t and $t + 1$, and because real money holdings in period t are necessary to purchase consumption goods in that period. Unlike the case of the consumption tax, what matters for the determination of current consumption is not the current devaluation rate, ϵ_t, but the future expected devaluation rate, ϵ_{t+1}. The reason is that period-t consumption is purchased with money balances that are held from period t to $t + 1$, and over this time interval their real value erodes at the rate ϵ_{t+1}. Notice also that the monetary friction does not affect the intratemporal allocation of expenditure across traded and nontraded goods. This is because both types of consumption are subject to the same cash-in-advance constraint.

All other equilibrium conditions of the model are as in the tax-reform economy. We can then define a competitive equilibrium in the cash-in-advance economy as a scalar λ_0 and sequences $\{c_t^T, p_t, d_t\}_{t=0}^{\infty}$ satisfying (11.6)–(11.8) and (11.21), given the initial debt position d_{-1} and a sequence of devaluation rates $\{\epsilon_t\}_{t=1}^{\infty}$ specified by the monetary authority.

The equilibrium sequence of real balances, m_t, can then be readily obtained by evaluating the cash-in-advance constraint (11.15) holding with equality at the equilibrium values of c_t^T, p_t, and $c_t^N = y^N$. Similarly, one could derive the equilibrium path of inflation. In this economy, households consume two types of goods: tradable and nontradable goods. Therefore the consumer price level is some average of the nominal prices of these two goods. It follows that consumer price inflation is some weighted average of inflation of tradables and inflation of nontradables. Inflation of tradables is given by the growth rate of P_t^T, which, by the law of one price and the assumption that P_t^{T*} is constant, is equal to $\epsilon_t - 1$. Inflation of nontradables is given by the growth rate of $P_t^N = p_t P_t^T$. It follows that up to changes in the relative price of nontradables, the inflation rate of nontradables also equals $\epsilon_t - 1$. Thus in the present economy, except in periods in which the relative price p_t changes, the inflation rate is equal to $\epsilon_t - 1$.

11.4.2 A Noncredible Exchange-Rate-Based Inflation-Stabilization Program

Consider now the effect of an imperfectly credible *exchange-rate-based inflation-stabilization program*. Specifically, suppose that in period 0, the central bank unexpectedly announces that it will permanently reduce the devaluation rate from ϵ^H to $\epsilon^L < \epsilon^H$. The public, however, disbelieves this announcement and instead is convinced that the devaluation rate will be low only until period T and will revert to ϵ^H thereafter. Formally, private agents believe that

$$\epsilon_t = \begin{cases} \epsilon^L & \text{for } 0 \le t \le T \\ \epsilon^H & \text{for } t > T. \end{cases} \tag{11.22}$$

As in the case of the tax-reform economy, we can characterize the equilibrium under imperfect credibility by assuming that the government announces a credible but temporary exchange-rate-based stabilization program in which ϵ_t follows the path given in equation (11.22) with certainty. The equilibrium dynamics triggered by the noncredible exchange-rate-based inflation-stabilization program are identical to those of the noncredible tax reform analyzed in Section 11.3. Thus the behavior of consumption, the trade balance, the current account, external debt, and the real exchange rate are the same as that depicted in Figure 11.1. The implied dynamics have much in common with those observed in Argentina in the early 1990s following the announcement of the Convertibility Plan (see Figure 11.2). Consumption booms, the trade balance deteriorates, and the real exchange rate appreciates.

11.5 Balance-of-Payments Crises

Thus far we have studied a noncredible exchange-rate-based inflation-stabilization program in which both the duration of the program, T, and the devaluation rate after its demise, ϵ^H, are exogenously given. Here we endogenize these two variables. The idea is to assume that the government runs a constant *primary fiscal deficit*. Under the stabilization program seignorage revenue is insufficient to finance the fiscal deficit. As a result, the government is forced to finance part of the deficit by drawing down foreign reserves. Because reserves are finite, the stabilization program is unsustainable. At some point, the government runs out of foreign reserves and must abandon the stabilization program. After the demise of the program, the fiscal deficit is financed via seignorage revenue, which requires a switch to a higher rate of devaluation. This switch causes a discrete fall in the demand for domestic currency, which makes private households run to the central bank to exchange local currency for foreign reserves. At this point, the central bank loses a discrete amount of its stock of foreign reserves. This currency run is known as a *balance-of-payments* (BOP) *crisis* and was first formalized by Krugman (1979).[3]

To facilitate the analysis, we make several modifications to the model studied in previous sections. First, we treat time as continuous. This assumption facilitates the characterization of the date at which the economy suffers the balance of payments crisis. Second, we assume that all goods are internationally traded. Extending the analysis to allow for non-tradable goods as in previous sections of this chapter is straightforward. Third, we replace the assumption of a cash-in-advance constraint with the assumption that money enters in the utility function. Finally, we assume that preferences are separable in consumption and

---

3. Krugman's analysis is an adaptation of a model of gold runs due to Salant and Henderson (1978).

real money balances. This last assumption simplifies the characterization of the equilibrium dynamics of aggregate spending in the run-up to the crisis.[4] The money-in-the-utility function model is due to Sidrauski (1967).

Specifically, consider an economy populated by a continuum of identical households with preferences defined over consumption of tradable goods and real money balances and described by the utility function

$$\int_0^\infty e^{-\rho t}[u(c_t^T) + v(m_t)]dt, \tag{11.23}$$

where, as before, c_t^T denotes consumption of tradables at time t, $m_t \equiv M_t/P_t^T$ denotes real money balances at time t, M_t denotes nominal money balances held at time t, and P_t^T denotes the nominal price of tradables at time t. The parameter $\rho > 0$ is a subjective discount factor, and $u(\cdot)$ and $v(\cdot)$ are increasing and concave instant subutility functions. Households are endowed with a constant stream of consumption goods (denoted by y^T) and receive a constant real transfer (denoted by g) from the government. Households can borrow or lend in world financial markets in a foreign-currency denominated bond that pays the constant interest rate r. The representative household's flow budget constraint is given by

$$\dot{d}_t \mathcal{E}_t = r d_t \mathcal{E}_t + P_t^T c_t^T + \dot{M}_t - P_t^T y^T - P_t^T g,$$

where d_t denotes foreign-currency denominated debt; and $\mathcal{E}_t$ denotes the nominal exchange rate, defined, as before, as the domestic-currency price of one unit of foreign currency. A dot on a variable denotes its time derivative. According to this constraint, the sources of debt are interest payments, $r d_t \mathcal{E}_t$; consumption, $+P_t^T c_t^T$; and the accumulation of money balances, $\dot{M}_t$. The value of the endowment, worth $-P_t^T y^T$, and the government transfer, worth $P_t^T g$, constitute the sources of wealth.

We continue to assume that the law of one price holds, that is, $P_t^T = \mathcal{E}_t P_t^{T*}$, where P_t^{T*} denotes the world price of the consumption good and is denominated in units of foreign currency. For simplicity assume that P_t^{T*} is constant and normalized to unity, so that $P_t^T = \mathcal{E}_t$. Let

$$\epsilon_t \equiv \frac{\dot{\mathcal{E}}_t}{\mathcal{E}_t}$$

denote the rate of depreciation, or rate of devaluation, of the local currency at time t. Then noting that

$$\frac{\dot{M}_t}{\mathcal{E}_t} = \dot{m}_t + \epsilon_t m_t,$$

we can write the flow budget constraint as

$$\dot{d}_t = r d_t + c_t^T + \dot{m}_t + \epsilon_t m_t - y^T - g. \tag{11.24}$$

---

4. Calvo (1987a) characterizes balance-of-payments crises in the context of a continuous-time version of the cash-in-advance economy of Section 11.4.

To avoid Ponzi-type games, assume that the household faces a terminal borrowing limit of the form $\lim_{t \to \infty} \exp(-\rho t) d_t \leq 0$.

The household chooses paths $\{c_t^T, m_t, d_t\}$ to maximize its lifetime utility function (11.23) subject to the flow budget constraint (11.24) and the no-Ponzi-game constraint. The optimality conditions associated with the household's problem are

$$\frac{u''(c_t^T)}{u'(c_t^T)} \dot{c}_t^T = \rho - r,$$

and

$$v'(m_t) = u'(c_t^T)(r + \epsilon_t).$$

The appendix to this chapter derives these conditions in detail. To avoid inessential dynamics in consumption, we assume that the subjective discount factor equals the interest rate, $\rho = r$. Then the first optimality condition implies that $\dot{c}_t^T = 0$, that is, consumption is constant over time. We can then write

$$c_t^T = c^T,$$

where c^T is a constant determined endogenously. The second optimality condition is a demand for money. It states that m_t depends negatively on the nominal interest rate, $r + \epsilon_t$, and positively on consumption, c_t^T. Solving for m_t and using the fact that $c_t^T = c^T$, we can write

$$m_t = L(\epsilon_t, c^T),$$

where the function $L(\cdot, \cdot)$ is decreasing in the first argument and increasing in the second.

The government holds noninterest-bearing reserves in foreign currency, which we denote by k_t, and prints domestic currency, M_t. In addition, the government runs a constant primary deficit of $g > 0$ units of tradable goods. The flow budget constraint of the government is given by

$$\dot{k}_t = \frac{\dot{M}_t}{\mathcal{E}_t} - g.$$

The first term on the right-hand side is the real value of the change in the money supply. Thus the above expression says that the change in foreign reserves equals the real value of money printing net of the primary deficit. Recalling that $\dot{M}_t / \mathcal{E}_t = \epsilon_t m_t + \dot{m}_t$, we can write the above expression as

$$\dot{k}_t = \epsilon_t m_t + \dot{m}_t - g. \tag{11.25}$$

Suppose that the government decides to peg the exchange rate in period 0. That is, $\epsilon^L = 0$. The government is committed to maintaining the peg as long as foreign reserves are above a certain floor, which we denote by k_L. As soon as foreign reserves hit this threshold, the government abandons the peg and begins to print enough money to finance the deficit. As long as the peg is maintained, the demand for money is constant and equal to $m_t = L(0, c^T)$. Thus we have that while the exchange-rate program is alive, $\dot{m}_t = 0$. Then combining the demand for money and the flow budget constraint of the government, we have that

$$\dot{k}_t = -g.$$

By pegging the exchange rate, the government relinquishes its sole source of revenue, seignorage. According to this expression, the stock of reserves is falling at the rate of g per period. The higher the fiscal deficit is, the faster the rate at which reserves will fall. This expression also shows that the peg cannot last forever. For in that case reserves would fall below the threshold k_L in finite time.

Let T denote the time at which the peg is abandoned. Then, $k_T = k_L$. We assume that starting at T, the government prints enough money to finance the primary deficit. This means that the stock of reserves stays at its lower bound k_L for all $t \geq T$.

An important element of the Krugman model is that the level of the nominal exchange rate cannot jump in period T. A perfectly anticipated discrete change in the nominal exchange rate—recall that agents are assumed to have perfect foresight—would induce a massive run against the domestic currency an instant before the crisis. Such a run would in turn anticipate the crisis. Continuing with this logic leads to a jump in the exchange rate in period 0. We assume that the government has enough reserves in period 0 to fend off such a run.

However, the devaluation rate can jump when the government runs out of reserves, since such a jump preserves the continuity of the level of the exchange rate. Let's first find the devaluation rate, ϵ^H, that allows the government to collect enough revenue to finance the deficit. This constant devaluation rate is associated with a constant level of real balances, $L(\epsilon^H, c^T)$. Then, noting that $\dot{k}_t = \dot{m}_t = 0$ for $t \geq T$, equation (11.25) implies that

$$\epsilon^H L(\epsilon^H, c^T) = g.$$

This expression states that the fiscal deficit must be financed with the inflation tax. The devaluation rate, ϵ^H, represents the inflation tax rate, and the demand for money, $L(\epsilon^H, c^T)$, represents the inflation tax base. The relationship between the inflation tax revenue, $\epsilon^H L(\epsilon^H, c^T)$, and the inflation tax rate, ϵ^H, is known as the inflation tax Laffer curve. In general, the above expression admits either two solutions or none. We assume it has two and take the one on the left side of the Laffer curve, as shown in Figure 11.3. It follows that the larger the fiscal deficit g is, the higher will be the devaluation rate ϵ^H necessary to finance it. Clearly, if g is positive, so is ϵ^H.

The fact that ϵ_t increases from 0 to ϵ^H at time T implies that at T there is a discrete decline in the demand for real balances from $L(0, c^T)$ to $L(\epsilon^H, c^T)$. Households get rid of this amount of money by running to the central bank to exchange domestic for foreign currency. The corresponding change in foreign reserves is given by

$$\Delta k_T = L(\epsilon^H, c^T) - L(0, c^T) < 0,$$

where Δ denotes change. This means that at $t = T$ the government loses a discrete amount of foreign reserves. This is what Krugman calls a balance-of-payments crisis. Figure 11.4 depicts the equilibrium dynamics of foreign reserves.

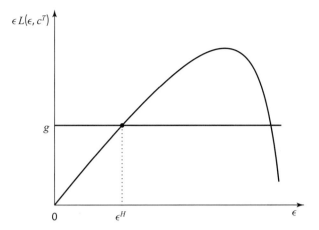

Figure 11.3 The inflation tax Laffer curve.

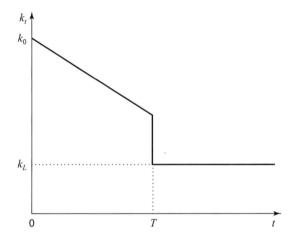

Figure 11.4 BOP crisis: Dynamics of foreign reserves.

Consider now the determination of the date, T, of the BOP crisis. The crisis takes place when the government has lost $k_0 - k_L$ units of foreign reserves, where k_0 denotes the foreign reserves at time 0 after the announcement of the peg.[5] Thus T must satisfy

---

5. At the instant the currency peg is announced, the central bank gains a discrete amount of reserves as the economy remonetizes in response to a fall in expected inflation. To see this, let $\epsilon^P > 0$ be the devaluation rate that was expected prior to the announcement of the peg. Then at the announcement, the demand for real balances increases from $L(\epsilon^P, c^T)$ to $L(0, c^T)$. This reliquefication is brought about by the public exchanging foreign currency for domestic currency at the central bank. As a result, the stock of foreign reserves held by the central bank jumps by $L(0, c^T) - L(\epsilon^P, c^T)$ at the moment of the announcement. This means that the stock of reserves an instant before the announcement of the peg is $k_0 - L(0, c^T) + L(\epsilon^P, c^T)$.

$$-(k_0 - k_L) = \int_0^T \dot{k} dt + \Delta k_T.$$

This expression can be written as

$$-(k_0 - k_L) = -gT + L(\epsilon^H, c^T) - L(0, c^T).$$

Solving for T we have

$$T = \frac{(k_0 - k_L) - [L(0, c^T) - L(\epsilon^H, c^T)]}{g}.$$

We note the following intuitive implications of this expression: (i) The higher is the fiscal deficit, g, the sooner the BOP crises will take place. (ii) The higher the initial stock of reserves and the lower the lower bound of reserves are, the later the crises will occur. (iii) The higher the interest elasticity of money demand is, the sooner the BOP crises will occur.

Summing up, the present model of balance-of-payments crises provides a theory of the duration and the long-run inflationary consequences associated with noncredible exchange-rate-based inflation-stabilization programs. At the root of the lack of credibility problem is a fiscal deficit that the policy authority is unable or unwilling to eliminate. The model makes a clear prediction about how reductions in the fiscal deficit can enhance credibility. Fiscal restraint slows down the drainage of foreign reserves, prolonging the life of the program, and it requires less seignorage to be financed after the program is abandoned, which implies a lower long-run rate of inflation. But the model cannot explain why a government would ever engage in an unsustainable inflation stabilization program, for, as shown earlier in the chapter, it predicts that a constant rate of devaluation welfare-dominates any temporary reduction. The answer to this question is likely to involve political economy considerations.

11.6 Discussion and Extensions

The framework developed in this chapter captures well a number of empirical regularities associated with the initial effects of inflation-stabilization programs. But it also misses some of them. For example, in the model, the adjustment of both consumption and the real exchange rate is instantaneous. The moment the inflation stabilization is announced, both variables jump up and then stay flat for the duration of the temporary plan. In contrast, the consumption booms and real appreciations observed in the initial phase of actual stabilization programs are gradual. Figure 11.2, for instance, shows that following the implementation of the Argentine Convertibility Plan in 1991, consumption and the real exchange rate adjusted gradually and continuously until 1994. This problem is not unique to the simple cash-in-advance model studied here. Uribe (2002) shows that a large class of standard optimizing models is unable to account for the empirical regularity that both consumption and the real exchange rate increase gradually in the initial phase of exchange-rate-based inflation-stabilization programs. In particular, models in this class predict that a gradual appreciation of the real exchange rate must necessarily be accompanied by a declining path of consumption. Uribe (2002) shows that one possible solution to this problem lies in the relaxation of the assumption of time separability in preferences. Specifically, under habit-forming preferences, temporary inflation-stabilization programs induce a positive comovement between consumption and the real exchange rate. The intuition behind this result is as follows. Habit formation is a form of consumption adjustment cost. Thus, naturally, the increase of consumption under habit formation is spread out over a number of periods. We have seen earlier in this chapter that the real exchange rate is an increasing function of tradable consumption. So if the latter variable adjusts gradually—as it does under habit formation—so will the real exchange rate.

Another difficulty of the simple framework studied in this chapter has to do with the response of output. By design, the endowment economy studied in this chapter is mute with respect to the response of output, employment, and investment to the announcement of inflation-stabilization programs. In reality, as in the Argentine Convertibility Plan of 1991 (Figure 11.2), the initial phase of inflation-stabilization programs is characterized by significant expansions in aggregate activity. Extensions of the model that allow for the use of money for the payment of factor services and for the purchase of capital goods (e.g., cash-in-advance constraints at the firm level or working capital constraints) can capture these supply-side effects (Roldós 1995; Uribe 1997; Lahiri 2001). More generally, this branch of the literature, which has come to be known as the supply-side hypothesis, offers an altogether alternative explanation for the initial expansionary effects of inflation-stabilization programs, which does not rely on the assumption of lack of credibility or temporariness. Instead a reduction in expected inflation, even if believed to be permanent, can foster employment and investment (and through wealth effects also private consumption) by reducing the opportunity cost of holding money at the firm level. For a comparative survey of the lack-of-credibility and supply-side theories, see Rebelo and Végh (1995).

We close by pointing out an important difference between exchange-rate-based inflation stabilization (the case studied here) and money-based inflation stabilization. The latter form of inflation stabilization consists of announcing a reduction in the money growth rate. Specifically, let $\mu_t \equiv M_t / M_{t-1}$ denote the (gross) growth rate of the money supply. A money-based inflation-stabilization program consists of announcing a lower path for μ_t. The difference between exchange-rate-based and a money-based inflation stabilization is in the policy instrument used by the central bank. Under exchange-rate-based stabilization, the central bank controls the path of the nominal exchange rate and lets the quantity of money be endogenously determined. Under money-based stabilization, the central bank controls the path of the money supply, and the nominal exchange rate is left to float. These two modalities of inflation stabilization can produce significant differences in an economy's adjustment following the inception of an anti-inflation policy. To see this, begin by noting that a fall in expected inflation causes the economy to remonetize (i.e., it induces households to rebuild their real money balances). Under exchange-rate-based stabilization, this remonetization happens quite naturally. At the specified nominal exchange rate, the central bank stands ready to exchange any quantity of foreign currency for domestic currency. So agents can quickly rebuild their money holdings by simply providing foreign reserves to the monetary authority in exchange for domestic money. In contrast, under a money-based stabilization program, the supply of money is controlled by the government. So the remonetization cannot occur by an increase in the money supply but must take place by a drop in the price level. Recall that $m_t = M_t / P_t^T$, so if the path of M_t is exogenously set by the government, m_t can increase only if P_t^T falls, that is, if the nominal exchange $\mathcal{E}_t$ falls. If the nominal price of nontradables, P_t^N, is sticky, the fall in $\mathcal{E}_t$ can cause an inefficient increase in the relative price of nontradables, $p_t = P_t^N / \mathcal{E}_t$, which can give rise to an excess supply of nontradables and unemployment as in the economy studied in Chapter 9.

The ease with which the economy remonetizes under exchange-rate-based stabilization is perhaps the reason virtually all real-world efforts to eliminate high inflation involve some sort of management of the nominal exchange rate. Calvo and Végh (1994) show that in the lack-of-credibility model with sticky prices, a money-based stabilization program causes an initial aggregate contraction. Uribe (1999) argues that pure money-based stabilization programs are virtually never observed. For most stabilization programs whether classified as exchange-rate-based or money-based feature an important initial increase in the money supply. For this reason Uribe (1999) analyzes a third category of stabilization program, namely, money-based with reliquefication programs. This is a money-based stabilization program that includes an initial injection of money by the central bank. Uribe (1999) shows that money-based programs with initial reliquefication avoid the initial contraction associated with (pure) money-based programs. Further, Uribe (1999) shows that money-based programs with reliquefication are equivalent to exchange-rate-based programs from a welfare point of view, and that both welfare-dominate pure money-based programs.

11.7 Appendix: The Hamiltonian

The household's problem posed in Section 11.5 is

$$\max \int_0^\infty e^{-\rho t} [u(c_t^T) + v(m_t)] dt$$

subject to

$$\dot{d}_t = r d_t + c_t^T + \dot{m}_t + \epsilon_t m_t - y^T - g,$$

and the no-Ponzi-game constraint $\lim_{t \to \infty} \exp(-\rho t) d_t \leq 0$. To find the first-order conditions associated with this maximization problem, we construct the following object, known as the Hamiltonian:

$$\mathcal{H}(c_t^T, d_t, m_t, \dot{d}_t, \dot{m}_t, \lambda_t)$$

$$\equiv e^{-\rho t} \left[u(c_t^T) + v(m_t) + \lambda_t [\dot{d}_t - r d_t - c_t^T - \dot{m}_t - \epsilon_t m_t + y^T + g] \right].$$

This expression is similar to the Lagrangian in discrete-time constrained optimization problems. In general, the first-order conditions of a Hamiltonian problem are

$$\frac{\partial \mathcal{H}(c_t^T, d_t, m_t, \dot{d}_t, \dot{m}_t, \lambda_t)}{\partial c_t^T} = 0,$$

$$\frac{\partial \mathcal{H}(c_t^T, d_t, m_t, \dot{d}_t, \dot{m}_t, \lambda_t)}{\partial d_t} - \frac{\partial^2 \mathcal{H}(c_t^T, d_t, m_t, \dot{d}_t, \dot{m}_t, \lambda_t)}{\partial \dot{d}_t \partial t} = 0,$$

$$\frac{\partial \mathcal{H}(c_t^T, d_t, m_t, \dot{d}_t, \dot{m}_t, \lambda_t)}{\partial m_t} - \frac{\partial^2 \mathcal{H}(c_t^T, d_t, m_t, \dot{d}_t, \dot{m}_t, \lambda_t)}{\partial \dot{m}_t \partial t} = 0,$$

and

$$\frac{\partial \mathcal{H}(c_t^T, d_t, m_t, \dot{d}_t, \dot{m}_t, \lambda_t)}{\partial \lambda_t} = 0,$$

where λ_t is a Hamilton multiplier associated with the flow budget constraint (see, e.g., Intriligator 1971). Note the general structure of the optimality conditions associated with stocks (d_t and m_t) on the one hand, and with flows (c_t^T and λ_t) on the other. Taking the first derivatives, the above optimality conditions become, respectively,

$$u'(c_t^T) = \lambda_t,$$

$$e^{-\rho t} \lambda_t r + \frac{\partial (e^{-\rho t} \lambda_t)}{\partial t} = 0,$$

$$e^{-\rho t} v'(m_t) - e^{-\rho t} \lambda_t \epsilon_t + \frac{\partial (e^{-\rho t} \lambda_t)}{\partial t} = 0,$$

and

$$\dot{d}_t = r d_t + c_t^T + \dot{m}_t + \epsilon_t m_t - y^T - g.$$

Taking the remaining derivatives gives

$$u'(c_t^T) = \lambda_t,$$

$$\frac{\dot{\lambda}_t}{\lambda_t} = \rho - r,$$

$$\frac{v'(m_t)}{\lambda_t} - \epsilon_t - \rho + \frac{\dot{\lambda}_t}{\lambda_t} = 0,$$

and

$$\dot{d}_t = r d_t + c_t^T + \dot{m}_t + \epsilon_t m_t - y^T - g.$$

(We repeat the entire set of optimality conditions for convenience). Differentiating the first of these optimality conditions yields $\dot{\lambda}_t = u''(c_t^T) \dot{c}_t^T$. Using this expression to eliminate $\dot{\lambda}_t$

and the first optimality condition to eliminate λ_t, we obtain

$$\frac{u''(c_t^T)}{u'(c_t^T)}\dot{c}_t^T = \rho - r,$$

$$v'(m_t) = u'(c_t^T)(r + \epsilon_t),$$

and

$$\dot{d}_t = rd_t + c_t^T + \dot{m}_t + \epsilon_t m_t - y^T - g,$$

which are the conditions presented in the body of the text.

11.8 Exercises

11.1 (Welfare Cost of Lack of Credibility) Consider a small open perfect-foresight economy populated by a large number of identical infinitely-lived consumers with preferences described by the utility function

$$\sum_{t=0}^{\infty} \beta^t \ln c_t,$$

where c_t denotes consumption, and $\beta \in (0, 1)$ denotes the subjective discount factor. Consumption is a composite good made of traded and nontradable goods, denoted c_t^T and c_t^N, respectively, via the aggregator function

$$c_t = \sqrt{c_t^T c_t^N}.$$

The sequential budget constraint of the representative household is given by

$$d_t^h = (1 + r)d_{t-1}^h + (1 + \tau_t)(c_t^T + p_t c_t^N) - w_t h_t - y^T - s_t,$$

where d_t^h denotes debt acquired in period t and maturing in $t + 1$, h_t denotes hours worked, τ_t is a proportional consumption tax, w_t denotes the real wage in terms of tradables, p_t denotes the relative price of nontradables in terms of tradables, $y^T = 1$ is an endowment of tradable goods, and s_t denotes a lump-sum transfer received from the government. The parameter r denotes the real interest rate and is assumed to satisfy $1 + r = \beta^{-1} = 1.04$. Debt is denominated in terms of tradables. Households are subject to the no-Ponzi-game constraint

$$\lim_{j \to \infty} \frac{d_{t+j}^h}{(1 + r)^j} \leq 0.$$

Assume that the household's initial debt position is nil ($d_{-1}^h = 0$). Households supply inelastically 1 unit of labor to the market each period. Suppose that the law of one price holds for tradables, so that $P_t^T = P_t^{T*}\mathcal{E}_t$, where P_t^T denotes the domestic-currency price of tradables; $\mathcal{E}_t$ denotes the nominal exchange rate, defined as the price of foreign currency in terms of domestic currency; and P_t^{T*} denotes the foreign-currency price of tradables. Assume that P_t^{T*} is constant and equal to unity for all t. Let W_t and P_t^N denote the nominal wage rate and the nominal price of nontradables, respectively. Then the real wage and the relative price of nontradables are defined as $w_t = W_t/P_t^T$ and $p_t = P_t^N/P_t^T$.

Firms in the nontraded sector produce goods by means of the linear technology $y_t^N = h_t$, where y_t^N denotes output of nontradables. Firms are price takers in product and labor markets, and there is free entry, so that all firms make zero profits at all times.

The government starts period 0 with no debt or assets outstanding and runs a balanced budget period by period, that is, $s_t = \tau_t(c_t^T + p_t c_t^N)$. The monetary authority pegs the exchange rate at unity, so that $\mathcal{E}_t = 1$ for all t.

Suppose that nominal wages are flexible and that before period 0 the economy was in a steady state with constant consumption of tradables and nontradables and no external debt.

1. Compute the equilibrium paths of c_t^T, w_t, W_t, p_t, the trade balance, and the current account under two alternative tax policies:

$$\text{policy 1:} \quad \tau_t = 0, \quad \forall t,$$

and

$$\text{policy 2:} \quad \tau_t = \begin{cases} 0 & 0 \leq t \leq 11 \\ 0.3 & t \geq 12. \end{cases}$$

2. Compute the welfare cost of policy 2 relative to policy 1, defined as the percentage increase in the consumption stream of a consumer living under policy 2 required to make him as well off as living under policy 1. Formally, the welfare cost of policy 2 relative to policy 1 is given by $\lambda \times 100$, where λ is implicitly given by

$$\sum_{t=0}^{\infty} \beta^t \ln[c_t^{p2}(1+\lambda)] = \sum_{t=0}^{\infty} \beta^t \ln c_t^{p1},$$

where c_t^{p1} and c_t^{p2} denote consumption in period t under policies 1 and 2, respectively.

11.2 (Welfare Cost of Lack of Credibility with Wage Rigidity) Modify the economy of exercise 11.1 by introducing downward nominal wage rigidity as in Chapter 9. Specifically, assume that $W_t \geq W_{t-1}$ for all $t \geq 0$.

Answer the questions of exercise 11.1 in this new environment. To this end, first compute W_{-1} under the assumption that before period 0 the economy was in a steady state with constant consumption of tradables and nontradables, full employment, no debt, and a nominal exchange rate equal to unity.

11.3 (Lack of Credibility and Tariff Reforms) How would your answers to exercises 11.1 and 11.2 change if τ_t was a tax only on consumption of tradables (i.e., a trade tariff)? Provide a quantitative answer and intuition.

11.4 (Nonequivalence of Temporariness and Lack of Credibility) In the body of this chapter, we established the equivalence of temporariness and lack of credibility in the context of a model with a consumption tax (with tradable and nontradable consumption taxed at the same rate). How does this equivalence result change in the economy of exercise 11.3, in which τ_t is a tax on tradable consumption only? Specifically, establish whether policy 2 induces the same equilibrium paths of consumption and the real exchange rate as policy 1 does when households incorrectly believe that the government will abandon this policy in period $T = 12$ in favor of policy 2. Consider separately the cases of flexible and downwardly rigid nominal wages.

11.5 (BOP Crisis with Linear Money Demand) Consider an economy in which the demand for money is of the form

$$L(\epsilon, c) = c - \frac{\epsilon_t}{2},$$

where ϵ_t denotes the devaluation rate, and c denotes a constant level of consumption. Suppose that c equals 2. Time is continuous, and the analysis starts at time 0. Let g denote a constant flow of government primary deficits. Suppose $g = 1.5$. At time 0, the government implements a currency peg. Let k_t denote the stock of (noninterest-bearing) foreign reserves held by the government. At time 0, and after any portfolio recomposition that the announcement of a currency peg might have caused, the level of reserves held at the central bank, k_0, equals 10. The government is determined to defend the peg until it runs out of reserves. At that point, it switches to a constant rate of devaluation, high enough to finance the deficit.

1. Calculate the rate of devaluation prevailing in this economy after the demise of the currency peg.
2. Calculate the loss of reserves suffered by the government at the time of the BOP crisis.
3. Calculate the length of the currency peg, denoted by T.
4. Assume alternatively that at time 0 everybody understands that when the government runs out of reserves, it will implement a fiscal reform whereby the primary deficit is fully eliminated. When does the government run out of reserves in this case? Is there a BOP crisis at time T, that is, does the government lose a discrete amount of reserves at time T? Provide intuition.

11.6 (BOP Crisis: A Numerical Example) Consider the model of BOP crises of Section 11.5. Suppose $c^T = y^T$, where y^T denotes output, assumed to be constant. Suppose that the initial stock of foreign reserves, k_0, is 10 percent of output; the lower bound on reserves, k_L, is 0; the fiscal deficit, g, is 2 percent of output; and the money demand function is given by $c^T(a - bi)$, with $a = 0.2$ and $b = 0.25$. Find the date of the BOP crisis, denoted T, and the devaluation rate after the BOP crisis, denoted by ϵ^H.

11.7 (BOP Crisis with Interest-Bearing Reserves) Consider the model of BOP crises of Section 11.5 but now assume that foreign reserves held by the central bank, k_t, earn interest at the rate r. Provide an implicit expression for the post-collapse rate of devaluation, ϵ^H, and derive an expression for the time of the crisis, T.

12

Financial Frictions and Aggregate Instability

In this chapter we study models in which external borrowing is limited by collateral. In some formulations, collateral is assumed to be a stock variable, such as the value of physical capital or the value of real estate. In other formulations, collateral takes the form of a flow variable, such as the stream of income. The collateral-constraint literature argues that during booms, increases in the price of collateral induce agents to borrow and spend excessively, which amplifies the expansionary phase of the cycle. During downturns, the argument continues, the price of collateral falls, forcing agents to deleverage, which aggravates the contraction. This fall in the price of collateral is known as a *Fisherian debt deflation,* after Fisher (1933), and the excessive borrowing during the boom phase of the cycle is known as *overborrowing.* Modern formulations of this argument in open economy macroeconomics have been developed by Auernheimer and García-Saltos (2000), Mendoza (2002, 2010), Uribe (2006, 2007), Lorenzoni (2008), Jeanne and Korinek (2010), Korinek (2011), Bianchi (2011), and Benigno et al. (2013, 2014), among others.

The theoretical models belonging to this literature predict the existence of a *pecuniary externality* in the market for external funds. The externality arises because the collateral constraint faced by individual agents depends on variables that are exogenous to them but endogenous to the economy as a whole. These variables can take various forms. In models in which the collateral is a stock, the variable that causes the externality is the market price of the stock. For instance, if the asset that serves as collateral is physical capital, then the price that causes the externality is Tobin's q, and if the asset used as collateral is real estate (as in mortgage contracts), then the externality originates in house prices. In models in which the collateral takes the form of a flow, the variable that causes the externality is the price of the different components of the flow in terms of units of debt. For example, if borrowing is limited by a fraction of total income, and income has a nontraded component, then the variable that causes the externality is the relative price of nontradables in terms of tradables (or the real exchange rate). The nature of the externality has to do with the fact that during booms the price of collateral is pushed up by the collective decisions of individual agents. Each agent understands that the increase in prices is inefficient (because

425

it leads to overborrowing) but can do nothing to prevent it because her consumption and savings are too small to affect market prices.

The pecuniary externality is not the only type of fragility caused by the introduction of collateral constraints in otherwise standard open economy models. A second type of instability, which has been given less attention in the literature, is the emergence of *multiplicity of equilibria*. Specifically, equilibria in which the economy is financially unconstrained may coexist with other equilibria with self-fulfilling Fisherian deflations and a limited ability of agents to allocate resources efficiently over time (Jeanne and Korinek 2010; Schmitt-Grohé and Uribe 2016b).

The main questions we wish to address in this chapter are: First, does the presence of collateral constraints affect the business-cycle properties of open economies? Second, do collateral constraints deepen the contractionary effects of large negative shocks? Third, do collateral constraints generate sizable welfare losses? Fourth, do collateral constraints lead to overborrowing or *underborrowing*? Fifth, how pervasive are self-fulfilling financial crises driven by arbitrary revisions in expectations in open economy models with stock and flow collateral constraints? Finally, we ask whether there exist *macroprudential policies* capable of inducing agents to internalize the pecuniary externality, and, if so, what they look like, and what type of policy rules can implement the allocation they support.

12.1 Stock Collateral Constraints

Consider a perfect-foresight small open economy populated by a large number of households with preferences given by the utility function[1]

$$\sum_{t=0}^{\infty} \beta^t \ln c_t,$$

where c_t denotes consumption, and $\beta \in (0, 1)$ denotes the subjective discount factor. The sequential budget constraint of the household is assumed to be of the form

$$c_t + d_t + q_t(k_{t+1} - k_t) = y_t + \frac{d_{t+1}}{1 + r}, \tag{12.1}$$

where d_t denotes debt acquired in period $t - 1$ and due in period t, k_t denotes the stock of physical capital in period t, q_t denotes the price of one unit of capital in terms of consumption in period t, y_t denotes output in period t, and $r > 0$ denotes a constant interest rate on debt. For simplicity, we assume a zero depreciation rate of physical capital. Output is produced with the technology

$$y_t = A_t k_t^{\alpha}, \tag{12.2}$$

where A_t is an exogenous and deterministic productivity factor, and $\alpha \in (0, 1)$ is a parameter.

Assume that borrowing is limited by a constant fraction $\kappa > 0$ of the value of physical capital. Formally, we assume

---

1. The presentation follows Schmitt-Grohé and Uribe (2016d).

$$d_{t+1} \le \kappa q_t k_{t+1}. \tag{12.3}$$

The parameter κ can be interpreted as the fraction of assets that lenders could seize from the borrower in the event of a default. Under this interpretation, the above borrowing constraint is an incentive compatibility restriction, which ensures that the borrower never walks away from his external debt obligations.[2]

The above collateral constraint pertains to the class of stock collateral constraints, because the pledgeable object, physical capital, is a stock. The source of the pecuniary externality is the price of capital, q_t, because it is taken as given by the individual household but is endogenously determined in equilibrium. An increase in the aggregate demand for capital drives up q_t, allowing the individual household to borrow more. Similarly, a fall in the aggregate demand for capital drives q_t down, which may force households to deleverage. Individual households understand this mechanism but fail to internalize it, because due to their atomistic nature they correctly realize that their own demand for capital is too small to affect its price q_t. This externality and its implications for prudential policy were first stressed in the context of an open economy model by Auernheimer and García-Saltos (2000).

The household chooses sequences $c_t > 0$, d_{t+1}, and $k_{t+1} \ge 0$ to maximize its lifetime utility subject to the sequential budget constraint (12.1), the production technology (12.2), and the collateral constraint (12.3), taking as given the sequence of prices q_t and the initial conditions d_0 and k_0. The Lagrangian associated with this optimization problem is

$$\mathcal{L} = \sum_{t=0}^{\infty} \beta^t \left\{ \ln c_t + \lambda_t \left[A_t k_t^{\alpha} + \frac{d_{t+1}}{1+r} - c_t - d_t - q_t(k_{t+1} - k_t) \right] \right. $$
$$\left. + \lambda_t \mu_t \left[\kappa q_t k_{t+1} - d_{t+1} \right] \right\},$$

where $\beta^t \lambda_t$ and $\beta^t \lambda_t \mu_t$ are the Lagrange multipliers associated with the sequential budget constraint and the collateral constraint, respectively. The associated first-order conditions with respect to c_t, d_{t+1}, and k_{t+1} are, respectively,

$$\frac{1}{c_t} = \lambda_t, \tag{12.4}$$

$$\lambda_t \left[\frac{1}{1+r} - \mu_t \right] = \beta \lambda_{t+1}, \tag{12.5}$$

and

$$\lambda_t q_t \left[1 - \kappa \mu_t \right] = \beta \lambda_{t+1} \left[q_{t+1} + \alpha A_{t+1} k_{t+1}^{\alpha-1} \right]. \tag{12.6}$$

Optimality condition (12.5) equates the marginal costs and benefits of increasing d_{t+1}. The marginal benefit is $1/(1+r)$ units of consumption in t, which is equivalent to $\lambda_t/(1+r)$

---

2. Alternatively, one could assume that borrowing is limited by the expected value of capital at the time debt is due. In this case, the right-hand side of the collateral constraint would be $\kappa q_{t+1} k_{t+1}$. Devereux, Young, and Yu (2015) pursue this avenue.

units of utility. In normal times (i.e., when the collateral constraint is not binding), the marginal cost of increasing d_{t+1} by one unit is the sacrifice of one unit of consumption in $t+1$, which is equivalent to $\beta\lambda_{t+1}$ units of utility. When the collateral constraint is binding, the marginal cost of an additional unit of debt increases by μ_t units of goods or $\lambda_t\mu_t$ units of utility, reflecting a shadow punishment for trying to increase debt when the household is up against the limit. Similarly, optimality condition (12.6) equates the marginal cost and benefit of purchasing an additional unit of capital. The marginal cost of capital is its price, q_t. During normal times, the marginal benefit of an additional unit of capital purchased in t is the additional output it generates in $t+1$, or the marginal product of capital, $\alpha A_{t+1}k_{t+1}^{\alpha-1}$, plus the price at which this additional unit of capital can be sold in period $t+1$, q_{t+1}. When the collateral constraint binds, the benefit of an additional unit of capital increases by $\kappa\mu_t q_t$, reflecting its contribution to relaxing the borrowing constraint.

The optimality conditions associated with the household's optimization problem also include the Kuhn-Tucker nonnegativity and slackness conditions

$$\mu_t \geq 0, \tag{12.7}$$

and

$$\mu_t\left(\kappa q_t k_{t+1} - d_{t+1}\right) = 0. \tag{12.8}$$

Because preferences display no satiation, the optimality conditions include the terminal condition

$$\lim_{t\to\infty}\frac{d_{t+1}}{(1+r)^t} = \kappa \lim_{t\to\infty}\frac{q_t k_{t+1}}{(1+r)^t}. \tag{12.9}$$

Exercise 12.1 asks you to show that if a set of sequences $\{c_t, d_{t+1}, k_{t+1}\}$ satisfies all optimality conditions but (12.9), then there exists a welfare-dominating set of feasible sequences, that is, sequences satisfying (12.1)–(12.3) that generate higher utility.

To facilitate the characterization of equilibrium, assume that the aggregate supply of capital is fixed and equal to $k > 0$. Therefore in equilibrium we have

$$k_t = k, \tag{12.10}$$

for all t. The price of capital must be nonnegative, that is, $q_t \geq 0$. In addition, we restrict attention to equilibria in which the price of capital does not display a bubble, that is, equilibria in which q_t grows at a rate strictly less than r. Formally, we impose

$$\lim_{t\to\infty}(1+r)^{-t}q_t = 0. \tag{12.11}$$

Conditions (12.9)–(12.11) imply that the present discounted value of debt must converge to zero:

$$\lim_{t\to\infty}(1+r)^{-t}d_t = 0.$$

In turn, this condition together with the sequential budget constraint (12.1) and the market-clearing condition (12.10) implies that $d_0 = \sum_{t=0}^{\infty}\frac{y_t-c_t}{(1+r)^t}$, which, as in many of the models analyzed earlier in this book, states that the present discounted value of future expected trade balances must cover the country's initial net external debt position. Finally, we assume that the subjective and market discount factors are equal:

$$\beta(1+r) = 1.$$

A (bubble-free) competitive equilibrium is then a set of sequences $c_t > 0$, d_{t+1}, $\mu_t \geq 0$, and $q_t \geq 0$ satisfying

$$d_0 = \sum_{t=0}^{\infty} \frac{y_t - c_t}{(1+r)^t}, \tag{12.12}$$

$$c_t + d_t = y_t + \frac{d_{t+1}}{1+r}, \tag{12.13}$$

$$\frac{1}{c_t}[1 - \mu_t(1+r)] = \frac{1}{c_{t+1}}, \tag{12.14}$$

$$\frac{q_t}{c_t}[1 - \kappa\mu_t] = \frac{\beta}{c_{t+1}}\left[q_{t+1} + \alpha\frac{y_{t+1}}{k}\right], \tag{12.15}$$

$$\mu_t\left(\kappa q_t k - d_{t+1}\right) = 0, \tag{12.16}$$

$$d_{t+1} \leq \kappa q_t k, \tag{12.17}$$

and

$$\lim_{t \to \infty}(1+r)^{-t}q_t = 0, \tag{12.18}$$

given d_0 and the exogenous sequences A_t and $y_t \equiv A_t k^\alpha$. Equation (12.14) together with the requirement that $c_t > 0$ implies that $\mu_t < 1/(1+r) < 1$.

12.1.1 The Steady-State Equilibrium

Suppose that the productivity factor A_t is constant over time and equal to A for all $t \geq 0$, where A is a positive parameter. Then the path of output is also constant and equal to $y_t = y \equiv Ak^\alpha$. In this subsection we show that under these conditions, there exists a steady state equilibrium, that is, an equilibrium in which all variables are constant over time.

A steady-state equilibrium is a set of constant sequences $c_t = c^* > 0$, $d_{t+1} = d^*$, $\mu_t = \mu^* \geq 0$, and $q_t = q^* \geq 0$ that satisfy equilibrium conditions (12.12)–(12.18) given d_0. What does the steady state look like? Because consumption is constant over time, equation (12.14) implies that $\mu^* = 0$. This means that in the steady state the economy is not borrowing constrained. Then equation (12.15) becomes $q_t = \beta q_{t+1} + \beta\alpha y/k$. Since $\beta \in (0, 1)$, the unique stationary solution to this expression is

$$q^* = \frac{\alpha y/k}{r} > 0, \tag{12.19}$$

which intuitively says that the steady-state price of capital equals the present discounted value of current and future marginal products of capital.

Evaluating the sequential budget constraint (12.13) in any period $t > 0$ implies that the steady-state level of consumption is given by

$$c^* = y - \frac{r}{1+r}d^*.$$

This is a familiar characteristic of open economy models in the steady state. It says that households consume their permanent income, given by the sum of nonfinancial income, y, and interest income, $-rd^*/(1+r)$. Using the above expression to eliminate c_0 from the sequential budget constraint in period 0 yields

$$d^* = d_0.$$

Thus the steady-state level of debt depends on (is actually equal to) the level of debt inherited from the past in period 0. Because the net debt position is constant in the steady state, we have that the steady-state current account, denoted ca^*, is nil:

$$ca^* = 0.$$

The steady-state trade balance, $tb^* \equiv y - c^*$, equals the interest obligations on external debt:

$$tb^* = \frac{r}{1+r}d^*.$$

Finally, it is natural to ask what levels of debt are sustainable in the steady state. Taken together, the above expression for steady-state consumption and the requirement that consumption be positive impose the following upper bound on external debt:

$$d_0 < \frac{1+r}{r}y, \tag{12.20}$$

which is a natural debt limit, above which servicing the debt would cause households to starve. The collateral constraint introduces a second upper bound on debt, given by

$$d_0 \leq \kappa q^* k = \kappa \frac{\alpha y}{r}. \tag{12.21}$$

Comparing the debt bounds (12.20) and (12.21), we have that as long as $\kappa < 1$, the latter will be the more restrictive bound. Throughout this section, we assume, as in much of the related literature, that

$$\kappa < 1.$$

This restriction says that leverage cannot exceed 100 percent. It then follows that the maximum value of debt sustainable in the steady state is given by condition (12.21). Any level of debt satisfying this condition can be supported as a steady-state equilibrium.

12.1.2 Frictionless Adjustment to Regular Shocks

An important theme of the collateral-constraint literature is that this type of financial friction affects the adjustment of economies to large, unusual shocks but not to regular shocks. We illustrate this principle by characterizing the equilibrium dynamics implied by the present model in response to regular and large negative productivity shocks. The analysis will make clear what constitutes a regular shock and a large shock in the present environment.

Suppose that the economy was in a steady state until period -1. Suppose also that in period 0 the productivity factor A_t unexpectedly falls from A to $A^L < A$ and returns to A permanently starting in period 1. This sequence of productivity shocks gives rise to the following path for output:

$$
y_t = \begin{cases} y^L \equiv A^L k^\alpha & \text{for } t = 0 \\ y \equiv Ak^\alpha > y^L & \text{for } t > 0. \end{cases}
$$

The question we wish to answer here is under what conditions the adjustment to the negative productivity shock will be frictionless. By a frictionless adjustment we mean one that would occur if the collateral constraint were not in place. The equilibrium conditions of the frictionless economy are (12.12)–(12.15) and (12.18), with $\mu_t = 0$ for all t.

Let c_t^{nc} denote the equilibrium level of consumption in period t in the economy without the collateral constraint (nc for no collateral constraint). Then equation (12.14) implies that

$$
c_t^{nc} = c^{nc},
$$

for all $t \geq 0$, where c^{nc} is a constant. So equilibrium consumption is perfectly smooth in the economy without the collateral constraint. This is a consequence of the assumption that $\beta(1+r) = 1$. Evaluating the intertemporal resource constraint (12.12) at $c_t = c^{nc}$ for all $t \geq 0$ implies that c^{nc} is given by

$$
c^{nc} = c^* - \frac{r}{1+r}(y - y^L) < c^*,
$$

for all $t \geq 0$, where, as before, $c^* = y - r/(1+r)d_0$ denotes the level of consumption that would have occurred in the absence of the negative productivity shock in period 0. Now using the sequential resource constraint (12.13), we obtain a constant equilibrium path of external debt given by

$$
d_t^{nc} = d^{nc} \equiv d_0 + y - y^L > d_0,
$$

for all $t \geq 1$. In period 0, both the current account and the trade balance deteriorate:

$$
ca_0^{nc} = -\frac{y - y^L}{1+r} < 0,
$$

and

$$
tb_0^{nc} = tb^* - \frac{y - y^L}{1+r} < tb^*.
$$

These results are reminiscent of those obtained in Chapter 2. Because the productivity shock is temporary, the household borrows an amount close to the output shock $(y - y^L)$ to smooth consumption. More precisely, the household borrows $(y - y^L)/(1 + r)$. This increases debt in period 1 by exactly $y - y^L$. The household finds it optimal to pay the interest on the additional debt every period but not the principal, so consumption falls slightly by the increased interest service, $r(y - y^L)/(1 + r)$.

Finally, because by definition, in the economy without the collateral constraint $\mu_t = 0$, equation (12.15) implies that the price of capital is unchanged by the productivity shock, we have

$$q_t^{nc} = q^{nc} \equiv q^*,$$

for all t.

Under what conditions does the equilibrium in the economy without the collateral constraint coincide with the equilibrium in the economy with the collateral constraint? For this to be the case, it is necessary that the collateral constraint (12.17) be satisfied when evaluated at d^{nc} and q^{nc}, that is, it is necessary that

$$d^{nc} \leq \kappa k q^*.$$

Using the solution for d^{nc} obtained above yields the condition

$$y - y^L \leq \kappa q^* k - d_0. \tag{12.22}$$

The right-hand side of this expression is the slack in the collateral constraint prior to period 0. The left-hand side is the output contraction in period 0. Thus an output contraction in period 0 induces a frictionless adjustment if it is smaller than the slack in the collateral constraint prior to the shock. It follows that the adjustment to an output contraction is more likely to be frictionless the smaller is the contraction itself; the smaller is the level of debt prior to the contraction, d_0; and the less severe is the financial friction (i.e., the larger is κ). In the context of this model, we will refer to contractions that satisfy (12.22) as regular contractions.

12.1.3 Adjustment to Large Shocks: Fisherian Debt Deflations and Deleveraging

Continue to assume that the economy was in a steady state until period -1. But now assume that the contraction of output in period 0, $y - y^L$, is so large that condition (12.22) is not satisfied, so that

$$y - y^L > \kappa q^* k - d_0. \tag{12.23}$$

In the context of the present model, we define a large contraction as one that satisfies the above inequality.

What does the equilibrium look like when the economy is hit by a large negative shock? We wish to show that a large negative output shock causes a Fisherian deflation (i.e., a fall in the price of capital, q_t) and deleveraging (i.e., a reduction in net external debt, d_t). The first thing to note is that the collateral constraint must bind in at least one period, that is, μ_t must be strictly positive and condition (12.3) must hold with equality for some $t \geq 0$. To see

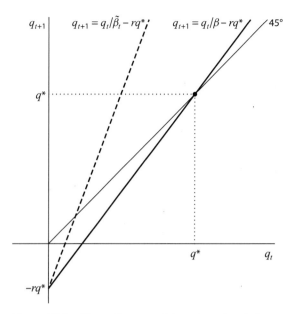

Figure 12.1   Phase diagram of the price of capital.

this, suppose on the contrary that $\mu_t = 0$ for all t. Then by the debt Euler equation (12.14), c_t is constant over time, which implies, by the intertemporal resource constraint (12.12), that $c_t = c^{nc}$. The sequential budget constraint (12.13) then yields $d_{t+1} = d^{nc}$, and the capital Euler equation (12.15) yields $q_t = q^*$ for all $t \geq 0$. But by condition (12.23), this allocation violates the collateral constraint in period 0. This establishes that in response to a large negative output shock, μ_t must be positive in at least one period.

Consider now the equilibrium value of capital, q_t, in the period in which μ_t is strictly positive. To this end, rewrite the capital Euler equation (12.15) as

$$q_{t+1} = \tilde{\beta}_t^{-1} q_t - rq^*, \qquad (12.24)$$

where $\tilde{\beta}_t$ is given by

$$\tilde{\beta}_t \equiv \beta \frac{1 - (1+r)\mu_t}{1 - \kappa \mu_t}.$$

Note that $0 < \tilde{\beta}_t \leq \beta$, that $\tilde{\beta}_t = \beta$ when $\mu_t = 0$, and that $\tilde{\beta}_t < \beta$ when $\mu_t > 0$ (recall that we are assuming that $\kappa < 1$ and that $r > 0$). According to this expression, in determining their demand for assets (in this case physical capital), households behave as if they became more impatient in periods in which the collateral constraint binds. Figure 12.1 displays the phase diagram of the price of capital in the space (q_t, q_{t+1}). The heavy solid line corresponds to the case $\tilde{\beta}_t = \beta$, and the dashed line to the case $\tilde{\beta}_t < \beta$. When $\tilde{\beta}_t = \beta$, the stationary state of q_t is given by q^*. It is clear from the phase diagram that, regardless of the value of $\tilde{\beta}_t$, a value of q_t larger than q^* would trigger an explosive path. In principle, a growing path of q_t could be consistent with equilibrium if it does not violate the no-bubble constraint (12.18). It turns out, however, that this constraint is violated for any initial condition $q_0 > q^*$. To see this, note that since $1/\tilde{\beta}_t \geq 1 + r$, it suffices to show that any path of q_t with initial condition $q_0 > q^*$ violates the no-bubble constraint for $\tilde{\beta}_t = \beta$. Now evaluate (12.24) at $\tilde{\beta}_t = \beta$, divide both sides by $(1 + r)^{t+1}$, and sum for $T - 1$ periods to get

$$\sum_{t=0}^{T-1} (\tilde{q}_{t+1} - \tilde{q}_t) = -\frac{rq^*}{1+r} \sum_{t=0}^{T-1} \frac{1}{(1+r)^t},$$

where $\tilde{q}_t \equiv q_t/(1+r)^t$ is the present discounted value of the price of capital. This object must converge to zero for the no-bubble constraint to be satisfied. We can write the above expression as

$$\tilde{q}_T - q_0 = -\frac{rq^*}{1+r} \sum_{t=0}^{T-1} \frac{1}{(1+r)^t}.$$

Letting $T \to \infty$ in the above expression, we obtain

$$\lim_{T \to \infty} \frac{q_T}{(1+r)^T} = q_0 - q^*.$$

It follows that the no-bubble constraint is violated for any initial condition $q_0 > q^*$. As we will see shortly, however, $q_0 < q^*$ does not necessarily lead to a violation of the no-bubble constraint or of the nonnegativity constraint on q_t, because in that case, changes in $\tilde{\beta}_t$ can prevent q_t from imploding.

So far we have established that in equilibrium $q_t \leq q^*$, for all $t \geq 0$, and that a large negative output shock in period 0 causes the collateral constraint to bind in at least one period. It remains to show that when the collateral constraint binds, q_t and d_{t+1} fall.

Let $T \geq 0$ denote the first period in which μ_t is strictly positive. This means that $\tilde{\beta}_T^{-1} > \beta^{-1} > 1$. It then follows from equation (12.24) that if q_T were to equal q^*, then q_{T+1} would be strictly greater than q^*, which, by the arguments given above, would be inconsistent with equilibrium. It follows that q_T must be strictly less than q^*. From periods 0 to $T - 1$, $\tilde{\beta}_t = \beta$. Therefore, in period $T - 1$, equation (12.24) becomes

$$q_{T-1} = \frac{1}{1+r} q_T + \frac{r}{1+r} q^*,$$

which says that q_{T-1} is a weighted average of q_T and q^*. Since $q_T < q^*$, it follows that $q_{T-1} < q^*$. By induction we have that

$$q_0 < q^*.$$

This establishes an important prediction of the present model, namely, that a large contraction in output is necessarily accompanied by a Fisherian deflation.

Furthermore, both debt and consumption fall in period 0 relative to the values they would have taken in the absence of the collateral constraint. To see this, note that the debt Euler equation (12.14) and the fact that $\mu_t \geq 0$ for all t imply that in any equilibrium, consumption is nondecreasing from period 0 on. The debt Euler equation and the fact that

$\mu_T > 0$ also imply that consumption must increase in period $T + 1$, that is, $c_{T+1} > c_T$. Since $\mu_t = 0$ for all $t < T$, we have, again by the debt Euler equation, that consumption is constant over this period: $c_t = c_T$ for $t \leq T$. Now, by the intertemporal resource constraint (12.12), the present discounted value of consumption must be the same in the economy with the collateral constraint and in the economy without that constraint. So we have two paths of consumption with the same present discounted value, one of which is flat (the one associated with the economy without the collateral constraint), and the other is nondecreasing and strictly increasing in at least one period (the one associated with the economy with the collateral constraint). It must therefore be the case that the initial value of the latter consumption path is strictly lower than the initial value of the former path. That is, c_0 must be strictly smaller than c_0^{nc}. The sequential budget constraint (12.13) evaluated at $t = 0$ then directly implies that d_1 must be strictly less than d_1^{nc}. This establishes that a large negative output shock in period 0 causes deleveraging in that period. It also follows that the economy with a collateral constraint experiences smaller deteriorations of the trade balance and current account deteriorations relative to the economy without the collateral constraint: $ca_0 > ca_0^{nc}$ and $tb_0 > tb_0^{nc}$.

In summary, we have shown that the presence of a collateral constraint causes a Fisherian deflation, debt deleveraging, and an amplification of the contraction in aggregate demand in response to a large negative output shock. The intuition behind this central result is as follows. In response to a temporary negative output shock, households would like to borrow to smooth consumption. If the shock is large enough, the desired level of debt will exceed the borrowing limit $\kappa q^* k$. From an individual point of view, the household has an incentive to sell capital, because one unit of capital sells for q^* units of consumption goods. However, the household cannot increase consumption by quite this amount, because reducing capital by one unit tightens the collateral constraint by κq^* units, so the household must use this amount to reduce debt, leaving $(1 - \kappa) q^*$ units for additional consumption. Now, every household wants to sell capital. This situation is known as a fire sale. But this is impossible in equilibrium, because the stock of capital is fixed. For the capital market to clear, the price of capital, q_t, must fall—that is, a Fisherian debt deflation must occur. If the collateral constraint was binding or close to binding before the shock (i.e., d_0 close to $\kappa q^* k$), then the fall in q_0 would force households to reduce their net debt positions, $d_1 < d_0$; that is to say, it would force households to deleverage. This is exactly the opposite of what happens in the absence of a collateral constraint. In that case, a large negative output shock induces an increase in household indebtedness.

Once the output shock is over (period 1), the economy can reach an equilibrium in which q_t returns to its steady-state value q^*, and debt is forever equal to d_1. To see that this is the case, notice that in such an equilibrium the collateral constraint would not bind after period 0, because $d_t = d_1 = \kappa q_0 k < \kappa q^* k$, for all $t \geq 1$. This means that $\mu_t = 0$, for $t \geq 1$, which by the Euler equation (12.14) implies that consumption is also constant. Notice that the country emerges from the financial crisis stronger than it entered: after period 0, consumption is permanently higher, debt is permanently lower, and the collateral constraint may be more relaxed. However, this strength comes at a cost, because the fall in consumption in period 0 reduces lifetime welfare.

12.2 Stock Collateral Constraints and Self-Fulfilling Financial Crises

The equilibrium in economies with collateral constraints is inherently fragile. A problem that plagues this type of economies is that under plausible parameterizations, the equilibrium may fail to be unique. The possibility of equilibrium multiplicity in open economy models with a stock collateral constraint was first identified by Jeanne and Korinek (2010), who present a heuristic analysis of sufficient conditions for uniqueness. The theoretical contribution of this section is to establish conditions for the existence of multiple equilibria. Essentially the problem that arises is that if an unconstrained equilibrium exists, often a second equilibrium exists in which the collateral constraint is binding. In the equilibrium with the binding collateral constraint, negative beliefs bring the price of capital down, causing a tightening of the collateral constraint. In turn, the decline in the value of collateral forces agents to deleverage, leading to a fire sale of capital. Because the stock of capital is fixed, the fire sale depresses asset prices, validating the negative beliefs.

For simplicity, assume that $y_t = y$ for all $t \geq 0$, where $y > 0$ is a constant. Suppose also that

$$d_0 < \kappa q^* k,$$

where q^* is the steady-state price of capital given in equation (12.19). This restriction guarantees that the initial level of debt does not violate the collateral constraint when $q_0 = q^*$. Then the analysis presented in Section 12.1.1 implies that there exists an equilibrium in which the economy is at a steady state starting in period 0. In this equilibrium, $c_t = c^* \equiv y - d_0 r/(1 + r) > 0$, $d_t = d_0$, $q_t = q^*$, and $\mu_t = 0$ for all $t \geq 0$. Along this equilibrium path, the collateral constraint never binds. We therefore refer to this equilibrium as the unconstrained equilibrium. We wish to show that in general there exists a second equilibrium in which the collateral constraint binds in period 0. In this second equilibrium, the economy suffers a Fisherian deflation and debt deleveraging in the initial period. In addition, the real allocation is welfare inferior to the one associated with the unconstrained equilibrium. We refer to this second equilibrium as the constrained equilibrium.

In the constrained equilibrium we consider here, the economy reaches a steady state in period 1. To see that a steady-state equilibrium starting in period 1 exists, recall from Section 12.1.1 that the only requirement for the existence of a steady-state equilibrium starting in period 1 is that the collateral constraint be satisfied. This is indeed the case, because $d_{t+1} = d_1 = \kappa q_0 k \leq \kappa q^* k = \kappa q_t k$ for all $t \geq 1$. The first equality follows from the assumption that the economy is in a steady state starting in period 1, the second follows from our assumption that the collateral constraint is binding in period 0, the weak inequality follows from the upper bound $q_t \leq q^*$ derived earlier, and the last equality from the fact that in a steady-state equilibrium $q_t = q^*$ for all t.

Taking into account that the economy reaches a steady state in period 1, the complete set of equilibrium conditions, equations (12.12)–(12.18), collapses to the following system of five equations plus an inequality in the five unknowns, $c_0 > 0$, $c_1 > 0$, d_1, $q_0 \geq 0$, and $\mu_0 \geq 0$:

$$d_0 = \frac{1+r}{r}y - \frac{c_1}{r} - c_0, \tag{12.25}$$

$$c_1 = y - \frac{r}{1+r}d_1, \tag{12.26}$$

$$\frac{1}{c_0}[1 - (1+r)\mu_0] = \frac{1}{c_1}, \tag{12.27}$$

$$\frac{q_0}{c_0}(1 - \kappa\mu_0) = \frac{\beta}{c_1}(q^* + \alpha y/k), \tag{12.28}$$

and

$$\mu_0(\kappa q_0 k - d_1) = 0, \tag{12.29}$$

with

$$d_1 \leq \kappa q_0 k. \tag{12.30}$$

Now solve (12.25)–(12.28) for q_0 as a function of d_1 to obtain

$$\kappa q_0 k = \kappa q^* k \left[\frac{(1+r)c^* + d_1 - d_0}{(1+r)c^* + (\kappa - r)(d_1 - d_0)} \right]. \tag{12.31}$$

Figure 12.2 displays with a heavy solid line the graph of $\kappa q_0 k$ as a function of d_1 implied by this equation. The locus $\overline{CC}$ is the collection of pairs $(d_1, \kappa q_0 k)$ that guarantee that equilibrium conditions (12.25)–(12.28) are satisfied. Recalling that $1 + r > 1 > \kappa$, it can readily be shown that $\overline{CC}$ is upward sloping. Also, $\overline{CC}$ crosses the point $(d_0, \kappa q^* k)$, which is labeled A in the figure. Note that point A lies above the 45° line, reflecting the assumption that $d_0 \leq \kappa q^* k$. We have already shown that $d_1 = d_0$ represents a steady-state equilibrium. To see that there may exist a second equilibrium, begin by noting that all points of $\overline{CC}$ that lie on or above the 45° line satisfy the collateral constraint (12.30). Consider now the value of d_1 at which the locus $\overline{CC}$ crosses the horizontal axis. This value of d_1 is denoted by $\underline{d}$ in the figure. Suppose that, as shown in the figure, $\underline{d}$ is positive. (We will discuss shortly conditions for this to be the case.) Then $\overline{CC}$ must necessarily cross the 45° line at some level of debt in the open interval $(\underline{d}, d_0)$. This value of d_1 is denoted by d_c, and the intersection point is marked with the letter B in the figure. Because B is on $\overline{CC}$ and on the 45° line, it satisfies equilibrium conditions (12.25)–(12.28) and the collateral constraint (12.30). Moreover, at B the collateral constraint holds with equality, which means that the slackness condition (12.29) is satisfied. To establish that point B represents an equilibrium, it remains to show that $d_1 = d_c$ implies that $c_0 > 0$, $c_1 > 0$, and $\mu_0 \geq 0$. To this end, note that the numerator of the bracketed expression in equation (12.31) is $(1+r)c_0$. At $d_1 = \underline{d}$, the numerator is nil, so $(1+r)c_0 = 0$. At $d_1 = d_0$, $(1+r)c_0 = (1+r)c^*$. Since by (12.25) and (12.26), c_0 is increasing in d_1, it follows that at $d_1 = d_c$, $(1+r)c_0$ must be strictly positive and less than $(1+r)c^*$. It follows that $d_1 = d_c$ implies that $0 < c_0 < c^*$. Also, $d_c < d_0$ implies, by the sequential resource constraint (12.26), that $c_1 > c^*$. So we have that $d_1 = d_c$ implies that $0 < c_0 < c^* < c_1$. The debt Euler equation (12.27) then implies that μ_0 is positive.

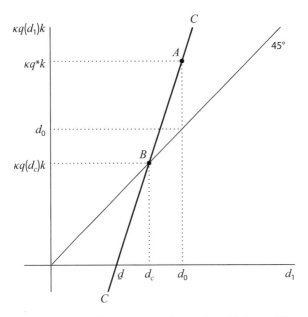

Figure 12.2   Collateral constraints and multiple equilibria.

This establishes the existence of a second equilibrium in which $q_0 < q^*$ and $d_1 < d_0$, that is, an equilibrium with a Fisherian deflation and debt deleveraging that coexists with the unconstrained equilibrium. We have shown that a sufficient condition for the constrained equilibrium to coexist with the unconstrained equilibrium is that $\underline{d}$ be positive. Since $\underline{d} = (1 + r)(d_0 - y)$, this condition is satisfied provided that $d_0/y > 1$. This is not an unrealistic requirement. Suppose that the time unit is one quarter. Then the sufficient condition for the existence of a self-fulfilling financial crisis is satisfied as long as net foreign debt is greater than 25 percent of annual output. This result shows that, in the present model, higher external debt makes economies more vulnerable to financial crises driven by nonfundamental revisions in expectations. More generally, in this economy, bad fundamentals make the economy more prone to nonfundamental crises. Finally, the fact that the path of consumption in the self-fulfilling crisis is not flat implies that it is welfare inferior to the flat path associated with the unconstrained equilibrium. Thus a benevolent social planner would always prefer the unconstrained equilibrium to the constrained one. In this sense, we can say that in the constrained equilibrium, the economy underborrows.

12.3 Flow Collateral Constraints

Many studies of open economies with collateral constraints assume that the object that serves as collateral is a flow rather than a stock. We will focus on the case in which tradable and nontradable output have collateral value, which is the type of flow collateral constraint most frequently studied in the related literature. Under this formulation, the source of pecuniary externalities is the relative price of nontradable goods in terms of tradables, or the real exchange rate. The narrative of how this externality may amplify the business cycle is as follows. A positive shock that expands aggregate demand pushes the price of nontradables up, raising the value of collateral and easing access to credit, which in turn amplifies the expansion in aggregate demand. At the same time, a negative shock that reduces aggregate demand leads to a decline in the relative price of nontradables, making the value of nontradable output in terms of tradable goods fall and the collateral constraint tighten, which deepens the contraction.

Like stock collateral constraints, flow collateral constraints create an externality because individual households fail to internalize the effect of their borrowing decision on the relative price of nontradables and hence on the value of their own collateral. As a result, this environment has the potential to generate inefficient credit booms and busts in equilibrium. The amount of amplification brought about by the pecuniary externality depends crucially on the amount of precautionary savings generated in the economy. The larger the level of savings is, the smaller the amplification effect will be, since households are less likely to be caught with a binding collateral constraint. Thus the amount of amplification induced by collateral constraints is ultimately a quantitative question.

Flow collateral constraints involving the value of tradable and nontradable output were introduced in open economy models by Mendoza (2002). The externality that emerges when debt is denominated in tradable goods but leveraged on nontradable income and the consequent room for macroprudential policy was emphasized by Korinek (2011) in the context of a three-period model. Bianchi (2011) extended the Korinek model to an infinite-horizon framework and derived quantitative predictions for optimal prudential policy. Schmitt-Grohé and Uribe (2016b) show that models with flow collateral constraints display self-fulfilling crises and underborrowing.

Consider a small open endowment economy in which households have preferences of the form

$$E_0 \sum_{t=0}^{\infty} \beta^t U(c_t), \tag{12.32}$$

where c_t denotes consumption in period t, $U(\cdot)$ denotes an increasing and concave period utility function, $\beta \in (0, 1)$ denotes a subjective discount factor, and E_t denotes the expectations operator conditional on information available in period t. We assume that the period utility function takes a CRRA form,

$$U(c) = \frac{c^{1-\sigma} - 1}{1 - \sigma},$$

with $\sigma > 0$. As in Chapters 8 and 9, we assume that consumption is a composite of tradable and nontradable goods:

$$c_t = A(c_t^T, c_t^N), \tag{12.33}$$

where c_t^T denotes consumption of tradables in period t, and c_t^N denotes consumption of nontradables in period t. We assume that the Armington aggregator takes a CES form:

$$A(c^T, c^N) = \left[a c^{T\,1-1/\xi} + (1-a) c^{N\,1-1/\xi} \right]^{1/(1-1/\xi)},$$

with $a \in (0, 1)$ and $\xi > 0$. Households are assumed to have access to a single, one-period, risk-free, internationally traded bond denominated in terms of tradable goods that pays the exogenous interest rate r_t when held from period t to $t + 1$. The household's sequential budget constraint is given by

$$c_t^T + p_t c_t^N + d_t = y_t^T + p_t y_t^N + \frac{d_{t+1}}{1 + r_t}, \tag{12.34}$$

where d_t denotes the amount of debt due in period t, and d_{t+1} denotes the amount of debt assumed in period t and maturing in $t + 1$. The variable p_t denotes the relative price of nontradables in terms of tradables, and y_t^T and y_t^N denote the endowments of tradables and nontradables, respectively. Both endowments are assumed to be exogenously given.

The collateral constraint takes the form

$$d_{t+1} \leq \kappa^T y_t^T + \kappa^N p_t y_t^N, \tag{12.35}$$

where $\kappa^T, \kappa^N > 0$ are parameters. Households internalize this borrowing limit. However, as for the case in which the value of capital is used as collateral, this borrowing constraint introduces an externality, because each individual household takes the real exchange rate, p_t, as exogenously determined, even though their collective desired absorption of tradable and nontradable goods is a key determinant of this relative price.

Households choose a set of processes $\{c_t^T, c_t^N, c_t, d_{t+1}\}$ to maximize (12.32) subject to (12.33)–(12.35), given the processes $\{r_t, p_t, y_t^T, y_t^N\}$ and the initial debt position d_0. The first-order conditions of this problem are (12.33)–(12.35) and

$$U'(A(c_t^T, c_t^N))A_1(c_t^T, c_t^N) = \lambda_t, \tag{12.36}$$

$$p_t = \frac{1 - a}{a} \left(\frac{c_t^T}{c_t^N} \right)^{1/\xi}, \tag{12.37}$$

$$\left(\frac{1}{1 + r_t} - \mu_t \right) \lambda_t = \beta E_t \lambda_{t+1}, \tag{12.38}$$

$$\mu_t \geq 0, \tag{12.39}$$

and

$$\mu_t(d_{t+1} - \kappa^T y_t^T - \kappa^N p_t y_t^N) = 0, \tag{12.40}$$

where $\beta^t \lambda_t$ and $\beta^t \lambda_t \mu_t$ denote the Lagrange multipliers on the sequential budget constraint (12.34) and the collateral constraint (12.35), respectively. The Euler condition (12.38) equates the marginal benefit of assuming more debt with its marginal cost. The interpretation of this equation is similar to that of its counterpart in the economy with a stock collateral constraint. During tranquil times, when the collateral constraint does not bind, one unit of debt payable in $t + 1$ increases tradable consumption by $1/(1 + r_t)$ units in period t, which increases utility by $\lambda_t/(1 + r_t)$. The marginal cost of an extra unit of debt assumed in period t and payable in $t + 1$ is the marginal utility of consumption in period $t + 1$ discounted at the subjective discount factor, $\beta E_t \lambda_{t+1}$. When the collateral constraint binds, a circumstance that we refer to as a financial crisis, the marginal utility of increasing debt falls to $[1/(1+r_t) - \mu_t]\lambda_t$, reflecting a shadow penalty for trying to increase debt when the collateral constraint is binding.

In equilibrium, the market for nontradables must clear:

$$c_t^N = y_t^N.$$

Then a competitive equilibrium is a set of processes $\{c_t^T, d_{t+1}, \mu_t\}$ satisfying

$$\left(\frac{1}{1+r_t} - \mu_t\right) U'(A(c_t^T, y_t^N)) A_1(c_t^T, y_t^N)$$

$$= \beta E_t U'(A(c_{t+1}^T, y_{t+1}^N)) A_1(c_{t+1}^T, y_{t+1}^N), \tag{12.41}$$

$$c_t^T + d_t = y_t^T + \frac{d_{t+1}}{1+r_t}, \tag{12.42}$$

$$d_{t+1} \leq \kappa^T y_t^T + \kappa^N \left(\frac{1-a}{a}\right) c_t^{T\,1/\xi} y_t^{N\,1-1/\xi}, \tag{12.43}$$

$$\mu_t \geq 0, \tag{12.44}$$

and

$$\mu_t \left[\kappa^T y_t^T + \kappa^N \left(\frac{1-a}{a}\right) c_t^{T\,1/\xi} y_t^{N\,1-1/\xi} - d_{t+1}\right] = 0, \tag{12.45}$$

given exogenous processes $\{r_t, y_t^T, y_t^N\}$ and the initial condition d_0.

The fact that c_t^T appears on the right-hand side of the equilibrium version of the collateral constraint (12.43) means that during contractions in which the absorption of tradables falls, the collateral constraint endogenously tightens. Individual agents do not take this effect into account in choosing their consumption plans. This is the nature of the pecuniary externality in this model.

From the perspective of the individual agent, equation (12.35) states that the higher the level of debt she takes on in period t, d_{t+1}, the closer she will come to hitting the borrowing limit. This is because she takes all objects on the right-hand side of (12.35) as exogenous. Moreover, from the individual's point of view, equation (12.35) defines a convex set of feasible debt choices, d_{t+1}. That is, if two debt levels d^1 and d^2 satisfy (12.35), then any weighted average $\alpha d^1 + (1-\alpha)d^2$, for $\alpha \in [0, 1]$, also satisfies this condition. From an equilibrium perspective, however, this ceases to be true in general. The reason is that the relative price of nontradables, p_t, which appears on the right-hand side of the collateral constraint (12.35), is increasing in consumption of tradables by equation (12.37), which, in turn, is increasing in d_{t+1} by the resource constraint (12.42). To see this, use equilibrium condition (12.42) to eliminate c_t^T from equilibrium condition (12.43) to obtain

$$d_{t+1} \leq \kappa^T y_t^T + \kappa^N \left(\frac{1-a}{a}\right) \left(y_t^T + \frac{d_{t+1}}{1+r_t} - d_t\right)^{1/\xi} y_t^{N\,1-1/\xi}. \tag{12.46}$$

It is clear from this expression that the right-hand side is increasing in the equilibrium level of external debt, d_{t+1}. Moreover, depending on the values assumed by the parameters κ^N, a, and ξ, the equilibrium value of collateral may increase more than one for one with d_{t+1}. In other words, instead of tightening the collateral constraint, an increase in debt may relax it. In this case the more indebted the economy becomes, the less leveraged it will be. As we will see shortly, this possibility can give rise to multiple equilibria and self-fulfilling drops in the value of collateral. Furthermore, if the intratemporal elasticity of substitution ξ is less than unity, which is the case of greatest empirical relevance for many countries (Akinci 2011), the equilibrium value of collateral is convex in the level of debt. This property may cause the emergence of two distinct values of d_{t+1} for which the collateral constraint binds, and two disjoint intervals of debt levels, for which the collateral constraint is slack.

12.4 Flow Collateral Constraints and Self-Fulfilling Financial Crises

The focus of this section is to characterize self-fulfilling financial crises under flow collateral constraints. The analysis follows Schmitt-Grohé and Uribe (2016b). For analytical convenience, assume that the CRRA period utility function and the CES aggregator function introduced above satisfy

$$\sigma = \frac{1}{\xi} = 2,$$

which, as argued in Chapter 9, is an empirically plausible case. We simplify the economy by assuming that the tradable and nontradable endowments and the interest rate are constant: $y_t^T = y^T$, $y_t^N = 1$, and $r_t = r$, for all t. Further, we assume that $a = 0.5$, $\kappa^T = \kappa^N \equiv \kappa$, and

$$\beta(1 + r) = 1.$$

Given these assumptions, the equilibrium conditions (12.41)–(12.45) can be written as

$$c_{t+1}^T \sqrt{1 - (1 + r)\mu_t} = c_t^T, \tag{12.47}$$

$$c_t^T + d_t = y^T + \frac{d_{t+1}}{1 + r}, \tag{12.48}$$

$$d_{t+1} \leq \kappa \left[y^T + \left(y^T + \frac{d_{t+1}}{1 + r} - d_t \right)^2 \right], \tag{12.49}$$

$$\mu_t \geq 0, \tag{12.50}$$

and

$$\mu_t \left\{ \kappa \left[y^T + \left(y^T + \frac{d_{t+1}}{1 + r} - d_t \right)^2 \right] - d_{t+1} \right\} = 0, \tag{12.51}$$

with d_0 given.

Let's first characterize conditions under which an equilibrium exists in which traded consumption and debt are constant for all $t \geq 0$, that is, an equilibrium in which $c_t^T = c_0^T$ and $d_t = d_0$ for all $t \geq 0$, where d_0 is given. We refer to this equilibrium as a steady-state

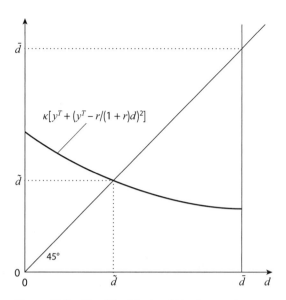

Figure 12.3 Feasible debt levels in the steady state under a flow collateral constraint.

equilibrium. By (12.47), in a steady-state equilibrium $\mu_t = 0$ for all t. This means that in a steady-state equilibrium the slackness condition (12.51) is also satisfied for all t.

When $d_{t+1} = d_t = d$, the collateral constraint (12.49) becomes

$$d \leq \kappa \left[y^T + \left(y^T - \frac{rd}{1+r} \right)^2 \right]. \tag{12.52}$$

We refer to this expression as the steady-state collateral constraint. Figure 12.3 displays the left- and right-hand sides of the steady-state collateral constraint (12.52) as a function of d. The left-hand side is the 45° line. The right-hand side, shown with the heavy solid line, is a quadratic expression with a minimum at the natural debt limit $\bar{d} \equiv y^T(1+r)/r$. At the natural debt limit, consumption of tradables is zero. This means that a steady-state equilibrium can exist only for initial values of debt less than $\bar{d}$. At $\bar{d}$, the right-hand side of the steady-state collateral constraint (12.52) equals κy^T, and the left-hand side equals $\bar{d} = y^T(1+r)/r$. We assume that $\kappa < (1+r)/r$, so that at $\bar{d}$ the left-hand side is larger than the right-hand side. This guarantees that the steady-state collateral constraint is violated at the natural debt limit, which makes the collateral constraint relevant in the long run. Let $\tilde{d} < \bar{d}$ be the value of d at which the steady-state collateral constraint (12.52) holds with equality, that is, the value of d at which the right-hand side of the steady-state collateral constraint crosses the 45° line, as indicated in the figure. Any initial value of debt, d_0, greater than $\tilde{d}$ violates the steady-state collateral constraint and therefore cannot be supported as a steady-state equilibrium. In contrast, any initial value of debt, d_0, less than or equal to $\tilde{d}$ satisfies the steady-state collateral constraint (12.52). Since we have already shown that a constant value of debt also satisfies all other equilibrium conditions, we have demonstrated that any initial value of debt less than or equal to $\tilde{d}$ can be supported as a steady-state equilibrium.

Is the steady-state equilibrium the only possible equilibrium? The answer is no. Consider an economy with an initial debt level $d_0 < \tilde{d}$, as shown in Figure 12.4. The figure reproduces from Figure 12.3 the right-hand side of the steady-state collateral constraint (12.52) with a heavy solid line and its left-hand side with a light solid line. Because in the graph the initial level of debt, d_0, satisfies $d_0 < \tilde{d}$, we have from the previous analysis that $d_t = d_0$ for all t can be supported as an equilibrium. Now consider the collateral constraint in period 0, given by

$$d \leq \kappa \left[y^T + \left(y^T + \frac{d}{1+r} - d_0 \right)^2 \right], \tag{12.53}$$

expressed as a function of the level of debt in period 1, denoted by d. We refer to expression (12.53) as the short-run collateral constraint. Figure 12.4 plots the right-hand side of the short-run collateral constraint with a dashed line. The left-hand side of the short-run collateral constraint is the 45° line and coincides with the left-hand side of the steady-state collateral constraint. The right-hand sides of the short-run and steady-state collateral constraints intersect when $d = d_0$ (point A in the figure). At point A, the right-hand side of the short-run collateral constraint (the dashed line) is upward sloping. To see this, note that at point A the slope is equal to $2\kappa/(1+r)(y^T - rd_0/(1+r)) > 2\kappa/(1+r)(y^T - r\tilde{d}/(1+r)) = 0$.

Because the right-hand side of the short-run collateral constraint is a quadratic function of d that opens upward, it must cross the 45° line to the left of d_0 either zero or two times. Suppose that it crosses the 45° line twice, as shown in Figure 12.4. This is possible for some parameter configurations.[3] At the crossing with the higher debt level, indicated by point B in the figure, the slope of the right-hand side of the short-run collateral constraint is positive. Thus at point B, c_0^T is positive, because the slope of the short-run collateral constraint is $2\kappa/(1+r)c_0^T$. We wish to show that point B can be supported as an equilibrium. The equilibrium we have in mind is one in which the economy deleverages in period 0 and reaches a steady state in period 1, that is, $d_t = d_1 < d_0$ for all $t > 0$. To establish this result, we must show that equilibrium conditions (12.47)–(12.51) are satisfied for all $t \geq 0$, with $c_t^T > 0$. We have already shown that $c_0^T > 0$ at point B. Now note that at point B the collateral constraint is binding in period 0, since the right-hand side of the short-run collateral constraint crosses the 45° line, which is the left-hand side of the short-run collateral constraint. Thus equilibrium conditions (12.49) and (12.51) are satisfied in period 0. Also, $d_1 < d_0$ and $d_1 = d_2$ imply that $c_0^T < c_1^T$, which can be verified by comparing the resource constraint (12.48) evaluated at $t = 0$ and $t = 1$. In turn, $c_0^T < c_1^T$ implies, by the Euler equation (12.47), that a strictly positive value of the Lagrange multiplier μ_0 makes the Euler equation hold with equality in period 0. Therefore, equilibrium condition (12.50) is sat-

---

3. A sufficient condition for the existence of two crossings of this type for some range of $d_0 < \tilde{d}$ is that the slope of the right-hand side of the short-run collateral constraint be larger than unity at $d = d_0 = \tilde{d}$. This condition is satisfied as long as $\kappa r/(1+r)(1 - \kappa r/(1+r))y^T > a/(1-a)((1+r)^2 - 1)/4$.

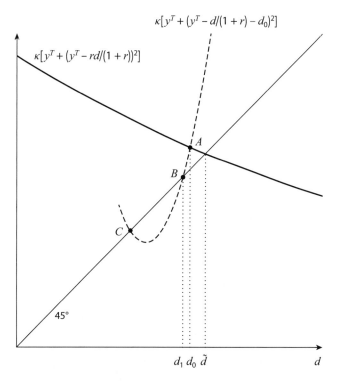

Figure 12.4 Multiple equilibria with flow collateral constraints.

isﬁed in period 0. This establishes that the debt level associated with point B satisfies all
equilibrium conditions in period 0. Since $d_1 < \tilde{d}$, we have, from the preceding analysis of
steady-state equilibria, that $d_t = d_1$ for all $t \geq 1$ can be supported as an equilibrium. This
completes the proof of the existence of multiple equilibria, one with $d_t = d_0$ for all $t \geq 0$
and the collateral constraint never binding, and another one with $d_1 < d_0$ and the collateral
constraint binding in period 0 and never binding thereafter. The latter equilibrium takes
place at a level of debt in period 1 at which, from an aggregate point of view, the collateral
constraint behaves perversely (in the sense that more borrowing would loosen rather than
tighten the borrowing restriction).

What is the intuition behind this second equilibrium? Imagine the economy being
originally in a steady state with debt constant and equal to d_0 (point A in Figure 12.4).
Unexpectedly, the public becomes pessimistic, and aggregate demand contracts. The contraction in aggregate demand means that households want to consume less of both types
of good, tradable and nontradable. Because nontradables are in fixed supply, their relative
price, p_0, must fall to bring about market clearing. As a result, the value of collateral, given
by $\kappa(y^T + p_0 y^N)$, also falls. This reduction in collateral is so large that it forces households
to deleverage. This generalized decline in the value of collateral represents the quintessential element of a financial crisis. To reduce their net debt positions, households must
cut spending, validating the initial pessimistic sentiments and making the financial crisis

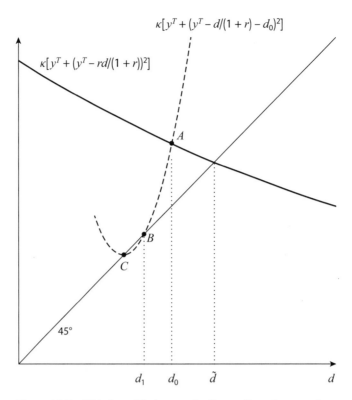

Figure 12.5   Third equilibrium under flow collateral constraints.

self-fulfilling. The contraction in aggregate demand and the fall in the relative price of nontradables imply that the self-fulfilling financial crisis occurs in the context of a current account surplus and a depreciation of the real exchange rate.

Figure 12.4 displays a short-run collateral constraint that crosses the 45° line once with a positive slope (point B) and once with a negative slope (point C). In this case point C cannot be an equilibrium, because it is associated with negative consumption in period 0, $c_0^T < 0$. To see this, recall that the slope of the short-run collateral constraint in period 0 is given by $2\kappa/(1+r)c_0^T$. So if the slope is negative, so is c_0^T.

However, if the short-run collateral constraint crosses the 45° line twice with a positive slope and before $\tilde{d}$, as shown in Figure 12.5, then a third equilibrium emerges (point C). The proof of this claim is identical to the one establishing that point B is an equilibrium. A third equilibrium of this type entails a larger drop in the value of collateral and more deleveraging than in the equilibrium associated with point B. This suggests that in the current environment self-fulfilling financial crises can come in different sizes.

12.5 Debt Dynamics in a Stochastic Economy with a Flow Collateral Constraint

In this section we characterize numerically the debt dynamics in a stochastic version of the flow collateral-constrained economy presented in Section 12.3. To this end, we assume a joint stochastic process for the tradable endowment and the country interest rate and calibrate the structural parameters of the model to match certain features of a typical emerging economy.

An equilibrium in the stochastic economy with a flow collateral constraint is a set of stationary processes c_t, c_t^T, d_{t+1}, λ_t, μ_t, p_t satisfying

$$c_t^T + d_t = y_t^T + \frac{d_{t+1}}{1+r_t}, \tag{12.54}$$

$$c_t = \left[a c_t^{T\,1-1/\xi} + (1-a) y^{N\,1-1/\xi} \right]^{\frac{1}{1-1/\xi}},$$

$$a c_t^{-\sigma} \left(\frac{c_t^T}{c_t} \right)^{-1/\xi} = \lambda_t,$$

$$\lambda_t \left[\frac{1}{1+r_t} - \mu_t \right] = \beta E_t \lambda_{t+1},$$

$$d_{t+1} \leq \kappa^T y_t^T + \kappa^N p_t y^N,$$

$$p_t = \frac{1-a}{a} \left(\frac{c_t^T}{y^N} \right)^{1/\xi},$$

$$\mu_t \left(\kappa^T y_t^T + \kappa^N p_t y^N - d_{t+1} \right) = 0,$$

and

$$\mu_t \geq 0,$$

given the joint process for (y_t^T, r_t) and the initial condition d_0. In these equilibrium conditions we are invoking market clearing in the nontradable sector, $c_t^N = y^N$, to replace consumption of nontradables with output of nontradables.

12.5.1 Calibration

We calibrate the model at a quarterly frequency. We assume that $\kappa^T = \kappa^N \equiv \kappa$, and set κ so that the upper limit of net external debt is 30 percent of annual output. This value is in line with those used in the quantitative literature on output-based collateral constraints (e.g., Bianchi 2011). Because the time unit in the model is a quarter, this calibration restriction implies a value of κ of 1.2 ($= 0.3 \times 4$). The calibration of all other parameters of the model follows the one adopted in Chapter 9. That is, we set $\beta = 0.9635$, $\sigma = 1/\xi = 2$, $a = 0.26$, and $y^N = 1$.

We assume that y_t^T and r_t follow the bivariate AR(1) process estimated in Chapter 9 for Argentine quarterly data for 1983:Q1–2001:Q4. We reproduce this estimate here for convenience:

$$\begin{bmatrix} \ln y_t^T \\ \ln \frac{1+r_t}{1+r} \end{bmatrix} = A \begin{bmatrix} \ln y_{t-1}^T \\ \ln \frac{1+r_{t-1}}{1+r} \end{bmatrix} + \epsilon_t, \tag{9.31 R}$$

Table 12.1   Calibration of the Constrained and Unconstrained Economies

Parameter	Value	Description
Structural parameters		
κ	1.2	Parameter of collateral constraint
σ	2	Inverse of intertemporal elasticity of consumption
β	0.9635	Quarterly subjective discount factor
r	0.0316	Steady-state quarterly country interest rate
ζ	0.5	Elasticity of substitution between tradables and nontradables
a	0.26	Share of tradables in CES aggregator
y^N	1	Nontradable output
y^T	1	Steady-state tradable output
Discretization of state space		
n_{y^T}	21	Number of grid points for $\ln y_t^T$, equally spaced
n_r	11	Number of grid points for $\ln[(1+r_t)/(1+r)]$, equally spaced
n_d	501	Number of grid points for d_t, equally spaced
$\left[\ln \underline{y}^T, \ln \overline{y}^T\right]$	$[-0.3858, 0.3858]$	Range for tradable output
$\left[\ln\left(\frac{1+\underline{r}}{1+r}\right), \ln\left(\frac{1+\overline{r}}{1+r}\right)\right]$	$[-0.0539, 0.0539]$	Range for interest rate
$[\underline{d}, \overline{d}]$	$[0, 3.5]$	Debt range for constrained economy
$[\underline{d}, \overline{d}]$	$[2, 8.3416]$	Debt range for unconstrained economy
$[\underline{d}, \overline{d}]$	$[0, 3.5]$	Debt range for Ramsey economy

Notes: The time unit is one quarter. The transition probability matrix for the joint process $\left(\ln y_t^T, \ln(1+r_t)/(1+r)\right)$ is stored in the file `tpm.mat` available online with the materials for this chapter on the book's Web site via http://press.princeton.edu/titles/11032.html.

where $\epsilon_t \sim N(\varnothing, \Sigma_\epsilon)$. The estimated parameters are

$$A = \begin{bmatrix} 0.79 & -1.36 \\ -0.01 & 0.86 \end{bmatrix}; \qquad \Sigma_\epsilon = \begin{bmatrix} 0.00123 & -0.00008 \\ -0.00008 & 0.00004 \end{bmatrix}; \qquad r = 0.0316.$$

Table 12.1 summarizes the calibration.

12.5.2 Equilibrium Selection

The numerical solution must take a stance on how to handle the possibility of indeterminacy of the rational expectations equilibrium of the type identified in Section 12.4. Failing to address this issue may result in nonconvergence of the numerical algorithms. The approach adopted here follows Schmitt-Grohé and Uribe (2016b). Specifically, we focus on two canonical equilibrium selection mechanisms suggested by the preceding theoretical analysis. We label these mechanisms (B) and (C) to indicate their relation to the corresponding points in Figure 12.5:

   (B) If for a given current state (y_t^T, r_t, d_t) there are one or more values of d_{t+1} for which all equilibrium conditions are satisfied, pick the largest one for which the collateral constraint is binding.

(C) If for a given current state (y_t^T, r_t, d_t) there are one or more values of d_{t+1} for which all equilibrium conditions are satisfied, pick the smallest one for which the collateral constraint is binding.

Criteria (B) and (C) favor self-fulfilling equilibria, as in points B and C in Figure 12.5, with (C) favoring larger crises. We could in principle adopt other equilibrium selection criteria, including ones in which *nonfundamental uncertainty* (*sunspot* realizations) affects the real allocation.

A second issue that needs to be tackled when approximating equilibrium policy functions is the possibility that for some current states (y_t^T, r_t, d_t), there exists no value of d_{t+1} that ensures both the satisfaction of the collateral constraint and positive consumption of tradables. These are in general high-debt states in which the individual deleveraging required to comply with the borrowing limit induces a level of traded consumption so low that collectively the price of nontradables falls to a point where the household fails to meet the collateral constraint even with zero tradable consumption. A third issue that must be explicitly dealt with when computing equilibrium allocations is to avoid debt choices that lead with positive probability to areas of the state space for which either consumption is nonpositive or the aggregate collateral constraint is violated in the future. We propose a solution algorithm that addresses the above two issues with a forward-looking computational approach we call "path-finder." The path-finder refinement of the solution algorithm facilitates convergence in the presence of nonconvexities in the aggregate feasible debt set.

12.5.3 Computation of Equilibrium

To approximate the equilibrium, we develop an Euler equation iteration procedure over a discretized state space. The appendix to Schmitt-Grohé and Uribe (2016b) describes the numerical algorithm in detail. The economy possesses two exogenous states, y_t^T and r_t, and one endogenous state, d_t. As in Chapter 9, we discretize $\ln y_t^T$ using 21 evenly spaced points in the interval $[\ln \underline{y}^T, \ln \overline{y}^T] = [-0.3858, 0.3858]$ and $\ln(1+r_t)/(1+r)$ using 11 evenly spaced points in the interval $\left[\ln\left(\frac{1+\underline{r}}{1+r}\right), \ln\left(\frac{1+\overline{r}}{1+r}\right)\right] = [-0.0539, 0.0539]$. We use 501 equally spaced points for d_t in the interval $[\underline{d}, \overline{d}] = [0, 3.5]$. This upper bound is below the natural debt limit of 8.3416, defined as the level of debt that could be supported with zero consumption of tradables if y_t^T takes forever its lowest possible value and r_t takes forever its highest possible value, that is, $\underline{y}^T(1+\overline{r})/\overline{r}$. Values of debt higher than 3.5 are never visited in the stochastic steady state, regardless of the equilibrium selection criterion adopted. Setting $\overline{d}$ equal to 3.5 therefore results in a more efficient use of the 501 debt grid points. The Matlab program `constrained.m` computes the equilibrium policy function, and `simu.m` produces simulated time series of variables of interest (both available on the book's Web site).

12.5.4 Equilibrium Debt Distributions

Figure 12.6 displays the unconditional distribution of external debt, d_t.[4] The different equilibrium selection criteria give rise to different debt distributions, revealing the presence of

---

4. To avoid clutter, the densities are smoothed out. Specifically, for each grid point d_i, the associated smoothed density is the average of the densities associated with points d_{i-19} to d_i for $i = 20, \ldots, 501$.

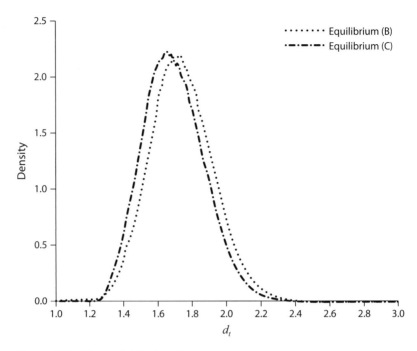

Figure 12.6   External debt densities.

Note: The Matlab replication program is `plotdu.m`, available on the book's Web site.

multiple equilibria.[5] The more pessimistic equilibrium selection criterion (C) (dash-dotted line in the figure), which favors large self-fulfilling debt crises, yields the debt distribution with a mean of 12.0 percent of annual output. The distribution of debt associated with selection criterion (B) (dotted line) is located to the right of the one associated with criterion (C), although the difference in the mean debt-to-output ratio is not large, 0.4 percentage points. However, if one were to attempt to compute the equilibrium assuming uniqueness, standard Euler-equation iteration procedures would in general not converge.

12.5.5 The Unconstrained Economy

For comparison, we also characterize numerically the equilibrium dynamics of an economy without a collateral constraint. We refer to this economy as the unconstrained economy. The unconstrained economy has no externalities. As a result, the competitive equilibrium coincides with the solution to a social planner problem of choosing processes c_t^T and d_{t+1} to maximize

$$E_0 \sum_{t=0}^{\infty} \beta^t U(A(c_t^T, y^N)),$$

5. Other parameterizations may deliver a unique equilibrium. Such is the case, for example, with the calibration adopted by Bianchi (2011); see exercise 12.8.

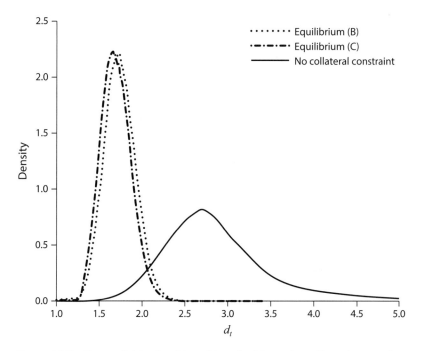

Figure 12.7 External debt densities with and without the collateral constraint.

Note: The Matlab replication program is `plotdu.m`, available on the book's Web site.

subject to the resource constraint (12.54) and some borrowing limit, such as the natural debt limit that rules out Ponzi schemes. Because the lifetime utility function is concave and the resource constraint is a convex set in tradable consumption and debt, the solution to the planner's problem is unique, unlike the situation encountered in the economy with the collateral constraint. Furthermore, the numerical approximation of the equilibrium is facilitated by the fact that the above planner's problem can be cast as a Bellman equation. Formally, the competitive equilibrium in the unconstrained economy solves

$$v(y^T, r, d) = \max_{c^T, d'} \left\{ U(A(c^T, y^N)) + \beta E\left[v(y^{T'}, r', d') \middle| y^T, r\right] \right\},$$

subject to

$$c^T + d = y^T + \frac{d'}{1+r},$$

where a prime superscript denotes next-period values.

Figure 12.7 displays the debt distribution associated with the unconstrained economy (solid line). For comparison, the figure reproduces from Figure 12.6 the debt densities that obtained in the economy with a collateral constraint under the two canonical equilibrium selection criteria. As expected, in the absence of the collateral constraint, the debt distribution shifts to the right. This is the case regardless of which equilibrium selection criterion is

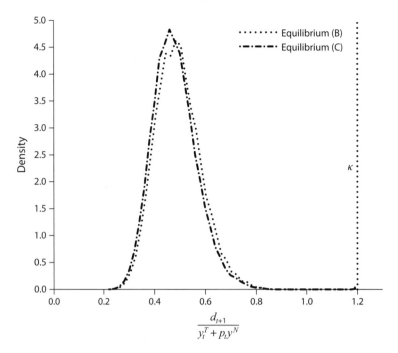

Figure 12.8   The equilibrium distributions of leverage.

Notes: (B) and (C) refer to the equilibrium selection criteria defined in Section 12.5.2. The Matlab replication program is `plot_leverage.m`, available on the book's Web site.

adopted. The mean debt level in the unconstrained economy is 66 percent higher than the ones associated with the constrained economies. This is also the case if one measures debt as a fraction of annual output. The mean debt-to-output ratio is 23 percent in annual terms in the economy without the collateral constraint and around 12 percent in the economies with the collateral constraint. It follows that the presence of the collateral constraint significantly limits the ability of households to borrow. More interestingly, the collateral constraint compresses the debt distribution around its mean. The unconditional standard deviation of debt is reduced by about 75 percent when the collateral constraint is introduced.

The fact that the debt distribution is severely displaced and compressed by the presence of the collateral constraint does not mean that the collateral constraint is hit frequently. It actually turns out that the contrary is the case. The collateral constraint almost never binds. On average, the constraint binds every 224 years under equilibrium selection criterion (B) and every 870 years under selection criterion (C).[6] This is illustrated in Figure 12.8, which displays the equilibrium distribution of the leverage ratio, defined as $d_{t+1}/(y_t^T + p_t y^N)$, under the two equilibrium selection criteria considered (B and C). As a reference, the figure also displays the leverage limit κ. Households choose to stay clear of the leverage upper

---

6. Financial crises can be made to occur more frequently by assuming that households are more impatient (i.e., by lowering the subjective discount factor β).

bound virtually all of the time. Households manage to avoid being caught with a binding constraint by engaging in precautionary savings. They save because, as we will see shortly, being up against the constraint leaves no room for smoothing income shocks and forces them to deleverage. This collective deleveraging causes the price of collateral to collapse, which reinforces the need to deleverage.

12.6 Financial Amplification

How do collateral constraints affect aggregate fluctuations? Do they amplify the business cycle? Table 12.2 addresses these questions by displaying unconditional second moments of macroeconomic indicators of interest in the economies with and without a collateral constraint (see columns labeled CC and No CC, respectively). For simplicity, results are shown for equilibrium selection criterion (C). The results are robust to adopting selection criterion (B). The amplitude of the business cycle—as measured by the unconditional standard deviations of output, consumption, the relative price of nontradables, and other variables of interest—is not increased by the presence of a collateral constraint. This result was first stressed by Mendoza (2010) in the context of a stock collateral constraint economy. The reason the presence of a collateral constraint does not produce an amplification of regular business cycles is that, because of precautionary savings, the collateral constraint is almost always slack. Serial correlations and correlations with output are also little changed by the presence of a collateral constraint, with the exception of the correlation of the current account with output. The results reported in Table 12.2 are important because they suggest that financial frictions of the type studied here are unlikely to explain the main difference between observed business cycles in emerging and advanced countries stressed in Chapter 1, namely, that the former are twice as volatile as the latter.

Table 12.2   No Amplification of Regular Business Cycles

Indicator	Standard Deviation			Serial Correlation			Correlation with Output		
	CC	No CC	R	CC	No CC	R	CC	No CC	R
Tradable output, y_t^T	0.12	0.12	0.12	0.94	0.94	0.94	0.97	0.95	0.96
Interest rate, r_t	0.02	0.02	0.02	0.90	0.90	0.90	−0.91	−0.92	−0.93
Output, $y_t^T + p_t y^n$	0.96	0.99	0.95	0.93	0.95	0.94	1.00	1.00	1.00
Consumption of tradables, c_t^T	0.15	0.16	0.15	0.92	0.95	0.94	0.99	0.99	0.99
Relative price of nontradables, p_t	0.85	0.87	0.83	0.92	0.95	0.94	1.00	1.00	1.00
Trade balance, tb_t	0.05	0.06	0.05	0.61	0.79	0.67	−0.65	−0.71	−0.63
Current account, ca_t	0.04	0.04	0.04	0.30	0.30	0.32	−0.27	0.13	−0.13
Capital control tax, τ_t (percent)			0.96			0.10			−0.11

Notes: All moments are unconditional. CC, collateral-constraint economy under equilibrium selection criterion (C) as defined in Section 12.5.2; No CC, economy without a collateral constraint; R, economy with Ramsey optimal capital control policy. The entries for the CC columns are virtually identical under equilibrium selection criterion (B). The Matlab replication program is table_r.m, available on the book's Web site.

But do collateral constraints play a more prominent role during large contractions? To address this question, we investigate the effect of collateral constraints during boom-bust cycles. We define a boom-bust cycle as in Chapter 10, that is, as a path of tradable output that starts below the mean, rises to one standard deviation above the mean over the following 10 quarters, and then falls to one standard deviation below the mean in the next 10 quarters. We date the beginning of the boom-bust cycle to be period -20, so that the peak occurs in period -10 and the trough in period 0. Between periods -10 and 0, tradable output falls by at least two standard deviations, or 24 percent. This is a severe contraction both in terms of depth and abruptness. The estimated driving process given in equation (9.31) delivers one boom-bust cycle every 130 years. Because y_t^T and r_t are estimated to be highly negatively correlated, we have that during a boom-bust cycle, the country interest rate is the mirror image of the endowment—that is, it falls rapidly during the boom and rises sharply during the bust. To obtain the typical boom-bust cycle, we generate artificial time series of length 1 million quarters, extract all windows containing a boom-bust cycle, and then average across windows.

Figure 12.9 displays the behavior of some variables of interest during a typical boom-bust cycle in the economy with a collateral constraint (solid line) and in the unconstrained economy (dashed line). The dynamics in both environments are quite similar, indicating a lack of amplification of boom-bust cycles due to collateral constraints. In particular, the paths of output, tradable consumption, the relative price of nontradables, and the trade balance are almost the same in the economies with and without the collateral constraint. The trade surplus is larger on average in the economy without the collateral constraint than in the economy with the constraint, because in the former economy the average debt level is higher, which requires dedicating more resources to interest service. The reason the collateral constraint fails to amplify boom-bust cycles is that it is typically highly slack during these episodes. The right panel of the third row of Figure 12.9 shows (dash-dotted line) the path of collateral, $\kappa(y_t^T + p_t y^N)$, and (solid line) the path of debt assumed in period t, d_{t+1}, in the collateral-constraint economy. Although the value of collateral falls significantly, by around 40 percent, the borrowing constraint is so slack that it never comes close to being binding. Given this, it is not too surprising that the paths of most macroeconomic indicators of interest are similar in the economies with and without the collateral constraint. Thus we conclude that collateral constraints do not amplify large boom-bust cycles. This result was first emphasized by Schmitt-Grohé and Uribe (2016c).

If a boom-bust cycle that is so severe that it occurs only once every 130 years cannot make the collateral constraint bind, what can? To answer this question, we proceed as in the analysis of a boom-bust cycle. Specifically, we simulate the economy for 1 million periods and collect all windows containing a binding collateral constraint. We continue to impose equilibrium selection criterion (C), but the results are robust to assuming criterion (B). The period in which the collateral constraint binds is denoted by 0. We refer to a period with a binding collateral constraint as a financial crisis. As mentioned earlier, under the present calibration and selection criterion, the model delivers financial crises quite infrequently, once every 870 years on average.

What drives the economy to a financial crisis and what happens when one occurs? Figure 12.10 displays (solid lines) the behavior of the economy during a typical financial

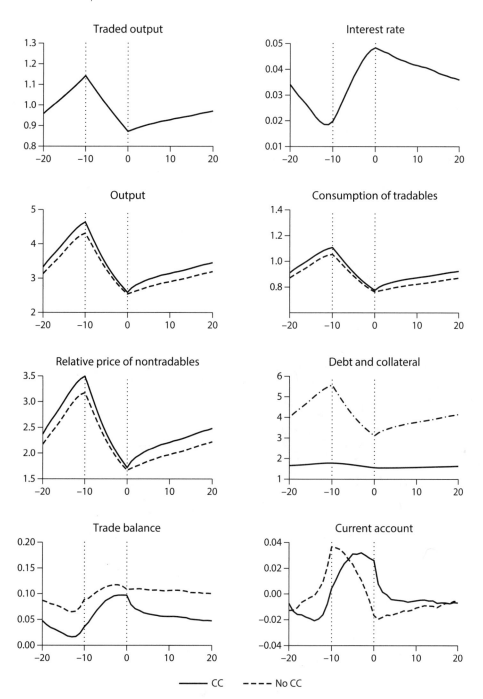

Figure 12.9 No amplification of boom-bust cycles.

Notes: CC, economy with the collateral constraint under equilibrium selection criterion (C), as defined in Section 12.5.2. The right panel in the third row plots for the CC economy debt (solid line) and collateral (dash-dotted) line. The Matlab replication program is `boom_bust.m`, available on the book's Web site.

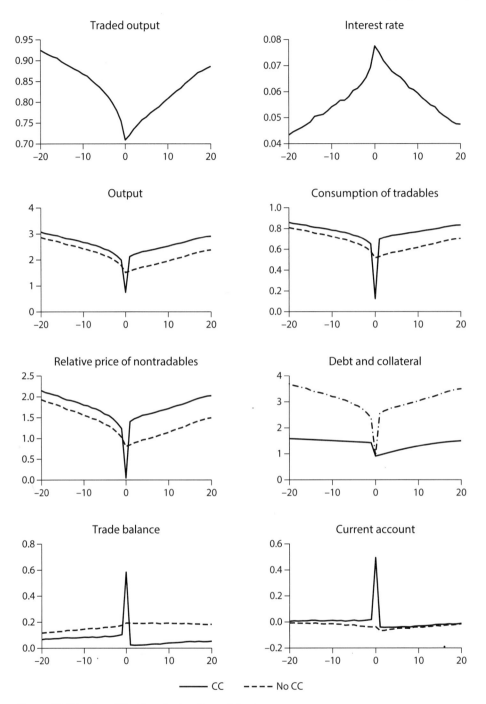

Figure 12.10 Amplification during financial crises.

Notes: CC, collateral-constraint economy under equilibrium selection criterion (C) as defined in Section 12.5.2. No CC, the economy without a collateral constraint. In the right panel in the third row, the heavy solid line corresponds to debt, d_{t+1}, in the CC economy, and the dashed-dotted line to the value of collateral, $\kappa(y_t^T + p_t y^N)$, in the CC economy. The Matlab replication program is typical_crisis.m, available on the book's Web site.

crisis. For comparison, it also shows (dashed lines) the equilibrium dynamics under the same 1 million realizations of the exogenous states y_t^T and r_t and the same initial condition d_0 in the economy without a collateral constraint. The first thing to notice is that a financial crisis occurs after a protracted period of large adverse output and interest-rate shocks. The top panels of the figure show that in the run-up to a financial crisis, tradable output contracts at an increasing pace for 5 years, reaching a trough of 30 percent below trend in the period of the crisis. Similarly, the country interest rate rises at an increasing rate, peaking at around 7.5 percent when the crisis occurs (or almost 30 percentage points per year). Because both y_t^T and r_t are mean reverting, the paths of these two driving forces represent a string of increasingly unlikely negative events.

A second notable characteristic of the equilibrium dynamics is the absence of a credit boom in the run-up to the crisis. The economy hits the collateral constraint because the value of collateral falls at an increasing rate up to the date of the crisis. This fall in the value of collateral has two components: the exogenous fall in tradable output and the endogenous fall in the relative price of nontradables. The latter occurs because aggregate demand falls continuously. In turn, the reduction in aggregate demand is caused by the fall in income (y_t^T) and the rise in the country interest rate (r_t). In the period of the crisis, the economy experiences yet another fall in tradable output and another increase in the interest rate. As before, both these shocks cause the value of collateral to fall. However, this time the constraint is binding, so all of the fall in collateral must be met by an equally large fall in debt (d_{t+1} falls by 30 percent between periods -1 and 0). To bring about the required deleveraging, households must severely cut spending, which drives the price of nontradables, p_t, into the ground. In turn, the collapse in the price of nontradables tightens the collateral constraint further, exacerbating the contraction in aggregate demand and thereby amplifying the crisis.

Although extremely large, the amplification effect is short lived. In Figure 12.10, the effect of the crisis lasts for just one period. The reason is that once the stock of debt is reduced in period 0, the collateral constraint is no longer tight in the future. Recall that d_t is a stock, so reducing it in period 0 has a lasting effect on the slackness of the collateral constraint.

To summarize, in this section we have shown that collateral constraints do not amplify regular business cycles. They do not amplify large boom-bust cycles either. This perhaps surprising finding is due to precautionary savings whereby households maintain debt levels low enough to stay clear of the collateral constraint. Collateral constraints do have a sizable albeit brief amplification effect when they bind, which occurs after long periods of extraordinarily adverse output and interest-rate shocks. It is worth stressing that, as just mentioned, the presence of the collateral constraint does not make the recession more protracted. This prediction of the model is at odds with existing empirical evidence suggesting that recessions that include a financial crisis tend to last longer (Reinhart and Rogoff 2014).

12.7 Optimal Capital Control Policy

The pecuniary externality created by the presence of the relative price of nontradables in the collateral constraint induces an allocation that is in general suboptimal—not only compared to the allocation that would result in the absence of a collateral constraint, but also relative to the best allocation possible among all those that satisfy the collateral constraint. As a result, the collateral constraint opens the door for welfare-improving policy intervention. We begin by studying capital controls, because they essentially represent a tax on external borrowing, which is the variable most directly affected by the pecuniary externality. In fact we will show that the optimal capital control policy fully internalizes the pecuniary externality, in the sense that it induces the representative household to behave as if it understood that its own borrowing choices influence the relative price of nontradables and therefore the value of collateral.

We assume, as we did in the economy with downward nominal wage rigidity of Chapters 9 and 10, that the government is benevolent in the sense that it seeks to maximize the well being of the representative household. Further, we assume that the government has the ability to commit to policy promises. In short, we characterize the Ramsey optimal capital control policy in the context of an open economy with a flow collateral constraint.[7]

Let τ_t be a proportional tax on debt acquired in period t. If τ_t is positive, it represents a proper capital control tax, whereas if it is negative, it is interpreted as a borrowing subsidy. The revenue from capital control taxes is given by $\tau_t d_{t+1}/(1 + r_t)$. We assume that the government consumes no goods and that it rebates all revenues from capital controls to the public in the form of lump-sum transfers (lump-sum taxes if $\tau_t < 0$), denoted by ℓ_t. The budget constraint of the government is then given by

$$\tau_t \frac{d_{t+1}}{1 + r_t} = \ell_t.$$

The household's sequential budget constraint now becomes

$$c_t^T + p_t c_t^N + d_t = y_t^T + p_t y^N + (1 - \tau_t)\frac{d_{t+1}}{1 + r_t} + \ell_t.$$

This expression makes it clear that the capital control tax distorts the borrowing decision of the household. In particular, the gross interest rate on foreign borrowing perceived by the private household is no longer $1 + r_t$ but instead $(1 + r_t)/(1 - \tau_t)$. All other things equal, the higher is τ_t, the higher will be the interest rate perceived by households. Thus by changing τ_t the government can encourage or discourage borrowing. All optimality conditions associated with the household's optimization problem (equations (12.36)–(12.40)) are unchanged, except for the debt Euler equation (12.38), which now takes the form

$$\left(\frac{1 - \tau_t}{1 + r_t} - \mu_t\right)\lambda_t = \beta E_t \lambda_{t+1}.$$

A competitive equilibrium in the economy with capital control taxes is then a set of processes c_t^T, d_{t+1}, λ_t, μ_t, and p_t satisfying

---

7. In the context of models with stock collateral constraints, the Ramsey optimal capital control policy may be time inconsistent. For an analysis of time-consistent capital control policy, see Jeanne and Korinek (2010), Bianchi and Mendoza (2013), and Devereux, Young, and Yu (2015).

$$c_t^T + d_t = y_t^T + \frac{d_{t+1}}{1 + r_t}, \tag{12.55}$$

$$d_{t+1} \leq \kappa \left[y_t^T + p_t y^N \right], \tag{12.56}$$

$$\lambda_t = U'(A(c_t^T, y^N)) A_1(c_t^T, y^N), \tag{12.57}$$

$$\left(\frac{1 - \tau_t}{1 + r_t} - \mu_t \right) \lambda_t = \beta E_t \lambda_{t+1}, \tag{12.58}$$

$$p_t = \frac{A_2(c_t^T, y^N)}{A_1(c_t^T, y^N)}, \tag{12.59}$$

$$\mu_t [\kappa (y_t^T + p_t y^N) - d_{t+1}] = 0, \tag{12.60}$$

and

$$\mu_t \geq 0, \tag{12.61}$$

given a policy process τ_t, exogenous driving forces y_t^T and r_t, and the initial condition d_0.

The benevolent government sets capital control taxes to maximize the household's lifetime utility subject to the restriction that the optimal allocation be supportable as a competitive equilibrium. It follows that all the above competitive equilibrium conditions are constraints of the Ramsey government's optimization problem. Formally, the Ramsey optimal competitive equilibrium is a set of processes τ_t, c_t^T, d_{t+1}, λ_t, μ_t, and p_t that solve the problem of maximizing

$$E_0 \sum_{t=0}^{\infty} \beta^t U(A(c_t^T, y^N)), \tag{12.62}$$

subject to (12.55)–(12.61), given processes y_t^T and r_t and the initial condition d_0. In the welfare function (12.62), we have replaced consumption of nontradables, c_t^N, with the endowment of nontradables, y^N, because the Ramsey planner takes into account that in a competitive equilibrium the market for nontradables clears at all times.

The above equilibrium conditions look like a formidable set of constraints. Fortunately, as in the optimal capital control problem of Chapter 10, it is possible to reduce considerably the set of constraints. In particular, it turns out that any processes c_t^T and d_{t+1} satisfy equilibrium conditions (12.55)–(12.61) if and only if they satisfy (12.55) and

$$d_{t+1} \leq \kappa \left[y_t^T + \frac{1 - a}{a} \left(\frac{c_t^T}{y^N} \right)^{\frac{1}{\xi}} y^N \right]. \tag{12.63}$$

To see this, suppose c_t^T and d_{t+1} satisfy (12.55) and (12.63). We must establish that (12.55)–(12.61) are also satisfied. Obviously, the resource constraint (12.55) holds. Now pick p_t to satisfy (12.59). This is possible, because the process c_t^T is given. Now use this expression to eliminate p_t from (12.56). The resulting expression is (12.63), establishing that (12.56) holds. Next pick λ_t to satisfy (12.57). Now set $\mu_t = 0$ for all t. It follows immediately that the slackness condition (12.60) and the nonnegativity condition (12.61) are satisfied. Finally, pick τ_t to ensure that (12.58) holds, that is,

$$\tau_t = 1 - \beta(1 + r_t)E_t \frac{U'(A(c_{t+1}^T, y^N))A_1(c_{t+1}^T, y^N)}{U'(A(c_t^T, y^N))A_1(c_t^T, y^N)}. \tag{12.64}$$

Next we need to show the reverse statement: processes c_t^T and d_{t+1} that satisfy (12.55)–(12.61) also satisfy (12.55) and (12.63). Obviously (12.55) is satisfied, and combining (12.56) with (12.59) yields (12.63). This completes the proof of the equivalence of the constraint sets (12.55)–(12.61) and (12.55) and (12.63).

We can then state the Ramsey problem as

$$\max_{\{c_t^T, d_{t+1}\}} E_0 \sum_{t=0}^{\infty} \beta^t U(A(c_t^T, y^N)) \tag{12.62 R}$$

subject to

$$c_t^T + d_t = y_t^T + \frac{d_{t+1}}{1 + r_t}, \tag{12.55 R}$$

$$d_{t+1} \leq \kappa \left[y_t^T + \frac{1-a}{a} \left(\frac{c_t^T}{y^N} \right)^{\frac{1}{\xi}} y^N \right]. \tag{12.63 R}$$

Comparing the levels of debt in the Ramsey equilibrium and in the unregulated equilibrium (i.e., the equilibrium without government intervention), we can determine whether the lack of optimal government intervention results in too much or too little debt. The case in which the economy borrows too much is known as overborrowing and the case in which the economy borrows too little as underborrowing. We turn to this issue next.

12.7.1 Overborrowing or Underborrowing? An Analytical Example

Consider the Ramsey optimal allocation in the perfect-foresight economy analyzed in Section 12.4. Suppose that the initial value of debt, d_0, satisfies $d_0 < \tilde{d}$, as shown in Figure 12.4. Since one possible competitive equilibrium is $d_t = d_0$ and $c_t^T = y^T - rd_0/(1 + r)$ for all $t \geq 0$, and since this equilibrium is the first best equilibrium (i.e., the equilibrium that would result in the absence of the collateral constraint), it also has to be the Ramsey optimal equilibrium. What is the capital control tax associated with the Ramsey optimal equilibrium? Take a look at equation (12.64). Since consumption of tradables is constant over time, it follows that $\tau_t = 0$ for all $t \geq 0$. Now compare the level of debt in the Ramsey optimal allocation with the one associated with the unregulated competitive equilibrium. Here we must take into account that there are two unregulated competitive equilibria. Suppose the unregulated competitive equilibrium happens to be the one in which the collateral constraint binds in period 0, shown with point B in Figure 12.4. In this case the unregulated economy underborrows at all times, since the level of debt at point B is less than the

Ramsey optimal level of debt, d_0. However, if the unregulated competitive equilibrium happens to be the unconstrained equilibrium (point A in the figure), then there is neither underborrowing nor overborrowing, since its associated level of debt coincides with the Ramsey optimal level, d_0. Thus in this economy, there is either underborrowing or optimal borrowing, depending on whether the competitive equilibrium happens to be the constrained or the unconstrained one.

12.7.2 Implementation

The Ramsey optimal policy is mute with regard to equilibrium implementation. In the context of the economy studied here, this means that the Ramsey optimal policy $\tau_t = 0$ does not guarantee that the competitive equilibrium will be the Ramsey optimal one (e.g., point A in Figures 12.4 and 12.5). In particular, the policy rule $\tau_t = 0$ for all t may result in an unintended competitive equilibrium, like point B in Figure 12.4 or points B or C in Figure 12.5. Thus a policy of setting $\tau_t = 0$ at all times may fail to implement the Ramsey optimal allocation. However, any capital control policy that succeeds in implementing the Ramsey optimal allocation must deliver $\tau_t = 0$ for all t in equilibrium. The difference between a policy that sets $\tau_t = 0$ under all circumstances and a policy capable of implementing the Ramsey optimal allocation is not the capital control tax that results in equilibrium, but the tax rates that would be imposed off equilibrium.

To shed light on the issue of implementation, we study a capital control feedback rule capable of bringing about the Ramsey optimal equilibrium. The analysis follows Schmitt-Grohé and Uribe (2016b). Specifically, consider the capital control policy

$$\tau_t = \tau(d_{t+1}, d_t),$$

satisfying $\tau(d, d) = 0$. According to this rule, capital controls depend not on the level of debt but on the magnitude of capital flows. Under this tax-policy rule, the Euler equation in period 0 (e.g., the combination of equations (12.57) and (12.58) evaluated at $t = 0$) becomes

$$\frac{c_1^T}{c_0^T} = \frac{1}{\sqrt{1 - \tau(d_1, d_0) - (1+r)\mu_0}}. \tag{12.65}$$

In the intended (Ramsey) equilibrium, we have that $c_1^T/c_0^T = 1$, $d_1 = d_0$, and $\mu_0 = 0$, so the Euler equation holds and $\tau(d_1, d_0) = 0$. This means that the proposed policy is consistent with the Ramsey optimal allocation.

But the same capital control policy can rule out the unintended equilibria. Recalling that c_0^T and c_1^T satisfy $c_0^T = y^T + d_1/(1+r) - d_0$ and $c_1^T = y^T - rd_1/(1+r)$, we can write the Euler equation (12.65) as

$$\frac{y^T - rd_1/(1+r)}{y^T + d_1/(1+r) - d_0} = \frac{1}{\sqrt{1 - \tau(d_1, d_0) - (1+r)\mu_0}}.$$

Now pick the policy function $\tau(\cdot, \cdot)$ in such a way that if a self-fulfilling crisis occurs and the economy deleverages, then the Euler equation holds only if μ_0 is negative. Specifically, set $\tau(d_1, d_0)$ to satisfy

$$\frac{y^T - rd_1/(1+r)}{y^T + d_1/(1+r) - d_0} < \frac{1}{\sqrt{1 - \tau(d_1, d_0)}},$$

for all $d_1 < d_0$.[8] Clearly this policy requires $\tau(d_1, d_0) > 0$ if $d_1 < d_0$. Under this capital control policy, the Euler equation would not hold for any value of d_1 less than d_0, since it would require $\mu_0 < 0$, which violates the nonnegativity constraint (12.61). This means that any equilibrium in which the economy deleverages is ruled out.

The capital control policy that rules out self-fulfilling crises and ensures that only the Ramsey optimal (and first-best) equilibrium emerges is one in which the policymaker is committed to imposing capital control taxes in the case of capital outflows, that is, if $d_1 < d_0$. This type of capital control policy serves as a metaphor for a variety of policies that are often contemplated in emerging countries during financial panics and that aim at temporarily restricting capital outflows, including restrictions on foreign exchange markets and repatriations of profits and dividends. In the present perfect-foresight economy, the mere threat of the imposition of capital control taxes in the case of capital outflows suffices to fend off self-fulfilling crises; thus such taxes never need to be deployed in equilibrium.

12.8 Overborrowing and Underborrowing: A Quantitative Analysis

We have shown analytically that the perfect-foresight economy of Section 12.4 may display underborrowing. Importantly, that analysis makes clear that the presence or absence of suboptimal borrowing critically depends on which equilibrium, of possibly multiple ones, materializes. The analysis further suggests that if the equilibrium selection criterion favors picking allocations in which the collateral constraint binds, then the unregulated equilibrium is likely to display underborrowing. Schmitt-Grohé and Uribe (2016b) show that this result extends to environments with uncertainty. In particular, under plausible calibrations, multiple equilibria exist, some displaying underborrowing. The following analysis draws on these results.

Consider the Ramsey optimal allocation in the calibrated stochastic economy of Section 12.5. The Ramsey optimal allocation is relatively easy to compute, because the Ramsey problem can be cast in the form of a Bellman equation problem. Specifically, the recursive version of the Ramsey problem of maximizing (12.62) subject to (12.55) and (12.63) is given by

$$v(y^T, r, d) = \max_{c^T, d'} \left\{ U(A(c^T, y^N)) + \beta E \left[v(y^{T'}, r', d') \middle| y^T, r \right] \right\},$$

subject to

$$c^T + d = y^T + \frac{d'}{1+r}$$

---

8. An example of a policy that satisfies this restriction is $\tau(d_1, d_0) = 1 - \left(\frac{y^T - rd_1/(1+r)}{y^T + d_1/(1+r) - d_0} + \alpha \right)^{-2}$, for any $\alpha > 0$.

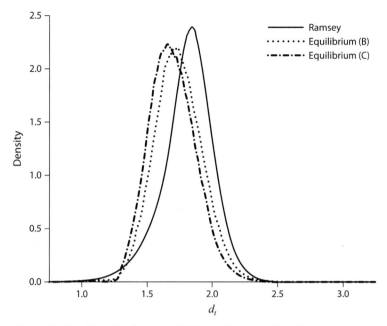

Figure 12.11 The distribution of debt under optimal capital controls.

Notes: (B) and (C) refer to the equilibrium selection criteria defined in Section 12.5.2. The replication program is `plotd_ramsey.m`, available on the book's Web site.

and

$$d' \leq \kappa \left[y^T + \frac{1-a}{a} \left(\frac{c^T}{y^N} \right)^{\frac{1}{\xi}} y^N \right],$$

where, as before, a prime superscript denotes next-period values. Although the constraints of this control problem may not represent a convex set in tradable consumption and debt, the fact that the Ramsey allocation is the result of a utility maximization problem implies that its solution is generically unique. The Matlab code `ramsey.m`, provided online with the materials for this chapter, solves for the Ramsey equilibrium. The calibration of the economy and the discretization of the state space are the same as those used for the unregulated economy, summarized in Table 12.1.

Figure 12.11 displays with a solid line the unconditional distribution of net external debt, d_t, under Ramsey optimal capital control policy. For comparison, the figure reproduces from Figure 12.6 the unconditional distributions of debt in the unregulated economy under the two equilibrium selection criteria defined in Section 12.5.2. Figure 12.11 shows that the analytical result of the previous section carries over to the stochastic economy. Namely, the unregulated economy may display underborrowing, in the sense that its debt distribution may lie to the left of the one associated with the Ramsey optimal capital control policy. This occurs when private agents coordinate on equilibria (B) or (C), both of which gravitate toward financial crises. The average annual debt-to-output ratio is 12.0 percent in the unregulated equilibrium (C), 12.4 percent in the unregulated equilibrium (B), and 13.1 percent in the Ramsey optimal equilibrium. The reason underborrowing occurs for equilibrium selection criteria (B) and (C) is that under these (pessimistic) expectations-coordination environments, households engage in a suboptimally high level of precautionary savings. In turn, precautionary savings is motivated by the fact that under equilibria (B) or (C) the economy is more fragile, as it is more prone to financial crises.

But the unregulated economy may also display overborrowing. Indeed the standard result stressed in the related quantitative literature on pecuniary externalities due to collateral constraints is overborrowing. For example, Bianchi (2011) finds that the unregulated economy holds on average an external debt that is 0.6 percentage points of output higher than the Ramsey optimal level. Under the present calibration, we could not detect an equilibrium displaying overborrowing. An important difference between Bianchi's calibration and the one considered here is the assumed time unit, which is a year in the former and a quarter in the latter. This is important, because it affects the value of the leverage parameter κ. This parameter is frequency dependent, because it links a stock, d_{t+1}, to a flow, $y_t^T + p_t y_t^N$. In both the present calibration and Bianchi's, the upper bound on leverage is one third of annual output. But this requires setting κ equal to 0.3 when the time unit is a year and equal to 1.2 when the time unit is a quarter. In turn, the value of κ affects the equilibrium sensitivity of collateral to the aggregate level of debt (see equation (12.46)). The larger is κ, the higher this sensitivity will be. Another parameter that is key in determining the sensitivity of collateral to debt in equilibrium is the intratemporal elasticity of substitution between tradables and nontradables, ξ. The larger is ξ, the less sensitive the equilibrium value of collateral to variations in debt will be. This parameter takes the value 0.83 in Bianchi's calibration and 0.5 in the present one. A third difference between the present model and the one studied by Bianchi is the battery of shocks considered. The present economy is driven by a mix of output and interest-rate shocks, whereas Bianchi's features only output shocks. This assumption is important, because interest-rate shocks have a more direct effect on the desired level of precautionary savings. We conjecture that the assumed time unit, the value of the intratemporal elasticity of substitution, and the assumed sources of uncertainty significantly affect the possibility of multiple equilibria and whether the model displays underborrowing or overborrowing.

An exception to the standard overborrowing result is Benigno et al. (2013), who obtain underborrowing by replacing the assumption of an endowment economy maintained in Bianchi (2011) with the assumption that output is produced with labor. In their production economy, the social planner sustains more debt than in the unregulated economy by engineering sectoral employment allocations conducive to elevated values of the collateral in terms of tradable goods. The underborrowing result obtained in this section is complementary but different from that of Benigno et al. Here underborrowing arises even in the context of an endowment economy and is due to an inefficiently high level of precautionary savings in an environment prone to self-fulfilling crises.

12.9 Is Optimal Capital Control Policy Macroprudential?

How does the Ramsey planner handle crisis situations? To address this question, we examine the behavior of the unregulated economy and the Ramsey economy around financial crises in the unregulated economy. For the unregulated economy, we assume equilibrium selection (C). Figure 12.12 displays (dashed line) the behavior of the Ramsey optimal economy near and during financial crises in the unregulated economy. The figure also reproduces from Figure 12.10 the behavior of the unregulated economy (solid line). The first thing to notice is that when the unregulated economy experiences a financial crisis (i.e., a binding collateral constraint), the Ramsey optimal economy typically does not. The unregulated economy experiences 287 financial crises every 1 million quarters, of which only 46 are also crises in the Ramsey economy. As a result, although the Ramsey economy experiences a downturn when the unregulated economy suffers from a financial crisis, the contraction is less severe.

How is the Ramsey planner able to avoid the financial crisis that would have taken place in the absence of optimal capital controls? The answer to this question is given in the bottom-right panel of Figure 12.12, which shows the behavior of the Ramsey optimal capital control tax. The planner increases capital controls markedly from 0 percent to 3.9 percent as the crisis becomes imminent. Recall that the capital control tax is indeterminate in periods in which the Ramsey economy is in a financial crisis. In these instances, we arbitrarily set τ_t to ensure that the Lagrange multiplier associated with the household's collateral constraint (μ_t) is nil. If we restrict attention to the 241 episodes in which the unregulated economy experiences a crisis but the Ramsey economy does not, the average level of τ_t at the time of the crisis is 3.6 percent.

The optimal capital control policy is hardly preemptive in nature, as it discourages borrowing only within a narrow window around what otherwise would have been a crisis. The fact that the Ramsey planner waits until economic fundamentals are significantly weakened before acting raises the question of whether optimal capital control policy is macroprudential in the present economic environment.

The term "macroprudential capital control policy" has been used in two ways in the related literature. One is to refer to a positive average capital control tax. The reason a positive average tax is considered macroprudential is that by discouraging external borrowing, it makes the economy less vulnerable to movements in the value of collateral. The second meaning of macroprudential capital controls refers to a policy regime that discourages capital inflows during booms and the reverse during busts. The idea here is that by curbing excessive borrowing when the economy is in good shape (especially when the value of collateral is high), policymakers can achieve a soft landing as the economy transitions to a contractionary phase of the cycle.

The present model delivers an optimal capital control policy that is not macroprudential in either of these two senses. The predicted unconditional mean of the capital control tax rate, τ_t, is virtually nil (0.002 percent), rendering the optimal capital control policy nonprudential under the first definition. This result is not independent of the specific assumed calibration and underlying sources of uncertainty. Bianchi (2011), for example, finds that the annual capital control tax is about 5 percent, or 1.25 per quarter.

To ascertain whether optimal capital control policy is prudential in a cyclical sense, Figure 12.13 displays the behavior of the economy with and without optimal capital controls during a large boom-bust cycle as defined in Section 12.6. The new information in Figure 12.13 is given by the behavior of the Ramsey economy (dashed-dotted lines). The dynamics of the unregulated economy (solid lines) are the same as those shown in

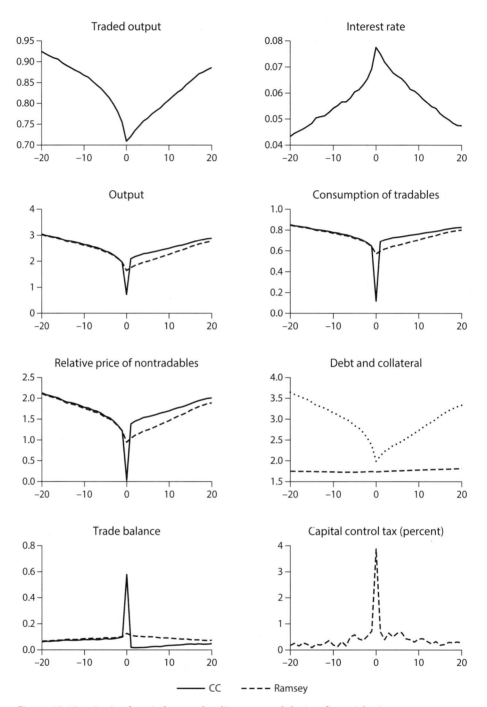

Figure 12.12   Optimal capital control policy near and during financial crises.

Notes: CC, the unregulated collateral-constrained economy under equilibrium selection criterion (C). The third panel on the right displays (dashed line) the level of debt, d_t, and (dotted
line) the value of collateral, $\kappa(y_t^T + p_t y^N)$ in the Ramsey economy. The replication program is
`typical_crisis_ramsey.m`, available on the book's Web site.

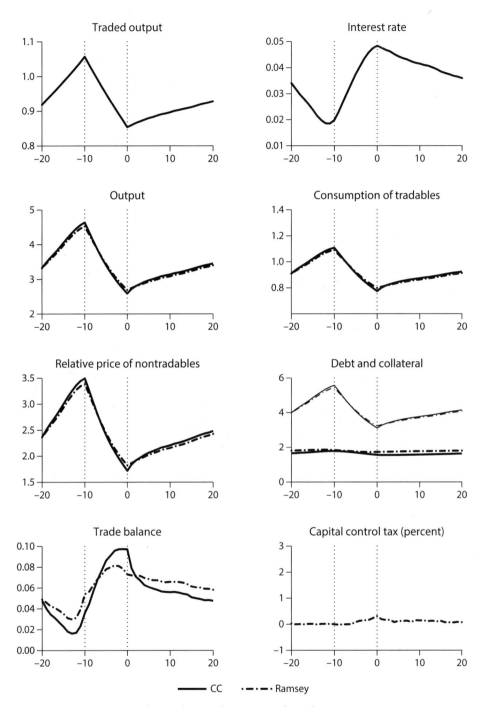

Figure 12.13   Are optimal capital controls macroprudential?

Notes: CC, unregulated collateral-constrained economy under equilibrium selection criterion (C). The third panel on the right displays (thick line) the level of debt, d_{t+1}, and (thin line) the value of collateral, $\kappa(y_t^T + p_t y^N)$. The replication file is `boom_bust_ramsey.m`, available on the book's Web site.

Figure 12.9. It is important to recall that the boom-bust cycle considered here is one of exceptionally large magnitude, since the economy is subject to a collapse from a one-standard-deviation boom to a one-standard-deviation trough in only 10 quarters, an event that in the present environment happens on average only once every 130 years. Nonetheless, the Ramsey dynamics are virtually identical to those implied by the unregulated economy. More importantly, the Ramsey planner makes virtually no use of capital controls at any point during the boom or the bust.

The preceding analysis suggests that optimal capital control policy is not counter-cyclical over boom-bust cycles. This result extends to regular business cycles. Table 12.2 shows that unconditional standard deviations, serial correlations, and contemporaneous correlations with output are largely the same in the unregulated economy and the Ramsey economy. Notably, capital control taxes display a small but negative correlation with output, indicating a lack of unconditional macroprudentiality.

The implied lack of cyclicality of optimal capital control policy resembles the actual behavior of capital controls during booms and busts documented in Fernández, Rebucci, and Uribe (2015) and discussed in Chapter 10 (see especially Figure 10.7).

12.10 Optimal Consumption Taxes

We have demonstrated that optimal capital controls can support the best constrained allocation. That is, they allow for full internalization of the pecuniary externality. In this section we show that a consumption tax levied on either nontradable or tradable goods can support an even more desirable allocation. Specifically, they can achieve the unconstrained allocation—that is, they allow the Ramsey planner to completely circumvent the collateral constraint. This result is due to Benigno et al. (2014).

Let τ_t^N be a proportional tax on nontradable consumption in period t. If τ_t^N is negative, it represents a subsidy. This tax generates government revenue in the amount $\tau_t^N p_t c_t^N$. We continue to assume that the government consumes no goods and that it rebates tax revenues in a lump-sum fashion. The government's budget constraint is then given by

$$\tau_t^N p_t c_t^N = \ell_t,$$

where, as before, ℓ_t denotes a lump-sum transfer if τ_t^N is positive or a lump-sum tax if τ_t^N is negative.

The consumption tax gives rise to the following sequential budget constraint on the household:

$$c_t^T + (1 + \tau_t^N) p_t c_t^N + d_t = y_t^T + p_t y^N + \frac{d_{t+1}}{1 + r_t} + \ell_t.$$

The first-order conditions associated with the household's optimization problem (equations (12.36)–(12.40)) remain the same, except for optimality condition (12.37), which now becomes

$$(1 + \tau_t^N) p_t = \frac{1 - a}{a} \left(\frac{c_t^T}{c_t^N} \right)^{1/\xi}.$$

This expression says that a tax on nontraded consumption distorts the allocation of private spending on tradable and nontradable goods by artificially increasing the perceived relative price of nontradables in terms of tradables. A competitive equilibrium in the economy with a tax on nontraded consumption goods is then a set of processes c_t^T, d_{t+1}, λ_t, μ_t, and p_t satisfying

$$c_t^T + d_t = y_t^T + \frac{d_{t+1}}{1+r_t}, \tag{12.66}$$

$$d_{t+1} \leq \kappa \left[y_t^T + p_t y^N \right], \tag{12.67}$$

$$\lambda_t = U'(A(c_t^T, y^N))A_1(c_t^T, y^N), \tag{12.68}$$

$$\left(\frac{1}{1+r_t} - \mu_t \right) \lambda_t = \beta E_t \lambda_{t+1}, \tag{12.69}$$

$$(1+\tau_t^N)p_t = \frac{A_2(c_t^T, y^N)}{A_1(c_t^T, y^N)}, \tag{12.70}$$

$$\mu_t[\kappa(y_t^T + p_t y^N) - d_{t+1}] = 0, \tag{12.71}$$

and

$$\mu_t \geq 0, \tag{12.72}$$

given a consumption-tax process τ_t^N; exogenous driving forces y_t^T and r_t; and the initial condition d_0.

The Ramsey optimal competitive equilibrium is a set of processes τ_t^N, c_t^T, d_{t+1}, λ_t, μ_t, and p_t that solves the problem of maximizing (12.62) subject to (12.66)–(12.72), given processes y_t^T and r_t and the initial condition d_0.

We show now that the processes c_t^T and d_{t+1} that solve the less constrained problem of maximizing (12.62) subject to (12.66) and some natural debt limit are feasible in the sense that they also satisfy the constraints of the Ramsey problem, equations (12.66)–(12.72). The first-order conditions of the less restricted problem are the resource constraint (12.66) and

$$\lambda_t^{LR} = U'(A(c_t^T, y^N))A_1(c_t^T, y^N),$$

and

$$\frac{\lambda_t^{LR}}{1+r_t} = \beta E_t \lambda_{t+1}^{LR},$$

where λ_t^{LR} denotes the Lagrange multiplier associated with the resource constraint in the less restricted problem. To see that this solution solves (12.66)–(12.72), note that it obviously satisfies (12.66). Now set $\lambda_t = \lambda_t^{LR}$ and $\mu_t = 0$. It follows immediately that (12.68), (12.69), (12.71), and (12.72) are satisfied. Next try $\tau_t^N = 0$, and set p_t to satisfy (12.70). Then check whether the collateral constraint (12.67) is satisfied. If it is, then we have found τ_t^N and p_t. Otherwise, set p_t to satisfy the collateral constraint (12.67) with equality and τ_t^N

to satisfy (12.70). This completes the proof that the solution to the less constrained problem is feasible. By necessity, the solution to the less restricted problem must achieve a level of welfare greater than or equal to the one associated with the Ramsey problem. It follows that the solution to the less restricted problem is indeed the Ramsey optimal allocation.

Notice that because the only constraint of the less restricted problem is the resource constraint, we have that the collateral constraint (12.67) no longer restricts the Ramsey allocation. This implies that the consumption tax can fully undo the limitations introduced by the collateral constraint, thereby achieving the unconstrained allocation characterized in Section 12.5.5. Intuitively, during a downturn that otherwise would become a crisis, the government inflates the relative price of nontradables by subsidizing spending on nontradables. In this way, it artificially increases the value of collateral and avoids a financial crisis. During tranquil periods, the government adopts a passive stance, keeping the subsidy at zero. It follows that the tax process is not prudential in nature, since it is activated only when doing nothing would cause a crisis.

But the Ramsey optimal tax process obtained above is not the only one that supports the unconstrained equilibrium. Exercise 12.10 asks you to show that the unconstrained allocation can also be achieved with a constant tax process $\tau_t^N = \tau^N$ for all t. Under this policy the government always keeps the price of nontradables sufficiently inflated to fend off crises. This tax process is more prudential in nature, since the government intervenes even in periods in which lack of intervention would not cause the collateral constraint to bind. Yet there is a sense in which it is not macroprudential, because it is perfectly acyclical. Finally, we note that the unconstrained equilibrium can also be supported by means of a tax on consumption of tradables and no taxation on nontradables. Unlike the case of nontradable taxation, the optimal tax on tradable consumption must in general be constant over time. This is the theme of exercise 12.11.

12.11 Aggregate Versus Individual Collateral Constraints

Thus far we have studied collateral constraints in which the individual household's debt is limited by the value of collateral. In reality, however, the amount that foreign lenders are willing to lend to a country is based on ratings assigned by credit-rating agencies, such as Standard & Poor's or Moody's. These agencies in turn base their rating decisions on macroeconomic indicators, such as debt-to-GDP ratios, not on each individual household's capacity to repay. It is often argued that this practice amplifies booms and busts, because it induces foreign lenders to provide funds indiscriminately during booms and to withdraw funding equally indiscriminately during contractions, without separating in each phase of the cycle the soundness of individual loans. To evaluate this view, we compare the following two types of collateral constraint:

$$d_{t+1} \leq \kappa [y_t^T + p_t y_t^N],$$

and

$$D_{t+1} \leq \kappa [y_t^T + p_t y_t^N], \tag{12.73}$$

where d_{t+1} denotes, as before, debt assumed by the individual household, and D_{t+1} denotes the aggregate per capita level of debt. The first constraint is the one we have been studying thus far and captures an environment in which foreign lenders base their loan decisions on each individual borrower's capacity to repay. The second constraint is new and is meant to formalize a situation in which foreign lenders regard the emerging country as a single investment opportunity and look only at aggregate variables when deciding whether to lend. The question is whether the two formulations give rise to different equilibrium distributions of debt, and in particular whether the one based on aggregate variables delivers more frequent financial crises (i.e., episodes in which the collateral constraint binds). The key difference between these two formulations is that the consumer internalizes the first collateral constraint, because it involves his own level of debt, but does not internalize the second one, because it features the cross-sectional average of debt, which is out of his control. The present analysis is based on Uribe (2006, 2007).

Consider the equilibrium associated with the aggregate collateral constraint (12.73). Because all variables that enter in this constraint are out of the control of the individual households, it does not enter as a constraint in their utility maximization problem. Therefore the household's problem consists of choosing process c_t^T, c_t^N, and d_{t+1} for $t \geq 0$ to maximize

$$E_0 \sum_{t=0}^{\infty} \beta^t U(A(c_t^T, c_t^N)),$$

subject to

$$c_t^T + p_t c_t^N + d_t = y_t^T + p_t y_t^N + \frac{d_{t+1}}{1 + r_t^d} + T_t,$$

where r_t^d denotes the domestic interest rate, which may differ from the country interest rate charged by foreign lenders, r_t. Specifically, when the collateral constraint (12.73) does not bind, domestic agents borrow less than the total amount of funds foreign lenders are willing to invest in the domestic economy. As a result, in this case the domestic interest rate equals the world interest rate: $r_t^d = r_t$. In contrast, when the collateral constraint binds, individual households compete for loans. At the country interest rate r_t, the demand for loans exceeds the value of collateral, $\kappa[y_t^T + p_t y_t^N]$, and consequently the domestic interest rate r_t^d rises to a point at which everybody is happy holding exactly $\kappa[y_t^T + p_t y_t^N]$ units of loans. The variable T_t denotes a lump-sum transfer to be specified below. The household is also subject to a no-Ponzi-game constraint of the form

$$\lim_{j \to \infty} E_t \frac{d_{t+j}}{\prod_{s=0}^{j-1}(1 + r_{t+s}^d)} \leq 0,$$

for all $t \geq 0$.

The first-order conditions of this problem are the sequential budget constraint, the no-Ponzi-game constraint holding with equality,

$$p_t = \frac{A_2(c_t^T, c_t^N)}{A_1(c_t^T, c_t^N)},$$

and

$$U'(A(c_t^T, c_t^N))A_1(c_t^T, c_t^N) = \beta(1 + r_t^d)E_t U'(A(c_{t+1}^T, c_{t+1}^N))A_1(c_{t+1}^T, c_{t+1}^N).$$

The interest-rate differential between the opportunity cost of funds to foreign lenders, r_t, and the domestic interest rate, r_t^d, creates a pure financial rent given by

$$\frac{D_{t+1}}{1+r_t}\left(\frac{1+r_t^d}{1+r_t}-1\right).$$

It is important to specify who appropriates this rent. There are two polar cases. In one, the financial rent is appropriated by domestic banks, which then distribute it to households in a lump-sum fashion. In this case, the emergence of rents does not represent a loss of resources for the country. In the second polar case, the rent is appropriated by foreign banks. In this case, the financial rent generates a resource cost for the domestic economy. Intermediate cases are also possible. Here we study the case in which the financial rent is appropriated domestically. Later we argue (following Uribe (2006, 2007), who analyzes both cases explicitly) that the other polar case, in which rents are appropriated by foreign lenders, delivers virtually identical results. Thus under the present formulation, we assume that the lump-sum transfer T_t satisfies

$$T_t = \frac{d_{t+1}}{1+r_t}\left(1-\frac{1+r_t}{1+r_t^d}\right).$$

Because all agents are identical, we have that in equilibrium,

$$D_t = d_t.$$

Also, as before, the market for nontradables must clear, $c_t^N = y_t^N$, for all $t \geq 0$. Combining the household's sequential budget constraint, the expression for transfers given above, the market clearing condition for nontradables, and the fact that $D_t = d_t$ yields the familiar resource constraint: $c_t^T + d_t = y_t^T + d_{t+1}/(1+r_t)$.

A competitive equilibrium in the economy with an aggregate collateral constraint is then a set of processes $\{c_t^T, d_{t+1}, r_t^d\}$ satisfying

$$\left(\frac{1}{1+r_t^d}\right)U'(A(c_t^T, y_t^N))A_1(c_t^T, y_t^N) = \beta E_t U'(A(c_{t+1}^T, y_{t+1}^N))A_1(c_{t+1}^T, y_{t+1}^N), \quad (12.74)$$

$$c_t^T + d_t = y_t^T + \frac{d_{t+1}}{1+r_t}, \quad (12.75)$$

$$d_{t+1} \leq \kappa y_t^T + \kappa \left(\frac{1-a}{a}\right)c_t^{T\,1/\xi}y_t^{N\,1-1/\xi}, \quad (12.76)$$

$$(r_t^d - r_t)\left[d_{t+1} - \kappa y_t^T - \kappa \left(\frac{1-a}{a}\right)c_t^{T\,1/\xi}y_t^{N\,1-1/\xi}\right] = 0, \quad (12.77)$$

and

$$r_t^d \geq r_t, \quad (12.78)$$

given exogenous processes y_t^T, r_t, and the initial condition d_0. Condition (12.77) is a slackness condition stating that if the collateral constraint is not binding, then the domestic interest rate must equal the world interest rate ($r_t^d = r_t$), and that if the domestic interest rate is strictly above the world interest rate ($r_t^d > r_t$), then the collateral constraint must be binding. Note that the resource constraint (12.75) features the world interest rate, r_t, and not the domestic interest rate, r_t^d. This is because we are assuming that the financial rent that emerges when the collateral constraint is binding stays in the country.

Consider now an environment in which the collateral constraint is imposed at the level of the individual household. This is the economy we studied in previous sections, so, for convenience, we can simply reproduce here the associated equilibrium conditions:

$$\left(\frac{1}{1+r_t} - \mu_t\right) U'(A(c_t^T, y_t^N)) A_1(c_t^T, y_t^N)$$

$$= \beta E_t U'(A(c_{t+1}^T, y_{t+1}^N)) A_1(c_{t+1}^T, y_{t+1}^N), \tag{12.41 R}$$

$$c_t^T + d_t = y_t^T + \frac{d_{t+1}}{1+r_t}, \tag{12.42 R}$$

$$d_{t+1} \leq \kappa y_t^T + \kappa \left(\frac{1-a}{a}\right) c_t^{T\,1/\xi} y_t^{N\,1-1/\xi}, \tag{12.43 R}$$

$$\mu_t \left[\kappa y_t^T + \kappa \left(\frac{1-a}{a}\right) c_t^{T\,1/\xi} y_t^{N\,1-1/\xi} - d_{t+1}\right] = 0, \tag{12.45 R}$$

and

$$\mu_t \geq 0, \tag{12.44}$$

where we have assumed that $\kappa^T = \kappa^N = \kappa$.

We wish to establish that the equilibrium behavior of external debt and consumption of tradables is identical in the economy with an aggregate collateral constraint and in the economy with an individual collateral constraint. That is, we want to show that the processes $\{d_{t+1}, c_t^T\}$ implied by the system (12.74)–(12.78) are identical to the ones implied by the system (12.41)–(12.44). To this end, we will show that by performing variable transformations, the system (12.41)–(12.44) can be written exactly like the system (12.74)–(12.78). Define the shadow interest rate $\tilde{r}_t$ as

$$\frac{1}{1+\tilde{r}_t} = \frac{1}{1+r_t} - \mu_t.$$

Note that μ_t must be nonnegative and less than $1/(1+r_t)$. This last property follows from the fact that, from equation (12.41), a value of μ_t greater than or equal to $1/(1+r_t)$ would imply that the marginal utility of consumption $U'(A(c_t^T, y_t^N)) A_1(c_t^T, y_t^N)$ is infinite or negative. It follows that $\tilde{r}_t$ is greater than or equal to r_t. Furthermore, it is straightforward to see that $\mu_t > 0$ if and only if $\tilde{r}_t > r_t$ and that $\mu_t = 0$ if and only if $\tilde{r}_t = r_t$.

We can therefore write the system (12.41)–(12.44) as

$$\left(\frac{1}{1+\tilde{r}_t}\right) U'(A(c_t^T, y_t^N)) A_1(c_t^T, y_t^N)$$

$$= \beta E_t U'(A(c_{t+1}^T, y_{t+1}^N)) A_1(c_{t+1}^T, y_{t+1}^N), \tag{12.79}$$

$$c_t^T + d_t = y_t^T + \frac{d_{t+1}}{1+r_t}, \tag{12.80}$$

$$d_{t+1} \leq \kappa y_t^T + \kappa \left(\frac{1-a}{a}\right) c_t^{T\,1/\xi} y_t^{N\,1-1/\xi}, \tag{12.81}$$

$$(\tilde{r}_t - r_t)\left[\kappa y_t^T + \kappa \left(\frac{1-a}{a}\right) c_t^{T\,1/\xi} y_t^{N\,1-1/\xi} - d_{t+1}\right] = 0, \tag{12.82}$$

and

$$\tilde{r}_t \geq r_t. \tag{12.83}$$

The systems (12.74)–(12.78) and (12.79)–(12.83) are identical and must therefore deliver identical equilibrium processes for d_{t+1} and c_t^T. This result demonstrates that whether the collateral constraint is imposed at the aggregate or the individual level, the real allocation is the same. In other words, the imposition of the collateral constraint at the aggregate level generates no overborrowing or underborrowing. What happens is that the market interest rate in the economy with the aggregate borrowing limit, r_t^d, conveys exactly the same signal as the Lagrange multiplier μ_t in the economy with the individual borrowing constraint.

If one assumes that the pure financial rents generated by the interest-rate differential accrue to foreign lenders, then under the aggregate collateral constraint the economy suffers resource losses every time r_t^d is larger than r_t. In this case, the economies with the aggregate and individual collateral constraints do not have identical equilibrium conditions. Nevertheless Uribe (2006, 2007) shows, using numerical methods, that the two economies deliver virtually identical real allocations. The reason is that, because the resource losses occur only when the collateral constraint binds and because the collateral constraint binds infrequently due to precautionary savings (see the analysis in Section 12.5), the resource losses are small in expected value and therefore generate negligible wealth effects. Uribe (2006, 2007) shows that this result extends to economies with stock collateral constraints like the one studied in Section 12.1.

12.12 Exercises

12.1 (Transversality Condition in Collateral-Constrained Economies) Consider the economy of Section 12.1. Show that if sequences c_t, d_{t+1}, and k_{t+1} satisfy optimality conditions (12.1)–(12.8) but not the transversality condition (12.9), then there exists a welfare dominating set of sequences that is also feasible (i.e., it satisfies (12.1)–(12.3)).

12.2 (Self-Fulfilling Financial Crises in a Two-Period Economy) Consider a two-period small open economy populated by identical households with preferences given by

$$\ln c_1 + \ln c_2,$$

where c_1 and c_2 denote consumption in periods 1 and 2, respectively. The household's budget constraints in periods 1 and 2 are, respectively,

$$d_2 = d_1 + c_1 + q(k_1 - k) - F(k),$$

and

$$c_2 = F(k_1) - d_2,$$

where d_1 denotes debt due in period 1 and d_2 the debt assumed in period 1 and due in period 2, k denotes an exogenous initial stock of capital, k_1 denotes capital purchased in period 1, q denotes the relative price of capital in terms of consumption, and $F(\cdot)$ is an increasing and concave production function. Implicit in the period-2 constraint is the requirement that the debt position at the end of period 2 be nil. Debt accumulation in period 1 is subject to the following collateral constraint:

$$d_2 \leq \kappa q k_1,$$

where $\kappa < 1$ is a parameter.

1. Derive the first-order conditions associated with the household's optimization problem.
2. Assume that the aggregate stock of capital is fixed. Derive the complete set of equilibrium conditions.
3. Characterize the range of initial debt positions, d_1, for which the collateral constraint does not bind in equilibrium.
4. Find sufficient conditions on the initial level of debt, d_1, for which the economy possesses multiple equilibria (in particular, at least one equilibrium in which the collateral constraint binds and one equilibrium in which it does not).

12.3 (Collateral Constraints and Impatient Consumers) The starting point of this exercise is the endowment economy with impatient households studied in exercise 2.11 of Chapter 2. Modify that environment by assuming that households are subject to a borrowing limit of the form

$$d_t \leq \bar{d}.$$

Consider two alternative scenarios: one in which this borrowing constraint is not binding in period 0 and one in which it is. Under both scenarios characterize the equilibrium paths of consumption, net external debt, and the trade balance.

12.4 (Financial Amplification) Consider the economy of Section 12.4, which features two equilibria, one in which the collateral constraint never binds (point A in Figure 12.4) and one in which the collateral constraint binds in period 0 (point B in the same figure). Suppose that the endowment of tradables, y_t^T, increases permanently in period 0. Suppose that the increase in y_t^T is sufficiently small to ensure that the constrained equilibrium continues to exist. Show that in the unconstrained equilibrium, traded consumption in period 0, c_0^T, increases one-for-one with y_0^T, whereas in the constrained equilibrium, c_0^T increases by more than one-for-one with y_0^T. Provide intuition. Comment on the responses of the trade balance, the current account, and the real exchange rate in the constrained and unconstrained equilibria.

12.5 (A Two-Period Economy with a Flow Collateral Constraint) Consider a two-period small open endowment economy populated by identical households with preferences given by

$$\ln c_1^T + \ln c_1^N + \beta \ln c_2^T,$$

where c_1^T and c_2^T denote consumption of traded goods in periods 1 and 2, respectively; c_1^N denotes consumption of nontraded goods in period 1; and $\beta \in (0, 1)$ is the subjective discount factor. The household's budget constraints in periods 1 and 2 are, respectively,

$$c_1^T + p_1 c_1^N = y_1^T + p_1 y_1^N + \frac{d_1}{1+r},$$

and

$$c_2^T + d_1 = y_2^T,$$

where p_1 denotes the relative price of nontradables in period 1; y_i^T denotes the endowment of tradables in period $i = 1, 2$; y_1^N denotes the endowment of nontradables in period 1; d_1 denotes debt due in period 2; and r denotes the interest rate at which the country can borrow internationally. Assume that $\beta(1 + r) = 1$. Implicit in the period-2 constraint is the requirement that the debt position at the end of period 2 be nil. Debt accumulation in period 1 is subject to the following flow collateral constraint:

$$\frac{d_1}{1+r} \leq \kappa [y_1^T + p_1 y_1^N],$$

where $0 < \kappa$ is a parameter.

1. Derive the first-order conditions associated with the household's optimization problem.
2. Derive the complete set of equilibrium conditions.
3. Find conditions on the structural parameters of the model (β, r, κ, y_1^T, y_2^T, and y_1^N) such that an equilibrium exists in which the collateral constraint is slack.
4. Under those conditions, does there also exist an equilibrium in which the collateral constraint is binding (i.e., an equilibrium with a self-fulfilling financial crisis)? If so, discuss whether there is underborrowing in the financial crisis and whether in the crisis the value of collateral suffers a Fisherian deflation.

12.6 (Overborrowing in a Two-Period Economy) Consider a two-period endowment economy populated by identical households with preferences defined over consumption of tradable and nontradable goods and described by the following utility function:

$$\ln c_1^T + \ln c_1^N + \ln c_2^T + \ln c_2^N,$$

where c_i^T and c_i^N denote, respectively, consumption of tradables and nontradables in period $i = 1, 2$. Households are born with no debts and receive endowments of tradables and nontradables in periods 1 and 2 denoted by y_i^T and y_i^N, respectively, for $i = 1, 2$. In period 1, households can borrow or lend in the international financial market in a one-period bond denominated in tradable goods that pays the world interest rate, $r > 0$. Assume that $(1 + r)y_1^T < y_2^T$. Borrowing is limited by two constraints. One is a no-Ponzi-game constraint that prevents households from holding any debt at the end of period 2. The other borrowing constraint takes the form of a flow collateral constraint. It limits the amount of debt a household can assume in period 1 to a fraction $\alpha > 0$ of the value of its endowment:

$$d_1 \leq \alpha(y_1^T + p_1 y_1^N),$$

where p_i denotes the relative price of nontradables in terms of tradables in period $i = 1, 2$. We will refer to increases in p_i as real exchange-rate appreciations and to decreases as real exchange-rate depreciations.

1. Compute the unconstrained equilibrium, defined as the equilibrium in which the collateral constraint is not imposed. Express the equilibrium values of c_1^T, c_1^N, d_1, and p_1 as functions of the underlying economic fundamentals (i.e., as functions of endowments and the world interest rate).

2. Derive a range of values of α, in terms of economic fundamentals, for which the collateral constraint binds.

3. Suppose α takes a value in the range derived in question 2. Compute the resulting constrained equilibrium. Again, express the equilibrium levels of consumption of each good, external debt, and the relative price of nontradables in period 1 as functions of the economic fundamentals.

4. Which of the two equilibria characterized above, the constrained or the unconstrained equilibrium, delivers a more appreciated real exchange rate? Provide intuition.

5. Derive a shadow domestic interest rate in the constrained equilibrium.

6. Now consider a benevolent social planner who, like households, faces the collateral constraint and the no-Ponzi-game constraint. Derive the unconstrained social planner's equilibrium (i.e., the social planner's equilibrium in which the collateral constraint is not imposed). Compare your answer to the one you obtained for the unconstrained competitive equilibrium.

7. Now assume that the planner in question 6 is also subject to the collateral constraint. Derive the constrained social planner's equilibrium, and compare it to the constrained competitive equilibrium.

8. Is there overborrowing in this economy? Provide intuition.

12.7 (Flow Collateral Constraints and Multiple Equilibria in a Calibrated Economy) Consider a calibrated version of the economy studied in Section 12.4. Specifically, following the calibration presented in Section 12.5, assume that the time unit is one quarter. Assume also that borrowing cannot exceed 30 percent of annual output, that is, set $\kappa^T = \kappa^N = 0.3 \times 4$. In addition, set $y^T = y^N = 1$, $\sigma = 1/\xi = 2$, $a = 0.26$, $r = 0.0316$, and $\beta = 1/(1+r)$.

1. Compute the natural debt limit, denoted $\bar{d}$.

2. Compute the debt level $\tilde{d}$, defined as the largest value of debt that can be supported as a steady-state equilibrium.

3. Compute the range of initial debt levels, $d_0 < \tilde{d}$, for which a second equilibrium exists with a self-fulfilling financial crisis in period 0 of the type studied in Section 12.4. Let $\underline{d}_0$ denote the lower bound of this range.

4. Calculate the value of d_1 associated with $\underline{d}_0$ in a self-fulfilling financial crisis. How much deleveraging does this imply (i.e., report $(d_1/\underline{d}_0 - 1) \times 100$)? What is the implied contraction in private consumption of tradables?

5. Characterize the range of values of d_0 larger than $\underline{d}_0$ and smaller than $\tilde{d}$ for which there are two equilibria with self-fulfilling financial crises in period 0 of the type studied in Section 12.4. Denote the upper bound of this range by $\hat{d}_0$. Solve analytically for $\hat{d}_0$ in terms of the structural parameters of the model, taking into account that $\sigma = 1/\xi$ and that $\beta(1+r) = 1$.

12.8 (A Stochastic Economy with a Unique Equilibrium) Consider the model economy with a flow collateral constraint of Section 12.5. Calibrate the model using the parameter values and shock process used by Bianchi (2011). Apply the Matlab program `constrained.m` to establish that the two equilibrium selection criteria (B) and (C) presented in Section 12.5.2 deliver identical policy functions.

12.9 (Time Unit and Equilibrium Indeterminacy) The stochastic economy with a flow collateral constraint of Section 12.5 is cast at a quarterly frequency. The purpose of the present exercise is to ascertain whether the model continues to display multiple equilibria when the time unit is set to 1 year. This alteration introduces profound changes in the economic environment. First, it means that households reoptimize consumption spending once a year instead of once a quarter. Second, it means that the collateral constraint must hold only year by year, instead of quarter by quarter. To carry out the change of frequency, answer the following questions.

1. List all parameters of the model (see Table 12.1) that are frequency dependent. Provide the new values corresponding to an annual frequency.

2. Simulate the quarterly version of the model (using the program `simu.m`) for 1 million periods to obtain artificial time series for y_t^T and r_t. Aggregate these time series to annual frequency. This should reduce their length to 250,000. Now use these artificial data to estimate a new transition probability matrix using 21 grid points for y_t^T and 11 points for r_t. Here you have to be careful and make sure that all variables are expressed in the correct units. (Be mindful of logs, deviations from

means, etc. . . . . Remember that the devil is in the details!) *Note:* To estimate the transition probability matrix, you can use the Matlab program `tpm.m`, available on the book's Web site (Schmitt-Grohé and Uribe 2009).

3. Finally, apply the Matlab program `constrained.m` to establish whether the two equilibrium selection criteria ((B) and (C)) presented in Section 12.5.2 deliver identical policy functions.

12.10 (Optimality of a Constant Tax on Nontradable Consumption) In Section 12.10, we characterized a time-varying subsidy on nontradable consumption that achieves the unconstrained equilibrium. Show that the unconstrained equilibrium can also be supported by a time-invariant subsidy on nontradable consumption.

12.11 (Optimality of a Constant Tax on Tradable Consumption) In Section 12.10 we showed that the unconstrained equilibrium can be supported by a subsidy on nontradable consumption financed by lump-sum taxes. Show that the unconstrained equilibrium can also be supported by a tax on tradable consumption financed with lump-sum taxes. Show that unlike the scheme based on nontradable taxation, the present scheme must feature a constant tax rate in general.

13

Sovereign Default

Why do countries pay their international debts? This is a fundamental question in open economy macroeconomics. A key distinction between international and domestic debts is that the latter are enforceable. Countries typically have in place domestic judicial systems capable of punishing defaulters. Thus one reason residents of a given country honor their debts with other residents of the same country is because creditors are protected by a government able and willing to apply force against delinquent debtors. At the international level the situation is quite different. There is no such thing as a supranational authority with the capacity to enforce financial contracts between residents of different countries. Defaulting on international financial contracts appears to have no legal consequences. If agents have no incentives to pay their international debts, then lenders should have no reason to lend internationally to begin with. Yet we do observe a significant amount of borrowing and lending across nations. It follows that international borrowers must have reasons to repay their debts other than pure legal enforcement.

Two main reasons are typically offered for why countries honor their international debts: economic *sanctions* and *reputation*. Economic sanctions may take many forms, such as seizures of a debtor country's assets located abroad, trade embargoes, and import tariffs and quotas. The use of force by one country or a group of countries to collect debt from another country was not uncommon until the beginning of the twentieth century. In 1902, an attempt by Great Britain, Germany, and Italy to collect the public debt of Venezuela by force prompted the Argentine jurist Luis-María Drago, who at the time was serving as minister of foreign affairs of Argentina, to articulate a doctrine stating that no public debt should be collected from a sovereign American state by armed force or through the occupation of American territory by a foreign power. The Drago doctrine was approved by the Hague Conference of 1907. Intuitively, the stronger is the ability of creditor countries to impose economic sanctions, the weaker will be the incentives for debtor countries to default.

A reputational motive to pay international debts arises when creditor countries have the ability to exclude from international financial markets those countries with a reputation of being defaulters. Being isolated from international financial markets is costly, as it precludes the use of the current account to smooth consumption over time in response to aggregate domestic income shocks. As a result, countries may choose to repay their debts simply to preserve access to international financing.

This chapter investigates whether the existing theories of *sovereign debt* are capable of explaining the observed levels of sovereign debt. Before plunging into theoretical models of country debt, however, we present some stylized facts about international lending and default that will guide us in evaluating the existing theories.

13.1 Empirical Regularities

In this section we take a look at the observed patterns of sovereign defaults and their relation to macroeconomic indicators of interest. We draw on existing empirical research and also provide some new evidence.

13.1.1 Frequency and Length of Defaults

How often do countries default? How long do countries take to resolve their debt disputes? To address these questions, we must first establish empirical definitions of default and of its resolution. Much of the data on sovereign default are produced by credit rating agencies, especially Standard & Poor's. Standard & Poor's defines default as the failure to meet a principal or interest payment on the due date (or within a specified grace period) contained in the original terms of a debt issue (Beers and Chambers 2006). This definition includes not only situations in which the sovereign simply refuses to pay interest or principal, but also situations in which it forces an exchange of old debt for new debt with less favorable terms than the original issue or it converts debt into a different currency of less than equivalent face value.

A country is considered to have emerged from default when it resumes payments of interest and principal, including arrears. But defaults often involve a debt renegotiation that culminates in a restructuring of debt contracts that may include the swap of old debt for new debt. For this reason, when such a settlement occurs and the rating agency concludes that no further near-term resolution of creditors' claims is likely, the sovereign is regarded as having emerged from default (Beers and Chambers 2006). This definition of re-emergence from default clearly requires a value judgment, as it involves the expectation on the part of the rating agency that no further disputes will emerge concerning the default in question. Such a judgment call may or may not turn out to be correct. For example, all rating agencies concluded that Argentina emerged from the 2001 default in 2005, when it restructured its $81.8 billion debt by issuing new instruments involving a haircut of 73 percent. However, in 2014 a small group of holdouts (i.e., bond holders that did not participate in the debt restructuring) won a lawsuit against Argentina in the United States. The country's refusal to comply with this ruling put it back into default status.

Table 13.1 displays empirical probabilities of default for nine emerging countries during 1824–2014. On average, the probability of default is 2.9 percent per year. That is, countries defaulted on average about once every 33 years. This empirical probability is computed by dividing the number of years in which default events occurred by the number of years in the sample (191 years). A related measure replaces the denominator in this ratio by the number of years in the sample in which the country is not in default status. This measure, which by construction delivers higher default probabilities, is given in the third column of the table. On average the default probability for the nine countries included in the table

Table 13.1   Frequency and Length of Sovereign Defaults, 1824–2014

| Country | Number of Defaults 1824–2014 | Probability of Default | | Years in State of Default per Default Episode |
		All Years	Years Not in default	
Argentina	5	0.026	0.035	10
Brazil	7	0.037	0.047	6
Chile	3	0.016	0.020	14
Colombia	7	0.037	0.058	10
Egypt	2	0.010	0.012	11
Mexico	8	0.042	0.056	6
Philippines	1	0.005	0.006	32
Turkey	6	0.031	0.037	5
Venezuela	10	0.052	0.079	6
Mean	5.4	0.029	0.039	11

Source: Calculations based on Reinhart, Rogoff, and Savastano (2003), table 1 for 1824–1999 and Table 13.19 for 2000–2014.

Notes: The sample includes only emerging countries with at least one external debt default or restructuring episode between 1824 and 1999. The 2014 selective default of Argentina with 1 percent of the holdout investors that did not enter the debt restructurings of 2005 and 2010 is not counted as a default event.

conditional on the country being in no-default standing is 3.9 percent. The difference between these two default probabilities can be sizable (as large as 2 percent), because when a country defaults it may remain in default status for a significant number of years.

The average number of years countries are in a state of default or restructuring after a default event is 11 years. If one assumes that while in a state of default countries have limited access to fresh funds from international markets, one would conclude that default causes countries to be in financial autarky for about a decade. But the connection between being in a state of default and being in financial autarky should not be taken too far. For being in state of default with one set of lenders does not necessarily preclude the possibility of obtaining new loans from other lenders with which the borrower has no unpaid debts. In this case, the period of financial autarky would be shorter than the period of being in default status. The converse can also be true. Suppose that foreign lenders choose to punish defaulters by excluding them from financial markets even after the delinquent country has come to an agreement with its creditors. In this case, the period of financial autarky could last longer than the period in default status. We discuss empirical estimates of exclusion periods in Section 13.2.1.

The information on frequency and length of default state provided in Table 13.1 spans a long period of time (from 1824 to 2014). In the past decades, however, international financial markets have experienced enormous changes, including an expansion in the set of sovereigns with access to international credit markets and the participation of small lenders. For this reason, it is of interest to ask whether the frequency and length of sovereign defaults

Table 13.2   Frequency and Length of Sovereign
Defaults: 1824–2014 Versus 1975–2014

Period	Probability of Default per Year	Years in State of Default per Default Episode
1824–2014	0.029	11
1975–2014	0.040	8

Source: Tables 13.1 and 13.19.

have changed. Table 13.19 in the appendix to this chapter displays data on the beginning and end of default episodes for all defaulters between 1975 and 2014. During this period 93 sovereigns defaulted at least once, and there were a total of 147 default episodes. This means that the empirical probability of default over the 40-year period 1975–2014 equals $147/(40 \times 93)$ or about 4 percent. Comparing this number with the one corresponding to the period 1824–2014 suggests that the default frequency has increased from three defaults to four defaults per century per country, conditional on the country having defaulted at least once. Table 13.19 also reveals that the average length of a default episode in the more recent sample period is 8 years, 3 years shorter than for the entire sample. We therefore conclude that in recent years, sovereign defaults have become more frequent but shorter. Table 13.2 summarizes these results.

Figure 13.1 displays the empirical probability distribution of the length of default episodes during 1975–2014. The distribution is strongly skewed to the right, which means that there are some default episodes that took very long to be resolved. For example, Table 13.19 documents that out of the 147 defaults recorded during 1975–2014, nine lasted longer than 30 years. The skewness of the distribution is reflected in a median of default length significantly lower than the mean, 5 versus 8 years. As pointed out by Tomz and Wright (2013), the shape of the empirical probability distribution resembles an exponential distribution. Assuming that the length of default episodes is a good proxy for the time of exclusion from international financial markets (for further discussion of this assumption, see Section 13.2.1), this suggests modeling the probability of a defaulter regaining access to financial markets as constant over time. As we will see in Section 13.6, this is precisely the way reentry is modeled in most quantitative models of sovereign default.

13.1.2 Haircuts

How large are defaults? Most existing theoretical models of default assume that when the country defaults, it does so on the entire stock of outstanding external debt. In reality, however, this is not the case. Typically countries default on a fraction of their outstanding debts. The resulting losses inflicted on creditors are called "haircuts."

Sturzenegger and Zettelmeyer (2008) measure haircuts as the percentage difference between the present values of old and new instruments discounted at market rates prevailing immediately after the debt exchange. They estimate haircuts for all major debt restructurings that occurred between 1998 and 2005. They find that haircuts are on average 40 percent. That is, after the default the creditor expects to receive a stream of payments with

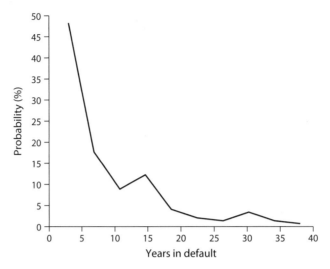

Figure 13.1   Distribution of the length of default episodes, 1975–2014.

Source: Table 13.19.

present discounted value 40 percent lower than prior to the default. At the same time, Sturzenegger and Zettelmeyer report a high dispersion of the size of haircuts ranging from 13 percent (Uruguay in 2003) to 73 percent (Argentina in 2005).

Other studies find similar results. Cruces and Trebesch (2013) use the same methodology to measure haircuts as Sturzenegger and Zettelmeyer but greatly expand the data set to include all debt restructurings with foreign banks and bond holders that took place between 1970 and 2010. The resulting data set covers 180 default episodes in 68 countries. They find that the average haircut is 37 percent, with a standard deviation of 22 percent. Benjamin and Wright (2013) use a constant rate of 10 percent to discount pre- and postrestructuring payments in their computation of haircuts. Their data set includes 90 default episodes in 73 countries from 1989 to 2006. Like the other two studies, these authors find an average haircut of 40 percent with a large associated dispersion.

13.1.3 Debt and Default

Table 13.3 displays average debt-to-GNP ratios during 1970–2000 for some emerging countries that defaulted on or restructured their external debt at least once between 1824 and 1999. The table also displays average debt-to-GNP ratios at the beginning of default or restructuring episodes. The data suggest that at the time of default, debt-to-GNP ratios are significantly above average. In effect, for the countries considered in the sample, the debt-to-GNP ratio at the onset of a default or restructuring episode was on average 14 percentage points of GNP above normal times. The information provided in the table is silent, however, about whether the higher debt-to-GNP ratios observed at the brink of default episodes result from a contraction in aggregate activity, or from a faster-than-average accumulation of debt in periods immediately preceding default, or both.

Table 13.3   Debt-to-GNP Ratios among Defaulters

Country	Average Debt-to-GNP Ratio	Debt-to-GNP Ratio in Year of Default
Argentina	37.1	54.4
Brazil	30.7	50.1
Chile	58.4	63.7
Colombia	33.6	—
Egypt	70.6	112.0
Mexico	38.2	46.7
Philippines	55.2	70.6
Turkey	31.5	21.0
Venezuela	41.3	46.3
Average	44.1	58.1

Source: Calculations based on Reinhart, Rogoff, and Savastano (2003), tables 3 and 6.

Notes: The sample includes only emerging countries with at least one external debt default or restructuring episode between 1824 and 1999. Debt-to-GNP ratios are averages over 1970–2000. Debt-to-GNP ratios at the beginning of a default episode are averages over the following default dates in the interval 1970–2002: Argentina, 1982 and 2001; Brazil, 1983; Chile, 1972 and 1983; Egypt, 1984; Mexico, 1982; Philippines, 1983; Turkey, 1978; and Venezuela, 1982 and 1995. Colombia did not register an external default or restructuring episode between 1970 and 2002.

13.1.4 Country Premia

Table 13.4 displays average country premia over a period starting on average in 1996 and ending in 2013. The country premium, or country spread, is the difference between the interest rate at which a country borrows in international financial markets and the interest rate at which developed countries borrow from one another. The average country premium for the nine countries included in the table is 5.5 percent per year.

Country spreads are much higher during periods in which countries are in default status than during periods of good financial standing. For this reason it is of interest to examine country spreads conditional on countries not being in default status. The sample period covered in Table 13.4 does contain a number of default events. Specifically, Argentina was in default from 2001 to 2005, and Venezuela was in default from 1995 to 1998 and then again in 2005. Thus column 2 of the table reports average spreads conditional on the country not being in default status. The corrected spreads are uniformly higher. For example, the Argentine spread was about half the size during periods not in default than over the entire sample (7.4 versus 15.8 percent).

13.1.5 Country Spreads and Default Probabilities: A Sample Mismatch Problem

Country spreads reflect default probabilities. In a world in which lenders are risk neutral, spreads should be on average equal to the probability of default. With partial default,

Table 13.4   Country Premia among Defaulters

| Country | *Average Country Spread (%)* | |
	All Years	Years Not in Default
Argentina	15.8	7.43
Brazil	5.61	5.61
Chile	1.44	1.44
Colombia	3.52	3.52
Egypt	2.46	2.46
Mexico	3.47	3.47
Philippines	3.49	3.49
Turkey	4.10	4.10
Venezuela	9.24	9.23
Average	5.5	4.5

Notes: The sample includes only emerging countries with at least one external debt default or restructuring episode between 1824 and 1999. Country spreads are measured using the EMBI Global index, produced by J.P. Morgan, and expressed as percentages, and are averages through 2013, with varying starting dates as follows: Argentina, 1994; Brazil, 1995; Chile, 2000; Colombia, 1998; Egypt, 2002; Mexico, 1994; Philippines, 1998; Turkey, 1997; and Venezuela, 1994. Average country spreads are computed over all available periods (first column) and over all periods during which the country is not in default (second column). Start and end dates of default episodes are taken from Table 13.19 in the appendix to this chapter.

spreads should be lower than default probabilities. Spreads in excess of default probabilities are hence an indication of risk aversion on the part of foreign lenders. For this reason, it is of interest to characterize empirically the spread-default-frequency differential. In Section 13.9 we revisit this issue from a theoretical perspective.

Computing the spread-default-frequency differential is not an easy task. The problem is that spreads and default data come in different sample sizes. For most countries data on interest-rate spreads are available only since the early 1990s. In contrast, data on default events go back to the early nineteenth century. As a result, often the empirical regularities involving interest-rate spreads and default frequency are based on a mix of short samples for the former and long samples for the latter. This is the case, for instance, when we compare the default frequencies reported in Table 13.1 with the average country spreads reported in Table 13.4.

This sample mismatch can sometimes lead to spurious conclusions regarding the relation between default frequency and average country spreads. For example, for Colombia Table 13.1 shows a default frequency of 5.8 percent, and Table 13.4 indicates that the average country spread is 3.52 percent, that is, the default frequency exceeds the country premium. The high default frequency obtains because Colombia defaulted quite frequently (seven times) between 1824 and 1935, but has not defaulted since then. At the same time, EMBI spread data for this country cover only 1997–2013, which contains no defaults and

Table 13.5   Default Probability and Country Spreads over a Common Sample

	Country Spread (%)	Default Probability (%)
Argentina	7.43	6.7
Brazil	5.61	0
Chile	1.44	0
Colombia	3.52	0
Egypt	2.56	0
Mexico	3.47	0
Philippines	3.49	0
Turkey	4.10	0
Venezuela	9.23	13.3
Mean	4.5	2.2

Source: Calculations based on Tables 13.4 and 13.19.

which is preceded by more than 60 years of good financial standing. It is reasonable to suspect that the sample mismatch introduces a negative bias in the spread-default-frequency differential. A similar problem is likely to affect Chile and Mexico. These two countries were quite unstable and displayed frequent economic crises until the end of the 1980s. Since then, however, both have implemented some structural reforms, including trade, fiscal, and monetary policy. Progress along this dimension has been widely recognized, as reflected, for instance, in both countries' accession to the Organisation for Economic Co-operation and Development (OECD). Not surprisingly, country spreads have been quite low in Chile and Mexico since the early 1990s, which is precisely the period spanned by the EMBI data set. In contrast, measures of default frequency based on long samples put in one bag periods of high and low instability. As a result, both Chile and Mexico display smaller country spreads than default probabilities (1.44 versus 2 percent for Chile and 3.5 versus 5.6 percent for Mexico). Again, in both these countries, the sample mismatch is likely to bias downwardly the spread-default-frequency differential.

To provide a partial correction to this problem, Table 13.5 displays empirical default frequencies computed over a country-specific sample given by the period for which both the EMBI and default event data are available. With this correction the average country spread is on average more than twice as large as the default frequency: 4.5 versus 2.2 percent. A weakness of this way of comparing spreads and default frequencies is the scarcity of data. It is therefore important to continue to reassess the validity of the stylized fact that country premia are significantly larger than default probabilities as more data become available.

13.1.6 Do Countries Default in Bad Times?

An important question in the theoretical literature on default is whether countries tend to dishonor their debt obligations during economic expansions or contractions. The reason is that different models produce opposite predictions in this regard. As a preview of the theory to come, consider the following two simple examples. Suppose first that a country that wishes to smooth consumption signs a contract with foreign investors that is state contingent. Specifically, suppose that the contract specifies that the country receives a transfer from the rest of the world if domestic output is below average and makes a payment to the rest of the world if domestic output is above average. Clearly, under this contract, incentives to default are highest when output is above average, since these are the states in which the country must make payments. The second example is one in which the country cannot sign state-contingent contracts. Instead, suppose that the sovereign borrows internationally and has to pay next period the amount borrowed plus a fixed amount in interest, regardless of the state of the domestic economy in the next period. In this case the incentive to default is likely to be strongest when output is low, because the cost of sacrificing consumption to service the debt is higher when consumption is already low due to the weak level of domestic output. Which of these two examples is favored by the data?

Figure 13.2 displays the typical behavior of output surrounding the default episodes listed in Table 13.19 in the appendix. Output is measured as percentage deviations of real GDP per capita from a log-quadratic trend.[1] The figure displays a window of 3 years before and after a default episode. The year of default is normalized to 0. The typical behavior of output surrounding a default episode is captured by computing the median of output period by period across the default episodes. The figure shows that defaults typically occur after long and severe economic contractions. Specifically, the typical country experiences a 6.5 percent contraction in output per capita in the 3 years leading up to default. This result suggests that the answer to the question posed in the title of this subsection is yes, countries default in bad times.

Some authors, however, arrive at a different conclusion. For example, Tomz and Wright (2007, 2013), using data from 1820 to 2005, argue that countries do default during bad times but that the supporting evidence is weak.[2] Tomz's and Wright's argument is based on two observations. First, they find that at the time of default, output is only about 1.5 percent below trend. This finding is in line with the results shown in Figure 13.2. However, note that by the time the economy reaches the period of default (period 0 in the figure), it has contracted by more than 5 percent between periods −3 and −1. The second reason Tomz and Wright argue that the evidence that countries default in bad times is weak is their finding that only 60 percent of the default episodes occur when output is below trend. This finding is also corroborated in the sample considered here. However, if one asks the question what fraction of the countries were contracting (i.e., experiencing output growth below trend growth) at the time of default, the answer is quite different. We find that 75 percent of the default episodes occur at a time in which output growth is below trend.

---

1. The trend was estimated over the longest available sample. Countries with less than 30 consecutive years of output observations were excluded. The longest output sample contains 54 observations ranging from 1960 to 2013. The shortest sample contains 33 output observations. The sample contains 105 default episodes.

2. Benjamin and Wright (2013) and Durdu, Nunes, and Sapriza (2013, table 4) arrive at similar conclusions using different samples.

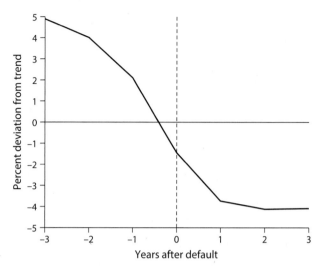

Figure 13.2   Output around default episodes.

Source: Output is from the database World Development Indicators, and default dates are from Table 13.19.

Notes: Output is measured as real per capita GDP, log quadratically detrended at annual frequency. Median across the default episodes is listed in Table 13.19. Countries with less than 30 consecutive years of output data were excluded, resulting in 105 default episodes during 1975–2014.

This finding further strengthens the conclusion that defaults occur in times of significant economic distress.

Note that the graph in Figure 13.2 flattens one period after default. This means that output growth returns to its long-run trend 1 year after default. Levy-Yeyati and Panizza (2011) were the first to identify the regularity in growth recovery. We note, however, that even 3 years after the default, the level of output remains 4 percent below trend. The broad picture that emerges from Figure 13.2 is that default marks the end of a large contraction and the beginning of a growth recovery, albeit not the beginning of a recovery in the level of output.

Figure 13.3 shows that the conclusion that countries default in bad times extends to variables other than output. The figure displays the cyclical components of private consumption, gross investment, the trade-balance-to-GDP ratio, and the real effective exchange rate. Private consumption contracts by as much as output (about 6 percent) in the run-up to default, and investment experiences a fall 3 times as large as output. At the same time, the trade balance is below average up until the year of default, when it experiences a reversal of about 2 percent. The bottom-right panel displays the behavior of the real exchange rate. This variable is defined in such a way that an increase means a real appreciation (i.e., the economy in question becomes more expensive than its trading partners). The figure shows that the real exchange rate depreciates significantly, by more than 4 percent, in the year of default. After the default, the real exchange rate begins to gradually appreciate.

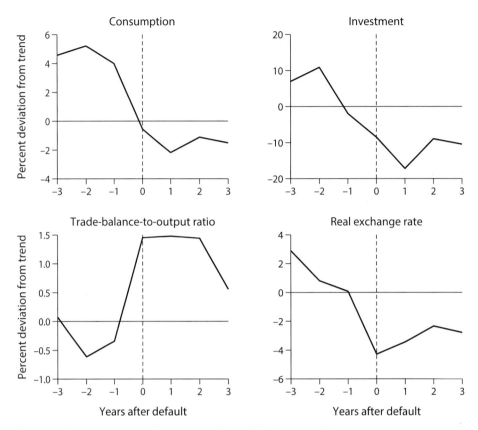

Figure 13.3   Consumption, investment, the trade balance, and the real exchange rate around default episodes.

Sources: Default dates are from Table 13.19 and all other variables from World Development Indicators.
Notes: The data are annual. Consumption, investment, and the real exchange rate are log-quadratically detrended. The trade-balance-to-output ratio is linearly detrended. The median is across all default episodes. Countries with less than 30 consecutive years of data were excluded. An increase in the real exchange rate indicates a real appreciation of the domestic currency.

13.2 The Cost of Default: Empirical Evidence

The empirical literature has identified three main sources of costs associated with sovereign default: exclusion from financial markets, output losses, and international trade sanctions.

13.2.1 Exclusion from Financial Markets

Do defaulting sovereigns lose access to credit markets on default? And, if so, how long does it take them to regain access? One possible approach to addressing this question is to assume that countries are excluded from credit markets as long as they are in default status. Using this approach, exclusion from credit markets begins in the year the default occurs, and re-access takes place in the year after the country re-emerges from default.

According to Table 13.2, for the sample 1975–2014, the average length of exclusion from international financial markets was 8 years. As mentioned earlier, however, this approach is a bit naive, because in principle nothing prevents foreign lenders from extending fresh loans to countries before or after their default disputes are settled. For instance, it took Argentina 11 years to settle its 1982 default (see Table 13.19 in the appendix). However, according to Gelos, Sahay, and Sandleris (2011), the country began to receive fresh external funds already in 1986. At the same time, and according to the same sources, Chile was in default status from 1983 to 1990 but was able to re-access international credit markets only in 1994.

Thus the arrival of new funds and the end of default status do not seem to always match, suggesting the importance of directly measuring the date on which countries are able to borrow again after a default. Gelos, Sahay, and Sandleris (2011) undertake this approach systematically by examining micro data on sovereign bond issuance and public syndicated bank loans during 1980–2000. As in most of the related literature (including this chapter), their measure of the year of default follows Beers and Chambers (2006). Their innovation is to measure resumption of access to credit markets as the first year after default in which the government borrows either in the form of bonds or syndicated loans and the stock of debt increases. The latter requirement is aimed at avoiding counting as re-access cases in which the country is simply rolling over an existing debt. It is not clear, however, that this requirement is appropriate. For the rolling over of existing debt is actually a manifestation of participation in international capital markets. Exclusion from financial markets is measured as the number of years between default and resumption. Gelos, Sahay, and Sandleris find that the mean exclusion period is 4.7 years—about half the length obtained by using the date of settlement as a proxy for re-access. However, this result is likely to be downwardly biased by the authors' decision to include only default episodes associated with resumptions happening within the sample. That is, countries that defaulted between 1980 and 2000 and had not regained access to credit markets by 2000 were excluded from the calculations. The bias is likely to be strong because the sample includes equal numbers of resumptions and no resumptions before 2000.[3] We therefore interpret the results reported in Gelos, Sahay, and Sandleris as suggesting that the period of exclusion from financial markets resulting from sovereign default is at least 4 years.

Using data from 1980 to 2005, Richmond and Dias (2009) also study the issue of exclusion after default. Their methodology differs from Gelos, Sahay, and Sandleris (2011) in three aspects. First, Richmond and Dias measure net borrowing using aggregate data. Second, and more importantly, they exclude from the definition of re-access situations in which an increase in borrowing reflects the capitalization of arrears.[4] Third, they count years of exclusion starting the year the country emerged from default, as opposed to the year in which the country entered into default. Their definition of re-access distinguishes the cases of partial and full re-access. Partial re-access is defined as the first year with positive

---

3. These authors also report a significant drop in the exclusion period from 4 to 2 years between the 1980s and the 1990s. This result is likely to be particularly affected by the bias reported in the body of the text.

4. It is not clear that increases in net foreign government debt due to the capitalization of arrears is not a reflection of re-access. For such situations may be the result of a successful negotiation between the lender and the debtor, culminating in the ability of the latter to tap international markets again.

Table 13.6   Estimates of Years of Exclusion from Credit Markets after Default

Measure	Partial Re-access (flows > 0)	Full Re-access (flows > 1% of GDP)	Sample Period
Length of default status (Table 13.19)*	8		1975–2014
First issuance of new debt			
Gelos, Sahay, and Sandleris (2011)*	4.7		1980–2000
· Richmond and Dias (2009)**	5.7	8.4	1980–2005
Adjusted Richmond and Dias (2009)*	13.7	16.4	1980–2005
Cruces and Trebesch (2013)**	5.1	7.4	1980–2010
Adjusted Cruces and Trebesch (2013)*	13.1	15.4	1980–2010
Average	9.8	15.9	

Note: Re-access is measured in years after the beginning of default (∗) or in years after the end of default (∗∗). Averages are taken over single-star lines.

aggregate flows to the public sector after the country has emerged from default. Full re-access is defined as the first year in which debt flows exceed 1 percent of GDP. They find that on average countries regain partial access to credit markets 5.7 years after emerging from default and full access 8.4 years after emerging from default. To make these numbers comparable with those reported by Gelos, Sahay, and Sandleris, we add the average number of years a country is in default, which according to Table 13.2 is 8 years. This adjustment is reasonable, because Richmond and Dias find that only a small fraction (less than 10 percent in their sample) of default episodes were associated with re-access while the country was in default. Thus, according to the adjusted estimate, countries regain partial access to international credit markets 13.7 years after default and full access 16.4 years after default.

Cruces and Trebesch (2013) extend and combine the data and criteria for market exclusion of Gelos, Sahay, and Sandleris (2011) and Richmond and Dias (2009). Their data on re-access cover 1980–2010. They find that on average countries regain partial access 5.1 years after emerging from default and full access 7.4 years after emerging from default. Introducing the same adjustment we applied to the Richmond and Dias estimates to measure exclusion from the beginning of the default episode, the estimates of Cruces and Trebesch imply that it takes defaulters on average 13.1 years to regain partial access and 15.4 years to gain full access after default. Table 13.6 summarizes the results of the estimates of exclusion we have discussed.

The studies covered here also analyze the determinants of the length of exclusion after default. Gelos, Sahay, and Sandleris (2011) find that the frequency of default is not a significant determinant of the length of exclusion. That is, markets seem to punish more or less equally one-time and serial defaulters. This finding lends support to an assumption along these lines maintained by most existing theories of sovereign default. Gelos, Sahay, and Sandleris also find that defaults that resolve quickly do not result in significant exclusion. Richmond and Dias (2009) find that excusable defaults (e.g., those following a natural disaster) are associated with reduced exclusion periods. Cruces and Trebesch (2013) provide evidence suggesting that lenders may use exclusion as a punishment, by documenting that restructurings involving higher haircuts (i.e., higher losses to creditors) are associated with significantly longer periods of capital market exclusion.

We close this discussion by pointing out that the existing attempts to measure exclusion do not incorporate distinctly supply and demand determinants of external credit. Since observed variations in debt are equilibrium outcomes, the lack of increase in debt need not be a reflection of supply restrictions related to sanctions. In this regard, the studies reviewed here may incorporate an upward bias in the estimates of the numbers of years a defaulter is excluded from international financial markets.

13.2.2 Output Losses

A standard assumption in theoretical models of sovereign debt is that default entails an output loss (see Section 13.6). This assumption helps the model economy to sustain a higher level of external debt in equilibrium. Some authors have attempted to empirically estimate this cost (see, e.g., Chuhan and Sturzenegger 2003; Borensztein and Panizza 2009; De Paoli, Hoggarth, and Saporta 2011; and Levy-Yeyati and Panizza 2011). The typical approach is to use cross-country panel data to run a standard growth regression augmented with variables capturing default. Borensztein and Panizza (2009), for example, estimate the following regression using data from 83 countries from 1972 to 2000:

$$\text{Growth}_{it} = \alpha + \beta X_{it} + \gamma \text{Default}_{it} + \sum_{j=0}^{3} \delta_j \text{DefaultB}_{it-j} + \epsilon_{it},$$

where Growth_{it} denotes the growth rate of real per capital GDP in country i from year $t - 1$ to year t in percent, X_{it} denotes a vector of controls typically used in growth regressions,[5] Default_{it} is a dummy variable taking the value 1 if country i is in default in year t and 0 otherwise, DefaultB_{it} is a dummy variable taking the value 1 if country i entered into default in period t, and ϵ_{it} is an error term. As in Table 13.19, the dates of entering and exiting default are based on data from Standard & Poor's.

Borensztein and Panizza (2009) estimate $\gamma = -1.184$ and $\delta_i = -1.388, 0.481, 0.337,$ 0.994 for $i = 0, 1, 2, 3$, respectively, with γ and δ_0 significant at confidence level of 5 percent or less. This estimate implies that the beginning of a default is accompanied by a 2.6 percent fall in the growth rate of output ($\gamma + \delta_0$). Subsequently, the growth rate recovers. However, the level of output never recovers, implying that default is associated with a permanent loss of output.

Figure 13.4 displays (dashed line) the logarithm of per capita output after a default implied by the Borensztein and Panizza regression. In the figure, the default is assumed to last for 5 years, the median length of the defaults reported in Table 13.19. The long-run growth rate is assumed to be 1.5 percent, and the default date is normalized to 0. For

---

5. The variables included in X_{it} are investment divided by GDP, population growth, GDP per capita in 1970, percentage of the population that completed secondary education, total population, lagged government consumption over GDP, an index of civil rights, the change in terms of trade, trade openness (defined as exports plus imports divided by GDP), a dummy variable (taking the value of one during a banking crisis), and three regional dummies (for sub-Saharan Africa, Latin America and the Caribbean, and transition economies).

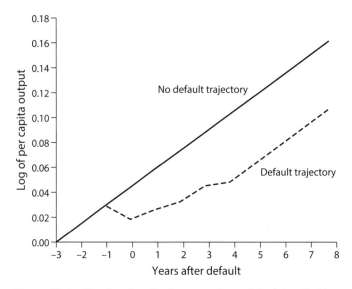

Figure 13.4   Simulated path of output after a default implied by
the Borensztein and Panizza (2009) regression.

comparison, the figure displays (solid line) the trajectory of output absent a default. After
an initial fall, output gradually regains its long-run growth rate of 1.5 percent. However, the
level of output remains forever 5.5 percent below the pre-default trajectory.

Taken at face value, the above regression results suggest an enormous cost of default.
But such regressions are likely to represent an upwardly biased estimate of the output cost
of default for two reasons. First, the regression may include an insufficient number of lags
in the default variables $Default_{it}$ and $DefaultB_{it}$. The former variable actually appears only
contemporaneously, and the latter with three lags. To the extent that the coefficients associated with these variables are positive, the gap between the no-default trajectory and the
default trajectory could be narrowed. Thus, adding more lags could be important, even
if they are individually estimated with low significance. Second and more fundamentally,
output growth and the default decision are endogenous variables, which may introduce a
bias in the coefficients of the default variables. For instance, if defaults tend to occur during
periods of low growth, then the estimated coefficient in the default variables may be negative even if default had no effect on growth. Thus, as stressed by Borensztein and Panizza
(2009) and others, regression results of the type presented here should be interpreted as
simply documenting a partial correlation between output growth and default.

Zarazaga (2012) proposes a growth accounting approach to gauge the output loss associated with default. He documents that the Argentine defaults of 1982 and 2001 were both
characterized by a peak in the capital-to-output ratio in the run-up to the default, followed
by a significant decline in the years after the default (see Figure 13.5). For instance, by 2002
the capital-to-output ratio had reached 1.9. Indeed, Zarazaga argues that a value of around
1.9 or higher is a normal long-run level for the capital-to-output ratio in emerging economies. Thus, his argument goes, absent any crisis, the capital-to-output ratio should have
remained at 1.9 or higher after 2002. However, after the default the capital-to-output ratio

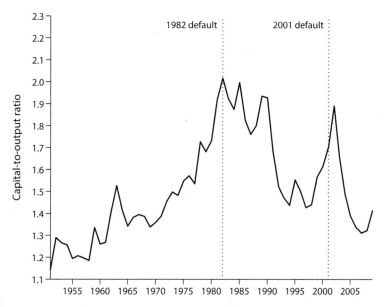

Figure 13.5   The capital-to-output ratio around default episodes: Argentina, 1951–2009.

Data source: Zarazaga (2012).

fell, reaching a trough of 1.35 in 2007. What is the fall in output per person associated with this loss of capital per unit of final production? Zarazaga assumes a production function of the form $y_t = k_t^{0.4}h_t^{0.6}$, where y_t denotes output, k_t denotes physical capital, and h_t denotes employment. This technology implies that the output-to-worker ratio, y_t/h_t, is linked to the capital-to-output ratio, k_t/y_t, by the relationship $y_t/h_t = (k_t/y_t)^{2/3}$. This means that if the capital-to-output ratio had not fallen between 2002 and 2007 (i.e., if k_t/y_t had not fallen from 1.9 to 1.35), output per worker in 2007 would have been 26 percent higher than it actually was ($[[1.9/1.35]^{2/3} - 1] \times 100$). Thus on average, between 2002 and 2007 output per worker was 13 ($= 26/2$) percent lower than it would have been had the capital output ratio not fallen. If one ascribes all of the fall in the capital-to-output ratio observed between 2002 and 2007 to the sovereign default of 2002, then one would conclude that the output cost of the default was 13 percent each year between 2002 and 2007. Further, because it takes time for the capital-to-output ratio to recover its long-run level, the 13 percent loss should continue for more years. Assuming that the recovery is as fast as the decline, the cost should be extended for another 5 years, that is, until 2012. In summary, this accounting suggests that the Argentine default of 2002 had an output cost of 13 percent per year per worker for 10 years, which is quite large.

    The 1982 default is not as clear cut as the default of 2001, because the capital-to-output ratio did not decline until late in the exclusion period (1982–1993). The capital-to-output ratio stayed at around 1.9 until 1990 and then fell to about 1.45 by 1996. It then took until 2002 to reach 1.9 again. Calculating the output loss following the same strategy applied to the 2002 default, we find that the output loss was 0 percent between 1982 and 1990 (8 years) and around 10 percent between 1990 and 2002 (12 years). On average, the output loss associated with the 1982 default was therefore 6 percent of output per worker per year for 20 years, which is also a large number.

It is important to keep in mind that these cost estimates hinge on the assumption that the entire decline in the capital-to-output ratio was caused by the defaults. To the extent that the fall in the capital-to-output ratio was in part driven by factors other than default, the cost estimates must be interpreted as an upper bound.

13.2.3 International Trade Sanctions

Default episodes are also associated with disruptions in international trade. Rose (2005) investigates this issue empirically. The question of whether default disrupts international trade is of interest because if for some reason trade between two countries is significantly diminished as a result of one country defaulting on its financial debts with other countries, then maintaining access to international trade could represent a reason countries tend to honor their international financial obligations. Rose estimates an equation of the form:

$$\ln T_{ijt} = \beta_0 + \beta X_{ijt} + \sum_{m=0}^{M} \phi_m ACRED_{ijt-m} + \epsilon_{ijt},$$

where T_{ijt} denotes the average real value of bilateral trade between countries i and j in period t. Rose identifies default with dates for which a country enters a debt-restructuring deal with the Paris Club. (The Paris Club is an informal association of creditor-country finance ministers and central bankers that meets to negotiate bilateral debt-rescheduling agreements with debtor-country governments.) The regressor $ACRED_{ijt}$ is a proxy for default. It is a binary variable taking the value one if either country in the pair (i, j) is involved with the other in a Paris-Club debt-restructuring deal in period t and zero otherwise. The main focus of Rose's work is the estimation of the coefficients ϕ_m.

Rose's empirical model belongs to the family of *gravity models*. The variable X_{ijt} is a vector of regressors including (current and possibly lagged) characteristics of the country pair ij at time t such as distance, combined output, combined population, combined area, sharing of a common language, sharing of land borders, being cosigners of a free trade agreement, and having had a colonial relationship. The vector X_{ijt} also includes country-pair-specific dummies and current and lagged values of a variable denoted IMF_{ijt} that takes the values 0, 1, or 2, respectively, if neither, one, or both countries i and j engaged in an IMF program at time t.

The data set used for the estimation of the model covers all bilateral trades between 217 countries from 1948 to 1997 at an annual frequency. The sample contains 283 Paris Club debt-restructuring deals. Rose finds sensible estimates of the parameters pertaining to the gravity model. Specifically, countries that are more distant geographically trade less, whereas high-income country pairs trade more. Countries that share a common currency, a common language, a common border, or membership in a regional free trade agreement trade more. Landlocked countries and islands trade less, and most of the colonial effects are large and positive. The inception of IMF programs is associated with a cumulative contraction in trade of about 10 percent over 3 years.

Default, as measured by the dummy variable $ACRED_{ijt}$, has a significant and negative effect on bilateral trade. Rose estimates the parameter ϕ_m to be on average about -0.07 (i.e.,

$\frac{\sum_{m=0}^{M} \phi_m}{1+M} = -0.07$) and the lag length, M, to be about 15 years. This means that entering into a debt-restructuring agreement with a member of the Paris Club leads to a decline in bilateral trade of about 7 percent per year for about 16 years. For instance, if trade in period -1 was 100 and the country enters a restructuring agreement with the Paris Club in period 0, then its trade in periods 0–15 will be on average 93. Thus the cumulative effect of default on trade is more than 1 year's worth of trade in the long run. Based on this finding, Rose concludes that one reason countries pay back their international financial obligations is fear of trade disruptions in the case of default.

Do the estimated values of ϕ_m really capture the effect of trade sanctions imposed by creditor countries on defaulting countries? Countries undergoing default or restructuring of their external financial obligations typically are subject to severe economic distress, which may be associated with a general decline in international trade that is unrelated to trade sanctions by the creditor country. If this is indeed the case, then the coefficients ϕ_m would be picking up the combined effects of trade sanctions and of general economic distress during default episodes. To disentangle these two effects, Martínez and Sandleris (2011) estimate the following variant of Rose's gravity model:

$$\ln T_{ijt} = \beta_0 + \beta X_{ijt} + \sum_{m=0}^{M} \phi_m ACRED_{ijt-m} + \sum_{m=0}^{M} \gamma_m DEBTOR_{ijt-m} + \epsilon_{ijt},$$

where $DEBTOR_{ijt-m}$ is a binary variable taking the value one if either country i or country j is a debtor country involved in a debt-restructuring deal in the context of the Paris Club in period t, and zero otherwise. Notice that, unlike variable $ACRED_{ijt}$, variable $DEBTOR_{ijt}$ is unity as long as one of the countries is a debtor involved in a restructuring deal with the Paris Club, regardless of whether the other country in the pair is the restructuring creditor. This regressor is meant to capture the general effect of default on trade with all trading countries, not just with those with which the debtor country is restructuring debt through the Paris Club.

In this version of the gravity model, evidence of trade sanctions would require a point estimate of $\sum_{m=0}^{M} \phi_m$ that is negative and significant, and evidence of a general effect of default on trade would require a negative and significant estimate of $\sum_{m=0}^{M} \gamma_m$. Martínez and Sandleris (2011) estimate $\sum_{m=0}^{15} \gamma_m$ to be -0.41. That is, when a country enters into default, its international trade with all countries falls by about 40 percent over 15 years. More importantly, they obtain a point estimate of $\sum_{m=0}^{15} \phi_m$ that is positive and equal to 0.01. The signs of the point estimates are robust to setting the number of lags, M, at 0, 5, or 10. This result would suggest the absence of trade sanctions if creditor countries acted in isolation against defaulters. However, if creditors behaved collectively by applying sanctions to defaulters regardless of whether they are directly affected, then the γ_m coefficients might in part be capturing sanction effects.

Martínez and Sandleris control for collective sanction effects by estimating two additional variants of the gravity model. One is of the form:

$$\ln T_{ijt} = \beta_0 + \beta X_{ijt} + \sum_{m=0}^{M} \phi_m CRED_{ijt-m} + \sum_{m=0}^{M} \gamma_m DEBTOR_{ijt-m} + \epsilon_{ijt},$$

where $CRED_{ijt}$ is a binary variable that takes the value one if either country in the pair (ij) is a debtor in a debt-restructuring deal with the Paris Club in period t and the other is a creditor, independently of whether it is renegotiating with the debtor country in the pair. Evidence of trade sanctions would require $\sum_{m=0}^{M} \phi_m$ to be negative and significant. The point estimate of $\sum_{m=0}^{M} \phi_m$ turns out to be sensitive to the lag length considered. At lag lengths of 0, 5, and 10 years the point estimate is positive and equal to 0.09, 0.19, and 0.01, respectively. But when the lag length is set at 15 years, the point estimate turns negative and equal to -0.19.

The third variant of Rose's gravity model considered by Martínez and Sandleris (2011) aims at disentangling the individual and collective punishment effects. It takes the form:

$$\ln T_{ijt} = \beta_0 + \beta X_{ijt} + \sum_{m=0}^{M} \phi_m ACRED_{ijt-m} + \sum_{m=0}^{M} \xi_m NACRED_{ijt-m}$$

$$+ \sum_{m=0}^{M} \gamma_m NOTCRED_{ijt-m} + \epsilon_{ijt}.$$

Here, $ACRED_{ijt}$, $NACRED_{ijt}$, and $NOTCRED_{ijt}$ are all binary variables taking the values one or zero. The variable $NACRED_{ijt}$ takes the value one if either country in the pair (ij) is a defaulter negotiating its debt in the context of the Paris Club in period t and the other country is a nonnegotiating Paris Club creditor (a nonaffected creditor). The variable $NOTCRED_{ijt}$ takes the value one if either country in the pair (ij) is a defaulter negotiating its debt in the context of the Paris Club in period t and the other country is not a creditor. In this variant of the model, evidence of individual and collective trade sanctions would require both $\sum_{m=0}^{M} \phi_m$ and $\sum_{m=0}^{M} \xi_m$ to be negative and significant. The cumulative effect of default on trade between defaulters and nonaffected creditors, given by $\sum_{m=0}^{M} \xi_m$, is consistently negative and robust across lag lengths. Specifically, it takes the values -0.0246, -0.2314, -0.4675, and -0.5629, at lag lengths of 0, 5, 10, and 15 years, respectively. However, the cumulative effect of default on trade between defaulters and directly affected creditors, given by $\sum_{m=0}^{M} \phi_m$, is again sensitive to the specified lag length, taking positive values at short and medium lag lengths and turning negative at long lag lengths. Specifically, the point estimate is 0.0631, 0.0854, 0.0119, and -0.3916 at lag lengths of 0, 5, 10, and 15, respectively.

We interpret the work of Martínez and Sandleris (2011) as suggesting that the importance of trade sanctions as a cost of default depends crucially on one's beliefs regarding the magnitude of the delay that creditors are able or willing to impose on defaulting debtors. If one believes that a reasonable period over which creditors apply trade sanctions to defaulting debtors is less than a decade, then the gravity model offers little evidence of trade sanctions on defaulters. Virtually all the observed decline in the bilateral trade of debtors after a default episode can be attributed to economic distress and not to punishment inflicted by creditors. However, if one believes that creditors have good memory and are capable of castigating defaulting debtors for many years (more than a decade) after a default episode, then the gravity model identifies a significant punishment component in the observed decline in bilateral trade following default episodes: about 50 percent of the trade volume cumulated over 15 years.

13.3 Default Incentives with State-Contingent Contracts

The focus of this section is to analyze the structure of international debt contracts when agents have access to state-contingent financial instruments but may lack commitment to honor debt obligations. The material in this section draws from the influential work of Grossman and Van Huyck (1988).

Consider a one-period economy facing a stochastic endowment given by

$$y = \bar{y} + \epsilon,$$

where $\bar{y} > 0$ is a constant, and ϵ is a mean-zero random variable with density $\pi(\epsilon)$ defined over the interval $[\epsilon^L, \epsilon^H]$. Thus $\bar{y}$ is the mean of the endowment process, and ϵ is an endowment shock satisfying

$$\int_{\epsilon^L}^{\epsilon^H} \epsilon \pi(\epsilon) d\epsilon = 0.$$

Assume that before ϵ is realized, the country can buy insurance against endowment shocks. This insurance is sold by foreign investors and takes the form of state-contingent debt contracts. Specifically, these debt contracts stipulate that the country must pay $d(\epsilon)$ units of goods to foreign lenders after the realization of the shock. The objective of the country is to pick the debt contract $d(\epsilon)$ optimally. This state-contingent payment can take positive or negative values. In states in which $d(\epsilon)$ is negative, the country receives a payment from foreign lenders; in states in which $d(\epsilon)$ is positive, the country makes payments to foreign lenders. Foreign lenders are assumed to be risk neutral, to operate in a perfectly competitive market, and to face an opportunity cost of funds equal to zero. These assumptions imply that debt contracts carrying an expected payment of zero are sufficient to ensure the participation of foreign investors. Formally, the zero-expected-profit condition, known as the participation constraint, can be written as

$$\int_{\epsilon^L}^{\epsilon^H} d(\epsilon) \pi(\epsilon) d\epsilon = 0. \tag{13.1}$$

The country seeks to maximize the welfare of its representative consumer, which is assumed to be of the form

$$\int_{\epsilon^L}^{\epsilon^H} u(c(\epsilon)) \pi(\epsilon) d\epsilon, \tag{13.2}$$

where $c(\epsilon)$ denotes consumption, and $u(\cdot)$ is a strictly increasing and strictly concave utility index. For the remainder of this section, we will use the terms "country" and "household" interchangeably. The household's budget constraint is given by

$$c(\epsilon) = \bar{y} + \epsilon - d(\epsilon). \tag{13.3}$$

We are now ready to characterize the form of the optimal external debt contract. We begin by considering the case in which the country can commit to honor its promises.

13.3.1 The Optimal Debt Contract with Commitment

Let's assume that after the realization of the endowment shock ϵ, the household honors any promises made before the occurrence of the shock. In this case, before the realization of the shock, the household's problem consists of choosing a state-contingent debt contract $d(\epsilon)$ to maximize

$$\int_{\epsilon^L}^{\epsilon^H} u(c(\epsilon))\pi(\epsilon)d\epsilon, \tag{13.2 R}$$

subject to the budget constraint

$$c(\epsilon) = \bar{y} + \epsilon - d(\epsilon) \tag{13.3 R}$$

and the participation constraint

$$\int_{\epsilon^L}^{\epsilon^H} d(\epsilon)\pi(\epsilon)d\epsilon = 0. \tag{13.1 R}$$

The Lagrangian associated with this problem can be written as

$$\mathcal{L} = \int_{\epsilon^L}^{\epsilon^H} \left[u(\bar{y} + \epsilon - d(\epsilon)) + \lambda d(\epsilon) \right] \pi(\epsilon)d\epsilon,$$

where λ denotes the Lagrange multiplier associated with the participation constraint (13.1). Note that λ is not state contingent. The first-order conditions associated with the representative household's problem are (13.1), (13.3), and

$$u'(c(\epsilon)) = \lambda.$$

Because the multiplier λ is independent of ϵ, this expression implies that consumption is also independent of ϵ. That is, the optimal debt contract achieves perfect consumption smoothing across states of nature. Multiplying both sides of the budget constraint (13.3) by $\pi(\epsilon)$ and integrating over the interval $[\epsilon^L, \epsilon^H]$ yields

$$c(\epsilon)\int_{\epsilon^L}^{\epsilon^H} \pi(\epsilon)d\epsilon = \bar{y}\int_{\epsilon^L}^{\epsilon^H} \pi(\epsilon)d\epsilon + \int_{\epsilon^L}^{\epsilon^H} \epsilon\pi(\epsilon)d\epsilon - \int_{\epsilon^L}^{\epsilon^H} d(\epsilon)\pi(\epsilon)d\epsilon.$$

In this step, we are using the fact that $c(\epsilon)$ is independent of ϵ. Since $\int_{\epsilon^L}^{\epsilon^H} \pi(\epsilon)d\epsilon = 1$, $\int_{\epsilon^L}^{\epsilon^H} \epsilon\pi(\epsilon)d\epsilon = 0$, and $\int_{\epsilon^L}^{\epsilon^H} d(\epsilon)\pi(\epsilon)d\epsilon = 0$, we have that

$$c(\epsilon) = \bar{y}.$$

That is, under the optimal contract, consumption equals the average endowment in all states. It then follows from the budget constraint (13.3) that the associated debt payments are exactly equal to the endowment shocks:

$$d(\epsilon) = \epsilon.$$

Under the optimal contract, domestic risk-averse households transfer all their income uncertainty to risk-neutral foreign lenders. They do so by receiving full compensation from foreign investors for any realization of the endowment below average and by transferring to foreign investors any amount of endowment in excess of the mean. Thus net payments to the rest of the world move one for one with the endowment:

$$d'(\epsilon) = 1.$$

The derivative of the debt contract with respect to the endowment shock is a convenient summary of how much insurance the contract provides. A unit slope is a benchmark that we will use to ascertain how much protection from output fluctuations the country can achieve through the optimal debt contract under alternative environments that vary in the amount of commitment the country has to honor debt and in the ability of foreign lenders to punish defaulters.

13.3.2 The Optimal Debt Contract without Commitment

In the economy under analysis, there are no negative consequences for not paying debt obligations. Moreover, debtors have incentives not to pay. In effect, in any state of the world in which the contract stipulates a payment to foreign lenders (i.e., in states in which the endowment is above average), the debtor country would be better off defaulting and consuming the resources it owes. After consuming these resources, the world simply ends, so debtors cannot be punished for having defaulted.

The perfect-risk-sharing equilibrium we analyzed in Section 13.3.1 was built on the premise that the sovereign can resist the temptation to default. What if this commitment to honoring debts were absent? Clearly, in our one-shot world, the country would default in any state in which the contract stipulates a payment to the rest of the world. It then follows that any debt contract must include the additional incentive-compatibility constraint

$$d(\epsilon) \leq 0, \tag{13.4}$$

for all $\epsilon \in [\epsilon^L, \epsilon^H]$. The representative household's problem then is to maximize

$$\int_{\epsilon^L}^{\epsilon^H} u(c(\epsilon))\pi(\epsilon)d\epsilon, \tag{13.2 R}$$

subject to

$$c(\epsilon) = \bar{y} + \epsilon - d(\epsilon), \tag{13.3 R}$$

$$\int_{\epsilon^L}^{\epsilon^H} d(\epsilon)\pi(\epsilon)d\epsilon = 0, \tag{13.1 R}$$

and

$$d(\epsilon) \leq 0. \tag{13.4 R}$$

Restrictions (13.1) and (13.4) state that debt payments must be zero on average and never positive. The only debt contract that can satisfy these two requirements simultaneously is clearly

$$d(\epsilon) = 0,$$

for all ϵ. This is a trivial contract stipulating no transfers of any sort in any state. It follows that under lack of commitment, international risk sharing breaks down. No meaningful debt contract can be supported in equilibrium. As a result, the country is in complete financial autarky and must consume its endowment in every state:

$$c(\epsilon) = \bar{y} + \epsilon,$$

for all ϵ. This consumption profile has the same mean as the one that can be supported with commitment, namely, $\bar{y}$. However, the consumption plan under commitment is constant across states, whereas the one associated with autarky inherits the volatility of the endowment process. It follows immediately that risk-averse households (i.e., households with concave preferences) are worse off in the financially autarkic economy. Formally, by the definition of concavity, we have that $u\left(\int_{\epsilon^L}^{\epsilon^H} (\bar{y} + \epsilon)\pi(\epsilon)d\epsilon\right) > \int_{\epsilon^L}^{\epsilon^H} u(\bar{y} + \epsilon)\pi(\epsilon)d\epsilon$. Put differently, commitment is welfare increasing.

Because in the economy without commitment international transfers are constant (and equal to zero) across states, we have that

$$d'(\epsilon) = 0.$$

This result is in sharp contrast with what we obtained under full commitment. In that case, the derivative of debt payments with respect to the endowment shock is unity at all endowment levels.

13.3.3 Direct Sanctions

Suppose that foreign lenders (or their representative governments) could punish defaulting sovereigns by seizing national property, such as financial assets or exports. One would expect that this type of action would deter borrowers from defaulting, at least as long as debt obligations do not exceed the value of the seizure. What is the shape of the optimal debt contract that emerges in this type of environment?

We model direct sanctions by assuming that in the case of default, lenders can seize $k > 0$ units of goods from the delinquent debtor. It follows that the borrower will honor all debts not exceeding k in value. Formally, this means that the incentive-compatibility constraint now takes the form

$$d(\epsilon) \leq k. \tag{13.5}$$

Under commitment, the optimal debt contract stipulates a maximum payment of ϵ^H. This means that if $k \geq \epsilon^H$, the optimal contract under commitment can be supported in an environment without commitment but with sanctions. At the opposite extreme, if $k = 0$, we are in the case with no commitment and no sanctions, and no payments can be supported in equilibrium, which results in financial autarky. Here our interest is to characterize the optimal debt contract in the intermediate case:

$$k \in (0, \epsilon^H).$$

The representative household's problem then consists of maximizing

$$\int_{\epsilon^L}^{\epsilon^H} u(c(\epsilon))\pi(\epsilon)d\epsilon, \tag{13.2 R}$$

subject to

$$c(\epsilon) = \bar{y} + \epsilon - d(\epsilon), \tag{13.3 R}$$

$$\int_{\epsilon^L}^{\epsilon^H} d(\epsilon)\pi(\epsilon)d\epsilon = 0, \tag{13.1 R}$$

and

$$d(\epsilon) \le k. \tag{13.5 R}$$

The Lagrangian associated with this problem can be written as

$$\mathcal{L} = \int_{\epsilon^L}^{\epsilon^H} \left\{ u(\bar{y} + \epsilon - d(\epsilon)) + \lambda d(\epsilon) + \gamma(\epsilon)[k - d(\epsilon)] \right\} \pi(\epsilon)d\epsilon,$$

where λ denotes the Lagrange multiplier associated with the participation constraint (13.1), and $\gamma(\epsilon)\pi(\epsilon)$ denotes the Lagrange multiplier associated with the incentive-compatibility constraint (13.5) in state ϵ (there is a continuum of such multipliers; one for each possible value of ϵ). The first-order conditions associated with the representative household's problem are (13.1), (13.3), (13.5), and

$$u'(c(\epsilon)) = \lambda - \gamma(\epsilon), \tag{13.6}$$

$$\gamma(\epsilon) \ge 0, \tag{13.7}$$

and the slackness condition,

$$(k - d(\epsilon))\gamma(\epsilon) = 0. \tag{13.8}$$

In states in which the incentive-compatibility constraint does not bind (i.e., when $d(\epsilon) < k$), the slackness condition (13.8) states that the Lagrange multiplier $\gamma(\epsilon)$ must vanish. It then follows from optimality condition (13.6) that the marginal utility of consumption equals λ for all states of nature in which the incentive-compatibility constraint does not bind. This means that consumption is constant across all states in which the incentive-compatibility constraint does not bind.

In turn, the budget constraint (13.3) implies that across states in which the incentive-compatibility constraint does not bind, payments to foreign lenders must differ from the endowment innovation ϵ by only a constant. Formally, we have that

$$d(\epsilon) = \bar{d} + \epsilon,$$

for all ϵ such that $d(\epsilon) < k$, where $\bar{d}$ is an endogenously determined constant.

Based on our analysis of the case with commitment, in which payments to the rest of the world take place in states of nature featuring positive endowment shocks, it is natural to conjecture that the optimal contract will feature the incentive-compatibility constraint binding at relatively high levels of income and not binding at relatively low levels of income. To see that this is indeed the case, let us show that if the incentive-compatibility constraint is not binding for some ϵ', then it is not binding for all $\epsilon'' < \epsilon'$. Formally, we wish to show that if $d(\epsilon') < k$ for some $\epsilon' \in (\epsilon^L, \epsilon^H)$, then $d(\epsilon'') < d(\epsilon')$ for any $\epsilon'' \in [\epsilon^L, \epsilon')$. The proof is by contradiction. Let $\epsilon'' \in [\epsilon^L, \epsilon')$. Suppose that $d(\epsilon'') \geq d(\epsilon')$. Then by the budget constraint (13.3), we have that $c(\epsilon'') = \bar{y} + \epsilon'' - d(\epsilon'') < \bar{y} + \epsilon' - d(\epsilon') = c(\epsilon')$. It follows from the strict concavity of the utility function that $u'(c(\epsilon'')) > u'(c(\epsilon'))$. Then by optimality condition (13.6), we have that $\gamma(\epsilon'') < \gamma(\epsilon')$. But $\gamma(\epsilon') = 0$ by the slackness condition (13.8) and the assumption that $d(\epsilon') < k$. So we have that $\gamma(\epsilon'') < 0$, which contradicts optimality condition (13.7).

It follows that there exists an $\bar{\epsilon}$ such that

$$d(\epsilon) = \begin{cases} \bar{d} + \epsilon & \text{for } \epsilon < \bar{\epsilon} \\ k & \text{for } \epsilon > \bar{\epsilon}. \end{cases} \tag{13.9}$$

We will show shortly that the debt contract described by this expression is indeed continuous in the endowment shock. That is, we will show that

$$d(\bar{\epsilon}) = \bar{d} + \bar{\epsilon} = k. \tag{13.10}$$

We will also show that this condition implies that the constant $\bar{d}$ is indeed positive. This means that under the optimal debt contract without commitment but with direct sanctions the borrower enjoys less insurance than in the case of full commitment. This is because in relatively low-endowment states (i.e., states in which the incentive-compatibility constraint does not bind) the borrower must pay $\bar{d} + \epsilon$, which is a larger sum than the one that is stipulated for the same state in the optimal contract with full commitment, given simply by ϵ.

To see that if condition (13.10) holds (i.e., if the optimal debt contract is continuous), then $\bar{d}$ is positive, write the participation constraint (13.1), which indicates that debt payments must be nil on average, as

$$0 = \int_{\epsilon^L}^{\bar{\epsilon}} (\bar{d} + \epsilon)\pi(\epsilon)d\epsilon + \int_{\bar{\epsilon}}^{\epsilon^H} k\pi(\epsilon)d\epsilon$$

$$= \int_{\epsilon^L}^{\bar{\epsilon}} (\bar{d} + \epsilon)\pi(\epsilon)d\epsilon + \int_{\bar{\epsilon}}^{\epsilon^H} (\bar{d} + \bar{\epsilon})\pi(\epsilon)d\epsilon$$

$$= \bar{d} + \int_{\epsilon^L}^{\bar{\epsilon}} \epsilon\pi(\epsilon)d\epsilon + \int_{\bar{\epsilon}}^{\epsilon^H} \bar{\epsilon}\pi(\epsilon)d\epsilon$$

$$= \bar{d} - \int_{\bar{\epsilon}}^{\epsilon^H} (\epsilon - \bar{\epsilon})\pi(\epsilon)d\epsilon.$$

Since $\bar{\epsilon} < \epsilon^H$, we have that[6]

$$\bar{d} > 0.$$

---

6. To see that $\bar{\epsilon} < \epsilon^H$, show that if $\bar{\epsilon} = \epsilon^H$, then (13.1) and (13.9) imply that $d(\epsilon) = \epsilon$, which violates the incentive-compatibility constraint (13.5) for all $\epsilon > k$.

In showing that $\bar{d}$ is positive, we made use of the conjecture that the debt contract is continuous in the endowment, that is, that $\bar{d} + \bar{\epsilon} = k$. We are now ready to establish this result. Using (13.9) to eliminate $d(\epsilon)$ from (13.3) and (13.1), the optimal contract sets $\bar{\epsilon}$ and $\bar{d}$ to maximize

$$\int_{\epsilon^L}^{\bar{\epsilon}} u(\bar{y} - \bar{d})\pi(\epsilon)d\epsilon + \int_{\bar{\epsilon}}^{\epsilon^H} u(\bar{y} + \epsilon - k)\pi(\epsilon)d\epsilon, \qquad (13.11)$$

subject to

$$\int_{\epsilon^L}^{\bar{\epsilon}} (\bar{d} + \epsilon)\pi(\epsilon)d\epsilon + [1 - F(\bar{\epsilon})]k = 0, \qquad (13.12)$$

where $F(\bar{\epsilon}) \equiv \int_{\epsilon^L}^{\bar{\epsilon}} \pi(\epsilon)d\epsilon$ denotes the probability that ϵ is less than $\bar{\epsilon}$. Now differentiate (13.11) with respect to $\bar{d}$ and $\bar{\epsilon}$ and set the result equal to zero. Also differentiate (13.12). The resulting expressions are, respectively,

$$-u'(\bar{y} - \bar{d})F(\bar{\epsilon})d\bar{d} + [u(\bar{y} - \bar{d}) - u(\bar{y} + \bar{\epsilon} - k)]\pi(\bar{\epsilon})d\bar{\epsilon} = 0, \qquad (13.13)$$

and

$$[\bar{\epsilon} - k + \bar{d}]\pi(\bar{\epsilon})d\epsilon + F(\bar{\epsilon})d\bar{d} = 0. \qquad (13.14)$$

Combining equations (13.13) and (13.14), we obtain the optimality condition

$$-u'(\bar{y} - \bar{d})[k - \bar{d} - \bar{\epsilon}] + [u(\bar{y} - \bar{d}) - u(\bar{y} + \bar{\epsilon} - k)] = 0. \qquad (13.15)$$

Conditions (13.12) and (13.15) represent a system of two equations in the two unknowns, $\bar{\epsilon}$ and $\bar{d}$. Clearly, equation (13.15) is satisfied for any pair $(\bar{\epsilon}, \bar{d})$ such that $\bar{d} + \bar{\epsilon} = k$. That is, any continuous contract from the family defined in (13.9) satisfies the optimality condition (13.15). We now need to show that there exists a continuous contract that satisfies (13.12). To this end, replace $\bar{d}$ in (13.12) by $k - \bar{\epsilon}$ to obtain

$$k = \int_{\epsilon^L}^{\bar{\epsilon}} (\bar{\epsilon} - \epsilon)\pi(\epsilon)d\epsilon.$$

The function $(\bar{\epsilon} - \epsilon)\pi(\epsilon)$ is nonnegative for $\epsilon \le \bar{\epsilon}$, which means that the right-hand side of this expression is a continuous, nondecreasing function of $\bar{\epsilon}$. Moreover, the right-hand side takes the value 0 at $\bar{\epsilon} = \epsilon^L$ and the value ϵ^H for $\bar{\epsilon} = \epsilon^H$. Since the sanction k belongs to the interval $(0, \epsilon^H)$, we have that there is at least one value of $\bar{\epsilon}$ that satisfies the above expression. We have therefore established that there exists at least one continuous debt contract that satisfies the two optimality conditions (13.12) and (13.15). Clearly, if the density function $\pi(\epsilon)$ is strictly positive for all $\epsilon \in (\epsilon^L, \epsilon^H)$, then there is a unique continuous contract that satisfies both optimality conditions.

Our analysis shows that the case with no commitment and direct sanctions falls in between the case with full commitment and the case with no commitment and no direct sanctions. In particular, payments to foreign creditors increase one for one with the endowment shock for $\epsilon < \bar{\epsilon}$ (as in the case with full commitment), and they are independent of the endowment shock for ϵ larger than $\bar{\epsilon}$ (as in the case without commitment and no direct sanctions):

$$d'(\epsilon) = \begin{cases} 1 & \epsilon < \bar{\epsilon} \\ 0 & \epsilon > \bar{\epsilon}. \end{cases}$$

Note also that if the sanction is sufficiently large—specifically, if $k > \epsilon^H$—then $\bar{\epsilon} > \epsilon^H$ and the optimal contract is identical to the one that results in the case of full commitment. In contrast, if creditors are unable to impose sanctions ($k = 0$), then $\bar{\epsilon} = \epsilon^L$ and the optimal contract stipulates financial autarky as in the case with neither commitment nor direct sanctions. It follows, perhaps paradoxically, that the larger the ability of creditors to punish debtor countries in case of default, the higher will be the welfare of the debtor countries themselves.

Finally, it is of interest to compare the consumption profiles across states in the model with commitment and in the model with direct sanctions and no commitment. Figure 13.6 provides a graphical representation of this comparison. In the model with commitment, consumption is perfectly smooth across states and equal to the average endowment. As mentioned earlier, in this case the risk-averse debtor country transfers all of the risk to risk-neutral lenders. In the absence of commitment, consumption smoothing is a direct function of the ability of the lender to punish debtors in the case of default. Consumption is flat in low-endowment states (from ϵ^L to $\bar{\epsilon}$) and increasing in the endowment in high-endowment states (from $\bar{\epsilon}$ to ϵ^H). The reduced ability of the risk-averse agent to transfer risk to risk-neutral lenders is reflected in two features of the consumption profile. First, the profile is no longer flat across all states of nature. Second, the flat segment of the consumption profile is lower than the level of consumption achieved under full commitment. This means that in the case with sanctions but no commitment, although households are protected by a safety net ($\bar{y} - \bar{d}$) below which consumption cannot fall no matter how severe the contraction of their income is, this safety net is more precarious than the one provided by full commitment ($\bar{y} > \bar{y} - \bar{d}$).

Finally, a consequence of our assumption that asset markets are complete is that the punishment is never imposed in equilibrium. The incentive-compatibility constraint ensures that the amount of payments contracted in each state of nature never exceeds the possible punishment. As a result, in equilibrium, the debtor never has an incentive to default.

13.3.4 Reputation

Suppose now that creditors do not have access to direct sanctions to punish debtors who choose to default. Instead, assume that creditors have the ability to exclude delinquent debtors from financial markets. Because financial autarky entails the cost of an elevated consumption volatility, financial exclusion has the potential to support international lending. Debtor countries pay their obligations to maintain their performing status.

Clearly the model we have in mind here can no longer be a one-period model like the one studied thus far. Time is at the center of any reputational model of debt. Accordingly,

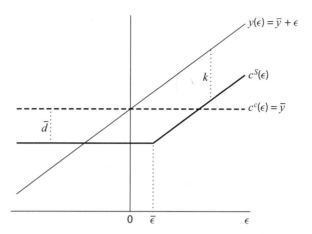

Figure 13.6 Consumption profiles under full commitment and no commitment with direct sanctions.

Note: $c^c(\epsilon)$ and $c^s(\epsilon)$ denote the levels of consumption in state ϵ under commitment and sanctions, respectively, $y(\epsilon) \equiv \bar{y} + \epsilon$ denotes output, and ϵ denotes the endowment shock.

we assume that the debtor country lives forever and each period receives an endowment equal to $\bar{y} + \epsilon$, where $\bar{y}$ is a positive constant, and ϵ is a mean-zero random variable with a time-invariant density $\pi(\epsilon) > 0$ over the continuous support $[\epsilon^L, \epsilon^H]$. For simplicity, we assume that the country cannot transfer resources intertemporally via a storage technology or financial markets.

If the country defaulted in the present or in the past, it is considered to be in bad financial standing. Suppose that foreign lenders punish countries that are in bad financial standing by perpetually excluding them from international financial markets. Let $v^b(\epsilon)$ denote the welfare of a country that is in bad financial standing. Then we have that $v^b(\epsilon)$ is given by

$$v^b(\epsilon) \equiv u(\bar{y} + \epsilon) + \beta \int_{\epsilon^L}^{\epsilon^H} v^b(\epsilon')\pi(\epsilon')d\epsilon'$$

$$= u(\bar{y} + \epsilon) + \frac{\beta}{1 - \beta} \int_{\epsilon^L}^{\epsilon^H} u(\bar{y} + \epsilon')\pi(\epsilon')d\epsilon'.$$

Consider designing a debt contract with the following characteristics. (i) Payments are state contingent, but time independent. That is, the contract stipulates that in any state ϵ, the country must pay $d(\epsilon)$ to foreign lenders independently of history. (ii) The contract is incentive compatible, that is, in every state and date, the country prefers to pay its debt rather than default. (iii) The contract satisfies the participation constraint (13.1) period by period. That is, for each date, the expected value of payments to foreign lenders across states must be equal to zero.

In any date and state, the country can be either in good or bad financial standing. We denote by $v^g(\epsilon)$ the welfare of a country that enters the period in good standing and by $v^c(\epsilon)$ the welfare of a country that enters the period in good standing and chooses to honor its external obligations in that period. Then, we have that

$$v^c(\epsilon) \equiv u(\bar{y} + \epsilon - d(\epsilon)) + \beta \int_{\epsilon^L}^{\epsilon^H} v^g(\epsilon')\pi(\epsilon')d\epsilon', \qquad (13.16)$$

and

$$v^g(\epsilon) = \max\{v^b(\epsilon), v^c(\epsilon)\}.$$

The incentive-compatibility constraint requires that the country prefer to honor its debt, or, formally, that

$$v^c(\epsilon) \geq v^b(\epsilon). \qquad (13.17)$$

The above two expressions then imply that

$$v^g(\epsilon) = v^c(\epsilon).$$

This equation implies that in equilibrium, countries never default. As we will see shortly, this will not be the case in models with incomplete financial markets. The above expression can be used to eliminate $v^g(\epsilon)$ from (13.16) to get

$$v^c(\epsilon) = u(\bar{y} + \epsilon - d(\epsilon)) + \beta \int_{\epsilon^L}^{\epsilon^H} v^c(\epsilon')\pi(\epsilon')d\epsilon'.$$

Iterating this expression forward yields

$$v^c(\epsilon) = u(\bar{y} + \epsilon - d(\epsilon)) + \frac{\beta}{1-\beta} \int_{\epsilon^L}^{\epsilon^H} u(\bar{y} + \epsilon' - d(\epsilon'))\pi(\epsilon')d\epsilon'.$$

We can then rewrite the incentive-compatibility constraint (13.17) as

$$u(\bar{y} + \epsilon - d(\epsilon)) + \frac{\beta}{1-\beta} \int_{\epsilon^L}^{\epsilon^H} u(\bar{y} + \epsilon' - d(\epsilon'))\pi(\epsilon')d\epsilon' \geq u(\bar{y} + \epsilon)$$

$$+ \frac{\beta}{1-\beta} \int_{\epsilon^L}^{\epsilon^H} u(\bar{y} + \epsilon')\pi(\epsilon')d\epsilon'. \qquad (13.18)$$

This restriction must hold for every state ϵ.

Before continuing with the characterization of the optimal debt contract, it is instructive to see what factors make the first-best contract, $d(\epsilon) = \epsilon$, fail in the present environment without commitment. Evaluating the above incentive-compatibility constraint at the first-best contract and rearranging terms, we obtain

$$u(\bar{y} + \epsilon) - u(\bar{y}) \leq \frac{\beta}{1 - \beta}[u(\bar{y}) - Eu(\bar{y} + \epsilon)],$$

where $Eu(\bar{y} + \epsilon) \equiv \int_{\epsilon^L}^{\epsilon^H} u(\bar{y} + \epsilon)\pi(\epsilon)d\epsilon$ denotes the expected value of the period utility under financial autarky. The left-hand side of this expression measures the short-run gains of defaulting, whereas the right-hand side (which is positive because of the assumption of strict concavity of the period utility index) measures the long-run costs of default. The short-run gains have to do with the extra utility derived from above-average realizations of the current endowment, and the long-run costs of default are associated with the lack of consumption smoothing that defaulters must endure under financial autarky.

The above expression shows that the first-best debt contract may not be implementable on reputational grounds alone, because it may violate the incentive-compatibility constraint in certain states. In general, incentives to default are stronger the larger the current realization of the endowment, ϵ. In particular, under the first-best debt contract, default could take place in states in which the endowment is above average ($\epsilon > 0$). Also, the more impatient the debtor is (i.e., the lower β is), the larger becomes the incentive to default. Intuitively, an impatient debtor does not place much value on the fact that future expected utility is higher under the first-best contract than under financial isolation. In addition, all other things being equal, less risk-averse countries have stronger incentives to default on the first-best debt contract. It follows from this analysis that the first-best contract is in general not incentive compatible in the absence of commitment, even if creditors could use financial isolation as a discipline device. Let's get back, then, to the characterization of the optimal incentive-compatible debt contract.

Because the debt contracting problem is stationary, in the sense that the contract must be time independent, it suffices to maximize the period utility index,

$$\int_{\epsilon^L}^{\epsilon^H} u(\bar{y} + \epsilon - d(\epsilon))\pi(\epsilon)d\epsilon,$$

subject to the participation constraint (13.1) and the incentive-compatibility constraint (13.18). The Lagrangian associated with this problem is

$$
\begin{aligned}
\mathcal{L} = & \int_{\epsilon^L}^{\epsilon^H} u(\bar{y} + \epsilon - d(\epsilon))\pi(\epsilon)d\epsilon \\
& + \lambda \int_{\epsilon^L}^{\epsilon^H} d(\epsilon)\pi(\epsilon)d\epsilon \\
& + \int_{\epsilon^L}^{\epsilon^H} \gamma(\epsilon) \left[u(\bar{y} + \epsilon - d(\epsilon)) + \frac{\beta}{1 - \beta} \int_{\epsilon^L}^{\epsilon^H} u(\bar{y} + \epsilon' - d(\epsilon'))\pi(\epsilon')d\epsilon' \right. \\
& \left. \qquad -u(\bar{y} + \epsilon) - \frac{\beta}{1 - \beta} \int_{\epsilon^L}^{\epsilon^H} u(\bar{y} + \epsilon')\pi(\epsilon')d\epsilon' \right] \pi(\epsilon)d\epsilon,
\end{aligned}
$$

where λ and $\pi(\epsilon)\gamma(\epsilon)$ denote the Lagrange multipliers on (13.1) and (13.18), respectively. The first-order conditions associated with the problem of choosing the transfer schedule $d(\epsilon)$ are (13.1), (13.18),

$$u'(\bar{y} + \epsilon - d(\epsilon)) = \frac{\lambda}{1 + \gamma(\epsilon) + \frac{\beta}{1-\beta}\int_{\epsilon^L}^{\epsilon^H} \gamma(\epsilon')\pi(\epsilon')d\epsilon'}, \qquad (13.19)$$

$$\gamma(\epsilon) \geq 0,$$

and the slackness condition,

$$\gamma(\epsilon)\left[u(\bar{y} + \epsilon - d(\epsilon)) + \frac{\beta}{1-\beta}\int_{\epsilon^L}^{\epsilon^H} u(\bar{y} + \epsilon' - d(\epsilon'))\pi(\epsilon')d\epsilon' - u(\bar{y} + \epsilon) \right.$$

$$\left. - \frac{\beta}{1-\beta}\int_{\epsilon^L}^{\epsilon^H} u(\bar{y} + \epsilon')\pi(\epsilon')d\epsilon' \right] = 0. \qquad (13.20)$$

In states in which the incentive-compatibility constraint (13.18) is not binding, the slackness condition (13.20) stipulates that the Lagrange multiplier $\gamma(\epsilon)$ must vanish. It follows that in these states, the optimality condition (13.19) becomes

$$u'(\bar{y} + \epsilon - d(\epsilon)) = \frac{\lambda}{1 + \frac{\beta}{1-\beta}\int_{\epsilon^L}^{\epsilon^H} \gamma(\epsilon')\pi(\epsilon')d\epsilon'}. \qquad (13.21)$$

Because the right-hand side of this expression is independent of the current value of ϵ, we have that the marginal utility of consumption must be constant across states in which the incentive compatibility constraint does not bind. This, in turn, implies that consumption is constant across these states, and that transfers are of the form $d(\epsilon) = \bar{d} + \epsilon$, where $\bar{d}$ is a constant. Over these states, consumption and payments to or from the rest of the world behave exactly as in the case with direct sanctions: domestic risk-averse agents transfer their endowment shock plus a constant to risk-neutral foreign lenders.

In states in which the incentive-compatibility constraint (13.18) is binding, consumption is greater than or equal to consumption in states in which the incentive-compatibility constraint is not binding. To see this, notice that because $\gamma(\epsilon) \geq 0$ for all ϵ, the right-hand side of (13.19) is smaller than or equal to the right-hand side of (13.21). It then follows from the concavity of the period utility function that consumption must be higher in states in which the incentive-compatibility constraint is binding.

It is again natural to expect that the incentive-compatibility constraint will bind in high-endowment states and that it will not bind in low-endowment states. The intuition is, again, that the debt contract should stipulate payments to the rest of the world in high-endowment states and transfers from the rest of the world to the domestic households in low-endowment states, creating the largest incentives to default in high-endowment states. To see that this intuition is correct, consider an ϵ_1 for which the incentive-compatibility constraint is not binding, that is, $\gamma(\epsilon_1) = 0$. Consider now any endowment $\epsilon_2 < \epsilon_1$. We wish to show that $\gamma(\epsilon_2) = 0$. The proof is by contradiction. Suppose that $\gamma(\epsilon_2) > 0$. The analysis of the previous paragraph implies that $c(\epsilon_2) > c(\epsilon_1)$ and hence that $\epsilon_2 - d(\epsilon_2) > \epsilon_1 - d(\epsilon_1)$. This in turn implies that as the endowment shock falls from ϵ_1 to ϵ_2, the left-hand side of the incentive-compatibility constraint (13.18) increases and its right-hand side decreases. This means that (13.18) must hold with strict inequality at ϵ_2. It follows that the slackness condition (13.20) is violated, which shows that $\gamma(\epsilon_2)$ cannot be positive. It follows from this analysis that there exists a threshold level of the endowment shock $\bar{\epsilon} \leq \epsilon^H$ such that the incentive-compatibility constraint binds for all $\epsilon > \bar{\epsilon}$ and does not bind for all $\epsilon < \bar{\epsilon}$. That is,

$$\gamma(\epsilon) \begin{cases} = 0 & \text{for } \epsilon < \bar{\epsilon} \\ > 0 & \text{for } \epsilon > \bar{\epsilon}. \end{cases}$$

Consider the question of how the optimal transfer $d(\epsilon)$ varies across states in which the collateral constraint is binding. Does it increase as one moves from low- to high-endowment states, and by how much? To address these questions, let us examine the incentive-compatibility constraint (13.18) holding with equality:

$$u(\bar{y} + \epsilon - d(\epsilon)) + \frac{\beta}{1-\beta} \int_{\epsilon^L}^{\epsilon^H} u(\bar{y} + \epsilon' - d_{\epsilon'}) \pi(\epsilon') d\epsilon'$$

$$= u(\bar{y} + \epsilon) + \frac{\beta}{1-\beta} \int_{\epsilon^L}^{\epsilon^H} u(\bar{y} + \epsilon') \pi(\epsilon') d\epsilon'. \tag{13.22}$$

Notice that in this expression the terms $\frac{\beta}{1-\beta} \int_{\epsilon^L}^{\epsilon^H} u(\bar{y} + \epsilon' - d_{\epsilon'}) \pi(\epsilon') d\epsilon'$ and $\frac{\beta}{1-\beta} \int_{\epsilon^L}^{\epsilon^H} u(\bar{y} + \epsilon') \pi(\epsilon') d\epsilon'$ are both independent of the current endowment shock ϵ. Only the first terms on the right- and left-hand sides of (13.22) change with the current level of endowment. Differentiating (13.22) with respect to the current endowment, ϵ, yields

$$d'(\epsilon) = \frac{u'(\bar{y} + \epsilon - d(\epsilon)) - u'(\bar{y} + \epsilon)}{u'(\bar{y} + \epsilon - d(\epsilon))}.$$

Because the incentive-compatibility constraint binds only when the risk-averse agent must make payments ($d(\epsilon) > 0$)—there are no incentives to default when the country receives income from the foreign agent—and because the utility index is strictly concave, it follows that $u'(\bar{y} + \epsilon - d(\epsilon)) > u'(\bar{y} + \epsilon)$ in all states in which the incentive-compatibility constraint binds. This implies that when the incentive-compatibility constraint binds, we have

$$0 < d'(\epsilon) < 1.$$

That is, payments to the foreign lender increase with the level of income, but less than one for one.

It might seem counterintuitive that as the current endowment increases, the payment to creditors that can be supported without default also increases. After all, the higher is the current level of endowment, the higher will be the level of current consumption that can be achieved on default. The intuition behind the direct relation between income and payments

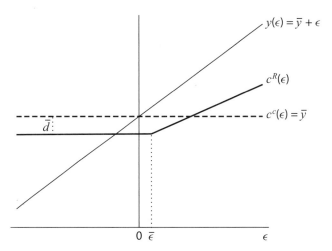

Figure 13.7 Consumption profiles under full commitment and no commitment in a reputational model of debt.

Note: $c^c(\epsilon)$ and $c^R(\epsilon)$ denote the levels of consumption in state ϵ under commitment and no commitment, respectively; $y(\epsilon) \equiv \bar{y} + \epsilon$ denotes output; and ϵ denotes the endowment shock.

is that *given* a positive level of current payments, $d(\epsilon) > 0$, a small increase in current endowment, ϵ, raises the current-period utility associated with not defaulting, $u(\bar{y} + \epsilon - d(\epsilon))$, by more than it raises the utility associated with the alternative of defaulting, $u(\bar{y} + \epsilon)$. (This is because the period utility function is assumed to be strictly concave.) It follows that in states in which $d(\epsilon) > 0$, the higher is the current endowment, the higher will be the level of payments to foreign lenders that can be supported without inducing default. This does not mean that default incentives are weaker the higher the level of the endowment becomes. Recall that the analysis in this paragraph is restricted to states in which the incentive-compatibility constraint is binding. The incentive-compatibility constraint tends to bind in relatively high-endowment states.

The positive slope of the payment schedule with respect to the endowment (when the incentive-compatibility constraint is binding) presents a contrast to the pattern that emerges in the case of direct sanctions. In the direct-sanction economy, when the incentive-compatibility constraint binds, payments equal the maximum punishment k, which implies that the slope of the payment schedule equals zero.

Finally, the fact that for the present reputational model the slope of the payment schedule is positive but less than one implies that when the incentive-compatibility constraint is binding, consumption is strictly increasing in the endowment. Figure 13.7 plots the consumption schedule as a function of the endowment shock.

13.4 Default Incentives with Non-State-Contingent Contracts

In a world with complete financial markets, optimal risk-sharing arrangements stipulate positive payoffs in low-income states and negative payoffs in high-income states. In this way, the optimal financial contract facilitates a smooth level of consumption across states of nature. An implication of this result is that default incentives are stronger in high-income states and weaker in low-income states. In the real world, however, as documented earlier in this chapter, countries tend to default during economic contractions. One goal of this section is to explain this empirical regularity. To this end, we remove the assumption that financial markets are complete. Indeed, we focus on the polar case of a single non-state-contingent asset. In this environment, debts assumed in the current period impose financial obligations in the next period that are independent of whether income in that period is high or low. The debtor is no longer able to design debt contracts that carry a high interest rate in good states and a low interest rate in bad states. As a result, debtors facing high debt obligations and low endowments will have strong incentives to default. The pioneer model of Eaton and Gersovitz (1981), which we study in this section, represents the first formalization of this idea. Our version of the Eaton-Gersovitz model follows Arellano (2008).

13.4.1 The Eaton-Gersovitz Model

Consider a small open economy populated by a large number of identical individuals. Preferences are described by the utility function,

$$E_0 \sum_{t=0}^{\infty} \beta^t u(c_t),$$

where c_t denotes consumption in period t, u is a period utility function assumed to be strictly increasing and strictly concave, and $\beta \in (0, 1)$ is a parameter denoting the subjective discount factor. Throughout our analysis, we will use the terms "household," "country," and "government" interchangeably. We have in mind an arrangement in which the government makes all decisions concerning international borrowing and default in a benevolent fashion. Each period $t \geq 0$, the representative country is endowed with y_t units of consumption goods. This endowment is assumed to be exogenous, stochastic, and i.i.d., with a distribution featuring a bounded support $Y \equiv [\underline{y}, \bar{y}]$.

At the beginning of each period, the country can be either in good financial standing or in bad financial standing. If the country is in bad financial standing, then it is prevented from borrowing or lending in financial markets. As a result, the country is forced to consume its endowment. Formally, consumption under bad financial standing is given by

$$c = y.$$

We drop the time subscript in expressions where all variables are dated in the current period.

If the country is in good financial standing, it can choose to default on its debt obligations or to honor its debt. If it chooses to default, then it immediately acquires a bad financial status. If it chooses to honor its debt, then it maintains its good financial standing until the beginning of the next period. If the country is in good standing and chooses not to default, its budget constraint is given by

$$c + d = y + q(d')d', \tag{13.23}$$

where d denotes the country's debt due in the current period, d' denotes the debt acquired in the current period and due in the next period, and $q(d')$ denotes the market price of the country's debt. Note that the price of debt depends on the amount of debt acquired in the current period and due next period, d', but not on the level of debt acquired in the previous period and due in the current period, d. This is because the default decision in the next period depends on the amount of debt due then. Notice also that $q(\cdot)$ is independent of the current level of output. This is because of the assumed i.i.d. nature of the endowment, which implies that its current value conveys no information about future expected endowment levels. If instead we had assumed that y was serially correlated, then bond prices would depend on the current level of the endowment, since it would be informative of the state of the business cycle—and hence of the probability of default—next period.

We assume that "bad financial standing" is an absorbent state. This means that once the country falls into bad standing, it remains in that status forever. The country acquires a bad standing when it defaults on its financial obligations. The value function associated with bad financial standing is denoted by $v^b(y)$ and is given by

$$v^b(y) = u(y) + \beta E(v^b(y')).$$

Here, y' denotes next period's endowment, and E denotes the expectations operator.

If the country is in good standing, the value function associated with continuing to participate in capital markets by honoring its current debts is denoted by $v^c(d, y)$ and is given by

$$v^c(d, y) = \max_{d'} \left\{ u(y + q(d')d' - d) + \beta E(v^g(d', y')) \right\},$$

subject to

$$d' \leq \bar{d},$$

where $v^g(d, y)$ denotes the value function associated with being in good financial standing and is given by

$$v^g(d, y) = \max\{v^b(y), v^c(d, y)\}.$$

The parameter $\bar{d} > 0$ is a debt limit that prevents agents from engaging in Ponzi games. In this economy, the country chooses to default when servicing the debt entails a cost in terms of forgone current consumption that is larger than the inconvenience of living in financial autarky forever. It is then reasonable to conjecture that default is more likely the larger the level of debt and the lower the current endowment. In what follows, we demonstrate that this intuition is in fact correct. We do so in steps.

13.4.2 The Default Set

The default set contains all endowment levels at which a country chooses to default given a particular level of debt. We denote the default set by $D(d)$. Formally, the default set is defined by

$$D(d) = \{y \in Y : v^b(y) > v^c(d, y)\}.$$

Because it is never in the agent's interest to default when its asset position is nonnegative (or $d \leq 0$), it follows that $D(d)$ is empty ($D(d) = \emptyset$) for all $d \leq 0$.

The trade balance is given by $tb \equiv y - c$. The budget constraint (13.23) then implies that

$$tb = d - q(d')d'.$$

The following proposition shows that at debt levels for which the default set is not empty, an economy that chooses not to default will run a trade surplus.

Proposition 13.1 If $D(d) \neq \emptyset$, then $tb = d - q(d')d' > 0$ for all $d' \leq \bar{d}$.

Proof The proof is by contradiction. Suppose that $D(d) \neq \emptyset$ and that $q\left(\widehat{d}\right)\widehat{d} - d \geq 0$ for some $\widehat{d} \leq \bar{d}$. Then we have

$$v^c(d, y) \equiv \max_{d' < \bar{d}} \left\{ u(y + q(d')d' - d) + \beta E(v^g(d', y')) \right\}$$

$$\geq u(y + q(\widehat{d})\widehat{d} - d) + \beta E(v^g(\widehat{d}, y'))$$

$$\geq u(y) + \beta E(v^b(y'))$$

$$\equiv v^b(y),$$

for all $y \in Y$. But if $v^c(d, y) \geq v^b(y)$ for all possible endowments, then the default set must be empty ($D(d) = \emptyset$), which contradicts the assumptions of the proposition. In the above expression, the first inequality follows from the definition of a maximum. The second inequality holds because, by assumption, $q(\widehat{d})\widehat{d} - d \geq 0$ and because, by definition, $v^g(\widehat{d}, y') \geq v^b(y')$. ∎

The object $q(d')d' - d$ represents the trade balance deficit (i.e., $q(d')d' - d = c - y$) for a country that chooses to continue to pay its debt. Thus the proposition states that a country with a level of debt that puts it at risk of default ($D(d) \neq \emptyset$) and that chooses to continue to participate in the financial market will devote part of its current endowment to servicing the debt, by running a trade balance surplus. Put differently, the proposition states that the economy runs trade deficits only when its debt position is such that the probability of default is nil ($D(d) = \emptyset$). This result is robust to assuming that the endowment is serially correlated (see exercise 13.10).

We now establish that in this economy the country tends to default in bad times. Specifically, we show that if a country with a certain level of debt and income chooses to default, then it will also choose to default at the same level of debt and a lower level of income. In other words, if the default set is not empty then it is indeed an interval with lower bound given by the lowest endowment level $\underline{y}$.

Proposition 13.2 If $y_1 \in D(d)$ and $\underline{y} \leq y_2 < y_1$, then $y_2 \in D(d)$.

Proof Suppose $D(d) \neq \emptyset$. Consider any $y \in Y$ such that $y \in D(d)$. Let $v_y^b(y) \equiv \partial v^b(y)/\partial y$ and $v_y^c(d, y) \equiv \partial v^c(d, y)/\partial y$. By the envelope theorem, $v_y^b(y) = u'(y)$

and $v_y^c(d, y) = u'(y + q(d')d' - d)$. By proposition 13.1, we have that $q(d')d' - d < 0$ for all $d' \leq \bar{d}$. This implies, by strict concavity of u, that $u'(y + q(d')d' - d) > u'(y)$. It follows that $v_y^b(y) - v_y^c(d, y) < 0$, for all $y \in D(d)$. That is, $v^b(y) - v^c(d, y)$ is a decreasing function of y for all $y \in D(d)$. This means that if $v^b(y_1) > v^c(d, y_1)$, then $v^b(y_2) > v^c(d, y_2)$ for $\underline{y} \leq y_2 < y_1$. Equivalently, if $y_1 \in D(d)$, then $y_2 \in D(d)$ for any $\underline{y} \leq y_2 < y_1$.

An alternative proof that does not rely on the differentiability of the value function is as follows.

$$v^b(y_2) - v^c(d, y_2)$$

$$= u(y_1) - u(y_1) + u(y_2) + \beta E v^b(y') - \max_{d'}\{u(y_2 + q(d')d' - d) + \beta E v^c(d', y')\}$$

$$= u(y_2) - u(y_1) + v^b(y_1) - \max_{d'}\{u(y_2 + q(d')d' - d) + \beta E v^c(d', y')\}$$

$$= u(y_2) - u(y_1) + v^b(y_1) - \max_{d'}\{u(y_2 + q(d')d' - d)$$

$$\quad - u(y_1 + q(d')d' - d) + u(y_1 + q(d')d' - d) + \beta E v^c(d', y')\}$$

$$\geq u(y_2) - u(y_1) + v^b(y_1) - \max_{d'}\{u(y_2 + q(d')d' - d) - u(y_1 + q(d')d' - d)\}$$

$$\quad - \max_{d'}\{u(y_1 + q(d')d' - d) + \beta E v^c(d', y')\}$$

$$= u(y_2) - u(y_1) + v^b(y_1) - u(y_2 + q(\tilde{d})\tilde{d} - d) + u(y_1 + q(\tilde{d})\tilde{d} - d)$$

$$\quad - \max_{d'}\{u(y_1 + q(d')d' - d) + \beta E v^c(d', y')\}$$

$$= [u(y_1 + q(\tilde{d})\tilde{d} - d) - u(y_2 + q(\tilde{d})\tilde{d} - d)] - [u(y_1) - u(y_2)] + v^b(y_1) - v^c(d, y_1)$$

$$> v^b(y1) - v^c(d, y_1)$$

$$> 0,$$

where $\tilde{d}$ is the value of d' that maximizes $\{u(y_2 + q(d')d' - d) - u(y_1 + q(d')d' - d)\}$. The first inequality holds because we are distributing the max operator. The second inequality holds because u is concave. And the third inequality follows because, by assumption, $y_1 \in D(d)$. ∎

We have shown that the default set is an interval with a lower bound given by the lowest endowment $\underline{y}$. We now show that the default set $D(d)$ is a larger interval, the larger the stock of debt becomes. Put differently, the higher the debt is, the larger the probability of default will be.

Proposition 13.3   If $D(d) \neq \emptyset$, then $D(d)$ is an interval, $[\underline{y}, y^*(d)]$, where $y^*(d)$ is increasing in d if $y^*(d) < \bar{y}$.

Proof We already proved that the default set $D(d)$ is an interval. By definition, every $y \in D(d)$ satisfies $v^b(y) - v^c(d, y) > 0$. At the same time, we showed that

$v_y^b(y) - v_y^c(d, y) < 0$ for all $y \in D(d)$. It follows that $y^*(d)$ is given either by $\bar{y}$ or (implicitly) by $v^b(y^*(d)) = v^c(d, y^*(d))$. Differentiating this expression yields

$$\frac{dy^*(d)}{dd} = \frac{v_d^c(d, y^*(d))}{v_y^b(y^*(d)) - v_y^c(d, y^*(d))},$$

where $v_d^c(d, y) \equiv \partial v^c(d, y)/\partial d$. We have shown that $v_y^b(y^*(d)) - v_y^c(d, y^*(d)) < 0$. Using the definition of $v_d^c(d, y)$ and applying the envelope theorem, it follows that $v_d^c(d, y^*(d)) = -u'(y^*(d) + q(d')d' - d) < 0$. We then conclude that

$$\frac{dy^*(d)}{dd} > 0,$$

as stated in the proposition. ∎

Summarizing, we have obtained two important results: First, given the stock of debt, default is more likely the lower the level of output becomes. Second, the larger is the stock of debt, the higher the probability of default will be. These two results are in line with the stylized facts presented earlier in this chapter, indicating that countries default in bad times (see Figures 13.2 and 13.3) and that at the time of default countries tend to display above-average debt-to-GNP ratios (see Table 13.3).

13.4.3 Default Risk and the Country Premium

We now characterize the behavior of the country interest-rate premium in this economy. Let the world interest rate be constant and equal to $r^* > 0$. We assume that foreign lenders are risk neutral and perfectly competitive. It follows that the expected rate of return on the country's debt must equal r^*. If the country does not default, foreign lenders receive $1/q(d')$ units of goods per unit lent. If the country does default, foreign lenders receive nothing. Equating the world interest rate to the expected rate of return on the domestic debt, one obtains

$$1 + r^* = \frac{\text{Prob}\left\{y' \geq y^*(d')\right\}}{q(d')}.$$

The numerator on the right-hand side of this expression is the probability that the country will not default next period. Letting $F(y)$ denote the cumulative density function of the endowment shock, we can write

$$q(d') = \frac{1 - F(y^*(d'))}{1 + r^*}.$$

This expression states that the gross country premium, $1/[q(d')(1 + r^*)]$, equals the inverse of the probability of repayment, or approximately one plus the probability of default. Hence the net country premium is approximately equal to the probability of default. The above expression implies that the derivative of the price of debt with respect to next period's debt is given by

$$\frac{dq(d')}{dd'} = \frac{-F'(y^*(d'))y^{*'}(d')}{1+r^*} \le 0.$$

The inequality follows because by definition $F' \ge 0$ and because, by proposition 13.3, $y^{*'}(d') \ge 0$. It follows that the country spread, given by the difference between $1/q(d')$ and $1 + r^*$, is nondecreasing in the stock of debt. We summarize this result in the following proposition.

> **Proposition 13.4** The country spread, given by $1/q(d') - 1 - r^*$, is nondecreasing in the stock of debt.

13.5 Saving and the Breakdown of Reputational Lending

A key assumption of the reputational model of sovereign debt is that when a country defaults, foreign lenders coordinate to exclude it from the possibility of borrowing or lending in international financial markets. At first glance, it might seem that what is important is that defaulters be precluded from borrowing in international financial markets. Why should defaulting countries not be allowed to save? Bulow and Rogoff (1989b) have shown that prohibiting defaulters from lending to foreign agents, or from holding a positive net foreign asset position, is crucial for the reputational model to work. If delinquent countries were not allowed to borrow but could run current account surpluses, no lending at all could be supported on reputational grounds alone.

To illustrate this insight in a simple setting, consider a deterministic economy. Suppose that a reputational equilibrium supports a path for external debt given by $\{d_t\}_{t=0}^{\infty}$, where d_t denotes the level of external debt assumed in period t and due in period $t + 1$.[7] Assume that default is punished with perpetual exclusion from borrowing in international financial markets, but that saving in these markets is allowed after default. This assumption and the fact that the economy operates under perfect foresight imply that any reputational equilibrium featuring positive debt in at least one date must be characterized by no default. To see this, notice that if the country defaults at some date $T > 0$, then no foreign investor would want to lend to this country in period $T - 1$, since default would occur for sure one period later. Thus, $d_{T-1} \le 0$. In turn, if the country is excluded from borrowing starting in period $T - 1$, then it will have no incentives to honor any debts outstanding in that period. As a result, no foreign investor would be willing to lend to the country in period $T - 2$. That is, $d_{T-2} \le 0$. Continuing with this logic, we arrive at the conclusion that default in period T implies no debt at any time. That is, $d_t \le 0$ for all $t \ge 0$.

It follows from this result that in an equilibrium with positive external debt the interest rate must equal the world interest rate, $r^* > 0$, because the probability of default is nil. The

---

7. For an example of a deterministic model with sovereign debt supported by reputation, see Eaton and Fernández (1995).

country premium is therefore also nil. The evolution of the equilibrium level of debt is then given by

$$d_t = (1+r^*)d_{t-1} - tb_t, \tag{13.24}$$

for $t \geq 0$, where $tb_t \equiv y_t - c_t$ denotes the trade balance in period t. Assume that the endowment path $\{y_t\}_{t=0}^{\infty}$ is bounded. Let $d_T > 0$ be the maximum level of external debt in this equilibrium sequence.[8]

That is, $d_T \geq d_t$ for all $t \geq -1$. Does it pay for the country to honor this debt? The answer is no. The reason is that the country could default in period $T + 1$—and therefore be excluded from borrowing internationally forever thereafter—and still be able to maintain a level of consumption no lower than the one that would have obtained in the absence of default. To see this, let $\tilde{d}_t$ for $t > T$ denote the post-default path of external debt (or external assets if negative). Let the debt position acquired in the period of default be

$$\tilde{d}_{T+1} = -tb_{T+1},$$

where tb_{T+1} is the trade balance prevailing in period $T + 1$ under the original debt sequence $\{d_t\}$. By (13.24) we have that $-tb_{T+1} = d_{T+1} - (1+r^*)d_T$, which implies that

$$\tilde{d}_{T+1} = d_{T+1} - (1+r^*)d_T. \tag{13.25}$$

Because by assumption $d_T \geq d_{T+1}$ and $r^* > 0$, we have that

$$\tilde{d}_{T+1} < 0.$$

That is, in period $T + 1$ the country can achieve the same level of trade balance (and hence consumption) under the default strategy as under the no-default strategy, without having to borrow internationally. Let the external debt position in period $T + 2$ in the default strategy be

$$\tilde{d}_{T+2} = (1+r^*)\tilde{d}_{T+1} - tb_{T+2},$$

where, again, tb_{T+2} is the trade balance prevailing in period $T + 2$ under the original (no default) debt sequence $\{d_t\}$. Using (13.24) and (13.25), we can rewrite the above expression as

$$\tilde{d}_{T+2} = d_{T+2} - (1+r^*)^2 d_T < 0.$$

The inequality follows because by assumption, $d_{T+2} \leq d_T$ and $r^* > 0$. We have shown that the defaulting strategy can achieve the no-default level of trade balance in period $t + 2$ without requiring any international borrowing. Continuing in this way, one obtains that

---

8. Exercise 13.11 asks you to derive the main result of this section when a maximal debt level does not exist.

the no-default sequence of trade balances, tb_t, for $t \geq T + 1$, can be supported by the debt path $\tilde{d}_t$ satisfying

$$\tilde{d}_t = d_t - (1 + r^*)^{t-T} d_T,$$

which is strictly negative for all $t \geq T + 1$. The fact that the entire post-default debt path is negative implies that the country could also implement a post-default path of trade balances $\tilde{tb}_t$ satisfying $\tilde{tb}_t \leq tb_t$ for $t \geq T + 1$ and $\tilde{tb}_{t'} < tb_{t'}$ for at least one $t' \geq T + 1$ and still generate no positive debt at any date $t \geq T + 1$. This new path for the trade balance would be strictly preferred to the no-default path, because it would allow consumption to be strictly higher than under the no-default strategy in at least one period and to be at least as high as under the no-default strategy in all other periods (recall that $tb_t = y_t - c_t$). It follows that it pays for the country to default immediately after reaching the largest debt level d_T.

But we showed that default in this perfect foresight economy implies zero debt at all times. Therefore, no external debt can be supported in equilibrium. In other words, allowing the country to save in international markets after default implies that no equilibrium featuring strictly positive levels of debt can be supported on reputational grounds alone. For simplicity, we derived this breakdown result using a model without uncertainty. But the result also holds in a stochastic environment (see Bulow and Rogoff 1989b).

13.6 Quantitative Analysis of the Eaton-Gersovitz Model

The reputational model of default analyzed in Section 13.4 has been subject to intense quantitative scrutiny. However, as formulated there, the model is too stylized to capture salient features of actual defaults. To give the model a chance to match the data, researchers have enriched it along a number of dimensions. Three basic features that can be found in virtually all quantitative models are serial correlation of the endowment process, a finite exclusion period from international credit markets after default, and an output cost of default. These features render the model less analytically tractable, but a full characterization of the equilibrium dynamics is possible using numerical methods.

13.6.1 Serial Correlation of the Endowment Process

We begin by introducing the assumption that the endowment process has an autoregressive component. Specifically, assume that the variable y_t has the AR(1) law of motion

$$\ln y_t = \rho \ln y_{t-1} + \sigma_\epsilon \epsilon_t, \tag{13.26}$$

where ln denotes the natural logarithm; $\rho \in [0, 1)$ is a parameter denoting the serial correlation of the endowment process; $\sigma_\epsilon > 0$ is a parameter denoting the standard deviation of the innovations to the endowment process; and ϵ_t is an i.i.d. random variable following a standard normal distribution, $\epsilon_t \sim N(0, 1)$. When $\rho = 0$, this process nests as a special case the i.i.d. specification assumed in Sections 13.3 and 13.4. At the other extreme, Aguiar and Gopinath (2006) consider an endowment process that is nonstationary in levels but follows an AR(1) law of motion in growth rates, as in the small open endowment economy studied in Chapter 2, Section 2.4.

A theoretical implication of assuming a serially correlated output process is that now the price of debt assumed in period t and due in period $t + 1$ is no longer only a function of the amount of debt assumed in t, d_{t+1}, but also of the current endowment, y_t. The reason is that, as we have seen, the price of debt in t depends on the expected value of default in $t + 1$. In turn, the decision to default in $t + 1$ depends on that period's output, y_{t+1}. When the output process is serially correlated, y_t provides information on y_{t+1}, and therefore affects the current price of debt. So we can write the price of debt as $q(y_t, d_{t+1})$.

13.6.2 Finite Exclusion Period

A second ubiquitous generalization of the default model is to assume that on default, the country is not perpetually excluded indefinitely from international credit markets. This assumption makes the model more realistic, as defaulting countries are not excluded from international financial markets indefinitely. As discussed in Section 13.2.1, depending on the empirical strategy, the typical exclusion period is estimated to last between 4.7 and 13.7 years (see Table 13.6).

The assumption of permanent exclusion on default is typically replaced with the assumption that after default the country regains access to financial markets with constant probability $\theta \in [0, 1)$ each period. This assumption implies that the average exclusion period is $1/\theta$ periods. To see this, assume that the first period of exclusion is the period of default. Then the probability that the country will be excluded for exactly 1 period is θ. The probability that the country will be excluded for exactly 2 periods is $(1 - \theta)\theta$. In general, the probability of being excluded for exactly j periods is given by $(1 - \theta)^{j-1}\theta$. Thus we have

$$\text{Average exclusion period} = 1 \times \theta + 2 \times (1 - \theta)\theta + 3 \times (1 - \theta)^2\theta + \ldots$$

$$= \theta \sum_{j=1}^{\infty} j(1 - \theta)^{j-1}$$

$$= \frac{1}{\theta}. \tag{13.27}$$

Most calibrations of the default model use an estimate of the left-hand side of this expression (the average length of the exclusion period) to identify the value of θ (see, e.g., the calibration strategy presented below in Section 13.6.5).

The assumption of a constant probability of reentry regardless of how long the country has been excluded from credit markets has some empirical support. As shown in Figure 13.1, the empirical distribution of the length of time defaulters are in default status resembles that of an exponential distribution.

The larger θ is, the quicker the country will regain credit access after default. As a result, θ affects the model's predictions regarding default frequency, average risk premium, and the amount of debt that can be sustained in equilibrium. The assumed specification of reentry nests as a special case—$\theta = 0$, the setup studied earlier—in which financial autarky is an absorbent state.

It is common to assume that when the country regains good financial standing, it starts with no external obligations. As we saw in Section 13.1.2, this assumption is unrealistic. There we documented that available estimates indicate that the typical haircut is about 40 percent of the external debt. Later in Section 13.11 we discuss theoretical studies that attempt to make the default model more realistic in this regard.

13.6.3 Output Cost of Default

As it turns out, exclusion by itself is not enough punishment for defaulting countries, in the sense that it is unable to support empirically realistic levels of external debt.[9] For this reason, a third generalization of the standard Eaton-Gersovitz model that has become commonplace in quantitative applications is the introduction of direct output costs of default. Typically the output cost of default is assumed to be exogenously given. Thus, on default, countries are assumed to be punished not only by being excluded from international credit markets but also by losing part of their endowment for the duration of their bad standing status. The empirical work surveyed in Section 13.2.2 provides strong evidence that defaults are associated with sizable and protracted contractions in output. However, as discussed there, the direction of causality has not yet been established.

Assume that the endowment received by the country is not y_t but $\tilde{y}_t \leq y_t$, where $\tilde{y}_t$ is defined as

$$\tilde{y}_t = \begin{cases} y_t & \text{if the country is in good standing} \\ y_t - L(y_t) & \text{if the country is in bad standing,} \end{cases}$$

where $L(y_t)$ is an output loss function assumed to be positive and nondecreasing. The introduction of this type of direct cost affects the model's predictions along two dimensions. First, it discourages default and therefore tends to increase the amount of debt sustainable in equilibrium and to reduce the risk premium. Second, it discourages default in good states of nature (i.e., when y_t is high). This is because the higher y_t is, the higher will be the output loss in case of default, as $L(y_t)$ is positive and nondecreasing.

This way of modeling output losses caused by default is, however, ad hoc, as it is not based on microfoundations. There have been some attempts at endogenizing this feature of the model. Mendoza and Yue (2012), for example, assume that imported inputs require working-capital financing. Default causes an increase in the cost of working capital, inducing an endogenous inefficient substitution toward domestic inputs. Na et al. (2014) study a model with downward nominal wage rigidity. Under suboptimal exchange-rate policy, such as a currency peg, default causes an endogenous increase in unemployment, which results in an inefficiently low level of output.

We assume the following specification for the loss function $L(y_t)$:

$$L(y_t) = \max\{0, a_0 + a_1 y_t + a_2 y_t^2\}. \tag{13.28}$$

---

9. We demonstrate this point in Section 13.6.11 below, where we show that with exclusion as the only punishment, the maximum predicted level of debt is zero.

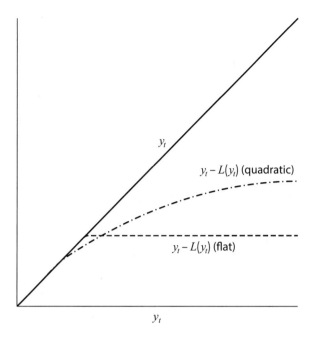

y_t

$y_t - L(y_t)$ (quadratic)

$y_t - L(y_t)$ (flat)

y_t

Figure 13.8   Output cost of default.

This specification encompasses a number of cases of interest. For example, Arellano (2008) assumes that when the country is in bad standing, it loses any endowment above a certain threshold, $\bar{y}$, that is,

$$y_t - L(y_t) = \begin{cases} y_t & \text{if } y_t < \bar{y} \\ \bar{y} & \text{if } y_t \geq \bar{y}. \end{cases} \tag{13.29}$$

Figure 13.8 displays (dashed line) the endowment net of the output cost as a function of the endowment itself for the Arellano specification. This specification obtains as a special case of (13.28) when one sets $a_0 = -\bar{y}$, $a_1 = 1$, and $a_2 = 0$.

Chatterjee and Eyigungor (2012) adopt a two-parameter specification of the output loss function, in which the output loss is quadratic at sufficiently large values of y_t. This case obtains by setting $a_0 = 0$, $a_1 < 0$, and $a_2 > 0$ in (13.28). Figure 13.8 displays (dash-dotted line) the endowment net of output cost under the Chatterjee-Eyigungor specification.

13.6.4 The Model

With these three modifications, the Eaton-Gersovitz model of Section 13.4 changes as follows. The value of continuing to participate in financial markets, $v^c(d, y)$, is the solution to the Bellman equation

$$v^c(d, y) = \max_{d'} \left\{ u(y + q(d', y)d' - d) + \beta E_y v^g(d', y') \right\},$$

where E_y denotes the expectations operator conditional on y, and $v^g(d, y)$ is the value of being in good financial standing. As before, we drop time subscripts and denote variables dated next period with a prime.

The value of being in bad financial standing is given by

$$v^b(y) = u(y - L(y)) + \beta\theta E_y v^g(0, y') + \beta(1 - \theta)E_y v^b(y').$$

The value of being in good financial standing, $v^g(d, y)$, is given by

$$v^g(d, y) = \max\{v^c(d, y), v^b(y)\}.$$

Finally, given the assumption that foreign lenders are risk neutral, the price of debt must satisfy

$$q(d', y) = \frac{\text{Prob}_y\{v^c(d', y') \geq v^b(y')\}}{1 + r^*}, \tag{13.30}$$

where Prob_y denotes probability conditional on y; and r^* is the risk-free real interest rate, assumed to be constant.

The country interest rate, denoted by r, is given by the inverse of the price of debt minus one:

$$r \equiv \frac{1}{q(d', y)} - 1.$$

In turn, the country premium (or country spread) is defined as the difference between the country interest rate, r, and the world interest rate r^*:

$$\text{country premium} = r - r^*.$$

13.6.5 Calibration and Functional Forms

Obtaining quantitative predictions of the model requires assigning functional forms to preferences and technologies and assigning numerical values to the structural parameters. We begin by assuming that one period in the model corresponds to one quarter (of a year). We adopt a CRRA form for the period utility function,

$$u(c) = \frac{c^{1-\sigma} - 1}{1 - \sigma},$$

and set the intertemporal elasticity of substitution, σ, at 2, as in much of the related literature. We set the world interest rate, r^*, to 1 percent per quarter.

The remaining parameters are calibrated to match characteristics of the Argentine economy. To calibrate the probability of reentry, θ, we revisit the evidence on the average exclusion period presented in Section 13.2.1. Consider first measuring the exclusion period by the number of years a country is in default status. According to Table 13.19 in the appendix to this chapter, after the 1982 default, Argentina was in default status until 1993, or 11 years. And after the 2001 default, Argentina was in default status until 2005, or 4 years.

Thus, on average, Argentina was in default status for 7.5 years. Consider now measuring the end of the exclusion period by the first year of issuance of new debt. Cruces and Trebesch (2013, table A.2) find that for both Argentine defaults, the first period of issuance of new debt coincided with the end of default status, also suggesting an average exclusion period of 7.5 years. However, Gelos, Sahay, and Sandleris (2011, table A.7) estimate that after the default of 1982, Argentina was able to issue new debt in 1986, resulting in an exclusion period of only 4 years. Their sample does not include the exit from the 2001 default. A simple average of the above estimates, $(7.5 + 7.5 + 4)/3$, yields 6.33 years. We round this number to 6.5 years. Applying the formula in equation (13.27), this estimate yields a value of θ of 0.0385 at a quarterly frequency. This value is the same as the one used in Chatterjee and Eyigungor (2012).

We use data from Argentina to estimate the output process. Choosing a proxy for y_t is complicated by the fact that in the model, output is fully traded internationally. In reality, a large fraction of the goods and services produced by any country is nontraded. We choose to proxy y_t by a measure of tradable output. In turn, as in Chapter 9, we measure tradable output as the sum of GDP in agriculture, forestry, fishing, mining, and manufacturing in Argentina from 1983:Q1 to 2001:Q4. We obtain the cyclical component of output by removing a quadratic trend. The OLS estimate of (13.26) is then

$$\ln y_t = 0.9317 \ln y_{t-1} + 0.037 \, \epsilon_t. \tag{13.31}$$

The data used in the estimation are in the Matlab file `Plgdp_traded.mat`. The estimated process is quite persistent, with a serial correlation of 0.93. It is also quite volatile. The implied unconditional standard deviation of output is 10 percent. Such a volatile process gives risk-averse domestic agents a strong incentive to use the current account to smooth consumption over time.

Following Chatterjee and Eyigungor (2012), we consider a two-parameter specification of the output loss function by setting $a_0 = 0$ in equation (13.28). We set $a_1 = -0.35$ and $a_2 = 0.4403$, which are the values assigned in Na et al. (2014). Also following these authors, we calibrate β, the subjective discount factor, at 0.85. Together with the rest of the parameter values, the chosen value for the triplet (a_1, a_2, β) produces the following three equilibrium implications: (i) the average debt-to-GDP ratio in periods of good financial standing is about 60 percent per quarter, (ii) the frequency of default is 2.6 times per century, and (iii) the average output loss is 7 percent per year conditional on being in financial autarky. These three targets are empirically justified as follows.

(i) The net external debt in Argentina over the inter-default period 1994–2001 fluctuated around 30 percent of GDP (Lane and Milesi-Ferretti 2007). At the same time, the haircuts in the 1982 and 2001 defaults were on average about 50 percent (Cruces and Trebesch 2013).[10] Since the Eaton-Gersovitz model assumes that the country defaults on 100 percent of the debt, we assume that only 50 percent of the country's external debt is unsecured and

---

10. Since 1975, Argentina has restructured its debt four times: in August 1985, August 1987, April 1993, and April 2005. The corresponding haircuts were, respectively, 0.303, 0.217, 0.325, and 0.768, and the amounts of debt on which these haircuts were applied were, respectively, 9.9, 29.5, 28.5, and $60.6 billion. Therefore the debt-weighted average haircut is 50.7 percent.

Table 13.7   Calibration of the Default Model

Item	Value	Description
Parameter		
σ	2	Inverse of intertemporal elasticity of consumption
β	0.85	Quarterly subjective discount factor
r^*	0.01	World interest rate
θ	0.0385	Probability of reentry
a_0	0	Parameter of output loss function
a_1	−0.35	Parameter of output loss function
a_2	0.4403	Parameter of output loss function
ρ	0.9317	Serial correlation of $\ln y_t$
σ_ϵ	0.037	Standard deviation of innovation ϵ_t
Discretization of State Space		
n_y	200	Number of output grid points (equally spaced in logs)
n_d	200	Number of debt grid points (equally spaced)
$[\underline{y}, \overline{y}]$	[0.6523,1.5330]	Output range
$[\underline{d}, \overline{d}]$	[0,1.5]	Debt range

Note: The time unit is one quarter.

thus target an annual debt-to-GDP ratio of 15 percent, or a quarterly debt-to-GDP ratio of 60 percent.

(ii) The predicted average frequency of default of 2.6 times per century is in line with the Argentine experience since the late nineteenth century. Table 13.1 implies that Argentina defaulted 5 times between 1824 and 2014. That is, 5 defaults over 191 years, or 2.6 times per century.

(iii) The implied average output loss of 7 percent per year for the duration of the default status is in the lower range of our estimates based on Zarazaga's methodology for calculating output losses in the Argentine defaults of 1982 and 2001 (see the discussion in Section 13.2.2).

The assumed value of β is low compared to the values used in models without default but is not uncommon in models à la Eaton-Gersovitz (see, e.g., Mendoza and Yue 2012).

Table 13.7 summarizes the calibration of the model.

13.6.6 Computation

We approximate the equilibrium dynamics by value-function iteration over a discretized state space. The AR(1) process for $\ln y_t$ given in equation (13.26) takes on continuous values, because the innovation ϵ_t is assumed to be normally distributed. We discretize this process using 200 equally spaced points for $\ln y_t$. The first and last values of the grid for $\ln y_t$ are set to ± 4.2 times the unconditional standard deviation of the estimated process. Given the assumed normality of the process, the probability that (the log of) an output observation falls outside this range is less than 10^{-4}. The values of σ_ϵ and ρ given in equation (13.31) imply an unconditional standard deviation of $\ln y_t$ of $0.037/\sqrt{1 - 0.9317^2}$ or 0.102. Thus the first and last points of the grid for $\ln y_t$ are ± 0.427.

To construct the transition probability matrix of the process $\ln y_t^T$, we apply the iterative procedure proposed by Schmitt-Grohé and Uribe (2009). Specifically, we simulate a time series of length 10 million drawn from the process (13.31). We associate each observation in the time series with one of the 200 possible discrete values of $\ln y_t$ by distance minimization. The resulting discrete-valued time series is used to compute the probability of transitioning from a particular discrete state in one period to a particular discrete state in the next period. Given the discretized series of draws, the algorithm proceeds as follows. Start with a 200 × 200 matrix of zeros. Suppose the first draw is element i of the grid and the second draw is element j of the grid. Then add 1 to element (i, j) of the 200 × 200 matrix. Now suppose that the third draw is element k of the grid. Then add 1 to element (j, k) of the 200 × 200 matrix. Continue in this way until draw 10^7. Then divide each row of the 200 × 200 matrix by the sum of its 200 elements. The resulting matrix is the transition probability matrix we wished to estimate. It captures well the covariance matrices of orders 0 and 1. It is available in the file `tpm.mat` and the Matlab code used to compute it is available in the file `tpm.m` on the book's Web site via http://press.princeton.edu/titles/11032 .html.[11]

Finally, the stock of net external debt, d_t, is also a continuous state of the model. We discretize this variable with a grid of 200 equally spaced points starting at 0 and ending at 1.5. These two values were chosen by a trial-and-error procedure. Widening the grid did not produce significant changes in the shape and position of the debt distribution. The Matlab code `eg.m` computes the equilibrium policy functions.

13.6.7 Quantitative Predictions of the Eaton-Gersovitz Model

Table 13.8 displays selected empirical and theoretical first and second moments. By design, the model closely matches the average default frequency and the average quarterly debt-to-GDP ratio. But the model also does quite well at replicating moments that were not targeted in the calibration. Specifically, it explains the observed volatility and countercyclicality of the country premium, as well as its positive correlation with the trade-balance-to-GDP ratio. The countercyclicality of default risk is intuitive. The lower is output, the harder it will be for the country to give up goods to service the debt. This result is also in line with the theoretical analysis of Section 13.4. There we proved that the default set is an interval, implying that (all other things being equal) if the country defaults at a certain level of the endowment, it also defaults at all other lower levels. The quantitative model studied here features an additional incentive not to default when output is high that is absent in the canonical model of Section 13.4—namely an output cost of default, $L(y)$, that increases more than proportionally with the level of y.

The positive correlation between the trade balance and the country premium is also in line with the analytical results of Section 13.4. Proposition 13.1 shows that in any period in which the default risk is positive, the trade balance must also be positive. Intuitively, when the country is at risk of default, foreign lenders demand that the economy makes an effort to improve its financial situation by at least paying part of the interest due.

---

11. An alternative method for computing the transition probability matrix of the exogenous state is the quadrature-based method proposed by Tauchen and Hussey (1991).

Table 13.8   Selected First and Second Moments: Data and Model Predictions

Source	Default Frequency	$E(d/y)$	$E(r - r^*)$	$\sigma(r - r^*)$	corr$(r - r^*, y)$	corr$(r - r^*, tb/y)$
Data	2.6	58.0	7.4	2.9	−0.64	0.72
Model	2.7	59.0	3.5	3.2	−0.54	0.78

Notes: Data moments are from Argentina over the inter-default period 1994:Q1–2001:Q3, except for the default frequency, which is calculated for 1824–2014. The variable d/y denotes the quarterly debt-to-GDP ratio in percent, $r - r^*$ denotes the country premium, in percent per year, y denotes (quarterly detrended) output, and tb/y denotes the trade-balance-to-GDP ratio. The symbols E, σ, and corr denote, respectively, the mean, the standard deviation, and the correlation. In the theoretical model, all moments, with the exception of the default frequency, are conditional on the country being in good financial standing. Theoretical moments were computed by running the Matlab script `statistics_model.m`.

The model, however, explains only half the observed average country premium in Argentina (3.5 versus 7.4 percent per year). Indeed, in the context of the present model, it is impossible to explain both the observed average frequency of default and the observed average country premium. This is because in the model the average country premium is approximately equal to the average frequency of default. To see this, note that the country premium, $r - r^* \equiv 1/q(d', y) - (1 + r^*)$, is approximately equal to $\ln\left[\frac{1}{q(d', y)(1+r^*)}\right]$. Then from equation (13.30) we have that

$$r - r^* \approx \ln\left[\frac{1}{q(d', y)(1 + r^*)}\right]$$

$$= \ln\left[\frac{1}{\text{Prob\{repayment in } t + 1 \text{ given information in } t\}}\right]$$

$$= \ln\left[\frac{1}{1 - \text{Prob\{default in } t + 1 \text{ given information in } t\}}\right]$$

$$\approx \text{Prob\{default in } t + 1 \text{ given information in } t\}. \tag{13.32}$$

According to this expression, the model can explain either the average country premium or the average frequency of default, but not both at the same time, unless both moments are the same in the data.[12]

A natural question to ask is why the frequency of default and the average country premium are so different in the data. One reason for the discrepancy, discussed in Section 13.1.5, is the sample mismatch problem. The average country premium is based on relatively few observations, namely the 31 quarters covering 1994:Q1–2001:Q3. In contrast, the default frequency is computed for a much longer sample, spanning 1824–2014.

---

12. The frequency of default reported in Table 13.8 is defined as the number of defaults per 100 years, whereas the probability of default that appears on the right-hand side of the above expression, Prob{default in $t + 1$ given information in t}, indicates the average number of defaults per 100 years of good financial standing. In the model, these two moments are quite similar, 2.7 and 3.2, respectively.

The sample mismatch problem could introduce a bias in the measured spread-default-frequency differential, because the structure of the economy could have changed substantially over time. For it could be possible that the default frequency has increased in the past few decades, rendering inappropriate the use of a long historical sample. Consider, for instance, the default history of Argentina over the past four decades. Between 1975 and 2014, Argentina defaulted twice, in 1982 and in 2001, which implies a default frequency of 5 defaults per 100 years. This number is almost twice as large as the one based on the sample 1824–2014.

There are also theoretical reasons, not captured in the present model, for a discrepancy between the average country premium and the frequency of default. We derived the result that the default frequency is approximately equal to the country premium under the assumptions that when the government defaults it does so on the totality of debt (no partial default), and that foreign lenders are risk neutral. Consider the case of partial default. Specifically, assume that if the country decides to default, it still honors a fraction $\lambda \in (0, 1)$ of its obligations. In this case, the price of debt must satisfy

$$q(d', y) = \frac{\lambda \, \mathrm{Prob}_y\{v^c(d', y') < v^b(y')\} + \mathrm{Prob}_y\{v^c(d', y') \geq v^b(y')\}}{1 + r^*}.$$

A derivation similar to the one presented for equation (13.32) yields that the country premium, $r - r^*$, satisfies

$$r - r^* \approx (1 - \lambda) \, \mathrm{Prob}\{\text{default in } t + 1 \text{ given information in } t\}. \qquad (13.33)$$

That is, the size of the haircut, $1 - \lambda$, is a wedge between the country premium and the probability of default. Note, however, that this wedge makes the country premium smaller than the probability of default—which is intuitive, because the fact that the country honors a fraction of the debt no matter what implies that lenders require less compensation than in the case of full default. But this makes the puzzle even worse, since in the data the premium exceeds the default risk.

Finally, altering the assumption of risk-neutral lenders may also break the equality result. Lizarazo (2013) shows that this is indeed the case by augmenting an otherwise standard Eaton-Gersovitz model with the assumption of risk-averse lenders. She shows that for plausible calibrations this assumption increases the predicted average country spread substantially without significantly affecting the average probability of default. The reason for the predicted increase in the country spread is that in this type of environment, the country spread is the sum of two compensations, one for the possibility of default and a second one necessary to induce risk-sensitive creditors to accept the default risk. Lizarazo's result relies on the assumption that default has a sizable negative wealth effect on the creditor. In Section 13.9, we show that under the realistic assumption that the emerging country is too small to affect the wealth of the creditor country (and hence the world interest rate), the model implies a near zero spread-default-frequency differential, even under high degrees of risk aversion on the part of foreign lenders.

The Eaton-Gersovitz model captures some of the standard regularities emphasized in the business-cycle literature, as shown in Table 13.9. One is the excess volatility of

Table 13.9   Data and Model Predictions: Additional Business-Cycle Statistics

Source	$\sigma(c)/\sigma(y)$	$\sigma(tb/y)/\sigma(y)$	corr(c, y)	corr$(tb/y, y)$
Data				
Emerging countries	1.23	0.69	0.72	−0.51
Argentina	1.11	0.48	0.75	−0.87
Model	1.22	0.57	0.88	−0.14

Notes: Data moments for emerging countries and Argentina are taken from Chapter 1, Tables 1.6 and 1.9, respectively. The symbols c and y denote the log deviation from trend, tb/y denotes the trade-balance-to-output ratio, and σ and corr denote, respectively, standard deviation and correlation.

consumption. In Chapter 1 we documented that in emerging countries consumption is at least as volatile as output. The model predicts that consumption is 1.22 times as volatile as output, which is in line with the values of 1.23 and 1.11 observed in emerging countries and Argentina, respectively. The reason for the predicted excess volatility of consumption is that during periods of good financial standing, the country is buffeted by large movements in the interest rate due to cyclical variations in default risk, which causes consumption to move significantly over the business cycle. During periods of bad financial standing, movements in consumption mimic exactly the movements in the endowment net of the output loss, which makes these two variables equally volatile.

Further, the model can explain well the observed relative volatility of the trade-balance-to-output ratio relative to the volatility of output (0.57 in the model versus 0.69 in emerging countries and 0.48 in Argentina). The model is equally successful in matching the procyclicality of consumption, as measured by its correlation with output (0.88 in the model versus 0.72 and 0.75 in emerging countries and Argentina, respectively). Finally, although the model captures the countercyclicality of the trade balance qualitatively, as it correctly predicts a negative correlation of the trade-balance-to-output ratio with output, it significantly underpredicts its magnitude (the correlation of tb/y with y is −0.14 in the model versus −0.51 and −0.87 in emerging countries and Argentina, respectively). The predicted countercyclicality of the trade balance is a step forward relative to an identical model without default risk. In Chapter 2 we saw that in the absence of default, positive temporary output shocks induce an increase in savings and therefore an improvement in the trade balance. Thus the model without default risk predicts a procyclical trade balance. The presence of default risk makes the interest rate countercyclical (see Table 13.8), because in the Eaton-Gersovitz model default incentives are weak when output is high and strong when output is low. In turn, the countercyclicality of the interest rate makes savings countercyclical, allowing for the possibility that the trade balance itself become countercyclical.

13.6.8 Dynamics Around a Typical Default Episode

What happens around default episodes? To answer this question, we simulate 1.1 million time periods from the theoretical model. After discarding the first 0.1 million periods, we identify all periods in which a default occurs and extract a window of 12 quarters prior to default and 12 quarters after default. Finally, we compute the median period by period across all windows and normalize the period of default to 0. Figure 13.9 presents the behavior of the economy around the typical default episode. Defaults occur after a sudden contraction in output. As shown in the top-left panel, y is at its mean level of unity until three quarters prior to default. Then, three consecutive negative shocks push y 1.3 standard deviations below normal. One may wonder whether a fall in traded output of slightly more than one standard deviation squares with a predicted average default frequency of only 2.7 per century (see Table 13.8). The reason it does is that the sequence of output shocks is what matters. The probability of traded output falling from its mean value to 1.3 standard deviations below mean in only three quarters is much lower than the unconditional probability of traded output being 1.3 standard deviations below mean.

In period 0, the government defaults, triggering a loss of output $L(y_t)$, as shown by the difference between the solid and dashed lines in the top-left panel. After the default, output begins to recover. Thus the period of default coincides with the trough of the contraction in output, y_t. Therefore the model captures the empirical regularity regarding the cyclical behavior of output around default episodes documented in Figure 13.2 and first identified by Levy-Yeyati and Panizza (2011), according to which default marks the end of a contraction and the beginning of a recovery.

As can be seen in Figure 13.9, the model predicts that the country does not smooth out the temporary decline in the endowment. Instead, the country sharply reduces consumption, by 14 percent. The contraction in consumption is actually larger than the contraction in the endowment, so that the trade balance improves. In fact, the trade balance surplus is large enough to generate a slight decline in the level of external debt. These dynamics seem at odds with the quintessential dictum of the intertemporal approach to the balance of payments, according to which countries should finance temporary declines in income by external borrowing. The country deviates from this prescription because foreign lenders raise the interest-rate premium prior to default. The bottom-right panel of Figure 13.9 shows that the country spread doubles from 3 to 6 percent per year in the run-up to default. This increase in the cost of credit discourages borrowing and induces agents to postpone consumption.

13.6.9 Goodness of Approximation of the Eaton-Gersovitz Model

We used the quantitative predictions of the Eaton-Gersovitz model to gauge its ability to explain observed patterns of default and country-spread dynamics and their comovement with other macroeconomic indicators. Because the model does not have a closed-form solution, its quantitative predictions are based on an approximation. As a result, the validity of the model evaluation requires trust in the accuracy of the approximate solution. The question of how close the approximation is to the true solution is impossible to answer with certainty because the latter is unknown. One way to address this issue is based on the reasonable assumption that as the number of grid points is increased, the approximate solution gets closer to the true solution. This suggests an accuracy test consisting of examining how stable the quantitative predictions of the model are to varying the number of grid points.

Hatchondo, Martínez, and Sapriza (2010) find that the numerical solution of the Eaton-Gersovitz model deteriorates significantly when the endowment grid is coarsely

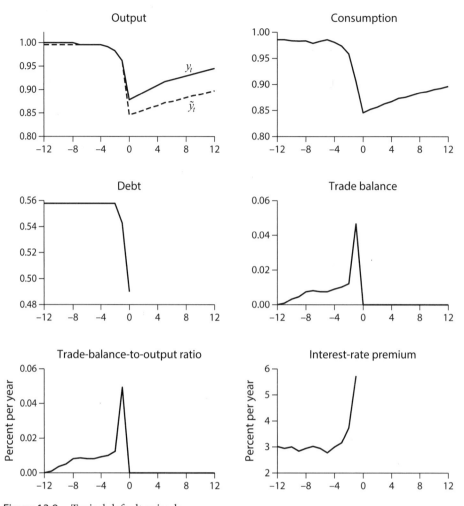

Figure 13.9   Typical default episode.

Notes: Solid lines display medians of 25-quarter windows centered on default episodes occurring in an artificial time series of 1 million quarters. The default date is normalized to 0. The figure is produced by running the Matlab script `typical_default_episode.m`, available on the book's Web site.

specified. The deterioration affects primarily the volatility and comovement of the country premium. To check the validity of their result in the context of the present parameterization of the Eaton-Gersovitz model, in Table 13.10 we present the predictions of the model for several alternative grid specifications. Consider an approximation based on an endowment grid containing 25 equally spaced points, 8 times coarser than the baseline grid specification, which contains 200 equally spaced endowment points. A specification with 25 grid points is of interest because it is representative of the one used in most early quantitative default studies (e.g., Arellano 2008; Aguiar and Gopinath 2006). The table shows that the coarser approximation affects mostly the correlation of the country premium with output

Table 13.10   Approximating the Eaton-Gersovitz Model: Accuracy Tests

	Grid Points		Default				Correlation	
	n_y	n_d	Frequency	$E(d/y)$	$E(r - r^*)$	$\sigma(r - r^*)$	$(r - r^*, y)$	$(r - r^*, tb/y)$
Data			2.6	58.00	7.4	2.9	−0.64	0.72
Model [1]	200	200	2.67	59.00	3.47	3.21	−0.54	0.78
Model	25	200	2.30	69.43	3.01	4.20	−0.28	0.44
Model	400	200	2.63	58.64	3.43	3.12	−0.55	0.82
Model	200	400	2.65	59.46	3.44	3.13	−0.55	0.83
Model	400	400	2.65	59.46	3.44	3.13	−0.55	0.83

Notes: Data moments are from Argentina over the inter-default period 1994:Q1–2001:Q3, except for the default frequency, which is calculated for 1824–2014. The variable d/y denotes the quarterly debt-to-GDP ratio in percent, $r - r^*$ denotes the country premium, in percent per year, y denotes (quarterly detrended) output, and tb/y denotes the trade-balance-to-GDP ratio. The symbols E and σ denote, respectively, the mean and the standard deviation. The symbols n_y and n_d denote the number of grid points for the endowment and debt, respectively. In the theoretical model, all moments are conditional on the country being in good financial standing. Theoretical moments were computed by running the Matlab script statistics_model.m after appropriately adjusting the number of grid points in eg.m.
[1] Baseline grid specification.

and with the trade-balance-to-output ratio. Although the sign is preserved, the magnitude of both correlations falls to about half. Also affected are the standard deviation of the country premium and the average debt-to-output ratio. The former is an entire percentage point higher than under the baseline grid specification and the latter is 10 percentage points higher.

A natural question to ask is whether the predictions of the model also change as one increases the number of endowment points above the baseline value of 200. Table 13.10 shows that this is not the case. All first and second moments displayed are quite stable as the number of endowment grid points is doubled from 200 to 400. Furthermore, the predictions for the baseline grid specification do not change substantially as one doubles the number of debt grid points from 200 to 400 either holding constant or doubling the number of endowment grid points. We therefore conclude that the baseline grid specification (with 200 points for the endowment and 200 points for debt) yields a reasonable numerical approximation to the equilibrium dynamics of the Eaton-Gersovitz model studied here.

13.6.10 Alternative Output Cost Specification

Thus far we have assumed a two-parameter specification of the output cost function $L(y_t)$ that is quadratic above some level of output. Another form that is often used in the default literature is one in which during periods of bad financial standing, all output beyond a certain threshold is lost. This specification is given in equation (13.29) and illustrated with a dashed line in Figure 13.8. As mentioned earlier, it is a special case of the three-parameter quadratic form given in (13.28) that arises when the coefficient of the constant term, a_0, takes a negative value; the coefficient of the linear term, a_1, is unity; and the coefficient of the quadratic term, a_2, is nil.

Table 13.11   The Eaton-Gersovitz Model: Alternative Output Cost Specification

Source	Default Frequency	$E(d/y)$	$E(r - r^*)$	$\sigma(r - r^*)$	$\text{corr}(r - r^*, y)$	$\text{corr}(r - r^*, tb/y)$
Data	2.6	58.0	7.4	2.9	−0.64	0.72
Model						
Quadratic						
(baseline)	2.7	59.0	3.5	3.2	−0.54	0.78
Flat	2.8	59.9	3.5	4.2	−0.43	0.74
Flat and $n_y = 25$	2.4	71.4	3.1	5.7	−0.26	0.48

Notes: See also notes to Table 13.8. Quadratic refers to the baseline specification, $L(y) = \max(0, -0.35y + 0.4403y^2)$. Flat refers to the specification $L(y) = \max(0, -0.88 + y)$.

To make the calibration of the model under this cost function comparable to the one associated with the baseline (quadratic) specification, we set β and a_0, respectively, to match the average debt-to-output ratio and the average default frequency observed in Argentina. This yields $\beta = 0.875$ and $a_0 = -0.88$. That the present specification features one less parameter than the quadratic specification means that one targeted empirical statistic must be left out. In this case, it is the average output cost during periods of bad financial standing. The present parameterization delivers an average output cost of default of 8.3 percent of the endowment per period for the duration of the bad financial status. This number is larger than the one corresponding to the baseline calibration (7 percent) but is still in the range estimated for Argentina by Zarazaga (2012), which we discussed in Section 13.2.2.

The predictions of the model are displayed in Table 13.11. For comparison, the table reproduces from Table 13.8 the empirical moments and the moments predicted by the baseline model. Overall, the model with a flat post-default endowment performs as well as the model with quadratic post-default output (baseline model). Moreover, as one makes the output grid coarser (n_y is reduced from 200 to 25), the model deteriorates along the same dimensions as it does under the quadratic specification, namely, by overpredicting the volatility of the country spread and by underpredicting the correlation of the spread with output and the correlation of the spread with the trade-balance-to-output ratio.

A third specification of the output loss function, employed in a number of existing studies, is of the form

$$L(y) = a_1 y,$$

with $a_1 \in (0, 1)$. Under this formulation, the output cost of default is proportional to the endowment level. Unlike the two specifications considered thus far, the present one does not punish default relatively more when the endowment is high than when it is low. Exercise 13.12 explores the quantitative implications of this formulation and in particular the way it affects the model's ability to explain why countries default in bad times.

13.6.11 The Quantitative Importance of Output Costs of Default

The original formulation of the Eaton-Gersovitz model (Eaton and Gersovitz 1981) contemplates a single cost of default, namely, exclusion from international financial markets.

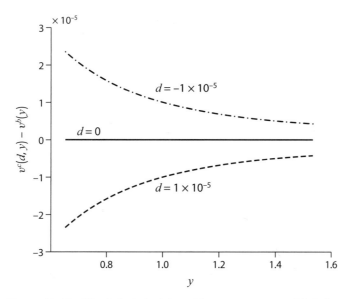

Figure 13.10   The default decision without output cost of default.

As explained earlier, quantitative analyses of this model invariably include an output cost of default, embodied in the function $L(y)$. The main purpose of this source of cost of default is to support realistic levels of debt in equilibrium.

To highlight the role of the output cost of default, we now consider the case $L(y) = 0$ for all y, by setting $a_0 = a_1 = a_2 = 0$ in equation (13.28). The debt grid is set to range from -0.001 to 0.001 with 200 equally spaced points. All other parameters of the model are set at their baseline values shown in Table 13.7. Using this parameterization, the model is unable to support any debt in equilibrium. The intuition for this result is that in the absence of an output cost of default, the only cost of debt repudiation is financial autarky, which makes it impossible for the country to use the current account to smooth output shocks. However, we know from the work of Lucas (1987) that the welfare cost of consumption volatility is quite small, which suggests that the cost of financial autarky is small. However, the benefit of default is a permanent increase in consumption, as the obliteration of the external debt frees up resources that would have otherwise been allocated to service external obligations. Under the current calibration, this benefit outweighs the cost for all values of debt and income.

Figure 13.10 displays the default decision in the vicinity of zero debt. It plots $v^c(d, y) - v^b(y)$ as a function of output for three different values of debt. The solid line corresponds to the case of zero debt. In this case, the country is indifferent between defaulting and not defaulting at any level of output. This can only be the case if the country assigns no value to the possibility of accessing financial markets. The dashed line displays the case of debt positive and equal to 10^{-5}, which is the smallest possible debt value in the grid. For this value of debt, the value of continuing to participate in credit markets is below the value of being in bad financial standing for all levels of output, meaning that the country defaults with probability one. Finally, the dashed-dotted line shows the case of a level of debt equal to -10^{-5}, the smallest possible level of assets in the grid. Obviously, in this case the value of not defaulting exceeds the value of defaulting at all levels of output.

We conclude that incorporating some sort of output loss due to default is essential for the empirical performance of the Eaton-Gersovitz model.

13.6.12 The Quantitative Irrelevance of Exclusion

The quintessential element of the Eaton-Gersovitz model is that default is punished by exclusion from international credit markets. In the original formulation of the model, this feature allows for the existence of debt in equilibrium in an environment in which the country cannot commit to repay. Quantitative implementations of the Eaton-Gersovitz model have introduced an additional cost of default in the form of an output loss. Here we gauge the quantitative relevance of the exclusion assumption. To this end, we remove exclusion from the quantitative model analyzed thus far, keeping all other features unchanged.

Specifically, suppose now that even if a country is in bad financial standing because it defaulted, it can still borrow and save internationally. Continue to assume, however, that if a country defaults, it suffers the output cost of default $L(y)$ until it exogenously exits default status with probability θ each period. Under this modification, the model changes as follows. The value of being in good financial standing and continuing to honor financial obligations, $v^{gc}(d, y)$, is the solution to the Bellman equation

$$ v^{gc}(d, y) = \max_{d'} \left\{ u(y + q^g(d', y)d' - d) + \beta E_y v^g(d', y') \right\}, $$

where, as before, E_y denotes the expectations operator conditional on y, $v^g(d, y)$ is the value of being in good financial standing, and $q^g(d', y)$ denotes the price of debt if the country ends the period in good financial standing.

The value of defaulting, $v^d(y)$, is given by

$$ v^d(y) = \max_{d'} \left\{ u(y - L(y) + q^b(d', y)d') + \beta \theta E_y v^g(d', y') + \beta(1 - \theta) E_y v^b(d', y') \right\}, $$

where $v^b(d, y)$ denotes the value of being in bad financial standing. Note that the value of defaulting is independent of whether the country started the period in good or bad financial standing.

The value of being in good financial standing is then given by

$$ v^g(d, y) = \max\{v^{gc}(d, y), v^d(y)\}. $$

When the country ends the period in good financial standing, the price of debt satisfies

$$ q^g(d', y) = \frac{\mathrm{Prob}_y\{v^{gc}(d', y') \geq v^d(y')\}}{1 + r^*}, $$

where, as before, Prob_y denotes probability conditional on y, and r^* is the constant risk-free real interest rate.

Suppose now that the country is in bad standing. Then it must pay the output cost, so that its income is $y - L(y)$. Contrary to the standard model, we assume that the country

Table 13.12   The Quantitative Irrelevance of Exclusion: Selected First and Second Moments

Source	Default Frequency	$E(d/y)$	$E(r - r^*)$	$\sigma(r - r^*)$	corr$(r - r^*, y)$	corr$(r - r^*, tb/y)$
Data	2.6	58.0	7.4	2.9	−0.64	0.72
Model						
Baseline	2.7	59.0	3.5	3.2	−0.54	0.78
No exclusion	3.0	53.1	4.0	3.6	−0.61	0.77

Notes: See notes to Table 13.8. The predictions of the theoretical model under no exclusion are produced by running the Matlab script `statistics_model_no_exclusion.m`, available on the book's Web site.

can access international financial markets even when it is in bad financial standing. The value of being in bad financial standing and continuing to service the debt, v^{bc}, is

$$v^{bc}(d, y)$$
$$= \max_{d'} \left\{ u(y - L(y) + q^b(d', y)d' - d) + \beta\theta E_y v^g(d', y') + \beta(1 - \theta)E_y v^b(d', y') \right\}.$$

The value of being in bad financial standing is then given by

$$v^b(d, y) = \max\{v^{bc}(d, y), v^d(y)\}.$$

The reason $v^b(d, y)$ may not always be equal to $v^d(y)$ is that a country in bad standing may have assets $d < 0$, in which case it will never default. The price of debt in periods of bad financial standing, $q^b(d', y)$, is given by

$$q^b(d', y) = \frac{\theta \; \text{Prob}_y\{v^{gc}(d', y') \geq v^d(y')\} + (1 - \theta) \, \text{Prob}_y\{v^{bc}(d', y') \geq v^d(y')\}}{1 + r^*}.$$

As in the baseline case, we solve this version of the model numerically using state-space methods and employing the baseline parameter values shown in Table 13.7. The approximation is performed using the Matlab script `eg_no_exclusion.m`.

Table 13.12 presents the predictions of this version of the model. For comparison it reproduces the data moments and the theoretical moments predicted by the baseline model. The model in which default is not punished by exclusion from financial markets behaves remarkably similar to the baseline model. Specifically, the no-exclusion model can support about the same amount of debt as the model with exclusion. The mean debt-to-output ratio in times of good financial standing is 53 percent per quarter in the no-exclusion model, slightly below the value of 59 percent predicted by the baseline model. This means that exclusion can support a level of debt of 6 percent of quarterly output, whereas the direct output cost, $L(y)$, explains a level of debt of 53 percent of quarterly output. The average country premium in times of good standing is predicted to be 4.0 percent in the no-exclusion model compared to 3.5 percent in the baseline case. The volatility of the country premium and the correlation of the country premium with output and the trade-balance-to-output ratio are also little changed. The model predicts that on average the country defaults 3 times per century compared to a default frequency of 2.7 times per century predicted by the baseline model.

We conclude that exclusion from credit markets plays a negligible role for the quantitative performance of the Eaton-Gersovitz model. The main mechanism supporting debt in equilibrium is the output loss associated with default.

13.6.13 The Role of Discounting

The predictions of the Eaton-Gersovitz model are particularly sensitive to the assumed value for the subjective discount factor β. One reason is that the lower β is, the higher will be the household's appetite for present consumption and therefore the higher the demand for debt. Under commitment the equilibrium level of debt grows higher as β is decreased. With default risk this relationship becomes more complex, because foreign lenders take into account the household's impatience when determining the supply of funds to the borrowing country. Thus β affects not only the demand for debt but also the supply of funds to the country.

A second channel through which β affects the predictions of the Eaton-Gersovitz model is through its effect on the costs of default. The reason is that default condemns agents to financial autarky and to an output loss for multiple periods. The more agents care about the future (i.e., the higher is β) the larger the present value of these two types of cost will be. We should therefore expect that the frequency of default falls as β is increased. In turn, a lower frequency of default should be associated with a lower country premium. This incentivizes households to borrow more, which means that we should expect a higher equilibrium level of debt during periods of good standing.

Table 13.13 displays the predictions of the model for values of β of 0.85, 0.90, and 0.95. Recall that the baseline value is 0.85. The table confirms the intuition given above. The default frequency falls from 2.7 defaults per century to 0.4 defaults as β rises from 0.85 to 0.95. The mirror image of this fall in the frequency of default is a drop in the average country premium from 3.5 percent per year to 0.5 percent. Concurrently, the average debt-to-output ratio during periods of good standing increases from 59 percent per quarter to 87.8 percent. These results suggest that the equilibrium level of debt is increasing in β, which is the opposite of what happens under commitment.

13.6.14 Changing the Volatility of the Endowment Process

An increase in the volatility of the income process has two effects on the predictions of the model. One is that agents are more frequently exposed to large negative income shocks; as a result they have a higher incentive to default. This should drive up the default frequency and the country premium. The second effect is that increased uncertainty induces a rise in precautionary savings and consequently a fall in the desired level of external debt. Table 13.14 displays the predictions of the model for three values of σ_ϵ, the standard deviation of the innovation to the (log of the) endowment process, the baseline value of 0.037, a lower value of 0.03, and a higher value of 0.045. The latter two values represent a change in the standard deviation of the log of output of ± 20 percent. The table shows that, in line with the

Table 13.13 Sensitivity Analysis: The Effects of Varying β

Source	Default Frequency	$E(d/y)$	$E(r-r^*)$	$\sigma(r-r^*)$	corr$(r-r^*, y)$	corr$(r-r^*, tb/y)$
Data	2.6	58.0	7.4	2.9	−0.64	0.72
Model						
$\beta = 0.85$[1]	2.7	59.0	3.5	3.2	−0.54	0.78
$\beta = 0.90$	1.4	71.4	1.6	2.0	−0.52	0.78
$\beta = 0.95$	0.4	87.8	0.5	0.9	−0.51	0.71

Notes: Data moments are from Argentina over the inter-default period 1994:Q1–2001:Q3, except for the default frequency, which is calculated for 1824–2014. The variable d/y denotes the quarterly debt-to-GDP ratio in percent, $r - r^*$ denotes the country premium, in percent per year, y denotes (quarterly detrended) output, and tb/y denotes the trade-balance-to-GDP ratio. The symbols E, σ, and corr denote, respectively, the mean, the standard deviation, and the correlation. In the theoretical model, all moments, with the exception of the default frequency, are conditional on the country being in good financial standing. Theoretical moments were computed by running the Matlab script `statistics_model.m`.
[1] Baseline value.

Table 13.14 Sensitivity Analysis: The Effects of Varying σ_ϵ

Source	Default Frequency	$E(d/y)$	$E(r-r^*)$	$\sigma(r-r^*)$	corr$(r-r^*, y)$	corr$(r-r^*, tb/y)$
Data	2.6	58.0	7.4	2.9	−0.64	0.72
Model						
$\sigma_\epsilon = 0.030$	2.1	72.6	2.6	2.3	−0.56	0.85
$\sigma_\epsilon = 0.037$[1]	2.7	59.0	3.5	3.2	−0.54	0.78
$\sigma_\epsilon = 0.045$	3.0	49.7	4.2	4.0	−0.49	0.74

Note: See notes to Table 13.13.
[1] Baseline value.

intuition provided above, the frequency of default and the country premium rise from 2.1 times per century and 2.6 percent per year, respectively, to 3.0 times per century and 4.2 percent per year as σ_ϵ increases from 0.03 to 0.045. At the same time, the average net external debt in periods of good financial standing falls from 72.6 percent of quarterly output to 49.7 percent.

13.6.15 Time-Varying Volatility, Country Spreads, and Default

The preceding analysis concerns the effect of permanent changes in output volatility. But changes in volatility can also be temporary. Indeed, it has been documented that emerging countries experience important changes in volatility over the business cycle (Fernández-Villaverde et al. 2011). Seoane (2014) studies the effect of time-varying output volatility on the equilibrium behavior of country spreads and default in the context of the Eaton-Gersovitz model. He begins by documenting a positive correlation between output volatility and country spreads for four peripheral European countries (Greece, Italy, Portugal, and Spain). Then Seoane augments the Eaton-Gersovitz model to allow for time-varying volatility in the endowment process. In particular, he formulates the following law of motion for the natural logarithm of the endowment:

$$\ln y' = \rho \ln y + e^{\sigma'} \epsilon',$$

with

$$\sigma' - \bar{\sigma} = \rho_\sigma (\sigma - \bar{\sigma}) + \sigma_\mu \mu',$$

where ϵ and μ are normally distributed i.i.d. innovations with mean zero and unit variance. Here e^σ is a time-varying volatility with a log-normal distribution with serial correlation ρ_σ. Seoane estimates the above law of motion separately for Greece, Italy, Portugal, and Spain using quarterly data on output for 1980–2011. Estimates are quite homogeneous across countries. The average estimated parameter values are $\bar{\sigma} = -4.55$, $\rho = 0.989$, $\rho_\sigma = 0.95$, and $\sigma_\mu = 0.16$. Seoane finds that when fed with a process of this type, the Eaton-Gersovitz model predicts a positive correlation between output volatility and the country spread, which is in line with the data. He also reports that this correlation is larger in the data (around 0.6 for the four European countries mentioned above) than in the model (below 0.2). Taken together this result and those presented in Table 13.14 suggest that the positive link between output volatility and spreads predicted by the Eaton-Gersovitz model holds for both permanent and transitory changes in output volatility.

13.6.16 Varying the Persistence of the Output Process

Table 13.15 displays the predictions of the model for different values of ρ, the parameter measuring the first-order autocorrelation of the endowment process. The changes in ρ are variance preserving. That is, changes in ρ are accompanied by adjustments in σ_ϵ (the standard deviation of the innovation to the endowment process) to ensure that the unconditional variance of (the log of) the endowment is constant at its baseline value. The table displays predicted moments for values of ρ ranging from 0 to 0.97. For low values of ρ the frequency of default and the country premium are small. This is because when the endowment process is not highly serially correlated, following negative shocks, the endowment is expected to recover quickly to values at which the output cost of default is nonzero (recall that $L(y)$ is increasing in y). As a result the economy defaults infrequently. In contrast, when the endowment process is highly serially correlated, negative income shocks are expected to persist over time, causing the economy to default more frequently in bad states. Because the frequency of default is low for low values of ρ, the economy is able to borrow more, resulting in relatively high equilibrium levels of debt. This negative relationship between ρ and the level of debt is broken at very high values of ρ (above 0.94). When the endowment is highly persistent, positive shocks are expected to last for a very long time. Because the output loss associated with default is high conditional on the endowment being high, the foreign lenders charge low interest-rate premia, inducing the economy to take on relatively high levels of debt. At the same time, conditional on the endowment being low, the economy defaults more frequently, because bad states are expected to persist. Thus

Table 13.15 Sensitivity Analysis: The Effects of Varying ρ

Source	Default Frequency	$E(d/y)$	$E(r-r^*)$	$\sigma(r-r^*)$	corr$(r-r^*, y)$	corr$(r-r^*, tb/y)$
Data	2.6	58.0	7.4	2.9	−0.64	0.72
Model						
$\rho = 0$	0.1	274.1	0.1	0.1	−0.68	0.65
$\rho = 0.5$	0.2	176.5	0.2	0.2	−0.68	0.67
$\rho = 0.75$	0.7	104.3	0.8	0.6	−0.57	0.66
$\rho = 0.85$	1.48	74.0	1.7	1.4	−0.52	0.73
$\rho = 0.9317$[1]	2.7	59.0	3.5	3.2	−0.54	0.78
$\rho = 0.95$	2.8	59.7	3.8	3.5	−0.58	0.85
$\rho = 0.97$	2.8	67.3	3.7	3.7	−0.62	0.85

Note: See notes to Table 13.13.
[1] Baseline value.

at high values of ρ the model predicts a paradoxical mix of high debt and high default frequency.

13.7 The Welfare Cost of Lack of Commitment

Lacking commitment to repay debt results in an equilibrium in which the country holds less debt than it would choose to hold under commitment. Thus in the absence of other distortions, lack of commitment is welfare decreasing. In the calibrated version of the Eaton-Gersovitz model of Section 13.6, this cost turns out to be extremely large. The reason is that under that calibration, consumers are highly impatient relative to the risk-free interest rate. The subjective discount rate, $1/\beta - 1$, is 17.7 percent per quarter, compared with a risk-free interest rate of 1 percent per quarter. Private households do not place a high value on future consumption and prefer to spend much of their lifetime wealth on current consumption. As a result, with full commitment, the equilibrium displays a high level of debt of 65.88, which is about 100 times larger than the average debt under lack of commitment. In this regard, imperfect enforcement of international debt contracts manifests itself in equilibrium as a borrowing constraint. In the present calibration, this endogenous borrowing constraint is quite severe.

The model economy under commitment is simple. Welfare, denoted $v^{\text{com}}(d, y)$, is given by

$$v^{\text{com}}(d, y) = \max_{d'} \left\{ u(y + d'(1+r^*)^{-1} - d) + \beta E_y v^{\text{com}}(d', y') \right\},$$

subject to a no-Ponzi-game constraint of the form $d' < \bar{d}$, where the limit $\bar{d}$ is finite but can be set arbitrarily large. The solution to this Bellman equation delivers the equilibrium processes for debt and welfare. Equilibrium consumption, denoted c^{com}, is then derived residually from the resource constraint as $c^{\text{com}} = y + d'/(1+r^*) - d$.

Given the state of the economy, (d, y), we define the welfare cost of lack of commitment as the proportional increase in the level of consumption under lack of commitment necessary to make the representative agent as well off as under commitment. Letting c_t^{nocom} denote consumption under lack of commitment, the welfare cost of no commitment, denoted by $\Lambda(d_t, y_t)$, is given by

$$E_0 \sum_{t=0}^{\infty} \beta^t \frac{\left(c_t^{\text{com}}\right)^{1-\sigma} - 1}{1 - \sigma} = E_0 \sum_{t=0}^{\infty} \beta^t \frac{\left[(1 + \Lambda(d_0, y_0))c_t^{\text{nocom}}\right]^{1-\sigma} - 1}{1 - \sigma}.$$

Solving for $\Lambda(d, y)$ yields

$$\Lambda(d, y) = \left[\frac{v^{\text{com}}(d, y)(1 - \sigma)(1 - \beta) + 1}{v^{\text{nocom}}(d, y)(1 - \sigma)(1 - \beta) + 1}\right]^{\frac{1}{1-\sigma}} - 1,$$

where $v^{\text{nocom}}(d, y)$ denotes the welfare level under no commitment to repay, which corresponds to $v^g(d, y)$ if the country is in good financial standing or to $v^b(y)$ if the country is in bad standing. Notice that because both d and y are random variables, so is the welfare cost of lack of commitment, $\Lambda(d, y)$.

We are interested in the distribution of $\Lambda(d, y)$ when the pair (d, y) is drawn from the distribution induced by the economy with lack of commitment. The resulting distribution allows us to compute moments of the welfare gains of migrating from the economy with no commitment to repay debt to the economy with commitment. These moments take into account the effect of the transitional dynamics involved in the migration from one economy to the other.

We find that the unconditional mean of the welfare cost of lack of commitment is 273 percent, that is, $100 \times E\Lambda(d, y) = 273$. This is an enormous value. It means that the consumption stream of an individual living in the economy without commitment must almost quadruple for her to be as well off as living in the economy with commitment to repay debts. The totality of this welfare cost is due to the transitional dynamics of switching from no commitment to commitment. Along this transition, debt increases from a mean of 0.59 to a mean of 65.88, and consumption declines from a mean of 0.98 to a mean of 0.36. Of course along this transition, consumption is temporarily much higher than 0.98. Figure 13.11 shows the typical transition paths for consumption and the stock of debt from the equilibrium with lack of commitment to the equilibrium with commitment. The typical transition path is the mean of 10,000 transition paths, each starting at a pair (d, y) drawn from the ergodic distribution under lack of commitment. As shown in the left panel of the figure, at the beginning of the typical transition, consumption rises to about 6 and stays above its no-commitment mean for 25 quarters. The high consumption in the early transition is financed with external debt, which increases 100 fold in 25 quarters.

It is clear from this analysis that the transitional dynamics are the key determinant of the welfare gains of commitment. Consider a naive approach to welfare evaluation, consisting of computing the unconditional welfare in each economy separately. Because in the stationary state average consumption in the commitment economy is one third as high as consumption in the no-commitment economy, one would erroneously conclude that lack of commitment is welfare improving.

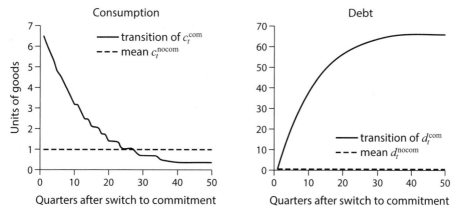

Figure 13.11   Transition from no commitment to commitment.

13.8 Decentralization of the Eaton-Gersovitz Model

The Eaton-Gersovitz model is cast in terms of a social planner's problem. A benevolent government aims to maximize the lifetime welfare of households. In doing so, it chooses how much to borrow, when to default, and how much the household should consume each period. The household itself makes no relevant decisions. It does not participate in financial markets, nor in goods markets, but it passively consumes the goods it receives from the government each period.

In this section, we wish to think about optimal sovereign default (i.e., about the government's decision to repudiate the country's external obligations) in an environment in which private households participate in credit markets and choose optimally how much to consume each period. In this new environment, the government retains only the decisions to default and to conduct fiscal policy. A central question that we will address is whether there exist fiscal instruments that the government can use to induce households to undertake borrowing and consumption decisions that mimic the social planner's allocation. This exercise is known as the decentralization of the social planner's equilibrium.

The government may need fiscal instruments to alter the behavior of private households, because the former internalizes that the interest rate faced by the country in international financial markets depends on its net external debt position, but households do not. Individual households are too small for their borrowing to affect the country's credit conditions. By applying fiscal distortions, the government makes its borrowing decisions and the private sector's coincide. We will show that the social planner's equilibrium can be decentralized via capital controls. An interesting by-product of characterizing the decentralized equilibrium is that it will allow us to back out the optimal fiscal policy. That is, we can deduce the capital control policy that induces households to carry out the planner's desired debt and consumption decisions.

Clearly, using the present approach, we must build the economy from the private sector up. Accordingly we begin by studying the household's problem. The exposition that follows draws from Na et al. (2014).

13.8.1 Households

Consider an economy populated by a large number of identical households with preferences described by the utility function

$$E_0 \sum_{t=0}^{\infty} \beta^t u(c_t). \tag{13.34}$$

Households can borrow and lend in credit markets using a non-state-contingent bond with price q_t^d. Households can commit to repay their debts. Their sequential budget constraint is of the form

$$c_t + d_t = (1 + \tau_t^y)\tilde{y}_t + (1 - \tau_t^d)q_t^d d_{t+1}, \tag{13.35}$$

where τ_t^y is an income subsidy (a tax if negative), and τ_t^d is a tax (a subsidy if negative) on debt. Households choose processes for consumption and debt to maximize their utility function subject to the above sequential budget constraint and the natural debt limit, which prevents them from engaging in Ponzi schemes. The optimality conditions associated with this problem are (13.35), the no-Ponzi-game constraint, and

$$u'(c_t)(1 - \tau_t^d)q_t^d = \beta E_t u'(c_{t+1}).$$

13.8.2 The Government

Default decisions are assumed to be made by the government. Each period the country can be either in good financial standing or in bad financial standing. If it is in good financial standing, it can choose to honor its international debts or default. Let I_t be a binary variable taking the value one if the country is in good standing in period t and chooses to honor its debt and zero if it is in bad standing. If the country defaults in period t, it immediately acquires bad financial standing, and I_t takes the value zero. If the country is in bad standing in period t, it regains good standing in period $t + 1$ with constant and exogenous probability θ, and maintains its bad financial standing with probability $1 - \theta$.

When the country is in bad financial standing, it is excluded from international financial credit markets and is therefore unable to borrow or lend internationally. We then have that

$$(1 - I_t)d_{t+1} = 0. \tag{13.36}$$

In periods in which the country is in bad standing ($I_t = 0$), the government confiscates any payments of households to foreign lenders and returns the proceeds to households via income subsidies. The government also uses the income subsidy to rebate the proceeds from the debt tax. The resulting sequential budget constraint of the government is then given by

$$\tau_t^y \tilde{y}_t = \tau_t^d q_t^d d_{t+1} + (1 - I_t)d_t. \tag{13.37}$$

Let q_t denote the price of debt charged by foreign lenders to domestic borrowers during periods in which the government maintains good financial standing. As before, the price of debt, q_t, must satisfy the condition that the expected return of lending to the domestic country equals the opportunity cost of funds:

$$q_t = \frac{\text{Prob}\{I_{t+1} = 1 | I_t = 1\}}{1 + r^*}.$$

This expression can be equivalently written as

$$I_t \left[q_t - \frac{E_t I_{t+1}}{1 + r^*} \right] = 0.$$

13.8.3 Competitive Equilibrium

Because all domestic households are identical, there is no borrowing or lending among them. This means that in equilibrium the household's net asset position equals the country's net foreign asset position. This in turn implies that the debt tax, τ_t^d, can be interpreted as a capital control tax. Because external debt is nil when the country is in bad standing, the value of τ_t^d in periods of bad standing is immaterial. Without loss of generality, we set $\tau_t^d = 0$ when $I_t = 0$, that is,

$$(1 - I_t)\tau_t^d = 0. \tag{13.38}$$

As before, the endowment received by the household, $\tilde{y}_t$, is given by

$$\tilde{y}_t = \begin{cases} y_t & \text{if } I_t = 1 \\ y_t - L(y_t) & \text{otherwise.} \end{cases} \tag{13.39}$$

In any period t in which the country is in good financial standing, the domestic price of debt, q_t^d, must equal the price of debt offered by foreign lenders, q_t:

$$I_t(q_t^d - q_t) = 0. \tag{13.40}$$

Combining (13.35)–(13.37), (13.39), and (13.40) yields the following market-clearing condition:

$$c_t = y_t - (1 - I_t)L(y_t) + I_t[q_t d_{t+1} - d_t].$$

A competitive equilibrium is a set of stochastic processes $\{c_t, d_{t+1}, q_t, q_t^d\}$ satisfying

$$c_t = y_t - (1 - I_t)L(y_t) + I_t[q_t d_{t+1} - d_t], \tag{13.41}$$

$$(1 - I_t)d_{t+1} = 0, \tag{13.42}$$

$$(1 - \tau_t^d)q_t^d u'(c_t) = \beta E_t u'(c_{t+1}), \tag{13.43}$$

$$I_t(q_t^d - q_t) = 0, \tag{13.44}$$

and

$$I_t \left[q_t - \frac{E_t I_{t+1}}{1 + r^*} \right] = 0, \tag{13.45}$$

given processes $\{y_t, \tau_t^d, I_t\}$ and the initial condition d_0.

13.8.4 Equilibrium under Optimal Capital Control Policy

Here we characterize the optimal default and capital control policies. When the government can choose freely the capital control tax, τ_t^d, the competitive equilibrium can be written in the following more compact form.

> **Proposition 13.5 (Competitive Equilibrium When τ_t^d Is Unrestricted)** When the government can choose τ_t^d freely, stochastic processes $\{c_t, d_{t+1}, q_t\}$ can be supported as a competitive equilibrium if and only if they satisfy
>
> $$c_t = y_t - (1 - I_t)L(y_t) + I_t[q_t d_{t+1} - d_t], \qquad (13.41\ \mathrm{R})$$
>
> $$(1 - I_t)d_{t+1} = 0, \qquad (13.42\ \mathrm{R})$$
>
> and
>
> $$I_t\left[q_t - \frac{E_t I_{t+1}}{1 + r^*}\right] = 0, \qquad (13.45\ \mathrm{R})$$
>
> given processes $\{y_t, I_t\}$ and the initial condition d_0.
>
> **Proof** The only nontrivial step involved in establishing this proposition is to show that if processes $\{c_t, d_{t+1}, q_t\}$ satisfy conditions (13.41), (13.42), and (13.45), then they also satisfy the remaining conditions defining a competitive equilibrium, namely, conditions (13.43) and (13.44). To see this, proceed as follows. When I_t equals 1, set q_t^d to satisfy (13.44) and set τ_t^d to satisfy (13.43). When I_t equals 0, set $\tau_t^d = 0$ (recall convention (13.38)) and set q_t^d to satisfy (13.43). ∎

The government is assumed to be benevolent. It chooses a default policy I_t to maximize the welfare of the representative household subject to the constraint that the resulting allocation can be supported as a competitive equilibrium. The Eaton-Gersovitz model imposes an additional restriction on the default policy: the government has no commitment to honor past promises regarding debt payments or defaults. The lack of commitment opens the door to time inconsistency. For this reason the Eaton-Gersovitz model assumes that the government has the ability to commit to a default policy that makes the default decision in period t an invariant function of the minimum set of aggregate states of the competitive equilibrium of the economy in period t. The states appearing in the conditions of the competitive equilibrium listed in proposition 13.5 are the endowment, y_t, and the stock of net external debt, d_t. Thus we impose the condition that the default decision in period t is a time-invariant function of y_t and d_t. We can then define the Eaton-Gersovitz problem as follows.

> **Definition 13.1 (Equilibrium in the Eaton-Gersovitz Model)** An equilibrium in the Eaton-Gersovitz model is a set of processes $\{c_t, d_{t+1}, q_t, I_t\}$ that maximizes

$$E_0 \sum_{t=0}^{\infty} \beta^t u(c_t), \qquad\qquad\qquad (13.34 \text{ R})$$

subject to

$$c_t = y_t - (1 - I_t)L(y_t) + I_t[q_t d_{t+1} - d_t], \qquad (13.41 \text{ R})$$

$$(1 - I_t)d_{t+1} = 0, \qquad\qquad\qquad (13.42 \text{ R})$$

$$I_t\left[q_t - \frac{E_t I_{t+1}}{1 + r^*}\right] = 0, \qquad\qquad\qquad (13.45 \text{ R})$$

and to the constraint that if $I_{t-1} = 1$, then I_t is an invariant function of y_t and d_t; and if $I_{t-1} = 0$, then $I_t = 0$ except when reentry to credit markets occurs exogenously, and to the natural debt limit, given the initial conditions d_0 and I_{-1}.

The equilibrium in the Eaton-Gersovitz model is generically unique. To see this, note that the equilibrium is the solution to an optimization problem. This means that if there were more than one equilibrium, all of them should deliver the same level of welfare. To understand this result, it is important to note that I_t and q_t are objects that are chosen as part of the optimization problem that defines the equilibrium and that the participation constraint (13.45) is one of the constraints of that optimization problem.

Moreover, the Eaton-Gersovitz problem is time consistent, because none of the constraints contains a conditional expectation of a future nonpredetermined endogenous variable. To see that this is true for constraint (13.45), notice that by the restrictions imposed on the default decision, I_{t+1} depends only on y_{t+1} and d_{t+1}, and that d_{t+1} is chosen in period t.

Proposition 13.6 (Uniqueness and Time Consistency of the Eaton-Gersovitz Equilibrium) The equilibrium in the Eaton-Gersovitz model is generically unique and time consistent.

A further implication of the restrictions imposed on the default decision I_t and of the assumption that output follows an AR(1) process is that, by equation (13.45), the price of debt depends only upon y_t, and d_{t+1}; hence we can write equation (13.45) as

$$I_t\left[q_t - q(y_t, d_{t+1})\right] = 0. \qquad\qquad\qquad (13.46)$$

13.8.5 The Optimal-Policy Equilibrium as a Decentralization of the Eaton-Gersovitz Model

We now show that the optimal default policy problem given in definition 13.1 is identical to the Eaton-Gersovitz model presented in Section 13.6.4. To this end, we express the optimal policy problem in recursive form as follows. If the country is in good financial standing in period t, $I_{t-1} = 1$, then the value of continuing to service the external debt, denoted by

$v^c(d_t, y_t)$ (i.e., the value of setting $I_t = 1$), is given by

$$v^c(d_t, y_t) = \max_{\{c_t, d_{t+1}\}} \{u(c_t) + \beta E_t v^g(d_{t+1}, y_{t+1})\}, \tag{13.47}$$

subject to

$$c_t + d_t = y_t + q(y_t, d_{t+1})d_{t+1}, \tag{13.48}$$

where $v^g(d_t, y_t)$ denotes the value of being in good financial standing at the beginning of period t. The constraint (13.48) results from evaluating (13.41) and (13.46) at $I_t = 1$ and using the latter to eliminate q_t from the former.

The value of being in bad financial standing in period t, denoted $v^b(y_t)$, is given by

$$v^b(y_t) = \left\{u(y_t - L(y_t)) + \beta E_t \left[\theta v^g(0, y_{t+1}) + (1-\theta)v^b(y_{t+1})\right]\right\}.$$

This equation results from expressing the utility function (13.34) in recursive form, evaluating (13.41) at $I_t = 0$ to eliminate c_t from the period utility function, and taking into account that the expected value of future lifetime utility is conditional on $I_t = 0$.

In any period t in which the economy is in good financial standing, it has the option to either continue to service its debt obligations or to default. It follows that the value of being in good standing in period t is given by

$$v^g(d_t, y_t) = \max \left\{v^c(d_t, y_t), v^b(y_t)\right\}.$$

In a period into which the government enters with good standing, $I_{t-1} = 1$, it chooses to default whenever the value of continuing to participate in financial markets is smaller than the value of being in bad financial standing, $v^c(d_t, y_t) < v^b(y_t)$. Therefore, in periods in which $I_t = 1$, we have that $E_t I_{t+1} = \text{Prob}\{v^c(y_{t+1}, d_{t+1}) \geq v^b(y_{t+1})|y_t\}$. It follows that when $I_t = 1$, equilibrium condition (13.45) can be written as

$$q_t = \frac{\text{Prob}_y\{v^c(y_{t+1}, d_{t+1}) \geq v^b(y_{t+1})\}}{1 + r^*}.$$

Combining this expression with (13.46), we obtain

$$q(y_t, d_{t+1}) = \frac{\text{Prob}_y\{v^c(y_{t+1}, d_{t+1}) \geq v^b(y_{t+1})\}}{1 + r^*},$$

which is condition (13.30) of Section 13.6.4. We have therefore demonstrated the equivalence between the optimal default policy problem in the decentralized equilibrium as stated in definition 13.1 and the optimal default policy problem in the Eaton-Gersovitz model as stated in Section 13.6.4. We highlight this result in the following proposition.

Proposition 13.7 (Decentralization) Sovereign default models in the tradition of Eaton and Gersovitz (1981) can be interpreted as the centralized version of competitive economies with default risk and optimal capital control policy.

The need for capital controls in the decentralization of Eaton-Gersovitz-style models arises from the fact that the government internalizes the effect of aggregate external debt on the

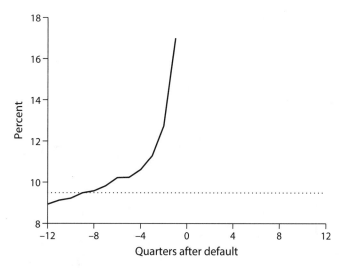

Figure 13.12   Optimal capital controls around the typical default episode.

Note: The solid line displays the median of 25-quarter windows centered around default episodes that occurred in an artificial time series of 1 million quarters. The default date is normalized to 0. The dotted line displays the unconditional median. The figure is produced by running the Matlab script `typical_default_episode.m`, available on the book's Web site.

country premium, whereas individual agents take the country premium as exogenously given.

13.8.6 Capital Control Dynamics

Figure 13.12 displays the dynamics of optimal capital controls around the typical default episode using the baseline calibration (Table 13.7). Since the optimal capital control policy is the one that supports the social planner's equilibrium, the capital controls shown in the figure are associated with the dynamics for the other variables of the model displayed in Figure 13.9. The government increases capital controls sharply from 9 to 17 percent in the three quarters prior to the default. This increase in capital control taxes increases the effective interest rate faced by households. In this way, the government makes private agents internalize the increased sensitivity of the interest-rate premium with respect to debt as the debt crisis nears. The debt elasticity of the country premium is larger in the run-up to the default, because foreign lenders understand that the lower output is, the higher the incentive to default will be, as the output loss that occurs on default, $L(y_t)$, decreases in absolute and relative terms as y_t falls. This capital control tax is implicitly present in every default model à la Eaton-Gersovitz. Analyzing the decentralized version of the model, as we did in this section, makes its presence explicit.

13.8.7 Optimal Default Policy without Capital Controls

The decentralization of the Eaton-Gersovitz model studied thus far relies on the government having access to tax instruments (e.g., capital controls) to induce households to make consumption and borrowing decisions mimicking the ones that are optimal from the social planners' perspective. Suppose instead that the government makes the optimal default decision as before but does not have the ability to set fiscal instruments optimally. In this case the borrowing decisions of the households may differ from the socially optimal ones. The reason is that in this environment, the decision to default resides with the government and therefore depends on the aggregate level of debt of the economy. As a result the interest foreign lenders charge to the country also depends on the aggregate stock of debt. Individual households are too small to affect the aggregate level of debt, and so they take the interest rate as independent of their own borrowing decisions. Collectively, however, the borrowing decisions of the households do affect the aggregate level of debt and hence the interest rate. The model without capital controls therefore features a pecuniary externality. Kim and Zhang (2012) quantitatively characterize debt and default dynamics in this environment.

The Eaton-Gersovitz model with the pecuniary externality is of interest, because in practice the interest rate charged to private borrowers in emerging markets depends on aggregate macroeconomic indicators rather than on individual agents' ability to repay. For instance, it has been documented that foreign lenders rely heavily on the assessments of credit-rating agencies of countries' ability to repay. And, in turn, such assessments are based on macroeconomic indicators. See, for instance, Ferri and Liu (2003), Agca and Celasun (2012), and Borensztein, Cowan, and Valenzuela (2013).

In the economy studied here—in which private households make borrowing decisions, and the government makes default decisions and cannot apply fiscal instruments to support the socially optimal level of borrowing—a competitive equilibrium is a set of stochastic processes $\{c_t, d_{t+1}, q_t, q_t^d\}$ satisfying (13.41)–(13.45), given $\tau_t^d = 0$, processes $\{y_t, I_t\}$, and the initial condition d_0. Taking these equilibrium conditions as constraints, the benevolent government chooses the default decision, I_t, to maximize the lifetime utility of the representative household.

To state the problem in recursive form, we follow Kim and Zhang (2012) and distinguish the individual household debt position, d, from the aggregate level of debt, denoted by D. At the household level, the welfare function in periods in which the government continues to service the debt is given by

$$v^c(d, y, D') = \max_{d'} u(y + q(D', y)d' - d)$$

$$+ \beta E_y \left[\delta(D', y')v^b(y') + (1 - \delta(D', y'))v^c(d', y', D'') \right],$$

subject to

$$D'' = \Gamma(D', y'),$$

where D'' denotes the aggregate level of debt assumed in the next period and due in two periods after the current period. The function $\delta(D', y')$ is an indicator that takes the value one if the government defaults given D' and y' and zero otherwise. Notice that now the value function of the individual household features a third argument, the aggregate level of debt, D', due in the next period. The reason this variable affects welfare is that it affects the price of debt in the current period, the probability that the government will default in the next period, and the aggregate level of debt in the next period. Note that although households take the aggregate level of debt as given, they understand its law of motion, as given in the constraint of this problem. The function $\Gamma(D', y')$ is taken as given by the households but is endogenously determined in equilibrium.

The welfare of the individual households in periods in which the country is in bad financial standing is given by

$$v^b(y) = u(y - L(y)) + \beta E_y \left[\theta v^c(0, y', D'') + (1 - \theta)v^b(y') \right].$$

The solution to this problem delivers value functions, $v^c(d, y, D')$ and $v^b(y)$, and a decision rule for debt, $d' = \gamma(d, y, D')$.

Because all agents are identical and assuming that there is a continuum of households with measure one, we have that in any competitive equilibrium the aggregate and individual levels of debt must equal each other:

$$d = D.$$

The decision to default is determined by the benevolent government to maximize the lifetime utility of the representative household. That is,

$$\delta(D, y) = \begin{cases} 1 & \text{if } v^b(y) > v^c(D, y, \Gamma(D, y)) \\ 0 & \text{otherwise.} \end{cases}$$

As before, with risk-neutral lenders the price of debt must satisfy

$$q(D', y) = \frac{1 - E_y \delta(D', y')}{1 + r^*}.$$

This completes the presentation of the model. The emergence of the third endogenous state variable, D, makes the computation of equilibrium more demanding both in terms of computer memory and time. Kim and Zhang (2012) calibrate the model to Argentina using similar values to those that appear in Table 13.7, except that they assume a flat specification for the post-default output, $y - L(y)$, by setting $a_0 = -0.9$, $a_1 = 1$, and $a_2 = 0$.

What differences should we expect between the equilibrium allocations with and without the pecuniary externality (i.e., with and without optimal capital controls)? Because households do not internalize that the interest rate is an increasing function of their own demand for debt, one would expect an increase in the demand schedule for debt. All other things being equal, such a shift in the demand for debt should imply higher levels of debt and higher interest rates in equilibrium. However, a striking finding of Kim and Zhang (2012) is that although the equilibrium interest rate does increase significantly as expected, the equilibrium quantity of debt is not significantly higher in the equilibrium with the externality than in the equilibrium without the externality. Thus the pecuniary externality does not necessarily induce overborrowing. The reason for the lack of overborrowing is that the externality shifts up the supply schedule of credit, $q(D', y)$, leading to a reduction in the supply of funds to the country for each level of the country interest rate. In other words, for given levels of debt, D', and current output, y, the probability of default next period is higher in the economy with the externality than in the economy without the externality. This shift in the supply schedule of funds offsets the increase in the demand schedule for funds, making it possible that the externality may or may not lead to over-borrowing. However, the country interest rate and the equilibrium frequency of default increase unambiguously with the introduction of the pecuniary externality.

13.9 Risk-Averse Lenders

Observed country spreads tend to be larger than observed default probabilities. Using data from nine emerging countries, Tables 13.1 and 13.4 document an average country premium of 4.5 percent per year and a default frequency of 3.9 percent per year, implying an average spread-default-frequency differential of 60 basis points. The spread-default-frequency differential is more pronounced when one corrects for the sample mismatch problem identified in Section 13.1.5. As Table 13.5 shows, after applying this correction, the differential increases to 230 basis points.

In contrast, as established earlier in this chapter, the Eaton-Gersovitz model with risk-neutral lenders predicts that the average country premium must equal the probability of default, or that the spread-default-frequency differential must be zero (see equation (13.32)). In fact, we established that under the empirically relevant assumption of partial default, the model predicts that the country premium is smaller than the probability of default, or that the spread-default-frequency differential is negative (see equation (13.33)).

One possible way to drive a wedge between the country spread and the probability of default is to introduce risk aversion on the part of foreign lenders. In this case, foreign investors will not just require that the expected return on emerging country debt be the same as the risk-free rate. In addition, they will need to be compensated for the default risk involved in investing in emerging markets.

Consider the Eaton-Gersovitz model of Section 13.6.4. Suppose now, however, that foreign lenders are risk averse. In particular, assume that their utility function is given by

$$E_0 \sum_{t=0}^{\infty} \tilde{\beta}^t u(\tilde{c}_t),$$

where $\tilde{\beta} \in (0, 1)$ is the foreign lender's subjective discount factor; $\tilde{c}_t$ denotes consumption of foreign lenders; and u is the foreign lender's period utility function, which takes the CRRA form

$$u(\tilde{c}) = \frac{\tilde{c}^{1-\tilde{\sigma}} - 1}{1 - \tilde{\sigma}},$$

where $\tilde{\sigma} > 0$ is a parameter representing the foreign lender's coefficient of relative risk aversion. Let

$$m' \equiv \tilde{\beta} \left(\frac{\tilde{c}'}{\tilde{c}} \right)^{-\tilde{\sigma}}$$

denote the foreign lender's intertemporal marginal rate of consumption substitution. (As usual, we are dropping the time subscript and using a prime to denote next-period values.) The variable m' can be interpreted as a pricing kernel, as it indicates the value of one unit of consumption delivered in a particular state in the next period in terms of current consumption. We assume that the emerging country is too small to affect the pricing kernel in the rest of the world. In other words, we assume that changes in the return of the emerging country's debt have no wealth effect on foreign lenders. As a result of this assumption, the pricing kernel m' is independent of economic conditions in the emerging economy.[13]

Let g' denote the gross growth rate of foreign consumption between the current period and the next:

$$g' \equiv \frac{\tilde{c}'}{\tilde{c}}.$$

We assume that g' follows a univariate AR(1) process of the form

$$\ln\left(\frac{g'}{\bar{g}}\right) = \rho_g \ln\left(\frac{g}{\bar{g}}\right) + \mu', \tag{13.49}$$

where $\bar{g} > 0$ and $|\rho_g| < 1$ are constant parameters, and μ' is a normally distributed disturbance with mean 0 and variance σ_μ^2. The parameter $\bar{g}$ denotes the average gross growth rate of foreign consumption. Note that g, denoting the gross growth rate of foreign consumption between the previous and the current period, is in the current information set, whereas g' and μ' are in next period's information set.

The foreign lender's optimality condition associated with investing in emerging-country debt is

$$q = E\{m'I'|I = 1, y, g, d'\}, \tag{13.50}$$

where, as before, q denotes the price of the emerging country's debt, y denotes the endowment, d denotes the emerging country's debt, and I is an indicator function that takes the value one if the emerging country is in good standing in the current period and chooses to honor its debt and zero otherwise.

The world pricing kernel m can be used to price other financial assets. Of particular interest is the price of a risk-free asset. Specifically, the risk-free interest rate, r^*, which in the standard Eaton-Gersovitz model is taken to be constant, is now time varying and satisfies

$$1 = (1 + r^*)E\{m'|g\}. \tag{13.51}$$

For $\rho_g \neq 0$, $E\{m'|g\}$ depends on g, which is a random variable. As a result, r^* is also a random variable. When $\tilde{\sigma}$ equals 0, foreign lenders are risk neutral, and $m = \tilde{\beta}$. In this case,

---

13. Alternatively, one could assume that the emerging country is large enough to affect the world's pricing kernel. Lizarazo (2013) pursues this alternative.

the risk-free interest rate r^* is constant over time and is equal to $\tilde{\beta}^{-1} - 1$. Thus the present formulation nests the baseline Eaton-Gersovitz model with risk-neutral lenders studied in Section 13.6 as a special case.

To derive an expression for the country premium, define the gross country interest rate, $1 + r$, as

$$1 + r = \frac{1}{q}.$$

Then the gross country premium is given by $(1+r)/(1+r^*)$. Combining the Euler equations (13.50) and (13.51), we can express the gross country premium in periods in which the emerging country is in good financial standing ($I = 1$) as

$$\frac{1+r}{1+r^*} = \frac{E\{m'|g\}}{E\{m'I'|y, g, d'\}}.$$

Now use the fact that $E\{m'I'|y, g, d'\} = \text{Cov}(m', I'|y, g, d') + E\{m'|g\}E\{I'|y, g, d'\}$ to obtain

$$\frac{1+r}{1+r^*} = \frac{E\{m'|g\}}{\text{Cov}(m', I'|y, g, d') + E\{m'|g\}E\{I'|y, g, d'\}}.$$

Recalling that $E\{m'|g\} = 1/(1+r^*) > 0$ and that $E\{I'|y, g, d'\} = 1 - \text{Prob}\{\text{default in } t + 1|y, g, d'\}$, we can write the gross country premium as

$$\frac{1+r}{1+r^*} = \frac{1}{(1+r^*)\text{Cov}(m', I'|y, g, d') + 1 - \text{Prob}\{\text{default in } t + 1|y, g, d'\}}.$$

Taking logs on both sides of this expression yields

$$r - r^* \approx \text{Prob}\{\text{default in } t + 1|y, g, d'\} - (1+r^*)\text{Cov}(m', I'|y, g, d'),$$

which implies that the country premium will exceed the probability of default if and only if the conditional covariance between the pricing kernel and the decision to repay is negative. Finally, averaging over all states in which the emerging country is in good financial standing and chooses to repay ($I = 1$), we obtain

$$E(r - r^*) > \text{Prob}\{\text{default in } t + 1\} \text{ if and only if } \text{Cov}(m', I') < 0.$$

According to this expression, the more negative is the covariance between the world pricing kernel and the decision to repay, the larger the average spread-default-frequency differential will be. Although the world pricing kernel m is an exogenous stochastic process, its covariance with the decision to repay, I, need not be nil. The reason is that m determines the world interest rate, and therefore it affects the emerging country's cost of external funds and its decision to default or repay.

How large is the spread-default-frequency differential induced by the assumption of risk-averse foreign lenders in the context of the Eaton-Gersovitz model? To answer this question, we next characterize the predictions of a calibrated version of the present model.

With risk-averse foreign lenders, the model contains one additional exogenous state variable, namely, g, which makes the computation of equilibrium more time consuming. Before plunging into computations, we present the equations describing the model in recursive form.

The value of continuing to honor the debt for the emerging country is now given by

$$v^c(y, g, d) = \max_{d'} \left\{ u(y + qd' - d) + \beta E_{y,g} v^g(y', g', d') \right\}.$$

The value of being in bad financial standing is given by

$$v^b(y, g) = u(y - L(y)) + \beta \left[\theta E_{y,g} v^g(y', g', 0) + (1 - \theta) E_{y,g} v^b(y', g') \right].$$

The value of being in good financial standing is given by

$$v^g(y, g, d) = \max\{v^c(y, g, d), v^b(y, g)\}.$$

The price of debt satisfies the participation constraint,

$$q = E_{y,g}\{m' I(v^c(y', g', d') \geq v^b(y', g'))\},$$

where $I(v^c(y', g', d') \geq v^b(y', g'))$ is an indicator function taking the value one if $v^c(y', g', d') \geq v^b(y', g')$ and zero otherwise, and m' is the pricing kernel defined as

$$m' = \tilde{\beta} \left(g' \right)^{-\tilde{\sigma}}.$$

The model closes with the law of motion of the gross growth rate of foreign consumption:

$$\ln\left(\frac{g'}{\bar{g}}\right) = \rho_g \ln\left(\frac{g}{\bar{g}}\right) + \mu'. \tag{13.49 R}$$

We calibrate all parameters common to the baseline specification (the one with risk-neutral foreign lenders) using the values displayed in Table 13.7. We estimate the process for the growth rate of world consumption given in equation (13.49) by using data on nominal U.S. per capita consumption expenditures on nondurables and services during 1948:Q1–2013:Q4, deflated using the U.S. GDP deflator. The estimated values of ρ_g and σ_μ are, respectively, 0.2553 and 0.0055. We discretize this process using 100 equally spaced grid points in $\ln(g/\bar{g})$ with upper/lower bounds equal to ± 0.0237. The stock of external debt, d_t, is discretized with a grid of 100 equally spaced points in the interval $[0, 1.5]$. We set $\tilde{\sigma}$ equal to 2, which implies the same coefficient of relative risk aversion in the emerging country as in the rest of the world. We also consider a case with highly risk-averse foreign lenders by setting $\tilde{\sigma}$ to 5. We calibrate the growth-adjusted discount factor $\tilde{\beta}\bar{g}^{-\tilde{\sigma}}$ to 0.990041 per quarter, to ensure that the unconditional mean of the risk-free interest rate, $Er^* = E\left\{\frac{1}{\tilde{\beta}\bar{g}^{-\tilde{\sigma}} E\{(g'/\bar{g})^{-\tilde{\sigma}}|g\}}\right\} - 1$, is 1 percent per quarter, as in the baseline economy. Note that the calibraton of the model does not require information on $\tilde{\beta}$ and $\bar{g}$ individually but only on the growth-adjusted discount factor $\tilde{\beta}\bar{g}^{-\tilde{\sigma}}$.

Table 13.16   Predictions of the Eaton-Gersovitz Model with Risk-Averse Lenders

	Default Frequency						
$\tilde{\sigma}$	All Periods	Periods in Good Standing	$E(d/y)$	$E(r - r^*)$	$\sigma(r - r^*)$	corr$(r - r^*, y)$	corr$(r - r^*, tb/y)$
0	2.7	3.2	59.0	3.5	3.2	−0.54	0.78
2	2.8	3.4	58.3	3.6	3.5	−0.54	0.70
5	2.7	3.3	58.0	3.6	3.4	−0.55	0.75

Notes: The variable d/y denotes the quarterly debt-to-output ratio in percent, $r - r^*$ denotes the country premium in percent per year, y denotes (quarterly detrended) output, and tb/y denotes the trade-balance-to-output ratio. The symbols E, σ, and corr denote, respectively, the mean, the standard deviation, and the correlation. All moments are conditional on the country being in good financial standing. Theoretical moments were computed by running the Matlab script `statistics_modelral.m`, available on the book's Web site.

Table 13.16 presents the predictions of the Eaton-Gersovitz model with risk-averse foreign lenders ($\tilde{\sigma} = 2$ and 5). For comparison, the table also presents the predictions of the baseline model with risk-neutral lenders ($\tilde{\sigma} = 0$). The key message of the table is that the assumption of risk-averse foreign lenders has quantitatively negligible effects on the predictions of the Eaton-Gersovitz model. In particular, the assumption of risk-averse foreign lenders does not change the prediction of a near-zero spread-default-frequency differential.

The insensitivity of the endogenous variables of the model to changes in foreign risk aversion is remarkable, because the volatility of the world interest rate (not shown in Table 13.16) does increase significantly with $\tilde{\sigma}$. Specifically, the standard deviation of r^* is 0, 1.2, and 3.0 percent per year for $\tilde{\sigma}$ equal to 0, 2, and 5, respectively. Why is it then that this sizable increase in the volatility of the world interest rate does not affect the domestic economy? The reason is that this is an economy with highly impatient agents, who can borrow much less than what they would like to borrow under commitment. As a result, the present model behaves quite similarly to one in which the agent is up against a borrowing constraint most of the time. In such a setting, the price of credit is not very allocative, and hence variation thereof does not affect much consumption or borrowing decisions. This result is likely to change in a setting with default and more patient consumers.

13.10 Long-Term Debt and Default

In the preceding analysis, we assumed that external debt has a maturity of one period. In addition, in the calibration of the model, a period is meant to represent a quarter of a year. This means that the totality of the debt has a maturity of one quarter. This assumption is clearly unrealistic. For example, Broner, Lorenzoni, and Schmukler (2013) report that of the foreign-currency denominated bonds issued by Argentina between 1993 and 2003, 91 percent had a maturity longer than 3 years, and 51 percent had a maturity longer than 9 years. A similar pattern holds for other emerging countries. In this section, we introduce long-term debt into the Eaton-Gersovitz model and then ask whether the amended model can still account quantitatively for observed debt and spread dynamics. We begin by presenting two tractable models of long-term debt and default that preserve the number of states of the Eaton-Gersovitz model. Later we extend the model to allow for an endogenous choice of maturity structure.

13.10.1 A Random-Maturity Model

Here we present the long-term debt specification introduced by Chatterjee and Eyigungor (2012). Consider a sovereign bond with the following characteristics. With probability $\lambda \in [0, 1]$ the bond matures next period and pays out one unit of the consumption good. With probability $1 - \lambda$ the bond does not mature and pays a coupon equal to $z > 0$ units of consumption. The country is assumed to hold a portfolio with a continuum of this type of bond. The realization of maturity is independent across bonds. Hence, if the country has d units of debt outstanding, a share λ will mature each period with certainty and the remaining share $1 - \lambda$ will not. The nonmaturing bonds trade at the price q per unit. Because a newly issued bond is indistinguishable from an existing bond that did not mature, the ex-coupon price of old bonds and new bonds must be equal. Provided the debtor does not default, d units of debt pay $[\lambda + (1 - \lambda)(z + q)]d$ units of consumption. If the debtor defaults, the bond pays zero.

The main difference between the models with long-term and one-period debt is that long-term debt results in a state-contingent payoff, which may provide hedging against income risk to the borrower. Specifically, the payoff on the long-term bond, $\lambda + (1 - \lambda)(z + q)$, depends on q, which is state dependent. In particular, in periods of low income, q is likely to be low, resulting in an ex post low interest rate paid by the borrower. Because periods of low income are associated with low consumption, the long-term bond provides insurance against income risk. In contrast, the payoff on a one-period bond is unity and hence non-state contingent, providing no insurance against income risk. Therefore we should expect that, all other things being equal, the borrower will hold more debt if debt is long term rather than short term.

Introducing this new asset structure into the Eaton-Gersovitz model of Section 13.6.4 is straightforward. It only requires modifying the Bellman equation for the value of continuing to service the debt and the participation constraint for foreign lenders. As before, let $v^c(d, y)$ denote the value of continuing to service the debt. With long-term debt the value of continuation is given by

$$v^c(d, y) = \max_{d', c} \left\{ u(c) + \beta E_y v^g(d', y') \right\},$$

subject to

$$c = y - \lambda d - (1 - \lambda)z \, d + q(d', y)(d' - (1 - \lambda)d). \tag{13.52}$$

The value of being in bad financial standing is unchanged:

$$v^b(y) = u(y - L(y)) + \beta \theta E_y v^g(0, y') + \beta(1 - \theta)E_y v^b(y').$$

The value of being in good financial standing, $v^g(d, y)$, is then

$$v^g(d, y) = \max\{v^c(d, y), v^b(y)\}.$$

Finally, we continue to assume that foreign lenders are risk neutral. Therefore the expected one-period return on long-term debt must equal the one-period risk-free rate:

$$1 + r^* = \frac{E_y \left\{ I(v^c(d', y') \geq v^b(y')) \left[\lambda + (1 - \lambda)(z + q(d'', y')) \right] \right\}}{q(d', y)}, \quad (13.53)$$

where $I(v^c(d', y') \geq v^b(y'))$ is an indicator function that takes the value one if $v^c(d', y') \geq v^b(y')$ and zero otherwise, and d'' denotes the debt chosen in the next period, which is a function of d' and y'.

An appealing feature of the random-maturity model is that it allows for long-term debt without expanding the state space. Specifically, as in the case of one-period debt, the state variables are the current endowment, y, and the stock of debt, d. Further, the random-maturity model nests the one-period debt model as a special case when λ equals unity, that is, when 100 percent of the debt matures each period.

Chatterjee and Eyigungor (2012) calibrate this model to Argentina. They set $\lambda = 0.05$ to capture an average maturity of debt of 20 quarters. To see how the parameter λ relates to the average maturity of debt, notice that the fraction of the current stock of debt that will mature after exactly one period is λ. The fraction of the current debt that will mature in exactly two periods is $(1 - \lambda)\lambda$. In general, the fraction of the current debt that will mature in exactly j periods is $(1 - \lambda)^{j-1}\lambda$. This means that the average maturity of the current debt is $1 \times \lambda + 2 \times (1 - \lambda)\lambda + 3 \times (1 - \lambda)^2\lambda + \ldots$, or

$$\text{average maturity of debt} = \frac{1}{\lambda}.$$

Thus a value of λ of 0.05 implies an average maturity of debt of 20 quarters. The parameter z is set to 0.03 to match an annual coupon rate of 12 percent.

The remaining parameters are similar to those appearing in Table 13.7, with the exception of β, a_1, and a_2. Chatterjee and Eyigungor calibrate these parameters to match an external debt-to-output ratio of 70 percent per quarter, an average interest-rate spread of 8.15 per year, and a standard deviation of the interest-rate spread of 0.0443. This strategy yields $\beta = 0.954$, $a_1 = -0.188$, and $a_2 = 0.246$. The performance of this calibrated long-term debt model is at least as good as the performance of the baseline model presented in Section 13.6. An appealing property of the long-term debt model is that to match key statistics associated with debt and default, it does not require making households very impatient (compare the value of β of 0.85 in the baseline model versus 0.954 in the long-term debt model). The low value of β required by the baseline model is not necessarily unrealistic, since no direct evidence on this parameter is available. However, the value of 0.954 is more in line with values used in business-cycle studies outside the default literature. The reason the model with long-term debt can support the same amount of debt as the model with one-period debt and at the same time feature a higher value of the discount factor is related to the intuition given above, namely, that long-term debt provides insurance against endowment shocks. On the downside, the model with long-term debt shares with the baseline model a tight relationship between the average country premium and the default frequency, and therefore it has a hard time explaining the fact that these two moments are different in the data.

13.10.2 A Perpetuity Model

Following Hatchondo and Martínez (2009), we now introduce long-duration debt into the Eaton-Gersovitz model in the form of a bond that pays a coupon with decaying value at perpetuity. Specifically, consider a bond that sells at the price q measured in terms of consumption goods and promises a stream of payments of δ^{j-1} units of goods, where $j = 1, 2, \ldots$ denotes the number of periods after issuance. The parameter δ lies in the interval $[0, 1+r^*)$. Let s denote the number of bonds issued in the current period and s_j, for $j = 1, 2, \ldots$, denote the number of bonds issued j periods prior to the current period. The debt service due in the current period, denoted by d, is given by the sum of all coupon payments associated with bonds issued in the past:

$$d = s_1 + \delta s_2 + \delta^2 s_3 + \ldots.$$

Similarly, the debt service in the next period, denoted by d', is given by

$$d' = s + \delta s_1 + \delta^2 s_2 + \ldots.$$

Combining these two expressions, we obtain the following law of motion of debt services:

$$d' = \delta d + s.$$

Then the budget constraint of the country conditional on continuing to service the debt is given by

$$c + d = y + q(d', y)[d' - \delta d].$$

The maturity of debt in the present model is infinity, because a perpetuity never matures. However, a concept related to maturity is duration. The duration of a bond is given by the average time to maturity of payments. In the present formulation bonds pay δ^{j-1} units of goods in period $j = 1, 2, \ldots$ after issuance. The present value of all payments discounted at the risk-free rate r^* is given by $\sum_{j=1}^{\infty}(1+r^*)^{-j}\delta^{j-1} = 1/(1+r^*-\delta)$. This means that the bond pays a fraction $(1+r^*)^{-j}\delta^{j-1}(1+r^*-\delta)$ of total (discounted) payments in period j. Therefore the average time to maturity of payments is given by $(1+r^*-\delta)\sum_{j=1}^{\infty} j(1+r^*)^{-j}\delta^{j-1} = (1+r^*)/(1+r^*-\delta)$. In other words,

$$\text{duration} = \frac{1+r^*}{1+r^*-\delta}.$$

This expression is quite intuitive. Suppose, for example, that δ is zero. In this case, the bond makes a single payment one period after issuance, and the duration is one period. In the polar case that $\delta \to 1+r^*$, the bond makes a payment with a present value of 1 every period ad infinitum, and its duration becomes infinitely large. In general, the larger is δ, the larger the duration of the bond will be.

The remaining features of the model are familiar. The value of continuing to service the debt, $v^c(d, y)$, is

$$v^c(d, y) = \max_{\{d', c\}} \left\{ u(c) + \beta E_y v^g(d', y') \right\},$$

subject to

$$c + d = y + q(d', y)(d' - \delta d). \tag{13.54}$$

Assume, as before, that if the government defaults, it does so on its entire debt obligations. On default, the country loses access to financial markets and suffers the output loss, $L(y)$. Access to credit markets is regained with constant probability θ each period. Then the value of being in bad financial standing is

$$v^b(y) = u(y - L(y)) + \beta \theta E_y v^g(0, y') + \beta(1 - \theta) E_y v^b(y').$$

Also unchanged is the value of being in good financial standing, $v^g(d, y)$:

$$v^g(d, y) = \max\{v^c(d, y), v^b(y)\}.$$

Continuing to assume that foreign lenders are risk neutral, the expected one-period return on long-term debt must equal the one-period risk-free rate. Consider first the case of long-term debt issued in the current period. In this case, the participation constraint is

$$1 + r^* = \frac{E_y \left\{ I(v^c(d', y') \geq v^b(y')) \left[1 + \delta q(d'', y') \right] \right\}}{q(d', y)}. \tag{13.55}$$

The numerator of the fraction appearing on the right-hand side of this expression, $1 + \delta q(d'', y')$, is next period's payoff of a perpetuity issued in the current period conditional on no default. The payoff consists of two terms. The first term is unity, which is the first coupon payment. The second term, $\delta q(d'', y')$, is the price next period of a perpetuity issued in the current period. Notice that from the next period on, the stream of coupon payments of a perpetuity issued in the current period is δ times the stream of coupon payments of a perpetuity issued in the next period. Therefore the price in the next period of a perpetuity issued in the current period must be δ times the price of a perpetuity issued next period, or $\delta q(d'', y')$, which is the second term in the numerator.

The participation constraint (13.55) also holds for perpetuities issued k periods prior to the current period, for $k = 1, 2, \ldots$. The current period price of such a perpetuity is $\delta^k q(d', y)$, and the payoff tomorrow conditional on no default is $\delta^k + \delta^{k+1} q(d'', y')$. Therefore the participation constraint is

$$1 + r^* = \frac{E_y \left\{ I(v^c(d', y') \geq v^b(y')) \left[\delta^k + \delta^{k+1} q(d'', y') \right] \right\}}{\delta^k q(d', y)},$$

which is the same as equation (13.55).

This completes the Eaton-Gersovitz model expanded to allow for long-duration debt in the form of a perpetuity.

13.10.3 The Perpetuity Model as a Special Case of the Random-Maturity Model

The structure of the perpetuity model is similar to that of the random-maturity model presented in Section 13.10.1. Indeed, the random-maturity model nests the perpetuity model as a special case when $\delta < 1$. Specifically, setting $\lambda = 1 - \delta$ and $z = 1$ renders the random-maturity model identical to the perpetuity model. This is straightforward to show. Using this parameterization, the budget constraint and the lender participation constraint of the random-maturity model (equations (13.52) and (13.53)) become identical to their respective counterparts in the perpetuity model (equations (13.54) and (13.55)). All other equations are common to both models. We summarize this result in the following statement:

random-maturity model with $\lambda = 1 - \delta$ and $z = 1 \Rightarrow$ perpetuity model.

In turn, it can be readily verified that the perpetuity model nests the one-period debt model in the special case that $\delta = 0$, that is, in the special case in which the perpetuity pays only one coupon of one unit of consumption goods in the first period after issuance.

13.10.4 Endogenous Choice of Maturity

A characteristic common to the random-maturity and the perpetuity models of long-term debt is that both have a single maturity or duration of debt. In reality, sovereigns issue debt with various maturities. It is therefore of interest to consider environments with more than one maturity and to compare their predictions to observed movements in the maturity structure of debt and in the term structure of country spreads.

Broner, Lorenzoni, and Schmukler (2013), using weekly observations on foreign-currency sovereign bond prices and bond issuance for 11 emerging countries during 1990–2009, identify the following three stylized facts:

1. During crises, issuance of new debt shifts toward relatively shorter maturities. In particular, issuance of short-term bonds (less than 3 years in maturity) is not significantly affected during crises. But medium- and long-term issuance (longer than 3-year bonds) decreases sharply.[14]

2. On average, the risk premium on long-term bonds exceeds the risk premium on short-term bonds (the term structure of country spreads is upward sloping). For example, the average difference between the risk premia of 12-year and 3-year maturities is around 3 percent.

3. During crises the cost of long-term borrowing increases relative to the cost of short-term borrowing. The difference between the risk premium on long-term bonds and the risk premium on short-term bonds is 30 percent during crisis, but less than 1 percent otherwise.

---

14. Broner, Lorenzoni, and Schmukler date the beginning of a crisis when the 9-year spread is 300 basis points above its average level over the past 6 months. They date the end of a crisis when the 9-year spread falls below the threshold of 300 basis points above average for more than 4 weeks. Spreads are defined as the difference between the return on emerging-market bonds and the return on comparable U.S. or German bonds.

Why do we observe a shortening of maturities during crises? One line of research (e.g., Rodrik and Velasco 2000; Cole and Kehoe 1996) argues that the accumulation of short-term debt may cause rollover problems that can lead the country to a debt crisis. Under this hypothesis, the causality direction is from the shortening of maturities to crises. Often this type of analysis is taken to suggest policies conducive to maintaining a relatively long maturity structure of sovereign debt. An alternative explanation for the observed shortening of maturities during crises is that it is optimal for countries to shift new issuance of debt to shorter maturities in response to adverse economic conditions. In this case, the causality runs from crises to maturity, and a policy of lengthening the maturity structure could be counterproductive. For example, Bi (2006) and Arellano and Ramanarayanan (2012) find that the Eaton-Gersovitz model augmented with multiple maturities predicts an optimal shortening of maturities during crises. In what follows, we study this explanation in more detail.

The intuition for why the maturity structure shortens in times of crisis in the Eaton-Gersovitz default model is that short-term debt enhances the country's incentive to repay. The following simple example, adapted from Arellano and Ramanarayanan (2012) illustrates this incentive-enhancing role of short-term debt.[15] Consider a three-period economy with linear preferences given by

$$U(c_0, c_1, c_2) = c_0 + \beta c_1 + \beta^2 c_2,$$

where c_i denotes consumption in period $i = 0$, 1, 2, and $\beta \in (0, 1)$ denotes the subjective discount factor. Suppose that the endowment is 0 in period 0 and $y > 0$ in periods 1 and 2. Suppose that the world interest rate, r^*, is zero and that the economy starts period 0 with no debt. Because preferences are linear in consumption and because agents discount future utility at a rate higher than the world interest rate, $\beta(1 + r^*) < 1$, the first-best allocation is to concentrate all consumption in period 0, that is, to set $c_0 = 2y$ and $c_1 = c_2 = 0$. Suppose that the country can borrow and lend in international markets using a two-period, zero coupon bond or a one-period bond. Suppose further that default results in a complete loss of current and future endowments.

There are two independent maturity structures that implement the first-best allocation. One is in period 0 to borrow y units long term and y units short term. Under this strategy, in period 1, the endowment is used to retire the short-term bond, and in period 2 the endowment is used to retire the long-term bond. The second strategy is to borrow $2y$ units short term in period 0, use the endowment in period 1 to pay off half the debt and roll over the remaining debt by borrowing y units short term. In period 2, the endowment is used to retire the outstanding short-term debt. Both these asset portfolios can be supported in equilibrium even though the government lacks commitment to repay its debts. Notice that both strategies contain short-term debt issued in period 0 and maturing in period 1. In contrast, any strategy that achieves the first-best allocation under commitment but involves no issuance of short-term debt in period 0 is unsupportable in equilibrium in the absence of commitment. Consider, for example, a case in which in period 0 the country is-

---

15. Jeanne (2009) and Rodrik and Velasco (2000) present models with a similar flavor.

sues $2y$ units of long-term debt and 0 units of short-term debt. In period 1, the government saves the endowment in short-term bonds. In period 2, the government uses its savings and its endowment to retire all long-term debt. This asset allocation would, however, result in default in period 2. This is because in period 1 the government could consume the endowment rather than saving it. This would increase utility by βy relative to the first-best allocation. In period 2 the government fails to meet its obligations and defaults, losing its endowment. Period-2 consumption is zero, as in the first-best allocation. Hence lifetime utility under default is higher than under repayment. Foreign lenders understand this and therefore would refuse to lend long term in period 0. International lending breaks down. It follows that the issuance of short-term debt in period 0 is necessary to create incentives for the country not to default.

The simple example presented above suggests that short-term debt may allow for international lending in situations in which otherwise it would break down. To the extent that during crises the value of commitment increases, the desirability of shortening the maturity of debt should also increase. To see how a crisis can lead to a shift in maturity toward the short run, consider modifying the previous example to allow for curvature in the period utility index. Specifically, suppose that now the lifetime utility function is of the form

$$U(c_0, c_1, c_2) = \ln(c_0) + \beta \ln(c_1) + \beta^2 \ln(c_2).$$

Suppose further that the endowment equals $y_0 > 0$ in period 0 and $y > 0$ in periods 1 and 2. Suppose that initially $y_0 = y$. Assume that all other features of the economy are as before. The first-best allocation now features a declining path of consumption, $c_1 = \beta c_0$, $c_2 = \beta^2 c_0$, and $c_0 = (y_0 + 2y)/(1 + \beta + \beta^2)$. Consider implementing this allocation with a debt issuance in period 0 of $s = y - c_1$ units of short-term debt and $\ell = y - c_2$ units of long-term debt. Suppose now that the country suffers a crisis that lowers y_0 and leaves the endowments in periods 1 and 2 unchanged. Clearly the crisis causes c_0 to fall, $\Delta c_0 < 0$. In turn the change in short-term borrowing, Δs, is positive and equal to $\Delta s = -\beta \Delta c_0$, and the change in long-term borrowing, $\Delta \ell = -\beta^2 \Delta c_0 < \Delta s$, is also positive but less than the change in short-term borrowing. Thus the crisis leads to a shortening of the maturity structure.

The above two examples illustrate the importance of short-term debt as a vehicle to create incentives to repay debt, especially during crises. However, they do not make the case for the desirability of long-term debt. For in both examples, the first-best allocation can be supported even in the absence of long-term debt by borrowing short term in both periods. The reason long-term debt has no advantage over short-term debt in the above two examples is the lack of uncertainty. The benefit of long-run debt is that it provides a hedge against shocks to the short-term interest rate. This hedging property manifests itself in the fact that an increase in short-term rates makes borrowing more expensive, but at the same time lowers the value of outstanding long-term debt, which compensates the borrower for the elevation in the cost of funds. Arellano and Ramanarayanan (2012) present a generalization of the log-preference economy of the previous paragraph with uncertainty. In their environment the optimal allocation under lack of commitment to repay features consumption smoothing across states in period 1 and across nondefault states in period 2. Implementing this allocation requires the use of long-term debt, in the sense that in the absence of long-term debt, the optimal allocation is no longer implementable.

What does a calibrated version of the Eaton-Gersovitz model with short- and long-term debt predict for the behavior of debt maturities and interest-rate spreads over the business cycle? Arellano and Ramanarayanan (2012) combine the model with one-period debt of Section 13.6.4 and the model with a perpetuity of Section 13.10.2. In the resulting economy the duration of debt is endogenous. It lies between 1 period (the duration of one-period debt) and $(1 + r^*)/(1 + r^* - \delta)$ periods (the duration of the perpetuity). The government determines optimally the average duration of outstanding debt by setting the quantities of one-period debt and perpetuities each period. The model is calibrated at an annual frequency using Brazilian data. The risk-free interest rate, r^*, is set to 3.2 percent per year and the rate of decay of the coupon payment, δ, to 0.936. The resulting duration of the perpetuity is 10.75 years.

The calibrated model captures the fact that the average duration of new issuance shortens during crisis. Specifically, the model predicts that when the 1-year spread is below its median, the average duration of newly issued debt is 4.9 years, whereas when the spread is above its median, the average duration falls to 3.7 years. Arellano and Ramanarayanan (2012) report that in the data, the corresponding numbers are 8.2 and 5.8 years, respectively.

In addition, the model predicts that long-term borrowing becomes relatively cheaper than short-term borrowing during crises. Specifically, it implies that when the short-term spread is below its median value, the average long-term spread is 1.5 percentage points above the average short-term spread. That is, when the short-term spread is low, the term structure of spreads is upward sloping. At the same time, the model predicts that when the short-term spread is above its median value, then the average long-term spread is 1.6 percentage points below the average short-term spread. That is, according to the model, during crises the term structure of country spreads not only becomes less steep, it also becomes downward sloping.

The predicted inversion of the term structure of spreads during crises is quite intuitive in the logic of the Eaton-Gersovitz model. The increase in the short-term spread during a crisis is the consequence of an elevated risk of default. Because the model displays reversion to the mean, future expected short-term spreads must display a declining path. Since the long-term spread is roughly an average of current and future expected spreads, it must be lower than the current short-term spread during a crisis.

Is the predicted inversion of the term structure of country spreads duing crises borne out in the data? This question turns out to be difficult to answer, because different empirical studies come to different conclusions about the behavior of the slope of the term structure of country spreads during crises. For instance, as discussed above (see stylized fact (3) near the start of this section), Broner, Lorenzoni, and Schmukler (2013) find that the term structure of spreads steepens during periods of high spreads. That is, long-term debt becomes relatively more expensive during crises. Arellano and Ramanarayanan (2012) find that the average slope of the term structure of country spreads is the same whether one conditions on the short-term spread being above or below its median value. These two pieces of empirical evidence are at odds with the predictions of the model. However, Arellano and Ramanarayanan also report that conditional on the short-term spread being extremely high (in the top decile), the average slope of the term structure of spreads is slightly negative at −0.7 percentage points, which is more in line with the inversion predicted by the model.

The Eaton-Gersovitz model with endogenous maturity discussed here also predicts that the slope of the term structure of country spreads must be about zero on average. This is a direct consequence of the assumption that foreign lenders are risk neutral. In contrast, the observed country-spread curve is on average upward sloping. As mentioned above, Broner, Lorenzoni, and Schmukler (2013) estimate an average difference between spreads on 3-year and 12-year maturities of 3 percentage points, and Arellano and Ramanarayanan (2012) estimate an average difference between 1-year and 10-year maturities of 1.8 percentage points.

The fact that during crises the maturity structure shortens and the term structure of country spreads steepens has led some authors to propose models in which the shortening of maturity is driven by credit supply factors rather than by credit demand factors, as is the case in the Eaton-Gersovitz model. In particular, Broner, Lorenzoni, and Schmukler (2013) present a model in which foreign creditors are risk averse, as in Lizarazo (2013). In their model, an exogenous increase in the degree of risk aversion induces foreign creditors to expand the supply of more liquid short-term securities, resulting in a steeper term structure of country spreads and a shortening of the maturity structure.

13.11 Debt Renegotiation

The standard Eaton-Gersovitz model assumes that on default the debtor country repudiates all its outstanding external debt. That is, it assumes that the haircut is always 100 percent. In reality, however, haircuts are rarely that large. Section 13.1.2 documents that the average observed haircut is around 40 percent. One way to bring the predictions of the Eaton-Gersovitz model closer to the data in this regard is to assume that on default the debtor country engages in a renegotiation process with foreign lenders. The haircut is then the outcome of such renegotiation, and its magnitude will depend on the bargaining power of borrowers and lenders as well as on the fundamentals of the economy. Contributions in this area include Bulow and Rogoff (1989a), Bi (2008), Yue (2010), D'Erasmo (2011), Guimaraes (2011), and Benjamin and Wright (2013).

In this section we extend the baseline Eaton-Gersovitz model of Section 13.6.4 to allow for debt renegotiation. In the model, renegotiation takes the form of a Nash bargaining game between the debtor country and foreign lenders. The model has the following distinctive features. First, after default renegotiation determines the amount of debt the country will owe on reentry. Second, the renegotiation can feature multiple restructurings, depending on the evolution of the state of economic fundamentals over the renegotiation period. Third, after default the length of the exclusion period is not dictated by the requirement that the debtor clears up all of its arrears. This feature of the model is motivated by the fact that in reality countries emerge from default with positive amounts of external debt outstanding. Fourth, the length of the exclusion period has endogenous and exogenous components. The exogenous component is as in the baseline Eaton-Gersovitz model of Section 13.6.4.

The endogenous component arises because the debtor may choose to restructure its debt during the exclusion period. This feature introduces an endogenous positive correlation between the size of the haircut and the length of the exclusion period. And fifth, the model generates a secondary market for distressed debt. This implication captures the empirical fact that observed debt prices during periods of default status are lower than during normal times but not zero as predicted by the standard Eaton-Gersovitz model.

13.11.1 The Eaton-Gersovitz Model with Debt Renegotiation

The problem of a country in good financial standing that chooses to service its debt is as in the standard Eaton-Gersovitz model. Specifically, the value of continuing to participate in credit markets, $v^c(d, y)$, solves the Bellman equation

$$v^c(d, y) = \max_{d'} \left\{ u(y + q(d', y)d' - d) + \beta E_y v^g(d', y') \right\},$$

where, as before, $v^g(d, y)$ denotes the value of being in good financial standing. If the country starts the current period in good financial standing and decides to default and renegotiate, it is assumed to be excluded from borrowing and lending starting in the current period, with constant and exogenous reentry probability θ beginning in the next period. During exclusion, the country suffers the output loss $L(y)$. Contrary to what we have assumed thus far, on reentry the country owes debt in the amount $\tilde{d}$, which is the result of a renegotiation that took place in the period in which the country defaulted. The value of being in bad standing, denoted $v^b(\tilde{d}, y)$, is given by

$$v^b(\tilde{d}, y) = u\left(y - L(y)\right) + \theta \beta E_y v^g(\tilde{d}, y') + (1 - \theta)\beta E_y v^b(\tilde{d}, y').$$

We assume that if the country decides to default and not renegotiate, then it is condemned to permanent financial autarky and a permanent output loss of $L(y)$ per period. Thus the value of defaulting without renegotiation, denoted by $v^a(y)$, is given by

$$v^a(y) = u(y - L(y)) + \beta E_y v^a(y').$$

Renegotiation is a mechanism to distribute surpluses between the debtor country and the foreign lenders in case of default. The surplus of the debtor country is the difference between the value of defaulting and renegotiating and the value of defaulting and not renegotiating, $v^b\left(\tilde{d}, y\right) - v^a(y)$. This difference is always nonnegative, because a renegotiating debtor can replicate the autarky allocation by always defaulting on reentry. We express the debtor surplus in terms of goods by dividing it by the marginal utility of consumption under autarky. This marginal utility is the value of goods in terms of utility when the country defaults, regardless of whether it renegotiates. Thus the surplus of the debtor expressed in terms of consumption goods is given by

$$\text{surplus of the debtor country} = \frac{v^b\left(\tilde{d}, y\right) - v^a(y)}{u'(y - L(y))}.$$

The surplus of foreign lenders is the difference between the value of the restructured debt, $q^b(\tilde{d}, y)\tilde{d}$, and the payment received by the lender in the absence of renegotiation, which is zero. The variable $q^b(\tilde{d}, y)$ denotes the price of distressed debt, that is, the price of debt when the country is in bad financial standing. Formally, the surplus of foreign lenders is given by

$$\text{surplus of foreign lenders} = q^b(\tilde{d}, y)\tilde{d}.$$

The outcome of the renegotiation is the level of restructured debt, $\tilde{d}$, which is assumed to be determined by generalized Nash bargaining with exogenous parameter $\alpha \in [0, 1]$. Specifically, $\tilde{d}$ maximizes the following Cobb-Douglas function:

$$\tilde{d} = \arg\max{}_x \left[\frac{v^b(x, y) - v^a(y)}{u'(y - L(y))} \right]^\alpha \left[q^b(x, y)x \right]^{1-\alpha}.$$

The parameter α measures the bargaining power of the borrower. The higher is α, the stronger the negotiating power of the debtor country will be. The level of the restructured debt, $\tilde{d}$, is a function of current output, y, but does not depend upon the level of debt the country defaults on, d. Therefore we have that

$$\text{restructured debt} = \tilde{d}(y).$$

Notice that nothing prevents $\tilde{d}(y)$ from being bigger than d, the debt defaulted on. When positive, we interpret the difference $\tilde{d}(y) - d$ as the threat of additional punishment, such as punitive interest, should the country declare cessation of payments. An alternative formulation, not pursued here, would be to impose the constraint $x \le d$ in the above bargaining problem.

The value of default with renegotiation is then given by

$$v^d(y) \equiv v^b(\tilde{d}(y), y),$$

which implies that the value of default and restructuring is independent of the size of the default. Note that both the haircut, $d - \tilde{d}(y)$, and the recovery rate, $\tilde{d}(y)/d$, do depend on the level of debt defaulted on. In particular, the model predicts that the size of the haircut is increasing with the level of debt, d.

A country in good financial standing has the option either to continue servicing the debt or to default. It follows that the value of being in good standing is given by

$$v^g(d, y) = \max\{v^c(d, y), v^d(y)\}.$$

As in the model without renegotiation, foreign lenders are assumed to be risk neutral and perfectly competitive. To derive a recursive representation of the price of debt, it is convenient to define the indicator function $I(d, y)$, which takes the value one if a country in good standing chooses to default and renegotiate and zero otherwise:

$$I(d, y) \equiv \begin{cases} 1 & \text{if } v^c(d, y) \ge v^d(y) \\ 0 & \text{otherwise.} \end{cases}$$

Then the price of debt in periods in which the country is in good standing and chooses to continue to be engaged in credit markets, denoted by $q(d', y)$, satisfies the following participation constraint:

$$1 + r^* = \frac{E_y I(d', y') + E_y[1 - I(d', y')](\tilde{d}(y')/d')q^b(\tilde{d}(y'), y')}{q(d', y)}.$$

The left-hand side is the opportunity cost of funds for lenders, given by the gross risk-free interest rate, $1 + r^*$. The right-hand side is the expected return on the emerging country debt. A key difference with the model without renegotiation is that now in the case of default, the return of one unit of debt purchased prior to default is not zero, but takes the value $(\tilde{d}(y')/d')q^b(\tilde{d}(y'), y')$, where $\tilde{d}(y')/d'$ is the recovery rate, and $q^b(\tilde{d}(y'), y')$ is the price of restructured debt. Because a unit of distressed debt represents a promise to pay one unit of consumption on reentry, the price of a unit of distressed debt, $q^b(\tilde{d}, y)$, must satisfy

$$1 + r^*$$
$$= \frac{(1 - \theta)E_y q^b(d', y') + \theta E_y I(d', y') + \theta E_y[1 - I(d', y')](\tilde{d}(y')/d')q^b(\tilde{d}(y'), y')}{q^b(d', y)}.$$

The numerator on the right-hand side has three components. The first component is the expected payoff of restructured debt when the debtor country does not reenter financial markets next period. The second term is the expected payoff when the debtor gets to reenter and chooses to honor its debt obligations. And the third term corresponds to the expected payoff when the debtor gets to reenter and chooses to default again, generating another renegotiation and debt restructuring.

The above expression embodies a key difference with the model without renegotiation. In the absence of renegotiation, the price of debt when the country is in bad standing is zero, $q^b(d', y) = 0$. But here, this price is in general positive, because the creditor expects to recover part of the distressed debt outstanding. A second property of the current model that is evident from the above participation constraint is that although the probability of reentry, θ, is exogenous, the duration of the exclusion period has an endogenous component. This is because when the country receives the exogenous signal allowing it to reenter, it can choose to remain in bad financial standing, thereby endogenously extending the exclusion period. This option is never exercised in the model without renegotiation, because in that model, by assumption, the country always reenters with zero outstanding debt and hence has no incentive to default at that point. The present model nests the standard Eaton-Gersovitz model in the special case in which all bargaining power lies with the debtor ($\alpha = 1$; see exercise 13.15).

13.11.2 Quantitative Predictions of the Debt-Renegotiation Model

To facilitate comparison of the quantitative predictions of the model with debt renegotiation and those of the standard Eaton-Gersovitz model studied in Section 13.6.4, we set the

Table 13.17   The Eaton-Gersovitz Model with Debt Renegotiation:
Properties of Predicted Haircuts

			Haircut h (%)	
Min(h)	Max(h)	Mean(h)	Standard Deviation(h)	Correlation(h, L)
26.8	56.4	40.3	5.0	0.06

Notes: L denotes the length of the exclusion period. The parameter α takes the
value 0.55. All other parameter values are as in Table 13.7. The Matlab script to
produce this table is `statistics_modelr.m`, available on the book's Web site.

values of all parameters common to both models to those given in Table 13.7.[16] The present
model features a single additional parameter relative to the model without renegotiation,
namely α, the parameter governing the bargaining power of the borrower. We set α to 0.55,
to match the observed average haircut of 40 percent (see Section 13.1.2). Matlab code to
solve the present model is available on the book's Web site. Policy functions are produced
by the program `egr.m`, simulated time series are computed by the program `simur.m`, and
predicted moments are produced by the program `statistics_modelr.m`.

Table 13.17 displays the predictions of the model concerning the behavior of its novel
variable, namely, the haircut:

$$h \equiv 1 - \frac{\tilde{d}(y)}{d}.$$

The haircut is a random variable whose mean, as indicated above, is pinned down to about
40 percent by appropriate choice of the bargaining weight α. The range of haircuts predicted
by the model varies from 27 to 56 percent, with a standard deviation of 5, which is lower
than its empirical counterpart of about 22 (see Section 13.1.2). The model also displays
a positive but modest correlation between the size of the haircut and the length of the
exclusion period. The sign of this correlation is in line with the data (see, e.g., Benjamin and
Wright 2013). The positive comovement between the size of the haircut and the length of
the exclusion period arises because occasionally the country finds it optimal to restructure
its debt while in bad financial standing, which causes both the size of the accumulated
haircut and the exclusion period to be larger.

Table 13.18 presents the predictions of the debt-renegotiation model regarding default,
debt, and the country spread. For comparison, the table reproduces from Table 13.8 the
predictions of the standard Eaton-Gersovitz model, which corresponds to the case $\alpha = 1$.
The debt renegotiation model supports more debt in equilibrium than the standard Eaton-
Gersovitz model (0.87 versus 0.59). The reason is that debt renegotiation establishes a floor
to how much lenders can lose in the event of default. This floor is on average 40 percent of
the initial investment. As a result, they are more willing to lend to the emerging economy,

---

16. An alternative strategy is to recalibrate the model to meet the targets imposed in Section 13.6.5. This is the
subject of exercise 13.16.

Table 13.18   The Eaton-Gersovitz Model with Debt Renegotiation: Predicted First and Second Moments

Model	Default Frequency	$E(d/y)$	$E(r - r^*)$	$\sigma(r - r^*)$	$\text{corr}(r - r^*, y)$	$\text{corr}(r - r^*, tb/y)$
Baseline	3.2	59.0	3.5	3.2	−0.54	0.78
Renegotiation	3.7	86.6	2.8	2.7	−0.53	0.80

Notes: Baseline refers to the standard Eaton-Gersovitz model of Section 13.6.4. In the debt-renegotiation model, the parameter α takes the value 0.55. All other parameter values are as in Table 13.7. The variable d/y denotes the quarterly debt-to-output ratio in percent; $r - r^*$ denotes the country premium in percent per year; y denotes output; and tb/y denotes the trade-balance-to-output ratio. The symbols E, σ, and corr denote, respectively, the mean, the standard deviation, and the correlation. All moments are conditional on the country being in good financial standing. The Matlab script to produce this table is `statistics_modelr.m`, available on the book's Web site.

which results in lower spreads and higher debt. The model predicts a negative spread-default-frequency differential (i.e., that the spread is on average lower than the default frequency). To a large extent, this is because the model features partial default in equilibrium. For the intuition behind this connection, see the discussion surrounding equation (13.33). The negative spread-default-frequency differential induced by debt renegotiation is at odds with the data: as discussed in Section 13.1.5, observed spread-default-frequency differentials are typically positive. The predictions of the model regarding the volatility and cyclicality of the country spread are similar to those of the standard Eaton-Gersovitz model.

It is of interest to analyze the effects of varying the parameter α governing the bargaining power of the debtor. Figure 13.13 shows that as α increases from 0 to 1, the size of the average haircut increases, reaching 100 percent when the borrower has all the bargaining power. At first glance this result is intuitive, because in the short run a higher haircut represents more resources available to the borrower for consumption. However, the shift of bargaining power from the lender to the borrower has additional equilibrium effects, because lenders incorporate the increase in the size of haircuts into the price of debt. As shown in the bottom-right panel of the figure, lenders charge a higher country premium for higher average haircuts, which raises the cost of borrowing for the debtor. This effect should induce the borrower to choose a smaller haircut. In equilibrium, however, the first effect dominates, and the haircut increases with the bargaining power of the borrower. Because the average haircut increases with bargaining power, lenders reduce the supply of funds as α increases, causing less lending in equilibrium, as shown in the top-right panel of the figure. Finally, as the bargaining power of borrowers increases, they find it optimal to default less frequently (bottom-left panel of the figure). This is because, over time, a given desired reduction in the level of debt can be achieved either by defaulting often and imposing small haircuts or by defaulting less frequently and imposing larger haircuts.

In summary, the main payoff of enriching the Eaton-Gersovitz model with debt renegotiation is the emergence of an endogenous and empirically realistic haircut. In addition, the model with renegotiation is able to support more debt in equilibrium. On the downside, the model with renegotiation exacerbates the difficulties of the standard Eaton-Gersovitz model to generate positive spread-default-frequency differentials.

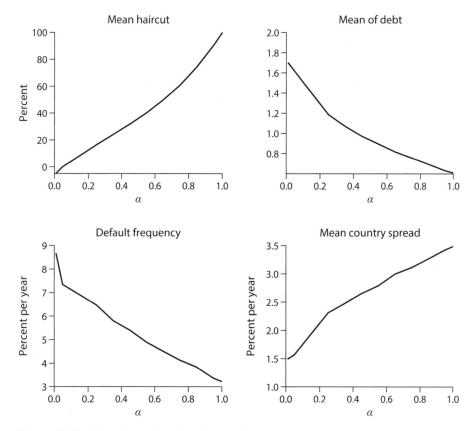

Figure 13.13   The effect of varying the bargaining power, α.

13.12 Default and Monetary Policy

All of the models of default we have studied thus far are cast in real terms. In those frameworks, there is no room for monetary or exchange-rate policy to matter. However, as we will see shortly, the data suggest that a significant relationship exists between default and exchange rates. To make room for monetary policy, in this section we introduce nominal rigidities into the Eaton-Gersovitz default model. We use this augmented model to characterize the equilibrium dynamics of default, devaluation, and employment under optimal and suboptimal exchange-rate policies. The analysis that follows draws from Na et al. (2014).

13.12.1 The Twin Ds

A strong link exists between sovereign default and devaluation in emerging countries. Reinhart (2002), using data for 58 countries for 1970–1999, estimates that the unconditional probability of a large devaluation (25 percent or higher) in any 24-month period is 17 percent. At the same time, she estimates that conditional on the 24-month period containing a default event, the probability of a large devaluation increases to 84 percent. Reinhart refers to this phenomenon as the "Twin Ds."

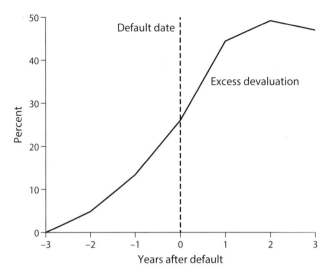

Figure 13.14   Excess devaluation around default, 1975–2013.

Source: Default dates are taken from Table 13.19. Exchange rates are from the World Bank's World Development Indicators, code: `PA.NUS.FCRF`.

Notes: The solid line displays the median of the cumulative devaluation rate between years −3 and +3 conditional on default in year 0 minus the unconditional median of the cumulative devaluation rate between years −3 and +3. Conditional medians are taken across 7-year windows centered on a default episode. The sample contains 116 default episodes between 1975 and 2013 in 70 countries. Unconditional medians are taken over all 7-year windows in the sample.

Figure 13.14 provides further evidence of the Twin Ds phenomenon. It displays the median excess depreciation of the nominal exchange rate for 116 sovereign defaults that occurred in 70 countries during 1975–2013. The nominal exchange rate is expressed as the price of one U.S. dollar in units of local currency. The exchange rate devalues when the price of a dollar increases in terms of domestic currency. The figure shows that in a 7-year window the exchange rate depreciates 45 percent more if the window contains a default event than if it does not. Figure 13.15 displays the behavior of the nominal exchange rate during six well-known default episodes. In all cases, sovereign default is accompanied by large devaluations of the domestic currency.

Next we build a model in which the Twin Ds emerge endogenously as an optimal policy outcome. That is, we will ask the question of whether it is optimal for a benevolent government to couple defaults with large devaluations.

13.12.2 A Model of the Twin Ds

The Twin Ds phenomenon suggests some connection between the decision to default and the decision to devalue. Here we build a model in which this connection results from combining lack of commitment to repay sovereign debt, as in the Eaton-Gersovitz model studied earlier in this chapter, and downward nominal wage rigidity, as in the model of Chapter 9. A prediction of the resulting model is that the country chooses to default when

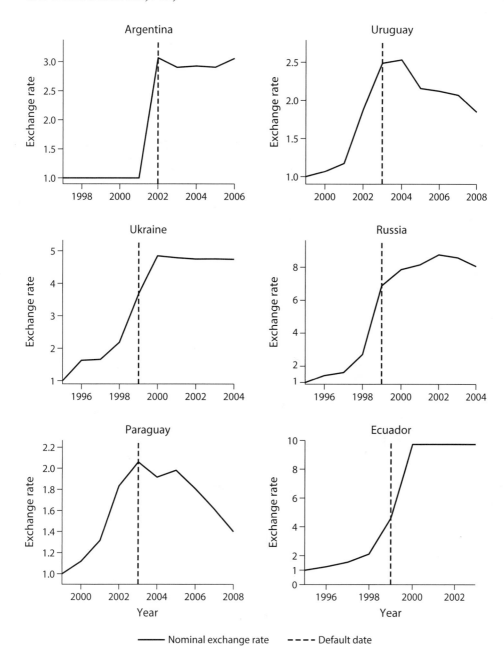

Figure 13.15 The Twin Ds: Six examples.

Notes: Exchange rates are nominal dollar exchange rates, annual average, first observation normalized to unity.
Data sources: Default dates, appendix to this chapter, section 13.13. Nominal exchange rates, WDI.

aggregate demand is depressed. In turn, when aggregate demand is low, so is the demand for labor. Full employment then requires real wages to fall. However, given the downward rigidity of nominal wages, a fall in the real wage can occur only if the government erodes the purchasing power of the nominal wage via a devaluation. Hence, in these circumstances, it is optimal for the government to devalue. The model therefore predicts that it is optimal for the government to combine default with currency devaluation. In this way the Twin Ds phenomenon emerges endogenously as an optimal outcome in this environment.

Consider an economy populated by a large number of identical households with preferences described by the utility function

$$E_0 \sum_{t=0}^{\infty} \beta^t U(c_t). \tag{13.56}$$

The consumption good is a composite of tradable consumption, c_t^T, and nontradable consumption, c_t^N. The aggregation technology is of the form

$$c_t = A(c_t^T, c_t^N), \tag{13.57}$$

where A is an increasing, concave, and linearly homogeneous function. The presence of nontradable goods is one of the differences between the present setup and the default model analyzed in previous sections.

The sequential budget constraint of the household is given by

$$P_t^T c_t^T + P_t^N c_t^N + \mathcal{E}_t d_t = P_t^T \tilde{y}_t^T + W_t h_t + (1 - \tau_t^d) q_t^d \mathcal{E}_t d_{t+1} + F_t + \Phi_t,$$

where P_t^T denotes the nominal price of tradable goods; P_t^N is the nominal price of nontradable goods; $\mathcal{E}_t$ is the nominal exchange rate, defined as the domestic-currency price of one unit of foreign currency; $\tilde{y}_t^T$ denotes the household's endowment of traded goods; W_t is the nominal wage rate; h_t is hours worked; τ_t^d is a tax on debt; F_t denotes a lump-sum transfer received from the government; and Φ_t denotes nominal profits from the ownership of firms. Households are assumed to be subject to the natural debt limit, which prevents them from engaging in Ponzi schemes. The variable $\tilde{y}_t^T$ is stochastic and is taken as given by the household.

Assume that the law of one price holds for tradables. Specifically, letting P_t^{T*} denote the foreign-currency price of tradables, the law of one price implies that

$$P_t^T = P_t^{T*} \mathcal{E}_t.$$

Further, assume that the foreign-currency price of tradables is constant and normalized to unity: $P_t^{T*} = 1$. Thus we have that the nominal price of tradables equals the nominal exchange rate:

$$P_t^T = \mathcal{E}_t.$$

Let $p_t \equiv P_t^N/\mathcal{E}_t$, $w_t \equiv W_t/\mathcal{E}_t$, $f_t \equiv F_t/\mathcal{E}_t$, and $\phi_t \equiv \Phi_t/\mathcal{E}_t$ denote, respectively, the relative price of nontradables, the real wage rate, real lump-sum transfers, and real profits, all expressed in terms of tradables. Then the sequential budget constraint of the household can be written as

$$c_t^T + p_t c_t^N + d_t = \tilde{y}_t^T + w_t h_t + (1 - \tau_t^d)q_t^d d_{t+1} + f_t + \phi_t. \qquad (13.58)$$

Households supply inelastically $\bar{h}$ hours to the labor market each period. However, sometimes they are unable to sell all the hours they supply. Hence hours worked, h_t, satisfies

$$h_t \leq \bar{h}. \qquad (13.59)$$

Households take h_t as given.

Households choose contingent plans $\{c_t, c_t^T, c_t^N, d_{t+1}\}$ to maximize the lifetime utility function (13.56) subject to (13.57)–(13.59) and the natural debt limit, taking as given p_t, w_t, h_t, ϕ_t, q_t^d, τ_t^d, f_t, and $\tilde{y}_t^T$. The optimality conditions associated with this problem are (13.57)–(13.59), the natural debt limit, and

$$\frac{A_2(c_t^T, c_t^N)}{A_1(c_t^T, c_t^N)} = p_t,$$

$$\lambda_t = U'(c_t) A_1(c_t^T, c_t^N),$$

and

$$(1 - \tau_t^d)q_t^d \lambda_t = \beta E_t \lambda_{t+1},$$

where λ_t denotes the Lagrange multiplier associated with (13.58).

Nontraded output, denoted y_t^N, is produced by perfectly competitive firms with the production technology

$$y_t^N = F(h_t). \qquad (13.60)$$

The function F is assumed to be strictly increasing and strictly concave. Firms choose the amount of labor input to maximize profits, which are given by

$$\Phi_t \equiv P_t^N F(h_t) - W_t h_t. \qquad (13.61)$$

The optimality condition associated with this problem is $P_t^N F'(h_t) = W_t$. Dividing both sides by $\mathcal{E}_t$ yields

$$p_t F'(h_t) = w_t.$$

As in the model of Chapter 9, we introduce downward nominal wage rigidity by imposing a lower bound on nominal wage growth of the form

$$W_t \geq \gamma W_{t-1},$$

where $\gamma > 0$ is a parameter governing the degree of downward nominal wage rigidity. In what follows, we assume that γ is less than unity. We impose the condition that at every point in time, wages and employment must satisfy the slackness condition:

$$(\bar{h} - h_t)\left(W_t - \gamma W_{t-1}\right) = 0.$$

Default decisions are assumed to be made by the government and are modeled along the lines of the decentralized Eaton-Gersovitz model of Section 13.8. Accordingly, the exclusion from international credit markets when the country is in bad financial standing $(I_t = 0)$ is formalized by the expression

$$(1 - I_t)d_{t+1} = 0. \tag{13.62}$$

As in Section 13.8, the sequential budget constraint of the government is

$$f_t = \tau_t^d q_t^d d_{t+1} + (1 - I_t)d_t. \tag{13.63}$$

The first term on the right-hand side reflects the assumption that the government rebates the proceeds from the debt tax in a lump-sum fashion to households. And the second term captures the assumption that in periods in which the country is in bad standing $(I_t = 0)$, the government confiscates any payments of households to foreign lenders and returns the proceeds to households in a lump-sum fashion.

With risk-neutral foreign lenders the price of debt charged by foreign lenders to the country, q_t, must obey the participation constraint:

$$I_t\left[q_t - \frac{E_t I_{t+1}}{1 + r^*}\right] = 0.$$

As explained in Section 13.8, the domestic price of debt, q_t^d, equals q_t when the country is in good financial standing $(I_t = 1)$ but is in general different from q_t when the country is in financial autarky $(I_t = 0)$.

In equilibrium the market for nontraded goods must clear at all times. That is, the condition

$$c_t^N = y_t^N \tag{13.64}$$

must hold for all t.

We assume that $\ln y_t^T$ obeys the law of motion,

$$\ln y_t^T = \rho \ln y_{t-1}^T + \mu_t,$$

where μ_t is an i.i.d. innovation with mean zero and variance σ_μ^2, and $|\rho| \in [0, 1)$ is a parameter. The variable $\tilde{y}_t^T$ is defined as the endowment net of the output loss associated with default:

$$\tilde{y}_t^T = \begin{cases} y_t^T & \text{if } I_t = 1 \\ y_t^T - L(y_t^T) & \text{otherwise.} \end{cases} \tag{13.65}$$

In any period t in which the country is in good financial standing and chooses to honor its debt $(I_t = 1)$, the domestic price of debt, q_t^d, must equal the price of debt offered by foreign lenders, q_t, that is,

$$I_t(q_t^d - q_t) = 0. \tag{13.66}$$

When the country is in bad financial standing ($I_t = 0$), the value of τ_t^d is immaterial. This is because in these periods, external debt is nil. Therefore without loss of generality, we set $\tau_t^d = 0$ when $I_t = 0$, that is,

$$(1 - I_t)\tau_t^d = 0. \tag{13.67}$$

Combining (13.58), (13.60), (13.61), (13.62), (13.63), (13.64), (13.65), and (13.66) yields the following market-clearing condition for traded goods:

$$c_t^T = y_t^T - (1 - I_t)L(y_t^T) + I_t[q_t d_{t+1} - d_t].$$

Finally, let

$$\epsilon_t \equiv \frac{\mathcal{E}_t}{\mathcal{E}_{t-1}}$$

denote the gross devaluation rate of the domestic currency. We are now ready to define a competitive equilibrium.

Definition 13.2 (Competitive Equilibrium) A competitive equilibrium is a set of stochastic processes $\{c_t^T, h_t, w_t, d_{t+1}, \lambda_t, q_t, q_t^d\}$ satisfying

$$c_t^T = y_t^T - (1 - I_t)L(y_t^T) + I_t[q_t d_{t+1} - d_t], \tag{13.68}$$

$$(1 - I_t)d_{t+1} = 0, \tag{13.69}$$

$$\lambda_t = U'(A(c_t^T, F(h_t)))A_1(c_t^T, F(h_t)), \tag{13.70}$$

$$(1 - \tau_t^d)q_t^d \lambda_t = \beta E_t \lambda_{t+1}, \tag{13.71}$$

$$I_t(q_t^d - q_t) = 0, \tag{13.72}$$

$$\frac{A_2(c_t^T, F(h_t))}{A_1(c_t^T, F(h_t))} = \frac{w_t}{F'(h_t)}, \tag{13.73}$$

$$w_t \geq \gamma \frac{w_{t-1}}{\epsilon_t}, \tag{13.74}$$

$$h_t \leq \bar{h}, \tag{13.75}$$

$$(h_t - \bar{h})\left(w_t - \gamma \frac{w_{t-1}}{\epsilon_t}\right) = 0, \tag{13.76}$$

and

$$I_t\left[q_t - \frac{E_t I_{t+1}}{1 + r^*}\right] = 0, \tag{13.77}$$

given processes $\{y_t^T, \epsilon_t, \tau_t^d, I_t\}$ and initial conditions w_{-1} and d_0.

When the government can choose freely ϵ_t and τ_t^d, the competitive equilibrium can be written in a more compact form, as stated in the following proposition.

Proposition 13.8 (Competitive Equilibrium When ϵ_t and τ_t^d Are Unrestricted) When the government can choose ϵ_t and τ_t^d freely, stochastic processes $\{c_t^T, h_t, d_{t+1}, q_t\}$ can be supported as a competitive equilibrium if and only if they satisfy (13.68), (13.69), (13.75), and (13.77), given processes $\{y_t^T, I_t\}$ and the initial condition d_0.

Proof The "only if" part of this proposition is trivial, since processes that satisfy the complete set of equilibrium conditions—that is, conditions (13.68)–(13.77)—must obviously satisfy a subset thereof. Establishing the "if" part of the proposition amounts to showing that if processes $\{c_t^T, h_t, d_{t+1}, q_t\}$ satisfy conditions (13.68), (13.69), (13.75), and (13.77), then they also satisfy the remaining conditions defining a competitive equilibrium, namely, conditions (13.70)–(13.74) and (13.76). To see this, pick λ_t to satisfy (13.70). When I_t equals one, set q_t^d to satisfy (13.72) and set τ_t^d to satisfy (13.71). When I_t equals zero, set $\tau_t^d = 0$ (recall convention (13.67)), and set q_t^d to satisfy (13.71). Set w_t to satisfy (13.73). Set ϵ_t to satisfy (13.74) with equality. This implies that the slackness condition (13.76) is also satisfied. This establishes proposition 13.8. ∎

13.12.3 Optimality of the Full-Employment Devaluation Policy

The benevolent government in this economy then chooses a set of processes $\{c_t^T, h_t, d_{t+1}, q_t, I_t\}$ that maximizes

$$E_0 \sum_{t=0}^{\infty} \beta^t U(A(c_t^T, F(h_t))), \tag{13.78}$$

subject to the compact version of the equilibrium conditions:

$$c_t^T = y_t^T - (1 - I_t)L(y_t^T) + I_t[q_t d_{t+1} - d_t], \tag{13.68 R}$$

$$(1 - I_t)d_{t+1} = 0, \tag{13.69 R}$$

$$h_t \leq \bar{h}, \tag{13.75 R}$$

and

$$I_t\left[q_t - \frac{E_t I_{t+1}}{1 + r^*}\right] = 0. \tag{13.77 R}$$

Notice that h_t enters only in the objective function (13.78) and the constraint (13.75). Because U, A, and F are all strictly increasing, the solution to the optimal policy problem clearly must feature full employment at all times: $h_t = \bar{h}$.

Once h_t is set at $\bar{h}$ for all t, the above optimization problem becomes identical to the canonical Eaton-Gersovitz model. This becomes evident if one rewrites the above optimization problem in recursive form, as we did in Section 13.8. We have therefore established that real models of sovereign default in the tradition of Eaton and Gersovitz (1981) can be interpreted as the centralized version of economies with default risk, downward nominal wage rigidity, optimal capital controls, and optimal devaluation policy. Unlike the family of real Eaton-Gersovitz models, however, the present model delivers precise predictions regarding the optimal behavior of the nominal devaluation rate. In particular, the present formulation allows us to answer the question of whether it is optimal to couple defaults with large devaluations—that is, whether the Twin Ds phenomenon emerges as an optimal outcome.

In Chapter 9 we showed that the optimal exchange-rate policy is indeed a family given by the devaluation rates satisfying $\epsilon_t \geq \gamma \frac{w_{t-1}}{\omega(c_t^T)}$, where $\omega(c_t^T)$ denotes the full-employment real wage, defined as

$$\omega(c_t^T) \equiv \frac{A_2(c_t^T, F(\bar{h}))}{A_1(c_t^T, F(\bar{h}))} F'(\bar{h}).$$

According to these expressions, under optimal policy the government must devalue in periods in which consumption of tradables experiences a sufficiently large contraction. To the extent that during contractions of this type the government finds it optimal to default, the current model predicts that devaluations and default happen together. From the family of optimal devaluation policies, we now select the one that stabilizes nominal wages, which are the source of nominal rigidity in the present model. Specifically, we assume a devaluation rule of the form

$$\epsilon_t = \frac{w_{t-1}}{\omega(c_t^T)}. \tag{13.79}$$

A property of this devaluation rule is that it fully stabilizes the nominal wage rate and guarantees price and exchange-rate stability in the long run (exercise 13.14 asks you to show this).

13.12.4 Default Dynamics under Optimal Devaluation Policy and Currency Pegs

We now explore quantitatively the dynamics of the model around defaults under two polar exchange-rate policies, the optimal policy and a currency peg. Where applicable, the parameterization of the model mimics that of the real Eaton-Gersovitz model presented in Section 13.6 (see Table 13.7). In particular, we set the parameters of the AR(1) process y_t^T equal to the corresponding parameters defining the process y_t. The present model, however, has a richer structure than the standard Eaton-Gersovitz model of Section 13.6, as it features an additional sector (the nontraded sector) and nominal rigidities. We parameterize these aspects of the model as in the model in Chapter 9 with nontradables and downward nominal wage rigidity. In particular, we assume that the aggregator function takes the CES form

$$A(c^T, c^N) = \left[a(c^T)^{1-\frac{1}{\xi}} + (1-a)(c^N)^{1-\frac{1}{\xi}} \right]^{\frac{1}{1-\frac{1}{\xi}}}$$

and that the production function of nontradables takes the isoelastic form $F(h_t) = h_t^\alpha$, with $\xi = 0.5$, $a = 0.26$, and $\alpha = 0.75$.

Because the intra- and intertemporal elasticity of consumption substitution, ξ and $1/\sigma$, respectively, are equal to each other, the equilibrium behavior of I_t, d_t, q_t, c_t^T, and

τ_t^d are the same as those implied by the real Eaton-Gersovitz model characterized in Sections 13.6 and 13.8.[17] This is because the optimal exchange-rate policy fully neutralizes the distortions introduced by downward nominal wage rigidity. Hours worked are always at the full employment level, $\bar{h}$, which we normalize to unity. Given these equilibrium processes, the wage rate, w_t, and the optimal devaluation rate, ϵ_t, can be readily obtained from equations (13.73) and (13.79), respectively.

Figure 13.16 displays (solid lines) the behavior of the model economy around a typical default episode under the optimal exchange-rate policy. The construction of the figure follows the methodology described in Section 13.6. As explained above, the dynamics of all variables but the devaluation rate and the real wage are as in the flexible-wage model (see Figures 13.9 and 13.12). The typical default event is accompanied by a large devaluation of the local currency of about 40 percent. The model thus captures the Twin Ds phenomenon identified by Reinhart (2002) and documented in Figure 13.14. The purpose of this devaluation is to inflate away the real value of wages, thereby facilitating employment in the nontraded sector. Indeed, Figure 13.16 shows that under the optimal exchange-rate policy the real wage falls sharply by about 40 percent around the default date. In this way, the monetary authority ensures that the external debt crisis does not spill over to the labor market.

It is of interest to compare the default dynamics under optimal devaluation policy with those resulting under a currency peg, because some of the observed debt crises have taken place in the context of fixed exchange rates (e.g., Greece in 2012 and Cyprus in 2013). Figure 13.16 displays (dashed lines) the predicted dynamics around the typical default episode under a currency peg. In this case, the monetary authority has its hands tied and is unable to inflate away the real value of wages through a devaluation. As a result, real wages remain high, and the debt crisis spreads to the labor market in the form of massive unemployment, which at the time of the default rises to almost 20 percent. This effect is reminiscent of the high levels of unemployment observed during the debt crisis in the periphery of the eurozone following the global contraction of 2008.

The inability of the pegging country to prevent external crises from spreading to the domestic labor market generates incentives for the government to boost the domestic absorption of consumption goods. One way to achieve this is to default and use resources that were previously allocated to servicing the external debt. It follows that in the model, peggers have additional incentives to default compared to countries following the optimal devaluation policy. Foreign lenders respond to this elevated incentive to default by reducing the supply of credit. Consequently the model predicts a much lower equilibrium level of debt under a peg. The unconditional mean of debt under a peg is 20 percent of traded output per quarter versus 60 percent under the optimal exchange-rate policy.

The present section establishes that the standard Eaton-Gersovitz model can be viewed as a decentralized economy in which households and firms transact in goods, services, and

---

17. One might wonder why the restriction $\xi = 1/\sigma$ is necessary to ensure the same quantitative behavior of the present model under optimal exchange-rate policy and the model of Section 13.6.4. The reason is that only under this restriction is the derivative of $U(A(c_t^T, F(\bar{h})))$ with respect to c_t^T proportional to the corresponding derivative of $U(c_t)$.

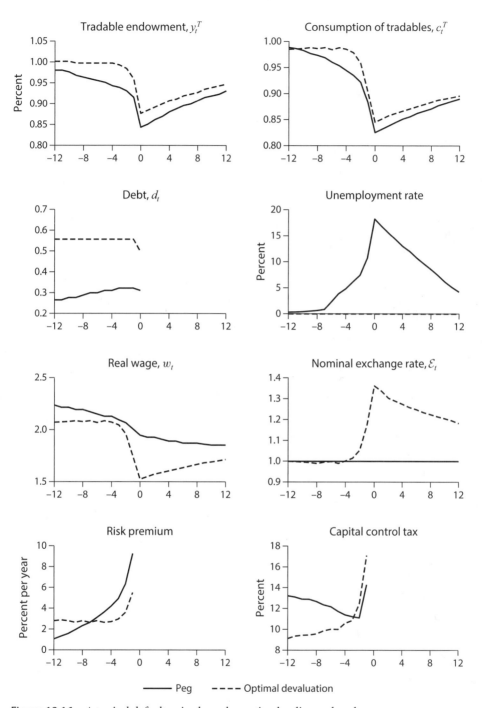

Figure 13.16   A typical default episode under optimal policy and under a peg.

Notes: Lines display medians of 25-quarter windows centered on default episodes occurring in an artificial time series of 1 million quarters. The default date is normalized to 0.

credit markets and in which prices suffer from nominal rigidity. This way of viewing the Eaton-Gersovitz model allows one to think about the joint properties of optimal default and optimal exchange-rate policy. In this regard, the section presents a model in which both default and large devaluations occur in tandem under optimal policy, which explains the Twin Ds regularity observed in the data. The approach of this section also allows for the analysis of default dynamics when the monetary authority follows suboptimal policy. In particular, the results of the section establish that under a currency peg, optimal defaults are accompanied by large levels of involuntary unemployment, as observed in the periphery of the eurozone in the wake of the global contraction of 2008.

13.13 Appendix: Sovereign Default Dates, 1975–2014

Default dates for the period 1975 to 2006 are from Beers and Chambers (2006). Default dates after 2006 are from Beers and Nadeau (2014), based on information on sovereign default on foreign currency bank loans, foreign currency bonds, or local currency debt. If Beers and Chambers (2006) list a country in default in 2006 (the last observation in that study), then Beers and Nadeau (2014) is consulted to establish the date the country emerged from default. Additional default date information is obtained from Chambers and Gurwitz (2014) and from Tudela et al. (2014).

Table 13.19 Sovereign Default Episodes, 1975–2014

Country	Start of Default	End of Default	Data Source
Albania	1991	1995	BC, table 7
Algeria	1991	1996	BC, table 7
Angola	1976	1976	BC, table 4
Angola	1985	2003	BC, table 7
Antigua and Barbuda	1996	2011	BC, table 7; BN
Argentina	1982	1993	BC, table 6
Argentina	2001	2005	BC, table 6
Belize	2006	2007	CG, table 2
Belize	2012	2013	CG, table 2
Bolivia	1980	1984	BC, table 6
Bolivia	1986	1997	BC, table 6
Bosnia and Herzegovina	1992	1997	BC, table 7
Brazil	1983	1994	BC, table 6
Bulgaria	1990	1994	BC, table 6
Burkina Faso	1983	1996	BC, table 6
Cameroon	1985	2004	BC, table 4
Cape Verde	1981	1996	BC, table 7
Central African Republic	1981	1981	BC, table 7

a. Most recent available observation (not necessarily emerged from default).
Sources: BC, Beers and Chambers (2006); BN, Beers and Nadeau (2014); CG, Chambers and Gurwitz (2014); TDMOVP, Tudela et al. (2014).

Table 13.19 *(continued)*

Country	Start of Default	End of Default	Data Source
Central African Republic	1983	2012 [a]	BC, table 7; BN
Chile	1983	1990	BC, table 6
Congo, Democratic Republic	1976	2010	BC, table 7; BN
Congo, Republic	1983	2012 [a]	BC, table 7; BN
Costa Rica	1981	1990	BC, table 4
Côte d'Ivoire	1983	1998	BC, table 7
Côte d'Ivoire	2000	2013 [a]	BC, table 7; BN
Croatia	1992	1996	BC, table 6
Cuba	1982	2013 [a]	BC, table 7; BN
Cyprus	2013	2013	CG, table 2
Dominica	2003	2005	BC, table 7
Dominican Republic	1975	2001	BC, table 4
Dominican Republic	2005	2005	CG, table 2
Ecuador	1982	1995	BC, table 6
Ecuador	1999	2000	BC, table 6
Ecuador	2008	2009	CG, table 2
El Salvador	1981	1996	BC, table 4
Ethiopia	1991	1999	BC, table 7
Gabon	1986	1994	BC, table 7
Gabon	1999	2005	BC, table 7
Gambia	1986	1990	BC, table 7
Ghana	1979	1979	BC, table 4
Ghana	1982	1982	BC, table 4
Ghana	1987	1987	BC, table 6
Greece	2012	2012	CG, table 2
Grenada	2004	2005	CG, table 2
Grenada	2012	2012	CG, table 2
Grenada	2013	2014 [a]	CG, table 2
Guatemala	1986	1986	BC, table 4
Guatemala	1989	1989	BC, table 6
Guinea	1986	1988	BC, table 7
Guinea	1991	1998	BC, table 7
Guinea-Bissau	1983	1996	BC, table 7
Guyana	1979	1979	BC, table 7
Guyana	1982	2006	BC, table 7
Haiti	1982	1994	BC, table 7
Honduras	1981	2006	BC, table 7; BN
Indonesia	1999	2000	CG, table 2
Indonesia	2002	2002	CG, table 2
Iran	1978	1995	BC, table 7
Iraq	1987	2006	BC, table 7; BN
Jamaica	1978	1979	BC, table 6
Jamaica	1981	1985	BC, table 6
Jamaica	1987	1993	BC, table 6
Jamaica	2010	2010	CG, table 2

a. Most recent available observation (not necessarily emerged from default).
Sources: BC, Beers and Chambers (2006); BN, Beers and Nadeau (2014); CG, Chambers and Gurwitz (2014); TDMOVP, Tudela et al. (2014).

Table 13.19 *(continued)*

Country	Start of Default	End of Default	Data Source
Jamaica	2013	2013	CG, table 2
Jordan	1989	1993	BC, table 6
Kenya	1994	1998	BC, table 4
Kenya	2000	2000	BC, table 4
Kuwait	1990	1991	BC, table 4
Liberia	1981	2010	BC, table 7; BN
Macedonia	1992	1997	BC, table 6
Madagascar	1981	2002	BC, table 6
Malawi	1982	1982	BC, table 7
Malawi	1988	1988	BC, table 7
Mali	2012	2012 [a]	CG, table 2
Mauritania	1992	1996	BC, table 7
Mexico	1982	1990	BC, table 6
Moldova	1998	1998	BC, table 7
Moldova	2002	2002	BC, table 7
Mongolia	1997	2000	BC, table 4
Morocco	1983	1983	BC, table 6
Morocco	1986	1990	BC, table 6
Mozambique	1980	1980	BC, table 6
Mozambique	1983	1992	BC, table 6
Myanmar	1984	1984	BC, table 5
Myanmar	1987	1987	BC, table 5
Myanmar	1997	2012 [a]	BC, table 7; BN
Nicaragua	1979	2008	BC, table 7; BN
Niger	1983	1991	BC, table 7
Nigeria	1982	1992	BC, table 6
Nigeria	2001	2001	BC, table 6
Nigeria	2004	2005	BC, table 6
Pakistan	1999	1999	CG, table 2
Panama	1983	1996	BC, table 6
Paraguay	1986	1992	BC, table 6
Paraguay	2003	2004	CG, table 2
Peru	1978	1978	BC, table 6
Peru	1980	1980	BC, table 6
Peru	1983	1997	BC, table 4
Philippines	1983	1992	BC, table 6
Poland	1981	1994	BC, table 6
Romania	1981	1983	BC, table 6
Romania	1986	1986	BC, table 6
Russian Federation	1991	1997	BC, table 6
Russian Federation	1998	2000	BC, table 6
Rwanda	1995	1995	BC, table 5
São Tomé and Príncipe	1987	1994	BC, table 7
Senegal	1981	1985	BC, table 6

a. Most recent available observation (not necessarily emerged from default).
Sources: BC, Beers and Chambers (2006); BN, Beers and Nadeau (2014); CG, Chambers and Gurwitz (2014); TDMOVP, Tudela et al. (2014).

Table 13.19 *(continued)*

Country	Start of Default	End of Default	Data Source
Senegal	1990	1990	BC, table 6
Senegal	1992	1996	BC, table 6
Serbia	1992	2004	BC, table 6
Seychelles	2000	2002	BC, table 6
Seychelles	2008	2009	CG, table 2; BN
Sierra Leone	1983	1984	BC, table 7
Sierra Leone	1986	1995	BC, table 7
Sierra Leone	1997	1998	BC, table 5
Slovenia	1992	1996	BC, table 6
Solomon Islands	1995	2011	BC, table 5; BN
South Africa	1985	1987	BC, table 6
South Africa	1989	1989	BC, table 6
South Africa	1993	1993	BC, table 6
South Korea	1974	2013[a]	BC, table 7; BN
South Sudan	1979	2013[a]	BC, table 7; BN
St. Kitts and Nevis	2011	2013[a]	TDMOVP
Suriname	2000	2002	BC, table 4
Tanzania	1984	2004	BC, table 7
Togo	1979	1980	BC, table 7
Togo	1982	1984	BC, table 7
Togo	1988	1988	BC, table 7
Togo	1991	1997	BC, table 7
Trinidad and Tobago	1988	1989	BC, table 6
Turkey	1978	1979	BC, table 6
Turkey	1982	1982	BC, table 6
Uganda	1980	1993	BC, table 7
Ukraine	1998	2000	BC, table 6
Uruguay	1983	1985	BC, table 6
Uruguay	1987	1987	BC, table 6
Uruguay	1990	1991	BC, table 6
Uruguay	2003	2003	CG, table 2
Venezuela	1983	1988	BC, table 6
Venezuela	1990	1990	BC, table 6
Venezuela	1995	1998	BC, table 4
Venezuela	2005	2005	CG, table 2
Vietnam	1975	1975	BC, table 4
Vietnam	1985	1998	BC, table 6
Yemen	1985	2001	BC, table 7
Zambia	1983	1994	BC, table 7
Zimbabwe	1965	1980	BC, table 7
Zimbabwe	2000	2012[a]	BC, table 7; BN

a. Most recent available observation (not necessarily emerged from default).
Sources: BC, Beers and Chambers (2006); BN, Beers and Nadeau (2014); CG, Chambers and Gurwitz (2014); TDMOVP, Tudela et al. (2014).

13.14 Exercises

13.1 (Default Clusters) Sturzenegger and Zettelmeyer (2006) argue that default episodes tend to happen in clusters. Devise an empirical strategy and use the information provided in Table 13.19 to ascertain whether the data provided there supports or contradicts their finding.

13.2 (Capital-to-Output Ratio Around Defaults) Figure 13.5 shows that the capital-to-output ratio in Argentina peaked in the run-up to the defaults of 1982 and 2001 and fell significantly thereafter. This exercise aims at establishing whether this finding holds more generally.

1. Use the World Development Indicators database to download data on real GDP per capita and real gross capital formation per capita (i.e., investment). The primary series to use here are GDP per capita in constant local currency units (NY.GDP.PCAP.KN) and gross capital formation in percentage of GDP (NE.GDI.TOTL.ZS). Let Y_{it} and I_{it} denote, respectively, real per capita output and real per capita investment in country i in year t.

2. For each country, compute the average growth rate of real per capita output, denoted by g_i (i.e., $g_i = 0.02$ means 2 percent).

3. Assume that the capital stock in country i evolves according to

$$K_{it+1} = (1 - \delta)K_{it} + I_{it}, \tag{13.80}$$

   where δ denotes the depreciation rate, which is assumed to be the same in all countries. Use this expression to construct a time series for capital. Set $\delta = 0.1$ (or 10 percent). You need an initial value for the capital stock, K_{i1}. Assume that $K_{i2} = (1 + g_i)K_{i1}$, that is, assume that between periods 1 and 2, the capital stock grew at the average growth rate of the economy. Use this assumption, equation (13.80), and I_{i1} to obtain K_{i1}.

4. Now use K_{i1}, the time series I_{it}, and iterations on equation (13.80) to derive a time series for K_{it}.

5. For each country i, use the time series for capital, K_{it}, and output, Y_{it}, to construct a time series for the capital-to-output ratio, K_{it}/Y_{it}.

6. Combine the data on the capital-to-output ratio with the data on default dates from Table 13.19 to produce a figure (in the spirit of Figure 13.2) displaying the typical behavior of the (demeaned) capital-to-output ratio around default episodes.

7. Discuss to what extent the behavior of the capital-to-output ratio pre- and postdefault in Argentina is representative of what happens during the typical default episode.

13.3 (No Excessive Punishment) In Section 13.3.3 we studied an environment in which creditors seize k units of goods from delinquent debtors. This threat could be viewed as excessive punishment in some states, because it implies that creditors will take away k

units of goods even if the size of the defaulted debt is smaller than k. A more compelling assumption is that the punishment takes the form $\min\{k, d(\epsilon)\}$, where $k \in (0, \epsilon^H)$, and $d(\epsilon)$ denotes the debt obligation in state ϵ. Show that the analysis of Section 13.3.3 goes through under this assumption.

13.4 (Proportional Sanctions) In the model with direct sanctions of Section 13.3.3, replace the assumption of a constant sanction k with the assumption of a proportional sanction $k(\epsilon) \equiv \alpha(\bar{y} + \epsilon)$. Characterize the optimal debt contract. How does it compare with the case of constant sanctions?

13.5 (Moral Sanctions) Consider another variant of the model with direct sanctions of Section 13.3.3. Suppose that direct sanctions are not possible, that is, $k = 0$. Instead, assume that defaulting countries experience a self-inflicted moral punishment. Specifically, assume that the utility of the country that defaults in state ϵ is given by $u(y + \epsilon) - m$, where $m > 0$ is a parameter defining the severity of the moral punishment.

1. Write the incentive-compatibility constraint.
2. Characterize the optimal debt contract $d(\epsilon)$, and compare it to the one corresponding to the case of direct sanctions.

13.6 (State-Contingent Sanctions) Consider a one-period economy facing a stochastic endowment given by $y = \bar{y} + \epsilon$, where $\bar{y} > 0$ is a constant, and ϵ is a mean-zero random variable with density $\pi(\epsilon)$ defined over the interval $[\epsilon^L, \epsilon^H]$. Before ϵ is realized the country can buy state-contingent contracts, $d(\epsilon)$, from foreign investors who are risk neutral and who face an opportunity cost of funds of zero. The participation constraint for foreign lenders is $\int_{\epsilon_L}^{\epsilon^H} d(\epsilon)\pi(\epsilon)d\epsilon = 0$. The country cannot commit to repay. In case of default, foreign creditors impose state-contingent sanctions, $k(\epsilon)$. Assume that $k(\epsilon) = \max\{0, \epsilon - \alpha\}$ and that $0 \le \alpha < \epsilon^H$. The objective of the country is to pick the debt contract optimally. Welfare of the representative household is given by $\int_{\epsilon_L}^{\epsilon^H} u(c(\epsilon))\pi(\epsilon)d\epsilon$, where $c(\epsilon)$ denotes consumption, and $u(\cdot)$ is a strictly increasing and strictly concave function. The budget constraint of the household, conditional on honoring its debt, is $c(\epsilon) = \bar{y} + \epsilon - d(\epsilon)$.

1. Explain in words the difference between the type of sanctions described above and constant sanctions, $k(\epsilon) = k > 0$, with $0 < k < \epsilon^H$. Which specification can potentially provide more insurance, and why?
2. Assume that $\alpha = 0$. Find the optimal debt contract, $d(\epsilon)$. Find the contingent plan for consumption, $c(\epsilon)$. Provide an intuitive explanation for your findings.
3. For the remainder of this problem assume that $\alpha > 0$. Characterize the optimal debt contract, $d(\epsilon)$, and provide a verbal discussion of its properties. Proceed as follows. Find the incentive compatibility constraint. State the maximization problem that the country solves to find the optimal debt contract. State the Lagrangian of the problem. State the optimality conditions. Then characterize the optimal debt contract.

4. Characterize the optimal consumption plan, $c(\epsilon)$, and provide an intuitive interpretation of your findings.

5. Compare and contrast your findings to the case of a constant and positive sanction, $k = \alpha$. Which specification of sanctions provides more insurance, and why?

13.7 (Nonzero Opportunity Cost of Lending) Consider yet another variant of the model with direct sanctions of Section 13.3.3. Suppose that the opportunity cost of funds of foreign lenders is not zero but positive and equal to the constant, r. Suppose first that the borrowing country does not have the option of not writing a debt contract with foreign lenders.

1. What restrictions on k and r do you need to impose to guarantee the existence of a nonautarkic equilibrium?

2. Write the participation constraint.

3. Characterize the optimal debt contract, $d(\epsilon)$, and compare it to the one corresponding to the case of zero opportunity costs.

4. How do the answers to questions 2 and 3 change if the borrowing country is assumed to have the option of not writing a contract with foreign lenders?

13.8 (Reputation, Complete Asset Markets, and Reentry) Extend the reputational model of Section 13.3.4 by allowing for the possibility of regaining access to international capital markets after default. Specifically, assume that with constant probability $\delta \in (0, 1)$ defaulters can reenter capital markets the next period.

1. Derive the value function of a country in bad financial standing, $v^b(\epsilon)$, as a function of current and future expected values of $u(\bar{y} + \epsilon)$ and $u(\bar{y} + \epsilon - d(\epsilon))$ only.

2. Write down the incentive-compatibility constraint.

3. Write down the optimization problem of the country and its associated Lagrangian.

4. Derive the optimality conditions of the country's problem.

5. Show that all results of Section 13.3.4 pertaining to the reputation model hold under this extension.

6. It is intuitively obvious that if $\delta = 1$, lending breaks down, since in this case lenders have no way to punish delinquent debtors. Show this result formally.

13.9 (The Current Account in the Eaton-Gersovitz Model) Show that in the default model of Section 13.4, the current account, denoted by ca, can be written as $ca = q(d)d - q(d')d'$.

13.10 (Default Risk and Trade Balance Surpluses with Correlated Shocks) Show that proposition 13.1 holds when the endowment process is assumed to be serially correlated.

13.11 (Breakdown of Reputational Lending) Consider a perfect-foresight endowment economy in which an equilibrium sequence of net external debt $\{d_t\}_{t=-1}^{\infty}$ is supported on reputational grounds when saving in international markets is not allowed after default. Suppose that this sequence contains no maximal element but has a positive least upper bound, $\bar{d}$. Show that the reputational equilibrium with debt breaks down if the country is allowed to save in international financial markets after default.

13.12 (Proportional Output Loss Function) Modify the Eaton-Gersovitz model of Section 13.6.4 to allow for a proportional output loss function of the form $L(y) = a_1 y$. Calibrate a_1 to match an average output loss due to default of about 7 percent of output per period conditional on the country being in bad financial standing. Use appropriately modified versions of the Matlab scripts `eg.m` and `simu.m`, or write your own code, to produce quantitative predictions of the model along the lines of Tables 13.8 and 13.9 and Figure 13.9. Discuss your findings, paying particular attention to how the present output loss specification affects the model's ability to predict that countries default in bad times.

13.13 (Duration in the Random-Maturity Model) Consider the sovereign debt model with random maturity studied in Section 13.10.1.

1. Compute the duration of the current portfolio of debt.
2. Compute the duration of a single bond in the current portfolio of debt.

13.14 (Optimality of Wage Stability) Show that the devaluation rule given in equation (13.79) is optimal, that it implies a constant nominal wage rate at all times, and that it induces nontrending paths for the nominal exchange rate, the nominal price of nontradables, and the consumer price level.

13.15 (Eaton-Gersovitz Model As Special Case of Debt-Renegotiation Model) Consider the debt-renegotiation model of Section 13.11. Investigate analytically whether for $\alpha = 1$, the equilibrium dynamics collapse to those of the standard Eaton-Gersovitz model studied in Section 13.6.

13.16 (Recalibration of the Debt-Renegotiation Model) In the model of debt renegotiation studied in Section 13.11, calibrate the parameters β, a_1, a_2, and α to match a quarterly debt-to-output ratio of 60 percent in periods of good financial standing, a default frequency of 2.6 times per century, an average output cost of 7 percent per period conditional on being in bad standing, and an average haircut of 40 percent. Discuss the differences with the calibration used in Section 13.11.2, with emphasis on the parameters β and α. Use the Matlab scripts `egr.m`, `simur.m`, and `statistics_modelr.m` (or your own code) to produce tables and graphs like those presented in Section 13.11.2. Discuss your findings.

References

Abel, Andrew, "Asset Prices under Habit Formation and Catching Up with the Joneses," *American Economic Review* 80, 1990, 38–42.

Agca, Senay, and Oya Celasun, "Sovereign Debt and Corporate Borrowing Costs in Emerging Markets," *Journal of International Economics* 88, 2012, 198–208.

Aguiar, Mark, and Gita Gopinath, "Defaultable Debt, Interest Rates and the Current Account," *Journal of International Economics* 69, 2006, 64–83.

——, "Emerging Market Business Cycles: The Cycle is the Trend," *Journal of Political Economy* 115, 2007, 69–102.

Aguirre, Ezequiel, "Business Cycles in Emerging Markets and Implications for the Real Exchange Rate," Ph.D. dissertation, Columbia University, New York, 2011.

Akinci, Özge, "A Note on the Estimation of the Atemporal Elasticity of Substitution between Tradable and Nontradable Goods," manuscript, Columbia University, New York, February 2, 2011.

——, "Global Financial Conditions, Country Spreads, and Macroeconomic Fluctuations in Emerging Countries," *Journal of International Economics* 91, 2013, 358–371.

Arellano, Cristina, "Default Risk and Income Fluctuations in Emerging Economies," *American Economic Review* 98, 2008, 690–712.

Arellano, Cristina, and Ananth Ramanarayanan, "Default and the Maturity Structure in Sovereign Bonds," *Journal of Political Economy* 120, 2012, 187–232.

Armington, Paul, "A Theory of Demand for Products Distinguished by Place of Production," *International Monetary Fund Staff Papers* 16, January 1969, 159–176.

Auernheimer, L., and R. García-Saltos, "International Debt and the Price of Domestic Assets," IMF Working Paper wp/00/177, October 2000.

Barattieri, Alessandro, Susanto Basu, and Peter Gottschalk, "Some Evidence on the Importance of Sticky Wages," *American Economic Journal: Macroeconomics* 6, January 2014, 70–101.

Beers, David T., and John Chambers, "Default Study: Sovereign Defaults at 26-Year Low, to Show Little Change in 2007," Global Credit Portal, RatingsDirect, Standard & Poor's, September 18, 2006.

Beers, David T., and Jean-Sébastien Nadeau, "Introducing a New Database of Sovereign Defaults," Technical Report 101, Bank of Canada, Ottawa, February 2014.

Benigno, Gianluca, Huigang Chen, Christopher Otrok, Alessandro Rebucci, and Eric R. Young, "Financial Crises and Macro-Prudential Policies," *Journal of International Economics* 89, 2013, 453–470.

———, "Optimal Capital Controls and Real Exchange Rate Policies: A Pecuniary Externality Perspective," CEPR Discussion Paper 9936, Center for Economic and Policy Research, Washington, DC, April 2014.

Benjamin, David, and Mark L. J. Wright, "Recovery before Redemption: A Theory of Delays in Sovereign Debt Renegotiations," working paper, University of California, Los Angeles, 2013.

Bi, Ran, "Debt Dilution and Maturity Structure of Sovereign Bonds," manuscript, University of Maryland, College Park, February 2006.

———, "Beneficial Delays in Debt Restructuring Negotiations," manuscript, University of Maryland, College Park, 2008.

Bianchi, Javier, "Overborrowing and Systemic Externalities in the Business Cycle," *American Economic Review* 101, 2011, 3400–3426.

Bianchi, Javier, and Enrique G. Mendoza, "Optimal Time-Consistent Macroprudential Policy," NBER Working Paper 19704, National Bureau of Economic Research, Cambridge, MA, December 2013.

Blanchard, Olivier, "Debt, Deficits, and Finite Horizons," *Journal of Political Economy* 93, 1985, 223–247.

Blanchard, Olivier J., Jean-Paul L'Huillier, and Guido Lorenzoni, "News, Noise, and Fluctuations: An Empirical Exploration," *American Economic Review* 103, 2013, 3045–3070.

Blundell, Richard, and Thomas H. MaCurdy, "Labor Supply: A Review of Alternative Approaches," in O. Ashenfelter and D. Card (eds.), *Handbook of Labor Economics*, Vol. 3, Amsterdam: North-Holland, 1999, 1559–1695.

Boldrin, Michele, Lawrence J. Christiano, and Jonas Fisher, "Asset Pricing Lessons for Modeling Business Cycles," *American Economic Review* 91, 2001, 149–166.

Borensztein, Eduardo, and Ugo Panizza, "The Costs of Sovereign Default," *IMF Staff Papers* 56, 2009, 683–741.

Borensztein, Eduardo, Kevin Cowan, and Patricio Valenzuela, "Sovereign Ceilings 'Lite'? The Impact of Sovereign Ratings on Corporate Ratings," *Journal of Banking and Finance* 37, 2013, 4014–4024.

Boz, Emine, Christian Daude, and Bora Durdu, "Emerging Market Business Cycles: Learning about the Trend," *Journal of Monetary Economics* 58, 2011, 616–631.

Broda, Christian, "Terms of Trade and Exchange Rate Regimes in Developing Countries," *Journal of International Economics* 63, 2004, 31–58.

Broner, Fernando A., Guido Lorenzoni, and Sergio L. Schmukler, "Why Do Emerging Economies Borrow Short Term?" *Journal of the European Economic Association* 11(S1), 2013, 67–100.

Bulow, Jeremy, and Kenneth Rogoff, "A Constant Recontracting Model of Sovereign Debt," *Journal of Political Economy* 97, 1989a, 155–178.

———, "Sovereign Debt: Is to Forgive to Forget?" *American Economic Review* 79, 1989b, 43–50.

Burstein, Ariel, Martin Eichenbaum, and Sergio Rebelo, "Large Devaluations and the Real Exchange Rate," *Journal of Political Economy* 113, 2005, 742–784.

Calderón, César, and Rodrigo Fuentes, "Characterizing the Business Cycles of Emerging Economies," Policy Research Working Paper 5343, World Bank, Washington, DC, June 2010.

Calvo, Guillermo A., "Staggered Prices in a Utility-Maximizing Framework," *Journal of Monetary Economics* 12, 1983, 383–398.

———, "Temporary Stabilization: Predetermined Exchange Rates," *Journal of Political Economy* 94, 1986, 1319–1329.

———, "Balance of Payments Crises in a Cash-in-Advance Economy," *Journal of Money, Credit and Banking* 19, 1987a, 19–32.

———, "On the Costs of Temporary Policy," *Journal of Development Economics* 27, 1987b, 245–261.

Calvo, Guillermo A., and Carlos Végh, "Exchange Rate Based Stabilization under Imperfect Credibility," in H. Frisch and A. Worgotter (eds.), *Open Economy Macroeconomics,* London: Macmillan, 1993, 3–28.

———, "Credibility and the Dynamics of Stabilization Policy: A Basic Framework," in Christopher A. Sims (ed.), *Advances in Econometrics,* Sixth World Congress, Cambridge: Cambridge University Press, 1994, 377–420.

Campbell, John Y., "Does Saving Anticipate Declining Labor Income? An Alternative Test of the Permanent Income Hypothesis," *Econometrica* 55, 1987, 1249–1273.

Cardia, Emanuela, "The Dynamics of a Small Open Economy in Response to Monetary, Fiscal, and Productivity Shocks," *Journal of Monetary Economics* 28, 1991, 411–434.

Chambers, John, and Zev Gurwitz, "Default Study: Sovereign Defaults and Rating Transition Data, 2013 Update," RatingsDirect, Standard & Poor's, April 18, 2014.

Chang, Roberto, and Andrés Fernández, "On the Sources of Aggregate Fluctuations in Emerging Economies," *International Economic Review* 54, 2013, 1265–1293.

Chatterjee, Satyajit, and Burcu Eyigungor, "Maturity, Indebtedness, and Default Risk," *American Economic Review* 102, 2012, 2674–2699.

Chuhan, P., and F. Sturzenegger, "Default Episodes in the 1980s and 1990s: What Have We Learned?" manuscript, Universidad Torcuato Di Tella, Buenos Aires, Argentina, November 24, 2003.

Cline, William R., *International Debt Reexamined*, Washington, DC: Institute for International Finance, 1995.

Cline, William R., and Kevin S. Barnes, "Spreads and Risk in Emerging Market Lending," Research Paper 97-1, Institute for International Finance, Washington, DC, 1997.

Clower, Robert W., "A Reconsideration of the Microfoundations of Money," *Western Economic Journal* 6, 1967, 1–9.

Cole, Harold L., and Timothy J. Kehoe, "A Self-Fulfilling Model of Mexico's 1994–1995 Debt Crisis," *Journal of International Economics* 41, 1996, 309–330.

Constantinides, George M., "Habit Persistence: A Resolution of the Equity Premium Puzzle," *Journal of Political Economy* 1990, 98, 519–543.

Corsetti, Giancarlo, Luca Dedola, and Sylvain Leduc, "International Risk Sharing and the Transmission of Productivity Shocks," *Review of Economic Studies* 75, 2008, 443–473.

Cruces, Juan J., and Christoph Trebesch, "Sovereign Defaults: The Price of Haircuts," *American Economic Journal: Macroeconomics* 5, 2013, 85–117.

Daly, Mary, Bart Hobijn, and Brian Lucking, "Why Has Wage Growth Stayed Strong?" *FRBSF Economic Letter* 2012-10, April 2012, 1–5.

De Paoli, Bianca, Glenn Hoggarth, and Victoria Saporta, "Chapter 8: Output Costs of Sovereign Default," in Robert W. Kolb (ed.), *Sovereign Debt: From Safety to Default,* Hoboken, NJ: John Wiley & Sons, 2011, 23–31.

D'Erasmo, Pablo, "Government Reputation and Debt Repayment in Emerging Economies," manuscript, University of Texas, Austin, 2011.

Devereux, Michael B., Eric R. Young, and Changhua Yu, "A New Dilemma: Capital Controls and Monetary Policy in Sudden Stop Economies," NBER Working Paper 21791, National Bureau of Economic Research, Cambridge, MA, December 2015.

Dornbusch, Rüdiger, "Expectations and Exchange Rate Dynamics," *Journal of Political Economy* 84, 1976, 1161–1176.

Durdu, Bora, Ricardo Nunes, and Horacio Sapriza, "News and Sovereign Default Risk in Small Open Economies," *Journal of International Economics* 91, September 2013, 1–17.

Eaton, J., and R. Fernández, "Sovereign Debt," in G. Grossman and K. Rogoff (eds.), *Handbook of International Economics III*, Amsterdam: Elsevier Science, 1995, 2031–2077.

Eaton, Jonathan, and Mark Gersovitz, "Debt with Potential Repudiation: Theoretical and Empirical Analysis," *Review of Economic Studies* 48, 1981, 289–309.

Edwards, Sebastian, "LDC Foreign Borrowing and Default Risk: An Empirical Investigation," *American Economic Review* 74, 1984, 726–734.

Eichengreen, Barry, and Ashoka Mody, "What Explains Changing Spreads on Emerging-Market Debt: Fundamentals or Market Sentiment?" NBER Working Paper 6408, National Bureau of Economic Research, Cambridge, MA, February 1998.

Eichengreen, Barry, and Jeffrey Sachs, "Exchange Rates and Economic Recovery in the 1930s," *Journal of Economic History* 45, 1985, 925–946.

Eichengreen, Barry, Ricardo Hausmann, and Hugo Panizza, "The Pain of Original Sin," in Barry Eichengreen and Ricardo Hausmann (eds.), *Other People's Money: Debt Denomination and Financial Instability in Emerging Market Economies,* Chicago: University of Chicago Press, 2005, 13–47.

Engel, Charles, and John H. Rogers, "How Wide Is the Border?" *American Economic Review* 86, 1996, 1112–1125.

Erceg, Christopher J., and Andrew T. Levin, "Imperfect Credibility and Inflation Persistence," *Journal of Monetary Economics* 50, 2003, 915–944.

Erceg, Christopher J., Dale W. Henderson, and Andrew T. Levin, "Optimal Monetary Policy with Staggered Wage and Price Contracts," *Journal of Monetary Economics* 46, 2000, 281–314.

Farhi, Emmanuel, and Ivan Werning, "Dealing with the Trilemma: Optimal Capital Controls with Fixed Exchange Rates," manuscript, MIT, Cambridge, MA, June 2012.

Farhi, Emmanuel, Gita Gopinath, and Oleg Itskhoki, "Fiscal Devaluations," *Review of Economic Studies* 81, 2014, 725–760.

Fehr, Ernst, and Lorenz Goette, "Robustness and Real Consequences of Nominal Wage Rigidity," *Journal of Monetary Economics* 52, 2005, 779–804.

Fernández, Andrés, Andrés González, and Diego Rodríguez, "Sharing a Ride on the Commodities Roller Coaster: Common Factors in Business Cycles of Emerging Economies," mimeo, Inter-American Development Bank, Washington, DC, March 2015.

Fernández, Andrés, Alessandro Rebucci, and Martín Uribe, "Are Capital Controls Countercyclical?" *Journal of Monetary Economics* 76, 2015, 1–14.

Fernández, Andrés, Stephanie Schmitt-Grohé, and Martín Uribe, "World Shocks, World Prices, and Business Cycles: An Empirical Investigation," *Journal of International Economics,* forthcoming.

Fernández-Villaverde, Jesús, Pablo Guerrón-Quintana, Juan Rubio-Ramírez, and Martín Uribe, "Risk Matters: The Real Effects of Volatility Shocks," *American Economic Review* 101, 2011, 2530–2561.

Ferri, Giovanni, and Li-Gang Liu, "How Do Global Credit-Rating Agencies Rate Firms from Developing Countries?" *Asian Economic Papers* 2, September 2003, 30–56.

Fisher, Irving, "The Debt-Deflation Theory of Great Depressions," *Econometrica* 1, 1933, 337–357.

Fons, Jerome, Richard Cantor, and Christopher Mahoney, "Understanding Moody's Corporate Bond Ratings and Rating Process," Rating Policy, Global Credit Research, Moody's Investors Service, New York, May 2002.

Fortin, Pierre, "The Great Canadian Slump," *Canadian Journal of Economics* 29, 1996, 761–787.

Frankel, Jeffrey, "Monetary Policy in Emerging Markets," in Benjamin M. Friedman and Michael Woodford (eds.), *Handbook of Monetary Economics,* Vol. 3B, Amsterdam: North-Holland, 2011, 1439–1520.

Friedman, Milton, "The Case for Flexible Exchange Rates," in Milton Friedman (ed.), *Essays in Positive Economics,* Chicago: University of Chicago Press, 1953, 157–203.

Friedman, Milton, and Anna Schwartz, *A Monetary History of the United States, 1867–1960,* Princeton, NJ: Princeton University Press, 1963.

Gagnon, Étienne, "Price Setting during Low and High Inflation: Evidence from Mexico," *Quarterly Journal of Economics* 124, 2009, 1221–1263.

García-Cicco, Javier, Roberto Pancrazi, and Martín Uribe, "Real Business Cycles in Emerging Countries?" *American Economic Review* 100, 2010, 2510–2531.

Gelos, R. Gaston, Ratna Sahay, and Guido Sandleris, "Sovereign Borrowing by Developing Countries: What Determines Market Access?" *Journal of International Economics* 83, 2011, 243–254.

Gertler, Mark, Christopher Huckfeldt, and Antonella Trigari, "Unemployment Fluctuations, Match Quality, and the Wage Cyclicality of New Hires," NBER Working Paper 22341, National Bureau of Economic Research, Cambridge, MA, June 2016.

González Rozada, Martín, Pablo Andrés Neumeyer, Alejandra Clemente, Diego Luciano Sasson, and Nicholas Trachter, "The Elasticity of Substitution in Demand for Non-tradable Goods in Latin America: The Case of Argentina," IDB Research Network Working Paper R-485, Inter-American Development Bank, Washington, DC, August 2004.

Gottschalk, Peter, "Downward Nominal-Wage Flexibility: Real or Measurement Error?" *Review of Economics and Statistics* 87, 2005, 556–568.

Greenwood, Jeremy, Zvi Hercowitz, and Gregory Huffman, "Investment, Capacity Utilization, and the Real Business Cycle," *American Economic Review* 78, 1988, 402–417.

Grossman, Herschel I., and John B. Van Huyck, "Sovereign Debt as a Contingent Claim: Excusable Default, Repudiation, and Reputation," *American Economic Review* 78, 1988, 1088–1097.

Guimaraes, Bernardo, "Sovereign Default: Which Shocks Matter?" *Review of Economic Dynamics* 14, 2011, 553–576.

Gust, Christopher, Sylvain Leduc, and Nathan Sheets, "The Adjustment of Global External Balances: Does Partial Exchange-Rate Pass-Through to Trade Prices Matter?" *Journal of International Economics* 79, 2009, 173–185.

Hall, Robert, "Stochastic Implications of the Life Cycle–Permanent Income Hypothesis: Theory and Evidence," *Journal of Political Economy* 86, 1978, 971–987.

Hamilton, James D., *Time Series Analysis,* Princeton, NJ: Princeton University Press, 1994.

Harberger, Arnold C., "Currency Depreciation, Income, and the Balance of Trade," *Journal of Political Economy* 58, 1950, 47–60.

Hatchondo, Juan Carlos, and Leonardo Martínez, "Long-Duration Bonds and Sovereign Defaults," *Journal of International Economics* 79, 2009, 117–125.

Hatchondo, Juan Carlos, Leonardo Martínez, and Horacio Sapriza, "Quantitative Properties of Sovereign Default Models: Solution Methods Matter," *Review of Economic Dynamics* 13, 2010, 919–933.

Hodrick, Robert, and Edward C. Prescott, "Postwar U.S. Business Cycles: An Empirical Investigation," *Journal of Money, Credit, and Banking* 29, 1997, 1–16.

Holden, Steinar, and Fredrik Wulfsberg, "Downward Nominal Wage Rigidity in the OECD," *B.E. Journal of Macroeconomics: Advances* 8, 2008, Article 15.

International Monetary Fund, "Recent Experiences in Managing Capital Inflows: Cross-Cutting Themes and Possible Framework," IMF Policy Paper, Washington, DC, February 2011.

Intriligator, Michael D., *Mathematical Optimization and Economic Theory,* Englewood Cliffs, NJ: Prentice-Hall, 1971.

Jeanne, Olivier, "Debt Maturity and the International Financial Architecture," *American Economic Review* 99, 2009, 2135–2148.

Jeanne, Olivier, and Anton Korinek, "Managing Credit Booms and Busts: A Pigouvian Taxation Approach," NBER Working Paper 16377, National Bureau of Economic Research, Cambridge, MA, 2010.

Justiniano, Alejandro, and Bruce Preston, "Can Structural Small Open Economy Models Account for the Influence of Foreign Disturbances?" *Journal of International Economics* 81, 2010, 61–74.

Justiniano, Alejandro, Giorgio Primiceri, and Andrea Tambalotti, "Investment Shocks and Business Cycles," *Journal of Monetary Economics* 57, 2010, 132–145.

Kamin, Steven, and Karsten von Kleist, "The Evolution and Determinants of Emerging Market Credit Spreads in the 1990s," BIS Working Paper 68, Bank of International Settlements, Basel, May 1999.

Kaur, Supreet, "Nominal Wage Rigidity in Village Labor Markets," manuscript, Columbia University, New York, January 15, 2012.

Keynes, John Maynard, "The Economic Consequences of Mr. Churchill," Donald Moggridge (ed.), *The Collected Writings of John Maynard Keynes*, Vol. IX, 1972 (1925), New York: St. Martin's, 207–230.

Kim, Yun Jung, and Jing Zhang, "Decentralized Borrowing and Centralized Default," *Journal of International Economics* 88, 2012, 121–133.

King, Robert G., Charles I. Plosser, and Sergio T. Rebelo, "Production, Growth, and Business Cycles II. New Directions," *Journal of Monetary Economics* 21, 1988, 309–341.

Klein, Paul, "Using the Generalized Schur Form to Solve a Multivariate Linear Rational Expectations Model," *Journal of Economic Dynamics and Control* 24, 2000, 1405–1423.

Korinek, Anton, "Excessive Dollar Borrowing in Emerging Markets: Balance Sheet Effects and Macroeconomic Externalities," University of Maryland, College Park, July 2011.

Kose, M. Ayhan, "Explaining Business Cycles in Small Open Economies: 'How Much Do World Prices Matter?'" *Journal of International Economics* 56, 2002, 299–327.

Krueger, Alan B., and Andreas I. Mueller, "Time Use, Emotional Well-Being, and Unemployment: Evidence from Longitudinal Data," *American Economic Review* 102, 2012, 594–599.

Krugman, Paul R., "A Model of Balance of Payments Crises," *Journal of Money, Credit and Banking* 11, 1979, 311–325.

Kuroda, Sachiko, and Isamu Yamamoto, "Are Japanese Nominal Wages Downwardly Rigid? (Part I): Examinations of Nominal Wage Change Distributions," Bank of Japan, *Monetary and Economic Studies,* August 2003, 1–29.

Lahiri, Amartya, "Exchange Rate Based Stabilizations under Real Frictions: The Role of Endogenous Labor Supply," *Journal of Economic Dynamics and Control* 25, 2001, 1157–1177.

Lane, Philip R., and Gian Maria Milesi-Ferretti, "The External Wealth of Nations Mark II: Revised and Extended Estimates of Foreign Assets and Liabilities, 1970–2004," *Journal of International Economics* 73, 2007, 223–250.

Laursen, Svend, and Lloyd A. Metzler, "Flexible Exchange Rates and the Theory of Employment," *Review of Economics and Statistics* 32, 1950, 281–299.

Levy-Yeyati, Eduardo, and Ugo Panizza, "The Elusive Costs of Sovereign Defaults," *Journal of Development Economics* 94, 2011, 95–105.

Lizarazo, Sandra Valentina, "Default Risk and Risk Averse International Investors," *Journal of International Economics* 89, 2013, 317–330.

Lorenzoni, Guido, "Inefficient Credit Booms," *Review of Economic Studies* 75, 2008, 809–833.

Lucas, Robert E. Jr., "Equilibrium in a Pure Currency Economy," *Economic Inquiry* 18, 1980, 203–220.

———, *Models of Business Cycles,* Cambridge, MA: Basil Blackwell, 1987.

Martínez, José V., and Guido Sandleris, "Is It Punishment? Sovereign Default and the Decline in Trade," *Journal of International Money and Finance* 30, 2011, 909–930.

McIntyre, K. H., "Can Non-traded Goods Solve the 'Comovement Problem?'" *Journal of Macroeconomics* 25, 2003, 169–196.

Mendoza, Enrique, "Real Business Cycles in a Small-Open Economy," *American Economic Review* 81, 1991, 797–818.

———, "The Terms of Trade, the Real Exchange Rate, and Economic Fluctuations," *International Economic Review* 36, 1995, 101–137.

———, "Credit, Prices, and Crashes: Business Cycles with a Sudden Stop," in Sebastian Edwards and Jeffrey A. Frankel (eds.), *Preventing Currency Crises in Emerging Markets,* Chicago: University of Chicago Press, 2002, 335–392.

———, "Sudden Stops, Financial Crises and Leverage," *American Economic Review* 100, 2010, 1941–1966.

Mendoza, Enrique G., and Vivian Z. Yue, "A General Equilibrium Model of Sovereign Default and Business Cycles," *Quarterly Journal of Economics* 127, 2012, 889–946.

Miyamoto, Wataru, and Thuy Lan Nguyen, "The Role of Common Shocks in Small Open Economies between 1900 and 2006: A Structural Estimation," *International Economic Review,* forthcoming.

———, "Understanding the Cross Country Effects of U.S. Technology Shocks," working paper, Bank of Canada, Ottawa, September 16, 2014.

Monacelli, Tommaso, "Into the Mussa Puzzle: Monetary Policy Regimes and the Real Exchange Rate in a Small Open Economy," *Journal of International Economics* 62, 2004, 191–217.

Mundell, Robert, "Capital Mobility and Stabilization Policy under Fixed and Flexible Exchange Rates," *Canadian Journal of Economics* 29, 1963, 475–485.

Mussa, Michael, "Nominal Exchange Regimes and the Behavior of Real Exchange Rates: Evidence and Implications," *Carnegie-Rochester Conference Series on Public Policy* 25, 1986, 117–214.

Na, Seunghoon, "Business Cycles and Labor Income Shares in Emerging Economies," manuscript, Columbia University, New York, April 2015.

Na, Seunghoon, Stephanie Schmitt-Grohé, Martín Uribe, and Vivian Z. Yue, "A Model of the Twin Ds: Optimal Default and Devaluation," NBER Working Paper 20314, National Bureau of Economic Research, Cambridge, MA, July 2014.

Nakamura, Emi, and Jon Steinsson, "Five Facts about Prices: A Reevaluation of Menu Cost Models," *Quarterly Journal of Economics* 123, 2008, 1415–1464.

Nason, James M., and John H. Rogers, "The Present-Value Model of the Current Account Has Been Rejected: Round Up the Usual Suspects," *Journal of International Economics* 68, 2006, 159–187.

Neumeyer, Pablo A., and Fabrizio Perri, "Business Cycles in Emerging Markets: The Role of Interest Rates," *Journal of Monetary Economics* 52, 2005, 345–380.

Obstfeld, Maurice, "Aggregate Spending and the Terms of Trade: Is There a Laursen-Metzler Effect?" *Quarterly Journal of Economics* 97, 1982, 251–270.

OECD (Organization of Economic Co-operation and Development), "Trade in Value-Added: Concepts, Methodologies and Challenges," Joint OECD-WTO Note, Paris, 2012.

Otto, Glenn, "Terms of Trade Shocks and the Balance of Trade: There Is a Harberger-Laursen-Metzler Effect," *Journal of International Money and Finance* 22, 2003, 155–184.

Ravn, Morten O., and Harald Uhlig, "On Adjusting the Hodrick-Prescott Filter for the Frequency of Observations," *Review of Economics and Statistics* 84, 2002, 371–380.

Rebelo, Sergio, and Carlos A. Végh, "Real Effects of Exchange-Rate-Based Stabilization: An Analysis of Competing Theories," in Ben S. Bernanke and Julio J. Rotemberg (eds.), *NBER Macroeconomics Annual 1995*, Cambridge, MA: MIT Press, 1995, 125–174.

Reinhart, Carmen M., "Default, Currency Crises, and Sovereign Credit Ratings," *World Bank Economic Review* 16, 2002, 151–170.

Reinhart, Carmen M., and Kenneth S. Rogoff, "Recovery from Financial Crises: Evidence from 100 Episodes," *American Economic Review: Papers & Proceedings* 104, 2014, 50–55.

Reinhart, Carmen M., Kenneth Rogoff, and Miguel Savastano, "Debt Intolerance," *Brookings Papers on Economic Activity* 2003(1), 2003, 1–74.

Richmond, Christine, and Daniel A. Dias, "Duration of Capital Market Exclusion: An Empirical Investigation," manuscript, University of California, Los Angeles, July 2009.

Rodrik, Dani, and Andrés Velasco, "Short Term Capital Flows," in Boris Pleskovic and Joseph E. Stiglitz (eds.), *Annual World Bank Conference on Development Economics 1999*, Vol. 1, Washington, DC: World Bank Group, 2000, 59–90.

Roldós, Jorge E., "Supply-Side Effects of Disinflation Programs," *IMF Staff Papers* 42, 1995, 158–183.

Rose, Andrew K., "One Reason Countries Pay Their Debts: Renegotiation and International Trade," *Journal of Development Economics* 77, 2005, 189–206.

Salant, Stephen W., and Dale W. Henderson, "Market Anticipations of Government Policies and the Price of Gold," *Journal of Political Economy* 86, 1978, 627–648.

Schindler, Martin, "Measuring Financial Integration: A New Data Set," *IMF Staff Papers* 56, 2009, 222–238.

Schmitt-Grohé, Stephanie, "The International Transmission of Economic Fluctuations: Effects of U.S. Business Cycles on the Canadian Economy," *Journal of International Economics* 44, 1998, 257–287.

Schmitt-Grohé, Stephanie, and Martín Uribe, "Closing Small Open Economy Models," *Journal of International Economics* 61, 2003, 163–185.

———, "Solving Dynamic General Equilibrium Models Using a Second-Order Approximation to the Policy Function," *Journal of Economic Dynamics and Control* 28, 2004, 755–775.

———, "Optimal, Simple, and Implementable Monetary and Fiscal Rules," *Journal of Monetary Economics* 54, 2007, 1702–1725.

———, "Finite-State Approximation of VAR Processes: A Simulation Approach," manuscript, Columbia University, New York, 2009.

———, "Managing Currency Pegs," *American Economic Review, Papers and Proceedings* 102, 2012a, 192–197.

———, "What's News in Business Cycles," *Econometrica* 80, 2012b, 2733–2764.

———, "Downward Nominal Wage Rigidity, Currency Pegs, and Involuntary Unemployment," *Journal of Political Economy* 124, 2016a, 1466–1514.

———, "Multiple Equilibria in Open Economy Models with Collateral Constraints: Overborrowing Revisited," NBER Working Paper 22264, National Bureau of Economic Research, Cambridge, MA, 2016b.

———, "Is Optimal Capital-Control Policy Countercyclical In Open-Economy Models With Collateral Constraints?" NBER Working Paper 22481, National Bureau of Economic Research, Cambridge, MA, 2016c.

———, "Adjustment to Small, Large, and Sunspot Shocks in Open Economies with Stock Collateral Constraints," NBER Working paper 22971, National Bureau of Economic Research, Cambridge, MA, 2016d.

———, "How Important Are Terms of Trade Shocks?" *International Economic Review*, forthcoming.

Seoane, Hernán D., "Time-Varying Volatility, Default and the Sovereign Risk Premium," manuscript, Universidad Carlos III de Madrid, March 17, 2014.

Shousha, Samer, "Macroeconomic Effects of Commodity Booms and Busts," manuscript, Columbia University, New York, October 2015.

Sidrauski, Miguel, "Rational Choice and Patterns of Growth in a Monetary Economy," *American Economic Review, Papers and Proceedings* 57, 1967, 534–544.

Sims, Christopher, "Solving Linear Rational Expectations Models," *Computational Economics* 20, 2001, 1–20.

Smets, Frank, and Raf Wouters, "Shocks and Frictions in US Business Cycles: A Bayesian DSGE Approach," *American Economic Review* 97, 2007, 586–606.

Stock, James H., and Mark W. Watson, "Business Cycle Fluctuations in US Macroeconomic Time Series," in John B. Taylor and Michael Woodford (eds.), *Handbook of Macroeconomics*, Amsterdam: Elsevier Science, 1999, 3–64.

Stockman, Alan C., "Real Exchange Rate Variability under Pegged and Floating Nominal Exchange Rate Systems: An Equilibrium Theory," *Carnegie-Rochester Conference Series on Public Policy* 29, 1988, 259–294.

Stockman, Alan C., and Linda L. Tesar, "Tastes and Technology in a Two-Country Model of the Business Cycle: Explaining International Comovements," *American Economic Review* 85, 1995, 168–185.

Sturzenegger, Federico, and Jeromin Zettelmeyer, *Debt Defaults and Lessons from a Decade of Crises*, Cambridge, MA: MIT Press, 2006.

———, "Haircuts: Estimating Investor Losses in Sovereign Debt Restructurings, 1998–2005," *Journal of International Money and Finance* 27, 2008, 780–805.

Svensson, Lars E. O., and Assaf Razin, "The Terms of Trade and the Current Account: The Harberger-Laursen-Metzler Effect," *Journal of Political Economy* 91, 1983, 97–125.

Tauchen, George, and Robert Hussey, "Quadrature-Based Methods for Obtaining Approximate Solutions to Nonlinear Asset Pricing Models," *Econometrica* 59, 1991, 371–396.

Tomz, Michael, and Mark L. J. Wright, "Do Countries Default in 'Bad Times'?" *Journal of the European Economic Association* 5, 2007, 352–360.

———, "Empirical Research on Sovereign Debt and Default," *Annual Review of Economics* 5, 2013, 247–272.

Tudela, Merxe, Elena Duggar, Albert Metz, Bart Oosterveld, and Anne Van Praagh, "Sovereign Default and Recovery Rates, 1983–2013," Credit Policy Research, Moody's Investor Service, New York, April 11, 2014.

Uribe, Martín, "Exchange Rate Based Inflation Stabilization: The Initial Real Effects of Credible Plans," *Journal of Monetary Economics* 39, 1997, 197–221.

———, "Comparing the Welfare Costs and Initial Dynamics of Alternative Inflation Stabilization Policies," *Journal of Development Economics* 59, 1999, 295–318.

———, "The Price-Consumption Puzzle of Currency Pegs," *Journal of Monetary Economics* 49, 2002, 533–569.

———, "On Overborrowing," *American Economic Review, Papers and Proceedings* 96, 2006, 417–421.

———, "Individual Versus Aggregate Collateral Constraints and the Overborrowing Syndrome," NBER Working Paper 12260, National Bureau of Economic Research, Cambridge, MA, May 2007.

Uribe, Martín, and Z. Vivian Yue, "Country Spreads and Emerging Countries: Who Drives Whom?" *Journal of International Economics* 69, 2006, 6–36.

Uzawa, H., "Time Preference, the Consumption Function and Optimum Asset Holdings," in J. N. Wolfe (ed.), *Value, Capital and Growth: Papers in Honor of Sir John Hicks,* Edinburgh: University of Edinburgh Press, 1968, 485–504.

Whalley, John, *Trade Liberalization among Major World Trading Areas,* Cambridge, MA: MIT Press, 1985.

Winkelmann, Liliana, and Rainer Winkelmann, "Why Are the Unemployed So Unhappy? Evidence from Panel Data," *Economica* 65, 1998, 1–15.

Woodford, Michael, *Interest and Prices: Foundations of a Theory of Monetary Policy,* Princeton, NJ: Princeton University Press, 2003.

Yue, Vivian Z., "Sovereign Default and Debt Renegotiation," *Journal of International Economics* 80, 2010, 176–187.

Yun, Tack, "Nominal Price Rigidity, Money Supply Endogeneity, and the Business Cycle," *Journal of Monetary Economics* 37, 1996, 345–370.

———, "Optimal Monetary Policy with Relative Price Distortions," *American Economic Review* 95, 2005, 89–109.

Zarazaga, Carlos, "Default and Lost Opportunities: A Message from Argentina for Euro-Zone Countries," *Federal Reserve Bank of Dallas, Economic Letter* 7, 2012, 1–4.

Zellner, Arnold, *An Introduction to Bayesian Inference in Econometrics,* New York: Wiley, 1971.

Index